HALLIWELL'S
SCREEN GREATS

By the same author

Halliwell's Film Guide
Halliwell's Filmgoer's Companion
Halliwell's Television Companion (with Philip Purser)
The Filmgoer's Book of Quotes
Halliwell's Movie Quiz
Mountain of Dreams
The Clapperboard Book of the Cinema
    (with Graham Murray)
Halliwell's Hundred
Halliwell's Harvest
The Ghost of Sherlock Holmes (fiction)
Seats in All Parts: Half a Lifetime at the Movies
Return to Shangri-La (fiction)
The Dead That Walk
Double Take and Fade Away

HALLIWELL'S
SCREEN GREATS

Leslie Halliwell

GRAFTON BOOKS

A Division of the Collins Publishing Group

LONDON GLASGOW
TORONTO SYDNEY AUCKLAND

Grafton Books
A Division of the Collins Publishing Group
8 Grafton Street, London W1X 3LA

Published by Grafton Books 1988

This selection copyright © Leslie Halliwell 1988

ISBN 0–261–10090–4

Printed in Great Britain by
Collins Glasgow.

Preface

Making the selections—more than a thousand of them—for this abstract of *Halliwell's Film Guide* was a labour that surprised even me. There were fewer films than I had expected which could be called great in the absolute and unchallengeable sense, even though many were great in their time or had elements of greatness still lingering about them.

In the end I interpreted the word 'great' in a number of different ways. Great entertainment, to begin with: that brings in *Casablanca* and *A Night at the Opera*. Great in ambition and scope: *A Matter of Life and Death*, *Close Encounters of the Third Kind*, and so on. Great in historical importance, or in the artistic development of the cinema: and so we include *The Battleship Potemkin* and *Orphée*. Great in box office receipts: *Star Wars* and *Jaws*. Great in the controversy they stirred: *Last Year in Marienbad* and *2001: A Space Odyssey*. Great, finally, in aiming high and falling far, like *Heaven's Gate* and the Elizabeth Taylor *Cleopatra*. And somewhere among and between these categories you will find the films which are simply great by any standard, the ones which frequently turn up in 'best ten' lists: films like *Citizen Kane* and *The Maltese Falcon* and *In Which We Serve* and *The Grapes of Wrath* and *Les Enfants du Paradis*.

Hopefully the little book, by its unadulterated concentration on films of worth, may help you to realize the brilliant talent which has been available in so many departments of the cinema during its first hundred years of existence.

Leslie Halliwell
February 1988

Categories of film

 Adventure

 Comedy

 Documentary

 Drama

 Family/Children

 Fantasy

 Horror

 Musical

 Romance

 Spy/Thriller

 War

 Western

Explanatory Notes

Alphabetical order
This has caused occasional problems. Some books in formulating the sequence take the complete title into account, as though there were no gaps between words. We have always persevered with the old-fashioned word-at-a-time arrangement: for instance, all the titles starting with *In*, including *In Which We Serve*, are used up before one goes on to titles such as *Indiscreet* or *Intolerance*. Hyphenated or apostrophized words are counted as one word. Compressions such as *Dr* and *St* are treated as though they had been spelled out, as *Doctor* and *Saint*. *Mac* and *Mc* are regarded as interchangeable under *Mac*.

Publicity tags   These were used in the original promotion for the film and, in the manner of trailers, precede the entry.

Category symbols   See earlier list for definitions.

Country of origin   First item after symbol on second line.

Year of release   Comes after country of origin, and is intended to be the year in which the film was first shown. If it was made earlier and held back, I have tried to indicate the fact. Dating is sometimes an onerous task, and the result debatable; please be sympathetic.

Running time   In minutes, signified by 'm'. So far as possible this is the original release time. Very many films are cut when they cross the water, sometimes by twenty minutes or more, but I have not tried to indicate this, as when the film appears on television a new print is usually taken from the original negative (but may be cut again). Remember, however, that an engineering function of British television results in an imperceptible speeding-up of projection and a consequent loss of one minute in every twenty-five. A hundred-minute film, therefore, will run only ninety-six minutes on the box.

Black and white or colour   I have given the colour process where known (it is not always stated these days) and I have coined the single word Eastmancolor to equate with Technicolor.

Other notable points   I have noted whether the film is in some special process (3–D, Vistavision, etc).

Production credit   The central credit on the third line is the production company. To the left, however, comes the distributor if different from the production company, in brackets if his rights subsequently lapsed. To the right is the actual producer, except for early thirties films in which he was seldom credited. He is also in brackets unless he has a stake in the production, in which case he follows an oblique.

Alternative title   This is given on a separate line, usually with a note of the country in which it was used. If no such fine line exists, I have used the formula *aka* (also known as).

Synopsis   Self-explanatory, with brevity and accuracy the keynote.

Assessment   Again very brief, so flippancy will inevitably be suspected. Not so, but for more considered judgements look for books which have more space.

Writer credit *(w)* It seems to me that this is, at least sometimes, more important than the director credit, and as script in any case precedes direction, it comes first in this book. The author of the screenplay is always given; if this derives from a novel, play or story, this is given next, together with the original author.

Director credit *d.*

Photography credit *ph.*

Music credit *(m)* This means the composer of the background music score. Sometimes there is only a music director *(md)* who orchestrates library or classical music.

Other credits Production designer *(pd)*, music and lyrics *(m / ly)*, art director *(ad)*, special effects *(sp)*, editor *(ed)*, etc, are given when they seem important and can be found. In some cases it has not been possible to track down all the credits one would wish.

Cast The principal actors are given, where possible, roughly in order of importance. I have stopped before the bit parts, and given fewer names in the case of foreign films, where the actors tend to be less well known.

Italics These denote a contribution of a particularly high standard.

Comments from critics To over half the items I have appended brief quotes from well-known professional critics, sometimes because they wittily confirm my own findings, and sometimes because they disagree with me entirely. I hope these will be enjoyable and illuminating; the absence of a quote casts no reflection whatever on the film, only on my own ability as a researcher.

Additional notes   Any other significant remarks about the film are given after the symbol †.

Academy Awards   Awards (AA) and also nominations (AAN) are listed for all principal categories, including acting, direction, photography, music score, songs and best picture.

A

À Bout de Souffle

France 1959 90m bw
SNC (Georges de
Beauregard)
aka: *Breathless*

A young car thief kills a policeman
and goes on the run with his
American girl friend. Casual,
influential, New Wave reminiscence
of both *Quai des Brumes* and
innumerable American gangster
thrillers. (The film is dedicated to
Monogram.)

*w François Truffaut d Jean-Luc
Godard ph Raoul Coutard
m Martial Solal*

Jean-Paul Belmondo, Jean Seberg,
Daniel Boulanger, Jean-Pierre
Melville.

'A film all dressed up for rebellion
but with no real tangible territory on
which to stand and fight.'—*Peter
John Dyer*

À Nous la Liberté

France 1931 95m bw
Tobis
US title: *Freedom for Us*

A factory owner is blackmailed
about his past, and helped by an old
prison friend, with whom he finally
takes to the road.
Operetta-style satirical comedy with
leftish attitudes, and several famous
sequences later borrowed by Chaplin
for *Modern Times*. In terms of sheer
film flair, a revelation, though the
plot has its tedious turns.

*wd René Clair ph Georges Périnal
m Georges Auric pd Lazare
Meerson*

Raymond Cordy, Henri Marchand,
Rolla France, Paul Olivier.

'Different from the usual run . . .
easily understandable even to those
who do not know French.'—*Variety*

'He demonstrates that sound
pictures can be as fluid as silents

were, and the picture is rightly
considered a classic.'—*Pauline Kael,
1970s*

'Jeepers! the creepers are after
somebody—and guess who!
More howls than you can shake
a shiver at!!!'

Abbott and Costello Meet Frankenstein

US 1948 83m bw
U-I (Robert Arthur)
GB title: *Abbott and Costello Meet
the Ghosts*

Two railway porters deliver crates
containing the Frankenstein
monster, Dracula, and the Wolf
Man.
Fairly lively spoof which put an end
to Universal's monsters for a while.
Good typical sequences for the stars,
a few thrills, and some good lines.
Dracula to Costello, lovingly: 'What
we need is young blood . . . and
brains . . .'

*w Robert Lees, Frederic I. Rinaldo,
John Grant d Charles Barton
ph Charles van Enger m Frank
Skinner*

*Bud Abbott, Lou Costello, Bela
Lugosi, Lon Chaney Jnr*, Glenn
Strange, Lenore Aubert, Jane
Randolph.

WOLF MAN:'You don't understand.
Every night when the moon is full, I
turn into a wolf.'

COSTELLO: 'You and fifty million
other guys!'

† Probably the Abbott and Costello
film which survives best.

Abe Lincoln in Illinois

US 1940 110m bw
RKO (Max Gordon)
GB title: *Spirit of the People*

Episodes in the political and
domestic life of Abraham Lincoln.
Pleasant, muted, careful film based

on a Broadway success: generally
informative and interesting.

w Grover Jones, *play* Robert E.
Sherwood d John Cromwell
ph James Wong Howe m Roy Webb

Raymond Massey, Ruth Gordon,
Gene Lockhart, Mary Howard,
Dorothy Tree, Minor Watson,
Howard da Silva

'If you want attitudes, a five gallon
hat, famous incidents, and One
Nation Indivisible, they're all here.
As a picture and as a whole, it just
doesn't stick.'—*Otis Ferguson*

AAN: Raymond Massey, James
Wong Howe

'The wonder film of the century,
about the most romantic figure
who ever lived!'
Abraham Lincoln
US 1930 97m bw
UA / D. W. Griffith
An account of Lincoln's entry into
politics and his years of power.
Rather boring even at the time, this
straightforward biopic has the virtues
of sincerity and comparative fidelity
to the facts.

w Stephen Vincent Benet, Gerrit
Lord *d D. W. Griffith ph* Karl
Struss *m* Hugo Riesenfeld
pd William Cameron Menzies

Walter Huston, Una Merkel, Edgar
Dearing, Russell Simpson, Henry B.
Walthall

'A startlingly superlative
accomplishment, one rejuvenating a
greatest Griffith . . . one smooth roll
of literally pulsating passion, pathos,
laughter . . . it should be his greatest
contribution to the
exhibitor.'—*Variety*

'It brings to us—with a curious
finality of disappointment, a
sentimental sense of the closing of a
chapter—the impression of a
director who has nowhere made a
valid contact with the condition of
the screen today.'—*C. A. Lejeune*

'A treasure trove of magnificent
moments.'—*MFB, 1973*

'Dull, episodic, overlong . . . it is
difficult to understand why

contemporary critics were so
impressed.'—*Anthony Slide, 70s*

Ace in the Hole
US 1951 111m bw
Paramount (Billy Wilder)
aka: *The Big Carnival*
In order to prolong the sensation
and boost newspaper sales, a
self-seeking journalist delays the
rescue of a man trapped in a cave.
An incisive, compelling melodrama
taking a sour look at the American
scene; one of its director's
masterworks.

w Billy Wilder, Lesser Samuels,
*Walter Newman d Billy Wilder
ph* Charles B. Lang Jnr *m* Hugo
Friedhofer

Kirk Douglas (Chuck Tatum), Jan
Sterling (Lorraine), *Porter Hall*
(Boot), Bob Arthur (Herbie),
Richard Benedict (Leo), Ray Teal
(Sheriff), Frank Cady (Federber)

LORRAINE to Tatum: 'I've met
some hard-boiled eggs, but
you—you're twenty minutes!'

LORRAINE: 'I don't go to church.
Kneeling bags my nylons.'

TATUM to editor: 'I've done a lot of
lying in my time. I've lied to men who
wear belts. I've lied to men who
wear suspenders. But I'd never be so
stupid as to lie to a man who wears
both belt and suspenders.'

TATUM, dying, to editor: 'How'd
you like to make a thousand dollars
a day, Mr Boot? I'm a
thousand-dollar-a-day
newspaperman. You can have me
for nothing.'

'Few of the opportunities for
irony, cruelty and horror are
missed.'—*Gavin Lambert*

'Style and purpose achieve for the
most part a fusion even more
remarkable than in *Sunset
Boulevard*.'—*Penelope Houston*

'As stimulating as black
coffee.'—*Richard Mallett, Punch*

'Americans expected a cocktail
and felt I was giving them a shot of
vinegar instead.'—*Billy Wilder*

'Some people have tried to claim
some sort of satirical brilliance for it,

but it's really rather nasty, in a sociologically pushy way.'—*New Yorker, 1980*

'A brilliant arrangement of cause and effect . . . unique as a mirror of the morbid psychology of crowds . . . revolting but incontrovertibly true.'—*New York Times*

AAN: script

Across the Pacific

US 1942 99m bw
Warner (Hal B. Wallis)
Just before Pearl Harbor, an army officer is cashiered by arrangement in order to contact pro-Japanese sympathizers.
Hasty, easy-going and very enjoyable hokum, partly ship-set and successfully reteaming three stars of *The Maltese Falcon*.

w Richard Macauley, *serial* Aloha Means Goodbye by Robert Carson d John Huston ph Arthur Edeson m Adolph Deutsch

Humphrey Bogart (Rick Leland), *Mary Astor* (Alberta Marlow), *Sydney Greenstreet* (Dr Lorenz), *Sen Yung* (Joe Totsuiko); and Charles Halton, Monte Blue, Richard Loo, Chester Gan, Kam Tong

'A spy picture which tingles with fearful uncertainties and glints with the sheen of blue steel.'—*Bosley Crowther*

† Huston was called up before the film was completed, and allegedly reshaped the script before leaving in order to put the hero in an impossible situation. Direction was eventually completed by Vincent Sherman.

Adam's Rib

US 1949 101m bw
MGM (Lawrence Weingarten)
Husband and wife lawyers are on opposite sides of an attempted murder case.
A superior star vehicle which also managed to introduce four promising personalities; slangily written and smartly directed, but perhaps a shade less funny than it once seemed.

w Ruth Gordon, Garson Kanin d George Cukor ph George J. Folsey m Miklos Rozsa

Spencer Tracy, Katharine Hepburn, David Wayne, Tom Ewell, Judy Holliday, Jean Hagen, Hope Emerson, Clarence Kolb

'Hepburn and Tracy are again presented as the ideal US Mr and Mrs of upper-middle income. This time, as well as being wittily urbane, both are lawyers.'—*Time*

'It isn't solid food but it certainly is meaty and juicy and comically nourishing.'—*Bosley Crowther*

† A 1972 TV series of the same title provided a boring imitation, with Ken Howard and Blythe Danner.

The Adventurer

US 1917 21m approx (24 fps) bw silent
Mutual
An escaped convict rescues two wealthy women from drowning and is invited to their home.
Hilarious early Chaplin knockabout, with his physical gags at their most streamlined.

wd Charles Chaplin ph William C. Foster, Rollie Totheroh

Charles Chaplin, Edna Purviance, Eric Campbell, Henry Bergman

The Adventures of Don Juan

US 1949 110m
Technicolor
Warner (Jerry Wald)
GB title: *The New Adventures of Don Juan*
A reformed 17th-century rake saves his queen from the machinations of her first minister. Expensive, slightly uneasy, but generally very entertaining swashbuckler with elements of self-spoofery. Flynn's last big-budget extravaganza.

w George Oppenheimer, Harry Kurnitz d Vincent Sherman ph Elwood Bredell m Max Steiner

Errol Flynn, Viveca Lindfors, Romney Brent, Robert Douglas, Alan Hale, Ann Rutherford, Robert Warwick, Jerry Austin, Douglas

Kennedy, Una O'Connor, Aubrey Mather, Raymond Burr

'A lavish film on a truly magnificent scale.'—*The Times*

The Adventures of Mark Twain

US 1944 130m bw
Warner (Jesse L. Lasky)

The life of America's foremost humorous writer, from a Mississippi riverboat to his becoming an honorary fellow of Oxford University.

Conventional biopic, quite watchable and with unusual side turnings, but eventually lacking the zest of the subject.

w Harold M. Sherman, Alan le May, Harry Chandler *d* Irving Rapper *ph* Sol Polito *m* Max Steiner

Fredric March, Alexis Smith, Donald Crisp, Alan Hale, C. Aubrey Smith, John Carradine, William Henry, Robert Barrat, Walter Hampden

'It's not that it's much worse than most cinematized biographies, because it does have its good moments. It's just that once more biographical inaccuracy is rampant, and once more the best dramatic possibilities have been overlooked, so it's hard to think of anything new, in the line of protest, to say.'—*David lardner, New Yorker*

AAN: Max Steiner

'Only the rainbow can duplicate its brilliance!'

The Adventures of Robin Hood

US 1938 102m
Technicolor
Warner (Hal B. Wallis)

Rebel outlaw Robin Hood outwits Guy of Gisbourne and the Sheriff of Nottingham, and saves the throne for the absent King Richard. A splendid adventure story, rousingly operatic in treatment, with dashing action highlights, fine comedy balance, and incisive acting all round. Historically notable for its use of early three-colour Technicolor; also for convincingly recreating Britain in California.

w Seton I. Miller, Norman Reilly Raine d William Keighley, Michael Curtiz ph Tony Gaudio, Sol Polito, Howard Green m Erich Wolfgang Korngold ad Carl Jules Weyl

Errol Flynn (Sir Robin of Locksley), *Basil Rathbone* (Sir Guy of Gisbourne), *Claude Rains* (Prince John). Olivia de Havilland (Maid Marian), *Alan Hale* (Little John), Patric Knowles (Will Scarlet), *Eugene Pallette* (Friar Tuck), *Ian Hunter* (King Richard), *Melville Cooper* (Sheriff of Nottingham), Una O'Connor (Bess), Herbert Mundin (Much the Miller's Son), Montagu Love (Bishop of Black Canons), Howard Hill (Captain of Archers)

PRINCE JOHN: 'Any objections to the new tax, from our Saxon friends?'

ROBIN to Gisbourne during duel: 'Did I upset your plans?'

GISBOURNE: 'You've come to Nottingham once too often!'

ROBIN: 'When this is over, my friend, there'll be no need for me to come again!'

PRINCE JOHN: 'Ho, varlets, bring Sir Robin food! Such insolence must support a healthy appetite!'

ROBIN: 'It's injustice I hate, not the Normans!'

'Magnificent, unsurpassable . . . the film is lavish, brilliantly photographed, and has a great Korngold score.'—*NFT, 1974*

'Mostly the picture is full of movement, some of it dashing in fine romantic costume style, some of it just sprightly. The excitement comes from fast action – galloping steeds, men swinging Tarzan-like from the trees, hurling tables and chairs, rapid running swordplay, the sudden whiz of Robin's arrows coming from nowhere to startle his enemies—more than from any fear that Robin might be worsted. Somehow the whole thing has the air of being a costume party, a jolly and rather athletic one, with a lot of well-bred Englishmen playing at being in the greenwood.'—*James Shelley Hamilton, National Board of Review*

† At the time of its release this was Warners' most expensive film, costing more than two million dollars. Chico, California, stood in for Sherwood Forest; the archery contest was shot at Bush Gardens, Pasadena. Curtiz took over direction when it was felt that the action lacked impact.

AA: Erich Wolfgang Korngold; Carl Jules Weyl
AAN: best picture

The Adventures of Robinson Crusoe
Mexico 1953 89m Pathecolor
Tepeyac (Oscar Dancigers, Henry F. Ehrlich)
A 17th-century mariner is shipwrecked on an uninhabited tropical island.
Fascinating version of a famous story, with only one character on screen until the belated arrival of Friday and the escape to civilization. Subtle and compelling, with only the colour unsatisfactory.

w Luis Bunuel, Phillip Roll, novel Daniel Defoe d Luis Bunuel ph Alex Phillips m Anthony Collins

Dan O'Herlihy, James Fernandez
'A film of which the purity, the tense poetic style, evokes a kind of wonder.'—*Gavin Lambert*
'Free of that deadly solicitude which usually kills off classics.'—*New Yorker, 1977*
AAN: Dan O'Herlihy

The Adventures of Sherlock Holmes
US 1939 83m bw
TCF (Gene Markey)
GB title: *Sherlock Holmes*
Moriarty sends Holmes on a false trail while he plots to steal the Crown jewels.
Highly engaging piece of Hollywood Victoriana, with all elements perfect except for an unconvincing plot.

w Edwin Blum, William Drake d Alfred Werker ph Leon Shamroy m Cyril Mockridge

Basil Rathbone (Holmes), *Nigel Bruce* (Dr Watson), *George Zucco* (Moriarty), Ida Lupino (Ann Brandon), Alan Marshal (Jerrold Hunter), Terry Kilburn (Billy), E. E. Clive (Inspector Bristol), Henry Stephenson (Sir Ronald Ramsgate), Mary Gordon (Mrs Hudson)
'The "elementary my dear Watson" type of dialogue is soft-pedalled for more modern phrases or understandable patter.'—*Variety*
'Told with more movie art per foot than seven reels of anything the intellectual men have been finding good this whole year or more.'—*Otis Ferguson*

† This was the second and last of Rathbone's costume outings as Holmes, and the one in which he sang a comic song in disguise.

The Adventures of Tom Sawyer
US 1938 91m Technicolor
David O. Selznick (William H. Wright)
Small-town Mississippi boy tracks down a murderer, Injun Joe.
Set-bound but excellent version of the children's classic by Mark Twain.

w John Weaver d Norman Taurog ph James Wong Howe, Wilfrid Cline m Max Steiner ad William Cameron Menzies

Tommy Kelly (Tom), *May Robson* (Aunt Polly), Walter Brennan (Muff Potter), Victor Jory (Injun Joe), Victor Kilian (Sheriff), Jackie Moran (Huckleberry Finn), Ann Gillis (Becky Thatcher), Donald Meek (Sunday School Superintendent), Margaret Hamilton (Mrs Sawyer), Marcia Mae Jones (Mary Sawyer)
'Another Selznick box office clean-up, an attraction destined for extended first runs, repeat bookings and heavy matinée take.'—*Variety*
'The familiar characters emerge in all their old amiability, the atmosphere is there and so is the excitement.'—*MFB*

'Should make Mark Twain
circulate in his grave like a trout in a
creel.'—*Otis Ferguson*

'Another Selznick International
box office clean-up . . . that there
exists a broad audience for films
whose essential appeal is to the
family trade has always been true.
Snow White touched a source of
almost unlimited audience draw:
Tom Sawyer follows to the same
customers.'—*Variety*

'Are the men and women of
  Washington really like this?'
Advise and Consent
👯 US 1962   139m   bw
 🗡 Panavision
Columbia / Alpha-Alpina / Otto
Preminger
The President's choice of an
unpopular secretary of state leads to
divisions in the Senate and the
blackmail and suicide of a senator.
Absorbing political melodrama from
a novel which aimed to lift the lid off
Washington. Many character actors
make their mark, but the
harsh-contrast photography seems
misjudged.

w Wendell Mayes, *novel* Allen
Drury *d* Otto Preminger *ph* Sam
Leavitt *m* Jerry Fielding *titles* Saul
Bass

Don Murray, *Charles Laughton*,
Henry Fonda, Walter Pidgeon, Lew
Ayres, Edward Andrews, Burgess
Meredith, Gene Tierney, Franchot
Tone, George Grizzard, Paul Ford,
Peter Lawford, Inga Swenson, Will
Geer
  'The result is supremely
ambivalent, a battle between
fascinatingly real props and
procedures and melodramatically
unreal characters and
situations.'—*Peter John Dyer*
  'The parade of people helps to
take one's mind off the overwrought
melodrama.'—*New Yorker, 1980*

An Affair to Remember
🎞 US 1957   114m
   Eastmancolor Cinemascope
TCF (Leo McCarey)

An ex-nightclub singer falls in love
with a wealthy bachelor on a
transatlantic liner, but an accident
prevents her from attending their
subsequent rendezvous.
Remake of *Love Affair*, a
surprisingly successful mixture of
smart lines, sentiment and tears, all
applied with style and assurance.

w Delmer Daves, Leo McCarey
d Leo McCarey *ph* Milton Krasner
m Hugo Friedhofer

*Cary Grant, Deborah Kerr, Cathleen
Nesbitt*, Richard Denning, Neva
Patterson
  'A lush slice of Hollywood
romanticism.'—*MFB*
  '90 masterly minutes of entrancing
light comedy and 25 beastly minutes
of beastly, melodramatic,
pseudo-tragic guff.'—*Paul Dehn*
AAN: Milton Krasner; Hugo
Friedhofer; title song (*m* Harry
Warren, *ly* Harold Adamson, Leo
McCarey)

'They never dreamed of being in
  each other's arms, yet the
  mystic spell of the jungle swept
  them to primitive, hungry
  embrace! The greatest
  adventure a man ever had . . .
  with a woman!'
The African Queen
✂ GB 1951   103m
 🎞 Technicolor
IFD / Romulus-Horizon (Sam
Spiegel)
In 1915, a gin-drinking river trader
and a prim missionary make odd
companions for a boat trip down a
dangerous river, culminating in an
attack on a German gunboat.
Despite some unfortunate studio sets
mixed in with real African footage
achieved through great hardship by
all concerned, this is one of those
surprising films that really work, a
splendidly successful mixture of
comedy, character and adventure.

w James Agee, novel C. S. Forester
*d John Huston ph Jack Cardiff
m Allan Gray*

Humphrey Bogart (Charlie Allnutt),
Katharine Hepburn (Rose Sayer),
Robert Morley (The Rev. Samuel
Sayer), Peter Bull (Captain),
Theodore Bikel (2nd Officer)

ROSE: 'I never dreamed that any
experience could be so stimulating!'

'Entertaining but not entirely
plausible or original.'—*Robert Hatch*

'The movie is not great art but it is
great fun, essentially one long,
exciting, old-fashioned movie
chase.'—*Time*

'A Technicolor Cook's Tour of
jungle wonders, enriched by
performances unmatched by
anything Hepburn or Bogart have
yet contributed to the screen.'—*Cue*

† Peter Viertel's book, *White Hunter
Black Heart*, is basically about
Huston during the making of this
film.

AA: Humphrey Bogart
AAN: James Agee; John Huston;
Katharine Hepburn

The Agony and the Ecstasy

US 1965   140m   De Luxe
Todd-AO

TCF / International Classics Inc
(Carol Reed)

Pope Julius II persuades
Michelangelo to leave his sculptures
and paint the ceiling of the Sistine
Chapel.

Dully reverent comic strip approach
to art and history; generally heavy
going, but good looking.

w Philip Dunne, *novel* Irving Stone
d Carol Reed ph Leon Shamroy
m Alex North pd John de Cuir

Charlton Heston, Rex Harrison,
Diane Cilento, Harry Andrews,
Alberto Lupo, Adolfo Celi.

JULIUS:'You dare to dicker with your
pontiff?'

'The vulgarity of the whole
concept has none of the joyfully
enthusiastic philistinism of a de
Mille; rather its tone is a dry, almost
cynical, condescension.'—*Brenda
Davies*

'All agony, no ecstasy.'—*Judith
Crist*

'Not a strong and soaring drama
but an illustrated lecture of a slow
artist at work.'—*Bosley Crowther*

† Michelangelo was apparently both
a dwarf and a homosexual. He is
played by Charlton Heston.

AAN: Leon Shamroy; Alex North

'The play that startled the nation!'
Ah, Wilderness

US 1935   101m   bw
MGM (Hunt Stromberg)

Problems of a small-town family at
the turn of the century.

Well-acted, affectionately
remembered version of a play later
musicalized as *Summer Holiday*. The
commercial success of this film led to
the Hardy family series.

w Albert Hackett, Frances
Goodrich, *play* Eugene O'Neill
d Clarence Brown ph Clyde de
Vinna m Herbert Stothart

Wallace Beery, Lionel Barrymore,
Eric Linden, Spring Byington,
Mickey Rooney, Aline MacMahon,
Charley Grapewin, Cecilia Parker,
Frank Albertson, Bonita Granville

'A job of picture making, in
craftsmanship and feeling, that is
wonderful to see.'—*Otis Ferguson*

'That it is a fine artistic effort will
not be denied anywhere, but for the
public at large it will need all the
boosting it can get.'—*Variety*

Airplane

US 1980   88m   Metrocolor
Paramount / Howard W. Koch
(Jan Davison)

A former pilot gets his nerve back
when called upon to land a
passenger plane because the crew all
have food poisoning.

Arthur Hailey's play *Flight into
Danger* and the film *Zero Hour*
which was made from it get the zany
parody treatment in this popular
movie which is often funny but
sometimes merely crude. It rang the
box office bell more loudly than
most expensive epics of its year.

wd Jim Abrahams, David and Jerry
Zucker ph Joseph Biroc m Elmer
Bernstein pd Ward Preston

Robert Stack, Lloyd Bridges, Robert Hays, Julie Hegerty, Peter Graves, Leslie Nielsen, Lorna Paterson, Ethel Merman, Kareem Abdul-Jabbar

'Parody may be the lowest form of humour, but few comedies in ages have rocked the laugh meter this hard.'—*Variety*

'It keeps going, like a dervish with skids on.'—*Derek Malcolm, Guardian*

'Proof that the cinema is alive and well and bursting with ingenuity.'—*David Hughes, Sunday Times*

'It's compiled like a jokebook and has the kind of pacing that goes with a laugh track.'—*Pauline Kael*

'All pretty juvenile really, though the relentless pace and sheer poor taste make up for a lack of originality.'—*Time Out, 1984*

Airport

US 1970   136m
Technicolor   Todd-AO
Universal / Ross Hunter (Jaque Mapes)

Events of one snowy night at a midwestern international airport, culminating in airborne melodrama when a mad bomber is killed and the damaged plane has to be talked down.

Glossy, undeniably entertaining, all-star version of a popular novel, with cardboard characters skilfully deployed in Hollywood's very best style.

w George Seaton, *novel* Arthur Hailey *d* George Seaton *ph* Ernest Laszlo *m* Alfred Newman

Burt Lancaster, Dean Martin, Jean Seberg, *Helen Hayes*, Van Heflin, Jacqueline Bisset, George Kennedy, Maureen Stapleton, Barry Nelson, Dana Wynter, Lloyd Nolan, Barbara Hale, Gary Collins, Jessie Royce Landis

'The best film of 1944.'—*Judith Crist*

'For sheer contentment there is nothing to beat the sight of constant catastrophe happening to others.'—*Alexander Walker*

'A *Grand Hotel* in the sky . . . every few years or so some more show-biz types would crowd onto a plane that would threaten to crash, collide with another, meet with terrorists, or otherwise be subjected to the perils of Pauline.'—*Les Keyser, Hollywood in the Seventies*

AA: Helen Hayes

AAN: best picture; George Seaton; Ernest Laszlo; Alfred Newman; Maureen Stapleton

The Alamo

US 1960   193m
Technicolor   Todd-AO
UA / John Wayne

In 1836 a small southern fort becomes the centre of Texas' fight for independence, but it is suddenly annihilated by a Mexican raid, and all its defenders killed.

Sprawling historical epic with many irrelevant episodes and distracting changes of mood.

w James Edward Grant *d* John Wayne *ph* William H. Clothier *m* Dmitri Tiomkin

John Wayne (as Crockett), Richard Widmark (Bowie), Laurence Harvey (Travis), Richard Boone (Houston), Frankie Avalon, Patrick Wayne, Linda Cristal, Chill Wills, Joseph Calleia

CROCKETT: 'Republic. I like the sound of the word. It means people can live free, talk free, go or come, buy or sell, be drunk or sober, however they choose. Some words give you a feeling. Republic is one of those words that makes me tight in the throat—the same tightness a man gets when his baby takes his first step or his first baby shaves and makes his first sound like a man. Some words can give you a feeling that makes your heart warm. Republic is one of those words.'

'Its sole redeeming feature lies in one of those crushing climaxes of total massacre which Hollywood can still pull off thunderingly well.'—*Peter John Dyer*

AAN: best picture; William H. Clothier; Dmitri Tiomkin; Chill

Wills; song 'The Green Leaves of Summer' (m Dmitri Tiomkin, ly Paul Francis Webster)

Alexander Nevsky

USSR 1938   112m   bw
Mosfilm

In 1242, Prince Alexander Nevsky defeats the invading Teutonic Knights in a battle on the ice of Lake Peipus.

A splendid historical pageant which shows the director at his most inventively pictorial and climaxes in a superb battle sequence using music instead of natural sound.

w Pyotr Pavlenko, Sergei Eisenstein d Sergei Eisenstein ph Edouard Tissé m Prokofiev ad I. Shpinel, N. Soloviov, K. Yeliseyev

Nikolai Cherkassov, Nikolai Okhlopkov, Andrei Abrikosov, Dmitri Orlov

'The picture will meet with good results wherever its political sentiments find established adherents. Otherwise it's almost nil for general appeal.'—Variety

'Superb sequences to cinematic opera that pass from pastoral to lamentation and end in a triumphal cantata.'—Georges Sadoul

'The colossus who conquered the world! The most colossal motion picture of all time!'

Alexander the Great

US 1956   135m
Technicolor Cinemascope
UA / Robert Rossen

The life and early death at thirty-three of the Macedonian warrior who conquered the entire known world.

Dour impassive epic which despite good intelligent stretches makes one long for Hollywood's usual more ruthless view of history.

wd Robert Rossen m Mario Nascimbene ph Robert Krasker ad Andrei Andreiev

Richard Burton, Fredric March, Danielle Darrieux, Claire Bloom, Barry Jones, Harry Andrews, Peter

Cushing, Stanley Baker, Michael Hordern, Niall MacGinnis

'Not a scene is held for a second longer than it is worth; greatness is pictured in constant dissolve.'—Alexander Walker

'Rossen has aimed for greatness and lost honourably.'—Andrew Sarris

Alexander's Ragtime Band

US 1938   106m   bw
TCF (Darryl F. Zanuck, Harry Joe Brown)

Between 1911 and 1939, two songwriters vie for the affections of a rising musical comedy star.

Archetypal chronicle musical with 26 songs; well-paced, smartly made, and bursting with talent.

w Kathryn Scola, Lamar Trotti, Richard Sherman d Henry King ph Peverell Marley m/ly Irving Berlin md Alfred Newman

Tyrone Power, Alice Faye, Don Ameche, Ethel Merman, Jack Haley, Jean Hersholt, Helen Westley, John Carradine, Paul Hurst, Wally Vernon, Ruth Terry, Eddie Collins, Douglas Fowley, Chick Chandler

'A grand filmusical which stirs and thrills, finding response in the American heart to memories of the exciting, sentimental and patriotic moments of the past quarter of a century.'—Variety

AA: Alfred Newman
AAN: best picture; Irving Berlin (for original story); Irving Berlin (for song, 'Now It Can Be Told')

Alfie

GB 1966   114m
Techniscope
Paramount / Sheldrake (Lewis Gilbert)

A Cockney Lothario is proud of his amorous conquests, but near-tragedy finally makes him more mature.

Garish sex comedy, an immense box office success because of its frankness and an immaculate performance from its star.

w Bill Naughton, from his play

d Lewis Gilbert *ph* Otto Heller
m Sonny Rollins

Michael Caine, Vivien Merchant,
Shirley Anne Field, Millicent
Martin, Jane Asher, Julia Foster,
Shelley Winters, Eleanor Bron,
Denholm Elliott

'Paramount thought it was a good
bet because it was going to be made
for 500,000 dollars, normally the sort
of money spent on executives' cigar
bills.'—*Lewis Gilbert*

AAN: best picture; Bill Naughton;
Michael Caine; Vivien Merchant;
title song

Algiers
US 1938 95m bw
Walter Wanger

A romantic Casbah thief makes the
mistake of falling in love.
Seminal Hollywood romantic drama
based closely on a French original,
Pepe le Moko, laughed at for years
because of the alleged line 'Come
with me to the Casbah' (which is
never actually said), it holds up
remarkably well in its fashion.

w John Howard Lawson, James M.
Cain *d* John Cromwell *ph* James
Wong Howe *m* Vincent Scott,
Mohammed Igorbouchen

Charles Boyer, Hedy Lamarr, *Sigrid
Gurie*, Gene Lockhart, *Joseph
Calleia*, Alan Hale, Johnny Downs

'A quality of sustained suspense
and excitement . . . there is nothing
makeshift about the
production.'—*Variety*

'Few films this season, or any
other, have sustained their mood
more brilliantly.'—*New York Times*

'The general tone is that of the
decent artistry we must demand and
enjoy in pictures, which should
someday be as respectable as books,
only more near and vivid.'—*Otis
Ferguson*

'This version is pure Hollywood,
sacrificing everything to glamour,
and the heavy make-up and studio
lighting make it seem so artificial one
can get giggly.'—*New Yorker, 1977*
† Remake: *Casbah*.

AAN: James Wong Howe; Charles
Boyer; Gene Lockhart

Alias Nick Beal
US 1949 93m bw
Paramount (Endre Boehm)
GB title: *The Contact Man*

A politician is nearly corrupted by a
mysterious stranger offering wealth
and power.
Highly satisfactory modern version
of *Faust*, done in gangster terms but
not eschewing a supernatural
explanation. Acting, photography
and direction all in the right key.

w Jonathan Latimer, *story* Mindret
Lord *d* John Farrow *ph* Lionel
Lindon *m* Franz Waxman

Ray Milland, Thomas Mitchell,
Audrey Totter, George Macready,
Fred Clark

'A picture for anyone who has ever
dreamed of a second chance!'
Alice Doesn't Live Here Any More
US 1974 112m Technicolor
Warner (David Susskind,
Audrey Maas)

A widow sets off with her young son
for Monterey and a singing career.
Realistically squalid and
foul-mouthed but endearing look at
a slice of America today, with firm
handling and excellent performances
in a surprisingly old-fashioned
theme.

w Robert Getchell *d* Martin
Scorsese *ph* Kent L. Wakeford
m various *pd* Toby Carr Rafelson

Ellen Burstyn, Alfred Lutter, Kris
Kristofferson, Billy Green Bush,
Diane Ladd, Lelia Goldoni, Jodie
Foster

'What Scorsese has done is to
rescue an American cliché from the
bland, flat but much more
portentous naturalism of such as
Harry and Tonto and restore it to an
emotional and intellectual
complexity through his particular
brand of baroque realism.'—*Richard
Combs*

'Full of funny malice and
breakneck vitality.'—*New Yorker*

'A tough weepie, redeemed by its picturesque locations and its eye for social detail.'—*Michael Billington, Illustrated London News*

AA: Ellen Burstyn

AAN: Robert Getchell; Diane Ladd

'In space, no one can hear you scream!'

Alien

GB 1979   117m
Eastmancolor Panavision
TCF/Brandywine (Walter Hill, Gordon Carroll, David Giler)

Astronauts returning to earth visit an apparently dead planet and are infected by a violent being which has unexpected behaviour patterns and eliminates them one by one. Deliberately scarifying and highly commercial shocker with little but its art direction to commend it to connoisseurs.

w Dan O'Bannon d Ridley Scott
ph Derek Vanlint, Denys Ayling
m Jerry Goldsmith chief designer H. R. Giger

Tom Skerritt, Sigourney Weaver, John Hurt, Veronica Cartwright, Harry Dean Stanton, Ian Holm, Yaphet Kotto

'A sort of inverse relationship to *The Thing* invites unfavourable comparisons.'—*Sight and Sound*

'Empty bag of tricks whose production values and expensive trickery cannot disguise imaginative poverty.'—*Time Out*

'It was not, as its co-author admitted, a think piece. The message he intended was simple: Don't close your eyes or it will get ya.'—*Les Keyser, Hollywood in the Seventies*

'The most provocative picture of the year!'

All About Eve

US 1950   138m   bw
TCF (Darryl F. Zanuck)

An ageing Broadway star suffers from the hidden menace of a self-effacing but secretly ruthless and ambitious young actress.

A basically unconvincing story with thin characters is transformed by a screenplay scintillating with savage wit and a couple of waspish performances into a movie experience to treasure.

wd Joseph L. Mankiewicz
ph Milton Krasner m Alfred Newman

Bette Davis (Margo Channing), George Sanders (Addison de Witt), Anne Baxter (Eve), Celeste Holm (Karen Richards), Thelma Ritter (Birdie), Gary Merrill (Bill Sampson), Hugh Marlowe (Lloyd Richards), Gregory Ratoff (Max Fabian), Marilyn Monroe (Miss Caswell), Barbara Bates (Girl at Mirror), Walter Hampden (Speaker at dinner)

MARGO: 'Fasten your seat belts, it's going to be a bumpy night!'

ADDISON: 'That I should want you at all suddenly strikes me as the height of improbability . . . you're an improbable person, Eve, but so am I. We have that in common. Also a contempt for humanity, an inability to love or be loved, insatiable ambition—and talent. We deserve each other.'

BIRDIE: 'The bed looks like a dead animal act.'

ADDISON: 'That's all television is, dear—just auditions.'

BIRDIE: 'What a story! Everything but the bloodhounds snappin' at her rear end!'

ADDISON: 'I have lived in the theatre as a Trappist monk lives in his faith. In it I toil not, neither do I spin. I am a critic and a commentator. I am essential to the theatre—as ants to a picnic, as the boll weevil to a cotton field.'

'The wittiest, the most devastating, the most adult and literate motion picture ever made that had anything to do with the New York Stage.'—*Leo Mishkin*

'The dialogue and atmosphere are so peculiarly remote from life that they have sometimes been mistaken for art.'—*Pauline Kael, 1968*

'Plenty of surface cynicism, but no detachment, no edge and no satire. Boiled down it is a plush backstage drama.'—*Richard Winnington*

'Long, but continuously, wonderfully entertaining in a way I had almost forgotten was possible for films.'—*Richard Mallett, Punch*

'Someone remarked of this witty, exaggerated, cruel and yet wildly funny film that the secret of its success was the extreme bad taste shown throughout by all concerned (though I hope they didn't mean to include Milton Krasner's tactful camerawork in this).'—*Basil Wright, 1972*

'The picture seemed long—though it was not by today's standards of length—and the crispness of the dialogue was not matched by equally crisp editing.'—*Hollis Alpert, 1962*

† The idea for the film came from a short story, 'The Wisdom of Eve', by Mary Orr.

AA: best picture; Joseph L. Mankiewicz (as writer); Joseph L. Mankiewicz (as director); George Sanders
AAN: Milton Krasner; Alfred Newman; Bette Davis; Anne Baxter; Celeste Holm; Thelma Ritter

All Quiet on the Western Front

US 1930 130m approx. bw Universal (Carl Laemmle Jnr)
In 1914, a group of German teenagers volunteer for action on the Western Front, but they become disillusioned, and none of them survives.
A landmark of American cinema and Universal's biggest and most serious undertaking until the sixties, this highly emotive war film with its occasional outbursts of bravura direction fixed in millions of minds the popular image of what it was like in the trenches, even more so than *Journey's End* which had shown the Allied viewpoint. Despite dated moments, it retains its overall power and remains a great pacifist work.

w Lewis Milestone, Maxwell Anderson, Del Andrews, George Abbott, *novel* Erich Maria Remarque d Lewis Milestone (in a manner reminiscent of Eisenstein and Lang) ph Arthur Edeson m David Broekman

Lew Ayres (Paul Baumer), Louis Wolheim (Katczinsky), Slim Summerville (Tjaden), John Wray (Himmelstoss), Raymond Griffith (Gerard Duval), Russell Gleason (Muller), Ben Alexander (Kemmerick), Beryl Mercer (Mrs Baumer)

TJADEN: 'Me and the Kaiser, we are both fighting. The only difference is, the Kaiser isn't here.'

KATCZINSKY: 'At the next war let all the Kaisers, Presidents and Generals and diplomats go into a big field and fight it out first among themselves. That will satisfy us and keep us at home.'

PAUL: 'We live in the trenches out there. We fight. We try not to be killed, but sometimes we are. That's all.'

'A magnificent cinematic equivalent of the book . . . to Mr Milestone goes the credit of effecting the similitude in united and dynamic picture terms. The sound and image mediums blend as one, as a form of artistic expression that only the motion screen can give.'—*National Board of Review*

'Nothing passed up for the niceties; nothing glossed over for the women. Here exhibited is war as it is, butchery. The League of Nations could make no better investment than to buy up the master-print, reproduce it in every language to be shown to every nation every year until the word war is taken out of the dictionaries.'—*Variety*

'A trenchant and imaginative audible picture . . . most of the time the audience was held to silence by its realistic scenes.'—*New York Times*

AA: best picture; Lewis Milestone (as director)
AAN: Lewis Milestone, Maxwell Anderson, Del Andrews, George Abbott; Arthur Edeson

All That Jazz
≋ US 1979   123m
Technicolor
TCF / Robert Alan Aurthur, Daniel
Melnick
A stage musical director pushes
himself too hard, and dies of a
surfeit of wine, women and work.
Self-indulgent,
semi-autobiographical tragi-comic
extravaganza complete with heart
operations and a recurring angel of
death. Flashes of brilliant talent
make it a must for Fosse fans.

w Robert Alan Aurthur, Bob Fosse
d Bob Fosse ph Giuseppe Rotunno
m Ralph Burns pd Philip
Rosenberg, Tony Walton

Roy Scheider, Jessica Lange, Ann
Rainking, Leland Palmer, Ben
Vereen, Cliff Gorman
    'Egomaniacal, wonderfully
choreographed, often
compelling . . . more an art item
than a broad commercial
prospect.'—Variety
    'An improbable mixture of crass
gags, song 'n' dance routines and
open heart surgery. Not for the
squeamish.'—Time Out
    'By the end I felt I'd learned more
about Fosse than I actually cared to
know.'—Daily Mail
    'High cholesterol hokum.
Enjoyable, but probably not good
for you.'—Pauline Kael, New Yorker

BFA: cinematography; editing (Alan
Heim); sound

All That Money Can Buy
⚞ US 1941   106m   bw
🎭 RKO / William Dieterle
(Charles L. Glett)
aka: The Devil and Daniel
Webster; Daniel and the Devil;
Here Is a Man

A hard-pressed farmer gives in to
the Devil's tempting, but is saved
from the pit by a famous lawyer's
pleading at his 'trial'.
A brilliant Germanic Faust set in
19th-century New Hampshire and
using historical figures, alienation
effects, comedy asides and the whole
cinematic box of tricks which

Hollywood had just learned again
through Citizen Kane. A magic act in
more ways than one.

w Dan Totheroh, based on The
Devil and Daniel Webster by
Stephen Vincent Benet d William
Dieterle ph Joseph August
m Bernard Herrmann ad Van Nest
Polglase sp Vernon L. Walker

Walter Huston ('Mr Scratch', a great
performance), James Craig, Anne
Shirley, Simone Simon, Edward
Arnold (Daniel Webster), Jane
Darwell, Gene Lockhart, John
Qualen, H. B. Warner

MR SCRATCH: 'A soul. A soul is
nothing. Can you see it, smell it,
touch it? No. Think of it—this
soul—your soul—a nothing, against
seven whole years of good luck! You
will have money and all that money
can buy.'
    'Some of those in the movie
industry who saw it restively called it
a dog; but some of them cried it was
another catapult hurling the cinema
up to its glorious destiny.'—Cecilia
Ager

AA: Bernard Herrmann
AAN: Walter Huston

'He thought he had the world by
    the tail—till it exploded in his
    face, with a bullet attached!'
All the King's Men
🎭 US 1949   109m   bw
X Columbia (Robert Rossen)
An honest man from a small town is
elected mayor and then governor,
but power corrupts him absolutely
and he ruins his own life and those
of his friends before being
assassinated.
Archetypal American political
melodrama based on the life of
southern senator Huey Long. The
background is well sketched in and
there are excellent performances,
but the overall narrative is rather
flabby.

w Robert Rossen, novel Robert
Penn Warren d Robert Rossen
ph Burnett Guffey m Louis
Gruenberg ad Sturges Carne

Broderick Crawford, John Ireland, Mercedes McCambridge, Joanne Dru, John Derek, Anne Seymour, Shepperd Strudwick.

'More conspicuous for scope and worthiness of intention than for inspiration.'—*Gavin Lambert*

'A superb pictorialism which perpetually crackles and explodes.'—*Bosley Crowther*

'Realism comes from within as well as without and the core of meaning that might have made this film a step forward from *Boomerang* does not exist amid all the courageous camera-work.'—*Richard Winnington*

'Broderick Crawford's Willie Stark might just make you feel better about the President you've got . . . By no means a great film, but it moves along.'—*Pauline Kael, New Yorker*

AA: best picture, Broderick Crawford; Mercedes McCambridge
AAN: Robert Rossen (as writer); Robert Rossen (as director); John Ireland

'The most devastating detective story of the century!'
All the President's Men
🐱🐱 US 1976   138m
  ✗ Technicolor
Warner/Wildwood (Robert Redford, Walter Coblenz)
A reconstruction of the discovery of the White House link with the Watergate affair by two young reporters from the *Washington Post*. An absorbing drama from the headlines which despite its many excellences would have been better with a more audible dialogue track, less murky photography and a clearer introduction of the characters concerned. The acting however is a treat.

w William Goldman, *book* Carl Bernstein, Bob Woodward *d* Alan J. Pakula *ph* Gordon Willis *m* David Shire *pd* George Jenkins
Robert Redford, Dustin Hoffman, Jason Robards Jnr, Martin Balsam, Hal Holbrook, Jack Warden, Jane Alexander, Meredith Baxter.

'It works as a detective thriller (even though everyone knows the ending), as a credible (if occasionally romanticized) primer on the prosaic fundamentals of big league investigative journalism, and best of all, as a chilling tone poem that conveys the texture of the terror in our nation's capital during that long night when an aspiring fascist regime held our democracy under siege.'—*Frank Rich, New York Post*

AA: William Goldman; Jason Robards Jnr
AAN: best picture; Alan J. Pakula; Jane Alexander

All This and Heaven Too
🐱🐱 US 1940   143m   bw
  ✗ Warner (Jack L. Warner, Hal B. Wallis)
A 19th-century French nobleman falls in love with his governess and murders his wife.
Romantic, melodramatic soap opera from a mammoth best seller; well made for those who can stomach it, with excellent acting and production values.

w Casey Robinson, *novel* Rachel Field *d* Anatole Litvak *ph* Ernest Haller *m* Max Steiner

Charles Boyer, Bette Davis, Barbara O'Neil, Virginia Weidler, Jeffrey Lynn, Helen Westley, Henry Daniell, Harry Davenport, Walter Hampden, George Coulouris, Janet Beecher, Montague Love
'Deserves extended runs and upped admissions . . . completely shorn of spectacle, but replete with finely drawn characters in absorbingly dramatic situations.'—*Variety*

AAN: best picture; Ernest Haller; Barbara O'Neil

Alone on the Pacific
✗ Japan 1963   104m
  ✗ Eastmancolor Cinemascope Ishihara-Nikkatsu (Akira Nakai)
original title: *Taiheiyo Hitoribochi*
A young man crosses from Osaka to San Francisco in a small yacht.
Fascinating Robinson Crusoe-like

exercise, with flashbacks to life on
dry land.

w Natto Wada, based on the
experiences of Kenichi Horie *d Kon
Ichikawa ph* Yoshihiro Yamazaki
m Yasushi Akatagawa, Tohru
Takemitsu

Yujiro Ishihara, Masayuki Mori,
Kinuyo Tanaka, Ruriko Asaoko
 'Wonderfully comic moments
emerge, but they never overshadow
the film's sheer pictorial
value.'—*Brenda Davies, MFB*

Amadeus
🏆🏆 US 1984   160m
X Technicolor Panavision
Saul Zaentz
Dying in 1823, the jealous composer
Salieri claims to have murdered
Mozart.
A musical legend performed with
success and economy on stage now
becomes an exciting baroque film,
like an opera in high-pitched
dialogue. Great to look at, and only
the American accents jar the ear.

w Peter Shaffer from his play
*d Milos Forman ph Miroslav
Ondricek md* Neville Marriner
*pd Patrizia Van Brandenstein
ed* Nena Danevic, Michael Chandler

F. Murray Abraham, Tom Hulce,
Elizabeth Berridge, Simon Callow,
Roy Dotrice, Christine Ebersole

AA: best picture, direction, F.
Murray Abraham, adapted
screenplay
AAN: Tom Hulce, photography,
editing, art direction
BFA: Miroslav Ondricek

Amarcord
🏆🏆 Italy/France 1973   123m
X Technicolor
FC Produzione/PECF (Franco
Cristaldi)
Memories of a small Italian town
during the fascist period.
A bizarre, intriguing mixture of fact,
fantasy and obscurity, generally
pleasing to watch though hardly
satisfying. The title means 'I
remember'.

w Federico Fellini, Tonino Guerra
d Federico Fellini ph Giuseppe
Rotunno *m Nino Rota ad* Danilo
Donati

Puppela Maggio, Magali Noel,
Armando Brancia, Ciccio Ingrassia
 'A rich surface texture and a sense
of exuberant melancholia.'—*Michael
Billington, Illustrated London News*
 'Peaks of invention separated by
raucous valleys of low
comedy.'—*Sight and Sound*
 'Some idea of attitudes within the
film business may be conveyed by
the fact that this witty, tender,
humane, marvellously photographed
picture has been booked into a
cinema with 132 seats.'—*Benny
Green, Punch*

AA: best foreign film
AAN: script; direction

The Amazing Dr Clitterhouse
🐕 US 1938   87m   bw
Warner (Robert Lord)
A criminologist researcher joins a
gangster's mob and becomes
addicted to crime.
Amusing, suspenseful, well acted
comedy-melodrama.

w John Huston, John Wexley,
play Barre Lyndon *d* Anatole
Litvak *ph* Tony Gaudio *m* Max
Steiner

Edward G. Robinson, Humphrey
Bogart, Claire Trevor, Allen
Jenkins, Gale Page, Donald Crisp,
Maxie Rosebloom
 'An unquestionable winner . . .
the picture inculcates a bit of the
sherlocking theme and modified
romance.'—*Variety*
 'The story is ingenious, but
Anatole Litvak and his
producing-acting crew have so
thoroughly kept the larky mood of it
while setting up the necessary mood
of interest and suspense that it is
hard to see where conception leaves
off and the shaping of it into motion
begins.'—*Otis Ferguson*

'Where were you in '62?'
American Graffiti
☻ US 1973   110m
   Techniscope
Universal / Lucasfilm / Coppola
Company (Francis Ford Coppola,
Gary Kurtz)

In 1962 California, four young men
about to leave for college gather for
a night's girl-chasing and
police-baiting.

Nostalgic comedy recalling many
sights and sounds of the previous
generation and carefully crystallizing
a particular time and place.
Successful in itself, it led to many
imitations.

*wd George Lucas ph Ron Eveslage,
Jan D'Alquen m popular songs*

Richard Dreyfuss, Ronny Howard,
Paul le Mat, Charlie Martin Smith,
Cindy Williams, Candy Clark,
Mackenzie Philips

AAN: best picture; George Lucas
(as writer); George Lucas (as
director); Candy Clark

An American in Paris
≋ US 1951   113m
   Technicolor
MGM (*Arthur Freed*)

A carefree young artist scorns a rich
woman's patronage and wins the
love of a gamine.

Altogether delightful musical
holiday, one of the highspots of the
Hollywood genre, with infectious
enthusiasm and an unexpected sense
of the Paris that was.

*w Alan Jay Lerner d Vincente
Minnelli ph Al Gilks, John Alton
m George Gershwin ly Ira
Gershwin ch Gene Kelly ad Cedric
Gibbons, Preston Ames*

*Gene Kelly, Oscar Levant, Nina
Foch, Leslie Caron, Georges Guetary*

Songs include 'I Got Rhythm';
'Embraceable You'; 'By Strauss';
''Swonderful'; 'Tra La La'; 'Our
Love Is Here to Stay'; 'Stairway to
Paradise'; 'Concerto in F'
(instrumental); 'An American in
Paris' (ballet)

'Too fancy and overblown, but the
principal performers are in fine form
and the Gershwin music keeps

everything good-spirited.'—*New
Yorker*, 1977

† Chevalier was originally paged for
the Georges Guetary role, but
turned it down because he lost the
girl. The production cost $2,723,903,
of which $542,000 went on the final
ballet.

AA: best picture; Alan Jay Lerner;
Al Gilks, John Alton; musical
arrangements (Saul Chaplin, Johnny
Green)
AAN: Vincente Minnelli

American Madness
☻☻ US 1932   80m   bw
   Columbia

When a bank failure threatens,
hundreds of small savers increase
their deposits to save the situation.

Vivid, overstressed topical
melodrama with crowd scenes typical
of its director's later output.

*w Robert Riskin d Frank Capra
ph Joseph Walker*

Walter Huston, Pat O'Brien, Kay
Johnson, Constance Cummings,
Gavin Gordon, Berton Churchill

'It's a money picture. That goes
both ways. It's about money and
banks and spells dough for the box
office. It's timely, topical, human,
dramatic, punchy and good
entertainment at one and the same
time.'—*Variety*

'The sequence of the mounting
panic and the storming of the bank
are effectively staged, but the
resolution is the usual Capra / Riskin
populist hokum.'—*New Yorker*,
1977

An American Romance
☻☻ US 1944   151m
   Technicolor
MGM (King Vidor)

The life of a European immigrant
who becomes a master of industry.

Mind-boggling pageant of the
American dream, coldly presented
and totally humourless. Its saving
grace is its smooth physical
presentation.

*w Herbert Dalmas, William Ludwig
d King Vidor ph Harold Rosson
m Louis Gruenberg*

Brian Donlevy, Ann Richards, John Qualen, Walter Abel, Stephen McNally

'A thousand chances to inform, excite or even interest have been flung away.'—*Richard Winnington*

'The whole aim of it is to boost The American Way.'—*Richard Mallett, Punch*

'Drama that happens around you every day—when the wild life of impetuous youth burns away age-old barriers!'
An American Tragedy
US 1931   95m   bw
Paramount
An ambitious young man murders his pregnant fiancée when he has a chance to marry a rich girl.
Dated but solidly satisfying adaptation of a weighty novel, more compelling than the 1951 remake *A Place in the Sun*.

wd Josef Von Sternberg, novel Theodore Dreiser ph Lee Garmes ad Hans Dreier

Phillips Holmes, *Sylvia Sidney*, Frances Dee, Irving Pichel, Frederick Burton, Claire McDowell

'It unreels as an ordinary programme effort with an unhappy ending . . . as Sternberg has seen fit to present it the celluloid structure is slow, heavy and not always interesting drama. Its box office success is very doubtful.'—*Variety*

'It is the first time, I believe, that the subjects of sex, birth control and murder have been put into a picture with sense, taste and reality.'—*Pare Lorentz*

'An aimless, lugubrious mess. The fireworks may dazzle to schoolboys of criticism, but they will add no permanent color to the motion picture.'—*Harry Alan Potamkin*

An American Werewolf in London
GB 1981   97m   Technicolor
Polygram / Lycanthrope
(Peter Guber, Jon Peters)
Two American tourists are bitten by a werewolf.
Curious but oddly endearing mixture of horror film and spoof, of comedy and shock, with everything grist to

its mill including tourist Britain and the wedding of Prince Charles. The special effects are notable, and signalled new developments in this field.

wd John Landis ph Robert Paynter m Elmer Bernstein sp Effects Associates, Rick Baker

David Naughton, Jenny Agutter, Griffin Dunne, John Woodvine
'The gear changes of tone and pace make for a very jerkily driven vehicle.'—*Sunday Times*

'The most amazing conspiracy the world has ever known, and love as it never happened to a man and woman before!'
Anastasia
US 1956   105m
Eastmancolor Cinemascope
TCF (Buddy Adler)
In 1928 Paris, a group of exiled White Russians claim to have found the living daughter of the Tsar, presumed executed in 1918; but the claimant is a fake schooled by a general, with whom she falls in love.
Slick, highly theatrical entertainment for the upper classes; it dazzles and satisfies without throwing any light on history.

w Arthur Laurents, play Marcelle Maurette, Guy Bolton d Anatole Litvak ph Jack Hildyard m Alfred Newman ad Andrei Andreiev, Bill Andrews
Ingrid Bergman (her Hollywood comeback after some years in Europe under a cloud for her 'immoral' behaviour), Yul Brynner, *Helen Hayes*, Martita Hunt, Akim Tamiroff, Felix Aylmer, Ivan Desny
'Little weight but considerable and urbane charm.'—*John Cutts*

AA: Ingrid Bergman
AAN: Alfred Newman

'Last year's number one best seller. This year's (we hope) number one motion picture!'
Anatomy of a Murder
US 1959   161m   bw
Cinemascope
Columbia / Carlyle / Otto Preminger

A small-town lawyer successfully defends an army officer accused of murdering a bartender who had assaulted his wife.

Overlong and over-faithful version of a highly detailed courtroom bestseller. The plot is necessarily equivocal, the characterizations overblown, but the trial commands some interest, and the use of 'daring' words in evidence caused controversy at the time.

w Wendell Mayes, *novel* Robert Traver *d* Otto Preminger *ph* Sam Leavitt *m* Duke Ellington *pd* Boris Leven

James Stewart, Ben Gazzara, Lee Remick, *Eve Arden*, Arthur O'Connell, *George C. Scott* (his first notable role, as the prosecutor), Kathryn Grant, Orson Bean, Murray Hamilton

† The trial judge was played by Joseph N. Welch, a real-life judge who had gained fame in 1954 by representing the army against Senator McCarthy.

AAN: best picture; Wendell Mayes; Sam Leavitt; James Stewart; Arthur O'Connell; George C. Scott

Anchors Aweigh
US 1945 139m Technicolor
MGM (Joe Pasternak)

Two sailors on leave in Los Angeles get involved with a small boy who wants to join the navy.

Rather droopy musical most notable as a forerunner of *On The Town*, though on much more conventional lines. Amiable performances, and a brilliant dance with a cartoon mouse, save the day.

w Isobel Lennart *d* George Sidney *ph* Robert Planck, Charles Boyle *principal songs* Jule Styne *ly* Sammy Cahn *m* George Stoll *pd* Cedric Gibbons

Frank Sinatra, Gene Kelly, Kathryn Grayson, Jose Iturbi, Sharon McManus, Carlos Ramirez, Dean Stockwell, Pamela Britton.

Songs include 'We Hate to Leave'; 'What Makes the Sun Set?'; 'The Charm of You'; 'I Begged Her'; 'I Fall in Love Too Easily'; 'The Worry Song'

AA: George Stoll

AAN: best picture; Robert Planck; Gene Kelly; song 'I Fall in Love Too Easily' (*m* Jule Styne, *ly* Sammy Cahn)

And Then There Were None
US 1945 97m bw
Popular Pictures / Harry M. Popkin (René Clair)
GB title: *Ten Little Niggers*

Ten people are invited to a house party on a lonely island, and murdered one by one.

A classic mystery novel is here adapted and directed with the utmost care to provide playful black comedy, stylish puzzlement, and some splendid acting cameos.

w Dudley Nichols, *novel* Agatha Christie (aka Ten Little Niggers) *d* René Clair *ph* Lucien Andriot *m* Mario Castelnuovo-Tedesco

Walter Huston, *Barry Fitzgerald*, *Louis Hayward*, June Duprez, *Ronald Young*, *Richard Haydn*, C. Aubrey Smith, Judith Anderson, Queenie Leonard, Mischa Auer

MISS BRENT: 'Very stupid to kill the only servant in the house. Now we don't even know where to find the marmalade.'

JUDGE QUINCANNON: 'Mr Owen could only come to the island in one way. It's perfectly clear. Mr Owen is one of us.'

ROGERS: 'Never in my life have I been accused of any crime, sir—and if that's what you think of me, I shan't serve any dinner.'

'Rich in the elements which have made mystery melodramas popular, yet not in the precise form of any previously made.'—*Hollywood Reporter*

'The efforts at sprightly, stylish comedy don't gain much momentum.'—*Pauline Kael, New Yorker, 70s*

Androcles and the Lion
US 1952 96m bw
RKO (Gabriel Pascal)

A slave takes a thorn from the paw of a lion which later, in the arena, refuses to eat him.

Shavian drollery, with interpolated discussions on faith, is scarcely ideal cinema material, but gusto in the performances keeps it going despite stolid direction.

w Chester Erskine, *play* Bernard Shaw d Chester Erskine ph Harry Stradling m Frederick Hollander ad Harry Horner

Alan Young, Jean Simmons, Robert Newton, Victor Mature, Maurice Evans (as Caesar), Reginald Gardiner, Elsa Lanchester, Alan Mowbray, Gene Lockhart

† Production had previously begun with Harpo Marx as Androcles and Rex Harrison as Caesar.

The Andromeda Strain
US 1970 131m
Technicolor Panavision
Universal / Robert Wise

Scientists work frantically to neutralize an infected village, knowing that the least infection will cause their laboratory to self-destruct.

Solemn and over-detailed but generally suspenseful thriller, with a sense of allegory about man's inhumanity to man.

w Nelson Gidding, *novel* Michael Crichton d Robert Wise ph Richard H. Kline m Gil Melle ad Boris Leven

Arthur Hill, David Wayne, James Olson, Kate Reid, Paula Kelly

Angel on My Shoulder
US 1946 101m bw
UA / Charles R. Rogers

The devil promises leniency to a dead gangster if he will return to earth and take over the body of a judge who is stamping out evil. Crude but lively fantasy on the tail-end of the *Here Comes Mr Jordan* cycle, and by the same author.

w Harry Segall, Roland Kibbee d Archie Mayo ph James Van Trees m Dmitri Tiomkin

Paul Muni, Claude Rains, Anne Baxter, Erskine Sanford, Hardie Albright

'The story is so imitative that it's hard to feel any more towards it than a mildly nostalgic regard.'–*Bosley Crowther*

Angels One Five
GB 1952 98m bw
Associated British (Templar)

A slice of life in an RAF fighter station during the Battle of Britain. Underplayed semi-documentary drama with stiff upper lips all round and the emphasis on characterization rather than action. A huge commercial success in Britain.

w Derek Twist d George More O'Ferrall ph Christopher Challis m John Wooldridge

Jack Hawkins, John Gregson, Michael Denison, Andrew Osborn, Cyril Raymond, Humphrey Lestocq, Dulcie Gray, Veronica Hurst

Angels with Dirty Faces
US 1938 97m bw
Warner (Sam Bischoff)

A Brooklyn gangster is admired by slum boys, but for their sake pretends to be a coward when he goes to the electric chair.

A shrewd, slick entertainment package and a seminal movie for all kinds of reasons. It combined gangster action with fashionable social conscience; it confirmed the Dead End Kids as stars; it provided archetypal roles for its three leading players and catapulted the female lead into stardom. It also showed the Warner style of film-making, all cheap sets and shadows, at its most effective.

w John Wexley, Warren Duff, *original story* Rowland Brown d Michael Curtiz ph Sol Polito m Max Steiner

James Cagney (gangster with redeeming features), *Pat O'Brien* (priest), *Humphrey Bogart* (gangster with no redeeming features), *The Dead End Kids*, *Ann Sheridan*, George Bancroft, Edward Pawley

'Should do fair business, but the picture itself is no bonfire.'—*Variety*

'A rousing, bloody, brutal melodrama.'—*New York Mirror*

AAN: Rowland Brown; Michael Curtiz; James Cagney

The Angry Silence

GB 1960 94m bw
British Lion / Beaver (Richard Attenborough, Bryan Forbes)

A worker who refuses to join an unofficial strike is 'sent to Coventry' by his mates; the matter hits national headlines, and the communists use it to their own advantage.
Irresistibly reminding one of a po-faced *I'm All Right Jack*, this remains a fresh and urgent film which unfortunately lost excitement in its domestic scenes.

w Bryan Forbes, *story* Michael Craig, Richard Gregson *d* Guy Green *ph* Arthur Ibbetson *m* Malcolm Arnold

Richard Attenborough, Michael Craig, Pier Angeli, Bernard Lee, Alfred Burke, Laurence Naismith, Geoffrey Keen

'Vastly entertaining as well as thought-provoking. Matter and manner are for once wholly in harmony.'—*Daily Mail*

AAN: Bryan Forbes

Animal Crackers

US 1930 98m bw
Paramount

Thieves covet a valuable oil painting unveiled at a swank party. An excuse for the Marx Brothers, and a lively one in patches, though sedate and stage bound in treatment. The boys are all in top form, and many of the dialogue exchanges are classics.

w Morrie Ryskind, from musical play by himself and *George F. Kaufman d* Victor Heerman *ph* George Folsey *m / ly* Bert Kalmar, Harry Ruby

Groucho, Chico, Harpo, Zeppo, *Margaret Dumont*, Lillian Roth,

Louis Sorin, Robert Greig, Hal Thompson

GROUCHO: 'You're the most beautiful woman I've ever seen, which doesn't say much for you.'

GROUCHO: 'One morning I shot an elephant in my pajamas. How he got into my pajamas I'll never know.'

GUESTS: 'Hooray for Captain Spaulding, the African explorer!'

GROUCHO: 'Did someone call me schnorrer?'

GUESTS: 'Hooray, hooray, hooray!'

ZEPPO: 'He went into the jungle, where all the monkeys *throw* nuts.'

GROUCHO: 'If I stay here, I'll *go* nuts.'

GUESTS: 'Hooray, hooray, hooray!
     He put all his reliance
     In courage and defiance
     And risked his life for
     science.'

GROUCHO: 'Hey, hey!'

MRS RITTENHOUSE: 'He is the only white man who covered every acre . . .'

GROUCHO: 'I think I'll try and make her . . .'

GUESTS: 'Hooray, hooray, hooray!'

'A hit on the screen before it opened, and in the money plenty.'—*Variety*

Animal Farm

GB 1955 75m Technicolor
Louis De Rochemont / Halas and Batchelor

Oppressed by the cruelty and inefficiency of their master, the animals take over a farm but find fresh tyrants among themselves. George Orwell's political fable—'all animals are equal but some animals are more equal than others'—is faithfully followed in this ambitious but rather disappointingly flat cartoon version.

w,p,d John Halas and Joy Batchelor *m* Matyas Seiber *voices* Maurice Denham

'A melodramatic fantasy that is mordant, tender and quixotic, shot with ironic humour.'—*New York Times*

Anna and the King of Siam
US 1946 128m bw
TCF (Louis D. Lighton)

In 1862 an English governess arrives in Bangkok to teach the 67 children of the king.

Unusual and lavish drama, tastefully handled and generally absorbing despite miscasting and several slow passages.

w Talbot Jennings, Sally Benson, *book* Margaret Landon *d* John Cromwell *ph Arthur Miller* *m* Bernard Herrmann *ad Lyle Wheeler, William Darling*

Irene Dunne, Rex Harrison, Linda Darnell, Gale Sondergaard, Lee J. Cobb, Mikhail Rasumny

'A film that never touches the imagination, a film that leaves the mind uninformed and the memory unburdened.'—*Richard Winnington*

'It's pitifully unauthentic, and not a very good movie either, but the story itself holds considerable interest.'—*Pauline Kael 70s*

AA: Arthur Miller
AAN: Talbot Jennings, Sally Benson; Bernard Herrmann; Gale Sondergaard

'Garbo talks!'
Anna Christie
US 1930 86m bw
MGM

A waterfront prostitute falls in love with a young seaman.

Primitive sound version of an earthy theatrical warhorse: it has a niche in history as the film in which Garbo first talked.

w Frances Marion, *play* Eugene O'Neill *d* Clarence Brown *ph* William Daniels

Greta Garbo, Charles Bickford, *Marie Dressler*, James T. Mack, Lee Phelps

'Great artistically and tremendous commercially . . . in all respects a wow picture.'—*Variety*

'A very talkie, uncinematic affair, more old-fashioned than the silent movies. If it were not so well acted it would be pretty tiresome.'—*National Board of Review*

AAN: Clarence Brown; William Daniels; Greta Garbo

Anna Karenina
US 1935 95m bw
MGM (David O. Selznick)

The wife of a Russian aristocrat falls for a dashing cavalry officer.

Well-staged but finally exasperating romantic tragedy, sparked by good performances and production.

w Clemence Dane, Salka Viertel, *novel* Leo Tolstoy *d Clarence Brown ph William Daniels* *m* Herbert Stothart

Greta Garbo (Anna), Fredric March (Vronsky), *Basil Rathbone* (Karenin), Freddie Bartholomew (Sergei), Maureen O'Sullivan (Kitty), May Robson (Countess), Reginald Owen (Silva), Reginald Denny (Yashvin)

'Cinch b.o. anywhere. In the foreign markets it should come close to establishing modern-day highs.'—*Variety*

'A dignified and effective drama which becomes significant because of that tragic, lonely and glamorous blend which is the Garbo personality.'—*André Sennwald*

'It reaches no great heights of tragedy or drama but rather moves forward relentlessly and a little coldly.'—*The Times*

† Previously filmed as a 1928 silent called *Love*, with Garbo and John Gilbert.

AAN: William Daniels

Anne of the Thousand Days
GB 1969 146m
Technicolor Panavision
Universal / Hal B. Wallis

Henry VIII divorces his wife to marry Anne Boleyn, but soon finds evidence of adultery.

A somewhat unlikely view of history, rather boringly presented on a woman's magazine level, but with occasional good moments from a cast of British notables.

w John Hale, Bridget Boland, *play* Maxwell Anderson *d* Charles

Jarrott *ph* Arthur Ibbetson *pd* Maurice Carter *m* Georges Delerue

Richard Burton, *Geneviève Bujold*, *John Colicos* (as Cromwell), Irene Papas, Anthony Quayle, Michael Hordern, Katharine Blake, Peter Jeffrey, William Squire, Esmond Knight, Nora Swinburne.

'The costumes, beautiful in themselves, have that unconvincing air of having come straight off the rack at Nathan's.'—*Brenda Davies*

'A decent dullness is, alas, the keynote.'—*Michael Billington, Illustrated London News*

'The quintessential work of art for people who haven't the foggiest notion of what art is.'—*John Simon*

'Intelligent from line to line, but the emotions supplied seem hypocritical, and the conception lacks authority . . . Burton's performance is colourless. It's as though he *remembered* how to act but couldn't work up much enthusiasm or involvement.'—*Pauline Kael*

AAN: best picture; John Hale, Bridget Boland; Arthur Ibbetson; Georges Delerue; Richard Burton; Geneviève Bujold; Anthony Quayle.

Annie Get Your Gun

US 1950 107m Technicolor MGM (Arthur Freed)

A young female hillbilly joins Frank Butler's sharpshooting act, and is sophisticated by her love for him. Gaudy, stagey, generally uninspired screen version of the famous musical show based remotely on a historical character of post-wild-west days. There is a lack of dancing, the direction is stodgy, and in general flair the production falls disappointingly below MGM's usual standard.

w Sidney Sheldon, *musical play* Herbert and Dorothy Fields *d* George Sidney *ph* Charles Rosher *m/ly* Irving Berlin *md* Adolph Deutsch, Roger Edens *ch* Robert Alton *ad* Cedric Gibbons, Paul Grosse

Betty Hutton, *Howard Keel*, Edward Arnold, J. Carrol Naish, Louis Calhern.

Songs include 'Colonel Buffalo Bill'; 'Doing What Comes Naturally'; 'The Girl That I Marry'; 'You Can't Get a Man with a Gun'; 'There's No Business Like Show Business'; 'My Defenses Are Down'; 'I'm an Indian Too'; 'I Got the Sun in the Morning'; 'Anything You Can Do'; 'They Say It's Wonderful'.

† The real Annie Oakley was born Phoebe Ann Oakley Mozie in 1860, and died in 1926. The role was to have been played by Judy Garland, who was fired after displays of temperament; also considered were Doris Day, Judy Canova and Betty Garrett.

†† Louis Calhern replaced Frank Morgan, who died during production

AA: music direction AAN: Charles Rosher

Annie Hall

US 1977 93m De Luxe UA/Jack Rollins-Charles H. Joffe (Fred T. Gallo)

Sub-title: *A Nervous Romance*

Against the neuroses of New York and Los Angeles, a Jewish comedian has an affair with a midwestern girl. Semi-serious collage of jokes and bits of technique, some of the former very funny and some of the latter very successful. For no very good reason it hit the box office spot and turned its creator, of whom it is very typical, from a minority performer to a superstar.

w Woody Allen, Marshall Brickman *d* Woody Allen *ph* Gordon Willis *m* various

Woody Allen, Diane Keaton, Tony Roberts, Carol Kane, Paul Simon, Shelly Duvall

ALLEN: 'Hey, don't knock masturbation. It's sex with someone I love.'

'The film's priceless vignettes about the difficulties in chitchatting with strangers, the awkward moments in family visits, and the frequent breakdowns in communication and failures in intimacy, its reminiscences about the palpable horrors of growing up in Brooklyn, and its comic encounters with lobsters in the kitchen or spiders in the bathroom, all seem like snapshots from Allen and Keaton's own romance.'—*Les Keyser, Hollywood in the Seventies*

† The narrative supposedly mirrors the real-life affair of the stars, who separated before the film came out. (Diane Keaton's family name is Hall.)

AA: best picture; script; direction; Diane Keaton
AAN: Woody Allen (as actor)

Anthony Adverse

US 1936 141m bw
Warner (Henry Blanke)
Adventures of an ambitious young man in early 19th-century America. A rousing spectacle of its day, from a bestselling novel, this award-winning movie quickly dated and now seems very thin and shadowy despite the interesting talents involved.

w Sheridan Gibney, *novel* Hervey Allen *d* Mervyn Le Roy *ph* Tony Gaudio *ad* Anton Grot *m* Erich Wolfgang Korngold

Fredric March, Olivia de Havilland, Gale Sondergaard, Edmund Gwenn, Claude Rains, Anita Louise, Louis Hayward, Steffi Duna, Donald Woods, Akim Tamiroff, Ralph Morgan, Henry O'Neill
'A bulky, rambling and indecisive photoplay which has not merely taken liberties with the letter of the original but with its spirit.'—*Frank S. Nugent, New York Times*
'In the dramatizing there is shown no relish or conviction, only a retentive memory for all the old clothes of show business.'—*Otis Ferguson*
'A lavish gold-leaf from Hervey Allen's book, an earnest cinema endeavour, taxing alike its studio's purse and artistry.'—*Douglas Gilbert, New York World Telegraph*

'The show is fairly glutted with plot and counter-plot and is apt to make one feel that one is witnessing a serial run off continuously at a single performance.'–*Howard Barnes, New York Herald Tribune*
'It goes on too long, otherwise it might have been the funniest film since *The Crusades*.'—*Graham Greene*

AA: Tony Gaudio; Erich Wolfgang Korngold; Gale Sondergaard
AAN: best picture; Anton Grot

'Movie-wise, there has never been anything like it—laugh-wise, love-wise, or otherwise-wise!'

The Apartment

US 1960 125m bw
Panavision
UA/Mirisch (Billy Wilder)
A lonely, ambitious clerk rents out his apartment to philandering executives and finds that one of them is after his own girl.
Overlong and patchy but agreeably mordant and cynical comedy with a sparkling view of city office life and some deftly handled individual sequences.

w Billy Wilder, I. A. L. Diamond *d* Billy Wilder *ph* Joseph La Shelle *m* Adolph Deutsch *ad* Alexander Trauner

Jack Lemmon (C. C. Baxter), Shirley Maclaine (Miss Kubelik), Fred MacMurray (Jeff D. Sheldrake), Ray Walston (Joe Dobisch), Jack Kruschen (Dr Dreyfuss), Joan Shawlee (Sylvia), Edie Adams (Miss Olsen), David Lewis (Al Kirkeby)

Baxter's opening narration: 'On November 1st, 1959, the population of New York City was 8,042,753. If you laid all these people end to end, figuring an average height of five feet six and a half inches, they would reach from Times Square to the outskirts of Karachi, Pakistan. I know facts like this because I work for an insurance company— Consolidated Life of New York. We are one of the top five companies in the country. Last year we wrote nine point three billion dollars worth of policies. Our home office has 31,259 employees, which is more than the entire population of Natchez, Mississippi, or Gallup, New Mexico. I work on the 19th floor—Ordinary Policy department—Premium Accounting division—Section W—desk number 861.'

BAXTER: 'Miss Kubelik, one doesn't get to be a second administrative assistant around here unless he's a pretty good judge of character, and as far as I'm concerned you're tops. I mean, decency-wise and otherwise-wise.'

BAXTER: 'You know, I used to live like Robinson Crusoe—shipwrecked among eight million people. Then one day I saw a footprint in the sand and there you were. It's a wonderful thing, dinner for two.'

MISS KUBELIK: 'Shut up and deal.' (*Last line of film*)

'Without either style or taste, shifting gears between pathos and slapstick without any transition.'—*Dwight MacDonald*

'Billy Wilder directed this acrid story as if it were a comedy, which is a cheat, considering that it involves pimping and a suicide attempt and many shades of craven ethics.'—*New Yorker, 1980*

AA: best picture; Billy Wilder, I. A. L. Diamond (as writers); Billy Wilder (as director)
AAN: Joseph La Shelle; Jack Lemmon; Shirley Maclaine; Jack Kruschen

Apocalypse Now
🎞 US 1979 153m
Technicolor Technovision
Omni Zoetrope (Francis Coppola)
A Vietnam captain is instructed to eliminate a colonel who has retired to the hills and is fighting his own war.
Pretentious war movie, made even more hollow-sounding by the incomprehensible performance of Brando as the mad martinet. Some vivid scenes along the way, and some interesting parallels with Conrad's

Heart of Darkness, but these hardly atone for the director's delusion that prodigal expenditure of time and money will result in great art. (The movie took so long to complete that it was dubbed *Apocalypse Later*.)

w John Milius, Francis Coppola
d Francis Coppola ph Vittorio Storaro m Carmine Coppola, Francis Coppola pd Dean Tavoularis

Martin Sheen, Robert Duvall, Frederic Forrest, Marlon Brando, Sam Bottoms, Dennis Hopper
'The characters are living through Vietnam as pulp adventure fantasy, as movie, as stoned humour.'—*New Yorker*

† Coppola admitted the following at the Cannes Film Festival: 'It's more of an experience than a movie. At the beginning there's a story. Along the river the story becomes less important and the experience more important.'

'Is Kitty a mother?'
Applause
🎭 US 1929 78m bw
Paramount (Jesse L. Lasky, Walter Wanger)
A vaudeville star gradually loses the love of her daughter.
Absorbing treatment of a hasbeen tearjerking theme, full of cinematic touches and with unusual use of New York locations.

w Garrett Fort, *novel* Beth Brown
d Rouben Mamoulian ph George Folsey

Helen Morgan, Joan Peers, Henry Wadsworth, Fuller Mellish Jnr
'An oasis of filmic sophistication in a desert of stage-bound early talkies.'—*William Everson, 1966*

'A cohesive, well integrated series of pictures. Its intensity, its sharp projection of tragedy, emerge from the eye of the camera; an omniscient, omnipresent eye that slides easily over the links of the story and emphasizes only the true and the relevant.'—*Thornton Delehanty, The Arts*

Arabesque

US 1966   118m
Technicolor Panavision
Universal (Stanley Donen)

An Oxford professor is asked by
Middle Eastern oil magnates to
decipher a hieroglyphic, and finds
afterwards that he is marked for
assassination.

The ultimate in sixties spy
kaleidoscopes, in which the working
out of the plot matters much less
than the stars, the jokes and the
lavish backgrounds. Fast moving,
amusing and utterly forgettable.

w Julian Mitchell, Stanley Price,
Pierre Marton, *novel* The Cipher by
Gordon Votler d Stanley Donen
ph Christopher Challis ad Reece
Pemberton m Henry Mancini

Gregory Peck, Sophia Loren, *Alan
Badel*, Kieron Moore, Carl Duering

'Nothing could look more "with
it", or somehow matter less.'—*MFB*

'A strikingly visual chase and
intrigue yarn.'—*Robert Windeler*

'All rather too flashy for
comfort.'—*Sight and Sound*

† Pierre Marton was a pen name for
Peter Stone.

'Here's the gay, glorious story of a
war correspondent and a war
ace . . . a romance that could
happen only in 1940!'

Arise My Love

US 1940   113m   bw
Paramount (Arthur Hornblow
Jnr)

American reporters in Europe and in
love survive the Spanish Civil War, a
wrathful editor in Paris and the
sinking of the *Athenia*.

Unique sophisticated entertainment
gleaned from the century's grimmest
headlines, ending with a plea against
American isolationism. A significant
and stylish comedy melodrama.

w *Charles Brackett*, Billy Wilder
d Mitchell Leisen ph Charles Lang
m Victor Young

Claudette Colbert, *Ray Milland*,
Walter Abel (who as the harassed
editor inaugurated his celebrated
line 'I'm not happy. I'm not happy at

all . . .'), Dennis O'Keefe, George
Zucco, Dick Purcell

'Against the background of
European fisticuffs, Paramount
brings forth a film of absorbing
romantic interest, proving that love
will find a way through the hazards
of air raids, torpedo attacks and
enemy invasions.'—*Variety*

† Joel McCrea was originally cast for
the Milland role.

AA: original story (Benjamin
Glazer, John S. Toldy)

AAN: Charles Lang; Victor Young

'It's a wonderful world, if you'll
only take the time to go around
it!'

Around the World in Eighty Days

US 1956   178m
Technicolor   Todd-AO
UA/Michael Todd

A Victorian gentleman and his valet
win a bet that they can go round the
world in eighty days.

Amiable large-scale pageant
resolving itself into a number of
sketches, which could have been
much sharper, separated by wide
screen spectacle. What was
breathtaking at the time seems
generally slow and blunted in
retrospect, but the fascination of
recognizing 44 cameo stars remains.
The film is less an exercise in
traditional skills than a tribute to its
producer's energy.

w James Poe, John Farrow, S. J.
Perelman, *novel* Jules Verne
d Michael Anderson, Kevin
McClory ph Lionel Lindon
m Victor Young titles Saul Bass

David Niven, Cantinflas, Robert
Newton, Shirley Maclaine, Charles
Boyer, Joe E. Brown, Martine
Carol, John Carradine, Charles
Coburn, *Ronald Colman*, Melville
Cooper, *Noel Coward*, Finlay
Currie, Reginald Denny, Andy
Devine, Marlene Dietrich, Luis
Dominguin, Fernandel, *John
Gielgud*, Hermione Gingold, Jose
Greco, Cedric Hardwicke, Trevor
Howard, Glynis Johns, *Buster
Keaton*, Evelyn Keyes, Beatrice

Lillie, Peter Lorre, Edmund Lowe, A. E. Matthews, Mike Mazurki, Tim McCoy, Victor McLaglen, John Mills, Alan Mowbray, Robert Morley, Jack Oakie, George Raft, Gilbert Roland, Cesar Romero, Frank Sinatra, *Red Skelton*, Ronald Squire, Basil Sidney, *Harcourt Williams*, Ed Murrow

'Michael Todd's "show", shorn of the ballyhoo and to critics not mollified by parties and sweetmeats, is a film like any other, only twice as long as most . . . the shots of trains and boats seem endless.'—*David Robinson*

AA: best picture; James Poe, John Farrow, S. J. Perelman; Lionel Lindon; Victor Young
AAN: Michael Anderson

The Arrangement
US 1969   127m
Technicolor Panavision
Warner/Athena (Elia Kazan)

A wealthy advertising man fails in a suicide attempt and spends his convalescence reflecting on his unsatisfactory emotional life.
A lush, all-American melodrama, rich in technique but peopled by characters who have nothing to say; the film makes no discernible point except as a well-acted tirade against the compromises of modern urban living.

wd Elia Kazan, from his own novel *ph* Robert Surtees *m* David Amram *pd* Malcolm C. Bert

Kirk Douglas, Faye Dunaway, Deborah Kerr, Richard Boone, Hume Cronyn.

'The sort of collage that won't fit together, no matter where you stand.'—*PS*

'As dead as a flower arrangement in an undertaker's parlour . . . all possible cinematic cleverness—usually yesterday's—are dragged out in an endless parade, to illustrate a senseless and banal story that reels from platitude to platitude.'—*John Simon*

Arsenic and Old Lace
US 1942 (released 1944)
118m   bw
Warner (Frank Capra)

Two dear, well-meaning old ladies invite lonely old men to their Brooklyn home, poison them with elderberry wine, and have their mad brother, who believes the corpses are yellow fever victims, bury them in the cellar. A homicidal nephew then turns up with bodies of his own.
A model for stage play adaptations, this famous black farce provided a frenzy of hilarious activity, and its flippant attitude to death was better received in wartime than would have been the case earlier or later. The director coaxes some perfect if overstated performances from his star cast, and added his own flair for perpetuating a hubbub.

w Julius J. and Philip G. Epstein, from the play by Joseph Kesselring with help from Howard Lindsay and Russell Crouse *d* Frank Capra *ph* Sol Polito *m* Max Steiner

Cary Grant (Mortimer Brewster), *Josephine Hull* (Abby Brewster), *Jean Adair* (Martha Brewster), Priscilla Lane (Elaine Harper), Raymond Massey (Jonathan Brewster), *John Alexander* (Teddy Brewster), Peter Lorre (Dr Einstein), James Gleason (Lt Rooney), Jack Carson (Officer O'Hara), Edward Everett Horton (Mr Witherspoon), Grant Mitchell (Reverend Harper)

MORTIMER: 'Insanity runs in my family. It practically gallops.'

MARTHA: 'One of our gentlemen found time to say "How delicious!" before he died . . .'

'I race cars, I play tennis, I fondle women, but I have weekends off and I am my own boss!'
Arthur
US 1981   97m   Technicolor
Warner/Orion (Robert Greenhut)

A rich New York layabout is forced to moderate his lifestyle in order to qualify for his inheritance.

An unattractive excuse for the star to do his drunk act. In effect his thunder was stolen by Gielgud as the valet who is not above a few choice four-letter words; but over the whole enterprise hung a pall of desperation. It is a sign of its times that it made a lot of money.

wd Steve Gordon ph Fred Schuler
m Burt Bacharach pd Stephen Hendrikson

Dudley Moore, John Gielgud, Liza Minnelli, Geraldine Fitzgerald, Jill Eikenberry, Stephen Elliott

'It comes as no surprise to find the funniest sequences packed into the first half-hour.'—Martyn Auty, MFB

'Gielgud may be the most poised and confident funnyman you'll ever see.'—New Yorker

'Arthur may be the surprise hit of 1981, but to me he's a pain in the neck.'—Margaret Hinxman, Daily Mail

AA: John Gielgud (supporting actor)
AAN: screenplay; Dudley Moore

Ashes and Diamonds
Poland 1958   104m   bw
Film Polski
original title: Popiol y Diament

A Polish partisan is confused by the apparent need to continue killing after the war is over. A chilling account of the intellectual contradictions to which war leads, and a moving and sensitive film in its own right.

wd Andrzej Wajda, novel Jerzy Andrzejewski ph Jerzy Wojcik
Zbigniew Cybulski, Ewa Krzyzanowska, Adam Pawlikowski

Ask a Policeman
GB 1938   82m   bw
Gainsborough (Edward Black)
In a small coastal village, incompetent policemen accidentally expose smugglers who are scaring the locals with a headless horseman legend.
One of the best comedies of an incomparable team, with smart

dialogue, good situations and a measure of suspense.

w Marriott Edgar, Val Guest, J. O. C. Orton d Marcel Varnel
ph Derek Williams

Will Hay, Moore Marriott, Graham Moffatt, Glennis Lorimer, Peter Gawthorne, Herbert Lomas, Charles Oliver

'A good laugh getter and safe second feature on any programme.'—Variety

The Asphalt Jungle
US 1950   112m   bw
MGM (Arthur Hornblow Jnr)
An elderly crook comes out of prison and assembles a gang for one last robbery.
Probably the very first film to show a 'caper' from the criminals' viewpoint (a genre which has since been done to death several times over), this is a clever character study rather than a thriller, extremely well executed and indeed generally irreproachable yet somehow not a film likely to appear on many top ten lists; perhaps the writer-director stands too far back from everybody, or perhaps he just needed Humphrey Bogart.

w Ben Maddow, John Huston, novel W. R. Burnett d John Huston ph Harold Rosson
m Miklos Rozsa

Sterling Hayden (Dix Handley), Louis Calhern (Alonzo D. Emmerich), Sam Jaffe (Doc Erwin Riedenschneider), Jean Hagen (Doll Conovan), James Whitmore (Gus Minissi), John McIntire (Police Commissioner Hardy), Marc Lawrence (Cobby), Marilyn Monroe (Angela Phinlay), Barry Kelley (Lt Ditrich)

RIEDENSCHNEIDER: 'Crime is a left-handed form of human endeavour.'

'Where this film excels is in the fluency of its narration, the sharpness of its observation of character and the excitement of its human groupings.'—Dilys Powell

'That Asphalt Pavement thing is full of nasty, ugly people doing nasty things. I wouldn't walk across the room to see a thing like that.'—*Louis B. Mayer* (who was head of the studio which made it)

† Apart from imitations, the film has been directly remade as *The Badlanders*, *Cairo* and *A Cool Breeze*.

AAN: Ben Maddow, John Huston (writers); John Huston (as director); Harold Rosson; Sam Jaffe

Assault on Precinct 13
US 1976   91m Metrocolor   Panavision
CKK (Joseph Kaufman)
Gang members on a vendetta attack a police station.
Violent but basically efficient and old-fashioned programmer which shows that not all the expertise of the forties in this then-familiar field has been lost.

wd/m John Carpenter *ph* Douglas Knapp

Austin Stoker, Darwin Joston, Laurie Zimmer, Martin West

'One of the most effective exploitation movies of the last ten years . . . Carpenter scrupulously avoids any overt socio-political pretensions, playing instead for laughs and suspense in perfectly balanced proportions.'—*Time Out*

At the Circus
US 1939   87m   bw
MGM (Mervyn Le Roy)
aka: *The Marx Brothers at the Circus*
A shyster lawyer and two incompetents save a circus from bankruptcy.
This film began the decline of the Marx Brothers; in it nothing is ill done but nothing is very fresh either apart from the rousing finale which shows just what professionalism meant in the old Hollywood. Highlights include Groucho singing about Lydia the tattooed lady, his seduction of Mrs Dukesbury, and the big society party.

w Irving Brecher *d* Edward Buzzell
ph Leonard M. Smith *m/ly* Harold

Arlen, E. Y. Harburg *m* Franz Waxman

Groucho, Chico, Harpo, Margaret Dumont, Florence Rice, Kenny Baker, Eve Arden, Nat Pendleton, Fritz Feld
Songs include 'Lydia', 'Two Blind Loves', 'Step up and Take a Bow'.

GROUCHO: 'I don't know what I'm doing here when I could be at home in bed with a hot toddy. That's a drink.'

'Rousing physical comedy and staccato gag dialogue . . . geared for fine b.o. and general audience appeal.'—*Variety*

'We must regretfully accept the fact that, thanks to the Metro millions, the Marx Brothers are finally imprisoned in the Hollywood world.'—*Graham Greene*

The Atonement of Gosta Berling
Sweden 1924   200m
approx (16 fps) bw silent
Svensk Filmindustri
original title: *Gosta Berlings Saga*
A pastor is defrocked for drinking, becomes a tutor, and has various love affairs.
Lumpy but often engrossing picturization of a famous novel, veering mostly into melodrama but finding its way to a happy ending.

w Mauritz Stiller, Ragnar Hylten-Cavallius, *novel* Selma Lagerlof *d* Mauritz Stiller *ph* Julius Jaenzon

Lars Hanson, Gerda Lundeqvist, Ellen Cederström, Mona Martensson, Jenny Hasselqvist, Otto Elg-Lundberg, Greta Garbo.

'Stiller was a master at unifying visual beauty and emotional effect; the complicated narrative is blurry, but there are sequences as lovely and expressive as any on film.'—*New Yorker, 1980*

† It was her small role in this film which led directly to Greta Garbo's American stardom.

Autumn Sonata

Sweden / West Germany / GB
1978   97m colour
Personafilm / ITC (Ingmar
Bergman)

When her lover dies, a concert
pianist visits the daughter she has
not seen for many years.

Typically Bergmanesque,
understated conversation piece with
no obvious happy ending for
anybody.

wd Ingmar Berman *ph* Sven
Nykvist *m* Chopin, Handel, Bach

Ingrid Bergman, Liv Ullmann,
Halvar Bjork

'Professional gloom.'—*Time*

'It fills these middle-class rooms
with the deep music of conflict and
reconciliation that must strike home
to any audiences in any culture or
society.'—*Jack Kroll, Newsweek*

AAN: script; Ingrid Bergman

L'Avventura

Italy / France 1960   145m
bw
Cino del Duca / PCE / Lyre (Amato
Pennasilico)

Young people on a yachting holiday
go ashore on a volcanic island. One
of them disappears; this affects the
life of the others, but she is never
found.

Aimless, overlong parable with lots
of vague significance; rather less
entertaining than the later *Picnic at
Hanging Rock*, it made its director a
hero of the highbrows.

w Michelangelo Antonioni, Elio
Bartolini, Tonino Guerra
d Michelangelo Antonioni ph Aldo
Scavarda *m* Giovanni Fusco

Monica Vitti, Lea Massari, Gabriele
Ferzetti, Dominique Blanchar,
James Addams, Lelio Luttazi

'A film of complete maturity,
sincerity and creative
intuition.'—*Peter John Dyer, MFB*

The Awful Truth

US 1937   90m   bw
Columbia (Leo McCarey)

A divorcing couple endure various
adventures which lead to
reconciliation.

Classic crazy comedy of the thirties,
marked by a mixture of
sophistication and farce and an
irreverent approach to plot.

wd Leo McCarey, play Arthur
Richman *ph* Joseph Walker
md Morris Stoloff

*Irene Dunne, Cary Grant, Ralph
Bellamy*, Alexander D'Arcy, Cecil
Cunningham, Molly Lamont, Esther
Dale, Joyce Compton

IRENE DUNNE: 'You've come back
and caught me in the truth, and
there's nothing less logical than the
truth.'

CARY GRANT: 'In the spring a young
man's fancy lightly turns to what he's
been thinking about all winter.'

'Fast, smart comedy that will
please everywhere and do strong
general biz.'—*Variety*

'The funniest picture of the
season.'—*Otis Ferguson*

'Among the ingredients the raising
powder is the important thing and
out of the oven comes a frothy bit of
stuff that leaves no taste in the
mouth and is easy on the
stomach.'—*Marion Fraser,World
Film News*

'Delightfully effective
entertainment.'—*Time Out, 1985*

† Remade 1953 as *Let's Do It Again*.

AA: Leo McCarey (as director)
AAN: best picture; script; Irene
Dunne; Ralph Bellamy

B

Babes in Arms
US 1939 96m bw
MGM (Arthur Freed)
The teenage sons and daughters of
retired vaudevillians put on a big
show. Simple-minded backstage
musical which marked the first
enormously successful teaming of its
two young stars.

w Jack McGowan, Kay Van Riper,
from the Broadway show by Rodgers
and Hart *d/ch* Busby Berkeley
ph Ray June *songs* Rodgers and
Hart and others *m* Roger Edens,
George Stoll

Judy Garland, *Mickey Rooney*,
Charles Winninger, Douglas
Macphail, Leni Lynn, June Preisser

Songs include 'Where or When';
'The Lady Is a Tramp'; 'Babes in
Arms'; 'I Cried for You'; 'God's
Country'; 'Good Morning'; 'You
Are my Lucky Star'
'A topflight filmusical
entertainment. It will click mightily
in the key deluxers, and roll up hefty
profits for exhibs in the subsequent
runs and smaller
situations.'—*Variety*

AAN: Roger Edens, George Stoll;
Mickey Rooney

Babes in Toyland
US 1934 77m bw
Hal Roach
aka: *Wooden Soldiers: March of
the Wooden Soldiers: Laurel and
Hardy in Toyland*
Santa Claus's incompetent assistants
accidentally make some giant
wooden soldiers, which come in
useful when a villain tries to take
over Toyland.
Comedy operetta in which the stars
have pleasant but not outstanding
material; the style and decor are
however sufficient to preserve the
film as an eccentric minor classic.

w Nick Grinde, Frank Butler,
original book/ly Glen MacDonough
d Gus Meins, Charles Rogers
ph Art Lloyd, Francis Corby
m Victor Herbert

Stan Laurel, Oliver Hardy,
Charlotte Henry, Henry Brandon,
Felix Knight, Florence Roberts,
Johnny Downs, Marie Wilson
'It is amusing enough to entertain
older persons who remember when
they were young.'—*Variety*

Babes on Broadway
US 1941 118m bw
MGM (Arthur Freed)
A sequel to *Babes In Arms*, in which
the kids get to Broadway and share
some disillusion. Inflated and less
effective than the original, but with
good numbers.

w Fred Finkelhoffe, Elaine Ryan
d/ch Busby Berkeley *ph* Lester
White *songs* Burton Lane and
Ralph Freed

Judy Garland, Mickey Rooney,
Virginia Weidler, Ray Macdonald,
Richard Quine, Fay Bainter
'Enough energy and enthusiasm to
make older people wish they were
young, and young people glad that
they are.'—*Monthly Film Bulletin*

† The Virginia Weidler role was
originally intended for Shirley
Temple, but TCF wouldn't loan her.
AAN: song 'How About You' (*m*
Burton Lane, *ly* Ralph Freed)

'19 years old and married . . . but
not really!'
Baby Doll
US 1956 116m bw
Warner/Elia Kazan
In the deep South, the child wife of a
broken-down cotton miller is
seduced by her husband's
revenge-seeking rival. An incisive,
cleverly-worked-out study of moral

and physical decay; whether it was worth doing is another question, for it's a film difficult to remember with affection.

wd Elia Kazan, *play* Tennessee Williams *ph* Boris Kaufman *m* Kenyon Hopkins *ad* Richard Sylbert

Karl Malden, Eli Wallach, Carroll Baker, Mildred Dunnock, Lonny Chapman

'Just possibly the dirtiest American-made motion picture that has ever been legally exhibited, with Priapean detail that might well have embarrassed Boccaccio.'—*Time*

'He views southern pretensions with sardonic humor, and builds an essentially minor story into a magnificently humorous study of the grotesque and the decadent.'—*Hollis Alpert*

'A droll and engrossing carnal comedy.'—*Pauline Kael, 1968*

'A film in which everything works: narration, casting, tempo, rhythm, dramatic tension.'—*Basil Wright, 1972*

† Another publicity tag read: 'Condemned by Cardinal Spellman!'

AAN: script; Boris Kaufman; Carroll Baker; Mildred Dunnock

'She climbed the ladder of success—wrong by wrong!'
Baby Face
US 1933   70m   bw
Warner (Ray Griffith)
Amorous adventures of an ambitious working girl.
Sharp melodrama very typical of its time, with fast pace and good performances.

w Gene Markey, Kathryn Scola, Mark Canfield (Darryl F. Zanuck) *d* Alfred E. Green *ph* James Van Trees

Barbara Stanwyck, George Brent, Donald Cook, Margaret Lindsay, Arthur Hohl, John Wayne, Henry Kolker, Douglass Dumbrille

'Blue and nothing else. It possesses no merit for general or popular appeal, is liable to offend

the family trade and can't count on any juve attendance.

'. . . This is reputed to be a remake on the first print, which was considered too hot. Anything hotter than this for public showing would call for an asbestos audience blanket.'—*Variety*

The Bachelor and the Bobbysoxer
US 1947   95m   bw
RKO (Dore Schary)
GB title: *Bachelor Knight*
A lady judge allows her impressionable young sister to get over her crush on an errant playboy by forcing them together.
Simple but unexpectedly delightful vehicle for top comedy talents, entirely pleasant and with several memorable moments.

w Sidney Sheldon *d* Irving Reis *ph* Robert de Grasse, Nicholas Musuraca *m* Leigh Harline

Cary Grant, Myrna Loy, Shirley Temple, *Ray Collins*, Rudy Vallee, *Harry Davenport*, Johnny Sands, Don Beddoe

'Sure-fire stuff guaranteed to do no conceivable harm . . . the audience laughed so loud I missed some of the lines.'—*Shirley O'Hara, New Republic*

AA: Sidney Sheldon

'Just ten tiny fingers and ten tiny toes . . . Trouble? Scandal? Gosh, nobody knows!'
Bachelor Mother
US 1939   82m   bw
RKO (B. G. De Sylva)
A shopgirl finds an abandoned baby and is thought to be its mother; the department store owner's son is then thought to be the father.
Blithely-scripted comedy which stands the test of time and provided several excellent roles.

w Norman Krasna *d* Garson Kanin *ph* Robert de Grasse *m* Roy Webb

Ginger Rogers, David Niven, Charles Coburn, Frank Albertson, E. E. Clive, Ernest Truex

'Carries some rather spicy lines aimed at the adult trade, but broad enough in implication to catch the fancy of general audiences . . . a surprise laugh hit that will do biz generally and overcome hot weather box office lethargy.'—*Variety*

'An excellent comedy, beautifully done.'—*Richard Mallett, Punch*

'This is the way farce should be handled, with just enough conviction to season its extravagances.'—*New York Times*

† Remade as *Bundle of Joy*.

AAN: Felix Jackson (for original story)

The Bachelor Party
US 1957   93m   bw
UA/Norma (Harold Hecht)
New York book-keepers throw a wedding eve party for one of their fellows, but drink only brings to the fore their own private despairs. Though the last half-hour lets it down, most of this is a brilliantly observed social study of New York life at its less attractive, and the acting matches the incisiveness of the script.

w Paddy Chayevsky, from his TV play *d Delbert Mann   ph Joseph La Shelle   m Alex North*
Don Murray, E. G. Marshall, Jack Warden, Philip Abbott, Larry Blyden, Patricia Smith, Carolyn Jones

AAN: Carolyn Jones

Back Street
US 1932   93m   bw
Universal (Carl Laemmle Jnr)
A married man has a sweet-tempered mistress who effaces herself for twenty years.
Popular version of a sudsy bestselling novel.

w Gladys Lehman, Lynn Starling, novel Fannie Hurst   d John M. Stahl   ph Karl Freund
Irene Dunne, John Boles, June Clyde, George Meeker, Zasu Pitts, Doris Lloyd

'Swell romance, a little tear-jerking, and a woman's picture—which means a money production.'—*Variety*

Back to the Future
US 1985   116m
Technicolor
Universal/Steven Spielberg (Bob Gale, Neil Canton)
With the help of a not-so-crazy scientist, a teenager goes back thirty years to make a man out of his dimwit father.
Lighthearted Twilight Zone fantasy which certainly pleased the international multitudes.

w Robert Zemeckis, Bob Gale   d Robert Zemeckis   ph Dean Cundey   m Alan Silvestri   pd Lawrence G. Paull   ed Arthur Schmidt, Harry Keramidas
Michael J. Fox, Christopher Lloyd, Crispin Glover, Lea Thompson, Claudia Wells

'Accelerates with wit, ideas, and infectious, wide-eyed wonder.'—*Variety*

AAN: original screenplay

'The story of a blonde who wanted to go places, and a brute who got her there—the hard way!'

The Bad and the Beautiful
US 1952   118m   bw
MGM (John Houseman)
A director, a star, a screenwriter and an executive recall their experiences at the hands of a go-getting Hollywood producer. Very much a Hollywood 'in' picture, this rather obvious flashback melodrama offers good acting chances and a couple of intriguing situations; never quite finding the style it seeks, it offers good bitchy entertainment along the way, and there are references back to it in *Two Weeks in Another Town*, made ten years later.

w Charles Schnee   d Vincente Minnelli   ph Robert Surtees   m David Raksin   ad Cedric Gibbons, Edward Carfagno
Kirk Douglas (Jonathan Shields), Lana Turner (Georgia Lorrison), Walter Pidgeon (Harry Pebbel), Dick Powell (James Lee Bartlow), Barry Sullivan (Fred Amiel), Gloria Grahame (Rosemary Bartlow),

Gilbert Roland (Victor Ribera), Leo G. Carroll (Henry Whitfield), Vanessa Brown (Kay Amiel), Paul Stewart (Syd Murphy)

'For all the cleverness of the apparatus, it lacks a central point of focus.'—*Penelope Houston*

'Clever, sharply observed little scenes reflect the Hollywood surface: the egotistic babble at a party, the affectations of European directors, the sneak preview, the trying on of suits for catmen in a B picture.'—*MFB*

'It is a crowded and colourful picture, but it is choppy, episodic and vague. There does not emerge a clear picture of exactly how movies are made.'—*Bosley Crowther*

AA: Charles Schnee; Robert Surtees; art direction; Gloria Grahame
AAN: Kirk Douglas

Bad Day at Black Rock

US 1954   81m
Eastmancolor Cinemascope
MGM (Dore Schary)

A one-armed stranger gets off the train at a sleepy desert hamlet and is greeted with hostility by the townsfolk, who have something to hide.

Seminal suspense thriller—the guilty town motif became a cliché—with a terse script and professional presentation. The moments of violence, long awaited, are electrifying.

w Millard Kaufman, story Bad Time at Hondo by Howard Briskin
d John Sturges *ph* William C. Mellor *m* André Previn

Spencer Tracy, Robert Ryan, Dean Jagger, Walter Brennan, Ernest Borgnine, Lee Marvin, Anne Francis, John Ericson, Russell Collins.

'A very superior example of motion picture craftsmanship.'—*Pauline Kael*

'The movie takes place within twenty-four hours. It has a dramatic unity, an economy of word and action, that is admirable in an age of flabby Hollywood epics that maunder on forever.'—*William K. Zinsser, New York Herald Tribune*

'The skill of some sequences, the mood and symbiosis between man and nature makes this film sometimes superior to *High Noon*.'—*G. N. Fenin*

AAN: Millard Kaufman; John Sturges; Spencer Tracy

Badlands

US 1973   94m
Consolidated Color
(Columbia)
Pressman / Williams / Badlands
(Terrence Malick)

A teenage girl and a young garbage collector wander across America leaving a trail of murder behind them.

A violent folk tale for moderns; very well put together if somewhat lacking in point, it quickly became a cult film.

wd Terrence Malick *ph* Brian Probyn, Tak Fujimoto, Stevan Larner *m* George Tipton

Martin Sheen, Sissy Spacek, Warren Oates, Ramon Bieri

'One of the finest literate examples of narrated cinema since the early days of Welles and Polonsky.'—*Jonathan Rosenbaum*

'So preconceived that there's nothing left to respond to.'—*New Yorker*

Ball of Fire

US 1942   111m   bw
Samuel Goldwyn
working title: *The Professor and the Burlesque Queen*

Seven professors compiling a dictionary give shelter to a stripteaser on the run from gangsters.

Rather overstretched but fitfully amusing romp inspired by *Snow White and the Seven Dwarfs*.

w Charles Brackett, Billy Wilder
d Howard Hawks *ph* Gregg Toland
m Alfred Newman

Barbara Stanwyck, Gary Cooper,

Oscar Homolka, Henry Travers, S. Z. Sakall, Tully Marshall, Leonid Kinskey, Richard Haydn, Aubrey Mather, Allen Jenkins, Dana Andrews, Dan Duryea

'It's played as if it were terribly bright, but it's rather shrill and tiresome.'—*New Yorker, 1982*

† Ginger Rogers was first choice for the Stanwyck role.

AAN: original story (Theodore Monroe, Billy Wilder); Alfred Newman; Barbara Stanwyck

Bambi

US 1942 72m Technicolor Walt Disney

The story of a forest deer, from the book by Felix Salten.

Anthropomorphic cartoon feature, one of Disney's most memorable and brilliant achievements, with a great comic character in Thumper the rabbit and a climactic forest fire sequence which is genuinely thrilling. A triumph of the animator's art.

supervisor David Hand *m* Frank Churchill, Edward Plumb

'The ultimate stag movie.'—*anon.*

AA: song 'Love Is a Song' (*m* Frank Churchill, *ly* Larry Morey)
AAN: Frank Churchill, Edward Plumb

The Band Wagon

US 1953 112m Technicolor
MGM (Arthur Freed)

A has-been Hollywood dancer joins forces with a temperamental stage producer to put on a Broadway musical.

Simple but sophisticated musical with the bare minimum of plot, told mostly in jokes, and the maximum of music and song. Numbers include those listed below, as well as a spoof Mickey Spillane ballet finale. Level of technical accomplishment very high.

w Adolph Green, Betty Comden d Vincente Minnelli ph Harry Jackson *songs* Howard Dietz, Arthur Schwarz *m* Adolph Deutsch

ad Cedric Gibbons, Preston Ames

Fred Astaire, Jack Buchanan, Oscar Levant, Cyd Charisse, Nanette Fabray

'The best musical of the month, the year, the decade, or for all I know of all time.'—*Archer Winsten*

† The Jack Buchanan character, Jeffrey Cordova, was first offered to Clifton Webb. It was loosely based on Jose Ferrer, who in the early fifties produced four Broadway shows all running at the same time, and acted in a fifth.

†† Songs include: 'A Shine on Your Shoes', 'By Myself', 'That's Entertainment', 'Dancing in the Dark', 'Triplets', 'New Sun in the Sky', 'I Guess I'll Have to Change My Plan', 'Louisiana Hayride', 'I Love Louisa', 'Girl Hunt' ballet.

AAN: Adolph Green, Betty Comden; Adolph Deutsch

The Bank Dick

US 1940 73m bw Universal

GB title: *The Bank Detective*

In Lompoc, California, a ne'er-do-well accidentally stops a hold-up, is made a bank detective, acquires deeds to a worthless mine and interferes in the production of a film. Imperfect, but probably the best Fields vehicle there is: the jokes sometimes end in mid-air, but there are delicious moments and very little padding. The character names are sometimes funnier than the script: they include Egbert Sousè (accent grave over the 'e'), J. Pinkerton Snoopington, Ogg Oggilbie and Filthy McNasty.

w Mahatma Kane Jeeves (W. C. Fields) *d* Eddie Cline *ph* Milton Krasner *md* Charles Previn

W. C. Fields, Franklin Pangborn, Shemp Howard, Jack Norton, Grady Sutton, Cora Witherspoon

'One of the great classics of American comedy.'—*Robert Lewis Taylor*

'When the man is funny he is terrific . . . but the story is makeshift, the other characters are stock types, the only pace discernible is the distance between drinks or the rhythm of the fleeting seconds it takes Fields to size up trouble coming and duck the hell out.'—*Otis Ferguson*

'Individualistic display of broad comedy . . . adequate program supporter.'—*Variety*

† Fields's writing nom-de-plume was allegedly borrowed from noble characters in old English plays he squirmed through as a youth. They kept saying: 'M'hat, m'cane, Jeeves.'

'The world's most beautiful animal!'
The Barefoot Contessa
US 1954   128m
Technicolor
UA / Figaro (Forrest E. Johnston)
A glamorous barefoot dancer in a Spanish cabaret is turned into a Hollywood star, but her sexual frustrations lead to a tragic end.
A fascinating farrago of addled philosophy and lame wisecracks, very typical of a writer-director here not at his best, decorated by a splendid gallery of actors and some attractive settings.

wd Joseph L. Mankiewicz *ph* Jack Cardiff *m* Mario Nascimbene

Humphrey Bogart (Harry Dawes), Ava Gardner (Maria Vargas), Edmond O'Brien (Oscar Muldoon), Marius Goring (Alberto Bravano), Valentina Cortesa (Eleonora Torlato-Favrini), Rossano Brazzi (Vincenzo Torlato-Favrini), Elizabeth Sellars (Jerry), Warren Stevens (Kirk Edwards), Franco Interlenghi (Pedro), Mari Aldon (Myrna)

HARRY: 'Life, every now and then, behaves as though it had seen too many bad movies, when everything fits too well—the beginning, the middle, the end—from fade-in to fade-out.'

'This example of the Higher Lunacy must vie with *Johnny Guitar* for the silliest film of the year.'—*Gavin Lambert*

'A trash masterpiece: a Cinderella story in which the prince turns out to be impotent.'—*Pauline Kael, 1968*

AA: Edmond O'Brien
AAN: Joseph L. Mankiewicz (as writer)

'Break the rules! Make love! Fall over laughing!'
Barefoot in the Park
US 1967   109m
Technicolor
Paramount / Hal B. Wallis
A pair of New York newlyweds rent a cold water flat at the top of a liftless building, and manage to marry the bride's mother to an eccentric neighbour.
Breezy but overlong adaptation of a stage play which succeeded through audience response to its one-liners, which on the screen sometimes fall flat. The people are nice, though.

w Neil Simon, from his play *d* Gene Saks *ph* Joseph La Shelle *m* Neal Hefti

Robert Redford (Paul Bratter), Jane Fonda (Corie Bratter), *Mildred Natwick* (Ethel Banks), *Charles Boyer* (Victor Velasco), Herb Edelman (Harry Pepper), Mabel Albertson (Aunt Harriet), Fritz Feld (restaurant owner)

ETHEL: 'Make him feel important. If you do that, you'll have a happy and wonderful marriage—like two out of every ten couples.'

ETHEL: 'I feel like we've died and gone to heaven—only we had to climb up.'

AAN: Mildred Natwick

'When poets love, heaven and earth fall back to watch!'
The Barretts of Wimpole Street
US 1934   109m   bw
MGM (Irving Thalberg)
TV title: *Forbidden Alliance*
Invalid Elizabeth Barrett plans to marry poet Robert Browning, against her tyrannical father's wishes.
Claustrophobic but well-acted adaptation of a stage play which has

become more forceful than history. Stilted now, but still better than the remake.

w Ernst Vajda, Claudine West, Donald Ogden Stewart, *play* Rudolf Besier *d* Sidney Franklin *ph* William Daniels *m* Herbert Stothart

Norma Shearer (Elizabeth Barrett), Fredric March (Robert Browning), *Charles Laughton* (Edward Moulton-Barrett), Maureen O'Sullivan (Henrietta), Katherine Alexander (Arabel), Una O'Connor (Wilson), Ralph Forbes (Captain Surtees-Cook), Ian Wolfe (Harry Bevan)

'Box office for all its celluloid lethargy . . . truly an actor's picture, with long speeches and verbose philosophical observations.'—*Variety*

AAN: best picture; Norma Shearer

Barry Lyndon
GB 1975   187m
Eastmancolor
Warner / Hawk / Peregrine (Stanley Kubrick)
Adventures of an 18th-century Irish gentleman of fortune.
A curiously cold-hearted enterprise, like an art gallery in which the backgrounds are sketched in loving detail and the human figures totally neglected; there is much to enjoy, but script and acting are variable to say the least, and the point of it all is obscure, as it certainly does not tell a rattling good story.

wd Stanley Kubrick, *novel* W. M. Thackeray *ph* John Alcott *md* Leonard Rosenman *pd* Ken Adam

Ryan O'Neal, Marisa Berenson, Patrick Magee, Hardy Kruger, Steven Berkoff, Gay Hamilton, Marie Kean, Murray Melvin, André Morell, Leonard Rossiter, Philip Stone, *narrator* Michael Hordern

'The motion picture equivalent of one of these very large, very expensive, very elegant and very dull books that exist solely to be seen on coffee tables.'—*Charles Champlin*

'Watching the movie is like looking at illustrations for a work that has not been supplied.'—*John Simon*

'All art and no matter: a series of still pictures which will please the retina while denying our hunger for drama. And far from re-creating another century, it more accurately embalms it.'—*Michael Billington, Illustrated London News*

AA: John Alcott; Leonard Rosenman
AAN: best picture; Stanley Kubrick (as writer); Stanley Kubrick (as director)

Battle of Britain
GB 1969   131m
Technicolor Panavision
UA / Spitfire (Harry Saltzman, Ben Fisz)
Summer 1940: England defends itself against aerial onslaught.
Plodding attempt to cover an historic event from too many angles and with too many guest stars, all indistinguishable from each other when masked in the cockpit during the repetitive and interminable dogfight sequences. On the ground, things are even duller.

w James Kennaway, Wilfrid Greatorex *d* Guy Hamilton *ph* Frederick A. Young *m* William Walton, Ron Goodwin

Laurence Olivier (as Dowding), Robert Shaw, Michael Caine, Christopher Plummer, Kenneth More, Susannah York, Trevor Howard, Ralph Richardson, Patrick Wymark, Curt Jurgens, Michael Redgrave, Nigel Patrick, Robert Flemyng, Edward Fox

Battle of the Bulge
US 1965   167m
Technicolor Ultra Panavision
Warner / United States Pictures (Sidney Harmon, Milton Sperling, Philip Yordan)
In December 1944, the Allies take longer than expected to win a land battle in the Ardennes because of a

crack Nazi Panzer commander. Bloody and unbowed war spectacle, quite literate and handsome but deafeningly noisy and with emphasis on strategy rather than character.

w Philip Yordan, Milton Sperling, John Melson *d* Ken Annakin *ph* Jack Hildyard *m* Benjamin Frankel

Henry Fonda, Robert Shaw, Robert Ryan, Telly Savalas, Dana Andrews, George Montgomery, Ty Hardin, Pier Angeli, Barbara Werle, Charles Bronson, James MacArthur, Werner Peters

The Battleship Potemkin

USSR 1925   75m approx (16 fps)   silent; sound version 65m
Goskino
original title: *Bronenosets Potemkin*

A partly fictitious account of the mutiny at Odessa, an episode in the 1905 revolution. (The film was made as part of the 20th anniversary celebrations.)
A textbook cinema classic, and masterpiece of creative editing, especially in the famous Odessa Steps sequence in which innocent civilians are mown down in the bloodshed; the happenings of a minute are drawn into five by frenzied cross-cutting. The film contains 1,300 separate shots, and was judged the best film ever made in 1948 and 1958 by a panel of international judges.

wd Sergei Eisenstein *ph* Edouard Tissé, V. Popov

A. Antonov, Grigori Alexandrov, Vladimir Barsky, Levshin

'Adventure at its boldest! Bogart at his best!'
Beat the Devil
GB 1953   100m   bw
Romulus / Santana (Jack Clayton)

In a small Mediterranean port, and subsequently on a boat bound for the African coast, oddly assorted travellers plan to acquire land known to contain uranium deposits. Unsatisfactory, over-talkative and inconsequential burlesque of the director's own *The Maltese Falcon* and *Across the Pacific*. Good fun was obviously had by the cast, but audiences were mostly baffled by the in-jokes, the extra-strange characters, and the lack of attention to pace, suspense and plot development.

w Truman Capote, John Huston, *novel* James Helvick *d* John Huston *ph* Oswald Morris *m* Franco Mannino

Humphrey Bogart (Billy Dannreuther), *Jennifer Jones* (Gwendolen Chelm), Gina Lollobrigida (Maria Dannreuther), *Edward Underdown* (Harry Chelm), Peter Lorre (O'Hara), Robert Morley (Petersen), *Ivor Barnard* (Major Ross), Bernard Lee (Inspector), Marco Tulli (Ravello)

GWENDOLEN: 'Harry, we must beware of these men. They're desperate characters. Not one of them looked at my legs.'

DANNREUTHER: 'Trouble with England, it's all pomp and no circumstance. You're very wise to get out of it, escape while you can.'

O'HARA: 'Time! Time! What is time? The Swiss manufacture it. The French hoard it, Italians want it. Americans say it is money. Hindus say it does not exist. Do you know what I say? I say time is a crook.'

'A potential treat emerged as a wet firecracker . . . the incidents remain on a naggingly arch and lagging verbal keel.'—*New York Times*

'Each of its cinematic clichés appears to be placed in the very faintest of mocking quotation marks.'—*Time*

'Only the phonies liked it. It's a mess!'—*Humphrey Bogart*

'The formula of *Beat the Devil* is that everyone is slightly absurd.'—*John Huston*

† James Helvick was the pseudonym of Claud Cockburn.

'Three against the world! Brothers and soldiers all!'

Beau Geste

US 1939   120m   bw
Paramount (William Wellman)

Three English brothers join the Foreign Legion, and die fighting the Arabs.

Spirited tale of derring-do, with the famous flashback opening of the desert fort defended by corpses. Style and acting generally satisfactory.

w Robert Carson   *d* William Wellman   *ph* Theodor Sparkuhl, Archie Stout   *m* Alfred Newman   *ad* Hans Dreier, Robert Odell

Gary Cooper, Ray Milland, Robert Preston, *Brian Donlevy*, J. Carrol Naish, Susan Hayward, Heather Thatcher, James Stephenson, Donald O'Connor, G. P. Huntley Jnr, Albert Dekker, Broderick Crawford

FOREWORD: 'The love of a man for a woman waxes and wanes like the moon, but the love of brother for brother is steadfast as the stars and endures like the word of the prophet . . .' *Arabian proverb*

MARKOFF: 'Keep shooting, you scum! You'll get a chance yet to die with your boots on!'

'Its melodrama is sometimes grim but never harrowing, its pace is close to hectic and its suspense is constant.'—*Herbert Cohn, Brooklyn Daily Eagle*

'A morbid picture, but I doubt whether any morality council will take action, the whole story being so wrapped up in the school colours—in comradeship and loyalty and breeding, and the pure girl left behind; morbid because the brutality has no relation whatever to the real world; it is uncriticized day-dreaming.'—*Graham Greene*

'A handsome treatment of a well-loved adventure tale.'—*New York Daily Mirror*

'Will do nominal biz, but lacks punch for smash proportions.'—*Variety*

† Shot in Buttercup Valley, west of Yuma.

†† The nasty sergeant, originally Lejeune, became Markoff to avoid offending the French.

AAN: Brian Donlevy; Hans Dreier, Robert Odell

La Beauté du Diable

Italy / France 1949   96m   bw
AYJM

The Faust story with the protagonists agreeing to change places.

Dazzling plot twists and cinematic virtuosity make this a richly enjoyable fantasy, though perhaps not among Clair's greatest works.

w René Clair, Armand Salacrou   *d* René Clair   *ph* Michel Kelber   *m* Roman Vlad   *ad* Léon Barsacq

Michel Simon, *Gérard Philipe*, Raymond Cordy, Nicole Besnard, Gaston Modot, Paolo Stoppa

'The screen explodes with rage and passion and greatness!'

Becket

GB 1964   149m
Technicolor Panavision (Paramount) Hal B. Wallis

Henry II leans on his boisterous Saxon friend Thomas à Becket, but when the latter is made first chancellor and then archbishop a rift between them widens and ends in Becket's assassination by Henry's over-eager knights. Jean Anouilh's bitter stage comedy is filmed literally and soberly as a rather anaemic epic, so that the point is lost and the edge blunted. The paucity of physical action causes good scenes to alternate with long stretches of tedium.

w Edward Anhalt   *d* Peter Glenville   *ph* Geoffrey Unsworth   *m* Laurence Rosenthal

Richard Burton, Peter O'Toole, Donald Wolfit, *John Gielgud*, Martita Hunt, Pamela Brown, Sian Phillips, Paolo Stoppa

'Handsome, respectable and boring.'—*John Simon*

AA: Edward Anhalt
AAN: best picture; Peter Glenville;

Geoffrey Unsworth; Laurence
Rosenthal; Richard Burton; Peter
O'Toole; John Gielgud

Becky Sharp

US 1935 83m Technicolor
(RKO) Kenneth MacGowan

An ambitious girl makes her way
into Regency society.

Chiefly notable as the first feature in
three-colour Technicolor, this rather
theatrical piece has its civilized
enjoyments and the director made a
few predictable cinematic
experiments; the overall effect,
however, is patchy.

w Francis Edward Faragoh, *play*
Landon Mitchell, *novel* Vanity Fair
by W. M. Thackeray *d Rouben
Mamoulian ph Ray Rennahan
m Roy Webb pd Robert Edmond
Jones*

Miriam Hopkins, *Cedric Hardwicke*,
Frances Dee, Billie Burke, Alison
Skipworth, Nigel Bruce, Alan
Mowbray, Colin Tapley, G. P.
Huntley Jnr

'Beautiful cinematographically but
weak on story. No cinch, and should
be sold on colour angle.'—*Variety*

'As pleasing to the eye as a fresh
fruit sundae, but not much
more.'—*Otis Ferguson*

'If colour is to be of permanent
importance a way must be found to
use it realistically, not only as a
beautiful decoration. It must be
made to contribute to our sense of
truth. The machine gun, the cheap
striped tie, the battered Buick and
the shabby bar will need a subtler
colour sense than the Duchess of
Richmond's ball, the girls of Miss
Pinkerton's Academy, the Marquess
of Steyne's dinner for two. Can
Technicolor reproduce with the
necessary accuracy the suit that has
been worn too long, the oily
hat?'—*Graham Greene*

AAN: Miriam Hopkins

The Bedford Incident

GB 1965 102m bw
Columbia/Bedford
Productions (James B. Harris)

A ruthlessly efficient US destroyer

captain in the Arctic chases a
Russian submarine and accidentally
fires an atomic weapon.

Gripping mixture of themes from *Dr
Strangelove* and *The Caine Mutiny*,
very tense and forceful, with
excellent acting.

w *James Poe, novel* Mark
Rascovitch *d James B. Harris
ph* Gilbert Taylor *m* Gerald
Schurrmann

Richard Widmark, Sidney Poitier,
James MacArthur, Eric Portman,
Wally Cox, Martin Balsam, Phil
Brown, Michael Kane, Garry
Cockrell, Donald Sutherland

The Beggar's Opera

GB 1952 94m Technicolor
British Lion/Imperadio
(Herbert Wilcox, Laurence Olivier)

A highwayman in Newgate jail
devises an opera based on his own
exploits.

Exuberant potted version of the 1728
low opera, generally likeable but
lacking a strong coherent approach
and marred by violent colour and
raggedly theatrical presentation. It
nearly but not quite comes off.

w Dennis Cannan, Christopher Fry,
opera John Gay *d* Peter Brook
ph Guy Green *ad* George
Wakhevitch, William C. Andrews
musical arrangement and additions
Arthur Bliss

Laurence Olivier, Stanley Holloway,
Dorothy Tutin, Daphne Anderson,
Mary Clare, George Devine, Athene
Seyler, Hugh Griffith, Margot
Grahame, Sandra Dorne, Laurence
Naismith

'The failure is equalled only by the
ambition.'—*Gavin Lambert*

'Getting there is half the fun;
  being there is all of it!'
Being There

US 1979 130m Metrocolor
Lorimar/North Star/CIP
(Andrew Braunsberg)

An illiterate gardener is taken for a
homespun philosopher and becomes
a national celebrity. Overlong
serio-comic parable hinging on a
somewhat dubious star performance.
Chance made it a popular urban

success, but few who saw it were enthused.

w Jerzy Kosinski, from his novel d Hal Ashby ph Dianne Schroeder m John Mandel pd Michael Haller

Peter Sellers, Shirley Maclaine, *Melvyn Douglas*, Jack Warden, Richard Dysart, Richard Basehart

BFA: screenplay

Belle de Jour

France / Italy 1967   100m Eastmancolor

Paris Film / Five Film (Robert and Raymond Hakim)

A surgeon's wife finds herself drawn to afternoon work in a brothel. Fascinating Bunuel mixture of fact and fantasy, impeccably woven into a rich fabric.

w *Luis Bunuel, Jean-Claude Carrière* d *Luis Bunuel ph Sacha Vierny* m none

Catherine Deneuve, Jean Sorel, Michel Piccoli, Genevieve Page, Pierre Clémenti

Les Belles de Nuit

France / Italy 1952   89m   bw Franco London / Rizzoli

A discontented music teacher dreams of beautiful women through the ages.

Charming but very slight dream fantasy with many of the master's touches. (He claims to have intended a comic *Intolerance*.)

wd *René Clair ph Armand Thirard, Robert Juilliard, Louis Née* m *Georges Van Parys* ad Léon Barsacq

Gérard Philipe, Gina Lollobrigida, Martine Carol, Magali Vendeuil, Paolo Stoppa, Raymond Bussières, Raymond Cordy

'Your heart will be wearing a smile!'

The Bells of St Mary's

US 1945   126m   bw RKO / Rainbow (Leo McCarey)

At a big city Catholic school, Father O'Malley and Sister Benedict indulge in friendly rivalry, and succeed in extending the school through the gift of a building. Sentimental and very commercial sequel to *Going My Way*, with the stars at their peak and the handling as cosy and well-paced as might be expected.

w Dudley Nichols d Leo McCarey ph George Barnes m Robert Emmett Dolan

Bing Crosby, Ingrid Bergman, Henry Travers, William Gargan, Ruth Donnelly, Rhys Williams, Una O'Connor, Eva Novak

'The picture is full of shrewd and pleasant flashes. It is also fascinating to watch as a talented, desperate effort to repeat the unrepeatable. But on the whole it is an unhappy film.'—James Agee

AAN: best picture; Leo McCarey; Robert Emmett Dolan; Bing Crosby; Ingrid Bergman; song 'Aren't You Glad You're You' (m Jimmy Van Heusen, ly Johnny Burke)

'The great decade (1915–25) of the progress of motion picture art reaches its summit! A cast of 125,000!'

'The inspired love of the prince of Hur for the gentle lovely Esther!'

Ben Hur

US 1926   170m approx (16 fps)   bw   (colour sequence)   silent

MGM

In the time of Christ, a Jew suffers mightily under the Romans. The American silent screen's biggest epic; the sea battle and the chariot race are its most famous sequences.

w Bess Meredyth, Carey Wilson, novel Lew Wallace d Fred Niblo ph Karl Struss, Clyde de Vinna, and others ad Horace Jackson, Ferdinand Pinney Earle

Ramon Novarro, Francis X. Bushman, Carmel Myers, May McAvoy, Betty Bronson

'Masterpiece of study and patience, a photodrama filled with artistry.'—*New York Times*

† Previously filmed in 1907.

Ben Hur
US 1959   217m
Technicolor   Camera 65
MGM (Sam Zimbalist)
Solid, expensive, surprisingly
unimaginative remake; generally less
sprightly than the silent version.

w Karl Tunberg   d William Wyler,
Andrew Marton ph Robert L.
Surtees *m* Miklos Rozsa
 ad William A. Horning, Edward
Carfagno

Charlton Heston, Haya Harareet,
Jack Hawkins, Stephen Boyd, Hugh
Griffith, Martha Scott, Sam Jaffe,
Cathy O'Donnell, Finlay Currie,
Frank Thring, Terence Longdon,
André Morell, George Relph
    'Watching it is like waiting at a
railroad crossing while an
interminable freight train lumbers
by, sometimes stopping
altogether.'—*Dwight MacDonald*
    'A Griffith can make a hundred
into a crowd while a Wyler can
reduce a thousand to a confused
cocktail party.'—*Ibid.*
    'The most tasteful and visually
exciting film spectacle yet produced
by an American company.'—*Albert
Johnson, Film Quarterly*
    'Spectacular without being a
spectacle . . . not only is it not
simple-minded, it is downright
literate.'—*Saturday Review*
    'A major motion picture
phenomenon.'—*Films in Review*
† The production cost four million
dollars, twice the maximum at the
time. Rock Hudson, Marlon Brando
and Burt Lancaster were all sought
in vain for the lead before Heston
was selected.

†† This version was subtitled 'A Tale
of the Christ'.

AA: best picture; William Wyler;
Robert L. Surtees; Miklos Rozsa;
Charlton Heston; Hugh Griffith
AAN: Karl Tunberg

Bend of the River
US 1952   91m   Technicolor
U-I (Aaron Rosenberg)
GB title: *Where the River Bends*
1880 wagon trains arrive in Oregon,

and the pioneers have trouble with
the local bad man. Good standard
western with pace and period
feeling.

w Borden Chase, *novel* Bend of the
Snake by William Gulick
d Anthony Mann *ph* Irving
Glassberg *m* Hans Salter

James Stewart, Arthur Kennedy,
Rock Hudson, Julia Adams, Lori
Nelson, Jay C. Flippen, Henry
Morgan, Royal Dano, Stepin Fetchit

Berlin, Symphony of a Great City
Germany 1927   78m   bw
silent
Fox-Europa
original title: *Berlin, die
    Symphonie einer Grosstadt*
An impression of the life of a city
from dawn to midnight, expressed by
cinematic montages, angles,
sequences, etc, and set to music.
A leader in the field of
'impressionistic' documentaries
which are now so familiar (*Rien que
les Heures* did a similar job for Paris
at around the same time), this still
has moments of poetry which have
seldom been equalled.

w Walter Ruttman, Karl Freund,
Carl Mayer d Walter Ruttman
ph Reimar Kuntze, Robert Baberske,
Laszlo Schäffer m Edmund Meisel
ed Walter Ruttman

The Bespoke Overcoat
GB 1956   33m   bw
Remus (Jack Clayton)
A clerk in a clothing warehouse is
refused a coat and asks a tailor
friend to make him one. But he dies
of cold and his ghost persuades the
tailor to steal the coat he deserved.
The story seems stiff, but the
production has a rich Dickensian feel
and may be the best short drama
filmed in Britain.

w Wolf Mankowitz, *story* Gogol
d Jack Clayton ph Wolfgang
Suschitzky m Georges Auric

Alfie Bass, David Kossoff
    'A triumph of talent, small means
and originality.'—*New Statesman*

The Best Man

US 1964   104m   bw
UA/Stuart Millar, Lawrence Turman

Two contenders for a presidential nomination seek the support of the dying ex-president.

Brilliant political melodrama, ingeniously adapted on a low budget from an incisive play, with splendid dramatic scenes, memorable performances and good convention detail.

w Gore Vidal from his play *d Franklin Schaffner ph* Haskell Wexler *m* Mort Lindsey

Henry Fonda, Cliff Robertson, *Lee Tracy*, Margaret Leighton, Edie Adams, Kevin McCarthy, *Shelley Berman*, Ann Sothern, Gene Raymond, Mahalia Jackson

'A fine opportunity to watch pros at work in a hard-hitting and cogent drama that seems to become more topical and have more relevance with each showing.'—*Judith Crist*

'Some of the wittiest lines since *Strangelove* . . . the acting fairly crackled with authenticity.'—*Isabel Quigly*

AAN: Lee Tracy

'Three wonderful loves in the best picture of the year!'
The Best Years of Our Lives

US 1946   182m   bw
Samuel Goldwyn

Three men come home from war to a small middle-American community, and find it variously difficult to pick up where they left off.

The situations and even some of the characters now seem a little obvious, but this was a superb example of high-quality film-making in the forties, with smiles and tears cunningly spaced, and a film which said what was needed on a vital subject.

w Robert Sherwood, novel Glory for Me by Mackinlay Kantor *d William Wyler ph Gregg Toland m* Hugo Friedhofer

Fredric March, Myrna Loy, Teresa Wright, Dana Andrews, Virginia Mayo, Cathy O'Donnell, *Hoagy Carmichael, Harold Russell* (a handless veteran whose only film this was), Gladys George, Roman Bohnen, Ray Collins

'One of the best pictures of our lives!'—*Variety*

'The result is a work of provocative and moving insistence and beauty.'—*Howard Barnes*

'One of the very few American studio-made movies in years that seem to me profoundly pleasing, moving and encouraging.'—*James Agee*

† In 1977 came a TV remake *Returning Home* but it did not lead to the expected series.

AA: best picture; Robert Sherwood; William Wyler; Hugo Friedhofer; Fredric March; Harold Russell

La Bête Humaine

France 1938   99m   bw
Paris Films (Robert Hakim)
aka: *The Human Beast; Judas Was a Woman*

A psychopathic train driver falls for a married woman, plans with her to kill her husband, but finally strangles her instead.

Curious melodrama with strong visual sequences, flawed by its ambivalent attitude to its hero-villain.

wd Jean Renoir, novel Emile Zola *ph Curt Courant m Joseph Kosma*

Jean Gabin, Simone Simon, Julien Carette, Fernand Ledoux, Jean Renoir

'French production at its best.'—*Variety*

'Marvellous atmosphere and a fine cast, but the material turns oppressive.'—*New Yorker, 1978*

'What is most deft is the way Renoir works the depot and the man's job into every scene—conversations on platforms, in washrooms and canteens, views from the station master's window over the steaming metal waste; the short sharp lust worked out in a wooden platelayer's shed among shunted trucks under the steaming rain.'—*Graham Greene*

† Remade in Hollywood as *Human Desire*.

Beverly Hills Cop
☺ US 1984 105m Technicolor
Paramount/Don Simpson/Jerry Bruckheimer

A Detroit cop races to Los Angeles to track down the killers of his best friend.

Filled with foul language and frenetic action, this rough-edged action comedy became one of the top box office grossers of its year. So much for its year.

w Daniel Petrie Jnr *d* Martin Brest *ph* Bruce Surtees *m* Harold Faltermeyer *pd* Angelo Graham *ed* Billy Weber, Arthur O. Coburn

Eddie Murphy, Judge Reinhold, Lisa Eilbacher, John Ashton, Ronny Cox, Steven Berkoff

† The role was originally tailored for Sylvester Stallone.

AAN: original screenplay

The Bible
❀❀ US/Italy 1966 174m De
✗ Luxe Dimension 150 (70mm)
TCF/Dino de Laurentiis (Luigi Luraschi)

Through the Old Testament from Adam to Isaac.

A portentous creation with whispered commentary gives way to a dull misty Eden with decorous nudes, a sprightly Noah's Ark, a spectacular Babel, a brooding Sodom and a turgid Abraham. The pace is killingly slow and the script has little religious sense, but the pictures are often pretty.

w Christopher Fry and others *d* John Huston *ph* Giuseppe Rotunno *m* Toshiro Mayuzumi *ad* Mario Chiari

Michael Parks (Adam), Ulla Bergryd (Eve), Richard Harris (Cain), *John Huston* (Noah), Stephen Boyd (Nimrod), George C. Scott (Abraham), Ava Gardner (Sarah), Peter O'Toole (the three angels)

'An Old Testament spectacular like any other.'—*David Robinson*

'At a time when religion needs all the help it can get, John Huston may have set its cause back a couple of thousand years.'—*Rex Reed*

AAN: Toshiro Mayuzumi

Bicycle Thieves
❀❀ Italy 1948 90m bw
✗ PDS-ENIC (Umberto Scarparelli)

original title: *Ladri di Biciclette*

An Italian workman, long unemployed, is robbed of the bicycle he needs for his new job, and he and his small son search Rome for it.

The epitome of Italian neo-realism, the slight human drama is developed so that it has all the force of *King Lear*, and both the acting and the backgrounds are vividly compelling.

w Cesare Zavattini *d* Vittorio de Sica *ph* Carlo Montuori *m* Alessandro Cicognini

Lamberto Maggiorani, Enzo Staiola

'A film of rare humanity and sensibility.'—*Gavin Lambert*

'A memorable work of art with the true flavour of reality. To see it is an experience worth having.'—*Richard Mallett, Punch*

'My idea is to de-romanticize the cinema.'—*Vittorio de Sica*

AA: best foreign film; Cesare Zavattini

Big Business
☺ US 1929 20m silent

Stan and Ollie fail to sell a Christmas tree to a belligerent householder. Classic silent comedy consisting largely of a brilliant tit-for-tat routine of reciprocal destruction, to which scripting, acting and editing equally combine. Laurel and Hardy, James Finlayson. Written by Leo McCarey and H. M. Walker; directed by James W. Horne; edited by Richard Currier; for Hal Roach.

'How much love, sex, fun and
friendship can a person take?'
'In a cold world, you need your
friends to keep you warm!'

The Big Chill

US 1983 105m Metrocolor
Columbia / Carson
Productions (Michael Shamberg)

University contemporaries try to
comfort each other after the death of
a friend.

Wry satirical comedy which seems to
be nostalgic for the sixties, but is
funny anyway.

w Lawrence Kasdan, Barbara
Benedek d Lawrence Kasdan
ph John Bailey m various pd Ida
Random ed Carol Littleton

Tom Berenger, Glenn Close, Jeff
Goldblum, William Hurt, Kevin
Kline, Mary Kay Place, Meg Tilly,
JoBeth Williams, Don Galloway

'The final impression left is of a
collage of small relishable
moments.'—Kim Newman, MFB

'An entertainment in which
humour and sentiment are finely
balanced and profundities are
artfully skirted.'—Sight and Sound

AAN: best picture; Glenn Close;
screenplay

The Big Country

US 1958 165m
Technirama
UA / Anthony / Worldwide
(William Wyler, Gregory Peck)

The Terrills and the Hannesseys feud
over water rights, and peace is
brought about only with the deaths
of the family heads.

Big-scale western with a few
pretensions to say something about
the Cold War. All very fluent,
star-laden and easy to watch.

w James R. Webb, Sy Bartlett,
Robert Wilder, novel Donald
Hamilton d William Wyler
ph Franz Planer m Jerome Moross

Gregory Peck, Jean Simmons,
Charlton Heston, Carroll Baker,
Burl Ives, Charles Bickford, Alfonso
Bedoya, Chuck Connors

AA: Burl Ives
AAN: Jerome Moross

'All the action you can take . . . all
the adventure you can wish
for!'

A Big Hand for the Little Lady

US 1966 96m Technicolor
Warner / Eden (Fielder Cook)

GB title: Big Deal at Dodge City
(though the action clearly takes
place in Laredo)

Five rich poker players are outwitted
by a family of confidence tricksters.

Diverting but thinly stretched
acting-piece from a much shorter TV
original; still, suspense builds nicely
until the disappointingly handled
revelation.

w Sidney Carroll, from his own TV
play d Fielder Cook ph Lee
Garmes m David Raksin

Henry Fonda, Joanne Woodward,
Jason Robards, Paul Ford, Kevin
McCarthy, Charles Bickford, Robert
Middleton, Burgess Meredith, John
Qualen

The Big Heat

US 1953 90m bw
Columbia (Robert Arthur)

A police detective's wife is killed by
a bomb meant for himself; he goes
undercover to track down the
gangsters responsible.

Considered at the time to reach a
new low in violence (boiling coffee
in the face), this dour little thriller
also struck a new note of realism in
crime films and produced one of
Glenn Ford's most typical
performances.

w Sydney Boehm, novel William P.
McGivern d Fritz Lang ph Charles
Lang m Arthur Morton- md Mischa
Bakaleinikoff

Glenn Ford, Gloria Grahame,
Alexander Scourby, Jocelyn Brando,
Lee Marvin, Jeanette Nolan, Peter
Whitney

'The main impression is of
violence employed arbitrarily,
mechanically and in the long run
pointlessly.'—Penelope Houston

'A hard cop and a soft
dame!'—publicity

The Big House

US 1930   88m   bw
MGM

Tensions in prison lead to an attempted breakout and a massacre. Archetypal prison melodrama and a significant advance in form for early talkies.

w Frances Marion d George Hill
ph Harold Wenstrom

Chester Morris, Wallace Beery, Robert Montgomery, Lewis Stone, Leila Hyams, George F. Marion, J. C. Nugent, Karl Dane

'Not a two-dollar talker, but virile, realistic melodrama, a cinch for any week-stand and hold-overable generally.'—Variety

'We all gave our roles the best that was in us, and the virility and truthfulness of the picture were more satisfying than anything else I've done.'—Chester Morris, 1953

† The role played by Wallace Beery had been intended for Lon Chaney, who died during preparation

AA: Frances Marion
AAN: best picture; Wallace Beery

'The epic of the American
   doughboy!'

The Big Parade

US 1925   115m approx (24 fps)   bw   silent
MGM

A young American enlists in 1917, learns the realities of war, is wounded but survives. Enormously successful commercially, this 'anti-war' film survives best as a thrilling spectacle and a well-considered piece of film-making.

w Lawrence Stallings, Harry Behn
d King Vidor ph John Arnold
m William Axt, David Mendoza

John Gilbert, Renee Adoree, Hobart Bosworth, Karl Dane, George K. Arthur

'The human comedy emerges from a terrifying tragedy.'—King Vidor

'A cinegraphically visualized result of a cinegraphically imagined thing . . . something conceived in terms of

a medium and expressed by that medium as only that medium could properly express it.'—National Board of Review

'The extraordinary impression of the rush of lorries, the queer terror of the woods . . . it was amazing how much fear could be felt in the mere continuous pace of movement.'—Bryher, Close Up

† The biggest grossing silent film of all.

The Big Sleep

US 1946   114m   bw
Warner (Howard Hawks)

Private eye Philip Marlowe is hired to protect General Sternwood's wild young daughter from her own indiscretions, and finds several murders later that he has fallen in love with her elder sister. Inextricably complicated, moody thriller from a novel whose author claimed that even he did not know 'who done it'. The film is nevertheless vastly enjoyable along the way for its slangy script, star performances and outbursts of violence, suspense and sheer fun.

w William Faulkner, Leigh Brackett, Jules Furthman, novel Raymond Chandler d Howard Hawks ph Sid Hickox m Max Steiner

Humphrey Bogart (Philip Marlowe), Lauren Bacall (Vivian Sherwood Rutledge), John Ridgely (Eddie Mars), Martha Vickers (Carmen Sternwood), Dorothy Malone (Proprietress), Regis Toomey (Bernie Ohls), Charles Waldron (General Sternwood), Charles D. Brown (Norris), Elisha Cook Jr (Harry Jones), Louis Jean Heydt (Joe Brody), Bob Steele (Canino), Peggy Knudsen (Mona Mars), Sonia Darrin (Agnes)

MARLOWE: 'My, my, my. Such a lot of guns around town and so few brains.'

GENERAL: 'You may smoke, too, I can still enjoy the smell of it. Nice thing when a man has to indulge his vices by proxy.'

VIVIAN: 'So you're a private detective. I didn't know they existed, except in books—or else they were greasy little men snooping around hotel corridors. My, you're a mess, aren't you?'

MARLOWE: 'I don't mind if you don't like my manners. I don't like 'em myself. They're pretty bad. I grieve over 'em on long winter evenings.'

GENERAL: 'If I seem a bit sinister as a parent, Mr Marlowe, it's because my hold on life is too slight to include any Victorian hypocrisy. I need hardly add that any man who has lived as I have and indulges for the first time in parenthood at the age of 55 deserves all he gets.'

MARLOWE: 'Speaking of horses . . . you've got a touch of class, but I don't know how far you can go.'

VIVIAN: 'A lot depends on who's in the saddle. Go ahead Marlowe, I like the way you work. In case you don't know it, you're doing all right.'

'A sullen atmosphere of sex saturates the film, which is so fast and complicated you can hardly catch it.'—*Richard Winnington*

'A violent, smoky cocktail shaken together from most of the printable misdemeanours and some that aren't.'—*James Agee*

'Harder, faster, tougher, funnier and more laconic than any thriller since.'—*NFT, 1974*

'Wit, excitement and glamour in generous doses.'—*Francis Wyndham*

A Bill of Divorcement
🎭 US 1932 76m bw
RKO / David O. Selznick
A middle-aged man, released from a mental institution, comes home and meets his strong-willed daughter. Pattern play which became a celebrated star vehicle; now very dated but the performances survive.

w Howard Estabrook, Harry Wagstaff Gribble, *play* Clemence Dane *d* George Cukor *ph* Sid Hickox *m* Max Steiner, W. Franke Harling

John Barrymore, Katharine Hepburn (her debut), Billie Burke, David Manners, Paul Cavanagh, Henry Stephenson, Elizabeth Patterson

'A money picture for all classes of houses . . . the most potent tear jerker in many a moon.'—*Variety*

'A very good picture, tender, emotional and intensely gripping.'—*Picturegoer*

Billy Liar
👹 GB 1963 98m bw
Cinemascope
Vic Films (Joe Janni)
In a drab North Country town, an undertaker's clerk lives in a world of fantasy.
Flawed only by its unsuitable Cinemascope ratio, this is a brilliant urban comedy of its time, seminal in acting, theme, direction and permissiveness. From a novel and play no doubt inspired by Thurber's Walter Mitty, it was later turned into a TV series and a successful stage musical, making Billy a universal figure of the period.

w Keith Waterhouse, Willis Hall, from KW's novel and their play *d* John Schlesinger *ph* Denys Coop *m* Richard Rodney Bennett

Tom Courtenay, Julie Christie, Wilfred Pickles, Mona Washbourne, *Ethel Griffies*, Finlay Currie. Rodney Bewes, Leonard Rossiter

Birdman of Alcatraz
🎭 US 1961 148m bw
UA / Hecht–Lancaster (Stuart Millar, Guy Trosper)
An imprisoned murderer makes a name for himself as an ornithologist. Overlong and rather weary biopic of Robert Stroud, who spent nearly sixty years in prison and became a *cause célèbre*. One cannot deny many effective moments, notably of direction, but it's a long haul.

w Guy Trosper, *book* Thomas E. Gaddis *d* John Frankenheimer *ph* Burnett Guffey *m* Elmer Bernstein

Burt Lancaster, Karl Malden, Thelma Ritter, Edmond O'Brien,

Betty Field, Neville Brand, Hugh
Marlowe, Telly Savalas, James
Westerfield

AAN: Burnett Guffey; Burt
Lancaster; Thelma Ritter; Telly
Savalas

'Suspense and shock beyond
    anything you have ever seen or
    imagined!'
The Birds
   US 1963   119m
   Technicolor
Universal / Alfred Hitchcock
In a Californian coastal area, flocks
of birds unaccountably make deadly
attacks on human beings.
A curiously absorbing work which
begins as light comedy and ends as
apocalyptic allegory, this piece of
Hitchcockery has no visible point
except to tease the audience and
provide plenty of opportunity for
shock, offbeat humour and special
effects (which despite the
drumbeating are not quite as good as
might be expected). The actors are
pawns in the master's hand.

w Evan Hunter, story Daphne du
Maurier d Alfred Hitchcock
ph Robert Burks sound consultant
Bernard Herrmann sp Lawrence A.
Hampton

Rod Taylor, Tippi Hedren, Jessica
Tandy, Suzanne Pleshette, Ethel
Griffies
  'Enough to make you kick the
next pigeon you come
across.'—Judith Crist
  'The dialogue is stupid, the
characters insufficiently developed to
rank as clichés, the story
incohesive.'—Stanley Kauffmann
  'We must sit through half an hour
of pachydermous flirtation between
Rod and Tippi before the seagull
attacks, and another fifteen minutes
of tedium . . . before the birds
attack again. If one adds later
interrelations between mother, girl
friend and a particularly repulsive
child actress, about two-thirds of the
film is devoted to extraneous
matters. Poe would have been
appalled.'—Dwight MacDonald

'The dawn of a new art!'
The Birth of a Nation
   US 1915   approx 185m (16
   fps) bw silent
Epoch (D. W. Griffith, Harry E.
Aitken)
Northern and southern families are
caught up in the Civil War.
The cinema's first and still most
famous epic, many sequences of
which retain their mastery despite
negro villains, Ku Klux Klan heroes,
and white actors in blackface.
Originally shown as The Clansman; a
shorter version with orchestral track
was released in 1931.

w D. W. Griffith, Frank E. Woods,
novel The Klansman by Thomas
Dixon Jnr d D. W. Griffith ph G.
W. Bitzer

Henry B. Walthall, Mae Marsh,
Miriam Cooper, Lillian Gish, Robert
Harron, Wallace Reid, Donald
Crisp, Joseph Henaberry, Raoul
Walsh, Eugene Pallette, Walter
Long
  'A film version of some of the
melodramatic and inflammatory
material contained in The Clansman
. . . a great deal might be said
concerning the sorry service
rendered by its plucking at old
wounds. But of the film as a film, it
may be reported simply that it is an
impressive new illustration of the
scope of the motion picture
camera.'—New York Times

The Bishop's Wife
   US 1947   108m bw
   Samuel Goldwyn
An angel is sent down to mend the
ways of a bishop whose absorption
with cathedral buildings has put him
out of touch with his wife and
parishioners.
Whimsical, stolid and protracted
light comedy saved by its actors and
its old-fashioned Hollywood style.

w Robert E. Sherwood, Leonardo
Bercovici, novel Robert Nathan
d Henry Koster ph Gregg Toland
m Hugo Friedhofer

Cary Grant, Loretta Young, David
Niven, Monty Woolley, James

Gleason, Gladys Cooper, Elsa Lanchester, Sara Haden, Regis Toomey

'It is the Protestant comeback to the deadly successful RC propaganda of *Going My Way* and *The Bells of St Mary's*. It surpasses in tastelessness, equals in whimsy and in technique falls well below those crooning parables. It is really quite a monstrous film.'—*Richard Winnington, News Chronicle*

'When a film undertakes to bring audiences a spiritual message, we wonder whether the director doesn't owe it to us to clothe such messages in less muddled characterizations and to dispense with caricature.'—*Scholastic Magazine*

'A sophisticated *Christmas Carol*.'—*Philip Hartung*

'As cheerful an invasion of the realm of conscience as we have seen.'—*New York Times*

† Director William A. Seiter was replaced when the film was half complete; this caused nearly one million dollars to be wasted.

AAN: best picture; Henry Koster; Hugo Friedhofer

The Bitter Tea of General Yen

US 1932 89m bw
Columbia (Walter Wanger)

An American lady missionary in Shanghai is captured by a Chinese warlord and falls in love with him. Arty miscegenation story which bids fair to become a cult film and certainly has a number of interesting sequences.

w Edward Paramore, *story* Grace Zaring Stone *d* Frank Capra *ph* Joseph Walker *m* W. Frank Harling

Barbara Stanwyck, Nils Asther, Toshia Mori, Walter Connolly, Gavin Gordon, Lucien Littlefield

'It is doubtful whether this picture can make the grade without support . . . photographic advantages cannot overcome the queer story.'—*Variety*

† The film chosen to open Radio City Music Hall.

'A journey that begins where everything ends!'

The Black Hole

US 1979 98m Technicolor
Technovision

Walt Disney (Ron Miller)

A research team in space is welcomed aboard a mysterious survey ship poised on the edge of a black hole.

The special effects are superb, though achieved through a general gloom which is barely acceptable. But the story is an ill-worked-out remake of *Twenty Thousand Leagues Under the Sea*, the characterization is ridiculously inept, and the final disclosure that black holes are doorways to hell sends one home rather bemused.

w Jeb Rosebrook, Gerry Day *d* Gary Nelson *ph* Frank Phillips *pd* Peter Ellenshaw *m* John Barry

Maximilian Schell, Robert Forster, Anthony Perkins, Joseph Bottoms, Yvette Mimieux, Ernest Borgnine

'As pastiche, it sounds promising; as drama, encumbered with references to Cicero and Goethe, it is merely tedious.'—*John Halford, MFB*

'Rated PG, but the only danger to children is that it may make them think that outer space is not much fun any more.'—*New Yorker*

'Unmasking America's brotherhood of butchery!'

Black Legion

US 1936 83m bw
Warner (Robert Lord)

A factory worker becomes involved with the Ku Klux Klan.

Social melodrama typical of its studio, and good of its kind.

w Robert Lord, Abem Finkel, William Wister Haines *d* Archie Mayo *ph* George Barnes

Humphrey Bogart, Erin O'Brien Moore, Dick Foran, Ann Sheridan, Robert Barrat, John Litel, Charles Halton

'Powerful story of the horror spread by the hooded order; Surefire man's picture.'—*Variety*

'An honest job of film work, and one of the most direct social pieces released from Hollywood.'—*Otis Ferguson*

AAN: Robert Lord (original story)

Black Narcissus
GB 1946   100m
Technicolor
GFD/The Archers (Michael Powell, Emeric Pressburger)
Anglo-Catholic nuns in the Himalayas have trouble with climate, morale, and one of their number who goes mad of sex frustration. An unlikely theme produces one of the cinema's most beautiful films, a visual and emotional stunner despite some narrative uncertainty.

wd Michael Powell, Emeric Pressburger, *novel* Rumer Godden *ph* Jack Cardiff *m* Brian Easdale

Deborah Kerr, David Farrar, Sabu, Jean Simmons, Kathleen Byron, Flora Robson, Esmond Knight, Jenny Laird, May Hallatt, Judith Furse

AA: Jack Cardiff

The Black Pirate
US 1926   76m approx (24 fps)   Technicolor   silent
Douglas Fairbanks
A shipwrecked mariner swears revenge on the pirates who blew up his father's ship.
Cheerful swashbuckler with the star in top form.

w Douglas Fairbanks, Jack Cunningham *d* Albert Parker *ph* Henry Sharp *ad* Oscar Borg, Dwight Franklin

Douglas Fairbanks, Billie Dove, Donald Crisp, Sam de Grasse

The Black Swan
US 1942   85m   Technicolor
TCF (Robert Bassler)
Morgan the pirate is made governor of Jamaica and enlists the help of his old friends to rid the Caribbean of buccaneers.
Rousing adventure story with comic asides: just what action hokum

always aimed to be, with a spirited gallery of heroes and villains and an entertaining narrative taken at a spanking pace.

w Ben Hecht, Seton I. Miller, *novel* Rafael Sabatini *d* Henry King *ph* Leon Shamroy *m* Alfred Newman

Tyrone Power, Maureen O'Hara, *Laird Cregar, Thomas Mitchell, George Sanders*, Anthony Quinn, George Zucco, Edward Ashley

AA: Leon Shamroy
AAN: Alfred Newman

'I'm a teacher. My pupils are the kind you don't turn your back on, even in class!'

The Blackboard Jungle
US 1955   101m   bw
MGM (Pandro S. Berman)
In a slum school, a teacher finally gains the respect of his class of young hooligans.
Seminal fifties melodrama more notable for its introduction of 'Rock Around the Clock' behind the credits than for any intrinsic interest.

wd Richard Brooks, *novel* Evan Hunter *ph* Russell Harlan *m* Bill Haley and the Comets

Glenn Ford, Anne Francis, Louis Calhern, Margaret Hayes, John Hoyt, Richard Kiley, Emile Meyer, Warner Anderson, Basil Ruysdael, *Sidney Poitier, Vic Morrow*, Rafael Campos

'It could just as well have been the first good film of this kind. Actually, it will be remembered chiefly for its timely production and release.'—*G. N. Fenin, Film Culture*

AAN: Richard Brooks (as writer); Russell Harlan

Blackmail
GB 1929   78m   bw
BIP (John Maxwell)
A Scotland Yard inspector finds that his girl is involved in a murder; he conceals the fact and is blackmailed. Hitchcock's first talkie is now a very hesitant entertainment but fully bears the director's stamp and will

reward patient audiences in several excitingly staged sequences.

w Alfred Hitchcock, Benn W. Levy, Charles Bennett, *play* Charles Bennett *d* Alfred Hitchcock *ph* Jack Cox *m* Campbell and Connelly

Anny Ondra, Sara Allgood, John Longden, Charles Paton, Donald Calthrop, Cyril Ritchard

'Hitchcock's ending was to have been ironic, the detective seeing the cell door shut on the arrested girl, going home and then being asked if he was going out with his girl friend that evening. His answer: "Not tonight." This was unacceptable commercially and a happy ending was substituted.'—*George Perry*

Blade Runner

US 1982   117m
Technicolor   Panavision
Warner / Ladd / Blade Runner Partnership (Michael Deeley, Ridley Scott)

Los Angeles, AD 2019; a licensed-to-kill policeman tracks down and destroys a group of intelligent robots who have hijacked a space shuttle and returned to earth.

Gloomy futuristic thriller, looking like a firework display seen through thick fog, and for all the tiring tricks and expense adding up to little more than an updated Philip Marlowe case.

w Hampton Fancher, David People, *novel* Do Androids Dream of Electric Sheep? by Philip K. Dick *d* Ridley Scott *ph* Jordan Cronenweth *pd* Lawrence G. Paull *m* Vangelis

Harrison Ford, Rutger Hauer, Sean Young, Edward James Olmos, M. Emmet Walsh, Daryl Hannah

'The sets are indeed impressive, but they are no compensation for a narrative so lame that it seems in need of a wheelchair.'—*Tom Milne, MFB*

'A richly detailed and visually overwhelming trip to 2019 which

sticks with you like a recurrent nightmare.'—*Sunday Times*

'A massive assault on the senses which seems to have been launched from a madhouse equipped with all computerized mod cons.'—*Daily Mail*

'Glitteringly and atmospherically designed; but ultimately mechanics win out over philosophizing.'—*Sight and Sound*

AAN: art direction; visual effects (Douglas Trumbull, Richard Yuricich, David Dryer)

Blessed Event

US 1932   84m   bw
Warner (Ray Griffith)

A gossip columnist gets himself into hot water.
Amusing vehicle for a fast-talking star, and quite an interesting historical document.

w Howard Green, *play* Manuel Seff, Forest Wilson *d* Roy del Ruth *ph* Sol Polito

Lee Tracy, Ned Sparks, Mary Brian, Dick Powell, Ruth Donnelly, Frank McHugh, Allen Jenkins

'A potential clean-up . . . a sustained hour and a half or so of smart entertainment.'—*Variety*

'Quick and pacy and very likeable.'—*Pauline Kael, 70s*

† A historically interesting note was small-part actress Emma Dunn's use of the expression 'Well I'll be damned', which was technically forbidden at the time.

Blind Alley

US 1939   68m   bw
Columbia

An escaped killer takes refuge in the home of a psychiatrist, who explores his subconscious and tames him.
Unusual lowercase thriller with effective dream sequences; it was much imitated.

w Michael Blankfort, Albert Duffy, *play* James Warwick *d* Charles Vidor *ph* Lucien Ballard *m* Morris Stoloff

Chester Morris, Ralph Bellamy, Ann

Dvorak, Melville Cooper, Rose
Stradner, Marc Lawrence

'Psychoanalysis of a criminal
provides a new twist to what would
otherwise be another crime picture
of general trend.'—*Variety*

'As un-Hollywood as anything that
has come from France this
year.'—*New York Daily News*

'Survive a sticky ten minutes and
you have a thriller of quite unusual
merit.'—*Graham Greene*

† Remake: *The Dark Past*.

Blindfold

US 1965   102m
Technicolor   Panavision
Universal (Marvin Schwarz)

A society psychiatrist is enlisted by
the CIA to make regular blindfold
journeys to a secret destination
where he treats a neurotic physicist.
Discovering that his contacts are
really enemy agents, he tracks down
the destination by sound and
guesswork, and routs the villains.
Lively spy spoof with rather too
much knockabout between the
Hitchcockian suspense sequences; it
has indeed the air of a script which
Hitchcock rejected, but provides
reliable entertainment.

w Philip Dunne, W. H. Menger,
novel Lucile Fletcher   *d* Philip
Dunne   *ph* Joseph MacDonald
m Lalo Schifrin

Rock Hudson, Claudia Cardinale,
Jack Warden, Guy Stockwell, Brad
Dexter

Blithe Spirit

GB 1945   96m   Technicolor
Two Cities / Cineguild (Anthony
Havelock-Allan)

A cynical novelist's second marriage
is disturbed when the playful ghost
of his first wife materializes during a
séance.
Direction and acting carefully
preserve a comedy which on its first
West End appearance in 1941
achieved instant classic status. The
repartee scarcely dates, and
altogether this is a most polished job
of film-making.

w Noel Coward, from his play
scenario David Lean, Anthony
Havelock-Allan, Ronald Neame
d David Lean   *ph* Ronald Neame
m Richard Addinsell

Rex Harrison, *Kay Hammond*,
Constance Cummings, *Margaret
Rutherford*, Hugh Wakefield, Joyce
Carey, Jacqueline Clark

† After seeing this, Noël Coward
reputedly told Rex Harrison: 'After
me you're the best light comedian in
the world.'

Blockade

US 1938   84m   bw
Walter Wanger

During the Spanish Civil War, a
peace-loving young farmer has to
take up arms to defend his land.
Much touted as Hollywood's first
serious contribution to international
affairs this dogged drama was in fact
so bland that audiences had difficulty
ascertaining which side it was on,
especially as neither Franco nor the
Fascists were mentioned. As a
romantic action drama, however, it
passed muster.

w John Howard Lawson   *d* William
Dieterle   *m* Werner Janssen
ph Rudolf Maté

Henry Fonda, Madeleine Carroll,
Leo Carrillo, John Halliday,
Vladimir Sokoloff, Robert Warwick,
Reginald Denny

'It misses any claim to greatness
because it pulls its punches . . . and
it's going to be tough to
sell.'—*Variety*

'The film has a curious unreality
considering the grim reality behind
it.'—*Frank S. Nugent*

'There is achieved a deadly numb
level of shameless hokum out of
which anything true or decent rises
only for a second to confound
itself.'—*Otis Ferguson*

† Original publicity carried this
disclaimer: NOTE: Care has been
taken to prevent any costume of the
production from being accurately
that of either side in the Spanish
Civil War. The story does not

attempt to favour any cause in the present conflict.

AAN: John Howard Lawson; Werner Janssen

Blockheads

☻ US 1938   60m   bw
    Hal Roach / Stan Laurel

Twenty years after World War I, Stan is still guarding a trench because nobody told him to stop. Olly takes him home to meet the wife, with disastrous consequences. The last first-class Laurel and Hardy comedy is shapeless but hilarious, a fragmented reworking of earlier ideas, all of which work beautifully. Gags include encounters with a tip-up truck and an automatic garage, and a brilliantly worked out sequence up and down several flights of stairs.

w James Parrott, Harry Langdon, Felix Adler, Charles Rogers, Arnold Belgard d John G. Blystone ph Art Lloyd m Marvin Hatley

Stan Laurel, Oliver Hardy, Billy Gilbert, Patricia Ellis, Minna Gombell, James Finlayson

'Hodge-podge of old-fashioned slapstick and hoke.'—*Variety*

AAN: Marvin Hatley

The Blood of a Poet

.♠: France 1930   58m   bw
🎬—Vicomte de Noailles
original title: *Le Sang d'un Poète*

Aspects of a poet's vision, taking place while a chimney is falling down.

An indescribable film full of striking imagery which may, or may not, be meaningful. Its author claims that it is not surrealist, but that label for most people will do as well as any other.

wd *Jean Cocteau* ph Georges Périnal m Georges Auric ad Jean Gabriel d'Aubonne

Lee Miller, Pauline Carton, Odette Talazac

'It must be placed among the classic masterpieces of the seventh art.'—*Revue du Cinéma*

Blow Up

.♠: GB 1966   110m
🎬—Eastmancolor
MGM / Carlo Ponti

A London fashion photographer thinks he sees a murder, but the evidence disappears.

Not a mystery but a fashionable think-in on the difference (if any) between fantasy and reality. Agreeable to look at for those who can stifle their irritation at the non-plot and non-characters; a huge audience was lured by flashes of nudity and the trendy 'swinging London' setting.

wd Michelangelo Antonioni ph Carlo di Palma m Herbert Hancock ad Assheton Gorton

David Hemmings, Sarah Miles, Vanessa Redgrave

AAN: Michelangelo Antonioni (as writer and director)

The Blue Angel

♠♦ Germany 1930   98m   bw
  X UFA (Erich Pommer)

A fuddy-duddy professor is infatuated with a tawdry night-club singer. She marries him but is soon bored and contemptuous; humiliated, he leaves her and dies in his old classroom.

A masterwork of late twenties German grotesquerie, and after a slowish beginning an emotional powerhouse, set in a dark nightmare world which could be created only in the studio. Shot also in English, it was highly popular and influential in Britain and America.

w Robert Liebmann, Karl Zuckmayer, Karl Vollmoeller, *novel* Professor Unrath by Heinrich Mann d Josef Von Sternberg ph Günther Rittau, Hans Schneeberger m Frederick Hollander (inc 'Falling in Love Again', 'They Call Me Wicked Lola') ad Otto Hunte, Emil Hasler

Emil Jannings, Marlene Dietrich (who was instantly catapulted to international stardom), Kurt Gerron, Hans Albers

'It will undoubtedly do splendidly –
in the whole of Europe and should
also appeal strongly in the States . . .
only fault is a certain ponderousness
of tempo which tends to
tire.'—*Variety*

The Blue Bird
US 1940 98m Technicolor
(bw prologue)
TCF (Gene Markey)

In a Grimm's Fairy Tale setting, the
two children of a poor woodcutter
seek the bluebird of happiness in the
past, the future and the Land of
Luxury, but eventually discover it in
their own back yard.

An imaginative and often chilling
script clarifies Maurice Maeterlinck's
fairy play, and the art direction is
outstanding, but the children are
necessarily unsympathetic and the
expensive production paled beside
the success of the more upbeat
Wizard of Oz, which was released
almost simultaneously. Slashed for
re-release, the only existing prints
now open with confusing abruptness
and no scene-setting before the
adventures begin.

*w Ernest Pascal d Walter Lang
ph* Arthur Miller, *Ray Rennahan
m* Alfred Newman

Shirley Temple, Johnny Russell,
Gale Sondergaard (as the cat), *Eddie
Collins* (as the dog), Nigel Bruce,
Jessie Ralph, Spring Byington, Sybil
Jason, Helen Ericson, Russell Hicks,
Al Shean, Cecilia Loftus

AAN: Arthur Miller, Ray Rennahan

'Tamed by a brunette—framed by
a blonde—blamed by the cops!'

The Blue Dahlia
US 1946 99m bw
Paramount (John Houseman)

A returning war veteran finds his
faithless wife murdered and himself
suspected.

Hailed on its first release as sharper
than average, this mystery suspenser
is now only moderately compelling
despite the screenplay credit;
direction and editing lack urgency
and the acting lacks bounce.

w Raymond Chandler d George
Marshall *ph* Lionel Lindon
m Victor Young

Alan Ladd, Veronica Lake, William
Bendix, Howard da Silva, Doris
Dowling, Tom Powers, Hugh
Beaumont, Howard Freeman, Will
Wright

'It threatens to turn into
something, but it never does.'—*New
Yorker, 1978*

'The picture is as neatly stylized
and synchronized, and as
uninterested in moral excitement, as
a good ballet; it knows its own
weight and size perfectly and carries
them gracefully and without
self-importance; it is, barring
occasional victories and noble
accidents, about as good a movie as
can be expected from the big
factories.'—*James Agee*

AAN: Raymond Chandler

The Blue Lamp
GB 1949 84m bw
Ealing (Michael Relph)

A young man joins London's police
force. The elderly copper who trains
him is killed in a shootout, but the
killer is apprehended.

Seminal British police film which
spawned not only a long line of
semi-documentary imitations but
also the twenty-year TV series *Dixon
of Dock Green* for which the shot PC
was happily revived. As an
entertainment, pacy but dated; more
important, it burnished the image of
the British copper for a generation
or more.

w T. E. B. Clarke d Basil Dearden
ph Gordon Dines *md* Ernest Irving

Jack Warner, Jimmy Hanley, Dirk
Bogarde, Meredith Edwards, Robert
Flemyng, Bernard Lee, Patric
Doonan, Peggy Evans, Gladys
Henson, Dora Bryan

'The mixture of coyness,
patronage and naive theatricality
which has vitiated British films for
the last ten years.'—*Gavin Lambert*

'A soundly made crime thriller
which would not be creating much of
a stir if it were American.'—*Richard
Mallett, Punch*

The Blue Max

US 1966   156m   De Luxe
Cinemascope
TCF (Christian Ferry)

In Germany after World War I an ambitious and skilful pilot causes the death of his comrades and steals the wife of his High Command superior, who eventually finds a means of revenge.

For once, an action spectacular not too badly let down by its connecting threads of plot, apart from some hilarious and unnecessary bedroom scenes in which the female star's bath towel seems to become conveniently adhesive.

w David Pursall, Jack Seddon, Gerald Hanley, *novel* Jack Hunter d John Guillermin *ph* Douglas Slocombe *m* Jerry Goldsmith

George Peppard, *James Mason*, Ursula Andress, Jeremy Kemp, Karl Michael Vogler, Anton Diffring, Derren Nesbitt

'Addicts of flying movies swear by this one, but for others, the monoplanes and biplanes can't smash or burn fast enough.'—*Pauline Kael*

The Boat

West Germany 1981   149m
Fujicolor
Columbia / Bavaria
Atelier / Radiant Film (Gunter Röhrbach)

original and US title: *Das Boot*

Adventures of a German U-boat during World War II.

Well-crafted but totally unsurprising saga of heroism and self-sacrifice; a decent view of war from the German side, designed to impress world markets. It did so only moderately.

wd Wolfgang Petersen *ph* Jost Vacano *m* Klaus Doldinger *pd* Rolf Zehetbauer

Jürgen Prochnow, Herbert Grönemeyer, Klaus Wennemann, Hubertus Bengsch, Martin Semmelrogge

AAN: direction; screenplay (adaptation); cinematography; editing; sound; sound editing.

Bob and Carol and Ted and Alice

US 1969   105m
Technicolor
Columbia / M. J. Frankovich (Larry Tucker)

Two California couples, influenced by a group therapy session advocating natural spontaneous behaviour, decide to admit their extra-marital affairs and narrowly avoid a wife-swapping party.

Fashionable comedy without the courage of its convictions: it starts and finishes very bashfully, but there are bright scenes in the middle. An attempt to extend it into a TV series was a failure.

w Paul Mazursky, Larry Tucker d Paul Mazursky *ph* Charles E. Lang *m* Quincy Jones

Natalie Wood, Robert Culp, Elliott Gould, Dyan Cannon, Horst Ebersberg

'An old-fashioned romantic comedy disguised as a blue picture.'—*Arthur Schlesinger Jnr*

AAN: Paul Mazursky, Larry Tucker; Charles E. Lang; Elliott Gould; Dyan Cannon

Bombshell

US 1933   91m   bw
MGM (Hunt Stromberg)

GB and aka title: *Blonde Bombshell*

A glamorous film star yearns for a new image. Crackpot farce which even by today's standards moves at a fair clip and enabled the star to give her best comedy performance.

w Jules Furthman, John Lee Mahin, *play* Caroline Francke, Mack Crane d Victor Fleming *ph* Chester Lyons, Hal Rosson

Jean Harlow, Lee Tracy, Frank Morgan, Franchot Tone, Pat O'Brien, Ivan Lebedeff, Una Merkel, Ted Healy, Isabel Jewell, C. Aubrey Smith, Louise Beavers, Leonard Carey, Mary Forbes

'Bound to click and the best legitimate comedy in a long time.'—*Variety*

'They're young . . . they're in love
. . . and they kill people!'
Bonnie and Clyde
US 1967   111m
Technicolor
Warner / Seven Arts / Tatira / Hiller
(*Warren Beatty*)

In the early thirties, a car thief and
the daughter of his intended victim
team up to become America's most
feared and ruthless bank robbers.
Technically brilliant evocation of
sleepy mid-America at the time of
the public enemies, using every kind
of cinematic trick including fake
snapshots, farcical interludes,
dreamy soft-focus and a jazzy score.
For all kinds of reasons a very
influential film which even made
extreme violence quite fashionable
(and very bloody it is).

*w David Newman, Robert Benton
d Arthur Penn ph Burnett Guffey
m Charles Strouse*, using 'Foggy
Mountain Breakdown' by Flatt and
Scruggs

Warren Beatty, Faye Dunaway,
Gene Hackman, Estelle Parsons,
Michael J. Pollard, Dub Taylor,
Denver Pyle, Gene Wilder

'It is a long time since we have
seen an American film so perfectly
judged.'—*MFB*

'. . . all to the rickety twang of a
banjo and a saturation in time and
place.'—*Judith Crist*

'The formula is hayseed comedy
bursting sporadically into
pyrotechnical bloodshed and laced
with sentimental
pop-freudianism.'—*John Simon*

'A film from which we shall date
reputations and innovations in the
American cinema.'—*Alexander
Walker*

AA: Burnett Guffey; Estelle Parsons
AAN: best picture; David Newman,
Robert Benton; Arthur Penn;
Warren Beatty; Faye Dunaway;
Gene Hackman; Michael J. Pollard

Boom Town
US 1940   120m   bw
MGM (Sam Zimbalist)

Two friendly oil drillers strike it rich.

Enjoyable four-star, big-studio
product of its time: world-wide
entertainment of assured success,
with a proven mix of romance,
action, drama and comedy.

w John Lee Mahin, *story* James
Edward Grant *d Jack Conway
ph* Harold Rosson *m* Franz
Waxman *ad* Cedric Gibbons

Clark Gable, Spencer Tracy,
Claudette Colbert, Hedy Lamarr,
Frank Morgan, Lionel Atwill, Chill
Wills

'Western high jinks, a wee child,
and courtroom speeches about
individual enterprise constitute the
various come-ons in a scrambled and
inept picture.'—*New York Herald
Tribune*

'More colourful action in the oil
fields and less agitation indoors
might have made it a great
picture.'—*Bosley Crowther*

AAN: Harold Rosson

Boomerang
US 1947   88m   bw
TCF (Louis de Rochemont)

In a New England town, a clergyman
is shot dead on the street. The DA
prevents an innocent man from
being convicted, but cannot track
down the guilty party.

Incisive real life thriller: based on a
true case, it was shot in an
innovative documentary style which
was much copied, and justice is not
seen to be done, though the
murderer is known to the audience.
A milestone movie of its kind.

w Richard Murphy *d* Elia Kazan
ph Norbert Brodine *m* David
Buttolph

Dana Andrews, Jane Wyatt, Lee J.
Cobb, Cara Williams, Arthur
Kennedy, Sam Levene, Taylor
Holmes, Robert Keith, Ed Begley

'A study of integrity, beautifully
developed by Dana Andrews against
a background of political corruption
and chicanery that is doubly
shocking because of its documentary
understatement.'—*Richard
Winnington*

'For the first time in many a moon we are treated to a picture that gives a good example of a typical small American city—the people, their way of living, their mode of government, the petty politics practised, the power of the press.'—*Frank Ward, National Board of Review*

AAN: Richard Murphy

Born Free
🎵 GB 1965   95m
Technicolor   Panavision
Columbia / Open Road (Carl Foreman) / High Road / Atlas (Sam Jaffe, Paul Radin)

A Kenyan game warden and his wife rear three lion cubs, one of which eventually presents them with a family.
Irresistible animal shots salvage this rather flabbily put together version of a bestselling book. An enormous commercial success, it was followed by the even thinner *Living Free*, by a TV series, and by several semi-professional documentaries.

w Gerald L. C. Copley, *book* Joy Adamson   *d* James Hill   *ph* Kenneth Talbot   *m* John Barry

Virginia McKenna, Bill Travers, Geoffrey Keen

AA: John Barry; title song (*m* John Barry, *ly* Don Black)

'A perfectly swell motion picture!'
Born Yesterday
👹 US 1950   103m   bw
Columbia (S. Sylvan Simon)
The ignorant ex-chorus girl mistress of a scrap iron tycoon takes English lessons, falls for her tutor, and politically outmanoeuvres her bewildered lover.
Pleasant film version of a cast-iron box office play, subtle and intelligent in all departments yet with a regrettable tendency to wave the flag.

w Albert Mannheimer, *play Garson Kanin   d George Cukor   ph* Joseph Walker   *m* Frederick Hollander

Judy Holliday, Broderick Crawford, William Holden, Howard St John

† The original choices for the Judy Holliday role were Rita Hayworth and Jean Parker (who had played it on tour).
AA: Judy Holliday
AAN: best picture; Albert Mannheimer; George Cukor

The Boston Strangler
🐟 US 1968   118m   De Luxe
Panavision
TCF (Robert Fryer)
A semi-factual account of the sex maniac who terrified Boston in the mid-sixties.
Ambitious *policier* rendered less effective by pretentious writing and flashy treatment, including multi-image sequences; the investigation is more interesting than the psychoanalysis.

w Edward Anhalt, *book* Gerold Frank   *d* Richard Fleischer   *ph* Richard Kline   *m* Lionel Newman

Henry Fonda, *Tony Curtis* (as the murderer), George Kennedy, Mike Kellin, Hurd Hatfield, Murray Hamilton, Sally Kellerman, Jeff Corey, George Voskovec

Boudu Sauvé des Eaux
👹 France 1932   87m   bw
Michel Simon / Jean Gehret
aka: *Boudu Saved from Drowning*
A scruffy tramp is not grateful for being rescued from suicide, and plagues the family who invite him to stay.
A minor classic of black comedy, interesting equally for its characterizations, its acting, and its film technique.

wd Jean Renoir, play René Fauchois   *ph* Marcel Lucien   *m* from Raphael and Johann Strauss

Michel Simon, Charles Grandval, Marcelle Hainia, Séverine Lerczinska, Jean Dasté, Jacques Becker

'A beautifully rhythmed film that makes one nostalgic for the period when it was made.'—*New Yorker, 1977*

The Bowery

US 1933 92m bw
Twentieth Century (Darryl F. Zanuck) (Raymond Griffith, William Goetz)

In nineties New York, two boisterous rivals settle their differences after one has jumped off the Brooklyn Bridge for a bet. Roistering saga of cross and double cross on the seamy side, splendidly vigorous in acting and treatment.

w Howard Estabrook, James Gleason d Raoul Walsh ph Barney McGill *m* Alfred Newman *ad Richard Day*

Wallace Beery, George Raft, Pert Kelton, Jackie Cooper, Fay Wray, Herman Bing

'It delivers as entertainment. It should draw by itself, while the cast will be a considerable help.'—*Variety*

'A model of skilful reconstruction and ingenious research.'—*Times*

'Fairly reeking with authentic, rowdy, hurdy-gurdy atmosphere . . . a grand evening of fun for everybody.'—*Photoplay*

† *The Bowery* was the first production of Twentieth Century.

†† Gable was sought for the Raft role, but proved unavailable.

'94 men must die to keep alive a dream—or a nightmare!'

The Boys From Brazil

US/GB 1978 124m De Luxe
ITC/Producer Circle (Martin Richards, Stanley O'Toole)

A renegade Nazi in hiding has a sinister plot to reconquer the world. Suspense fantasy firmly based on a gripping book; excellent performances, but a shade too long.

w Heywood Gould, novel Ira Levin d Franklin Schaffner *ph* Henri Dɪcaë *m* Jerry Goldsmith *pd* Gil Parrando

Gregory Peck, Laurence Olivier, James Mason, Lilli Palmer, Uta Hagen, Steven Guttenberg, Denholm Elliott, Rosemary Harris,

John Dehner, John Rubinstein, Anne Meara, David Hurst, Michael Gough

AAN: Jerry Goldsmith; Laurence Olivier

Boys' Town

US 1938 93m bw
MGM (John W. Considine Jnr)

The story of Father Flanagan and his school for juvenile delinquents. Well-made, highly successful, but sentimental crowd pleaser.

w John Meehan, Dore Schary, original story Eleanor Griffin, Dore Schary d Norman Taurog ph Sidney Wagner m Edward Ward

Spencer Tracy, Mickey Rooney, Henry Hull, Gene Reynolds, Sidney Miller, Frankie Thomas, Bobs Watson, Tommy Noonan

'More laughs than Laurel and Hardy! More thrills than *Test Pilot*! More tears than *Captains Courageous*!'—*publicity*

'A production that should build goodwill for the whole industry.'—*Variety*

AA: Eleanor Griffin, Dore Schary; Spencer Tracy
AAN: best picture; John Meehan, Dore Schary; Norman Taurog

Boys Will Be Boys

GB 1935 75m bw
Gaumont/Gainsborough (Michael Balcon)

An incompetent headmaster thwarts a jewel robber.
The first recognizable Will Hay vehicle, based in part on J. B. Morton's Narkover sketches.

w Will Hay, Robert Edmunds d William Beaudine ph Charles Van Enger m Louis Levy

Will Hay, Gordon Harker, Jimmy Hanley, Davy Burnaby, Norma Varden, Claude Dampier, Charles Farrell, Percy Walsh

'It is hard to see how his distinctive sketch writing could have found a satisfactory screen equivalent. Nevertheless, a good augury of the films to come.'—*Ray Seaton and Roy Martin, 1978*

'The monster demands a mate!'
The Bride of Frankenstein
US 1935   85–90m   bw
Universal (Carl Laemmle Jnr)
Baron Frankenstein is blackmailed by Dr Praetorious into reviving his monster and building a mate for it. *Frankenstein* was startlingly good in a primitive way; this sequel is the screen's sophisticated masterpiece of black comedy, with all the talents working deftly to one end. Every scene has its own delights, and they are woven together into a superb if wilful cinematic narrative which, of its gentle mocking kind, has never been surpassed.

w John L. Balderston, William Hurlbut d James Whale ph John Mescall m Franz Waxman

Boris Karloff, Colin Clive, *Ernest Thesiger*, Valerie Hobson, *E. E. Clive*, Dwight Frye, O. P. Heggie, Una O'Connor, *Elsa Lanchester* (as Mary Shelley and the monster's mate), Gavin Gordon (as Byron), Douglas Walton (as Shelley)

FRANKENSTEIN: 'I've been cursed for delving into the mysteries of life!'
'It is perhaps because Whale was by now master of the horror film that this production is the best of them all.'—*John Baxter, 1968*
'An extraordinary film, with sharp humour, macabre extravagance, and a narrative that proceeds at a fast, efficient pace.'—*Gavin Lambert, 1948*
'A great deal of art has gone into it, but it is the kind of art that gives the healthy feeling of men with their sleeves rolled up and working, worrying only about how to put the thing over in the best manner of the medium—no time for nonsense and attitudes and long hair.'—*Otis Ferguson*
† The regular release version runs 75m, having dropped part of the Mary Shelley prologue and a sequence in which the monster becomes unsympathetic by murdering the burgomaster.

†† The title was originally to have been *The Return of Frankenstein*.

'In the privacy of a girls' school he sought his prey—turning innocent beauty into a thing of unspeakable horror!'
Brides of Dracula
GB 1960   85m   Technicolor
U-I / Hammer / Hotspur
(Anthony Hinds)
Baron Meinster, a disciple of Dracula, is locked up by his mother; but a servant lets him out and he goes on the rampage in a girls' school.
The best of the Hammer *Draculas*, with plenty of inventive action, some classy acting and a good sense of place and period.

w Jimmy Sangster, Peter Bryan, Edward Percy d Terence Fisher ph Jack Asher m Malcolm Williamson

David Peel (as Meinster), *Peter Cushing*, Freda Jackson, *Martita Hunt*, Yvonne Monlaur, Andrée Melly, Mona Washbourne, Henry Oscar, Miles Malleson

'It spans a whole new world of entertainment!'
The Bridge on the River Kwai
GB 1957   161m
Technicolor   Cinemascope
Columbia / Sam Spiegel
British POWs in Burma are employed by the Japs to build a bridge; meanwhile British agents seek to destroy it.
Ironic adventure epic with many fine moments but too many centres of interest and an unforgivably confusing climax. It is distinguished by Guinness' portrait of the English CO who is heroic in his initial stand against the Japs but finally cannot bear to see his bridge blown up: and the physical detail of the production is beyond criticism.

w Carl Foreman, novel Pierre Boulle d David Lean ph Jack Hildyard m Malcolm Arnold

Alec Guinness (Colonel Nicholson),
Shears (William Holden), Jack
Hawkins (Major Warden), Sessue
Hayakawa (Colonel Saito), James
Donald (Major Clipton), Geoffrey
Horne (Lieut. Joyce), Andre Morell
(Col. Green), Percy Herbert
(Grogan)

'It may rank as the most rousing
adventure film inspired by the last
World War.'—*Alton Cook, New
York World Telegram*

† Cary Grant was originally sought
for the William Holden role.

AA: best picture; Carl Foreman
(credited as Michael Wilson); David
Lean; Jack Hildyard; Malcolm
Arnold; Alec Guinness
AAN: Sessue Hayakawa

A Bridge Too Far

US / GB 1977   175m
Technicolor   Panavision
UA / Joseph E. Levine (John
Palmer)

The story of the Allied defeat at
Arnhem in 1944.
Like all large-scale military films,
this one fails to make its tactics
clear, and its sober intent conflicts
with its roster of guest stars. For all
that, there are impressive moments
of acting and production.

w William Goldman, *book* Cornelius
Ryan *d* Richard Attenborough (and
Sidney Hayers) *ph* Geoffrey
Unsworth, *Harry Waxman, Robin
Browne m* John Addison
pd Terence Marsh

Dirk Bogarde, James Caan, Michael
Caine, Sean Connery, Edward Fox,
Elliott Gould, Gene Hackman,
Anthony Hopkins, Hardy Kruger,
Laurence Olivier, Ryan O'Neal,
Robert Redford, Maximilian Schell,
Liv Ullmann, Arthur Hill, Wolfgang
Preiss

'A film too long.'—*Anon.*

'So wearily, expensively
predictable that by the end the
viewer will in all likelihood be too
enervated to notice Attenborough's
prosaic moral epilogue.'—*John Pym,
MFB*

Brief Encounter

GB 1945   86m   bw
Cineguild (Anthony
Havelock-Allan, Ronald Neame)

A suburban housewife on her weekly
shopping visits develops a love affair
with a local doctor; but he gets a job
abroad and they agree not to see
each other again.
An outstanding example of good
middle-class cinema turned by sheer
professional craft into a masterpiece;
even those bored by the theme must
be riveted by the treatment,
especially the use of a dismal railway
station and its trains.

w Noel Coward, from his one-act
play *Still Life d David Lean
ph Robert Krasker m* Rachmaninov

Celia Johnson, Trevor Howard,
Stanley Holloway, Joyce Carey,
Cyril Raymond

'Both a pleasure to watch as a
well-controlled piece of work, and
deeply touching.'—*James Agee*

'Polished as is this film, its
strength does not lie in movie
technique, of which there is plenty,
so much as in the tight realism of its
detail.'—*Richard Winnington*

'A celebrated, craftsmanlike
tearjerker, and incredibly neat.
There's not a breath of air in
it.'—*Pauline Kael, 70s*

† A TV film version was made in
1975 by ITC, starring Richard
Burton and Sophia Loren and
directed by Alan Bridges. It was an
unqualified disaster.

AAN: script; David Lean; Celia
Johnson

Brighton Rock

GB 1947   92m   bw
Associated British / The
Boultings
US title: *Young Scarface*

The teenage leader of a racetrack
gang uses a waitress as alibi to cover
a murder, and marries her. He later
decides to be rid of her, but fate
takes a hand in his murder plot. A
properly 'seedy' version of Graham
Green's 'entertainment', very flashily
done for the most part but with a

trick ending which allows the
heroine to keep her illusions.

w Graham Greene, Terence
Rattigan *d John Boulting* *ph* Harry
Waxman *m* Hans May

Richard Attenborough, Hermione
Baddeley, *Harcourt Williams*,
William Hartnell, Alan Wheatley,
Carol Marsh

'The film is slower, much less
compelling, and, if you get me, less
cinematic than the book, as a child's
guide to which I hereby offer
it.'—*Richard Winnington*

'It proceeds with the efficiency,
the precision and the anxiety to
please of a circular saw.'—*Dilys
Powell*

Bringing Up Baby
US 1938 102m bw
RKO (Howard Hawks)

A zany girl causes a zoology
professor to lose a dinosaur bone
and a pet leopard in the same
evening.
Outstanding crazy comedy which
barely pauses for romance and ends
up with the whole splendid cast in
jail.

w Dudley Nichols, Hagar Wilde
d Howard Hawks *ph* Russell Metty
m Roy Webb

Katharine Hepburn, Cary Grant,
May Robson, Charles Ruggles,
Walter Catlett, Fritz Feld, Jonathan
Hale, Barry Fitzgerald

'Harum-scarum farce comedy . . .
definite box-office.'—*Variety*

'I am happy to report that it is
funny from the word go, that it has
no other meaning to recommend it
. . . and that I wouldn't swap it for
practically any three things of the
current season.'—*Otis Ferguson*

'It may be the American movies'
closest equivalent to Restoration
comedy.'—*Pauline Kael*

'Crazy comedies continue to
become crazier, and there will soon
be few actors and actresses left who
have no straw in their hair.'—*Basil
Wright*

† The dog George was played by
Asta from *The Thin Man* movies.

Broadway Bill
US 1934 104m bw
Columbia (Frank Capra)
GB title: *Strictly Confidential*

A cheerful horse trainer finds he has
a winner. Easygoing romantic
comedy with the energetic Capra
style in fairly full bloom.

w Robert Riskin, *story* Mark
Hellinger *d Frank Capra* *ph* Joseph
Walker

Warner Baxter, Myrna Loy, Walter
Connolly, Helen Vinson, Douglass
Dumbrille, Raymond Walburn,
Lynne Overman, Clarence Muse,
Margaret Hamilton, Paul Harvey,
Claude Gillingwater, Charles Lane,
Ward Bond

'The effect of capable direction is
discernible in every foot.'—*Variety*

'It will be a long day before we see
so little made into so much: it is gay
and charming and will make you
happy, and I am sorry to say I do not
know recommendations much
higher.'—*Otis Ferguson*

† Remade as *Riding High*.

'The pulsating drama of
   Broadway's bared heart speaks
   and sings with a voice to stir
   your soul!'
'The new wonder of the screen!'

Broadway Melody
US 1929 110m bw
(Technicolor scenes)
MGM (Lawrence Weingarten)

Chorus girls try to make it big on
Broadway. The screen's very first
musical, exceedingly primitive by the
standards of even a year later, but
rather endearing and with a splendid
score.

w James Gleason, Norman Houston,
Edmund Goulding *d* Harry
Beaumont *ph* John Arnold *songs*
Nacio Herb Brown, Arthur Freed

Charles King, Anita Page, Bessie
Love, Jed Prouty, Kenneth
Thomson, Mary Doran, Eddie Kane

'A basic story with some sense to
it, action, excellent direction, laughs,
a tear, a couple of great
performances and plenty of
sex.'—*Variety*

AAN: best picture; Harry Beaumont; Bessie Love

Broken Blossoms
US 1919   105m (16 fps)
bw   silent
UA/D. W. Griffith
In slummy Limehouse, a young Chinaman loves the daughter of a brute, who kills her; the Chinaman then kills him and commits suicide. Victorian-style melodrama presented by Griffith with all the stops out; sometimes striking, but very dated even on its first appearance.

wd D. W. Griffith, *story* The Chink and the Child in Thomas Burke's Limehouse Nights *ph* G. W. Bitzer

Lillian Gish, Donald Crisp, Richard Barthelmess

'This is a Limehouse which neither Mr Burke nor anybody else who knows his East End of London will be able to recognize . . . but *Broken Blossoms* is a genuine attempt to bring real tragedy onto the screen as opposed to machine-made drama, and for that Mr Griffith deserves the thanks of all who are convinced of the potentialities of the film.'—*The Times*

'I know of no other picture in which so much screen beauty is obtained . . . attributable to the Whistlerian fogs and shadows, with that dock in Limehouse recurring like some pedal point.'—*James Agate, 1928*

† Leslie Henson appeared in a parody, *Broken Bottles* in 1920.

The Brothers
GB 1947   98m   bw
GFD/Sydney Box
An orphan girl comes to a Skye fishing family at the turn of the century, and causes superstition, sexual jealousy and tragedy. Wildly melodramatic but good-looking open-air melodrama, a surprising and striking British film of its time.

w Muriel and Sydney Box, *novel* L. A. G. Strong *d* David Macdonald *ph* Stephen Dade

Patricia Roc, Maxwell Reed, *Duncan Macrae* (a splendidly malevolent performance), Will Fyffe, Andrew Crawford, Finlay Currie

'Heavy breathing, heavier dialect, and any number of quaint folk customs . . . the island and its actual inhabitants are all right; the rest is Mary Webb with hair on her chest.'—*James Agee*

Brothers in Law
GB 1957   97m   bw
British Lion/the Boultings
A young barrister has comic misdemeanours in and out of court. The lighter side of the law, from a bestseller by a judge; mechanically amusing and not in the same street as its predecessor *Private's Progress*, though it seemed hilarious at the time.

w Roy Boulting, Frank Harvey, Jeffrey Dell, *novel* Henry Cecil *d* John Boulting *ph* Max Greene *m* Benjamin Frankel

Ian Carmichael, Terry-Thomas, Richard Attenborough, *Miles Malleson*, *Eric Barker*, Irene Handl, John Le Mesurier, Olive Sloane, Kynaston Reeves

FOREWORD: If all the characters in this film were not fictitious—it would be alarming!

CLERK: 'You start with a blue robing bag, sir. Then if you do good work for counsel, he'll give you a red one. If at the end of seven years you haven't been given a red bag—use a suitcase.'

The Brothers Karamazov
US 1958   146m   Metrocolor
MGM/Avon (Pandro S. Berman)
In 19th-century Russia, the father of three sons is murdered and the wrong brother is found guilty. Decent but decidedly unenthralling Hollywood compression of a classic, faithful to the letter but not the spirit of the book, and with few memorable moments or performances.

w Richard Brooks, *novel* Fedor
Dostoievsky d Richard Brooks
ph John Alton *m* Bronislau Kaper
ad William A. Horning, Paul
Groesse

Yul Brynner, Maria Schell, Richard
Basehart, Claire Bloom, Lee J.
Cobb, Albert Salmi, William
Shatner, Judith Evelyn
  'A picture full of ferocity and
passion, with streaks of genius in the
lighting, mounting and
music.'—*News of the World*

† In 1968 came Ivan Pyryev's
massive 220m Russian version, little
seen in the west.

AAN: Lee J. Cobb

The Browning Version
🏵🏵 GB 1951 90m bw
    GFD / Javelin (Teddy Baird)
Retiring through ill health, a classics
master finds that he is hated by his
unfaithful wife, his headmaster and
his pupils. An unexpected act of
kindness gives him courage to face
the future.
A rather thin extension of a one-act
play, capped by a thank-you speech
which is wildly out of character.
Dialogue and settings are smooth,
but the actors are not really happy
with their roles.

w Terence Rattigan, from his play
d Anthony Asquith *ph* Desmond
Dickinson

Michael Redgrave, Jean Kent, Nigel
Patrick, Wilfrid Hyde White, Bill
Travers, Ronald Howard
  'If the sustained anguish of the
role does not allow Redgrave a great
deal of room to move around in, it
does give him a chance to show what
he can do in tight quarters, and that,
it turns out, is
considerable.'—*Pauline Kael, 70s*

Bugsy Malone
🏵 GB 1976 93m
  Eastmancolor
Rank / Bugsy Malone Productions
(David Puttnam, Allan Marshall)
New York 1929: gangster Fat Sam
fights it out with Dandy Dan, and
the best man wins the girl.
Extremely curious musical gangster

spoof with all the parts played by
children and the guns shooting ice
cream. Very professionally done, but
one wonders to whom it is supposed
to appeal.

wd Alan Parker *ph* Michael Seresin,
Peter Biziou *m* / *songs* Paul
Williams *pd* Geoffrey Kirkland

Scott Baio, Jodie Foster, Florrie
Digger, John Cassisi
  'If for nothing else, you would
have to admire it for the sheer
doggedness of its
eccentricity.'—*David Robinson, The
Times*
  'All the pizazz in the world
couldn't lift it above the level of
empty camp.'—*Frank Rich, New
York Post*
  'I only wish the British could make
adult movies as intelligent as this
one.'—*Michael Billington, Illustrated
London News*

AAN: Paul Williams

Bullitt
US 1968 113m
  Technicolor
Warner / Solar (Philip D'Antoni)
A San Francisco police detective
conceals the death of an
underground witness in his charge,
and goes after the killers himself.
Routine cop thriller with undoubted
charisma, distinguished by a splendid
car chase which takes one's mind off
the tedious plot.
Technical credits first class.

w Harry Kleiner, Alan R. Trustman,
novel Mute Witness by Robert L.
Pike *d Peter Yates ph* William A.
Fraker *m* Lalo Schifrin

Steve McQueen, Jacqueline Bisset,
Robert Vaughn, Don Gordon,
Robert Duvall, Simon Oakland
  'It has energy, drive, impact, and
above all, style.'—*Hollis Alpert*

Bunny Lake is Missing
GB 1965 107m bw
  Panavision
Columbia / Wheel (Otto
Preminger)
The 4-year-old illegitimate daughter
of an American girl in London

disappears and no one can be found
to admit that she ever existed.
A nightmarish gimmick story, with
more gimmicks superimposed along
the way to say nothing of a
*Psycho*ish ending; some of the
decoration works and makes even
the unconvincing story compelling,
while the cast is alone worth the
price of admission.

w John and Penelope Mortimer,
novel Evelyn Piper *d* Otto
Preminger *ph* Denys Coop *m* Paul
Glass *pd* Don Ashton *titles* Saul
Bass

Laurence Olivier, Carol Lynley, Keir
Dullea, Noel Coward, Martita Hunt,
Finlay Currie, Clive Revill, Anna
Massey, Lucie Mannheim
  'It has the enjoyable hallmarks of
really high calibre
professionalism.'—*Penelope
Houston*

The Burmese Harp
  Japan 1956   116m   bw
  Nikkatsu (Masayuki Takagi)
original title: *Biruma no tategoto*
A shell-shocked Japanese soldier
stays in the Burmese jungle to bury
the unknown dead.
Deeply impressive and horrifying
war film with an epic, folk-tale
quality, emphasized by superbly
controlled direction.

w Natto Wada, *novel* Michio
Takeyama *d* Kon Ichikawa
ph Minoru Yokoyama *m* Akira
Ifukube

Shoji Yasui, Rentaro Mikuni,
Tatsuya Mihashi

Bus Stop
  US 1956   96m
  Eastmancolor   Cinemascope
TCF (Buddy Adler)
TV title: *The Wrong Kind of Girl*
In a rodeo town, a simple-thinking
cowboy meets a café singer and asks
her to marry him.
Sex comedy-drama, a modest
entertainment in familiar American
vein, very well done but rather
over-inflated by its star.

w George Axelrod, *play* William
Inge *d* Joshua Logan *ph* Milton
Krasner *m* Alfred Newman, Cyril
Mockridge

Marilyn Monroe, Don Murray,
Betty Field, Arthur O'Connell,
Eileen Heckart, Robert Bray, Hope
Lange, Hans Conried, Casey Adams
  'The film demands of its principal
performers a purely physical display
of their bodies viewed as sexual
machinery.'—*David Robinson*

AAN: Don Murray

'Not that it matters, butt most of it
is true!'

Butch Cassidy and the Sundance
Kid
  US 1969   110m   De Luxe
  Panavision
TCF/Campanile (John Foreman)
A hundred years ago, two western
train robbers keep one step ahead of
the law until finally tracked down to
Bolivia.
Humorous, cheerful, poetic,
cinematic account of two
semi-legendary outlaws, winningly
acted and directed. One of the
decade's great commercial successes,
not least because of the song
'Raindrops Keep Fallin' on My
Head'.

w William Goldman *d* George Roy
Hill *ph* Conrad Hall *m* Burt
Bacharach

Paul Newman, Robert Redford,
Katharine Ross, Strother Martin,
Henry Jones, Jeff Corey, Cloris
Leachman, Ted Cassidy, Kenneth
Mars
  'A mere exercise in smart-alecky
device-mongering, chock-full of out
of place and out of period
one-upmanship, a battle of wits at a
freshman smoker.'—*John Simon*

AA: William Goldman; Conrad
Hall; Burt Bacharach; song
'Raindrops Keep Fallin' on My
Head' (*m* Burt Bacharach, *ly* Hal
David)
AAN: best picture; George Roy Hill

C

Cabaret

US 1972 123m
Technicolor
ABC Pictures / Allied Artists (Cy Feuer)

In the early thirties, Berlin is a hotbed of vice and anti-semitism. In the Kit Kat Klub, singer Sally Bowles shares her English lover with a homosexual German baron, and her Jewish friend Natasha has troubles of her own. This version of Isherwood's Berlin stories regrettably follows the plot line of the play *I am a Camera* rather than the Broadway musical on which it is allegedly based, and it lacks the incisive remarks of the MC, but the very smart direction creates a near-masterpiece of its own, and most of the songs are intact.

w Jay Presson Allen, from Goodbye to Berlin by Christopher Isherwood *d/ch* Bob Fosse *m* John Kander *ly* Fred Ebb *ph* Geoffrey Unsworth *md* Ralph Burns *pd* Rolf Zehetbauer

Liza Minnelli, Joel Grey, Michael York, Helmut Griem, Fritz Wepper, Marisa Berenson

'Film journals will feast for years on shots from this picture; as it rolled along, I saw page after illustrated page from a not-too-distant book called *The Cinema of Bob Fosse*.'—*Stanley Kauffmann*

AA: Bob Fosse (as director); Geoffrey Unsworth; Ralph Burns; Liza Minnelli; Joel Grey
AAN: best picture; Jay Presson Allen

'Broadway's big, fun-jammed music show is on the screen at last—crowded with stars and songs and spectacle in the famed MGM manner!'

Cabin in the Sky

US 1943 99m bw
MGM (Arthur Freed)

An idle, gambling husband is reformed by a dream of his own death, with God and Satan battling for his soul.

Consistently interesting, often lively, but generally rather stilted all-black musical which must have seemed a whole lot fresher on the stage. Still, a good try.

w Joseph Schrank, *musical play* Lynn Root *d* Vincente Minnelli *ph* Sidney Wagner *md* George Stoll *new songs: m* Harold Arlen, *ly* E. Y. Harburg *show songs: m* Vernon Duke, *ly* John Latouche, Ted Fetter

Eddie 'Rochester' Anderson, Ethel Waters, Lena Horne, Cab Calloway, Louis Armstrong, John W. Bublett

'Whatever its box office fate, a worthwhile picture for Metro to have made, if only as a step toward Hollywood recognition of the place of the colored man in American life.'—*Variety*

AAN: song 'Happiness Is Just a Thing Called Joe' (*m* Harold Arlen, *ly* E. Y. Harburg)
Other songs: 'Li'l Black Sheep'; 'Ain't It De Truth'; 'Dat Ole Debbil Consequence'; 'Honey in the Honeycomb'; 'Taking a Chance on Love'; 'In My Old Virginia Home'; 'Going Up'; 'Things Ain't What They Used to be'; 'Shine'

'See the sleepwalker, floating down the street, ripped from some nightmare! A street of misshapen houses with brooding windows, streaked by dagger strokes of light and darkened by blots of shadow! You will immediately feel the terror in the movements of that floating grotesque!' (American advertising)

The Cabinet of Dr Caligari

Germany 1919 90m approx (16 fps) bw silent
Decla-Bioscop (Erich Pommer)

A fairground showman uses a somnambulist for purposes of murder and is finally revealed to be the director of a lunatic asylum; but the whole story is only the dream of a madman.

Faded now, but a film of immense influence on the dramatic art of cinema, with its odd angles, stylized sets and hypnotic acting, not to mention the sting in the tail of its story (added by the producer).

*w Carl Mayer, Hans Janowitz
d Robert Wiene ph Willy Hameister
ad Hermann Warm, Walter Röhrig,
Walter Reiman*

Werner Krauss, Conrad Veidt, Lil Dagover, Friedrich Feher, Hans von Twardowski

'The first hundred shocks are the hardest.'—*New York Evening Post*, 1924

† The film cost 18,000 dollars to make.

'Days of magnificent adventure
. . . nights of maddest revelry
. . . a temptation in
Technicolor!'
Caesar and Cleopatra
GB 1945   135m
Technicolor
Rank / Gabriel Pascal
An elaborate screen treatment of Bernard Shaw's comedy about Caesar's years in Alexandria. Britain's most expensive film is an absurd extravaganza for which the producer actually took sand to Egypt to get the right colour. It has compensations however in the sets, the colour, the performances and the witty lines, though all its virtues are theatrical rather than cinematic and the play is certainly not a major work.

*w Bernard Shaw d Gabriel Pascal
ph F. A. Young, Robert Krasker,
Jack Hildyard, Jack Cardiff
m Georges Auric decor,
costumes Oliver Messel sets John
Bryan*

Claude Rains, Vivien Leigh, Cecil Parker, Stewart Granger, Flora Robson, Francis L. Sullivan,
Raymond Lovell, Anthony Harvey, Anthony Eustrel, Basil Sydney, Ernest Thesiger, Stanley Holloway, Leo Genn, Jean Simmons, Esmé Percy, Michael Rennie

'It cost over a million and a quarter pounds, took two and a half years to make, and well and truly bored one spectator for two and a quarter hours.'—*Richard Winnington*

'It is so wonderful as to make my other films look naive.'—*Bernard Shaw*

'When Rains played a small part he sometimes gave the impression that he was carrying the movie, but here his impish grin and his equanimity aren't enough.'—*Pauline Kael, 70s*

La Cage aux Folles
France / Italy 1978   91m
Eastmancolor
UA / PAA / Da Ma (Marcello Danon)
aka: *Birds of a Feather*
A homosexual nightclub owner is persuaded by his straight son to behave properly in front of his girl friend's parents, but chaos comes on the night of the party.
Internationally popular near-the-knuckle farce with excellent moments and some *longueurs*.

*w Francis Veber, Edouard Molinaro, Marcello Danon, Jean Poiret, play Jean Poiret d Edouard Molinaro ph Armando Nannuzzi
m Ennio Morricone*

Ugo Tognazzi, Michel Serrault, Michel Galabru, Claire Maurier, Remi Laurent

AAN: Edouard Molinaro (as director)

'As big as the ocean!'
The Caine Mutiny
US 1954   125m
Technicolor
Columbia / Stanley Kramer
Jealousies and frustrations among the officers of a peacetime destroyer come to a head when the neurotic captain panics during a typhoon and

is relieved of his post. At the resulting trial the officers learn about themselves.

Decent if lamely paced version of a bestseller which also made a successful play; the film skates too lightly over the characterizations and even skimps the courtroom scene, but there are effective scenes and performances.

w Stanley Roberts, *novel* Herman Wouk *d* Edward Dmytryk
ph Franz Planer *m* Max Steiner

Humphrey Bogart (Captain Queeg), Jose Ferrer (Lt Barney Greenwald), Van Johnson (Lt Steve Maryk), Fred MacMurray (Lt Tom Keefer), Robert Francis (Ensign Willie Keith), May Wynn (May), Tom Tully (Captain DeVriess), E. G. Marshall (Lt Cdr Challee), Lee Marvin (Meatball), Claude Akins (Horrible)

QUEEG: 'There are four ways of doing things on board my ship. The right way, the wrong way, the navy way, and my way. If they do things my way, we'll get along.'

QUEEG: 'Ah, but the strawberries! That's where I had them. They laughed and made jokes, but I proved beyond the shadow of a doubt, and with geometric logic, that a duplicate key to the wardroom icebox did exist. And I'd have produced that key if they hadn't pulled the *Caine* out of action. I know now they were out to protect some fellow officer.'

KEEFER: 'There is no escape from the *Caine*, save death. We're all doing penance, sentenced to an outcast ship, manned by outcasts, and named after the greatest outcast of them all.'

AAN: best picture; Stanley Roberts; Max Steiner; Humphrey Bogart; Tom Tully

Calamity Jane
US 1953 101m
Technicolor
Warner (William Jacobs)
Calamity helps a saloon owner friend find a star attraction, and wins the heart of Wild Bill Hickok.

Agreeable, cleaned-up, studio-set western musical patterned after *Annie Get Your Gun*, but a much friendlier film, helped by an excellent score.

w James O'Hanlon *d* David Butler
ph Wilfrid Cline *songs* Sammy Fain, *Paul Francis Webster* *md* Ray Heindorf *ch* Jack Donohue

Doris Day, *Howard Keel*, Allyn McLerie, Phil Carey, Dick Wesson, Paul Harvey

AA: song 'Secret Love' (*m* Sammy Fain, *ly* Paul Francis Webster)
AAN: Ray Heindorf

Call Me Madam
US 1953 114m
Technicolor
TCF (Sol C. Siegel)
A Washington hostess is appointed Ambassador to Lichtenberg and marries the foreign minister.
Studio-bound but thoroughly lively transcription of Irving Berlin's last big success, with most of the performers at their peak and some topical gags which may now be mystifying.

w Arthur Sheekman, *play* Howard Lindsay, Russel Crouse *m/ly* Irving Berlin *md* Alfred Newman
ph Leon Shamroy *d* Walter Lang
ch Robert Alton

Ethel Merman, *Donald O'Connor*, *George Sanders*, *Vera-Ellen*, Billy de Wolfe, Helmut Dantine, Walter Slezak, Steve Geray, Ludwig Stossel

AA: Alfred Newman

Call Northside 777
US 1948 111m bw
TCF (Otto Lang)
A Chicago reporter helps a washerwoman prove her son not guilty of murdering a policeman.
Overlong semi-documentary crime thriller based on a real case. Acting and detail excellent, but the sharp edge of *Boomerang* is missing.

w Jerome Cady, Jay Dratler
d Henry Hathaway *ph* Joe MacDonald *m* Alfred Newman

James Stewart, Lee J. Cobb, Helen Walker, *Kazia Orzazewski*, Betty Garde, Richard Conte

'A most satisfying thriller generously streaked with class.'—*Daily Mail*

'Absorbing, exciting, realistic.'—*Star*

Camelot

US 1967   181m
Technicolor   Panavision 70
Warner (Jack L. Warner)

King Arthur marries Guinevere, loses her to Lancelot, and is forced into war.

A film version of a long-running Broadway show with many excellent moments. Unfortunately the director cannot make up his mind whether to go for style or realism, and has chosen actors who cannot sing. The result is cluttered and overlong, with no real sense of period or sustained imagination, but the photography and the music linger in the mind.

w Alan Jay Lerner m Frederick Loewe d Joshua Logan ph Richard H. Kline pd/costumes John Truscott ad Edward Carere md Ken Darby, Alfred Newman

Richard Harris, Vanessa Redgrave, David Hemmings, Lionel Jeffries, Laurence Naismith, Franco Nero
Songs include 'The Merry Month of May'; 'Camelot'; 'If Ever I Would Leave You'; 'Take Me to the Fair'; C'est Moi'

'One wonders whether the fashion for musicals in which only the chorus can actually sing may be reaching its final stage.'—*MFB*

'Three hours of unrelieved glossiness, meticulous inanity, desperate and charmless striving for charm.'—*John Simon*

'The sets and costumes and people seem to be sitting there on the screen, waiting for the unifying magic that never happens.'—*New Yorker, 1977*

AA: art direction; costumes; music direction
AAN: cinematography

The Cameraman

US 1928   78m approx (24 fps)   bw   silent
MGM (Lawrence Weingarten)

In order to woo a film star, a street photographer becomes a newsreel cameraman.

Highly regarded chapter of farcical errors among the star's top features.

w Clyde Bruckman, Lex Lipton, Richard Schayer d Edward Sedgwick ph Elgin Lessley, Reggie Manning

Buster Keaton, Marceline Day, Harry Gribbon, Harold Goodwin

† The film was remade in 1948 for Red Skelton as *Watch the Birdie*, with Keaton sadly supervising the gags but getting no credit.

'You who are so young—where can you have learned all you know about women like me?'

Camille

US 1936   108m   bw
MGM (Irving Thalberg, Bernard Hyman)

A dying courtesan falls for an innocent young man who loves her, and dies in his arms.

This old warhorse is an unsuitable vehicle for Garbo but magically she carries it off, and the production is elegant and pleasing.

w Frances Marion, James Hilton, Zoe Akins, novel Alexandre Dumas d George Cukor ph William Daniels m Herbert Stothart

Greta Garbo, Robert Taylor, Lionel Barrymore, *Henry Daniell*, Elizabeth Allan, Lenore Ulric, Laura Hope Crews, Rex O'Malley, Jessie Ralph, E. E. Clive

'Pretty close to the top mark in showmanship, direction, photography and box office names.'—*Variety*

'The slow, solemn production is luxuriant in its vulgarity: it achieves that glamor which MGM traditionally mistook for style.'—*Pauline Kael, 1968*

'The surprise is to find a story that should by rights be old hat coming to such insistent life on the screen.'—*Otis Ferguson*

'It steadily builds up an impression of being a spectacle of manners and fashions, a socially true background for its characters to move against.'—*National Board of Review*

'Their lips meet for the first time . . . a superb thrill seared in your memory forever!'—*publicity*

'This is not death as mortals know it. This is but the conclusion of a romantic ritual.'—*Bosley Crowther*

AAN: Greta Garbo

The Candidate
🏵🏵 US 1972   110m
✗ Technicolor
Warner / Redford–Ritchie (Walter Coblenz)

A young Californian lawyer is persuaded to run for senator; in succeeding, he alienates his wife and obscures his real opinions.

Put together in a slightly scrappy but finally persuasive style, this joins a select band of rousing, doubting American political films.

w Jeremy Larner d Michael Ritchie ph Victor J. Kemper m John Rubinstein

Robert Redford, Peter Boyle, *Don Porter*, Allen Garfield, Karen Carlson, Quinn Redeker, Morgan Upton, *Melvyn Douglas*

'Decent entertainment . . . it is never boring, but it is never enlarging, informationally or emotionally or thematically.'—*Stanley Kauffmann*

AA: Jeremy Larner

A Canterbury Tale
🏵🏵 GB 1944   124m   bw
✗ Rank / Archers (Michael Powell, Emeric Pressburger)

A batty magistrate is unmasked by a land girl, an army sergeant and a GI. Curious would-be propaganda piece with Old England bathed in a roseate wartime glow, but the plot seems to have little to do with Chaucer. Indeed, quite what Powell and Pressburger thought they were

up to is hard to fathom, but the detail is interesting.

wd Michael Powell and Emeric Pressburger ph Erwin Hillier

Eric Portman, Sheila Sim, John Sweet, Dennis Price, Esmond Knight, Charles Hawtrey, Hay Petrie, George Merritt, Edward Rigby

'To most people the intentions of the film-makers remained highly mysterious; nor did this picture of the British administration of justice commend itself to the authorities, who showed some reluctance to encourage its export to our allies.'—*Basil Wright, 1972*

Captain Blood
✗✗ US 1935   119m   bw
✗ Warner (Harry Joe Brown)

A young British surgeon, wrongly condemned by Judge Jeffreys for helping rebels, escapes and becomes a Caribbean pirate.

Modestly produced but quite exhilarating pirate adventure notable for making a star of Errol Flynn. Direction makes the most of very limited production values.

w Casey Robinson, *novel* Rafael Sabatini d Michael Curtiz ph Hal Mohr m Erich Wolfgang Korngold ad Anton Grot

Errol Flynn, Olivia de Havilland, *Basil Rathbone*, Lionel Atwill, Guy Kibbee, Ross Alexander, Henry Stephenson, Forrester Harvey, Hobart Cavanaugh, Donald Meek.

'A lavish, swashbuckling saga of the Spanish Main . . . it can't fail at the wickets.'—*Variety*

'Here is a fine spirited mix-up with clothes and wigs which sometimes hark back to the sixteenth century and sometimes forward to the period of Wolfe . . . one is quite prepared for the culminating moment when the Union Jack breaks proudly, anachronistically forth at Peter Blood's masthead.'—*Graham Greene*

'Magnificently photographed, lavishly produced, and directed with consummate skill.'—*Picturegoer*

AAN: best picture

Captains Courageous

US 1937   116m   bw
MGM (Louis D. Lighton)

A spoiled rich boy falls off a cruise
liner and lives for a while among
fisherfolk who teach him how to live.

Semi-classic Hollywood family film
which is not all that enjoyable while
it's on but is certainly a good
example of the prestige picture of
the thirties. (It also happened to be
good box office.)

w John Lee Mahin, Marc Connelly,
Dale Van Every, *novel* Rudyard
Kipling d Victor Fleming
ph Harold Rosson m Franz
Waxman

Spencer Tracy, Lionel Barrymore,
Freddie Bartholomew, Mickey
Rooney, Melvyn Douglas, Charley
Grapewin, Christian Rub, John
Carradine, Walter Kingsford, Leo
G. Carroll, Charles Trowbridge

'Will not have to go begging for
patronage . . . one of the best
pictures of the sea ever
made.'—*Variety*

'Another of those grand jobs of
movie-making we have come to
expect from Hollywood's most
profligate studio.'—*Frank S. Nugent,
New York Times*

† 1977 brought a TV movie remake.

AA: Spencer Tracy
AAN: best picture; script

The Captain's Paradise

GB 1953   89m   bw
BL / London (Anthony
Kimmins)

The captain of a steamer plying
between Gibraltar and Tangier has a
wife in each port, one to suit each of
his personalities.

Over-dry comedy in which the idea
is much funnier than the script. One
is left with the memory of a pleasant
star performance.

w Alec Coppel, Nicholas Phipps
d Anthony Kimmins ph Ted Scaife
m Malcolm Arnold

Alec Guinness, Celia Johnson,
Yvonne de Carlo, Charles Goldner,
Miles Malleson, Bill Fraser, Nicholas
Phipps, Ferdy Mayne, George
Benson

AAN: original story (Alec Coppel)

The Captive Heart

GB 1946   108m   bw
Ealing (Michael Relph)

Stories of life among British officers
in a German POW camp, especially
of a Czech who has stolen the papers
of a dead Britisher.

Archetypal POW drama lacing an
almost poetic treatment with humour
and melodrama.

w Angus Macphail, Guy Morgan
d Basil Dearden ph Lionel Banes,
Douglas Slocombe m Alan
Rawsthorne

Michael Redgrave, *Jack Warner*,
Basil Radford, Mervyn Johns,
Jimmy Hanley, Gordon Jackson,
Ralph Michael, Derek Bond, Karel
Stepanek, Guy Middleton, Jack
Lambert, Gladys Henson, Rachel
Kempson, Meriel Forbes

'A warm, emotional intensely
human document, entitled to rate
among the best twenty films of the
last ten years.'—*News of the World*

The Card

GB 1952   91m   bw
Rank / British Film Makers
(John Bryan)
US title: *The Promoter*

A bright young clerk from the
potteries finds many ingenious ways
of improving his bank account and
his place in society.

Pleasing period comedy with the star
in a made-to-measure role and
excellent production values.

w Eric Ambler, *novel* Arnold
Bennett d Ronald Neame
ph Oswald Morris ad T. Hopwell
Ash m William Alwyn

Alec Guinness, Glynis Johns, Petula
Clark, *Valerie Hobson*, Edward
Chapman, Veronica Turleigh, Gibb
McLaughlin, Frank Pettingell

The Cardinal

US 1963   175m
Technicolor   Panavision 70
Gamma / Otto Preminger

A 1917 ordinand becomes a Boston
curate, a fighter of the Ku Klux
Klan, a Rome diplomat, and finally

gets a cardinal's hat.
Heavy-going documentary
melodrama with many interesting
sequences marred by lack of
cohesion, too much grabbing at
world problems, and
over-sensational personal asides.

w Robert Dozier, *novel* Henry
Morton Robinson *d Otto
Preminger ph* Leon Shamroy
m Jerome Moross *pd* Lyle Wheeler
titles Saul Bass

Tom Tryon, *Carol Lynley*, Dorothy
Gish, Maggie Macnamara, Cecil
Kellaway, John Saxon, *John Huston*,
Robert Morse, Burgess Meredith,
Jill Haworth, Raf Vallone, Tullio
Carminati, Ossie Davis, Chill Wills,
Arthur Hunnicutt, Murray
Hamilton, Patrick O'Neal, Romy
Schneider
   'Very probably the last word in
glossy dishonesty posturing as
serious art.'—*John Simon*
   'Mere and sheer wide screen
Technicolor movie.'—*Stanley
Kauffmann*

AAN: Otto Preminger; Leon
Shamroy; John Huston

Carmen
  Spain 1983 101m
  Eastmancolor
A rehearsal for the ballet *Carmen*
finds dancers playing out in reality
the parts of the drama. Enjoyable
but exhausting melodrama with
elements of *The Red Shoes*;
meticulous choreography and
direction are its chief assets. Antonio
Gades, Laura del Sol, Paco de
Lucia, Cristina Hoyos. Written by
Carlos Saura, Antonio Gades;
directed by *Carlos Saura*; for
Emiliano Piedra
Productions/Television Espanola.
'Extremely enjoyable, but lacks the
edge that would make it in any way
compelling.'—*Jill Forbes, MFB*

Un Carnet de Bal
  France 1937 135m bw
  Lévy/Strauss/Sigma
aka: *Life Dances On*
  rich widow seeks her partners at a

ball she remembers from her youth,
finding that they are all failures and
the ball is a village hop.
Considering its fame, this is a lumpy
porridge of a picture, good in parts
but often slow, pretentious and
banal. Its gallery of actors is,
however, unique.

w Jean Sarment, Pierre Wolff,
Bernard Zimmer, Henri Jeanson,
Julien Duvivier *d* Julien Duvivier
ph Michel Kelber, Philippe Agostini
m Maurice Jaubert

Marie Bell, Françoise Rosay, *Louis
Jouvet*, *Raimu*, *Harry Baur*,
Fernandel, *Pierre Blanchar*
   'Recent winner of the Mussolini
Cup is loaded with top names, but it
is not the film of the year . . . it tries
to take in too much and takes too
long to put across.'—*Variety*

† The film's international success
took Duvivier to Hollywood, where
he half-remade it as *Lydia* and went
on to other multi-story films such as
Tales of Manhattan and *Flesh and
Fantasy*.

'This is adult entertainment!'
The Carpetbaggers
  US 1964 150m
  Technicolor Panavision
Paramount/Embassy (Joseph E.
Levine)
A young playboy inherits an aircraft
business, becomes a megalomaniac
tycoon, and moves to Hollywood in
his search for power.
Enjoyable pulp fiction clearly
suggested by the career of Howard
Hughes. Lashings of old-fashioned
melodrama, quite well pointed by all
concerned.

w John Michael Hayes,
novel Harold Robbins *d Edward
Dmytryk ph* Joseph MacDonald
m Elmer Bernstein *ad* Hal Pereira,
Walter Tyler

George Peppard, Carroll Baker,
Alan Ladd (his last film), *Martin
Balsam*, Bob Cummings, Martha
Hyer, Elizabeth Ashley, Lew Ayres,
Ralph Taeger, Archie Moore, Leif
Erickson, Audrey Totter

'One of those elaborate conjuring tricks in which yards and yards of coloured ribbon are spread all over the stage merely to prove that the conjuror has nothing up his sleeve.'—*Tom Milne*

Carrie

US 1952   122m   bw
Paramount (William Wyler)
In the early 1900s a country girl comes to Chicago, loses her innocence and goes on the stage, meanwhile reducing a wealthy restaurant manager to penury through love for her.
A famous satirical novel is softened into an unwieldy narrative with scarcely enough dramatic power to sustain interest despite splendid production values. Heavy pre-release cuts remain obvious, and the general effect is depressing; but it is very good to look at.

w Ruth and Augustus Goetz, *novel* Sister Carrie by Theodore Dreiser   *d* William Wyler   *ph* Victor Milner   *m* David Raksin   *ad* Hal Pereira, Roland Anderson

Laurence Olivier, Jennifer Jones, Miriam Hopkins, Eddie Albert, Basil Ruysdael, Ray Teal, Barry Kelley, Mary Murphy
'Olivier is so impassioned and so painfully touching that everything else in the movie, including the girl whose story it's meant to be, fades into insignificance.'—*Variety*
'They shot the later episodes for the strongest dramatic effect only, despite the fact that the story had stopped following a melodramatic line and become a sociological study . . . each additional episode exploits the audience's hope that things will be brought to a satisfactory conclusion, but they never are.—*Films in Review*

Carrie

US 1976   98m   MGM-De Luxe
UA/Red Bank (Paul Monash)
A repressed teenager with remarkable mental powers takes a macabre revenge on classmates who taunt and persecute her.
Stylish but unattractive shocker which works its way up to a fine climax of gore and frenzy, and takes care to provide a final frisson just when the audience thinks it can safely go home.

w Laurence D. Cohen, *novel* Stephen King   *d* Brian de Palma   *ph* Mario Tosi   *m* Pino Donaggio

Sissy Spacek, *Piper Laurie*, Amy Irving, William Katt, John Travolta
'Combining Gothic horror, off hand misogyny and an air of studied triviality, *Carrie* is de Palma's most enjoyable movie in a long while, and also his silliest.'—*Janet Maslin, Newsweek*
'The horror is effective only once, and the attempts at humour are never very successful and come almost when one is inclined to be moved by somebody's plight, so that the non-jokes yield authentic bad taste.'—*John Simon, New York*
AAN: Sissy Spacek; Piper Laurie

'As big and timely a picture as ever you've seen! You can tell by the cast it's important! gripping! big!'

Casablanca

US 1942   102m   bw
Warner (*Hal B. Wallis*)
Rick's Café in Casablanca is a centre for war refugees awaiting visas for America. Rick abandons his cynicism to help an old love escape the Nazis with her underground leader husband.
Cinema par excellence: a studio-bound Hollywood melodrama which after various chances just fell together impeccably into one of the outstanding entertainment experiences of cinema history, with romance, intrigue, excitement, suspense and humour cunningly deployed by master technicians and a perfect cast.

w Julius J. Epstein, Philip G. Epstein, Howard Koch, from an unproduced play, Everybody Comes to Rick's, by Murray Burnett and Joan Alison *d Michael Curtiz ph Arthur Edeson m Max Steiner*

Humphrey Bogart (Rick Blaine), *Ingrid Bergman* (Ilse Lund), Paul Henreid (Victor Laszlo), *Claude Rains* (Captain Louis Renault), Sydney Greenstreet (Ferrari), Peter Lorre (Ugarte), S. Z. Sakall (Carl), *Conrad Veidt* (Major Strasser), *Dooley Wilson* (Sam), *Marcel Dalio* (Croupier) and Madeleine LeBeau, Joy Page, John Qualen, Ludwig Stossel, Leonid Kinskey, Helmut Dantine, Ilka Gruning
Songs: 'As Time Goes By', 'Knock on Wood'

RICK: 'I stick out my neck for nobody. I'm the only cause I'm interested in.'

LOUIS: 'How extravagant you are, throwing away women like that. Someday they may be scarce.'

RICK: Ilse, I'm no good at being noble, but it doesn't take much to see that the problems of three little people don't amount to a hill of beans in this crazy world. Someday you'll understand that. Not now. Here's looking at you, kid.'

RICK: 'I came to Casablanca for the waters.'
LOUIS: 'What waters? We're in the desert.'
RICK: 'I was misinformed.'

RICK: 'Louis, I think this is the beginning of a beautiful friendship.'

'A picture which makes the spine tingle and the heart take a leap . . . they have so combined sentiment, humour and pathos with taut melodrama and bristling intrigue that the result is a highly entertaining and even inspiring film.'—*New York Times*

'Its humour is what really saves it, being a mixture of Central European irony of attack and racy Broadway-Hollywood Boulevard cynicism.'—*Herman G. Weinberg*

'The happiest of happy accidents, and the most decisive exception to the *auteur* theory.'—*Andrew Sarris, 1968*

'A film which seems to have been frozen in time . . . the sum of its many marvellous parts far exceeds the whole.'—*NFT, 1974*

'It's far from a great film, but it has an appealingly schlocky romanticism, and you're never really pressed to take its melodramatic twists and turns seriously.'—*Pauline Kael, 70s*

† Originally named for the leads were Ronald Reagan, Ann Sheridan and Dennis Morgan.

AA: best picture; Julius J. and Philip G. Epstein, Howard Koch; Michael Curtiz
AAN: Arthur Edeson; Max Steiner; Humphrey Bogart; Claude Rains

Casque d'Or

France 1952   96m   bw
Speva / Paris
aka: *Golden Marie*
1898. In the Paris slums, an Apache finds passionate love but is executed for murder.
A tragic romance which on its first release seemed bathed in a golden glow and is certainly an impeccable piece of film-making.

w Jacques Becker, Jacques Companeez *d* Jacques Becker *ph* Robert Le Fèbvre *m* Georges Van Parys

Simone Signoret, Serge Reggiani, Claude Dauphin, Raymond Bussières, Gaston Modot

'Takes its place alongside *Le Jour Se Lève* among the masterpieces of the French cinema.'—*Karel Reisz*
'A screen alive with sensuousness and luminous figures.'—*Dilys Powell*

The Cat and the Canary

US 1927   84m (24 fps)
bw   silent
Universal
Greedy relatives assemble in an old house to hear an eccentric's will, and a young girl's sanity is threatened. Archetypal spooky house comedy horror, here given an immensely stylish production which influenced Hollywood through the thirties and was spoofed in *The Old Dark House*.

*w Alfred Cohn, Robert F. Hill,
play John Willard d Paul Leni
ph Gilbert Warrenton ad Charles D.
Hall*

Creighton Hale, Laura La Plante,
Forrest Stanley, Tully Marshall,
Flora Finch, Gertrude Astor, Arthur
Carewe

† Remade for sound by Rupert
Julian in 1930 as *The Cat Creeps*,
with Raymond Hackett, Helen
Twelvetrees and Jean Hersholt. This
title was also used for a grade Z 1946
second feature with a different plot.

The Cat and the Canary
US 1939 72m bw
Paramount (Arthur Hornblow
Jnr)
A superbly staged remake, briskly
paced, perfectly cast and lusciously
photographed.
The comedy-thriller par excellence,
with Bob Hope fresh and
sympathetic in his first big star part.

*w Walter de Leon, Lynn Starling
d Elliott Nugent ph Charles Lang
m Dr Ernst Toch ad Hans Dreier,
Robert Usher*

Bob Hope (Wally Campbell),
Paulette Goddard (Joyce Norman),
Gale Sondergaard (Miss Lu),
Douglass Montgomery (Charlie
Wilder), John Beal (Fred Blythe),
George Zucco (Lawyer Crosby),
Nydia Westman (Cicily), *Elizabeth
Patterson* (Aunt Susan), John Wray
(Hendricks)

CICILY: 'Do you believe people
come back from the dead?'

WALLY: 'Do you mean like
republicans?'

CICILY: 'Don't these big empty
houses scare you?'

WALLY: 'Not me, I was in
vaudeville.'

WALLY: 'I get goose pimples. Even
my goose pimples have goose
pimples.'

'The objective is carried out
briskly and to our complete
satisfaction.'—*New York Times*
'A top programmer for
upper-bracket bookings in the keys,

and will hit a consistent stride down
the line in the
subsequents.'—*Variety*
'Beautifully shot, intelligently
constructed.'—*Peter John Dyer,
1966*

Cat Ballou
US 1965 96m Technicolor
Columbia (Harold Hecht)
Young Catherine Ballou hires a
drunken gunfighter to protect her
father from a vicious gunman, but
despite her efforts he is shot, so she
turns outlaw.
Sometimes lively, sometimes
somnolent western spoof which
considering the talent involved
should have been funnier than it is.
The linking ballad helps.

*w Walter Newman, Frank R.
Pierson, novel Roy Chanslor d Eliot
Silverstein ph Jack Marta m Frank
de Vol*

Jane Fonda, *Lee Marvin*, Michael
Callan, Dwayne Hickman, Nat King
Cole, Stubby Kaye, Tom Nardini,
John Marley, Reginald Denny

'Uneven, lumpy, coy and
obvious.'—*Pauline Kael*

AA: Lee Marvin
AAN: Walter Newman, Frank R.
Pierson; Frank de Vol; song 'The
Ballad of Cat Ballou' (*m* Jerry
Livingston, *ly* Mack David)

'Kiss me and I'll claw you to
death!'
Cat People
US 1942 73m bw
RKO (*Val Lewton*)
A beautiful Yugoslavian girl believes
she can turn into a panther; before
she is found mysteriously dead,
several of her acquaintances are
attacked by such a beast.
The first of Lewton's famous horror
series for RKO is a slow starter but
has some notable suspense
sequences. It was also the first
monster film to refrain from showing
its monster.

*w De Witt Bodeen d Jacques
Tourneur ph Nicholas Musuraca
m Roy Webb*

Simone Simon, Kent Smith, Tom
Conway, Jane Randolph, Jack Holt
'(Lewton) revolutionized scare
movies with suggestion, imaginative
sound effects and camera angles,
leaving everything to the fear-filled
imagination.'—*Pauline Kael, 1968*

† *Curse of the Cat People* was a very
unrelated sequel.

Catch 22
US 1970 122m
Technicolor Panavision
Paramount / Filmways (John
Calley, Martin Ransohoff)

At a US Air Force base in the
Mediterranean during World War II,
one by one the officers are
distressingly killed; a survivor
paddles towards neutral Sweden.

Intensely black comedy, more so
than *M*A*S*H* and less funny,
effectively mordant in places but too
grisly and missing several tricks.

w Buck Henry, *novel* Joseph Heller
d Mike Nichols *ph* David Watkin
m none *d pd* Richard Sylbert

Alan Arkin, Martin Balsam, Richard
Benjamin, Art Garfunkel, Jack
Gilford, Buck Henry, Bob Newhart,
Anthony Perkins, Paula Prentiss,
Jon Voight, Martin Sheen, Orson
Welles

'There are startling effects and
good revue touches here and there,
but the picture keeps going on and
on, as if it were determined to
impress us.'—*New Yorker, 1977*

'As hot and heavy as the original
was cool and light.'—*Richard
Schickel*

'It goes on so long that it cancels
itself out, even out of people's
memories; it was long awaited and
then forgotten almost
instantly.'—*Pauline Kael*

'Dr Strangelove out of Alice in
Wonderland.'—*Daily Mail*

'A love that suffered and rose
    triumphant above the crushing
    events of this modern age! The
    march of time measured by a
    mother's heart!'
Cavalcade
US 1932 109m bw
Fox (Winfield Sheehan)

The story of an upper-class English
family between the Boer War and
World War I.

Rather static version of the famous
stage spectacular, very similar in
setting and style to TV's later
Upstairs Downstairs. Good
performances, flat handling.

w Reginald Berkeley, *play Noel
Coward d* Frank Lloyd *ph* Ernest
Palmer *war scenes* William
Cameron Menzies *ad* William
Darling *m* Louis de Francesco

Clive Brook, Diana Wynyard,
Ursula Jeans, Herbert Mundin, Una
O'Connor, Irene Browne, Merle
Tottenham, Beryl Mercer, Frank
Lawton, Billy Bevan

'Dignified and beautiful spectacle
that will demand respect.'—*Variety*

'If there is anything that moves the
ordinary American to uncontrollable
tears, it is the plight—the constant
plight—of dear old England . . . a
superlative newsreel, forcibly
strengthened by factual scenes, good
music, and wonderful
photography.'—*Pare Lorentz*

'Greater even than *Birth of a
Nation!*'—*Louella Parsons*

'An orgy of British
self-congratulation.'—*Pauline Kael,
'70s*

AA: best picture; Frank Lloyd;
William Darling
AAN: Diana Wynyard

'This is the only sport in the world
    where two guys get paid for
    doing something they'd be
    arrested for if they got drunk
    and did it for nothing.'
Champion
US 1949 99m bw
Stanley Kramer

An ambitious prizefighter alienates
his friends and family, and dies of
injuries received in the ring.
Interesting exposé of the fight
racket, presented in good cinematic
style and acted with great bravura.

w Carl Foreman, *story* Ring
Lardner *d Mark Robson ph* Franz
Planer *m* Dmitri Tiomkin

Kirk Douglas, Arthur Kennedy,

Marilyn Maxwell, Paul Stewart,
Ruth Roman, Lola Albright, Luis
Van Rooten

AAN: Carl Foreman; Franz Planer;
Dmitri Tiomkin; Kirk Douglas;
Arthur Kennedy

Charade

US 1964   113m
Technicolor
Universal/Stanley Donen
A Parisienne finds her husband
murdered. Four strange men are
after her, and she is helped by a
handsome stranger . . . but is he
hero, spy or murderer?
Smoothly satisfying sub-Hitchcock
nonsense, effective both as black
romantic comedy and macabre farce.

w Peter Stone d Stanley Donen
ph Charles Lang Jnr m Henry
Mancini

Cary Grant (sixty but concealing the
fact by taking a shower fully
clothed), Audrey Hepburn, Walter
Matthau, James Coburn, George
Kennedy, Ned Glass, Jacques Marin

   'One hesitates to be uncharitable
to a film like Charade, which seeks
only to provide a little innocent
merriment and make a pot of
money. . . . Of itself, it is a stylish
and amusing melodrama, but in the
context of the bloodlust that seems
unloosed in our land it is as sinister
as the villains who stalk Miss
Hepburn through the cobbled streets
of Paris.'—Arthur Knight

AAN: song 'Charade' (m Henry
Mancini, ly Johnny Mercer)

'The reckless lancers sweep on
   and on—so that a woman's
   heart might not be broken!
   You're not fighting a single
   legion—you're fighting the
   entire British army, Surat Khan!'
The Charge of the Light Brigade
US 1936   115m   bw
Warner (Hal B. Wallis, Sam
Bischoff)
An army officer deliberately starts
the Balaclava charge to even an old
score with Surat Khan, who's on the
other side.

Though allegedly 'based on the
poem by Alfred Lord Tennyson',
this is no more than a travesty of
history, most of it taking place in
India. As pure entertainment
however it is a most superior slice of
Hollywood hokum and the film
which set the seal on Errol Flynn's
superstardom.

w Michael Jacoby, Rowland Leigh
d Michael Curtiz ph Sol Polito, Fred
Jackman m Max Steiner

Errol Flynn, Olivia de Havilland,
Patric Knowles, Donald Crisp, C.
Aubrey Smith, David Niven, Henry
Stephenson, Nigel Bruce, C. Henry
Gordon, Spring Byington, E. E.
Clive, Lumsden Hare, Robert
Barrat, J. Carrol Naish

AAN: Max Steiner

'Two men chasing dreams of
   glory!'
Chariots of Fire
GB 1981   121m   colour
TCF/Allied Stars/Enigma
(David Puttnam)
In the 1924 Paris Olympics, a Jew
and a Scotsman run for Britain.
A film of subtle qualities, rather like
those of a BBC classic serial.
Probably not quite worth the
adulation it received, but full of
pleasant romantic touches and sharp
glimpses of the wider issues
involved.

w Colin Welland d Hugh Hudson
ph David Watkin m Vangelis

Ben Cross, Ian Charleson, Nigel
Havers, Nicholas Farrell, Daniel
Gerroll, Cheryl Campbell, Alice
Krige, John Gielgud, Lindsay
Anderson, Nigel Davenport, Ian
Holm, Patrick Magee
   'The whole contradictory bundle is
unexpectedly watchable.'—Jo
Imeson, MFB
   'A piece of technological lyricism
held together by the glue of
simple-minded heroic
sentiment.'—Pauline Kael

AA: best picture; Colin Welland;
Vangelis; costume design (Milera
Canonero)

AAN: Hugh Hudson; editing (Terry Rawlings); Ian Holm (supporting actor)
BFA: best picture; costume design; Ian Holm

'When he runs out of dumb luck he always has genius to fall back on!'

Charley Varrick
US 1973   111m
Technicolor
Universal (Don Siegel)

A bank robber discovers he has stolen Mafia money, and devises a clever scheme to get himself off the hook.

Sharp, smart, well-observed but implausible thriller, astringently handled and agreeably set in Californian backlands. Accomplished, forgettable entertainment.

w Howard Rodman, Dean Reisner, *novel* The Looters by John Reese *d* Don Siegel *ph* Michael Butler *m* Lalo Schifrin

Walter Matthau, Joe Don Baker, Felicia Farr, Andy Robinson, John Vernon, Sheree North, Norman Fell

'The narrative line is clean and direct, the characterizations economical and functional, and the triumph of intelligence gloriously satisfying.'—*Andrew Sarris*

Charley's Aunt
US 1941   81m   bw
TCF (William Perlberg)

GB title: *Charley's American Aunt*

For complicated reasons, an Oxford undergraduate has to impersonate his own rich aunt from Brazil (where the nuts come from).

Very adequate version of the Victorian farce, with all concerned in excellent form.

w George Seaton, *play* Brandon Thomas *d* Archie Mayo *ph* Peverell Marley *m* Alfred Newman *ad* Richard Day, Nathan Juran

Jack Benny, Kay Francis, James Ellison, Anne Baxter, *Laird Cregar*, Edmund Gwenn, Reginald Owen,

Richard Haydn, Arleen Whelan, Ernest Cossart

Charlie Bubbles
GB 1968   91m   Technicolor
Universal / Memorial (Michael Medwin, George Pitcher)

A successful novelist loathes the pointlessness of the good life and tries unsuccessfully to return to his northern working class background. A little arid and slow in its early stages, and with a rather lame end (our hero escapes by air balloon), this is nevertheless a fascinating, fragmentary character study with a host of wry comedy touches and nimbly sketched characters; in its unassuming way it indicts many of the symbols people lived by in the sixties.

w Shelagh Delaney *d* Albert Finney *ph* Peter Suschitsky *m* Mischa Donat

Albert Finney, Billie Whitelaw, Liza Minnelli, Colin Blakely, Timothy Garland, Diana Coupland, Alan Lake, Yootha Joyce, Joe Gladwin

'A modest thing, but like all good work in minor keys it has a way of haunting the memory.'—*Richard Schickel*

'The supreme deadweight is Liza Minnelli, whose screen debut proves easily the most inauspicious since Turhan Bey's.'—*John Simon*

The Chase
US 1966   135m
Technicolor   Panavision
Columbia / Sam Spiegel

When a convict escapes and heads for his small Texas home town, almost all the inhabitants are affected in one way or another. Expensive but shoddy essay in sex and violence, with Brando as a masochistic sheriff lording it over Peyton-Place-in-all-but-name. Literate moments do not atone for the general pretentiousness, and we have all been here once too often.

w Lillian Hellman, *novel* Horton Foote *d* Arthur Penn *ph* Joseph La Shelle *pd* Richard Day *m* John Barry

Marlon Brando, Jane Fonda, Robert
Redford, Angie Dickinson, Janice
Rule, James Fox, Robert Duvall, E.
G. Marshall, Miriam Hopkins,
Henry Hull

'The worst thing that has
happened to movies since Lassie
played a war veteran with
amnesia.'—*Rex Reed*

'Considering all the talent
connected with it, it is hard to
imagine how *The Chase* went so
haywire.'—*Philip T. Hartung*

Cheaper by the Dozen
⚫ US 1950   86m   Technicolor
TCF (Lamar Trotti)

Efficiency expert Frank Gilbreth and
his wife Lillian have twelve children,
a fact which requires mathematical
conduct of all their lives.
Amusing family comedy set in the
twenties, unconvincing in detail
though based on a book by two of
the children. A great commercial
success and a Hollywood
myth-maker. Sequel: *Belles on their
Toes*.

w Lamar Trotti, *book* Frank B.
Gilbreth Jnr, Ernestine Gilbreth
Carey *d Walter Lang ph* Leon
Shamroy *m* Cyril Mockridge
md Lionel Newman *ad* Lyle
Wheeler, Leland Fuller

Clifton Webb, Myrna Loy, Jeanne
Crain, Edgar Buchanan, Barbara
Bates, Betty Lynn, Mildred
Natwick, Sara Allgood

Cheyenne Autumn
🎞 US 1964   170m
Technicolor   Panavision 70
Warner/Ford-Smith (Bernard
Smith)

In the 1860s, Cheyenne Indians are
moved to a new reservation 1500
miles away; wanting aid, they begin
a trek back home, and various
battles follow.
Dispirited, shapeless John Ford
western with little of the master's
touch; good to look at, however,
with effective cameos, notably an
irrelevant and out-of-key comic one
featuring James Stewart as Wyatt
Earp.

w James R. Webb, *novel* Mari
Sandoz *d* John Ford *ph* William H.
Clothier *m* Alex North

Richard Widmark, Carroll Baker,
Karl Malden, *Dolores del Rio*, Sal
Mineo, Edward G. Robinson, *James
Stewart*, Ricardo Montalban, Gilbert
Roland, Arthur Kennedy, Patrick
Wayne, Elizabeth Allen, Victor
Jory, John Carradine, Mike
Mazurki, John Qualen, George
O'Brien

'Although one would like to praise
the film for its high-minded aims, it
is hard to forget how ponderous and
disjointed it is.'—*Moira Walsh*

'The acting is bad, the dialogue
trite and predictable, the pace
funereal, the structure fragmented
and the climaxes puny.'—*Stanley
Kauffmann*

AAN: William H. Clothier

The Childhood of Maxim Gorky
🎞 USSR 1938–40   bw
Soyuzdetfilm

Orphan Gorky is raised by his
grandparents, and becomes a ship's
cook and a painter before going on
to university.
This simple and direct story is told in
three beautifully detailed if rather
overlong films:
'The Childhood of Maxim Gorky':
101m
'Out in the World': 98m
'My Universities': 104m

w Mark Donskoi, I. Grudzev
d Mark Donskoi ph Pyotr
Yermolov *m* Lev Schwartz *ad* I.
Stepanov

Alexei Lyarsky, Y. Valbert, M.
Troyanovski, Valeria Massalitinova

Chimes at Midnight
🎞 Spain/Switz 1966   119m
bw

Internacional Films
Espanola/Alpine (Alessandro
Tasca)

aka: *Falstaff*

Prince Hal becomes King Henry V
and rejects his old friend Falstaff.
Clumsy adaptation of Shakespeare
with brilliant flashes and the usual

Welles vices of hasty production, poor synchronization and recording, etc. One wonders why, if he wanted to make a telescoped version of the plays, he did not spare the time and patience to make it better.

w Orson Welles *d* Orson Welles
ph Edmond Richard *m* Angelo Francesco Lavagnino

Orson Welles, Keith Baxter, John Gielgud (Henry IV), Margaret Rutherford (Mistress Quickly), Jeanne Moreau (Doll Tearsheet), Norman Rodway, Alan Webb, Marina Vlady, Tony Beckley, Fernando Rey

China Seas
US 1935 89m bw
MGM (Albert Lewin)
Luxury cruise passengers find themselves involved with piracy. Omnibus shipboard melodrama, tersely scripted and featuring a splendid cast all somewhere near their best; slightly dated but very entertaining.

w Jules Furthman, James Kevin McGuinness, *novel* Crosbie Garstin
d Tay Garnett *ph* Ray June
m Herbert Stothart

Clark Gable, Jean Harlow, Wallace Beery, Rosalind Russell, Lewis Stone, C. Aubrey Smith, Dudley Digges, Robert Benchley
'It will do double-barrelled duty, drawing business and providing ace entertainment.'—*Variety*
'The hell with art this time. I'm going to produce a picture that will make money.'—*Irving Thalberg*

Chinatown
US 1974 131m
Technicolor Panavision
Paramount / Long Road (Robert Evans)
In 1937, a Los Angeles private eye takes on a simple case and burrows into it until it leads to murder and a public scandal.
Pretentious melodrama which is basically no more serious than the Raymond Chandler mysteries from which it derives; the tragic ending is merely an irritation, and the title only allusive. Superficially, however, it is eminently watchable, with effective individual scenes and performances and photography which is lovingly composed though tending to suggest period by use of an orange filter.

w Robert Towne *d* Roman Polanski
ph John A. Alonso *m* Jerry Goldsmith *pd* Richard Sylbert

Jack Nicholson, Faye Dunaway, John Huston, Perry Lopez, John Hillerman, Roman Polanski, Darrell Zwerling, Diane Ladd

AA: Robert Towne
AAN: best picture; Roman Polanski; John A. Alonso; Jerry Goldsmith; Jack Nicholson; Faye Dunaway

'If you can't sleep at night, it isn't the coffee—it's the bunk!'
Christmas in July
US 1940 67m bw
Paramount
A young clerk and his girl win first prize in a big competition. Slightly unsatisfactory as a whole, this Preston Sturges comedy has echoes of Clair and a dully predictable plot line, but is kept alive by inventive touches and a gallery of splendid character comedians.

wd Preston Sturges *ph* Victor Milner *m* Sigmund Krumgold

Dick Powell, Ellen Drew, Ernest Truex, *Al Bridge*, Raymond Walburn, William Demarest
'The perfect restorative for battered humors and jangled nerves.'—*Bosley Crowther*
'Agreeable enough, but it lacks the full-fledged Sturges lunacy.'—*New Yorker, 1977*

'Secrets of a doctor as told by a doctor!'
The Citadel
GB 1938 113m bw
MGM (Victor Saville)
A young doctor has a hard time in the mining villages but is later

swayed by the easy rewards of a
Mayfair practice.
Solidly produced adaptation of a
bestseller; the more recent deluge of
doctors on television make it appear
rather elementary, but many scenes
work in a classical way. One of the
first fruits of MGM's British studios
which were closed by World War II.

w Elizabeth Hill, Ian Dalrymple,
Emlyn Williams, Frank Wead,
novel A. J. Cronin *d* King Vidor
ph Harry Stradling *m* Louis Levy

Robert Donat, Rosalind Russell,
Ralph Richardson, Emlyn Williams,
Penelope Dudley Ward, Francis L.
Sullivan

'General audience limited . . .
strong for the Anglo
market.'—*Variety*

'I think any doctor will agree that
here is a medical picture with no
Men in White hokum, no hysterical,
incredible melodrama, but with an
honest story, honestly told. And
that's a rare picture.'—*Pare Lorentz*

'We are grateful that a worthy
idea has been handled with
intelligence and imagination, that
Vidor has shown respect both for his
talent and for the sensibilities of the
audience.'—*Robert Stebbins*

'Numerous passages shine
brilliantly with those deft touches
that first brought Vidor to
prominence.'—*Variety*

'The pace of Hollywood, the
honest characterization of England's
best.'—*New York Times*

† The parts played by Russell and
Richardson were originally intended
for Elizabeth Allan and Spencer
Tracy

AAN: best picture; script; King
Vidor; Robert Donat

Citizen Kane

🏆🏆 US 1941   119m   bw
X RKO (Orson Welles)

A newspaper tycoon dies, and a
magazine reporter interviews his
friends in an effort to discover the
meaning of his last words.
A brilliant piece of Hollywood
cinema using all the resources of the
studio; despite lapses of
characterization and gaps in the
narrative, almost every shot and
every line is utterly absorbing both
as entertainment and as craft. See
The Citizen Kane Book by Pauline
Kael, and innumerable other
writings.

*w Herman J. Mankiewicz, Orson
Welles d Orson Welles ph Gregg
Toland m Bernard Herrmann
ad Van Nest Polglase sp Vernon L.
Walker*

Orson Welles (Kane), *Joseph Cotten*
(Jedediah Leland), *Dorothy
Comingore* (Susan Alexander),
Everett Sloane (Bernstein), *Ray
Collins* (Boss Jim Geddes), *Paul
Stewart* (Raymond), *Ruth Warrick*
(Emily Norton), *Erskine Sanford*
(Herbert Carter), *Agnes Moorehead*
(Kane's mother), *Harry Shannon*
(Kane's father), *George Coulouris*
(Walter Parks Thatcher), *William
Alland* (Thompson), *Fortunio
Bonanova* (music teacher)

'What is his name? It's Charlie
Kane! I'll bet you five you're not
alive if you don't know his name!'

NEWSREEL: 'Then, last week, as it
must to all men, death came to
Charles Foster Kane.'

BERNSTEIN: 'Old age . . . it's the
only disease you don't look forward
to being cured of.'

THOMPSON: 'Mr Kane was a man
who got everything he wanted, and
then lost it. Maybe Rosebud was
something he couldn't get, or
something he lost. Anyway, I don't
think it would have explained
everything. I don't think any word
can explain a man's life. No, I guess
Rosebud is just a piece in a jigsaw
puzzle . . . a missing piece.'

SUSAN: 'Forty-nine acres of
nothing but scenery and statues. I'm
lonesome.'

KANE: 'You're right, Mr Thatcher.
I did lose a million dollars last year.
I expect to lose a million dollars this
year. I expect to lose a million
dollars next year. You know, Mr
Thatcher, at the rate of a million

dollars a year, I'll have to close this place—in sixty years.'

KANE: 'I run a couple of newspapers. What do you do?'

BERNSTEIN: 'One day back in 1896 I was crossing over to Jersey on the ferry, and as we pulled out, there was another ferry pulling in, and on it there was a girl waiting to get off. A white dress she had on. She was carrying a white parasol. I only saw her for one second. She didn't see me at all, but I'll bet a month hasn't gone by since that I haven't thought of that girl.'

'On seeing it for the first time, one got a conviction that if the cinema could do that, it could do anything.'—*Penelope Houston*

'What may distinguish *Citizen Kane* most of all is its extracting the mythic from under the humdrum surface of the American experience.'—*John Simon, 1968*

'Probably the most exciting film that has come out of Hollywood for twenty-five years. I am not sure it isn't the most exciting film that has ever come out of anywhere.'—*C. A. Lejeune*

'At any rate Orson Welles has landed in the movies, with a splash and a loud yell.'—*James Shelley Hamilton*

'More fun than any great movie I can think of.'—*Pauline Kael, 1968*

'It is a fascinating picture, but because of its congestion of technical stunts, it fails to move us.'—*Egon Larsen*

'A quite good film which tries to run the psychological essay in harness with the detective thriller, and doesn't quite succeed.'—*James Agate*

AA: Herman J. Mankiewicz, Orson Welles (script)

AAN: best picture; Orson Welles (as director); Gregg Toland; Bernard Herrmann; Orson Welles (as actor)

City for Conquest

US 1940 106m bw
Warner (Anatole Litvak)

An East Side truck driver becomes a boxer but is blinded in a fight; meanwhile his composer brother gives up pop music for symphonies. Phony but oddly persuasive melodrama set in a studio in New York and heavily influenced by the pretensions of the Group theatre.

w John Wexley, *novel* Aben Kandel d Anatole Litvak ph Sol Polito, James Wong Howe m Max Steiner

James Cagney, Ann Sheridan, Frank Craven, Donald Crisp, *Arthur Kennedy*, Frank McHugh, George Tobias, Anthony Quinn, Jerome Cowan, Lee Patrick, Blanche Yurka, Thurston Hall.

'Sometimes we wonder whether it wasn't really the Warner brothers who got New York from the Indians, so diligent and devoted have they been in feeling the great city's pulse, picturing its myriad facets and recording with deep compassion the passing life of its seething population.'—*Bosley Crowther*

City Lights

US 1931 87m bw silent
(with music and effects)
(UA) Charles Chaplin

A tramp befriends a millionaire and falls in love with a blind girl. Sentimental comedy with several delightful sequences in Chaplin's best manner.

wd,m Charles Chaplin ph Rollie Totheroh, Mark Marlott, Gordon Pollock

Charles Chaplin, Virginia Cherrill, Harry Myers

'Chaplin has another good picture, but it gives indications of being short-winded, and may tire fast after a bombastic initial seven days . . . he has sacrificed speed to pathos, and plenty of it.'—*Variety*

'Even while laughing, one is aware of a faint and uneasy feeling that Chaplin has been pondering with more than a bit of solemnity on conventional story values, and it has led him further than ever into the realms of what is often called pathetic.'—*National Board of Review*

'Love and courage pitted against a ruthless hate!'

City Streets

US 1931 86m bw
Paramount (Rouben Mamoulian)

A gangster's daughter is sent to jail for a murder she did not commit, and on release narrowly escapes being 'taken for a ride'.

Tense, dated gangland melodrama of primary interest because of its director's very cinematic treatment.

w Max Marcin, Oliver H. P. Garrett, Dashiell Hammett, *story* Ladies of the Mob by Ernest Booth *d Rouben Mamoulian ph Lee Garmes*

Sylvia Sidney, Gary Cooper, Paul Lukas, Guy Kibbee, William (Stage) Boyd, Stanley Fields, Wynne Gibson

TYPICAL GANGSTER DIALOGUE OF THE TIME:

Who's running this show, anyhow?
—I am.
Who says so?
—I say so, for one. And when you talk to me, take that toothpick outa your mouth!

'So many brilliant touches that anyone who sees it will have to predict for Mamoulian a brilliant career.'—*Film Spectator*

'Too much attempt to artify hurts though the sophisticated treatment and elegant settings will help.'—*Variety*

'A love story in a gangster setting which got carried away into so much fancy expressionism and symbolism that it seems stylized out of all relationship to the actual world.'—*Pauline Kael, 70s.*

Civilization

US 1916 68m (1931 'sound' version) bw silent
Triangle

A mythical country starts war, but one of the principals has a vision of Christ on the battlefields and the king is persuaded to sign a peace treaty.

Surprisingly impressive parable showing this early director at his best; intended as a pacifist tract in the middle of World War I.

w C. Gardner Sullivan *d Thomas Ince ph* Irwin Willat

Enid Markey, Howard Hickman, J. Barney Sherry

Claudia

US 1943 92m bw
TCF (William Perlberg)

A middle-class husband helps his child-wife to mature.

Typical of the best of Hollywood's 'woman's pictures' of the period, this is a pleasant domestic comedy-drama featuring recognizably human characters in an agreeable setting.

w Morrie Ryskind, *novel* and *play* Rose Franken d Edmund Goulding *ph* Leon Shamroy m Alfred Newman

Dorothy McGuire (her film debut), *Robert Young*, *Ina Claire*, Reginald Gardiner, Olga Baclanova, Jean Howard, Elsa Janssen

'It won't leave a dry eye in the house.'—*Variety*

† Cary Grant was sought for the Robert Young part.

'The love affair that shook the world!'

Cleopatra

US 1934 101m bw
Paramount/Cecil B. de Mille

After Julius Caesar's death, Cleopatra turns her attention to Mark Antony.

More of the vices than the virtues of its producer are notable in this fustian epic, which is almost but not quite unwatchable because of its stolid pace and miscasting. Some of the action montages and the barge scene, however, are superb cinema.

w Waldemar Young, Vincent Lawrence *d Cecil B. de Mille ph* Victor Milner *m* Rudolph Kopp

Claudette Colbert, Henry Wilcoxon (Antony), Warren William (Caesar), Gertrude Michael, Joseph Schildkraut, Ian Keith, C. Aubrey Smith, Leonard Mudie, Irving Pichel, Arthur Hohl.

'He has certainly made the most sumptuous of Roman circuses out of Roman history . . . a constant succession of banquets, dancers, triumphs, and a fleet set on fire.'—*The Times*

'Gorgeous optically but mentally weak . . . a handpicked audience was polite but not over-enthusiastic.'—*Variety*

'A great cinematic achievement, a spectacle of breathtaking brilliance.'—*Daily Express*

'It is remarkable how Cecil B. de Mille can photograph so much on such a vast scale and still say nothing ... it reeks of so much pseudo-artistry, vulgarity, philistinism, sadism, that it can only be compared with the lowest form of contemporary culture: Hitlerism. This is the type of "culture" that will be fed to the audience of Fascist America.'—*Irving Lerner, 1968*

AA: Victor Milner
AAN: best picture

'The motion picture the world has been waiting for!'
Cleopatra
US 1963 243m De Luxe
Todd-AO
TCF (Walter Wanger)
The unsurprising story is told at inordinate length and dullness in this ill-starred epic, one of the most heralded, and mismanaged, in film history. (Its story is best told in the producer's *My Life with Cleopatra*.) The most expensive film ever made, for various reasons which do not appear on the screen.

w Joseph L. Mankiewicz, Ranald MacDougall, Sidney Buchman, and others d Joseph L. Mankiewicz (and others) ph Leon Shamroy m Alex North ad John de Cuir, Jack Martin Smith, and others

Elizabeth Taylor, Richard Burton, Rex Harrison, Pamela Brown, George Cole, Hume Cronyn, Cesare Danova, Kenneth Haigh, Andrew Keir, Martin Landau, Roddy McDowall, Robert Stephens

Francesca Annis, Martin Benson, Herbert Berghof, Grégoire Aslan, Richard O'Sullivan

'Whatever was interesting about it clearly ended up somewhere else: on the cutting room floor, in various hotel rooms, in the newspaper columns . . . it lacks not only the intelligent spectacle of *Lawrence of Arabia* but the spectacular unintelligence of a Cecil B. de Mille product . . .'—*John Simon*

'The small screen does more than justice to this monumental mouse.'—*Judith Crist*

'I only came to see the asp.'—*Charles Addams*

'Surely the most bizarre piece of entertainment ever to be perpetrated.'—*Elizabeth Taylor*

AA: Leon Shamroy
AAN: best picture; Alex North; Rex Harrison

The Clock
US 1945 90m bw
MGM (Arthur Freed)
GB title: *Under the Clock*
A girl meets a soldier at New York's Grand Central Station and marries him during his 24-hour leave. Everyone now seems far too nice in this winsome romance full of comedy cameos and real New York locations, but if you can relive the wartime mood it still works as a corrective to the Betty Grable glamour pieces.

w Robert Nathan, Joseph Schrank, *story* Paul and Pauline Gallico *d* Vincente Minnelli *ph* George Folsey *m* George Bassman

Judy Garland, Robert Walker, James Gleason, Lucile Gleason, Keenan Wynn, Marshall Thompson, Chester Clute

'Sweetly charming, if maybe too irresistible . . . fortunately the director fills the edges with comic characters.'—*New Yorker, 1978*

'The emotion may have been honest, but the method was too rich for my eyes, and the writing as used on the screen too weak for my mind.'—*Stephen Longstreet*

'Strictly a romance . . . safely told, disappointing and angering in the thought of the great film it might have been.'—*James Agee*

'Amazingly, it was all shot in the studio, using street sets and back projection; even the old Penn station, where so much of the action takes place, is a set.'—*Pauline Kael, 70s*

'We are not alone . . .'
Close Encounters of the Third Kind
US 1977   135m
Metrocolor   Panavision
Columbia/EMI (Julia and Michael Phillips)

A series of UFOs takes Indiana by surprise, and a workman is led by intuition and detection to the landing site which has been concealed from the public.

There's a lot of padding in this slender fantasy, which has less plot and much less suspense than *It Came from Outer Space* which was made on a tiny budget in 1955; but the technical effects are masterly though their exposure is over-prolonged, and the benevolent mysticism filled a current requirement of popular taste, accounting for the enormous box-office success of a basically flawed film. Much of the dialogue is inaudible.

wd Steven Spielberg *ph* Vilmos Zsigmond *m* John Williams *sp* Douglas Trumbull *pd* Joe Alves

Richard Dreyfuss, François Truffaut, Teri Garr, Melinda Dillon, Cary Guffey

'It somehow combines Disney and 1950s SF and junk food into the most persuasive (if arrested) version of the American dream yet.'—*Time Out*

† The cost of this film was estimated at 20,000,000 dollars.

†† In 1980 a 'special edition' was released with some success: this pared down the idiotic middle section and extended the final scenes of the space ship, including some new interiors.

††† This film used the largest set in film history: the inside of an old dirigible hangar.

Of the special edition, Derek Malcolm in the *Guardian* wrote: 'One is inclined to feel that with all the money at his disposal, Spielberg might have got it right the first time.'

AA: Vilmos Zsigmond
AAN: direction; John Williams; Melinda Dillon

The Cocoanuts
US 1929   96m   bw
Paramount (Walter Wanger, James R. Cown)

A chiselling hotel manager tries to get in on the Florida land boom. Considering its age and the dismal prints which remain, this is a remarkably lively if primitive first film by the Marxes, with some good routines among the excess footage.

w George S. Kaufman, Morrie Ryskind *d* Robert Florey, Joseph Santley *ph* George Folsey *m/ly* Irving Berlin

The Four Marx Brothers, Margaret Dumont, Oscar Shaw, Mary Eaton, Kay Francis, Basil Ruysdael

'The camerawork showed all the mobility of a concrete fire hydrant caught in a winter freeze.'—*Paul D. Zimmermann*

Cocoon
US 1985   117m   De Luxe
TCF/Zanuck-Brown (Lili Zanuck)

Aliens from another galaxy leave pods in the pool of a Florida retirement home, whose bathers are rejuvenated.

Unusual, amusing and sentimentally effective movie of the kind which gets hearty word-of-mouth recommendation.

w Tom Benedek *novel* David Saperstein *d* Ron Howard *ph* Don Peterman *m* James Horner *pd* Jack T. Collis *ed* Daniel Hanley, Michael J. Hill

Don Ameche, Wilford Brimley, Hume Cronyn, Brian Dennehy, Jack

Gilford, Steve Guttenberg, Maureen
Stapleton, Jessica Tandy, Gwen
Verdon

'A mesmerizing tale that's a
certified audience pleaser.'—*Variety*

AA: best supporting actor, Don
Ameche

The Colditz Story
GB 1954 97m bw
British Lion/Ivan Foxwell
Adventures of British POWs in the
German maximum security prison in
Saxony's Colditz Castle during
World War II.
Probably the most convincing of the
British accounts of POW life, with a
careful balance of tragedy and
comedy against a background of
humdrum, boring daily existence. A
TV series followed in 1972.

w Guy Hamilton, Ivan Foxwell,
book P. R. Reid *d* Guy Hamilton
ph Gordon Dines *m* Francis
Chagrin

John Mills, Eric Portman,
Christopher Rhodes, Lionel Jeffries,
Bryan Forbes, Ian Carmichael,
Richard Wattis, Frederick Valk,
Anton Diffring, Eugene Deckers,
Theodore Bikel

'It has all the realism, dignity and
courage of the men it
commemorates.'—*News of the
World*

The Color of Money
US 1986 119m DuArt
Touchstone (Irving Axelrod,
Barbara de Fina)
Twenty-five years later, the hero of
The Hustler teaches a young man his
skills.
Slackly told but consistently
enjoyable adventures of Fast Eddie
Felson in his older age.

w Richard Price, from characters in
the novel by Walter Tevis *d Martin
Scorsese ph* Michael Ballhaus
m Robbie Robertson

Paul Newman, Tom Cruise, Mary
Elizabeth Mastrantonio, Helen
Shaver, Bill Cobbs, John Turturro

The Comancheros
US 1961 107m De Luxe
Cinemascope
TCF (George Sherman)
A Texas Ranger and his gambler
prisoner join forces to clean up
renegade gunmen operating from a
remote armed compound.
Easy-going, cheerfully violent
western with lively roughhouse
sequences.

w James Edward Grant, Clair
Huffaker *d* Michael Curtiz
ph William H. Clothier *m* Elmer
Bernstein

John Wayne, Stuart Whitman,
Nehemiah Persoff, Lee Marvin, Ina
Balin, Bruce Cabot

The Company of Wolves
GB 1984 95m colour
ITC/Palace (Chris Brown,
Stephen Woolley)
A young girl dreams of wolves and
werewolves.
Fragmentary adult fantasy which had
an unexpected box office success,
chiefly because of its sexual
allusiveness, its clever make-up and
its pictorial qualities.

w Angela Carter, Neil Jordan, from
stories by Angela Carter *d Neil
Jordan ph* Bryan Loftus *m* George
Fenton *special make-up
effects* Christopher Tucker
pd Anton Furst

Angela Lansbury, David Warner,
Graham Crowden, Brian Glover,
Sarah Patterson, Micha Bergese,
Stephen Rea

Coney Island
US 1943 96m Technicolor
TCF (William Perlberg)
Two fairground showmen vie for the
affections of a songstress.
Brassy, simple-minded, entertaining
musical. Very typical of its time;
later remade as *Wabash Avenue*.

w George Seaton *d Walter Lang
ph* Ernest Palmer *songs* Leo Robin,
Ralph Rainger *m* Alfred Newman
ch Hermes Pan *ad* Richard Day,
Joseph C. Wright

Betty Grable, George Montgomery,
Cesar Romero, Charles Winninger,
Phil Silvers, Matt Briggs, Paul
Hurst, Frank Orth, Andrew
Tombes, Alec Craig, Hal K. Dawson

AAN: Alfred Newman

Confessions of a Nazi spy
🐾 US 1939   110m   bw
Warner (Robert Lord)

How G-men ferreted out Nazis in
the United States.

Topical exposé with all concerned in
top form; a semi-documentary very
typical of Warner product
throughout the thirties and forties,
from *G-Men* to *Mission to Moscow*
and *I Was a Communist for the FBI*:
well made, punchy, and smartly
edited, with a loud moral at the end.

w Milton Krims, John Wexley, from
materials gathered by former FBI
agent Leon G. Turrou *d* Anatole
Litvak *ph* Sol Polito *m* Max Steiner

Edward G. Robinson, Paul Lukas,
George Sanders, Francis Lederer,
Henry O'Neill, Lya Lys, James
Stephenson, Sig Rumann, Dorothy
Tree, Joe Sawyer.

'Its social implications are far
more important than the immediate
question of how much money the
release makes for Warner
Brothers.'—*Variety*

'The Warner brothers have
declared war on Germany with this
one . . . with this precedent there is
no way any producer could argue
against dramatizing any social or
political theme on the grounds that
he's afraid of domestic or foreign
censorship. Everybody duck.'—*Pare
Lorentz*

'Has a remarkable resemblance to
a full-length *Crime Does Not
Pay*.'—*David Wolff*

'One of the most sensational
movie jobs on record, workmanlike
in every respect and spang across the
headlines.'—*Otis Ferguson*

Conquest
🐾 US 1937   115m   bw
MGM (Bernard Hyman)
GB title: *Marie Walewska*

The life of Napoleon's most
enduring mistress.

Measured, dignified, and often
rather dull historical fiction,
lightened by excellent performances
and production.

w Samuel Hoffenstein, Salka
Viertel, S. N. Behrman, from a
Polish play dramatized by Helen
Jerome *d* Clarence Brown *ph* Karl
Freund *m* Herbert Stothart

Greta Garbo, *Charles Boyer*,
Reginald Owen, Alan Marshal,
Henry Stephenson, Dame May
Whitty, Leif Erickson

'For special first-run
openings—and then the clean
up.'—*Variety*

'Ornate, unexpectedly tasteful,
carefully detailed—and
lifeless.'—*Pauline Kael, 70s*

AAN: Charles Boyer

The Conversation
🐾🐾 US 1974   113m
Technicolor
Paramount / Francis Ford Coppola

A bugging device expert lives only
for his work, but finally develops a
conscience.

Absorbing but extremely difficult to
follow in detail, this personal, timely
(in view of Watergate), Kafkaesque
suspense story centres almost
entirely on director and leading
actor, who have a field day.

wd Francis Ford Coppola *ph* Bill
Butler *m* David Shire

Gene Hackman, John Cazale, Allen
Garfield, Frederick Forrest

'A private, hallucinatory study in
technical expertise and lonely
guilt.'—*Sight and Sound*

'A terrifying depiction of a
ransacked spirit.'—*New Yorker,
1977*

'Alert, truthful, unarty and
absolutely essential
viewing.'—*Michael Billington,
Illustrated London News*

AAN: best picture; Francis Ford
Coppola (as writer)

'What we've got here is a failure to communicate.'

Cool Hand Luke

US 1967 126m
Technicolor Panavision
Warner / Jalem (Gordon Carroll)

Sentenced to two years' hard labour with the chain gang, a convict becomes a legend of invulnerability but is eventually shot during an escape.

Allegedly a Christ-allegory, this well-made and good-looking film is only partially successful as an entertainment; slow stretches of soul-searching alternate with brutality, and not much acting is possible.

w Donn Pearce, Frank R. Pierson, *novel* Donn Pearce *d* Stuart Rosenberg *ph* Conrad Hall *m* Lalo Schifrin

Paul Newman, George Kennedy, Jo Van Fleet, J. D. Cannon, Lou Antonio, Robert Drivas, Strother Martin, Clifton James

AA: George Kennedy
AAN: Donn Pearce, Frank R. Pierson; Lalo Schifrin; Paul Newman

Le Corbeau

France 1943 92m bw
L'Atelier Français
US title: *The Raven*

Poison pen letters disturb a small provincial town.

Impressively characterized whodunnit with the usual French qualities of detail and discretion. Remade in Hollywood to less effect as *The Thirteenth Letter*.

w Louis Chavance *d* Henri-Georges Clouzot *ph* Nicholas Hayer *m* Tony Aubain

Pierre Fresnay, Pierre Larquey, Ginette Leclerc, Hélène Manson

'By no means as malign or as brilliant as it's cracked up to be, but a sour, clever, amusing job.'—*James Agee*

The Count of Monte Cristo

US 1934 114m bw
Edward Small / Reliance

After spending years in prison, Edmond Dantes escapes and avenges himself on those who framed him.

Classic swashbuckler, extremely well done with due attention to dialogue as well as action; a model of its kind and period.

w Philip Dunne, Dan Totheroh, Rowland V. Lee, *novel* Alexandre Dumas *d* Rowland V. Lee *ph* Peverell Marley *m* Alfred Newman

Robert Donat, Elissa Landi, Louis Calhern, Sidney Blackmer, Raymond Walburn, O. P. Heggie, William Farnum

'A near-perfect blend of thrilling action and grand dialogue.'—*Variety*

'How far should a woman go to redeem the man she loves?'

The Country Girl

US 1954 104m bw
Paramount (William Perlberg)

The wife of an alcoholic singer blossoms when he is stimulated into a comeback.

Theatrically effective but highly unconvincing, this rather glum stage success made a cold film, miscast with an eye on the box office.

w George Seaton, *play* Clifford Odets *d* George Seaton *ph* John F. Warren *m* Victor Young *songs* Ira Gershwin, Harold Arlen

Bing Crosby, Grace Kelly, William Holden, Anthony Ross, Gene Reynolds

'The dramatic development is not really interesting enough to sustain a film of the intensity for which it strives.'—*Karel Reisz*

'Rather inexplicably, this sado-masochist morass was one of the biggest box office hits of its year.'—*Pauline Kael, 70s*

AA: George Seaton (as writer); Grace Kelly
AAN: best picture; John F. Warren; Bing Crosby

The Court Jester

US 1955 101m
Technicolor Vistavision
Paramount / Dena (Melvin Frank, Norman Panama)

Opposition to a tyrannical king is provided by the Fox, but it is one of the rebel's meekest men who, posing as a jester, defeats the usurper.
One of the star's most delightful vehicles, this medieval romp has good tunes and lively action, not to mention an exceptional cast and the memorable 'chalice from the palace' routine.

wd Norman Panama, Melvin Frank ph Ray June songs Sylvia Fine, Sammy Cahn ad Hal Pereira, Roland Anderson

Danny Kaye, Glynis Johns, *Basil Rathbone*, Cecil Parker, *Mildred Natwick*, Angela Lansbury, Edward Ashley, Robert Middleton, Michael Pate, Alan Napier

'Too thrilling for words, so they set it to music!'

Cover Girl

US 1944   107m
Technicolor
Columbia (Arthur Schwartz)
The road to success for magazine cover models.
Wartime glamour musical with a stronger reputation than it really deserves apart from Kelly's solos; it does however manage a certain *joie de vivre* which should not be despised.

w Virginia Van Upp d Charles Vidor ph Rudolph Maté md Morris Stoloff, Carmen Dragon songs Jerome Kern, Ira Gershwin

Rita Hayworth, Gene Kelly, *Phil Silvers*, Lee Bowman, Jinx Falkenberg, Otto Kruger, Eve Arden, Ed Brophy
'Kelly and Silvers are better than Kelly and Hayworth, though she does look sumptuous, and her big smile could be the emblem of the period.'—*New Yorker, 1977*
'Much of it is not as fresh as it may seem; but its second-handedness and its occasional failures cannot obliterate the pleasure of seeing the work of a production company which obviously knows, cares about and enjoys what it is doing.'—*James Agee*

AA: Morris Stoloff, Carmen Dragon
AAN: Rudolph Maté; song 'Long Ago and Far Away'

Cries and Whispers

Sweden 1972   91m
Eastmancolor
Cinematograph (Ingmar Bergman)
original title: *Viskingar och Rop*
A young woman dying of cancer in her family home is tended by her two sisters.
Quiet, chilling, classical chapter of doom which variously reminds one of Chekhov, Tolstoy and Dostoievsky but is also essential Bergman. Tough but important viewing, it lingers afterwards in the mind like a picture vividly painted in shades of red.

wd Ingmar Bergman ph Sven Nykvist m Chopin and Bach

Harriet Andersson, Kari Sylwan, *Ingrid Thulin*, Liv Ullmann
'Harrowing, spare and perceptive, but lacking the humour that helps to put life and death into perspective.'—*Michael Billington, Illustrated London News*

AA: Sven Nykvist
AAN: best picture; Ingmar Bergman (as writer); Ingmar Bergman (as director)

Crime and Punishment

US 1935   88m   bw
Columbia
A student kills a pawnbroker and is tortured by remorse.
Heavy-going rendering of Dostoievsky with some pictorial interest.

w S. K. Lauren, Joseph Anthony d Josef Von Sternberg ph Lucien Ballard m Arthur Honegger md Louis Silvers

Peter Lorre, Edward Arnold, Tala Birell, Marian Marsh, Elizabeth Risdon, Mrs Patrick Campbell
'Will have to be sold, but should average fair takings.'—*Variety*

'He had tired of her—and for that
he was sorry! He was tied to
her—and for that he hated her!'

Crime Without Passion

US 1934   82m   bw
Paramount (Ben Hecht,
Charles MacArthur)

A lawyer is driven to commit
murder.

Effective melodrama notable for
then-new techniques which were
blended into the mainstream of
movie-making, and for the first
appearance in Hollywood of a smart
new writer-producer-director team.

wd Ben Hecht, Charles MacArthur,
from their story Caballero of the
Law *ph Lee Garmes sp Slavko
Vorkapitch*

Claude Rains, Margo, Whitney
Bourne, Stanley Ridges

'It turns a lot of established
motion picture conventions
topsy-turvy . . . shouldn't have much
trouble at the box office, and inside
the theatre it is safe.'—*Variety*

'The whole venture seems to take
a long stride forward for the
movies.'—*Otis Ferguson*

'A flamboyant, undisciplined, but
compulsively fascinating film
classic.'—*Peter John Dyer, 1966*

Crocodile Dundee

Australia 1986   102m
Kodacolour   Panavision
Paramount / Hoyts / Rimfire (John
Cornell)

An outback hero goes to Manhattan
and puts New Yorkers in their place.
Easygoing comedy with no real style,
which astounded the industry by
becoming one of America's most
popular films in 1986.

*w Paul Hogan, Ken Shadie d Peter
Faiman ph Russell Boyd m Peter
Best*

Paul Hogan, Linda Koslowski, John
Meillon, Mark Blum

Cromwell

GB 1970   141m
Technicolor   Panavision
Columbia / Irving Allen (Andrew
Donally)

An account of the rise of Cromwell
to power, the execution of Charles I,
and the Civil War.

Disappointingly dull schoolbook
history, with good production values
but glum handling.

*wd Ken Hughes ph Geoffrey
Unsworth m Frank Cordell
pd John Stoll*

Richard Harris, Alec Guinness,
Robert Morley, Dorothy Tutin,
Frank Finlay, Timothy Dalton,
Patrick Wymark, Patrick Magee,
Nigel Stock, Charles Gray, Michael
Jayston, Anna Cropper, Michael
Goodliffe

'It tries to combine serious
intentions with the widest kind of
popular appeal and falls unhappily
between the two. It will offend the
purists and bore the
kiddies.'—*Brenda Davies*

'Shakespeare spoiled us for this
sort of thing. We wait for great
speeches and witty remarks, for rage
and poetry, and we get dedicated
stodginess.'—*Pauline Kael*

AAN: Frank Cordell

'Sensational? No, it's dynamite!'

Crossfire

US 1947   86m   bw
RKO (Adrian Scott)

A Jew is murdered in a New York
hotel, and three soldiers are
suspected.

Tense, talky thriller shot entirely at
night with pretty full expressionist
use of camera technique; notable for
style, acting, experimentation, and
for being the first Hollywood film to
hit out at racial bigotry.

*w John Paxton, novel The Brick
Foxhole by Richard Brooks ph J.
Roy Hunt d Edward Dmytryk
m Roy Webb*

*Robert Young, Robert Mitchum,
Robert Ryan, Gloria Grahame, Paul
Kelly*, Sam Levene, Jacqueline
White, Steve Brodie

AAN: best picture; John Paxton;
Edward Dmytryk; Robert Ryan;
Gloria Grahame

The Cruel Sea

GB 1953   126m   bw
Ealing (Leslie Norman)

Life and death on an Atlantic
corvette during World War II.
Competent transcription of a
bestselling book, cleanly produced
and acted; a huge box office success.

w Eric Ambler, *novel* Nicholas
Monsarrat d Charles Frend
ph Gordon Dines, Jo Jago, Paul
Beeson m Alan Rawsthorne

Jack Hawkins, Donald Sinden,
Stanley Baker, John Stratton,
Denholm Elliott, John Warner,
Bruce Seton, Virginia McKenna,
Moira Lister, June Thorburn

'This is a story of the battle of the
Atlantic, a story of an ocean, two
ships and a handful of men. The men
are the heroes. The heroines are the
ships. The only villain is the sea—the
cruel sea—that man has made even
more cruel.'—*opening narration*

'One is grateful nowadays for a
film which does not depict war as
anything but a tragic and bloody
experience, and it is this quality
which gives the production its final
power to move.'—*John Gillett*

'Sensitivity, faithfulness, and
almost inevitable tedium.'—*Time
Out, 1984*

AAN: Eric Ambler

'Wonders to dazzle the human
imagination—in a flaming love
story set in titanic world
conflict!'

The Crusades

US 1935   127m   bw
Paramount / Cecil B. de Mille

Spurred by his wife Berengaria,
Richard the Lionheart sets off on his
holy wars.

Heavily tapestried medieval epic,
spectacular sequences being
punctuated by wodges of uninspired
dialogue. A true de Mille pageant.

w Harold Lamb, Waldemar Young,
Dudley Nichols d Cecil B. de Mille
ph Victor Milner sp Gordon
Jennings m Rudolph Kopp

Henry Wilcoxon, Loretta Young, C.
Aubrey Smith, Ian Keith, Katherine

de Mille, Joseph Schildkraut, Alan
Hale, C. Henry Gordon, George
Barbier, Montagu Love, Lumsden
Hare, William Farnum, Hobart
Bosworth, Pedro de Cordoba,
Mischa Auer

'Mr de Mille's evangelical films are
the nearest equivalent today to the
glossy German colour prints which
decorated mid-Victorian bibles.
There is the same lack of a period
sense, the same stuffy horsehair
atmosphere of beards and whiskers,
and, their best quality, a childlike
eye for detail.'—*Otis Ferguson*

'Cinema addicts by now have
some idea what to expect in a de
Mille version of the Holy Wars. *The
Crusades* should fufil all
expectations. As a picture it is
historically worthless, didactically
treacherous, artistically absurd.
None of these defects impairs its
entertainment value. It is a
hundred-million-dollar sideshow
which has at least three features to
distinguish it from the long line of
previous de Mille extravaganzas. It is
the noisiest; it is the biggest; it
contains no baths.'—*Time*

'Probably only de Mille could
make a picture like this and get away
with it. It's long, and slow, and the
story is not up to some of his
previous films, but the production
has sweep and spectacle.'—*Variety*

AAN: Victor Milner

Cry of the City

US 1948   96m   bw
TCF (Sol C. Siegel)

A ruthless gangster on the run is
pursued by a policeman who was
once his boyhood friend.

Very well produced but relentlessly
miserable New York thriller on the
lines of *Manhattan Melodrama* and
Angels with Dirty Faces.

w Richard Murphy, *novel* The Chair
for Martin Rome by Henry Helseth
d Robert Siodmak ph Lloyd
Aherne m Alfred Newman

Victor Mature, Richard Conte, Mimi
Agulia, Shelley Winters, Tommy
Cook, Fred Clark, Debra Paget

'When the city cries in a movie, it's with the desolate wail of police sirens and with rain-streaked sidewalks; but most of all with poetic justification.'—*Paul Taylor, Time Out, 1980*

Cry Terror

 US 1958 96m bw
MGM / Andrew Stone

As security against ransom money being delivered, an airline bomber kidnaps a family.

Unabashed suspenser which screws panic situations as far as they will go and farther.

wd Andrew Stone ph Walter Strenge *m* Howard Jackson

James Mason, Rod Steiger, Inger Stevens, Neville Brand, Angie Dickinson, Kenneth Tobey, Jack Klugman, Jack Kruschen

'The creature created by man is forgotten by nature!'
The Curse of Frankenstein
GB 1957 83m
Eastmancolor
Warner / Hammer (Anthony Hinds)

A lurid revamping of the 1931 *Frankenstein*, this time with severed eyeballs and a peculiarly unpleasant and uncharacterized creature, all in gory colour. It set the trend in nasty horrors from which we have all suffered since, and launched Hammer Studios on a long and profitable career of charnelry. But it did have a gruesome sense of style.

w Jimmy Sangster d Terence Fisher ph Jack Asher *m James Bernard ad* Ted Marshall

Peter Cushing, Christopher Lee, Hazel Court, Robert Urquhart, Valerie Gaunt, Noel Hood

Cynara

US 1933 78m bw
Samuel Goldwyn

A London barrister has an affair with a young girl who commits suicide when he goes back to his wife.

Solidly carpentered, effective star vehicle of the old school, now dated but preserving its dignity.

w Frances Marion, Lynn Starling, *novel* An Imperfect Lover by Robert Gore Brown *d* King Vidor *ph* Ray June *m* Alfred Newman

Ronald Colman, Kay Francis, Phyllis Barry, *Henry Stephenson*, Paul Porcasi

'The values it involves are wholly unlike those which US audiences are usually called upon to comprehend.'—*Time*

D

Dad's Army

GB 1971 95m Technicolor
Columbia/Norcon (John R. Sloan)

Misadventures of a number of elderly gents in Britain's wartime Home Guard.

Expanded big-screen version of the long-running TV series, a pleasant souvenir but rather less effective than was expected because everything is shown—the town, the Nazis, the wives—and thus the air of gentle fantasy disappears, especially in the face of much coarsened humour.

w Jimmy Perry, David Croft
d Norman Cohen ph Terry Maher
m Wilfred Burns

Arthur Lowe, *John Le Mesurier*, *John Laurie*, *James Beck*, Ian Lavender, *Arnold Ridley*, Liz Fraser, *Clive Dunn*, Bill Pertwee, Frank Williams, Edward Sinclair

The Dam Busters

GB 1954 125m bw
ABPC (Robert Clark)

In 1943 the Ruhr dams are destroyed by Dr Barnes Wallis' bouncing bombs.

Understated British war epic with additional scientific interest and good acting and model work, not to mention a welcome lack of love interest.

w *R. C. Sheriff, books* by Guy Gibson and Paul Brickhill
d Michael Anderson ph Eric Hillier m Leighton Lucas, *Eric Coates* sp George Blackwell

Michael Redgrave, Richard Todd, Basil Sydney, Derek Farr, Patrick Barr, Ernest Clark, Raymond Huntley, Ursula Jeans

Dames

US 1934 90m bw
Warner (Robert Lord)

A millionaire purity fanatic tries to stop the opening of a Broadway show.

Typical Warner musical of the period; its real *raison d'être* is to be found in the splendidly imaginative numbers at the finale, but it also gives very full rein to the roster of comic actors under contract at the time.

w Delmer Daves d Ray Enright
ch *Busby Berkeley* ph Sid Hickox, George Barnes m various

Joan Blondell, Hugh Herbert, Guy Kibbee, Zasu Pitts, Dick Powell, Ruby Keeler

'That Warners was able to fashion so zestful an entertainment under post-Haysian restrictions is a credit to the collective ingenuities of the studio artificers. . . . Swell entertainment, no matter how you slice it.'—*Variety*

† Originally intended as *Gold Diggers of 1934*.

The Damned

West Germany/Italy 1969
164m Eastmancolor
Praesidens/Pegaso
original title: *Götterdämmerung*

A family of German industrialists divides and destroys itself under Nazi influence.

A film which has been called baroque, Wagnerian, and just plain unpleasant; it is also rather a strain to watch, with exaggerated colour and make-up to match the rotting theme.

w Nicola Badalucco, Enrico Medioli, Luchino Visconti d *Luchino Visconti* ph Armando Nannuzzi, Pasquale de Santis m Maurice Jarre ad Enzo del Prato, Pasquale Romano

Dirk Bogarde, Ingrid Thulin, Helmut Berger, Renaud Verley, Helmut Griem, René Kolldehof, Albrecht Schönhals, Umberto Orsini

'One is left lamenting that such a quondam master of realism as Visconti is making his films look like operas from which the score has been inexplicably removed.'—*MFB*

'The ludicrous flailings of puny puppets in inscrutable wooden frenzies.'—*John Simon*

AAN: script

'This is your melody—you gave it to me. I'll never play it again without thinking of you!'

Dangerous Moonlight

GB 1941 98m bw
RKO (William Sistrom)
US title: *Suicide Squadron*

A Polish pianist escapes from the Nazis and loses his memory after flying in the Battle of Britain. Immensely popular wartime romance which introduced Richard Addinsell's Warsaw Concerto. Production values and script somewhat below par.

w Shaun Terence Young, Brian Desmond Hurst, Rodney Ackland *d* Brian Desmond Hurst *ph* Georges Périnal, Ronald Neame

Anton Walbrook, Sally Gray, Derrick de Marney, Cecil Parker, Percy Parsons, Keneth Kent, Guy Middleton, John Laurie, Frederick Valk

Dangerous When Wet

US 1953 95m Technicolor
MGM (George Wells)

An entire Arkansas family is sponsored to swim the English Channel.

A bright and lively vehicle for an aquatic star, who in one sequence swims with Tom and Jerry. Amusing sequences give opportunities to a strong cast.

w Dorothy Kingsley *d* Charles Walters *ph* Harold Rosson *md* George Stoll *songs* Johnny Mercer, Arthur Schwarz

Esther Williams, *Charlotte Greenwood*, *William Demarest*, Fernando Lamas, Jack Carson, Denise Darcel, Barbara Whiting

Dante's Inferno

US 1935 89m bw
TCF (Sol M. Wurtzell)

A ruthless carnival owner gets too big for his boots, and has a vision of hell induced by one of his own attractions.

Curiously unpersuasive melodrama with a moral, but the inferno sequence is one of the most unexpected, imaginative and striking pieces of cinema in Hollywood's history.

w Philip Klein, Robert Yost *d* Harry Lachmann *ph* Rudolph Maté *sp* Fred F. Sersen, Ralph Hammeras *sets* Willy Pogany, from drawings by Gustav Doré *m* Hugo Friedhofer, Samuel Kaylin, R. H. Bassett, Peter Brunelli

Spencer Tracy, Claire Trevor, Henry B. Walthall, Alan Dinehart, Scotty Beckett, Rita Hayworth (her first appearance, as a dancer)

'A pushover for vigorous exploitation . . . accentuate the inferno sequence and forget the rest, including the story.'—*Variety*

'We depart gratefully, having seen papier maché photographed in more ways than we had thought possible.'—*Robert Herring*

'One of the most unusual and effectively presented films of the thirties.'—*John Baxter, 1968*

'The spectacle is shattering.'—*Sunday Times*

'Immediately following the 10-minute picturization of Hell, the story reverts to its native dullness.'—*Variety*

The Dark At the Top of the Stairs

US 1960 124m
Technicolor
Warner (Michael Garrison)

Twenties small town drama about a young boy's awakening to the sexual tensions around him.

Archetypal family drama set in that highly familiar American street. The perfect essence of this playwright's work, with high and low spots, several irrelevancies, but a real feeling for the people and the place.

w Harriet Frank Jnr, Irving Ravetch, *play William Inge d* Delbert Mann *ph* Harry Stradling *m* Max Steiner

Robert Preston, Dorothy McGuire, Angela Lansbury, Eve Arden, Shirley Knight, Frank Overton, Lee Kinsolving, Robert Eyer

'Every time a woman turns her face away because she's tired or unwilling, there's someone waiting like me . . .'—*publicity*

† The curious title turns out to be a synonym for life, which one should never be afraid of.

AAN: Shirley Knight

'One twin loves—and one twin loves to kill!'

The Dark Mirror
US 1946 85m bw
International

A police detective works out which of identical twin girls is a murderer. Unconvincing but highly absorbing thriller with all credits plus; the best brand of Hollywood moonshine.

w Nunnally Johnson, *original story* Vladimir Posner *d* Robert Siodmak *ph* Milton Krasner *m* Dmitri Tiomkin

Olivia de Havilland, Lew Ayres, Thomas Mitchell, Garry Owen
'Smooth and agreeable melodrama . . . the detective work involves inkblot and word association tests and an amusingly sinister tandem of oscillating pens which register concealed emotions as one of the sisters talks.'—*James Agee*

AAN: Vladimir-Posner

Dark Passage
US 1947 106m bw
Warner (Jerry Wald)

A convicted murderer escapes from jail and proves his innocence. Loosely assembled, totally unconvincing star thriller which succeeds because of its professionalism, some good cameos, and a number of narrative tricks including subjective camera for the first half hour.

w Delmer Daves, *novel* David Goodis *d Delmer Daves ph* Sid Hickox *m* Franz Waxman

Humphrey Bogart, Lauren Bacall, Agnes Moorehead, Bruce Bennett, *Tom D'Andrea, Houseley Stevenson*
'An almost total drag.'—*New Yorker, 1977*

'Never a love so exquisite! She smiled at the cost, and bravely paid the reckoning when her heart's happy dancing was ended!'

Dark Victory
US 1939 106m bw
Warner (David Lewis)

A good-time society girl discovers she is dying of a brain tumour. A highly commercial tearjerker of its day, this glutinous star vehicle now works only fitfully.

w Casey Robinson, *play* George Brewer Jnr, Bertram Bloch *d* Edmund Goulding *ph* Ernest Haller *m* Max Steiner

Bette Davis, George Brent, Humphrey Bogart, Ronald Reagan, Geraldine Fitzgerald, Henry Travers, Cora Witherspoon, Dorothy Peterson

JUDITH (Bette Davis): 'Nothing can hurt us now. What we have can't be destroyed. That's our victory—our victory over the dark. It is a victory because we're not afraid.'
'If it were an automobile, it would be a Rolls-Royce with the very best trimmings.'—*Time*
'Will turn in a good account of itself at the box office, though not rating socko proportions.'—*Variety*
'A completely cynical appraisal would dismiss it all as emotional flim-flam . . . but it is impossible to be that cynical about it.'—*Frank S. Nugent*
'A gooey collection of clichés, but Davis slams through them in her nerviest style.'—*New Yorker, 1976*

† Remade 1963 as *Stolen Hours*, with Susan Hayward; 1975 as *Dark Victory* (TV movie) with Elizabeth Montgomery.

AAN: best picture; Bette Davis; Max Steiner

Dark Waters

US 1944   90m   bw
Benedict Bogeaus

Recovering from being torpedoed, an orphan girl visits her aunt and uncle in Louisiana and has some terrifying experiences.

Competent frightened-lady melodrama helped by its bayou surroundings. Possibly discarded by Hitchcock, but with sequences well in his manner.

w Joan Harrison, Marian Cockrell *d André de Toth* ph John Mescall *m Miklos Rozsa*

Merle Oberon, Franchot Tone, *Thomas Mitchell*, Fay Bainter, John Qualen, Elisha Cook Jnr, Rex Ingram

'When she was good she was very very good. When she was bad, she was . . .'

Darling

GB 1965   127m   bw
Anglo-Amalgamated / Vic / Appia (Joseph Janni, Victor Lyndon)

An ambitious young woman deserts her journalist mentor for a company director, an effeminate photographer and an Italian prince.

Fashionable mid-sixties concoction of smart swinging people and their amoral doings. Influential, put over with high style, and totally tiresome in retrospect.

w Frederic Raphael *d John Schlesinger* ph Ken Higgins *m John Dankworth*

Julie Christie, Dirk Bogarde, Laurence Harvey, Roland Curram, Alex Scott, Basil Henson, Pauline Yates

BOGARDE to Christie: 'Your idea of being fulfilled is having more than one man in bed at the same time.'

'As empty of meaning and mind as the empty life it's exposing.'—*Pauline Kael*

AA: Frederic Raphael; Julie Christie
AAN: best picture; John Schlesinger

'One of the greatest stories of love and adventure ever told is brought to the screen as Dickens himself would wish it!'

David Copperfield

US 1934   132m   bw
MGM (David O. Selznick)

Disliked by his cruel stepfather and helped by his eccentric aunt, orphan David grows up to become an author and eventually to marry his childhood sweetheart.

Only slightly faded after forty-five years, this small miracle of compression not only conveys the spirit of Dickens better than the screen has normally managed but is a particularly pleasing example of Hollywood's handling of literature and of the deployment of a great studio's resources. It also overflows with memorable character cameos, and it was a box office giant.

w Hugh Walpole, Howard Estabrook, *novel* Charles Dickens *d George Cukor* ph Oliver T. Marsh   *m* Herbert Stothart *montages* Slavko Vorkapitch *ad Cedric Gibbons*

Freddie Bartholomew (young David), *Frank Lawton* (David as a man), W. C. Fields (Micawber), *Roland Young* (Uriah Heep), *Edna May Oliver* (Aunt Betsy), *Lennox Pawle* (Mr Dick), *Basil Rathbone* (Mr Murdstone), Violet Kemble Cooper (Miss Murdstone), Maureen O'Sullivan (Dora), Madge Evans (Agnes), Elizabeth Allan (Mrs Copperfield), *Jessie Ralph* (Peggotty), Lionel Barrymore (Dan Peggotty), Hugh Williams (Steerforth), Lewis Stone (Mr Wickfield), *Herbert Mundin* (Barkis), Elsa Lanchester (Clickett), Jean Cadell (Mrs Micawber), Una O'Connor (Mrs Gummidge), John Buckler (Ham), Hugh Walpole (the Vicar), Arthur Treacher (donkey man)

'One of the best ensembles ever . . . unusually good production which will win general approval.'—*Variety*

'Though half the characters are absent, the whole spectacle of the book, Micawber always excepted, is conveyed.'—*James Agee*

'The most profoundly satisfying screen manipulation of a great novel that the camera has ever given us.'—*André Sennwald*

'Perhaps the finest casting of all time.'—*Basil Wright, 1972*

† Charles Laughton was originally cast as Micawber, but resigned from the role after two days of shooting. It was said at the time that 'he looked as though he were about to molest the child.'

AAN: best picture

Davy Crockett

US 1955   93m   Technicolor
Walt Disney

Episodes in the career of the famous Tennessee hunter and Indian scout who died at the Alamo.

Disjointed and naive but somehow very fresh and appealing adventures; made for American television (as 3 × 50m episodes) but elsewhere an enormous hit in cinemas.

w Tom Blackburn *d* Norman Foster *ph* Charles Boyle *m* George Bruns

Fess Parker, Buddy Ebsen, Basil Ruysdael, William Bakewell, Hans Conried, Kenneth Tobey, Nick Cravat

† 1956 sequel on similar lines: *Davy Crockett and the River Pirates*.

'There's no chance for a flight to get through, but one man—flying low, hedgehopping—might make it!'

The Dawn Patrol

US 1938   103m   bw
Warner (Hal B. Wallis)

In France during World War I, flying officers wait their turn to leave on missions which may mean death.

A remarkably early but trim and competent remake of the 1930 film, using much of the same aerial footage.

w Seton I. Miller, Dan Totheroh

d Edmund Goulding *ph* Tony Gaudio *m* Max Steiner

Errol Flynn, Basil Rathbone, David Niven, Melville Cooper, Donald Crisp, Barry Fitzgerald, Carl Esmond

'A powerful, red-corpuscled drama . . . geared for top grosses.'—*Variety*

'A great deal of self-pity and romanticism have gone into the making of this excellent ham sandwich.'—*Graham Greene*

A Day at the Races

US 1937   109m   bw
(blue-tinted ballet sequence)
MGM (Lawrence Weingarten)

The Marxes help a girl who owns a sanatorium and a racehorse.

Fashions in Marxism change, but this top quality production, though lacking their zaniest inspirations, does contain several of their funniest routines and a spectacularly well integrated racecourse climax. The musical and romantic asides are a matter of taste but delightfully typical of their time.

w Robert Pirosh, George Seaton, George Oppenheimer *d* Sam Wood *ph* Joseph Ruttenberg *m* Franz Waxman

Groucho, Chico, Harpo, Margaret Dumont, Maureen O'Sullivan, Allan Jones, *Douglass Dumbrille, Esther Muir, Sig Rumann*

'The money is fairly splashed about; the capitalists have recognized the Marx Brothers; ballet sequences, sentimental songs, amber fountains, young lovers. Easily the best film to be seen in London, but all the same I feel a nostalgia for the old cheap rickety sets.'—*Graham Greene*

Day for Night

France / Italy 1973   116m
Eastmancolor
Films du Carrosse / PECF / PIC
(Marcel Bébert)
original title: *La Nuit Américaine*

Frictions and personality clashes

beset the making of a romantic film in Nice.

Immensely enjoyable, richly detailed, insider's-eye-view of the goings-on in a film studio. A fun film with melodramatic asides.

w François Truffaut, Jean-Louis Richard, Suzanne Schiffman d François Truffaut ph Pierre-William Glenn m Georges Delerue

Jacqueline Bisset, Valentina Cortese, Jean-Pierre Aumont, Jean-Pierre Léaud, Dani, Alexandra Stewart, Jean Champion, François Truffaut, David Markham

'I thought I'd had my last dram of enjoyment out of the Pagliacci theme and studio magic, and Truffaut shows there's life in the old whirl yet.'—*Stanley Kauffmann*

'Made with such dazzling craftsmanship and confidence that you can never quite believe Truffaut's point that directing a movie is a danger-fraught experience.'—*Michael Billington, Illustrated London News*

† Graham Greene, as Henry Graham, played an insurance representative.

AA: best foreign film
AAN: script, François Truffaut (as director); Valentina Cortese

The Day of the Jackal
GB / France 1973   142m
Technicolor
Universal / Warwick / Universal France (John Woolf, David Deutsch)
British and French police combine to prevent an OAS assassination attempt on de Gaulle by use of a professional killer.

An incisive, observant and professional piece of work based on a rather clinical bestseller. Lack of a channel for sympathy, plus language confusions, are its main drawbacks.

w Kenneth Ross, *novel* Frederick Forsyth d Fred Zinnemann ph Jean Tournier m Georges Delerue

Edward Fox, Michel Lonsdale, Alan

Badel, Eric Porter, Cyril Cusack, Delphine Seyrig, Donald Sinden, Tony Britton, Timothy West, Olga Georges-Picot, Barrie Ingham, Maurice Denham, Anton Rodgers

'Before *Jackal* is five minutes old, you know it's just going to be told professionally, with no flavour and no zest.'—*Stanley Kauffmann*

'All plot, with scarcely a character in sight.'—*Michael Billington, Illustrated London News*

'A better than average thriller for those who haven't read the book.'—*Judith Crist*

'A rare lesson in film-making in the good old grand manner.'—*Basil Wright, 1972*

Day of Wrath
Denmark 1943   105m   bw
Palladium
original title: *Vredens Dag*
In a 17th-century village an old woman is burned as a witch and curses the pastor who judged her. He dies and his mother accuses her daughter-in-law, in love with another man, of using witchcraft to kill him. Harrowing, spellbinding melodrama with a message, moving in a series of Rembrandtesque compositions from one horrifying sequence to another. Depressing, but marvellous.

w Carl Dreyer, Poul Knudsen, Mogens Skot-Hansen, *play* Anne Pedersdotter by Hans Wiers Jenssen d Carl Dreyer ph Carl Andersson m Poul Schierbeck ad Erik Ases

Lis Fribert, Thorkild Roose, Lisbeth Movin, Sigrid Neiiendam, Preben Lerdoff Rye, Anna Svierkier

The Day the Earth Caught Fire
GB 1961   99m   bw with filters Dyaliscope
British Lion / Pax (Val Guest)
Nuclear tests knock the world off its axis and send it careering towards the sun.

A smart piece of science fiction told through the eyes of Fleet Street journalists and showing a sharp eye for the London scene. Rather exhaustingly talkative, but genuinely frightening at the time.

*w Wolf Mankowitz, Val Guest
d Val Guest ph* Harry Waxman
m Monty Norman

Edward Judd, Janet Munro, Leo
McKern, *Arthur Christiansen*
(ex-editor of the Daily Express),
Michael Goodliffe, Bernard Braden,
Reginald Beckwith, Austin Trevor,
Renée Asherson, Edward
Underdown

Days of Wine and Roses

US 1962   117m   bw
Warner (Martin Manulis)

A PR man becomes an alcoholic; his
wife gradually reaches the same
state, but he recovers and she does
not.

Smart satirical comedy confusingly
gives way to melodrama, then
sentimentality; quality is evident
throughout, but all concerned are
happiest with the first hour.

w J. P. Miller d Blake Edwards
ph Philip Lathrop m Henry Mancini

*Jack Lemmon, Lee Remick, Charles
Bickford, Jack Klugman,* Alan
Hewitt, Debbie Megowan, Jack
Albertson

AA: title song (*m Henry Mancini,
ly* Johnny Mercer)
AAN: Jack Lemmon; Lee Remick

'You may not like these people,
nor pity them, but you'll never
forget this picture!'

Dead End

US 1937   92m   bw
Samuel Goldwyn

A slice of life in New York's east
side, where slum kids and gangsters
live in a river street next to a luxury
apartment block.

Highly theatrical film of a highly
theatrical play, more or less
preserving the single set and
overcoming the limitations of the
script and setting by sheer cinematic
expertise. It is chiefly remembered,
however, for introducing the Dead
End Kids to a delighted world.

w Lillian Hellman, *play* Sidney
Kingsley *d* William Wyler *ph* Gregg
Toland *ad* Richard Day *m* Alfred
Newman

Joel McCrea, Sylvia Sidney,
Humphrey Bogart, Wendy Barrie,
Claire Trevor, Allen Jenkins,
Marjorie Main, James Burke, Ward
Bond, *The Dead End Kids* (Billy
Halop, Leo Gorcey, Bernard
Punsley, Huntz Hall, Bobby Jordan,
Gabriel Dell)

'Tense and accurate transcription,
but sordid and depressing . . . in for
a disappointing career.'—*Variety*

AAN: best picture; Gregg Toland;
Claire Trevor

Dead of Night

GB 1945   104m   bw
Ealing (Sidney Cole, John
Croydon)

An architect is caught up in an
endless series of recurring dreams,
during which he is told other
people's supernatural experiences
and finally murders the psychiatrist
who is trying to help him.

Chillingly successful and influential
compendium of the macabre,
especially effective in its low-key
handling of the linking sequence
with its circular ending.

w John Baines, Angus Macphail,
based on stories by themselves, H.
G. Wells, E. F. Benson
*d Cavalcanti, Charles Crichton,
Robert Hamer, Basil Dearden
ph* Douglas Slocombe, Stan Pavey
m Georges Auric ad Michael Relph

Mervyn Johns, Roland Culver, Mary
Merrall, Judy Kelly, Anthony Baird,
*Sally Ann Howes, Frederick Valk,
Googie Withers,* Ralph Michael,
Esmé Percy, Basil Radford,
Naunton Wayne, Miles Malleson,
Michael Redgrave, Hartley Power,
Elizabeth Welch

'In a nightmare within a nightmare
are contained five separate ghost
stories . . . they have atmosphere
and polish, they are eerie, they are
well acted.'—*Richard Winnington*

'One of the most successful blends
of laughter, terror and outrage that I
can remember.'—*James Agee*

'The five ghost stories accumulate
in intensity until the trap closes in
the surrealist climax.'—*Pauline Kael,
1968*

The Deadly Affair

GB 1966   106m
Technicolor
Columbia / Sidney Lumet

A Foreign Office man apparently commits suicide; his colleague is unconvinced and finally uncovers a spy ring.

Compulsive if heavy-going thriller from the sour-about-spies era, deliberately glum, photographed against the shabbiest possible London backgrounds in muddy colour. Solidly entertaining for sophisticated grown-ups.

w Paul Dehn, novel Call for the Dead by John Le Carré *d Sidney Lumet ph* Frederick A. Young *m* Quincy Jones

James Mason, Simone Signoret, Harry Andrews, Maximilian Schell, Harriet Andersson, Kenneth Haigh, *Max Adrian*, Robert Flemyng, Roy Kinnear, Lynn Redgrave

Dear Octopus

GB 1943   86m   bw
GFD / Gainsborough (Edward Black)

US title: *The Randolph Family*

Members of a well-to-do British family reunite for Golden Wedding celebrations.

Traditional upper-class British comedy drama, and very well done too, with opportunities for excellent character acting.

w R. J. Minney, Patrick Kirwan, *play Dodie Smith d* Harold French *ph* Arthur Crabtree

Margaret Lockwood, Michael Wilding, *Helen Haye, Frederick Leister, Celia Johnson, Roland Culver, Athene Seyler*, Basil Radford, Nora Swinburne, Jean Cadell, Kathleen Harrison, Ann Stephens, Muriel George, Antoinette Cellier, Graham Moffatt

Death in Venice

Italy 1971   128m
Technicolor Panavision
Warner / Alfa (Mario Gallo)

original title: *Morte a Venezia*

In a lush Venetian hotel one summer in the early years of the century, a middle-aged German composer on holiday falls for the charms of a silent young boy, and stays in the city too long to escape the approaching plague.

Incredibly extended and rather pointless fable enriched by moments of great beauty and directorial style; these do not quite atone for the slow pace or the muddled storyline.

w Luchino Visconti, Nicola Bandalucco, *novel* Thomas Mann *d* Luchino Visconti *ph* Pasquale de Santis *m* Gustav Mahler *md* Franco Mannino *ad* Ferdinando Scarfiotti

Dirk Bogarde, Bjorn Andresen, Silvana Mangano, Marisa Berenson, Mark Burns

'Maybe a story as elusive as *Death in Venice* simply can't be filmed. Visconti has made a brave attempt, always sensitive to the original; but it's finally not quite the same thing.'—David Wilson, MFB

'Camp and miscalculated from start to finish . . . a prime contender for the title Most Overrated Film of All Time.'—*Time Out, 1985*

'A salesman's got to dream—it comes with the territory!'
'One mistake—seen by his son—unleashes with overwhelming power the great drama of our day!'

Death of a Salesman

US 1951   112m   bw
Columbia (Stanley Kramer)

An ageing travelling salesman recognizes the emptiness of his life and commits suicide.

A very acceptable screen version of a milestone play which has become an American classic; stage conventions and tricks are cleverly adapted to cinematic use, especially when the hero walks from the present into the past and back again.

w Stanley Roberts, *play Arthur Miller d* Laslo Benedek *ph* Franz Planer *m* Alex North *md* Morris Stoloff

Fredric March, *Kevin McCarthy*, Cameron Mitchell, Mildred Dunnock, Howard Smith, Royal Beal, Jesse White

MRS LOMAN: 'Attention must finally be paid to such a man. He's not to be allowed to fall into his grave like an old dog.'

WILLY LOMAN: 'A salesman is somebody way up there in the blue, riding on a smile and a shoeshine . . .'

'Its time shifts with light, which were poetic in the theatre, seemed shabby in a medium that can dissolve time and space so easily.'—*Stanley Kauffmann*

AAN: Franz Planer; Alex North; Fredric March; Kevin McCarthy; Mildred Dunnock

---

'No woman ever loved such a man! The whole world waited while he made love!'
Death Takes a Holiday
US 1934 78m bw
Paramount (E. Lloyd Sheldon)
In the form of a mysterious prince, Death visits an Italian noble family to see why men fear him so.
A somewhat pretentious classic from a popular play of the twenties; interesting handling and performances, but a slow pace by modern standards.

w Maxwell Anderson, Gladys Lehman, Walter Ferris based on plays by Maxwell Anderson and Alberto Casella *d Mitchell Leisen* *ph* Charles Lang *ad* Ernst Fegte

Fredric March, Evelyn Venable, Sir Guy Standing, Katherine Alexander, Gail Patrick, Helen Westley, Kathleen Howard, Henry Travers, Kent Taylor
'Highly fantastic, but well done . . . likely to have greater appeal among the intelligentsia.'—*Variety*

Deception
US 1946 112m bw
Warner (Henry Blanke)
A European cellist returning to America after the war finds that his former girl friend has a rich and jealous lover.
Downcast melodrama made when its star was beginning to slide; today it seems irresistible bosh with a background of classical music, done with intermittent style especially by Claude Rains as the egomaniac lover.

w John Collier, *play* Monsieur Lamberthier by Louis Verneuil *d* Irving Rapper *ph* Ernest Haller *m* Erich Wolfgang Korngold

Bette Davis, *Claude Rains*, Paul Henreid, John Abbott, Benson Fong
'It's like grand opera, only the people are thinner . . . I wouldn't have missed it for the world.'—*Cecelia Ager*
'Exquisitely foolish: a camp classic.'—*New Yorker, 1977*

† Previously filmed in 1929 as *Jealousy*, with Fredric March and Jeanne Eagels.

The Deep
US 1977 124m Metrocolor Panavision
Columbia / EMI / Casablanca (Peter Guber)
Underwater treasure seekers off Bermuda clash with black villains seeking a lost consignment of morphine.
An expensive action picture which is singularly lacking in action and even in plot, but oozes with brutality and overdoes the splendours of submarine life, forty per cent of it taking place under water.

w Peter Benchley, Tracy Keenan Wynn, *novel* Peter Benchley *d* Peter Yates *ph* Christopher Challis, Al Giddings, Stan Waterman *m* John Barry *pd* Tony Masters

Jacqueline Bisset, Robert Shaw, Nick Nolte, Lou Gossett, Eli Wallach
'The ultimate disco experience . . . it dances on the spot for two hours, taking voodoo, buried treasure, morphine, violence and sea monsters in its stride.'—*Time Out*

'Peter Yates has knocked himself out doing masterly underwater action sequences in the service of a woefully crummy book.'—*Russell Davies, Observer*

The Deer Hunter
🔊 US 1978   182m
📺 Technicolor Panavision
Universal/EMI (Barry Spikings, Michael Deeley, Michael Cimino, John Peverall)

Three friends from a small Pennsylvania town go to fight in Vietnam.

The three-hour running time is taken up with crosscutting of a wedding, a deer hunt and a game of Russian roulette. Presumably the audience has to guess the point, if any; meanwhile it may be repelled by this long and savage if frequently engrossing film.

w Deric Washburn, *Story* Michael Cimino, Louis Garfinkle, Quinn K. Redeker and Washburn *d Michael Cimino ph* Vilmos Zsigmond *m* Stanley Myers

Robert De Niro, John Cazale, John Savage, Christopher Walken, Meryl Streep

'A hollow spectacle, less about war than its effect on a community, full of specious analogies, incoherent sentimentality and belief in its own self-importance.'—*Time Out*

AA: best picture; direction; Christopher Walken
AAN: Deric Washburn; Vilmos Zsigmond; Robert de Niro; Meryl Streep

Defence of the Realm
🎖 GB 1985   96m   colour
(Rank) Enigma/NFFC (David Puttnam) (Linda Miles)

A journalist tries to check the relationship between an MP and a Russian agent.

Efficient political melodrama, basically too old-fashioned to start a cult.

w Martin Stellman d David Drury ph Roger Deakins *m* Richard

Hartley *pd* Roger Murray-Leach *ed* Michael Bradsall

Gabriel Byrne, Greta Scacchi, Denholm Elliott, Ian Bannen, Fulton Mackay, Bill Paterson

BFA: best supporting actor, Denholm Elliott

The Defiant Ones
🐾 US 1958   96m   bw
Ⅹ UA/Stanley Kramer

A black and a white convict escape from a chain gang, still linked together but hating each other. Schematic melodrama with a moral, impeccably done and with good performances.

w Nathan E. Douglas, Harold Jacob Smith *d Stanley Kramer .ph* Sam Leavitt *m* Ernest Gold

Tony Curtis, Sidney Poitier, Theodore Bikel, Charles McGraw, Lon Chaney Jnr, King Donovan, Claude Akins, Lawrence Dobkin, Whit Bissell, Carl 'Alfalfa' Switzer, Cara Williams

'Probably Kramer's best picture. The subject matter is relatively simple, though "powerful"; the action is exciting; the acting is good. But the singleness of purpose behind it all is a little offensive.'—*Pauline Kael*

AA: Nathan E. Douglas, Harold Jacob Smith; Sam Leavitt
AAN: best picture; Stanley Kramer; Tony Curtis; Sidney Poitier; Theodore Bikel; Cara Williams

Deliverance
US 1972   109m   technicolor Panavision
Warner/Elmer Enterprises (John Boorman)

Four men spend a holiday weekend canoeing down a dangerous river, but find that the real danger to their lives comes from themselves and other humans.

Vigorous, meaningful, almost apocalyptic vision of man's inhumanity, disguised as a thrilling adult adventure.

w James Dickey, from his novel

d John Boorman *ph* Vilmos
Zsigmond *m* Eric Weissberg

Burt Reynolds, Jon Voight, Ned
Beatty, Ronny Cox, James Dickey

'There is fundamentally no view of
the material, just a lot of painful
grasping and groping.'—*Stanley
Kauffmann*

AAN: best picture; John Boorman

Demetrius and the Gladiators
US 1954   101m
Technicolor Cinemascope
TCF (Frank Ross)

A Greek slave who keeps Christ's
robe after the crucifixion is
sentenced to be one of Caligula's
gladiators and becomes involved in
Messalina's wiles.

Lively, efficient sequel to *The Robe*,
with emphasis less on religiosity than
on the brutality of the arena and our
hero's sexual temptations and
near-escapes. Good Hollywood
hokum.

w Philip Dunne *d* Delmer Daves
ph Milton Krasner *m* Franz
Waxman

Victor Mature, Susan Hayward,
Michael Rennie (as Peter), Debra
Paget, Anne Bancroft, Jay
Robinson, Barry Jones, William
Marshall, Richard Egan, Ernest
Borgnine

'An energetic attempt to fling the
mantle of sanctity over several more
millions of the entertainment
dollar.'—*The Times*

The Dentist
US 1932   19m   bw

Classic star short with W. C. Fields
working up briskly to a dentist
sketch in which he deals summarily
with a variety of patients. Directed
by Leslie Pearce; for
Paramount/Sennett.

Desert Victory
GB 1943   60m   bw
Ministry of
Information/British Army Film
Unit

Montgomery's army chases the Nazis
through Tripoli.

Classic war documentary.

w (anonymous) *d* David
MacDonald *speaker* James
Langdale Hodson *m* William
Alwyn *ed* A. Best, F. Clarke

'The greatest battle film of the
war . . . it puts the audience right in
the middle . . . Americans who see
this film will be anxiously waiting for
the next—and a US
equivalent.'—*Variety*

'A first rate work of art.'—*Time*

'The finest factual film ever
made.'—*Daily Telegraph*

'Profoundly moving, and fierce in
its impact upon imagination, eye and
ear.'—*Scotsman*

† A few shots were reconstructed in
the studio.

'Three people who loved each
  other very much!'
Design for Living
US 1933   88m   bw
Paramount (Ernst Lubitsch)

Two friends love and are loved by
the same worldly woman, and they
set up house together.

Elegant but miscast version of a
scintillating play, with all the sex and
the sting removed (at the insistence
of the Legion of Decency, then
coming into power). Ben Hecht
claimed to have removed all but one
line of Coward's dialogue: 'For the
good of our immortal souls!'

w Ben Hecht, *play* Noel Coward
d Ernst Lubitsch *ph* Victor Milner
m Nathaniel Finston *ad* Hans
Dreier

Gary Cooper, Fredric March,
Miriam Hopkins, Edward Everett
Horton, Franklin Pangborn, Isabel
Jewell

'Can't miss because it holds
plenty . . . an improvement on the
original.'—*Variety*

'A delightfully smart, crisp piece
of entertainment, cleverly conceived
and delightfully executed.'—*New
York American*

'A partial cleansing for the screen
of a stage story notorious for its
wealth and variety of moral code
infractions.'—*Martin Quigley*

The Desk Set

🙂 US 1957   103m
  Eastmancolor   Cinemascope
TCF (Henry Ephron)
GB title: *His Other Woman*
Ladies in a broadcasting company's
reference section are appalled when
an electronics expert is sent to
improve their performance.
Thin comedy, altered from a
Broadway success; patchy as a
whole, but with several splendid
dialogue scenes for the principals.

w Phoebe and Henry Ephron,
play William Marchant *d* Walter
Lang *ph* Leon Shamroy *m* Cyril
Mockridge

Spencer Tracy, *Katharine Hepburn*,
Joan Blondell, Gig Young, Dina
Merrill, Neva Patterson.
  'They lope through this trifling
charade like a couple of oldtimers
who enjoy reminiscing with simple
routines.'—*Bosley Crowther, New
York Times*

Desperate Journey

🦅 US 1942   109m   bw
  Warner (Hal B. Wallis)
Three POWs in Nazi Germany fight
their way back to freedom.
When you pit Errol Flynn against
the Nazis, there's no doubt who
wins; and the last line is 'Now for
Australia and a crack at those Japs!'
Exhilarating adventure for the
totally uncritical; professional
standards high.

w Arthur Horman *d Raoul Walsh*
ph Bert Glennon *m* Max Steiner

Errol Flynn, *Alan Hale*, Ronald
Reagan, Nancy Coleman, Raymond
Massey, Arthur Kennedy, Ronald
Sinclair, Albert Basserman, Sig
Rumann, Ilka Gruning, Pat
O'Moore
  'Yarn is an extreme strain on
anyone's credulity, and yet it's so
exciting that the preposterousness of
it all is only something to be thought
about on the way home from the
theatre.'—*Variety*
  'A 1942 treatment of *The Three
Musketeers*, packed with action,
shorn of romance, and utilizing the

Third Reich for terrain. Folks who
sacrifice reason for fast action and
the joy of seeing Nazis foiled, will
find it entirely gratifying.'—*New
York Times*

Destiny of a Man

🎭 USSR 1959   98m   bw
  Sovexportfilm / Mosfilm (G.
Kuznetsov)
original title: *Sudba Cheloveka*
During World War II a Russian is
captured by Nazis but escapes and
returns home only to find his family
dead.
Strikingly styled sob story whose
very glumness prevented it from
being hailed as a masterpiece; in
technique however it is in the best
Russian tradition.

w Y. Lukin, F. Shakhmagonov,
story Mikhail Sholokhov *d Sergei
Bondarchuk ph* Vladimir
Monakhov *m* V. Basnov

Sergei Bondarchuk, Zinaida
Kirienko, Pavlik Boriskin
  'Of all Soviet post-war films, this
will be looked on as the greatest and
most original work of the
period.'—*MFB*

'They make the fighting sinful
  west blaze into action before
  your eyes!'

Destry Rides Again

🤠 US 1939   94m   bw
  Universal (Joe Pasternak)
A mild-mannered sheriff finally gets
mad at local corruption and straps
on his guns.
Classic western which manages to
encompass suspense, comedy,
romance, tenderness, vivid
characterization, horseplay, songs
and standard western excitements,
without moving for more than a
moment from a studio main street
set. It starts with a sign reading
'Welcome to Bottleneck' and an
outburst of gunfire; it ends with
tragedy followed by a running joke.
Hollywood expertise at its very best.

W Felix Jackson, Gertrude Purcell,
Henry Myers, *novel* Max Brand
d George Marshall ph Hal Mohr

songs *Frederick Hollander, Frank Loesser m Frank Skinner*

James Stewart, Marlene Dietrich, Brian Donlevy, Charles Winninger, Samuel S. Hinds, Mischa Auer, Irene Hervey, Jack Carson, Una Merkel, Allen Jenkins, Warren Hymer, Billy Gilbert

'Makes the b.o. grade in a big way . . . just plain, good entertainment.'—*Variety*

'I think it was Lord Beaverbrook who said that Marlene Dietrich standing on a bar in black net stockings, belting out *See What the Boys in the Back Room Will Have*, was a greater work of art than the Venus de Milo.'—*Richard Roud*

† An early sound version in 1932 starred Tom Mix; *Frenchie* (1950) was a slight variation. See also *Destry*.

The Detective

US 1968   114m   De Luxe Panavision
TCF / Arcola / Millfield (Aaron Rosenberg)

A New York police detective fights crime and corruption.

Determinedly sleazy and 'frank' cop stuff, quite arrestingly narrated and with something to say about police methods. Good violent entertainment, with just a shade too many homosexuals and nymphomaniacs for balance.

w Abby Mann, novel Roderick Thorp *d Gordon Douglas ph* Joseph Biroc *m* Jerry Goldsmith

Frank Sinatra, Lee Remick, Jacqueline Bisset, Ralph Meeker, Jack Klugman, Horace MacMahon, Lloyd Bochner, William Windom, Tony Musante, Al Freeman Jnr, Robert Duvall

'It vacillates uncertainly between murder mystery, political allegory, and a psychological study of the hero.'—*Jan Dawson*

'A man whose wife was more woman than angel!'
Detective Story
US 1951   103m   bw
Paramount (William Wyler)

A day in a New York precinct police station, during which a detective of almost pathological righteousness discovers a stain on his family and himself becomes a victim of violence.

Clever, fluent transcription of a Broadway play with some of the pretensions of Greek tragedy; it could have been the negation of cinema, but professional handling makes it the essence of it.

w Philip Yordan, Robert Wyler, play Sidney Kingsley d William Wyler ph Lee Garmes

Kirk Douglas, Eleanor Parker, William Bendix, Cathy O'Donnell, George Macready, Horace MacMahon, Gladys George, *Joseph Wiseman, Lee Grant,* Gerald Mohr, Frank Faylen, Luis Van Rooten

'The admirably directed interaction of movement and talk all over the big room is what gives the thing its satisfying texture.'—*Richard Mallett, Punch*

AAN: Philip Yordan, Robert Wyler; William Wyler; Eleanor Parker; Lee Grant

The Devil and Miss Jones

US 1941   97m   bw
RKO / Frank Ross, Norman Krasna

A millionaire masquerades as a clerk in his own department store to investigate worker complaints. Attractive comedy with elements of the crazy thirties and the more socially conscious forties.

w Norman Krasna d Sam Wood *ph* Harry Stradling

Jean Arthur, *Charles Coburn,* Robert Cummings, Spring Byington, S. Z. Sakall, William Demarest

AAN: Norman Krasna; Charles Coburn

'Hell holds no surprises . . . for them!'

The Devils

🐾 GB 1970   111m
Technicolor   Panavision
Warner / Russo (Robert H. Solo, Ken Russell)

An account of the apparent demoniacal possession of the 17th-century nuns of Loudun, climaxing in the burning of their priest as a sorcerer.

Despite undeniable technical proficiency this is its writer-director's most outrageously sick film to date, campy, idiosyncratic and in howling bad taste from beginning to end, full of worm-eaten skulls, masturbating nuns, gibbering courtiers, plague sores, rats and a burning to death before our very eyes . . . plus a sacrilegious dream of Jesus. A pointless pantomime for misogynists.

wd Ken Russell, *play* John Whiting, *book* The Devils of Loudun by Aldous Huxley *ph* David Watkin *m* Peter Maxwell Davies *ad* Robert Cartwright

Vanessa Redgrave, Oliver Reed, Dudley Sutton, Max Adrian, Gemma Jones, Murray Melvin, Michael Gothard, Graham Armitage

'Ken Russell doesn't report hysteria, he markets it.'—*New Yorker, 1976*

'Russell's swirling multi-colored puddle . . . made me glad that both Huxley and Whiting are dead, so that they are spared this farrago of witless exhibitionism.'—*Stanley Kauffmann*

'A garish glossary of sado-masochism . . . a taste for visual sensation that makes scene after scene look like the masturbatory fantasies of a Roman Catholic boyhood.'—*Alexander Walker*

'It tells ALL about those Brontë sisters! . . . They didn't dare call it love—they tried to call it devotion!'

Devotion

🦇 US 1943 (released 1946)
107m   bw
Warner (Robert Buckner)

A highly romanticised account of the lives of the Brontë sisters and their brother Branwell. An enjoyably bad example of a big-budget Hollywood production which tampers with things it cannot understand, in this case life in a Yorkshire parsonage in Victorian times. An excuse is found to give the curate an Austrian accent to fit the available actor, but this and other *faux pas* are atoned for by the vividness of Emily's recurrent dream of death as a silhouetted man on horseback. In general, an interesting period piece in more senses than one.

w Keith Winter *d* Curtis Bernhardt *ph* Ernest Haller *m* Erich Wolfgang Korngold

Ida Lupino (Emily), Olivia de Havilland (Charlotte), Nancy Coleman (Anne), Arthur Kennedy (Branwell), Montagu Love (Revd Brontë), Paul Henreid (Revd Nicholls), Ethel Griffies (Aunt Branwell), Sidney Greenstreet (Thackeray), Eily Malyon, Forrester Harvey, Victor Francen

'I found it painless. I never got nearer to the subject than names and consequently it didn't hurt. But I would like to know who was devoted to whom and why.'—*Richard Winnington*

† More items from the extraordinary publicity campaign devised by Warners for this placid Victorian romance:

Emily: she ruled in that strange quiet house! None could resist the force of her will!

The man in black (i.e. the Revd Nicholls): he fled from her demands into her sister's arms!

Charlotte: the sweetness of love

and the meaning of torment—she learned them both together!

The 'friend'—the furious fat man (i.e. William Makepeace Thackeray): they couldn't fool him—they couldn't trust him!
†† Dialogue includes the celebrated exchange between two celebrated London literary figures:

THACKERAY: 'Morning, Dickens.'
DICKENS: 'Morning, Thackeray.'

Les Diaboliques
France 1954   114m   bw
Filmsonor (Henri-Georges Clouzot)
aka: *Diabolique; The Fiends*

A sadistic headmaster's wife and mistress conspire to murder him; but his body disappears and evidence of his presence haunts them.
Highly influential, suspenseful and scary thriller with a much-copied twist typical of its authors. Slow to start and shabby-looking as befits its grubby school setting, it gathers momentum with the murder and turns the screw with fine professionalism.

w Henri-Georges Clouzot, G. Geronimi, *novel* The Woman Who Was by Pierre Boileau and Thomas Narcejac d Henri-Georges Clouzot ph Armand Thirard m Georges Van Parys

Simone Signoret, Vera Clouzot, Charles Vanel, Paul Meurisse
'Scary, but so calculatedly sensational that it's rather revolting.'—*New Yorker, 1978*
'It depends very much on the intimate details of the seedy fourth-rate school, with its inadequate education and uneatable food, its general smell of unwashed children, hatred and petty perversions.'—*Basil Wright, 1972*
† Remade in 1976 as a TV movie, *Reflections of Murder*

'If a woman answers—hang on for dear life!'
Dial M For Murder
US 1954   105m
Warnercolor 3-D
Warner (Alfred Hitchcock)

An ageing tennis champion tries to arrange the death of his wife so that he will inherit, but his complex plan goes wrong.
Hitchcock did not try very hard to adapt this highly commercial play for the cinema, nor did he exploit the possibilities of 3-D. But for a one-room film with a not very exciting cast the film holds its grip pretty well.

w Frederick Knott, from his play d Alfred Hitchcock ph Robert Burks m Dmitri Tiomkin

Ray Milland, John Williams, Grace Kelly, Robert Cummings, Anthony Dawson
'All this is related with Hitchcock's ghoulish chic but everyone in it seems to be walking around with tired blood.'—*Pauline Kael, 1968*

A Diary for Timothy
GB 1945   40m   bw

A baby is born as the war ends, and the narrator ponders its future. Brilliant sentimental documentary, a summing up of the aims and feelings of Britain at the time. Written by E. M. Forster, speaker Michael Redgrave; directed by Humphrey Jennings; for Basil Wright/Crown Film Unit.

The Diary of a Country Priest
France 1950   120m   bw
Union Générale Cinématographique (Léon Carré)
original title: *Journal d'un Curé de Campagne*

A lonely young priest fails to make much impression in his first parish; and, falling ill, he dies alone. Striking, depressing, slow and austere, with little dialogue but considerable visual beauty; a very typical work of its director.

wd Robert Bresson, *novel* Georges Bernanos *ph* L. Burel *m* Jean-Jacques Grunenwald

Claude Laydu, Jean Riveyre, Armand Guibert, Nicole Ladmiral

The Diary of Anne Frank

US 1959 170m bw Cinemascope

TCF / George Stevens

In 1942, a family of Dutch Jews hides in an attic from the Nazis; just before the war ends they are found and sent to concentration camps. Based on the famous diaries of a girl who died at Auschwitz, this solemn adaptation is elephantine in its length, its ponderousness and its use of Cinemascope when the atmosphere is supposed to be claustrophobic.

w Frances Goodrich, Albert Hackett, from their play based on Anne Frank's diaries *d* George Stevens *ph* William C. Mellor *m* Alfred Newman

Millie Perkins, *Joseph Schildkraut, Shelley Winters, Ed Wynn*, Richard Beymer, Gusti Huber, Lou Jacobi, Diane Baker

AA: William C. Mellor; Shelley Winters

AAN: best picture; George Stevens; Alfred Newman; Ed Wynn

Diner

US 1982 110m Technicolor

MGM / SLM (Jerry Weintraub)

In 1959 Baltimore, college students congregate at their old meeting place and find themselves more occupied by adult problems than of yore. Generally amusing group character study, an awkward attempt to divine the meaning of life through the accumulation of detail. A little masterpiece of observation, for those with ears to hear; but not necessarily a great film.

wd Barry Levinson *ph* Peter Sova

m Bruce Brody, Ivan Kral *pd* Leon Harris *ed* Stu Linder

Steve Guttenberg, Daniel Stern, Mickey Rourke, Kevin Bacon, Timothy Daly, Ellen Barkin, Paul Reiser, Kathryn Dowling, Michael Tucker, Jessica James

AAN: original screenplay

Dinner at Eight

US 1933 113m bw MGM (David O. Selznick)

Guests at a society dinner party all find themselves in dramatic circumstances.

Artificial but compelling pattern play from a Broadway success.

w Frances Marion, Herman J. Mankiewicz, *play* George S. Kaufman, Edna Ferber *d* George Cukor *ph* William Daniels *m* William Axt

Marie Dressler, John Barrymore, Lionel Barrymore, Billie Burke, Wallace Beery, *Jean Harlow*, Lee Tracy, Edmund Lowe, Madge Evans, Jean Hersholt, Karen Morley, Louise Closser Hale, Phillips Holmes, May Robson, Grant Mitchell, Elizabeth Patterson

KITTY (Jean Harlow): 'You know, I read a book the other day. It's all about civilization or something—a nutty kind of a book. Do you know that the guy said machinery is going to take the place of every profession?'

CARLOTTA (Marie Dressler): 'Oh, my dear. That's something *you* need *never* worry about!'

'Marquee speaks for itself. It spells money, and couldn't very well be otherwise.'—*Variety*

'Damn them or praise them—you'll never forget them!'

The Dirty Dozen

US / Spain 1967 150m Metrocolor 70mm

MGM / Kenneth Hyman (Raymond Anzarut)

In 1944, twelve convicts serving life sentences are recruited for a commando suicide mission.

Professional, commercial but unlikeable slice of wartime thick ear; pretensions about capital punishment are jettisoned early on in favour of frequent and violent bloodshed. Much imitated, e.g. by *The Devil's Brigade*, *A Reason to Live*, *A Reason to Die*, etc.

w Nunnally Johnson, Lukas Heller *d* Robert Aldrich *ph* Edward Scaife *m* Frank de Vol

Lee Marvin, Ernest Borgnine, Robert Ryan, Charles Bronson, Jim Brown, John Cassavetes, George Kennedy, Richard Jaeckel, Trini Lopez, Telly Savalas, Ralph Meeker, Clint Walker, Robert Webber, Donald Sutherland

AAN: John Cassavetes

'You don't assign him to murder cases—you just turn him loose!'
Dirty Harry
US 1971 103m
Technicolor Panavision
Warner / Malpaso (Don Siegel)
A violently inclined San Francisco police inspector is the only cop who can bring to book a mad sniper. When the man is released through lack of evidence, he takes private revenge.
A savage cop show which became a cult and led to a spate of dirty cop movies, including two sequels, *Magnum Force* and *The Enforcer*. Well done for those who can take it.

w Harry Julian Fink, Rita M. Fink, Dean Riesner *d* Don Siegel *ph* Bruce Surtees *m* Lalo Schifrin

Clint Eastwood, Harry Guardino, Reni Santoni, John Vernon, Andy Robinson, John Larch, John Mitchum

The Discreet Charm of the Bourgeoisie
France / Spain / Italy 1972
105m Eastmancolor
Greenwich (Serge Silberman)
original title: *Le Charme Discret de la Bourgeoisie*
The efforts of a group of friends to dine together are continually frustrated.

A frequently hilarious, sometimes savage surrealist fable which makes all its points beautifully and then goes on twenty minutes too long. The performances are a joy.

w Luis Bunuel, Jean-Claude Carrière *d* Luis Bunuel *ph* Edmond Richard

Fernando Rey, Delphine Seyrig, Stéphane Audran, Bulle Ogier, Jean-Pierre Cassel, Paul Frankeur, Julien Bertheau
'A perfect synthesis of surreal wit and blistering social assault.'—*Jan Dawson, MFB*

AA: best foreign film
AAN: Luis Bunuel, Jean-Claude Carrière (script)

Dishonored
US 1931 91m bw
Paramount
An officer's widow turned streetwalker is hired by the German government as a spy.
Rather gloomy melodrama which helped to establish its star as a top American attraction; but the heavy hand of her Svengali, Von Sternberg, was already evident.

w Daniel H. Rubin *d* Josef Von Sternberg *ph* Lee Garmes *m* Karl Hajos

Marlene Dietrich, Victor McLaglen, Lew Cody, Gustav Von Seyffertitz, Warner Oland, Barry Norton, Wilfred Lucas
'Miss Dietrich rises above her director . . . should make the money grade of an A1 draw talker.'—*Variety*
'The most exciting movie I have seen in several months . . . yet I hope I may die young if I ever again have to listen to a manuscript so full of recusant, stilted, outmoded theatrical mouthings.'—*Pare Lorentz*
'The whole film has a kind of magnificent grandeur embellished, of course, by its shining central performance.'—*John Gillett, 1964*

DOA

US 1949 81m bw
Cardinal Pictures (Leo C. Popkin)

A businessman discovers that he has effectively been murdered by a slow-acting poison. In the few hours left to him he tracks down and kills his murderer, and confesses to the police.

Unusual and effective thriller, well photographed on location in San Francisco and Los Angeles.

w Russell Rouse, Clarence Greene d Rudolph Maté ph Ernest Laszlo m Dmitri Tiomkin

Edmond O'Brien, Luther Adler, Pamela Britton, William Ching

† Remade 1970 as Colour Me Dead, with Tom Tryon.

Dr Ehrlich's Magic Bullet

US 1940 103m bw
Warner (Wolfgang Reinhardt)
aka: The Story of Dr Ehrlich's Magic Bullet

A German scientist develops a cure for venereal disease.

Excellent period biopic: absorbing, convincing and extremely well put together.

w John Huston, Heinz Herald, Norman Burnside d William Dieterle ph James Wong Howe m Max Steiner

Edward G. Robinson, Ruth Gordon, Otto Kruger, Donald Crisp, Maria Ouspenskaya, Montagu Love, Sig Rumann, Donald Meek, Henry O'Neill, Albert Basserman, Edward Norris, Harry Davenport, Louis Calhern, Louis Jean Heydt

'A superb motion picture.'—Pare Lorentz

AAN: John Huston, Heinz Herald, Norman Burnside

Doctor in the House

GB 1954 91m
Eastmancolor
Rank (Betty Box)

Amorous and other misadventures of medical students at St Swithin's Hospital.

A comedy with much to answer for: several sequels and an apparently endless TV series. The original is not bad, as the students, though plainly over age, constitute a formidable mass of British talent at its peak.

w Nicholas Phipps, book Richard Gordon d Ralph Thomas ph Ernest Steward m Bruce Montgomery

Dirk Bogarde, Kenneth More, Donald Sinden, Donald Houston, Kay Kendall, Muriel Pavlow, James Robertson Justice, Geoffrey Keen

'Works its way with determined high spirits through the repertoire of medical student jokes.'—MFB

† Sequels, of increasing insanity and decreasing connection with the original characters, were: Doctor at Sea, Doctor at Large, Doctor in Love, Doctor in Distress, Doctor in Clover and Doctor in Trouble. Carry on Doctor and Carry on Again Doctor were horses of a different colour.

'Strange desires! Loves and hates and secret yearnings . . . hidden in the shadows of a man's mind!'

Doctor Jekyll and Mr Hyde

US 1931 98m bw
Paramount (Rouben Mamoulian)

A Victorian research chemist finds a formula which separates the good and evil in his soul; when the latter predominates, he becomes a rampaging monster.

The most exciting and cinematic version by far of the famous horror story; the make-up is slightly over the top, but the gas-lit London settings, the pace, the performances and clever camera and sound tricks make it a film to enjoy over and over again. Subjective camera is used at the beginning, and for the first transformation the actor wore various layers of make up which were sensitive to different colour filters and thus produced instant change.

w Samuel Hoffenstein, Percy Heath, novel Robert Louis Stevenson d Rouben Mamoulian ph Karl Struss ad Hans Dreier

Fredric March, Miriam Hopkins, Rose Hobart, Holmes Herbert, Halliwell Hobbes, Edgar Norton

'Promises abundant shocks and returns now that the fan public is horror conscious. Probably loses something on popular appeal by highbrow treatment.'—*Variety*

'As a work of cinematic imagination this film is difficult to fault.'—*John Baxter, 1968*

† The screenplay with 1,400 frame blow-ups was published in 1976 in the Film Classics Library (editor Richard J. Anobile).

†† The film was subsequently edited down to 80m, and this is the only version remaining.

AA: Fredric March
AAN: Samuel Hoffenstein, Percy Heath; Karl Struss

Dr Jekyll and Mr Hyde

US 1941   122m   bw
MGM (Victor Saville, Victor Fleming)

Curiously misconceived, stately, badly cast version with elaborate production including Freudian dream sequences. Always worth watching, but not a success.

w John Lee Mahin d Victor Fleming ph Joseph Ruttenberg m Franz Waxman

Spencer Tracy, Ingrid Bergman, Lana Turner, Ian Hunter, C. Aubrey Smith, Donald Crisp, Sara Allgood

'Not so much evil incarnate as ham rampant . . . more ludicrous than dreadful.'—*New York Times*

'A romantic gentleman by day—a love-mad beast at night!'—*publicity*

† Other versions: *The Two Faces of Dr Jekyll* (1960), *I Monster* (1970). Variations: *Daughter of Dr Jekyll* (1957), *Abbott and Costello Meet Dr Jekyll and Mr Hyde* (1954), *Son of Dr Jekyll* (1951), *The Ugly Duckling* (1960), *House of Dracula* (1945),

The Nutty Professor (1963), *Dr Jekyll and Sister Hyde* (1971).

AAN: Joseph Ruttenberg; Franz Waxman

Doctor Mabuse the Gambler

Germany 1922   101m (24 fps)   bw   silent
UFA (Erich Pommer)
original title: *Doktor Mabuse, der Spieler*

A criminal mastermind uses hypnotism and blackmail in his efforts to obtain world domination, but when finally cornered is discovered to be a raving maniac.

A real wallow in German post-war depression and melodrama, in the form of a Fu Manchu/Moriarty type thriller. Fascinating scene by scene, but by now a slightly tiresome whole.

w Thea Von Harbou, Fritz Lang, novel Norbert Jacques d Fritz Lang ph Carl Hoffman ad Otto Hunte, Stahl-Urach, Erich Kettelhut, Karl Vollbrecht

Rudolph Klein-Rogge, Alfred Abel, Gertrude Welcker, Lil Dagover, Paul Richter

† Originally issued in Germany in two parts, *Der Grosse Spieler* and *Inferno*, adding up to a much longer running time.

Doctor No

GB 1962   111m
Technicolor
UA/Eon (Harry Saltzman, Albert R. Broccoli)

A British secret service agent foils a master criminal operating in the West Indies.

First of the phenomenally successful James Bond movies, mixing sex, violence and campy humour against expensive sets and exotic locales. Toned down from the original novels, they expressed a number of sixties attitudes, and proved unstoppable box office attractions for nearly fifteen years. The first was, if not quite the best, reasonably representative of the series.

w Richard Maibaum, Johanna Harwood, Berkeley Mather, *novel* Ian Fleming *d* Terence Young *ph* Ted Moore *m Monty Norman*

Sean Connery, Ursula Andress, Jack Lord, Joseph Wiseman, John Kitzmiller, Bernard Lee, Lois Maxwell, Zena Marshall, Eunice Gayson, Anthony Dawson

† The subsequent titles were *From Russia with Love* (1963), *Goldfinger* (1964), *Thunderball* (1965), *You Only Live Twice* (1967), *On Her Majesty's Secret Service* (1969), *Diamonds Are Forever* (1971), *Live and Let Die* (1973), *The Man with the Golden Gun* (1974), *The Spy Who Loved Me* (1977), *Moonraker* (1979), *For Your Eyes Only* (1981), *Octopussy* (1983), *Never Say Never Again* (1984). Casino Royale (1967) was a Bond spoof made by other hands.

'The hot line suspense comedy!'
Dr Strangelove; or, How I Learned to Stop Worrying and Love the Bomb
GB 1963 93m bw
Columbia/Stanley Kubrick
(Victor Lyndon)
A mad USAF general launches a nuclear attack on Russia, and when recall attempts fail, and retaliation is inevitable, all concerned sit back to await the destruction of the world. Black comedy resolving itself into a series of sketches, with the star playing three parts (for no good reason): the US president, an RAF captain, and a mad German-American scientist. Historically an important film in its timing, its nightmares being those of the early sixties, artistically it clogs its imperishable moments by untidy narrative and unattractively contrasty photography.

w Stanley Kubrick, Terry Southern, Peter George, *novel* Red Alert by Peter George *d* Stanley Kubrick *ph* Gilbert Taylor *m* Laurie Johnson *ad* Ken Adam

Peter Sellers, George C. Scott, Peter Bull, Sterling Hayden, Keenan Wynn, Slim Pickens, James Earl Jones, Tracy Reed

GENERAL (George C. Scott): 'I don't say we wouldn't get our hair mussed, but I do say no more than ten to twenty million people killed.'

'Scarcely a picture of relentless originality; seldom have we seen so much made over so little.'—*Joan Didion*

† *Fail Safe*, which took the same theme more seriously, was released almost simultaneously.

AAN: best picture; script; Stanley Kubrick (as director); Peter Sellers

---

'A full moon was his signal to kill!'
Dr X
US 1932 82m Technicolor
Warner (Hal Wallis)
A reporter investigates a series of moon murders and narrows his search to one of several doctors at a medical college.
Fascinating, German-inspired, overblown and generally enjoyable horror mystery whose armless villain commits murders by growing limbs from 'synthetic flesh'.

w Earl Baldwin, Robert Tasker, *play* Howard W. Comstock, Allen C. Miller *d* Michael Curtiz *ph* Richard Tower, Ray Rennahan *md* Leo Forbstein

Lee Tracy, Lionel Atwill, Preston Foster, Fay Wray, George Rosener, Mae Busch, Arthur Edmund Carewe, John Wray

'The settings, lighting and final battle with the man-monster are quite stunning.'—*NFT, 1974*

'It almost makes Frankenstein seem tame and friendly.'—*New York Times*

'A love caught in the fire of revolution!'
Doctor Zhivago
US 1965 192m Metrocolor
Panavision 70
MGM/Carlo Ponti
A Moscow doctor is caught up in World War I, exiled for writing poetry, forced into partisan service and separated from his only love.

Beautifully photographed and meticulously directed, this complex epic has been so reduced from the original novel that many parts of the script simply do not make any kind of sense. What remains is a collection of expensive set pieces, great for looking if not listening.

w Robert Bolt, *novel* Boris Pasternak *d* David Lean *ph* Frederick A. Young *m* Maurice Jarre

Omar Sharif, Julie Christie, Rod Steiger, Alec Guinness, Rita Tushingham, Ralph Richardson, Tom Courtenay, Geraldine Chaplin, Siobhan McKenna, Noel Willman, Geoffrey Keen, Adrienne Corri

'A long haul along the road of synthetic lyricism.'—*MFB*

'David Lean's *Doctor Zhivago* does for snow what his *Lawrence of Arabia* did for sand.'—*John Simon*

'It isn't shoddy (except for the music); it isn't soap opera; it's stately, respectable, and dead. Neither the contemplative Zhivago nor the flow of events is intelligible, and what is worse, they seem unrelated to each other.'—*Pauline Kael*

AA: Robert Bolt; Frederick A. Young; Maurice Jarre
AAN: best picture; David Lean; Tom Courtenay

'West of Chicago there was no law! West of Dodge City there was no God!'
Dodge City
US 1939   104m Technicolor
Warner (Robert Lord)

An ex-soldier and trail boss helps clean up the west's great railroad terminus.

Standard, satisfying big-scale western with all clichés intact and very enjoyable, as is the soft, rich early colour. The story is plainly inspired by the exploits of Wyatt Earp.

w Robert Buckner *d* Michael Curtiz *ph* Sol Polito, Ray Rennahan *m* Max Steiner

Errol Flynn, Olivia de Havilland, Ann Sheridan, Bruce Cabot, Alan Hale, Frank McHugh, John Litel, Victor Jory, William Lundigan, Henry Travers, Henry O'Neill, Guinn Williams, Gloria Holden

'A lusty western packed with action including some of the dandiest mêlée stuff screened.'—*Variety*

'It looks programmed and underpopulated, though in an elegantly stylized way.'—*New Yorker, 1980*

Dodsworth
US 1936   101m   bw
Samuel Goldwyn

An American businessman takes his wife on a tour of Europe, and their lives are changed.
Satisfying, well-acted drama from a bestselling novel; production values high.

w Sidney Howard, *novel* Sinclair Lewis *d* William Wyler *ph* Rudolph Maté *m* Alfred Newman

Walter Huston, Mary Astor, Ruth Chatterton, David Niven, Paul Lukas, Gregory Gayę, *Maria Ouspenskaya*, Odette Myrtil, Spring Byington, John Payne.

'No one, I think, will fail to enjoy it, in spite of its too limited and personal plot, the sense it leaves behind of a very expensive, very contemporary, Bond Street vacuum flask.'—*Graham Greene*

'William Wyler has had the skill to execute it in cinematic terms, and a gifted cast has been able to bring the whole alive to our complete satisfaction.'—*New York Times*

'A smoothly flowing narrative of substantial interest, well-defined performances and good talk.'—*New York Times*

'An offering of dignity and compelling power to provide you with a treat you can rarely experience in a picture house.'—*Hollywood Spectator*

AAN: best picture; Sidney Howard; William Wyler, Walter Huston; Maria Ouspenskaya

Dog Day Afternoon

US 1975   130m
Technicolor
Warner / AEC (Martin Bregman,
Martin Elfland)

Two incompetent robbers are
cornered in a Brooklyn bank.
Recreation of a tragi-comic episode
from the newspaper headlines; for
half its length a fascinating and
acutely observed film which then
bogs itself down in a surplus of talk
and excessive sentiment about
homosexuality.

w Frank Pierson, *book* Patrick
Mann *d Sidney Lumet ph* Victor J.
Kemper *m* none

Al Pacino, John Cazale, *Charles
Durning*, Sully Boyar, James
Broderick, *Chris Sarandon*

'There is plenty of Lumet's vital
best here in a film that at least
glancingly captures the increasingly
garish pathology of our urban
life.'—*Jack Kroll*

'Scattered moments of wry
humour, sudden pathos and correct
observation.'—*John Simon*

'The mask of frenetic cliché
doesn't spoil moments of pure
reporting on people in
extremity.'—*New Yorker*

'A long and wearying case history
of the beaten, sobbing, despairing
and ultimately powerless
anti-hero.'—*Karyn Kay, Jump Cut*

'Full of galvanic mirth rooted in
human desperation.'—*Michael
Billington, Illustrated London News*

'Brisk, humorous and alive with
urban energies and angers fretting
through the 92 degree heat.'—*Sight
and Sound*

AA: Frank Pierson
AAN: best picture; Sidney Lumet;
Al Pacino; Chris Sarandon

La Dolce Vita

Italy / France 1960   173m
bw   Totalscope
Riama / Pathé Consortium
(Giuseppe Amato)
aka: *The Sweet Life*

A journalist mixes in modern Roman
high society and is alternately
bewitched and sickened by what he
sees.
Episodic satirical melodrama, a
marathon self-indulgent wallow with
a wagging finger never far away. Not
a successful whole, but full of choice
moments such as a statue of Christ
being flown by helicopter over the
city.

w Federico Fellini, Tullio Pinelli,
Ennio Flaiano, Brunello Rondi
d Federico Fellini ph Otello
Martelli *m* Nino Rota *ad* Piero
Gherardi

Marcello Mastroianni, Anita
Ekberg, Anouk Aimée, Alain Cuny,
Yvonne Furneaux, Magali Noel,
Nadia Gray, Lex Barker

'Its personification of various
familiar symbols—love, death,
purity, sin, reason and so on—never
succeeds in reflecting human values
or creating intellectual
excitement . . . Its actual
significance rests in the way its
(albeit specious) social attack has
stirred the imagination of other
Italian film-makers, as well as public
interest in their work.'—*Robert Vas,
MFB*

AAN: script; Federico Fellini

The Dolly Sisters

US 1945   114m
Technicolor
TCF (George Jessel)

The lives of a Hungarian sister act in
American vaudeville.
Fictionalized biographical musical,
only fair in the script department but
glittering to look at in superb colour,
and enriched by splendid production
values. Undoubtedly among the best
of its kind.

w John Larkin, Marian Spitzer
d Irving Cummings *ph* Ernest
Palmer *md* Alfred Newman,
Charles Henderson *songs* various
ch Seymour Felix *ad* Lyle Wheeler,
Leland Fuller

Betty Grable, June Haver, John
Payne, S. Z. Sakall, Reginald
Gardiner, Frank Latimore, Gene
Sheldon, Sig Rumann, Trudy
Marshall

AAN: song 'I Can't Begin to Tell You' (*m* Johnny Monaco, *ly* Mack Gordon)

Domenica d'Agosto
Italy 1950   75m   bw
Colonna (Sergio Amidei)
GB title: *Sunday in August*
Various Romans enjoy Sunday by the sea at Ostia.
Fragmented comedy-drama which succeeds in being charming throughout, every detail being freshly observed through an inquisitive eye

w Franco Brusati, Luciano Emmer, Giulio Macchi, Cesare Zavattini *d* Luciano Emmer *ph* Domenico Scala, Leonida Barboni, Ubaldo Marelli *m* Roman Vlad *ed* Jolanda Benvenuti

Anna Baldini, Franco Interlenghi, Elvy Lissiak, Massimo Serato, Marcello Mastroianni, Corrado Verga

Don Juan
US 1926   126m
(synchronized)   bw
Warner
Exploits of the famous lover and adventurer at Lucretia Borgia's court.
Lithe swashbuckler in the best silent tradition, but with a synchronized score (by William Axt) which made it a sensation and led directly to the talkie revolution.

w Bess Meredyth *d* Alan Crosland *ph* Byron Haskin

John Barrymore, Mary Astor, Warner Oland, Estelle Taylor, Myrna Loy, Phyllis Haver, Willard Louis, Montagu Love

Don't Look Now
GB 1973   110m
Technicolor
BL / Casey / Eldorado (Peter Katz)
After the death of their small daughter, the Baxters meet in Venice two old sisters who claim mediumistic connection with the dead girl. The husband scorns the idea, but repeatedly sees a little

red-coated figure in shadowy passages by the canals. When he confronts it, it proves to be a maniac dwarf who stabs him to death.
A macabre short story has become a pretentious and puzzling piece of high cinema art full of vague suggestions and unexplored avenues. Whatever its overall deficiencies, it is too brilliant in surface detail to be dismissed. Depressingly but fascinatingly set in wintry Venice, it has to be seen to be appreciated.

w Allan Scott, Chris Bryant, *story* Daphne du Maurier *d* Nicolas Roeg *ph* Anthony Richmond *m* Pino D'Onnagio *ad* Giovanni Soccol

Donald Sutherland, Julie Christie, Hilary Mason, Clelia Matania, Massimo Serrato
'The fanciest, most carefully assembled enigma yet seen on the screen.'—*New Yorker*
'A powerful and dazzling visual texture.'—*Penelope Houston*

'You can't kiss away a murder!'
Double Indemnity
US 1944   107m   bw
Paramount (Joseph Sistrom)
An insurance agent connives with the glamorous wife of a client to kill her husband and collect.
Archetypal *film noir* of the forties, brilliantly filmed and incisively written, perfectly capturing the decayed Los Angeles atmosphere of a Chandler novel but using a simpler story and more substantial characters. The hero/villain was almost a new concept.

w Billy Wilder, Raymond Chandler, *novel* James M. Cain *d* Billy Wilder *ph* John Seitz *m* Miklos Rozsa

Fred MacMurray, Barbara Stanwyck, Edward G. Robinson, Tom Powers, Porter Hall, Jean Heather, Byron Barr, Richard Gaines
Opening narration: Office memorandum. Walter Neff to Barton T. Keyes, Claims Manager, Los Angeles, July 16, 1938. Dear Keyes: I suppose you'll call this a

confession when you hear it. Well, I don't like the word confession. I just want to set you right about something you couldn't see because it was smack up against your nose . . . I killed Dietrichson. Me, Walter Neff, insurance salesman, 35 years old, unmarried, no visible scars. Until a while ago, that is . . .

'The sort of film which revives a critic from the depressive effects of bright epics about the big soul of America or the suffering soul of Europe and gives him a new lease of faith.'—*Richard Winnington*

'The most pared-down and purposeful film ever made by Billy Wilder.'—*John Coleman, 1966*

'Profoundly, intensely entertaining.'—*Richard Mallett, Punch*

'One of the highest summits of *film noir* without a single trace of pity or love.'—*Charles Higham, 1971*

AAN: best picture; script, direction; John Seitz; Miklos Rozsa; Barbara Stanwyck

'This woman inspired him—this woman feared him!'
A Double Life
US 1947   103m   bw
(Universal) Kanin Productions (Michael Kanin)
An actor playing Othello is obsessed by the role and murders a woman he imagines to be Desdemona.
An old theatrical chestnut (cf *Men Are Not Gods*) is decked out with smartish backstage dialogue but despite a pleasant star performance remains unrewarding if taxing, and the entertainment value of the piece is on the thin side considering the mighty talents involved.

w Ruth Gordon, Garson Kanin *d* George Cukor *ph* Milton Krasner *m* Miklos Rozsa

Ronald Colman, Shelley Winters, Signe Hasso, Edmond O'Brien, Millard Mitchell

AA: Miklos Rozsa; Ronald Colman
AAN: Ruth Gordon, Garson Kanin; George Cukor

'The strangest love a woman has ever known . . . a livid face bent over her in the ghostly mist!'
Dracula
US 1931   84m   bw
Universal (Carl Laemmle Jnr)
A Transylvanian vampire count gets his comeuppance in Yorkshire.
A film which has much to answer for. It started its star and its studio off on horror careers, and it launched innumerable sequels (see below). In itself, after two eerie reels, it becomes a pedantic and slow transcription of a stage adaptation, and its climax takes place offscreen; but for all kinds of reasons it remains full of interest.

w Garrett Fort, *play* Hamilton Deane, John Balderston, *novel* Bram Stoker *d* Tod Browning *ph* Karl Freund *m* Tchaikovsky

Bela Lugosi, Helen Chandler, David Manners, *Dwight Frye*, Edward Van Sloan

'Must have caused much uncertainty as to the femme fan reaction . . . as it turns out the signs are that the woman's angle is all right and that sets the picture for better than average money . . . it comes out as a sublimated ghost story related with all surface seriousness and above all with a remarkably effective background of creepy atmosphere.'—*Variety*

'A too literal adaptation of the play (*not* the book) results in a plodding, talkative development, with much of the vital action taking place off-screen.'—*William K. Everson*

'The mistiest parts are the best; when the lights go up the interest goes down.'—*Ivan Butler*

'It'll chill you and fill you with fears. You'll find it creepy and cruel and crazed.'—*New York Daily News*

† Later advertising variations concentrated on the horror element:
'In all the annals of living horror one name stands out as the epitome of evil! So evil, so fantastic, so degrading you'll

wonder if it isn't all a nightmare!
Innocent girls lured to a fate truly
worse than death!'

†† Lugosi was not the first choice for
the role of the Count. Ian Keith and
William Powell were strongly
favoured.

††† Sequels include *Dracula's
Daughter*, *Son of Dracula*; the later
Hammer sequence consists of
Dracula (see below), *Brides of
Dracula*, *Dracula Prince of
Darkness*, *Dracula Has Risen From
the Grave*, *Taste the Blood of
Dracula*, *Scars of Dracula*, *Dracula
AD 1972*, *The Satanic Rites of
Dracula*. Other associated films in
which the Count or a disciple
appears include *Return of the
Vampire* (1944), *House of
Frankenstein* (1945), *House of
Dracula* (1945), *Abbott and Costello
Meet Frankenstein* (1948), *The
Return of Dracula* (1958), *Kiss of the
Vampire* (1963), *The Fearless
Vampire Killers* (1967), *Count Yorga
Vampire* (1969), *Countess Dracula*
(1970), *Vampire Circus* (1970), *The
House of Dark Shadows* (1970),
Vampire Lovers (1971), *Blacula*
(1972), Minor potboilers are legion.

'Who will be his bride tonight?'
Dracula
🦇 GB 1958 82m Technicolor
   Hammer (Anthony Hinds)
US title: *Horror of Dracula*
A remake of the 1930 film.
Commendably brief in comparison
with the later Hammer films, this
was perhaps the best horror piece
they turned out as well as the most
faithful to its original. Decor and
colour were well used, and the
leading performances are striking.

*w Jimmy Sangster d Terence Fisher
ph Jack Asher m James Bernard
ad Bernard Robinson*

Peter Cushing (as Van Helsing),
Christopher Lee (as Dracula),
Melissa Stribling, Carol Marsh,
Michael Gough, John Van Eyssen,
Valerie Gaunt, Miles Malleson

Die Dreigroschenoper
🎞 Germany 1931 114m bw
   Warner / Tobis / Nero
US title: *The Threepenny Opera*
In turn-of-the-century London,
Mack the Knife marries the daughter
of the beggar king and runs into
trouble.
Heavy-footed but interesting
updating of *The Beggar's Opera*,
with splendid sets.

*w Bela Balazs, Leo Lania, Ladislas
Vajda*, from Bertolt Brecht's
version *d G. W. Pabst ph Fritz
Arno Wagner m Kurt Weill
ad Andrei Andreiev*

Lotte Lenya, Rudolf Forster, Fritz
Rasp, Caroline Neher, Reinhold
Schunzel, Valeska Gert, Vladimir
Sokoloff

† Brecht disliked the film and sued
the makers, but lost.
†† A French version was also
released under the title *L'Opéra de
Quat'sous*, with Albert Préjean.

'Every nightmare has a beginning.
   This one never ends!'
Dressed to Kill
🔪 US 1980 105m
   Technicolor
Filmways / Samuel Z.
Arkoff / Cinema 77 (George Litto)
A sexually disturbed matron under
analysis is murdered by a transvestite
slasher, who then goes after a
witness.
Occasionally brilliant, generally
nasty suspenser clearly derived from
many viewings of *Psycho*. Certainly
not for the squeamish.

*wd Brian de Palma ph Ralf Bode
m Pino Donaggio pd Gary Weist*

Michael Caine, Angie Dickinson,
Nancy Allen, Keith Gordon, Dennis
Franz
   'De Palma goes right for the
audience jugular . . . it fully milks
the boundaries of its "R"
rating.'—*Variety*
   'By casting a halo of excitement
around killing, a glow of degradation
around living, and linking the two in
a queasy, guilty partnership, de
Palma is asking us to celebrate the

joys of barbarism in a world already drunk on rape, torture, murder and war.'—*Sunday Times*

Drums along the Mohawk

US 1939   103m
Technicolor
TCF (Raymond Griffith)
Colonists survive Indian attacks in upstate New York during the Revolutionary War.
Patchy, likeable period adventure story with domestic and farming interludes; in its way a key film in the director's canon.

w Lamar Trotti, Sonya Levien, *novel* Walter Edmonds *d* John Ford *ph* Bert Glennon, Ray Rennahan *m* Alfred Newman

Claudette Colbert, Henry Fonda, *Edna May Oliver*, Eddie Collins, John Carradine, Dorris Bowdon, Jessie Ralph, Arthur Shields, Robert Lowery, Roger Imhof, Ward Bond

'Outdoor spec, a top-bracketer, though not in the smash division.'—*Variety*

'No one appears to know why the picture is being made, or what its point is, exactly.'—*Pauline Kael, 70s*

AAN: Edna May Oliver

Duel in the Sun

US 1946   135 or 138m
Technicolor
David O. Selznick
A half-breed girl causes trouble between two brothers.
Massive western, dominated and fragmented by its producer, who bought the best talent and proceeded to interfere with it, so that while individual scenes are marvellous, the narrative has little flow. The final gory shoot-up between two lovers was much discussed at the time.

w David O. Selznick, Oliver H. P. Garrett, *novel* Niven Busch *d* King Vidor (and others) *second unit* B. Reeves Eason, Otto Brower *ph* Lee Garmes, Harold Rosson, Ray Rennahan *m* Dmitri Tiomkin *ad* James Basevi *pd* J. McMillan Johnson

Jennifer Jones, Joseph Cotten, Gregory Peck, Lionel Barrymore, Lillian Gish, Walter Huston, Herbert Marshall, Charles Bickford, Tilly Losch, Joan Tetzel, Harry Carey, Otto Kruger, Sidney Backmer

'A knowing blend of oats and aphrodisiac.'—*Time*

'Cornographic is a word that might have been coined for it.'—*Daily Mail*

'As sexual melodrama with a spectacular background it is in its way remarkable.'—*New Statesman*

'A razzmatazz of thunderous naïvety simmering into a kind of majestic dottiness.'—*Basil Wright, 1972*

'A lavish, sensual spectacle, so heightened it becomes a cartoon of passion.'—*Pauline Kael, 70s*

† The uncredited directors included Joseph Von Sternberg, William Dieterle, B. Reeves Eason, and Selznick himself.

AAN: Jennifer Jones; Lillian Gish

Dumbo

US 1941   64m   Technicolor
Walt Disney
A baby circus elephant finds that his big ears have a use after all.
Delightful cartoon feature notable for set pieces such as the drunken nightmare and the crows' song.

w various *d* Ben Sharpsteen *m* Frank Churchill, Oliver Wallace

AA: music
AAN: song, 'Baby Mine' (*m* Frank Churchill, *ly* Ned Washington)

Dunkirk

GB 1958   135m   bw
MGM / Ealing (Michael Balcon)
In 1940 on the Normandy beaches, a small group gets detached from the main force.
Sober, small-scale approach to an epic subject; interesting but not inspiring, with performances to match.

w W. P. Lipscomb, David Divine *d* Leslie Norman *ph* Paul Beeson *m* Malcolm Arnold

John Mills, Richard Attenborough, Bernard Lee, Robert Urquhart, Ray Jackson

Dynamite

US 1929   129m   bw
MGM (Cecil B. de Mille)

In order to gain an inheritance, a socialite marries a man about to be executed . . . but he is reprieved. Dated but still dynamic social melodrama of the early talkie period.

w Jeanie Macpherson *d* Cecil B. de Mille *ph* Peverell Marley
m Herbert Stothart

Kay Johnson, Charles Bickford, Conrad Nagel, Julia Faye, Joel McCrea

'A pot-pourri of all previous de Mille efforts crammed into one picture.'—*Variety*

'Exuberant, wonderfully vigorous, the film skilfully evokes the look and character of the Jazz Age.'—*Charles Higham*

'An astonishing mixture, with artificiality vying with realism and comedy hanging on the heels of grim melodrama.'—*Mordaunt Hall, New York Times*

E

E.T.

US 1982　115m　De Luxe
Universal (Steven Spielberg, Kathleen Kennedy)

When an alien spacecraft is disturbed in a Los Angeles suburb, one of its crew members is left behind and befriended by a small boy.

Stupefyingly successful box office fairy tale by the current wonder kid Spielberg, taken to the world's heart because he dares to make films without sex, violence or bad language. This one could hardly be simpler, but it works; and the ailing cinema would love to know how to repeat the trick several times a year.

w Melissa Mathison d Steven Spielberg ph Allen Daviau m John Williams pd James D. Bissell creator of E.T. Carlo Rambaldi

Dee Wallace, Henry Thomas, Peter Coyote, Robert MacNaughton, Drew Barrymore, K. C. Martel

† E.T. = extra-terrestrial

AA: visual effects; music; sound
AAN: best picture; direction; original screenplay; cinematography; editing
BFA: best score

Each Dawn I Die

US 1939　84m　bw
Warner (David Lewis)

A crusading reporter is framed for manslaughter and becomes a hardened prisoner.

Efficient, vigorous yet slightly disappointing star vehicle; the talents are in the right background, but the script is wobbly.

w Norman Reilly Raine, Warren Duff, Charles Perry, novel Jerome Odlum d William Keighley ph Arthur Edeson m Max Steiner

James Cagney, George Raft, Jane Bryan, George Bancroft, Maxie Rosenbloom, Stanley Ridges, Alan Baxter, Victor Jory

'Rich in horror and brutality.'—*New York Sunday Mirror*

'In addition to its crackling screenplay, it is made memorable by the easy mastery of its two principals.'—*Time*

'Towards the end of the thirties Warners underworld pictures began to get hazy and high-minded, and in this one the pre-Second World War spiritual irradiation blurs the conventions of the prison genre.'—*Pauline Kael, 70s*

† Original title: *Killer Meets Killer*.

The Eagle

US 1925　80m approx (24 fps)　bw　silent
United Artists

A Cossack lieutenant turns masked outlaw when his father's lands are annexed.

Enjoyable romp in the wake of Robin Hood, the Scarlet Pimpernel and Zorro; the eye-flashing star is somewhere near his best.

w Hans Kraly, story Dubrowsky by Alexander Pushkin d Clarence Brown ph George Barnes

Rudolph Valentino, Vilma Banky, Louise Dresser

Earth

USSR 1930　63m approx (24 fps)　bw　silent
VUFKU

original title: *Zemlya*

Trouble results in a Ukrainian village when a landowner refuses to hand over his land for a collective farm.

The melodramatic little plot takes second place to lyrical sequences of rustic beauty, illustrating life, love and death in the countryside.

wd, ed Alexander Dovzhenko
ph Danylo Demutsky

Semyon Svashenko, Stephan
Shkurat, Mikola Nademsky, Yelena
Maximova

  'Stories in themselves do not
interest me. I choose them in order
to get the greatest expression of
essential social forms.'—*Dovzhenko*

  'A picture for filmgoers who are
prepared to take their cinema as
seriously as Tolstoy took the
novel.'—*James Agate*

Earthquake

US 1974   123m
Technicolor   Panavision
Universal / Jennings Lang / Mark
Robson

Various personal stories intertwine
in a Los Angeles earthquake.
Dreary drama with very variable
special effects, gimmicked up by
Sensurround. A box office bonanza.

w George Fox, Mario Puzo *d* Mark
Robson *ph* Philip Lathrop *m* John
Williams *pd* Alexander Golitzen
sp Albert Whitlock

Charlton Heston, Ava Gardner,
Lorne Greene, Marjoe Gortner,
Barry Sullivan, George Kennedy,
Richard Roundtree, Geneviève
Bujold, Walter Matthau (under the
alias of his real name)

  'The picture is swell, but it isn't a
cheat. It's an entertaining marathon
of Grade A destruction effects, with
B-picture stock characters spinning
through it.'—*Pauline Kael*

AAN: Philip Lathrop

'Of what a boy did . . . what a girl
  did . . . of ecstasy and revenge!'
'The most shocking revenge a girl
  ever let one brother take on
  another!'

East of Eden

US 1955   115m
Warnercolor   Cinemascope
Warner (Elia Kazan)

In a California farming valley in 1917
a wild adolescent rebels against his
stern father and discovers that his

mother, believed dead, runs a
nearby brothel.

Turgid elaboration of Genesis with
strong character but nowhere to go.
Heavily over-directed and rousingly
acted.

w Paul Osborn, *novel* John
Steinbeck *d Elia Kazan ph* Ted
McCord *m* Leonard Rosenman
ad James Basevi, Malcolm Bert

Raymond Massey, James Dean (his
first star role), Julie Harris, Dick
Davalos, *Jo Van Fleet*, Burl Ives,
Albert Dekker

  'The first distinguished production
in Cinemascope.'—*Eugene Archer*

AA: Jo Van Fleet
AAN: Paul Osborn; Elia Kazan;
James Dean

Easter Parade

US 1948   109m
Technicolor
MGM (Arthur Freed)

A song and dance man quarrels with
one partner but finds another.
A musical which exists only in its
numbers, which are many but
variable. All in all, an agreeable
lightweight entertainment without
the style to put it in the top class.

w Sidney Sheldon, Frances
Goodrich, Albert Hackett *d* Charles
Walters *ph* Harry Stradling
m/ly Irving Berlin md Roger
Edens, Johnny Green

Fred Astaire, Judy Garland, Ann
Miller, Peter Lawford, Clinton
Sundberg, Jules Munshin

  'The important thing is that Fred
Astaire is back, with Irving Berlin
calling the tunes.'—*Newsweek*

† Fred Astaire was actually second
choice, replacing Gene Kelly who
damaged an ankle.

AA: Roger Edens, Johnny Green

'Where there's smoke, there must
be somebody smoking!'
Easy Living
🐛 US 1937   91m   bw
Paramount (Arthur Hornblow
Jnr)
A fur coat is thrown out of a window
and lands on a typist . . .
Amusing romantic comedy with
farcical trimmings; it now stands
among the classic crazy comedies of
the thirties.

*w Preston Sturges d Mitchell Leisen
ph Ted Tetzlaff md Boris Morros*

Jean Arthur, Ray Milland, *Edward
Arnold*, Luis Alberni, Mary Nash,
Franklin Pangborn, William
Demarest, Andrew Tombes
    'Slapstick farce which does not
fulfil the box office possibilities of its
stars.'—*Variety*
    'Secretaries, millionaires, jokes,
sight gags, furies, attacks of cool
sense—there are always three things
going on at once.'—*New Yorker,
1977*

'A man went looking for America
and couldn't find it anywhere!'
Easy Rider
🐝 US 1969   94m   Technicolor
Columbia / Pando / Raybert
(Peter Fonda)
Two drop-outs ride across America
on motorcycles.
Happening to please hippies and
motor-cycle enthusiasts as well as
amateur politicians, this oddball
melodrama drew freakishly large
audiences throughout the world and
was much imitated though never
equalled in its casual effectiveness,
nor did promising careers ensue for
the actors mainly concerned.

*w Peter Fonda, Dennis Hopper,
Terry Southern d Dennis Hopper
ph Laszlo Kovacs m various
recordings*

Peter Fonda, Dennis Hopper, *Jack
Nicholson*
    '*Cinéma-vérité* in allegory
terms.'—*Peter Fonda*
    'Ninety-four minutes of what it is
like to swing, to watch, to be fond,

to hold opinions and to get killed in
America at this moment.'—*Penelope
Gilliatt*

AAN: script; Jack Nicholson

Easy Street
🐛 US 1917   22m approx   bw
silent
Mutual / Charles Chaplin
In a slum street, a tramp is reformed
by a dewy-eyed missionary, becomes
a policeman, and tames the local
bully.
Quintessential Chaplin, combining
sentimentality and social comment
with hilarious slapstick.

*wd Charles Chaplin ph William C.
Foster, Rollie Totheroh*

Charles Chaplin, Edna Purviance,
Albert Austin, Eric Campbell

Edge of the World
🐝🐝 GB 1937   80m   bw
GFD / Rock (Joe Rock)
Life, love and death on Foula, a
remote Shetland island.
Rare for its time, a vigorous location
drama in the Flaherty tradition;
sometimes naïve, usually
exhilarating.

*wd Michael Powell ph Ernest
Palmer and others m Lambert
Williamson*

Niall MacGinnis, Belle Chrystal,
John Laurie, Finlay Currie, Eric
Berry
    'Scant of plot and unlikely to be
hailed by the public at
large.'—*Variety*

'The love of a woman . . . the
courage of a fighting America
. . . lifted him from obscurity to
thrilling fame!'
Edison the Man
🐝🐝 US 1940   107m   bw
MGM (John W. Considine Jnr)
Edison struggles for years in poverty
before becoming famous as the
inventor of the electric light bulb.
Standard, well-made biopic
following on from *Young Tom
Edison*; reasonably absorbing, but
slightly suspect in its facts.

w Dore Schary, Talbot Jennings, Bradbury Foote, Hugo Butler *d* *Clarence Brown* *ph* Harold Rosson *m* Herbert Stothart

Spencer Tracy, Rita Johnson, Lynne Overman, Charles Coburn, Gene Lockhart, Henry Travers, Felix Bressart

AAN: Dore Schary, Hugo Butler (original story)

'10,965 pyramids! 5,337 dancing girls! One million swaying bulrushes! 802 sacred bulls!'

The Egyptian

US 1954   140m   De Luxe
Cinemascope
TCF (Darryl F. Zanuck)

In ancient Egypt an abandoned baby grows up to be physician to the pharaoh.

More risible than reasonable, sounding more like a parody than the real thing, this pretentious epic from a bestseller flounders helplessly between its highlights but has moments of good humour and makes an excellent example of the pictures they don't make 'em like any more.

w Philip Dunne, Casey Robinson, *novel* Mika Waltari *d* Michael Curtiz *ph* Leon Shamroy *m* Bernard Herrmann, Alfred Newman *ad* Lyle Wheeler, George W. Davis

Edmund Purdom, Victor Mature, *Peter Ustinov*, Bella Darvi, Gene Tierney, Michael Wilding, Jean Simmons, Judith Evelyn, Henry Daniell, John Carradine, Carl Benton Reid

'The novel . . . supplied the reader with enough occurrences and customs of Akhnaton's time . . . to hide some of the more obvious contrivances of the story. The film does not do this.'—*Carolyn Harrow, Films in Review*

AAN: Leon Shamroy

Eight and a Half

Italy 1963   138m   bw
Cineriz (Angelo Rizzoli)
original title: *Otto e Mezzo*

A successful film director on the verge of a nervous breakdown has conflicting fantasies about his life. A Fellini self-portrait in which anything goes. Some of it is fascinating, some not worth the trouble of sorting out.

w Federico Fellini, Ennio Flaiano, Tullio Pinelli, Brunello Rondi *d* *Federico Fellini* *ph* Gianni di Venanzo *m* Nino Rota *ad* Piero Gherardi

Marcello Mastroianni, Claudia Cardinale, Anouk Aimée, Sandra Milo, Rossella Falk, Barbara Steele, Madeleine Lebau

'The whole may add up to a magnificent folly, but it is too singular, too candid, too vividly and insistently alive to be judged as being in any way diminishing.'—*Peter John Dyer, MFB*

'Fellini's intellectualizing is not even like dogs dancing; it is not done well, nor does it surprise us that it is done at all. It merely palls on us, and finally appals us.'—*John Simon*

'A de luxe glorification of creative crisis, visually arresting but in some essential way conventional-minded.'—*Pauline Kael, 70s*

AAN: best foreign film; script; direction

El Cid

US / Spain 1961   184m
Super Technirama
Samuel Bronston

A legendary 11th-century hero drives the Moors from Spain. Endless glum epic with splendid action sequences as befits the high budget.

w Frederic M. Frank, Philip Yordan *d* Anthony Mann *ph* Robert Krasker *m* Miklos Rozsa

Charlton Heston, Sophia Loren, Raf Vallone, Geraldine Page, John Fraser, Gary Raymond, Herbert Lom, Hurd Hatfield, Massimo

Serato, Andrew Cruickshank, Michael Hordern, Douglas Wilmer, Frank Thring

AAN: Miklos Rozsa; song 'The Falcon and the Dove' (*m* Miklos Rozsa, *ly* Paul Francis Webster)

'The big one with the big two!'
El Dorado
US 1966   126m
Technicolor
Paramount / Laurel (Howard Hawks)
A gunfighter and a drunken sheriff tackle a villainous cattle baron. Easy-going, semi-somnolent, generally likeable but disappointing western . . . an old man's movie all round.

w Leigh Brackett, *novel* The Stars in their Courses by Harry Joe Brown *d* Howard Hawks *ph* Harold Rosson *m* Nelson Riddle

John Wayne, Robert Mitchum, James Caan, Charlene Holt, Michele Carey, Ed Asner, Arthur Hunnicutt, R. G. Armstrong, Paul Fix, Christopher George

'A rumbustious lament for the good days of the bad old west.'—*Tom Milne*

'A claustrophobic, careless and cliché-ridden thing, wavering constantly between campy self-deprecation and pretentious pomposity.'—*Richard Schickel*

'Wayne and Mitchum, parodying themselves while looking exhausted.'—*Pauline Kael, 70s*

The Elephant Man
US 1980   124m   bw
Panavision
EMI / Brooksfilms (Stuart Cornfield)
In 1884 London, a penniless man deformed by a rare illness is rescued by a doctor from a fairground freak show, and becomes a member of fashionable society.
A curious story which happens to be true; the film sets its scene superbly, has splendid performances and a fascinating make-up. Yet it fails to move quite as it should, perhaps because the central figure is treated as a horrific come-on, like the hunchback of Notre Dame.

w Christopher de Core, Eric Bergren, David Lynch, from various memoirs *d* David Lynch *ph* Freddie Francis *m* John Morris *pd* Stuart Craig

Anthony Hopkins, John Hurt, John Gielgud, Anne Bancroft, Freddie Jones, Wendy Hiller, Michael Elphick, Hannah Gordon

'If there's a wrong note in this unique movie—in performance, production design, cinematography or anywhere else—I must have missed it.'—*Paul Taylor, Time Out*

'In an age of horror movies this is a film which takes the material of horror and translates it into loving kindness.'—*Dilys Powell, Punch*

AAN: best film; screenplay; David Lynch; editing (Ann V. Coates); art direction (Stuart Craig, Bob Cartwright, Hugh Scaife); John Morris; costume design (Patricia Norris); John Hurt
BFA: best film; production design; John Hurt

The Empire Strikes Back
US 1980   124m
Eastmancolor   Panavision
TCF / Lucasfilm (Gary Kurtz)
The Rebel Alliance takes refuge from Darth Vader on a frozen planet.
More exhilarating interplanetary adventures, as mindless as *Star Wars* but just as enjoyable for aficionados.

w Leigh Brackett, Lawrence Kasdan, *story* George Lucas *d* Irvin Kershner *ph* Peter Suschitzky *m* John Williams *pd* Norman Reynolds

Mark Hamill, Harrison Ford, Carrie Fisher, Billy Dee Williams

'Slightly encumbered by some mythic and neo-Sophoclean overtones, but its inventiveness, humour and special effects are scarcely less inspired than those of its phenomenally successful predecessor.'—*New Yorker*

AAN: art direction
BFA: music

Les Enfants du Paradis

France 1945 195m bw
Pathé (Fred Orain, Raymond Borderic)

US title: *Children of Paradise*

In the 'theatre street' of Paris in the 1840s, a mime falls in love with the elusive Garance, but her problems with other men keep them apart.
A magnificent evocation of a place and a period, this thoroughly enjoyable epic melodrama is flawed only by its lack of human warmth and of a real theme. It remains nevertheless one of the cinema's most memorable films.

w Jacques Prévert d Marcel Carné ph Roger Hubert m Maurice Thiriet, Joseph Kosma, G. Mouque *ad Alexandre Trauner, Léon Barsacq, Raymond Gabutti*

Arletty, Jean-Louis Barrault, Pierre Brasseur, Marcel Herrand, Maria Casarès, Louis Salon, Pierre Renoir, Gaston Modot, Jane Marken

'A magnificent scenario . . . Prévert is as adept with wit as with poignancy . . . I don't believe a finer group of actors was ever assembled on film.'—*John Simon*

AAN: Jacques Prévert

'The first story of the double-fisted DA who tore apart the evil dynasty that peddled murder for a price!'

The Enforcer

US 1950 87m bw
United States Pictures (Milton Sperling)

GB title: *Murder, Inc*

A crusading District Attorney tracks down the leader of a gang which murders for profit.
Extremely suspenseful and well-characterized police yarn based on fact. One of the very best of its kind.

w Martin Rackin d Bretaigne Windust ph Robert Burks m David Buttolph

Humphrey Bogart, Everett Sloane, Zero Mostel, Ted de Corsia, Roy Roberts, King Donovan

'A tough, very slickly-made thriller with a host of fine character parts.'—*NFT, 1969*

'Absorbing and exciting, with little of the violence that so often disfigures films of this kind.'—*Richard Mallett, Punch*

'The first fifteen minutes is as powerful and rapid a sketch of tension as I can recall for seasons. The last fifteen might make Hitch weep with envy.'—*Observer*

The Entertainer

GB 1960 96m bw
BL / Bryanston / Woodfall / Holly (John Croydon)

A faded seaside comedian reflects on his failure as an entertainer and as a man.
Even with Olivier repeating his stage triumph, or perhaps because of it, this tragi-comedy remains defiantly theatrical and does not take wing on film.

w John Osborne, Nigel Kneale, *play* John Osborne *d* Tony Richardson *ph* Oswald Morris *m* John Addison

Laurence Olivier, Joan Plowright, Brenda de Banzie, *Roger Livesey*, Alan Bates, Shirley Anne Field, Albert Finney, Thora Hird, Daniel Massey

'No amount of deafening sound effects and speciously busy cutting can remove one's feeling that behind this distracting façade of heightened realism lurks a basic lack of confidence.'—*Peter John Dyer*

AAN: Laurence Olivier

Escape

US 1940 104m bw
MGM (Lawrence Weingarten)

reissue title: *When the Door Opened*

An American gets his mother out of a Nazi concentration camp before World War II.
Ingenious but somewhat slow-moving melodrama with an exciting climax and good production values.

w Arch Oboler, Marguerite Roberts, *novel* Ethel Vance *d* Mervyn Le Roy *ph* Robert Planck *m* Franz Waxman

Norma Shearer, Robert Taylor, *Conrad Veidt*, Nazimova, Felix Bressart, Albert Basserman, Philip Dorn, Bonita Granville

'It takes an hour to get started and makes just another feeble fable from headlines.'—*Otis Ferguson*

'Far and away the most dramatic and hair-raising picture yet made on the sinister subject of persecution in a totalitarian land.'—*Bosley Crowther, New York Times*

'One of the most poignant dramatic films of the year.'—*Modern Screen*

'The director takes forever to set up the manoeuvres, and the villain is so much more attractive than the hero that the whole thing turns into a feeble, overproduced joke.'—*Pauline Kael, 70s*

Evergreen
GB 1934 90m bw
Gaumont (Michael Balcon)

A star's daughter takes her mother's place, with romantic complications. Pleasant musical with more wit and style than might be expected.

w Emlyn Williams, Marjorie Gaffney, *play* Benn W. Levy *d* Victor Saville *ph* Glen MacWilliams *songs* Rodgers and Hart ('Dancing on the Ceiling', 'Dear Dear'); all other songs Harry Woods

Jessie Matthews, Sonnie Hale, Betty Balfour, Barry Mackay, Ivor McLaren, Hartley Power

'High up in the skyscraper beauty and power clash in conflict!'
Executive Suite
US 1954 104m bw
MGM (John Houseman)

When the president of a big company dies, the boardroom sees a battle for control.

First of the boardroom films of the fifties, a calculatedly commercial mixture of business ethics and domestic asides, with an all-star cast working up effective tensions.

w Ernest Lehman, *novel* Cameron Hawley *d* Robert Wise *ph* George Folsey

Fredric March, William Holden, June Allyson, *Barbara Stanwyck*, Walter Pidgeon, Shelley Winters, Paul Douglas, *Louis Calhern*, Dean Jagger, *Nina Foch*, Tim Considine

'Not a classic, not a milestone in movie making, but it does suggest a standard of product that could bring back to the box office those vast audiences long alienated by trivia.'—*Arthur Knight*

'The only trouble with all these people is that they are strictly two-dimensional. They give no substantial illusion of significance, emotion or warmth.'—*Bosley Crowther, New York Times*

† A TV series followed in 1976

AAN: George Folsey; Nina Foch

Exodus
US 1960 220m
Technicolor Super Panavision 70
UA/Carlyle/Alpha (Otto Preminger)

The early years of the state of Israel, seen through various eyes.

Heavy-going modern epic, toned down from a passionate novel.

w Dalton Trumbo, *novel* Leon Uris *d* Otto Preminger *ph* Sam Leavitt *m* Ernest Gold

Paul Newman, Eva Marie Saint, Ralph Richardson, Peter Lawford, Lee J. Cobb, Sal Mineo, John Derek, Hugh Griffith, Gregory Ratoff, Felix Aylmer, David Opatoshu, Jill Haworth, Alexandra Stewart, Martin Benson, Martin Miller

'Professionalism is not enough—after three and a half hours the approach seems more exhausting than exhaustive.'—*Penelope Houston*

† Jewish comedian Mort Sahl, invited by the director to a preview, is said to have stood up after three hours and said: 'Otto—let my people go!'

AA: Ernest Gold
AAN: Sam Leavitt; Sal Mineo

The Exorcist

US 1973 122m Metrocolor
Warner / Hoya (William Peter
Blatty)

A small girl is unaccountably
possessed by the devil and turned
into a repellent monster who causes
several violent deaths before she is
cured.

Spectacularly ludicrous mishmash
with uncomfortable attention to
physical detail and no talent for
narrative or verisimilitude. Its
sensational aspects, together with a
sudden worldwide need for the
supernatural, assured its enormous
commercial success.

w William Peter Blatty, from his
novel *d* William Friedkin *ph* Owen
Roizman *m* George Crumb and
others *pd* Bill Malloy

Ellen Burstyn, Max Von Sydow,
Jason Miller, Linda Blair, Lee J.
Cobb, Kitty Winn, Jack McGowran

'No more nor less than a blood
and thunder horror movie,
foundering heavily on the rocks of
pretension.'—*Tom Milne*

'*The Exorcist* makes no sense,
[but] if you want to be shaken, it will
scare the hell out of you.'—*Stanley
Kauffmann*

'It exploits the subject of diabolic
possession without telling you
anything about it . . . just a stylistic
exercise.'—*Michael Billington,
Illustrated London News*

'There is a little exposition, some
philosophy and theology, a quiet
interlude, and then pandemonium
reigns: rooms shake, heads turn full
circle on bodies, wounds fester,
vomit spews forth in bilious clouds
besmirching a saintly priest, a
possessed adolescent girl
masturbates bloodily on a crucifix as
she barks blasphemies and
obscenities, and hoary demons
freeze the soul.'—*Les Keyser,
Hollywood in the Seventies*

'I know how to do it. I just throw
everything at the audience and give
them a real thrill. That's what they
want. They don't want to go into a
theater and treat it like a book. They
don't even read books!'—*William
Peter Blatty*

† Published 1974: *The Story Behind
the Exorcist* by Peter Travers and
Stephanie Reiff.

AA: William Peter Blatty
AAN: best picture; William
Friedkin; Owen Roizman; Ellen
Burstyn; Jason Miller; Linda Blair

The Exterminating Angel

Mexico 1962 95m bw
Uninci Films 59 (Gustavo
Alatriste)

original title: *El Angel
Exterminador*

High society dinner guests find
themselves unable to leave the
room, stay there for days, and go
totally to the bad before the strange
spell is broken; when they go to
church to give thanks, they find
themselves unable to leave.
Fascinating surrealist fantasia on
themes elaborated with even more
panache in *The Discreet Charm of
the Bourgeoisie*. Nevertheless, one of
its director's key films.

wd Luis Bunuel (story assistance
from Luis Alcoriza) *ph* Gabriel
Figueroa *ad* Jesus Bracho

Silvia Pinal, Enrique Rambal,
Jacqueline Andere, Jose Baviera

'An unsound and unsightly
mixture of spurious allegory and
genuine craziness.'—*John Simon*

F

The Face
Sweden 1958   103m   bw
Svensk Filmindustri
original title: *Ansiktet;* US title:
The Magician
In 19th-century Sweden, a mesmerist
and his troupe are halted at a
country post to be examined by
three officials. Partly exposed as a
fraud, he takes a frightening
revenge.
A virtually indecipherable parable
which may be about the survival of
Christianity (and may not), this
wholly personal Bergman fancy has
to be enjoyed chiefly for its surface
frissons, for its acting and its look,
which are almost sufficient
compensation.

*wd Ingmar Bergman ph Gunnar
Fischer m Erik Nordgren*

Max Von Sydow, Ingrid Thulin,
Gunnar Bjornstrand, Naima
Wifstrand, Ake Fridell, Lars
Ekborg, Bengt Ekerot

A Face in the Crowd
US 1957   126m   bw
(Warner) Newton (Elia Kazan)
A small-town hick becomes a
megalomaniac when television turns
him into a cracker-barrel
philosopher.
Brilliantly cinematic melodrama of
its time which only flags in the last
lap and paints a luridly entertaining
picture of modern show business.

w Budd Schulberg, from his story
Your Arkansas Traveller *d Elia
Kazan ph Harry Stradling, Gayne
Rescher m Tom Glazer*

Andy Griffith, *Lee Remick*, *Walter
Matthau*, *Patricia Neal*, Anthony
Franciosa, Percy Waram, Marshall
Neilan

'Savagery, bitterness, cutting
humour.'—*Penelope Houston*
'If Kazan and Schulberg had been
content to make their case by
implication, it might have been a
completely sophisticated piece of
movie-making. Instead, everything is
elaborately spelled out, and the film
degenerates into preposterous liberal
propaganda.'—*Andrew Sarris*
'Some exciting scenes in the first
half, but the later developments are
frenetic, and by the end the film is a
loud and discordant mess.'—*Pauline
Kael, 70s*

Fail Safe
US 1964   111m   bw
Columbia/Max E.
Youngstein/Sidney Lumet
An American atomic bomber is
accidentally set to destroy Moscow,
and the president has to destroy New
York in retaliation.
Despite a confusing opening, this
deadly earnest melodrama gets
across the horror of its situation
better than the contemporaneous *Dr
Strangelove* which treated the same
plot as black comedy. Here the
details are both terrifying and
convincing.

*w Walter Bernstein, novel Eugene
Burdick, Harvey Wheeler d Sidney
Lumet ph Gerald Hirschfeld
m none*

Henry Fonda, Walter Matthau, Dan
O'Herlihy, Frank Overton, Fritz
Weaver, Edward Binns, Larry
Hagman, Russell Collins

'It will have you sitting on the
brink of eternity.'—*publicity*

The Fall of the Roman Empire
US/Spain 1964   187m
Technicolor   Ultra
Panavision 70
Samuel Bronston
After poisoning the Emperor Marcus
Auerelius his mad son Commodus
succumbs to dissipation and allows
Rome to be ravaged by pestilence
and the Barbarians.

Would-be distinguished epic with an
intellectual first hour; unfortunately
the hero is a priggish bore, the
villain a crashing bore, the heroine a
saintly bore, and the only interesting
character is killed off early. A
chariot race, a javelin duel, some
military clashes and a mass burning
at the stake keep one watching, and
the production values are high
indeed.

w Ben Barzman, Philip Yordan
 d Anthony Mann ph Robert
Krasker, John Moore m Dmitri
Tiomkin pd Venerio Colasanti

Alec Guinness, Christopher
Plummer, Stephen Boyd, James
Mason, Sophia Loren, John Ireland,
Eric Porter, Anthony Quayle, Mel
Ferrer, Omar Sharif
  'The film works from a restricted
palette, and the result is weirdly
restraining and severe, a dignified
curb on absurdities.'—John Coleman
† The forum set in this film is said to
be the largest ever built.

AAN: Dmitri Tiomkin

The Fallen Idol

GB 1948 94m bw
British Lion / London Films
(Carol Reed)
US title: The Lost Illusion
An ambassador's small son nearly
incriminates his friend the butler in
the accidental death of his shrewish
wife.
A near-perfect piece of small-scale
cinema, built up from clever nuances
of acting and cinematic technique.

w Graham Greene, from his story
The Basement Room d Carol Reed
 ph Georges Périnal m William
Alwyn

Ralph Richardson, Michèle Morgan,
Bobby Henrey, Sonia Dresdel, Jack
Hawkins
  'A short story has become a film
which is compact without loss of
variety in pace and shape.'—Dilys
Powell
  'It's too deliberate and hushed to
be much fun . . . you wait an extra
beat between the low-key lines of
dialogue.'—Pauline Kael, 70s

AAN: Graham Greene; Carol Reed

Family Portrait

GB 1950 24m bw
Festival of Britain / Wessex
(Ian Dalrymple)
A study of the English tradition and
spirit through history.
The last work of a director–poet; not
his most vivid movie, yet an accurate
distillation of the themes which
concerned him and of a dream-like
patriotism which now seems lost.

wd Humphrey Jennings ph Martin
Curtis ed Stewart MacAllister
 comm Michael Goodliffe
  'Perhaps the most polished in style
of all Jennings' films . . .
continuously fascinating, sharp and
evocative.'—MFB

Fanny and Alexander

Sweden / France / West
Germany
1982 / 188m / Eastmancolor
AB Cinematograph / Swedish Film
Institute / Swedish TV
One / Gaumont / Persona
Film / Tobis (Jorn Donner)
A well-to-do Uppsala family comes
together to celebrate Christmas
1907.
An interesting mixture of Dear
Octopus and Wild Strawberries turns
into something more akin to The
Face or The Night Comers. A kind of
Bergman compendium, and
impossible to describe exactly for
those who have not seen it.

wd Ingmar Bergman ph Sven
Nykvist m Daniel Bell pd Anna
Asp

Gunn Walgren, Ewa Froeling, Jarl
Kulle, Erland Josephson, Allan
Edwall, Boerje Ahlstedt, Mona
Malm, Gunnar Bjornstrand, Jan
Malmsjoe
  'It's as if Bergman's neuroses had
been tormenting him for so long that
he cut them off and went sprinting
back to Victorian health and
domesticity.'—New Yorker

AA: cinematography; best
foreign-language film; screenplay;
art direction; costume
AAN: direction

Fanny by Gaslight
🎭 GB 1944   108m   bw
🏹 GFD / Gainsborough (Edward Black)
US title: *Man of Evil*
The illegitimate daughter of a cabinet minister is saved from a lustful Lord.
Highly-coloured Victorian romantic melodrama, enjoyably put over with no holds barred and a pretty high budget for the time.

w Doreen Montgomery, Aimée Stuart, *novel* Michael Sadleir *d* Anthony Asquith *ph* Arthur Crabtree *m* Cedric Mallabey

James Mason, Phyllis Calvert, Stewart Granger, Wilfrid Lawson, John Laurie, Margaretta Scott, Stuart Lindsell, Jean Kent

'Seldom have I seen a film more agreeable to watch, from start to finish.'—*William Whitebait*

'Mr Asquith does not seem to have made much effort to freshen it by interesting treatment, so that the rare unusual device seems quite out of key among so much that is simple, obvious, hackneyed.'—*Richard Mallett, Punch*

† One of several costume melodramas patterned after the success of *The Man in Grey*.

Fantasia
🎬 US 1940   135m
🌀 Technicolor
Walt Disney
A concert of classical music is given cartoon interpretations. The pieces are:
  Bach: Toccata and Fugue in D Minor
  Tchaikovsky: The Nutcracker Suite
  Dukas: The Sorcerer's Apprentice
  Stravinsky: The Rite of Spring
  Beethoven: The Pastoral Symphony
  Ponchielli: Dance of the Hours
  Moussorgsky: Night on a Bare Mountain
  Schubert: Ave Maria
Brilliantly inventive for the most part, the cartoons having become classics in themselves. The least part (the Pastoral Symphony) can be forgiven

supervisor Ben Sharpsteen *md* Edward H. Plumb

Leopold Stokowski, the Philadelphia Orchestra, Deems Taylor

'Dull as it is towards the end, ridiculous as it is in the bend of the knee before Art, it is one of the strange and beautiful things that have happened in the world.'—*Otis Ferguson*

'It is ambitious, and finely so, and one feels that its vulgarities are at least unintentional.'—*James Agate*

† Multiplane cameras, showing degrees of depth in animation, were used for the first time.

Fantastic Voyage
🎬 US 1966   100m   De Luxe
🌀 Cinemascope
TCF (Saul David)
When a top scientist is shot and suffers brain damage, a team of doctors and a boat are miniaturized and injected into his blood stream . . . but one is a traitor.
Engagingly absurd science fiction which keeps its momentum but is somewhat let down by its decor.

w Harry Kleiner *d* Richard Fleischer *ph* Ernest Laszlo *m* Leonard Rosenman *ad* Dale Hennesy, Jack Martin Smith *sp* L. B. Abbott, Art Cruickshank, Emil Kosa Jnr

Stephen Boyd, Raquel Welch, Edmond O'Brien, Donald Pleasence, Arthur Kennedy, Arthur O'Connell, William Redfield

'The process shots are so clumsily matted . . . that the actors look as if a child has cut them out with blunt scissors.'—*Pauline Kael*

AA: art direction
AAN: Ernest Laszlo

Farewell My Lovely
🗿 US 1944   95m   bw
RKO (Adrian Scott)
aka: *Murder My Sweet*
A private eye searches for an ex-convict's missing girl friend.
A revolutionary crime film in that it

was the first to depict the genuinely seedy milieu suggested by its author. One of the first *films noirs* of the mid-forties, a minor masterpiece of expressionist film making, and a total change of direction for a crooner who suddenly became a tough guy.

w John Paxton, novel Raymond Chandler d Edward Dmytryk ph Harry J. Wild m Roy Webb

Dick Powell, Claire Trevor, Anne Shirley, *Mike Mazurki, Otto Kruger*, Miles Mander, Douglas Walton, Ralf Harolde, Don Douglas, Esther Howard

MARLOWE (Dick Powell): ' "Okay Marlowe," I said to myself. "You're a tough guy. You've been sapped twice, choked, beaten silly with a gun, shot in the arm until you're crazy as a couple of waltzing mice. Now let's see you do something really tough—like putting your pants on." '

MARLOWE: 'I caught the blackjack right behind my ear. A black pool opened up at my feet. I dived in. It had no bottom.'

MARLOWE: 'My fingers looked like a bunch of bananas.'

'A nasty, draggled bit of dirty work, accurately observed.'—*C. A. Lejeune*

A Farewell to Arms
US 1932   78m   bw
(Paramount) Frank Borzage
In World War I, a wounded American ambulance driver falls in love with his nurse.
Now very dated but important in its time, this romantic drama was one of the more successful Hemingway adaptations to be filmed.

w Benjamin Glazer, Oliver H. P. Garrett, novel Ernest Hemingway d Frank Borzage ph Charles Lang m W. Franke Harling

Gary Cooper, *Helen Hayes*, Adolphe Menjou, Mary Philips, Jack La Rue, Blanche Frederici, Henry Armetta

'Too much sentiment and not enough strength.'—*Mordaunt Hall, New York Times*

'Borzage has invested the war scenes with a strange, brooding expressionist quality . . . indeed, the overall visual style is most impressive.'—*NFT, 1974*

'Corking femme film fare at any angle or price.'—*Variety*

† Remade as *Force of Arms*.

AA: Charles Lang
AAN: best picture

'Now she's raising eyebrows instead of corn!'
The Farmer's Daughter
US 1947   97m   bw
David O. Selznick (Dore Schary)
The Swedish maid of a congressman becomes a political force.
Well-made Cinderella story with a touch of asperity and top notch production values and cast.

w Allen Rivkin, Laura Kerr d H. C. Potter ph Milton Krasner m Leigh Harline

Loretta Young, Joseph Cotten, *Ethel Barrymore*, Charles Bickford, Rose Hobart, Rhys Williams, Harry Davenport, Tom Powers

'Patricians, politicians, even peasants are portrayed with unusual perception and wit.'—*James Agee*

AA: Loretta Young
AAN: Charles Bickford

Farrebique
France 1947   85m   bw
L'Ecran Français / Les Films Etienne Lallier
Problems of a peasant family in central France.
Superbly-filmed semi-documentary, acted by a real family.

wd Georges Rouquier ph André Dantan m Henri Sauguet
'Definitely a film for posterity.'—*MFB*

Father Brown

♉ GB 1954 91m bw
(Columbia) Facet (Vivian A. Cox)

US title: *The Detective*

A Catholic clergyman retrieves a priceless church cross from master thief Flambeau.

Delightfully eccentric comedy based closely on the famous character, with a sympathetic if rather wandering script, pointed direction and some delicious characterizations. A thoroughly civilized entertainment.

w Thelma Schnee, *story* The Blue Cross by G. K. Chesterton *d* Robert Hamer *ph* Harry Waxman *m* Georges Auric

Alec Guinness, Joan Greenwood, Peter Finch, Sidney James, *Cecil Parker, Bernard Lee, Ernest Thesiger,* Marne Maitland

'It has wit, elegance, and kindly humour—all somewhat rare commodities in the 1954 cinema.'—*Star*

'The bride gets the thrills! Father gets the pills!'

Father of the Bride

♉ US 1950 93m bw
MGM (Pandro S. Berman)

A dismayed but happy father surveys the cost and chaos of his daughter's marriage.

Fragmentary but mainly delightful suburban comedy which finds Hollywood in its best light vein and benefits from a strong central performance.

w Frances Goodrich, Albert Hackett, *novel* Edward Streeter *d* Vincente Minnelli *ph* John Alton *m* Adolph Deutsch

Spencer Tracy, Joan Bennett, Elizabeth Taylor, Don Taylor, Billie Burke, Moroni Olsen, Leo G. Carroll, Taylor Holmes, Melville Cooper

'The idealization of a safe sheltered existence, the good life according to MGM: 24 carat complacency.'—*New Yorker, 1980*

Fear in the Night

🦇 US 1947 72m bw
Maxwell Shane

A man suffering from a strange nightmare discovers he has been hypnotized into committing a murder.

Intriguing small-scale puzzler later remade to less effect as *Nightmare.* Adequate performances and handling, but the plot's the thing.

wd Maxwell Shane *ph* Jack Grennhalgh *m* Rudy Schraeger

Paul Kelly, De Forrest Kelley, Ann Doran, Kay Scott

'A thrill a minute! A laugh a second! A comedy cyclone!'

Feet First

♉ US 1930 88m bw
Harold Lloyd

A shoe salesman gets entangled with crooks and has a narrow escape when hanging from the side of a building.

Very funny early talkie comedy, probably the comedian's last wholly satisfactory film.

w Lex Neal, Felix Adler, Paul Gerard Smith *d* Clyde Bruckman *ph* Walter Ludin, Henry Kohler

Harold Lloyd, Robert McWade, Barbara Kent

'That Lloyd was a bit pressed for laughs may be guessed from the fact that he is again dangling from the front of a skyscraper.'—*Variety*

La Femme du Boulanger

♉ France 1938 110m bw
Marcel Pagnol

aka: *The Baker's Wife*

Villagers put a stop to the infidelity of the baker's wife because her husband no longer has the heart to make good bread.

Best-known of Pagnol's rustic fables, this rather obvious and long-drawn-out joke is important because international critics hailed it as a work of art (which it isn't) and because it fixed an image of the naughty bucolic French.

wd Marcel Pagnol, *novel* Jean Le

Bleu by Jean Giono *ph* G. Benoit,
R. Lendruz, N. Daries *m* Vincent
Scotto

Raimu, Ginette Leclerc, Charles
Moulin, Charpin, Maximilienne
  'It is a long film with a small
subject, but the treatment is so
authentic that it seems over far too
soon, and the acting is
superb.'—*Graham Greene*

Fiddler on the Roof
US 1971 180m
Technicolor Panavision 70
UA/Mirisch (Norman Jewison)
In a pre-revolutionary Russian
village, Tevye the Jewish milkman
survives family and political
problems and when the pogroms
begin cheerfully emigrates to
America.
Self-conscious, grittily realistic
adaptation of the stage musical, with
slow and heavy patches in its grossly
overlong celebration of a vanished
way of life. The big moments still
come off well though the songs tend
to be thrown away and the
photography is unnecessarily murky.
w Joseph Stein, from his play and
Sholom Aleichem's story Tevye and
his Daughters
d Norman Jewison *ph* Oswald
Morris *m* Jerry Bock *md* John
Williams *pd* Robert Boyle
ly Sheldon Harnick

Topol; Norma Crane, Leonard Frey,
Molly Picon
  'Jewison hasn't so much directed a
film as prepared a product for world
consumption.'—*Stanley Kauffmann*
AA: Oswald Morris; John Williams
AAN: best picture; Norman Jewison
(as director); Topol; Leonard Frey

La Fin du Jour
France 1939 106m bw
Filmsonor/Regina
Tensions mount in a home for
retired actors.
Fascinating opportunity for three
fine actors to play off each other.
w Charles Spaak, Julien Duvivier
d Julien Duvivier *ph* Christian
Matras *m* Maurice Jaubert

*Michel Simon, Louis Jouvet, Victor
Francen*, Gabrielle Dorziat,
Madeleine Ozeray, Sylvie

Fire Over England
GB 1937 92m bw
London Films/Pendennis
(Erich Pommer)
Elizabeth I and her navy overcome
the Spanish Armada.
Though the film has a faded air and
the action climax was always a
bath-tub affair, the splendid cast
keeps this pageant afloat and
interesting.
w Clemence Dane, Sergei
Nolbandov, *novel* A. E. W. Mason
d William K. Howard *ph* James
Wong Howe *m* Richard Addinsell

Flora Robson, Laurence Olivier,
Leslie Banks, Vivien Leigh,
Raymond Massey, Tamara Desni,
Morton Selten, Lyn Harding, James
Mason
  'Should bring much artistic
acclaim but, outside of the urban
class spots, business will be stubborn
. . . if it had marquee strength it
would stand an excellent
chance.'—*Variety*
  'Pommer and Howard have done
one remarkable thing: they have
caught the very spirit of an English
public schoolmistress's vision of
history.'—*Graham Greene*
  'Swashbuckling nonsense, but with
a fine spirit.'—*Pauline Kael, 70s*

Fires Were Started
GB 1942 63m bw
Crown Film Unit (Ian
Dalrymple)
aka: *I Was a Fireman*
One day and night in the life of a
National Fire Service unit during the
London blitz.
Thoughtful, slow-moving, poetic
documentary originally intended as a
training film but generally released
to boost morale. Not its director's
finest work, but perhaps his most
ambitious.
wd Humphrey Jennings ph C.
Pennington-Richards *m* William
Alwyn

'An astonishingly intimate portrait of an isolated and besieged Britain . . . an unforgettable piece of human observation, affectionate, touching, and yet ironic.'—*Georges Sadoul*

'It transforms its observation into a personal, epic celebration of the courage and dignity of ordinary people in times of stress.'—*Time Out, 1984*

† The firemen were real firemen, but the scenes were re-enacted.

The First of the Few
GB 1942 117m bw
Melbourne / British Aviation
(Leslie Howard, George King, Adrian Brunel, John Stafford)
US title: *Spitfire*
The story of R. J. Mitchell who saw World War II coming and devised the Spitfire.
Low-key but impressive biopic with firm acting and good dialogue scenes. Production values slightly shaky.

w Anatole de Grunwald, Miles Malleson, Henry C. James, Katherine Strueby *d* Leslie Howard *ph* Georges Perinal *m* William Walton

Leslie Howard, David Niven, Rosamund John, Roland Culver, David Horne

'Full of action, Schneider Trophy races, test flying and flashes from the Battle of Britain.'—*Sunday Times*

Fitzcarraldo
West Germany 1982 158m colour
Werner Herzog / Project Filmproduktion / Zweite Deutsches Fernsehen / Wildlife Films, Peru
(Werner Herzog, Lucki Stipetic)
In Peru at the turn of the century, an eccentric Irishman succeeds against all odds in establishing an opera house in the jungle.
A strange and brilliant film centring on the hero's successful attempt to drag his massive boat from one river to another.

wd Werner Herzog *ph* Thomas Mauch *m* Popol Vuh

Klaus Kinski, Claudia Cardinale, Jose Lewgoy, Paul Hittscher

† 'Fitzcarraldo' is the nearest the natives can get to 'Fitzgerald'.

Five Easy Pieces
US 1970 98m Technicolor
Columbia / Bert Schneider
(Bob Rafelson, Richard Wechsler)
A middle-class drifter jilts his pregnant mistress for his brother's fiancée, but finally leaves both and hitches a ride to nowhere in particular.
Echoes of *Easy Rider*, *The Graduate* and *Charlie Bubbles* abound in this generally likeable but insubstantial modern anti-drama which at least takes place in pleasant surroundings and is firmly directed.

w Adrien Joyce *d* Bob Rafelson *ph* Laszlo Kovacs *m* various

Jack Nicholson, Karen Black, Susan Anspach, Lois Smith, Billy 'Green' Bush, Fannie Flagg

AAN: best picture; Adrien Joyce; Jack Nicholson; Karen Black

Five Fingers
US 1952 108m bw
TCF (Otto Lang)
The valet of the British ambassador in Ankara sells military secrets to the Germans, who pay him but never use the information.
Absorbing, lightweight film adaptation of a true story of World War II; civilized suspense entertainment with all talents contributing nicely.

w Michael Wilson, *book* Operation Cicero by L. C. Moyzich *d* Joseph L. Mankiewicz *ph* Norbert Brodine *m* Bernard Herrmann *ad* Lyle Wheeler, George W. Davis

James Mason, Danielle Darrieux, Michael Rennie, Walter Hampden, Oscar Karlweis, Herbert Berghof, John Wengraf, Michael Pate

'One of the highest, fastest and most absorbing spy melodramas since Hitchcock crossed the Atlantic.'—*Arthur Knight*

AAN: Michael Wilson; Joseph L. Mankiewicz

Five Graves to Cairo

US 1943   96m   bw
Paramount (Charles Brackett)
During the North Africa campaign,
British spies try to destroy Rommel's
secret supply dumps.
Intriguing spy melodrama set in a
desert hotel, a notable example of
Hollywood's ability to snatch
polished drama from the headlines.

w Charles Brackett, Billy Wilder,
play Lajos Biro *d* Billy Wilder
m Miklos Rozsa *ph* John Seitz

Franchot Tone, Anne Baxter, *Erich
Von Stroheim* (as Rommel), Akim
Tamiroff, Peter Van Eyck, Miles
Mander

'Von Stroheim has all the other
movie Huns backed completely off
the screen.'—*Variety*

'Billy Wilder must have had
something a little grander in mind:
the cleverness lacks lustre.'—*New
Yorker, 1978*

'A fabulous film fable, but it has
been executed with enough finesse to
make it a rather exciting pipe
dream.'—*Howard Barnes, New York
Herald Tribune*

† Locations representing the African
desert include California's Salton
Sea and Yuma, Arizona.

AAN: John Seitz

Flying Down to Rio

US 1933   89m   bw
RKO (Merian C. Cooper, Lou
Brock)
A dance band is a big success in Rio
de Janeiro.
A thin musical electrified by the
finale in which girls dance on the
wings of moving airplanes, and by
the teaming of Astaire and Rogers
for the first time. Now an irresistible
period piece.

w Cyril Hume, H. W. Hannemann,
Erwin Gelsey, *play* Anne Caldwell
d Thornton Freeland *ph* J. Roy
Hunt *m* Vincent Youmans
ly Edward Eliscu, Gus Kahn
ch Dave Gould

Dolores del Rio, Gene Raymond,
Raul Roulien, *Ginger Rogers, Fred
Astaire*, Blanche Frederici, Walter

Walker, Franklin Pangborn, Eric
Blore

'Its main point is the screen
promise of Fred Astaire . . . the
others are all hoofers after
him.'—*Variety*

Other songs: 'Music Makes Me';
'Orchids in the Moonlight'; 'Flying
Down to Rio'

AAN: song 'The Carioca'

Fog over Frisco

US 1934   68m   bw
Warner (Henry Blanke)
A San Francisco heiress gets herself
murdered.
Silly whodunnit highly notable for its
cinematic style, all dissolves, wipes
and quick takes. Probably the fastest
moving film ever made, and very
entertaining despite its plot
inadequacy.

w Robert N. Lee, *novel* George
Dyer *d* William Dieterle *ph* Tony
Gaudio *md* Leo F. Forbstein
ed Harold McLernon

Bette Davis, Donald Woods,
Margaret Lindsay, Lyle Talbot,
Hugh Herbert, Arthur Byron,
Robert Barrat, Douglass Dumbrille,
Henry O'Neill, Irving Pichel, Alan
Hale

'Another racketeering story, mild
in entertainment. No marked names
of strength.'—*Variety*

'It reveals those qualities of pace
and velocity and sharpness which
make the Hollywood product
acceptable even when the shallow
content of ideas makes you want to
scream.'—*Robert Forsythe*

'Its speed is artificially created by
pacing, wipes, opticals, overlapping
sound, camera movement and
placing of characters, and by its
habit of never having time really to
begin or end scenes.'—*William K.
Everson*

† Remade 1942 as *Spy Ship*, a
second feature.

Folies Bergère

US 1935   84m   bw
Twentieth Century (William
Goetz, Raymond Griffith)
GB title: *The Man from the Folies
Bergère*

A Parisian banker persuades a music hall artist to impersonate him, but the wife and girl friend become involved in the confusion.

Amusing star vehicle with inventive Berkeleyish numbers and some remarkably sexy dialogue.

w Bess Meredyth, Hal Long, *play* The Red Cat by Rudolph Lothar, Hans Adler *d* Roy del Ruth *ph* Barney McGill, Peverell Marley *md* Alfred Newman *ch* Dave Gould

Maurice Chevalier, Merle Oberon, Ann Sothern, Eric Blore

† Remade as *That Night in Rio*, with Don Ameche, and *On the Riviera*, with Danny Kaye.

Follow the Fleet

US 1936 110m bw
RKO (Pandro S. Berman)

Sailors on shore leave romance a couple of girl singers.

Amiable star musical which makes heavy weather of a listless and overlong script, but has good numbers for those who can wait.

w Dwight Taylor, *play* Shore Leave by Hubert Osborne, Allan Scott *d* Mark Sandrich *ph* David Abel *m/ly* Irving Berlin

Fred Astaire, *Ginger Rogers*, Randolph Scott, Harriet Hilliard, Astrid Allwyn, Harry Beresford, Lucille Ball, Betty Grable, Tony Martin

Songs: 'I'm Putting All My Eggs in One Basket'; 'We Saw the Sea'; 'Let's Face the Music and Dance'; 'Let Yourself Go'; 'But Where Are You?'; 'I'd Rather Lead a Band'; 'Get Thee Behind Me Satan'

'The running time is way overboard . . . dialogue is good and can be depended on for laughs, with the Astaire-Rogers dancing sure to do the rest. But cutting it would have helped a lot more.'—*Variety*

Foolish Wives

US 1921 85m approx (24 fps); originally much longer
bw silent
Universal

In Monte Carlo, a fake count seduces and blackmails rich women. Weird melodrama with memorable moments and a vast set; Stroheim's most vivid star performance and one of his most lavish productions.

wd Erich Von Stroheim *ph* Ben Reynolds, William Daniels *ad* Erich Von Stroheim, Richard Day

Erich Von Stroheim, *Mae Busch*, Maud George, Cesare Gravina

'A very superior piece of photoplay craftsmanship, original in ideas and treatment and deserving of higher rating than *Orphans of the Storm*, *Loves of Pharaoh*, *The Storm* and other second-class material which however brought forth applause and bravos from screen public and scribes.'—*Tamar Lane, What's Wrong with the Movies*

† The film was released in Latin America at a length of 6hrs 48m.

'Can you even think of missing it?'
Footlight Parade

US 1933 104m bw
Warner (Robert Lord)

A determined producer of cine-variety numbers gets the show going despite great difficulty. Classic putting-on-a-show musical distinguished by rapid-fire dialogue, New York setting, star performances and some of the best Busby Berkeley numbers.

w Manuel Seff, James Seymour *d* Lloyd Bacon *ch* Busby Berkeley *ph* Georges Barnes *ad* Anton Grot, Jack Okey *m/ly* Harry Warren, Al Dubin, Sammy Fain, Irving Fahal

James Cagney, Joan Blondell, Ruby Keeler, Dick Powell, Frank McHugh, Guy Kibbee, Ruth Donnelly, Hugh Herbert, Claire Dodd, Herman Bing

Songs: 'By a Waterfall'; 'Ah, the Moon Is Here'; 'Sitting on a Backyard Fence'; 'Shanghai Lil'; 'Honeymoon Hotel'

'1,000 surprises! 300 beauties! 20 big stars!'—*publicity*

'Bevies of beauty and mere males disport themselves in a Honeymoon Hotel, by (and in) a Waterfall, and over several acres of Shanghai.'
—*C. A. Lejeune*

† The Chester Kent studio was a take-off of Fanchon and Marco, who had just such a studio on Sunset Boulevard.

For Me and My Gal

 US 1942   104m   bw
MGM (Arthur Freed)

Just before World War I, a girl vaudevillian chooses between two partners.

A routine musical romance at the time of its production, this film now stands out because of its professional execution, its star value, and the fact that they don't make 'em like that any more.

w Richard Sherman, Sid Silvers, Fred Finkelhoffe   *d* Busby Berkeley   *ph* William Daniels   *md* Georgie Stoll, Roger Edens

Judy Garland, Gene Kelly, George Murphy, Marta Eggerth, Ben Blue, Richard Quine, Stephen McNally

'A touch of imagination and a deal more than a touch of energy.'—*The Times*

AAN: Georgie Stoll, Roger Edens

'168 minutes of breathless thrills and romance!'
For Whom the Bell Tolls

US 1943   168m
Technicolor
Paramount (Sam Wood)

An American joins partisan fighters in the Spanish Civil War and falls in love with a refugee girl before going on a suicide mission.

Portentous, solemn adventure story based on a modern classic but without much cinematic impetus despite careful handling and useful performances. It looks expensive, though.

w Dudley Nichols, *novel* Ernest Hemingway   *d* Sam Wood   *ph* Ray Rennahan   *m* Victor Young   *pd* William Cameron Menzies

Gary Cooper, Ingrid Bergman, Akim Tamiroff, Arturo de Cordova, *Katina Paxinou*, Vladimir Sokoloff, Mikhail Rasumny, Victor Varconi, Joseph Calleia, Alexander Granach

MARIA (Ingrid Bergman): 'I do not know how to kiss, or I would kiss you. Where do the noses go?'

'Everybody must have thought they were making a classic . . . but what with the typical Hollywood compromises, plus the political pressures from Spain and from Catholics—or the fears of such pressures—the whole thing became amorphous and confused.'—*Pauline Kael, 70s*

'The rhythm of this film is the most defective I have ever seen in a super-production . . . colour is very nice for costume pieces and musical comedies, and has a great aesthetic future in films, but it still gets fatally in the way of any serious imitation of reality.'—*James Agee*

AA: Katina Paxinou
AAN: best picture; Ray Rennahan; Victor Young; Gary Cooper; Ingrid Bergman; Akim Tamiroff

'More than a year in production!'
Forbidden Planet

US 1956   98m
Eastmancolor   Cinemascope
MGM (Nicholas Nayfack)

In AD 2200 a space cruiser visits the planet Altair Four to discover the fate of a previous mission.

Intriguing sci-fi with a plot derived from *The Tempest* and a Prospero who unwittingly creates monsters from his own id. High spirits and suspense sequences partially cancelled out by wooden playing from the younger actors and some leaden dialogue.

w Cyril Hume   *d* Fred M. Wilcox   *ph* George Folsey   *m* Louis and Bebe Barron   *ad* Cedric Gibbons, Arthur Lonergan

Walter Pidgeon, Anne Francis, Leslie Nielsen, Warren Stevens, Jack Kelly, Richard Anderson, Earl Holliman

'It's a pity they didn't lift some of Shakespeare's language.'—*New Yorker, 1977*

Force of Evil

US 1948   78m   bw
MGM / Enterprise (Bob Roberts)

A racketeer's lawyer finds that his boss has killed the lawyer's brother. Involved, atmospheric melodrama about the numbers racket, moodily and brilliantly photographed in New York streets, gloweringly well acted and generally almost as hypnotic as *Citizen Kane*.

w Abraham Polonsky, Ira Wolfert, *novel* Tucker's People by Ira Wolfert *d Abraham Polonsky ph George Barnes m David Raksin*

John Garfield, *Thomas Gomez,* Beatrice Pearson, Marie Windsor

'It credits an audience with intelligence in its ears as well as its eyes.'—*Dilys Powell*

A Foreign Affair

US 1948   116m   bw
Paramount (Charles Brackett)

A deputation of American politicians goes to visit post-war Berlin and a congresswoman finds herself in an emotional triangle with a captain and his German mistress. Bleakly sophisticated comedy from this team's headline-grabbing period; full of interest and amusement, it never quite sparkles enough to remove the doubtful taste.

w Charles Brackett, Billy Wilder, Richard Breen d Billy Wilder ph Charles Lang Jnr *m* Frederick Hollander

Jean Arthur, *Marlene Dietrich,* John Lund, *Millard Mitchell,* Peter Von Zerneck, Stanley Prager

'This deliberately cynical political farce . . . often seems on the verge of being funny, but the humour is too clumsily forced.'—*New Yorker, 1980*

AAN: script; Charles Lang Jnr

Foreign Correspondent

US 1940   120m   bw
Walter Wanger

An American journalist is sent to Europe in 1938 and becomes involved with spies.

Thoroughly typical and enjoyable Hitchcock adventure with a rambling script which builds up into brilliantly managed suspense sequences: an assassination, a windmill, an attempted murder in Westminster Cathedral, a plane crash at sea. The final speech was an attempt to encourage America into the war.

w Charles Bennett, Joan Harrison, James Hilton, Robert Benchley, from Personal History by Vincent Sheean *d Alfred Hitchcock ph Rudolph Maté m* Alfred Newman *sp* Lee Zavitz *ad* Alexander Golitzen *pd* William Cameron Menzies

Joel McCrea, *Laraine Day, Herbert Marshall, Albert Basserman, Edmund Gwenn, George Sanders, Eduardo Ciannelli, Robert Benchley, Harry Davenport,* Martin Kosleck

HAVERSTOCK (Joel McCrea): 'I've been watching a part of the world blown to pieces! I can't read the rest of the speech I had because the lights have gone out. It is as if the lights were out everywhere, except in America. Keep those lights burning there! Cover them with steel! Ring them with guns! Build a canopy of battleships and bombing planes around them! Hello, America! Hang on to your lights, they're the only lights left in the world!'

'If you have any interest in the true motion and sweep of pictures, watching that man work is like listening to music . . . If you would like a seminar in how to make a movie travel the lightest and fastest way, in a kind of beauty that is peculiar to movies alone, you can see this once, and then again to see what you missed, and then study it twice.'—*Otis Ferguson*

'The most excitingly shot and edited picture of the year.'—*Basil Wright*

'A masterpiece of propaganda, a first class production which no doubt will make a certain impression upon the broad masses of the people in enemy countries.'—*Joseph Goebbels*

'This juxtaposition of outright

melodramatics with deadly serious propaganda is eminently satisfactory . . . Hitchcock uses camera tricks, cinematic rhythm and crescendo to make his points.'—*Howard Barnes, New York Herald Tribune*

'Easily one of the year's finest pictures.'—*Time*

AAN: best picture; script; Rudolph Maté; Albert Basserman

Forever and a Day

US 1943 · 104m · bw
RKO (Herbert Wilcox, Victor Saville)

The history of a London house from 1804 to the blitz of World War II. Made for war charities by a combination of the European talents in Hollywood, this series of sketches was unavoidably patchy but gave good opportunities to several familiar performers and stands as a likeable quick reference to their work at this period.

w Charles Bennett, C. S. Forester, Lawrence Hazard, Michael Hogan, W. P. Lipscomb, Alice Duer Miller, John Van Druten, Alan Campbell, Peter Godfrey, S. M. Herzig, Christopher Isherwood, Gene Lockhart, R. C. Sherriff, Claudine West, Norman Corwin, Jack Hartfield, James Hilton, Emmet Lavery, Frederick Lonsdale, Donald Ogden Stewart, Keith Winter *ph* Robert de Grasse, Lee Garmes, Russell Metty, Nicholas Musuraca *m* Anthony Collins *d* René Clair, Edmund Goulding, Cedric Hardwicke, Frank Lloyd, Victor Saville, Robert Stevenson, Herbert Wilcox *ad* Albert D'Agostino, Lawrence Williams, Al Herman

Anna Neagle, Ray Milland, *Claude Rains*, C. Aubrey Smith, Dame May Whitty, Gene Lockhart, Edmund Gwenn, Ian Hunter, *Jessie Matthews*, *Charles Laughton*, Montagu Love, *Cedric Hardwicke*, Reginald Owen, *Buster Keaton*, Wendy Barrie, Ida Lupino, *Brian Aherne*, Edward Everett Horton, June Duprez, Eric Blore, Merle

Oberon, Una O'Connor, Nigel Bruce, *Roland Young*, *Gladys Cooper*, Robert Cummings, Richard Haydn, Elsa Lanchester, Sara Allgood, Robert Coote, Donald Crisp, Ruth Warrick, Kent Smith, Herbert Marshall, Victor McLaglen, many others in bit parts

'One of the most brilliant casts of modern times has been assembled to bolster up one of the poorest pictures.'—*James Agate*

'It is holding and entertaining . . . a production of outstanding quality.'—*CEA Film Report*

† The film is notable for having the longest-ever list of credited co-writers.

Fort Apache

US 1948 · 127m · bw
RKO (John Ford, Merian C. Cooper)

In the old west, a military martinet has trouble with his family as well as the Indians.

Rather stiff and unsatisfactory epic western which yet contains sequences in its director's best manner.

w Frank S. Nugent, *story* Massacre by James Warner Bellah *d* John Ford *ph* Archie Stout *m* Richard Hageman

Henry Fonda, John Wayne, Shirley Temple, Pedro Armendariz, Ward Bond, Irene Rich, George O'Brien, John Agar, Victor McLaglen, Anna Lee, Dick Foran, Guy Kibbee

'A visually absorbing celebration of violent deeds.'—*Howard Barnes*

'The whole picture is bathed in a special form of patriotic sentimentality: scenes are held so that we cannot fail to appreciate the beauty of the American past.'—*New Yorker, 1976*

'Shirley Temple and her husband handle the love interest as though they were sharing a soda fountain special, and there is enough Irish comedy to make me wish Cromwell had done a more thorough job.'—*James Agee*

Forty Ninth Parallel
GB 1941 123m bw
GFD / Ortus (John Sutro,
Michael Powell)
US title: *The Invaders*
In Canada, five stranded U-boat
men try to escape into the US.
Episodic, effective propaganda piece
which develops some nice
Hitchcockian touches and allows a
range of star actors to make impact.

*w Emeric Pressburger, Rodney
Ackland d Michael Powell ph* F. A.
Young *m* Ralph Vaughan Williams

Eric Portman, Laurence Olivier,
*Anton Walbrook, Leslie Howard,
Raymond Massey*, Glynis Johns,
Niall MacGinnis, Finlay Currie,
Raymond Lovell, John Chandos

'Some of the plotting and
characterization look rather rusty at
this remove, but the sense of
landscape and figures passing
through it remains authoritatively
dynamic.'—*Tony Rayns, Time Out,
1979*

'An admirable piece of work from
every point of view.'—*MFB*

AA: original story (Emeric
Pressburger)
AAN: best picture; script

'Mightier than Broadway ever
beheld.'
Forty-Second Street
US 1933 89m bw
Warner (Hal B. Wallis)
A Broadway musical producer has
troubles during rehearsal but reaches
a successful opening night.
Archetypal Hollywood
putting-on-a-show musical in which
the leading lady is indisposed and a
chorus girl is told to get out there
and come back a star. The clichés
are written and performed with great
zest, the atmosphere is convincing,
and the numbers when they come
are dazzlers.

w James Seymour, Rian James, novel
Bradford Ropes *d* Lloyd Bacon
ch Busby Berkeley *ph* Sol Polito
m / ly Al Dubin, Harry Warren

*Warner Baxter, Ruby Keeler, Bebe
Daniels*, George Brent, Una Merkel,
Guy Gibbee, Dick Powell, *Ginger
Rogers* (as Anytime Annie), *Ned
Sparks*, George E. Stone, Allen
Jenkins
Songs: 'Forty-Second Street';
'Shuffle Off to Buffalo'; 'Young and
Healthy'; 'You're Getting to Be a
Habit with Me'
(Warner Baxter): 'Sawyer, you listen
to me, and you listen hard. Two
hundred people, two hundred jobs,
two hundred thousand dollars, five
weeks of grind and blood and sweat
depend upon you. It's the lives of all
these people who've worked with
you. You've got to go on, and
you've got to give and give and give.
They've got to like you. Got to. Do
you understand? You can't fall
down. You can't because your
future's in it, my future and
everything all of us have is staked on
you. All right, now I'm through, but
you keep your feet on the ground
and your head on those shoulders of
yours and go out, and Sawyer,
you're going out a youngster but
you've got to come back a star!'

'The story has been copied a
hundred times since, but never has
the backstage atmosphere been so
honestly and felicitously
caught.'—*John Huntley, 1966*

'It gave new life to the clichés that
have kept parodists happy.'—*New
Yorker, 1977*

AAN: best picture

The Fountainhead
US 1949 114m bw
Warner (Henry Blanke)
An idealistic architect clashes with
big business.
Overripe adaptation of a rather silly
novel, full of Freudian symbols and
expressionist techniques with which
the star really can't cope; but an
enjoyable field day for the director
and the rest of the cast.

*w Ayn Rand, from her novel
d King Vidor ph Robert Burks
m* Max Steiner

Gary Cooper, *Patricia Neal,*

Raymond Massey, Kent Smith, Robert Douglas, Henry Hull, Ray Collins, Moroni Olson, Jerome Cowan

'If you like deep thinking, hidden meanings, plus pure modern architecture, then this is something for which you have been waiting a long time.'—*Screenland*

'The most bizarre movie in both Vidor's and Cooper's filmographies, this adaptation mutes Ms Rand's neo-Nietzschian philosophy of "objectivism" but lays on the expressionist symbolism with a "free enterprise" trowel.'—*Time Out, 1980*

Four Daughters
  US 1938   90m   bw
  Warner (Henry Blanke)

Domestic and romantic adventures of a small-town family.

Standard small-town hearth-fire hokum, impeccably done and really quite irresistible.

w Julius Epstein, Lenore Coffee, *novel* Sister Act by Fannie Hurst *d* Michael Curtiz *ph* Ernest Haller *m* Max Steiner

Claude Rains, John Garfield (a sensation in his first role), Priscilla Lane, Rosemary Lane, Lola Lane, Gale Page, Jeffrey Lynn, Frank McHugh, *May Robson*, Dick Foran

'It may be sentimental, but it's grand cinema.'—*New York Times*

'It simply, yet powerfully, brings into focus a panorama of natural but startling events.'—*Motion Picture Herald*

† An immediate sequel was required, but the Garfield character had been killed off, so to accommodate him a variation was written under the title *Daughters Courageous*; then came two proper sequels without him, *Four Wives* and *Four Mothers*. In 1955 the original was remade as *Young at Heart*.

AAN: best picture; script; Michael Curtiz; John Garfield

The Four Feathers
  GB 1939   130m
  Technicolor
London (Alexander Korda, Irving Asher)

During the Sudan campaign of the nineties, a stay-at-home receives four white feathers as a symbol of cowardice; but he goes undercover and becomes a hero.

Perfectly cast and presented, with battle scenes which have since turned up in a score of other films from *Zarak* to *Master of the World*; also a triumph of early colour.

w R. C. Sheriff, Lajos Biro, Arthur Wimperis *d* Zoltan Korda *ph* Georges Périnal, Osmond Borradaile, Jack Cardiff *m* Miklos Rozsa

John Clements, Ralph Richardson, C. Aubrey Smith, June Duprez, Allan Jeayes, Jack Allen, Donald Gray, Henry Oscar, John Laurie

'It cannot fail to be one of the best films of the year . . . even the richest of the ham goes smoothly down, savoured with humour and satire.'—*Graham Greene*

† Remade 1956 as *Storm over the Nile*.

The Four Horsemen of the Apocalypse
  US 1921   150m approx
  bw   silent
Metro

A young Argentinian fights for his father's country, France, in World War I.

Highly derivative dramatic spectacle, almost a pageant, from a fairly unreadable novel.

Despite its variable if exotic style, it made a star of Rudolph Valentino.

w June Mathis, *novel* Vicente Blasco-Ibanez *d* Rex Ingram *ph* John F. Seitz

Rudolph Valentino, Alice Terry, Nigel de Brulier, Alan Hale, Jean Hersholt, Wallace Beery

'A blend of exotic settings, striking composition, dramatic lighting, and colourful if sordid atmosphere.'—*Lewis Jacobs*

'Not only was it marvellously effective in its appeal to the eye, but the logical and dramatic unfolding of the basic story was a striking revelation of the valuable service that an expert scenario-writer may render to the professional writer of novels.'—*Edward S. Van Zile, That Marvel the Movie*

'Here's to our friends—and the strength to put up with them!'
The Four Seasons
US 1981   108m
Technicolor
Universal (Martin Bregman)
Three married couples take seasonal holidays together, and remain united despite various tensions.
Rueful sexual comedy which maintains considerable momentum and actually makes us laugh at its sympathetic characters.

wd Alan Alda *ph* Victor J. Kemper *m* Antonio Vivaldi

Alan Alda, Carol Burnett, Len Cariou, Sandy Dennis, Rita Moreno, Jack Weston, Bess Armstrong

'An odd mingling of perspicuity and histrionics . . . a real middle-of-the-road film.'—*Geoff Brown, MFB*
'Unfailingly amusing, touchingly honest, and in the end refreshingly decent.'—*Margaret Hinxman, Daily Mail*

Fourteen Hours
US 1951   92m   bw
TCF (Sol C. Siegel)
A man stands on the ledge of a tall building and threatens to jump.
Well-made documentary drama based on a true occurrence but given a happy ending. First class detail gives an impression of realism.

w John Paxton, *article* Joel Sayre *d* Henry Hathaway *ph* Joe MacDonald *m* Alfred Newman

Richard Basehart, Paul Douglas, Barbara Bel Geddes, Grace Kelly, Debra Paget, Agnes Moorehead, Robert Keith, Howard da Silva, Jeffrey Hunter, Martin Gabel, Jeff Corey

'A model of craftsmanship in all departments.'—*Penelope Houston*
'A highly enjoyable small scale picture, with a strength immensely greater than its size would suggest.'—*Richard Mallet, Punch*

Fra Diavolo
US 1933   90m   bw
MGM / Hal Roach
aka: *The Devil's Brother*
Two incompetent bandits are hired as manservants by a real bandit.
Auber's 1830 operetta becomes a vehicle for Laurel and Hardy, setting a pattern they followed with *Babes in Toyland* and *The Bohemian Girl*. They have excellent sequences, but overall the film lacks pace.

w Jeanie McPherson *d* Hal Roach, Charles Rogers *ph* Art Lloyd, Hap Depew *md* Le Roy Shield

Stan Laurel, Oliver Hardy, Dennis King, *James Finlayson*, Thelma Todd

'An early 19th-century comic opera doesn't make for particularly good film fare despite its hoking.'—*Variety*

'To have seen it is to wear a badge of courage!'
'A monster science created but could not destroy!'
Frankenstein
US 1931   71m   bw
Universal (Carl Laemmle Jnr)
A research scientist creates a living monster from corpses, but it runs amok.
Whole books have been written about this film and its sequels. Apart from being a fascinating if primitive cinematic work in its own right, it set its director and star on interesting paths and established a Hollywood attitude towards horror (mostly borrowed from German silents such as *The Golem*). A seminal film indeed, which at each repeated viewing belies its age.

w Garrett Fort, Francis Edward Faragoh, John L. Balderston, from the play by Peggy Webling and the

novel by Mary Wollstonecraft
Shelley *d James Whale ph Arthur
Edeson m* David Broekman
ad Charles D. Hall

Boris Karloff, Colin Clive, Mae
Clarke, John Boles, *Edward Van
Sloan, Frederick Kerr, Dwight Frye*

'Still the most famous of all horror
films, and deservedly so.'—*John
Baxter, 1968*

'The horror is cold, chilling the
marrow but never arousing
malaise.'—*Carlos Clarens*

† Direct sequels by the same studio
include *The Bride of Frankenstein,
Son of Frankenstein, Ghost of
Frankenstein, Frankenstein Meets the
Wolf Man, House of Frankenstein,
House of Dracula, Abbott and
Costello Meet Frankenstein*. The
later Hammer series, which told the
story all over again in gorier vein,
includes *The Curse of Frankenstein,
The Revenge of Frankenstein, The
Evil of Frankenstein, Frankenstein
Created Woman, Frankenstein Must
be Destroyed, Horror of
Frankenstein, Frankenstein and the
Monster from Hell*. Other
Frankenstein films date from as early
as 1908, and scores have been made
in various languages. *Young
Frankenstein* is a partly effective
spoof on the Hollywood series; *The
Munsters* was a sixties comedy series
for TV which used the monster as its
leading character in a domestic
setting.

†† Robert Florey is said to have
contributed to the script, having
been the first choice for director.

'Titans of terror, clashing in
    mortal combat!'
Frankenstein Meets the Wolf Man
    US 1943   73m   bw
    Universal (George Waggner)
Lawrence Talbot, the wolf man,
travels to Vasaria in the hope of a
cure, and finds the Frankenstein
monster being reactivated.
Once one recovered from the
bargain basement combination of
two monsters in one picture, this was

a horror comic with stylish
sequences, weakened by cuts in the
script and a miscast Bela Lugosi.

w Curt Siodmak *d Roy William
Neill ph* George Robinson *m* Hans
Salter

Lon Chaney Jnr, Ilona Massey, Bela
Lugosi (as the monster), Patric
Knowles, *Maria Ouspenskaya*

Freaks
    US 1932   64m   bw
    MGM (Tod Browning)
A lady trapeze artist marries a
midget, then poisons him for his
money; his abnormal friends take
revenge by turning her into a freak.
Made but disowned by MGM after
accusations of tastelessness, this
strident and silly melodrama has
dated badly but has sequences of
great power, especially the final
massing of the freaks, slithering to
their revenge in a rainstorm. It
would have been better as a silent;
the dialogue kills it.

w Willis Goldbeck, Leon Gordon,
novel Spurs by Tod Robbins *d Tod
Browning ph* Merrit B. Gerstad

Wallace Ford, Olga Baclanova, Leila
Hyams, Roscoe Ates

'Either too horrible or not
sufficiently so.'—*Variety*

'It is a skilfully presented
production but of a character which
in consideration of the
susceptibilities of mass audiences
should be avoided.'—*Martin Quigley*

'For pure sensationalism it tops
any picture yet produced.'—*Louella
Parsons*

'I want something that out-horrors
Frankenstein.'—*Irving Thalberg*

'Touching and funny and made
with a miraculous
delicacy.'—*Evening Standard, 1964*

'Doyle is bad news . . . but a good cop!'

The French Connection

🐾 US 1971   104m   De Luxe
TCF / Philip D'Antoni

New York police track down a consignment of drugs entering the country in a car.

Lively semi-documentary based on the true exploits of a tough cop named Eddie Egan who liked to break a few rules. Most memorable for a car chase scene involving an elevated railway, for showing the seamy side of New York more or less as it is, and for the most mumbled dialogue and the poorest sound track in years.

w Ernest Tidyman, *book* Robin Moore *d* William Friedkin *ph* Owen Roizman *m* Don Ellis

Gene Hackman, Roy Scheider, *Fernando Rey*, Tony Lo Bianco

AA: best picture; Ernest Tidyman; William Friedkin; Gene Hackman

AAN: Owen Roizman; Roy Scheider

'She was lost from the moment she saw him . . .'

The French Lieutenant's Woman

🎭 GB 1981   123m
Technicolor

UA / Juniper (Leon Clore)

In 1867 Lyme Regis, a gentleman forsakes his fiancée for the abandoned mistress of a French seaman.

Vaguely unsatisfactory and muddily coloured adaptation of a novel which set its thin story against the entire social background of the Victorian age as related to our own. The attempt to replace this by an equally thin modern story about actors playing the Victorian roles fails rather dismally; but the enterprise supplies points of interest along the way.

w Harold Pinter, *novel* John Fowles *d* Karel Reisz *ph* Freddie Francis *m* Carl Davis *pd* Assheton Gorton

Jeremy Irons, *Meryl Streep*, Leo McKern, Patience Collier, Peter Vaughan, Hilton McRae

'Pinter's reduction not only shears away the sliding historical perspective, but robs the narrative of its Victorian charisma.'—*Tom Milne, MFB*

'There are some lovely moments, and a few have magical undertones, but most of the picture might be taking place in a glass case.'—*Pauline Kael*

AAN: Harold Pinter; editing (John Bloom); Meryl Streep

BFA: best sound; Carl Davis; Meryl Streep

The Freshman

🎭 US 1925   75m (24 fps)
bw   silent

Harold Lloyd

An awkward college student accidentally becomes a star football player.

A rather slow but striking star vehicle with assured set-pieces. the football game climax was later used as the first reel of *Mad Wednesday*.

w Sam Taylor, Ted Wilde, Tim Whelan, John Grey *d* Fred Newmeyer, Sam Taylor *ph* Walter Lundin, Henry Kohler

Harold Lloyd, Jobyna Ralston, Brooks Benedict

Freud

🎭 GB 1962   140m   bw
U-I (Wolfgang Reinhardt)

Vienna 1885; Dr Sigmund Freud, a neurologist, uses hypnotism to treat hysteria, and finds new interest in the case of a boy whose hatred of his father springs from incestuous love of his mother, a failing which Freud finds in himself.

Earnest and competent biopic harking back to Warners' similar films of the thirties, with the addition of franker language. Generally absorbing, but undeniably hard tack.

w Charles Kaufman, Wolfgang Reinhardt *d* John Huston *ph* Douglas Slocombe *m* Jerry Goldsmith

Montgomery Clift, *Larry Parks*, Susannah York, Eileen Herlie, Susan Kohner, David McCallum

'The dream sequences, photographed mostly in negative or overexposure, belong not on the couch of Dr Freud but in the Cabinet of Dr Caligari.'—*John Simon*

'It is impossible, I would think, for any educated person to sit through *Freud* without bursting into laughter at least once.'—*Ernest Callenbach, Film Quarterly*

AAN: script; Jerry Goldsmith

Friday the Thirteenth
🎭 GB 1933   84m   bw
✗ Gainsborough (Michael Balcon)

Several people are involved in a bus crash, and we turn back the clock to see how they came to be there.

Highly competent compendium of comedies and dramas looking back to *The Bridge of San Luis Rey* and forward to the innumerable all-star films of the forties.

w G. H. Moresby-White, Sidney Gilliat, Emlyn Williams *d* Victor Saville *ph* Charles Van Enger

Sonnie Hale, Cyril Smith, *Eliot Makeham*, Ursula Jeans, *Emlyn Williams*, Frank Lawton, Belle Chrystal, *Max Miller*, Alfred Drayton, Edmund Gwenn, Mary Jerrold, Gordon Harker, *Robertson Hare*, Martita Hunt, Leonora Corbett, Jessie Matthews, Ralph Richardson

Friendly Persuasion
🎭 US 1956   139m   De Luxe
✗ AA (William Wyler)

At the outbreak of the Civil War, a family of Quakers has to consider its position.

Sentimental, homespun western fare, well done without being especially engrossing.

w Michael Wilson, *novel* Jessamyn West *d* William Wyler *ph* Ellsworth Fredericks *m* Dmitri Tiomkin

Gary Cooper, Dorothy McGuire, Anthony Perkins, Marjorie Main, Richard Eyer, Robert Middleton, Walter Catlett

'The material is a little tenuous . . . but Wyler's sure-handed direction constantly illuminates it with a humour, a gentle charm and a feeling for fundamental values that are rare indeed.'—*Moira Walsh, America*

AAN: best picture; Michael Wilson; William Wyler; Anthony Perkins; song 'Thee I Love' (*m* Dmitri Tiomkin, *ly* Paul Francis Webster)

From Here to Eternity
🎭 US 1953   118m   bw
✗ Columbia (Buddy Adler)

Life in a Honolulu barracks at the time of Pearl Harbor.

Cleaned up and streamlined version of a bestseller in which the mainly sexual frustrations of a number of unattractive characters are laid bare. As a production, it is Hollywood in good form, and certainly took the public fancy as well as establishing Sinatra as an acting force.

w Daniel Taradash, *novel* James Jones *d* Fred Zinnemann *ph* Burnett Guffey *m* George Duning

Burt Lancaster, Deborah Kerr, Frank Sinatra, Donna Reed, Ernest Borgnine, Montgomery Clift, Philip Ober, Mickey Shaughnessy

'This is not a theme which one would expect Zinnemann to approach in the hopeful, sympathetic mood of his earlier films; but neither could one expect the negative shrug of indifference with which he seems to have surrendered to its hysteria.'—*Karl Reisz, Sight and Sound*

† The story was remade for TV in 1979 as a six-hour mini-series.

†† Frank Sinatra got his key role after Eli Wallach dropped out.

AA: best picture; Daniel Taradash; Fred Zinnemann; Burnett Guffey; Frank Sinatra; Donna Reed
AAN: George Duning; Burt Lancaster; Deborah Kerr; Montgomery Clift

From Russia with Love
⚔ GB 1963 118m
Technicolor
UA/Eon (Harry Saltzman, Albert Broccoli)

A Russian spy joins an international crime organization and develops a plan to kill James Bond and steal a coding machine.

The second Bond adventure and possibly the best, with Istanbul and Venice for backdrops and climaxes involving a speeding train and a helicopter. Arrant nonsense with tongue in cheek, on a big budget.

w Richard Maibaum, Johanna Harwood, novel Ian Fleming
d Terence Young ph Ted Moore
m John Barry titles Robert Brownjohn

Sean Connery, Robert Shaw, Pedro Armendariz, Daniela Bianchi, Lotte Lenya, Bernard Lee, Eunice Gayson, Lois Maxwell

From This Day Forward
US 1946 95m bw
RKO (William L. Pereira)

After World War II, a New York couple think back to their early years in the poverty-stricken thirties.

Effective sentimental realism coupled with Hollywood professionalism made this film more memorable than it may sound.

w Hugo Butler, Garson Kanin, novel All Brides Are Beautiful by Thomas Bell d John Berry ph George Barnes m Leigh Harline

Joan Fontaine, Mark Stevens, Rosemary de Camp, Henry Morgan, Wally Brown, Arline Judge, Bobby Driscoll, Mary Treen

'Distinguished from the usual film about Young Love and Young Marriage by irony, poetry and realism.'—Richard Winnington

The Front Page
US 1931 101m bw
Howard Hughes

A Chicago reporter wants to retire and marry, but is tricked by his scheming editor into covering one last case.

Brilliant early talkie perfectly transferring into screen terms a stage classic of the twenties. Superficially a shade primitive now, its essential power remains.

w Bartlett Cormack, Charles Lederer, play Charles MacArthur, Ben Hecht d Lewis Milestone
ph Glen MacWilliams

Adolphe Menjou (Walter Burns), Pat O'Brien (Hildy Johnson), Mary Brian (Peggy), Edward Everett Horton (Bensinger), Walter Catlett (Murphy), George E. Stone (Earl Williams), Mae Clarke (Molly), Slim Summerville (Pincus), Matt Moore (Kruger), Frank McHugh (McCue)

'Sure money-getter . . . it will universally entertain and please.'—Variety

'The most riproaring movie that ever came out of Hollywood.'—Pare Lorentz

'It excelled most of the films of its day by sheer treatment. The speedy delivery of lines and business and the re-emphasis upon cutting as a prime structural element made the film a model of mobility for confused directors who did not know yet how to handle sound.'—Lewis Jacobs, The Rise of the American Film

† Remade 1940 as His Girl Friday.

AAN: best picture; Lewis Milestone; Adolphe Menjou

Funny Girl
US 1968 169m
Technicolor Panavision 70
Columbia/Rastar (Ray Stark)

Fanny Brice, an ugly Jewish girl from New York's east side, becomes a big Broadway star but loses her husband in the process.

Interminable cliché-ridden musical drama relieved by a few good numbers, high production gloss and the unveiling of a new powerhouse star.

w Isobel Lennart, from her play
d William Wyler ph Harry Stradling
md Walter Scharf m Jule Styne
ly Bob Merrill pd Gene Callahan

Barbra Streisand, Omar Sharif,
Walter Pidgeon, Kay Medford,
Anne Francis, Lee Allen, Gerald
Mohr, Frank Faylen

AA: Barbra Streisand
AAN: best picture; Harry Stradling;
Walter Scharf; Kay Medford; title
song

A Funny Thing Happened on the Way to the Forum

GB 1966   99m   De Luxe
UA / Quadrangle (Melvin
Frank)

In ancient Rome, a conniving slave
schemes to win his freedom.
Bawdy farce from a Broadway
musical inspired by Plautus but with
a New York Jewish atmosphere. The
film pays scant attention to the comic
numbers that made the show a hit,
but adds some style of its own,
including a free-for-all slapstick
climax.

w Melvin Frank, Michael Pertwee,
musical comedy Burt Shevelove,
Larry Gelbart *m / ly* Stephen
Sondheim *md* Ken Thorne
d Richard Lester *ph* Nicolas Roeg
pd Tony Walton *titles* Richard
Williams

Zero Mostel, Phil Silvers, Michael
Crawford, Jack Gilford, *Michael
Hordern*, Buster Keaton, Patricia
Jessel, Leon Greene, Beatrix
Lehmann

'Actors have to be very fast and
: very sly to make themselves felt
amid the flash and glitter of a
characteristic piece of Lester
film-mosaic.'—*John Russell Taylor*

'He proceeds by fits and starts and
leaves jokes suspended in mid-air
. . . like coitus interruptus going on
forever.'—*Pauline Kael*

AA: Ken Thorne

Fury

US 1936   94m   bw
MGM (Joseph L. Mankiewicz)

A traveller in a small town is
mistaken for a murderer and
apparently lynched; he escapes in a
fire but determines to have his
persecutors hanged for his murder.
Powerful drama which becomes
artificial in its latter stages but
remains its director's best American
film.

w Bartlett Cormack, Fritz Lang,
story Norman Krasna *d* Fritz Lang
ph Joseph Ruttenberg *m* Franz
Waxman

Spencer Tracy, Sylvia Sidney, Bruce
Cabot, Walter Abel, Edward Ellis,
Walter Brennan, Frank Albertson

'The surface of American life has
been rubbed away: *Fury* gets down
to the bones of the thing and shows
them for what they are.'—*C. A.
Lejeune*

'Since the screen began to talk, no
other serious film except *The Front
Page* has so clearly shown that here
is a new art and what this new art
can do.'—*John Marks*

'Everyday events and people
suddenly took on tremendous and
horrifying proportion; even the most
insignificant details had a pointed
meaning.'—*Lewis Jacobs*

G

G Men

US 1935 85m bw
Warner (Lou Edelman)

A young lawyer becomes a G-man to avenge the murder of his best friend, and finds himself tracking down another old friend who is a gangster. In the face of mounting criticism of their melodrama making heroes of gangsters, Warners pulled a clever switch by showing the same crimes from a different angle, that of the law enforcer. As an action show it became pretty good after a slow start.

w Seton I. Miller *d* William Keighley *ph* Sol Polito *md* Leo F. Forbstein

James Cagney, Ann Dvorak, Margaret Lindsay, Robert Armstrong, Barton MacLane, Lloyd Nolan, William Harrigan

'Cagney joins the government and cleans up the gangsters. Just loads of action, knocked off in bing-bang manner. Strong b.o.'—*Variety*

'The gangster is back, racing madly through one of the fastest melodramas ever made.'—*New York Sun*

'The headiest dose of gunplay that Hollywood has unleashed in recent months.'—*André Sennwald, New York Times*

'It is not violence alone which is in the air; there is also a skilfully contrived and well-maintained suspense, and throughout a feeling of respect for the men who are paid to die in the execution of necessary work.'—*The Times*

'A swell show: the construction is swift and staccato.'—*New York World Telegraph*

'Not for the kiddies, but see if your nerves are good.'—*Photoplay*

'Dangerous love in a desert paradise!'

The Garden of Allah

US 1936 80m Technicolor
David O. Selznick

A disenchanted socialist falls in love with a renegade monk in the Algerian desert.

Arty old-fashioned romantic star vehicle; great to look at, and marking a genuine advance in colour photography, but dramatically a bit of a drag.

w W. P. Lipscomb, Lynn Riggs, *novel* Robert Hichens *d* Richard Boleslawski *ph* W. Howard Greene, Harold Rosson *m* Max Steiner *ad* Sturges Carne, Lyle Wheeler, Edward Boyle

Marlene Dietrich, Charles Boyer, Basil Rathbone, Tilly Losch

'The last word in colour production, but a pretty dull affair.'—*Variety*

'Hopelessly dated folderol.'—*J. R. Parish*

'The juiciest tale of woe ever, produced in poshly lurid colour, with a Max Steiner score poured on top.'—*Judith Crist*

'Alas! my poor church, so picturesque, so noble, so superhumanly pious, so intensely dramatic. I really prefer the *New Statesman* view, shabby priests counting pesetas on their dingy fingers before blessing tanks.'—*Graham Greene*

† Previous, silent, versions had been made in 1917, with Tom Santschi and Helen Ware, and in 1927 with Ivan Petrovich and Alice Terry.

AA: photography
AAN: Max Steiner

Gaslight

GB 1939 88m bw
British National (John
Corfield)
US title: *Angel Street*

A Victorian schizophrenic drives his
wife insane when she seems likely to
stumble on his guilty secret of an old
murder and hidden rubies.

Modest but absolutely effective film
version of a superb piece of suspense
theatre.

w A. R. Rawlinson, Bridget Boland,
play Patrick Hamilton *d* Thorold
Dickinson *ph* Bernard Knowles
m Richard Addinsell

Anton Walbrook, *Diana Wynyard*,
Frank Pettingell, Cathleen Cordell,
Robert Newton, Jimmy Hanley

'The electric sense of tension and
mid-Victorian atmosphere are
entirely cinematic.'—*Sequence, 1950*

The Gay Desperado

US 1936 85m bw
Mary Pickford

An heiress is held for ransom by a
romantic bandit.

Very light, quite amusing,
sometimes irritatingly skittish
musical spoof sparked by the
director's ideas.

w Wallace Smith, *story* Leo Birinski
d Rouben Mamoulian *m* Alfred
Newman *ph* Lucien Andriot

Ida Lupino, Nino Martini, Leo
Carrillo, Harold Huber, Mischa
Auer

'Fairly diverting Mexican
western . . . it'll do spotty trade,
depending on locale.'—*Variety*

'One of the best light comedies of
the year . . . Mr Mamoulian's
camera is very
persuasive.'—*Graham Greene*

'While some of the show is
fetching, the ideas mostly misfire and
the spell is fitful and unsure.'—*Otis
Ferguson*

'It has the lightness of touch which
goes into the making of the perfect
meringue.'—*Basil Wright*

'The gayest of mad musicals!'
'The dance-mad musical triumph
of two continents!'
The Gay Divorcee

US 1934 107m bw
RKO (Pandro S. Berman)
GB title: *The Gay Divorce*

A would-be divorcee in a Brighton
hotel mistakes an author who loves
her for a professional co-respondent.

Wildly and hilariously dated comedy
musical with splendidly archaic
comedy routines supporting
Hollywood's great new dance team
in their first big success. Not much
dancing, but 'The Continental' is a
show-stopper.

w George Marion Jnr, Dorothy
Yost, Edward Kaufman, *musical
comedy* Dwight Taylor *d* Mark
Sandrich *ph* David Abel *md* Max
Steiner *songs* various *sp* Vernon
Walker *ad* Van Nest Polglase,
Carroll Clark

Fred Astaire, *Ginger Rogers*, *Edward
Everett Horton*, *Alice Brady*, *Erik
Rhodes*, *Eric Blore*, Lillian Miles,
Betty Grable

'Cinch box office anywhere and
certain of big foreign
grosses.'—*Variety*

'The plot is trivial French farce,
but the dances are among the
wittiest and most lyrical expressions
of American romanticism on the
screen.'—*New Yorker, 1977*

AA: song 'The Continental' (*m* Con
Conrad, *ly* Herb Magidson)
AAN: best picture; musical
adaptation (Ken Webb, Samuel
Hoffenstein)

'Everybody laughs but Buster!'
The General

US 1926 80m approx (24
fps) bw silent
UA/Buster Keaton (Joseph M.
Schenck)

A confederate train driver gets his
train and his girl back when they are
stolen by Union soldiers.

Slow-starting, then hilarious action
comedy, often voted one of the best
ever made. Its sequence of sight
gags, each topping the one before, is
an incredible joy to behold.

*w Al Boasberg, Charles Smith
d Buster Keaton, Clyde Bruckman
ph J. Devereux Jennings, Bert
Haines*

*Buster Keaton, Marion Mack, Glen
Cavander*

'It has all the sweet earnestness in
the world. It is about trains, frontier
America, flower-faced girls.'—*New
Yorker, 1977*

'The production itself is singularly
well mounted, but the fun is not
exactly plentiful . . . here he is more
the acrobat than the clown and his
vehicle might be described as a
mixture of cast iron and
jelly.'—*Mordaunt Hall, New York
Times*

† The story is based on an actual
incident of the Civil War, treated
more seriously in *The Great
Locomotive Chase.*

†† The screenplay with 1,400 freeze
frames was issued in 1976 in the Film
Classics Library (editor, Richard
Anobile).

The General Line
USSR 1929   90m (24 fps)
bw   silent
Sovkino
original title: *Staroye i Novoye;
aka: Old and New*

A country woman helps to start a
village co-operative.
A slight piece of propaganda, put
together with all of Eisenstein's
magnificent cinematic resources: the
cream separator demonstration is
one of the most famous montage
sequences in cinema history.

*wd Sergei Eisenstein co-d Grigori
Alexandrov ph Edouard Tissé.*

Marta Lapkina and a cast of
non-professionals

Genevieve
GB 1953   86m   Technicolor
GFD / Sirius (Henry Cornelius)
Two friendly rivals engage in a race
on the way back from the Brighton
veteran car rally.
One of those happy films in which
for no very good or expected reason
a number of modest elements merge

smoothly to create an aura of high
style and memorable moments. A
charmingly witty script, carefully
pointed direction, attractive actors
and locations, an atmosphere of
light-hearted British sex and a lively
harmonica theme turned it, after a
slowish start, into one of Britain's
biggest commercial hits and most
fondly remembered comedies.

*w William Rose d Henry Cornelius
ph Christopher Challis m Larry
Adler* (who also played it) *md Muir
Mathieson ad Michael Stringer*

*Dinah Sheridan, John Gregson, Kay
Kendall, Kenneth More, Geoffrey
Keen, Joyce Grenfell, Reginald
Beckwith, Arthur Wontner*

'One of the best things to have
happened to British films over the
last five years.'—*Gavin Lambert*

AAN: William Rose; Muir
Mathieson

'Now! It comes to the screen with
    nothing left unsaid and no
    emotion unstressed!'
Gentleman's Agreement
US 1947   118m   bw
TCF (Darryl F. Zanuck)
A journalist poses as a Jew in order
to write about anti-semitism.
Worthy melodrama which caused a
sensation at the time but as a film is
alas rather dull and self-satisfied.

*w Moss Hart, novel Laura Z.
Hobson d Elia Kazan ph Arthur
Miller m Alfred Newman*

Gregory Peck, Dorothy McGuire,
John Garfield, Celeste Holm, *Anne
Revere*, June Havoc, Albert Dekker,
Jane Wyatt, Dean Stockwell

AA: best picture; Elia Kazan;
Celeste Holm
AAN: Moss Hart; Gregory Peck;
Dorothy McGuire; Anne Revere

'It takes two to make it. The big
    two!'
The Getaway
US 1972   122m
Technicolor   Todd-AO 35
Solar / First Artists (David Foster,
Mitchell Brower)
A convict leaves jail and promptly

joins his wife in a bank robbery. Violent, amoral, terse and fast-moving action melodrama which generally holds the interest despite its excesses.

w Walter Hill, *novel* Jim Thompson *d* Sam Peckinpah *ph* Lucien Ballard *m* Quincy Jones

Steve McQueen, Ali MacGraw, Ben Johnson, Sally Struthers, Al Lettieri, Slim Pickens

'This pair have no mission or "meaning". As in all romances, *The Getaway* simply extracts one element of reality and dwells on it. Nor is the violence "American". Pictures like this don't fail overseas.'—*Stanley Kauffmann*

The Ghost Breakers

US 1940 85m bw
Paramount (Arthur Hornblow Jnr)

A girl inherits a West Indian castle and finds herself up to her neck in ghosts, zombies and buried treasure. Archetypal comedy horror, very well done; a follow-up to the success of *The Cat and the Canary*, and just about as entertaining.

w Paul Dickey, Walter de Leon, *play* Paul Dickey, Charles W. Goddard *d* George Marshall *ph* Charles Lang *m* Ernst Toch *ad* Hans Dreier

Bob Hope, Paulette Goddard, Paul Lukas, *Willie Best*, Richard Carlson, Lloyd Corrigan, Anthony Quinn, Noble Johnson, Pedro de Cordova

'Bob Hope can joke, apparently, even with a risen corpse.'—*Monthly Film Bulletin*

'Paramount has found the fabled formula for making audiences shriek with laughter and fright at one and the same time.'—*New York Times*

† Previously filmed in 1914 with H. B. Warner; in 1922 with Wallace Reid; and remade in 1953 as *Scared Stiff*.

The Ghost Goes West

GB 1935 85m bw
London Films (Alexander Korda)

When a millionaire buys a Scottish castle and transports it stone by stone to America, the castle ghost goes too.
Amusing whimsy which is always pleasant but never quite realizes its full potential; fondly remembered for its star performance.

w Robert E. Sherwood, Geoffrey Kerr, *story* Eric Keown *d* René Clair *ph* Harold Rosson *m* Mischa Spoliansky

Robert Donat, Jean Parker, Eugene Pallette, Elsa Lanchester, Ralph Bunker, Patricia Hilliard, Morton Selten

'Fine business likely in the keys, but not for the tanks.'—*Variety*

'Although the film is not cast in the fluid, rapidly paced style of Clair's typical work, it has a sly wit and an adroitness of manner that make it delightful.'—*André Sennwald, New York Times*

'It is typical of the British film industry that M. René Clair should be brought to this country to direct a Scottish film full of what must to him be rather incomprehensible jokes about whisky and bagpipes, humorous fantasy without any social significance, realistic observation, or genuine satire.'—*Graham Greene*

The Ghost of St Michael's

GB 1941 82m bw
Ealing (Basil Dearden)

A school is evacuated to the Isle of Skye, and the local ghost turns out to be an enemy agent. The star's schoolmaster character is here at its seedy best, and he is well supported in a comedy-thriller plot.

w Angus Macphail, John Dighton *d* Marcel Varnel *ph* Derek Williams

Will Hay, Claude Hulbert, Felix Aylmer, Raymond Huntley, Elliot Mason, Charles Hawtrey, John Laurie, Hay Petrie, Roddy Hughes, Manning Whiley

The Ghost Train

GB 1931 72m bw
Gainsborough (Michael Balcon)

Passengers stranded at a haunted station in Cornwall include a detective posing as a silly ass in order to trap smugglers.

Excellent early sound version of a comedy-thriller play which has not only been among the most commercially successful ever written but also provided the basic plot for many another comedy: *Oh Mr Porter*, *The Ghost of St Michael's*, *Back Room Boy*, *Hold That Ghost*, etc. Previously filmed as a silent in 1927, with Guy Newall.

w Angus Macphail, Lajos Biro, play Arnold Ridley d Walter Forde

Jack Hulbert, Cicely Courtneidge, Donald Calthrop, Ann Todd, Cyril Raymond, Angela Baddeley, Allan Jeayes

Ghostbusters

US 1984   105m
Metrocolor   Panavision
Columbia / Delphi (Ivan Reitman)
Unemployed academic parapsychologists set themselves up as ghostbusters and destroy several monstrous apparitions on the streets of New York.

Crude farce with expensive special effects. It took more money—millions more—than *Indiana Jones and the Temple of Doom*, which must say something about the age we live in.

w Dan Aykroyd, Harold Ramis d Ivan Reitman ph Laszlo Kovacs, Herb Wagreitch m Elmer Bernstein pd John De Cuir ed Sheldon Kahn, David Blewitt

Bill Murray, Dan Aykroyd, Harold Ramis, Sigourney Weaver, Rick Moranis, Annie Potts, William Atherton

Gigi

US 1958   119m
Metrocolor   Cinemascope
MGM (Arthur Freed)
In Paris in the nineties, a young girl is trained by her aunt to be a cocotte, but when married off to a rake she reforms him.

Delightfully set, costumed and performed, but oddly lacking dance numbers.

w / ly Alan Jay Lerner ˙ m Frederick Loewe d Vincente Minnelli ph Joseph Ruttenberg md André Previn pd / cost Cecil Beaton

Leslie Caron, Louis Jourdan, Maurice Chevalier, Hermione Gingold, Isabel Jeans, Jacques Bergerac, Eva Gabor, John Abbott

'It has the sureness expected when a group of the most sophisticated talents are able to work together on material entirely suited to them.'—*Penelope Houston*

AA: best picture; Alan Jay Lerner; Vincente Minnelli; Joseph Ruttenberg; André Previn; Cecil Beaton; Adrienne Fazan (editing); Preston Ames and Keogh Gleason (art directors); title song (*m* Frederick Loewe, *ly* Alan Jay Lerner); Maurice Chevalier (special award)

Gilda

US 1946   110m   bw
Columbia (Virginia Van Upp)
A gambler in a South American city resumes a love-hate relationship with an old flame . . . but she is now married to his dangerous new boss.

Archetypal Hollywood *film noir*, wholly studio-bound and the better for it, with dialogue that would seem risible if it did not happen to be dealt with in this style and with these actors, who keep the mood balanced between suspense and absurdity.

w Marion Parsonnet, story E. A. Ellington d Charles Vidor ph Rudolph Maté m Hugo Friedhofer md Morris Stoloff, Marlin Skiles

Rita Hayworth, Glenn Ford, George Macready, Steve Geray, Joseph Calleia, Joe Sawyer, Gerald Mohr, Ludwig Donath

'From a quietly promising opening the film settles into an intractable obscurity of narrative through which as in a fog three characters bite off at each other words of hate.'—*Richard Winnington*

Ginger and Fred

Italy / France / West Germany
1985   colour   126m
REA / Revcom / Stella / RAI
(Alberto Grimaldi)
An ageing pair of dancers is brought
out of retirement to appear on a TV
show.

Melancholy comedy with
resonances, chiefly taking the side of
age against youth, with 'Fred' as an
image of Fellini himself.

*w Federico Fellini, Tonino Guerra,
Tullio Pinelli d Federico Fellini
ph Tonino Delli Colli, Ennio
Guarnieri m Nicola Piovani
ad Dante Ferretti*

*Giulietta Masina, Marcello
Mastroianni*, Franco Fabrizi,
Frederick Von Ledenberg

The Glass Key

US 1942   85m   bw
Paramount (Fred Kohlmar)
A slightly corrupt but good-natured
politician is saved from being
implicated in a murder.
Finds some limited talents in their
best form, helped by a plot which
keeps one watching.

*w Jonathan Latimer d Stuart
Heisler ph Theodor Sparkuhl
m Victor Young*

*Brian Donlevy, Alan Ladd, Veronica
Lake*, Bonita Granville, *William
Bendix*, Richard Denning, Joseph
Calleia, Moroni Olsen

  MADVIG (Brian Donlevy): 'I'm
going to society. He's practically
given me the key to his house.'

  BEAUMONT (Alan Ladd): 'Yeah, a
glass key. Be sure it doesn't break
up in your hand.'

The Glass Menagerie

US 1950   107m   bw
Warner / Charles K. Feldman
(Jerry Wald)
A shy crippled girl seeks escape from
the shabby reality of life in St Louis
and from her mother's fantasies.
Pleasantly moody version of one of
its author's lighter and more
optimistic plays; fluent and
good-looking production,
memorable performances

*w Tennessee Williams (with Peter
Berneis) from his play d Irving
Rapper ph Robert Burks m Max
Steiner*

Gertrude Lawrence, Jane Wyman,
Kirk Douglas, Arthur Kennedy

The Glenn Miller Story

US 1954   116m
Technicolor
U-I (Aaron Rosenberg)
The life of the unassuming
trombonist and bandleader whose
plane disappeared during World War
II.
Competent musical heartwarmer
with a well-cast star and successful
reproduction of the Miller sound. A
big box office hit.

*w Valentine Davies, Oscar Brodney
d Anthony Mann ph William
Daniels md Henry Mancini, Joseph
Gershenson*

James Stewart, June Allyson, Harry
Morgan, Charles Drake, Frances
Langford, Louis Armstrong, Gene
Krupa

AAN: script; music direction

The Go-Between

GB 1970   116m
Technicolor
EMI / World Film Services (John
Heyman, Norman Priggen)
Staying at a stately home around the
turn of the century, 12-year-old Leo
carries love letters from a farmer to
his friend's sister.
A rather tiresome plot sustains a rich
picture of the Edwardian gentry, a
milieu with which however the
director is not at home and treats far
too slowly and tricksily.

*w Harold Pinter, novel L. P.
Hartley d Joseph Losey
ph Geoffrey Fisher m Michel
Legrand ad Carmen Dillon*

Alan Bates, Julie Christie, Michael
Redgrave, Dominic Guard, Michael
Gough, Margaret Leighton, Edward
Fox

'It's an almost palpable recreation of a past environment, and that environment is the film's real achievement, not the drama enacted within it.'—*Stanley Kauffmann*

AAN: Margaret Leighton

Go into Your Dance

US 1935 89m bw
Warner (Sam Bischoff)
GB title: *Casino de Paree*

A big-headed star gets his come-uppance and finds happiness. Moderate backstage musical notable for the only teaming of Jolson and Keeler, who were then married.

w Earl Baldwin *d* Archie Mayo *ph* Tony Gaudio, Sol Polito *songs* Harry Warren, Al Dubin

Al Jolson, Ruby Keeler, Glenda Farrell, Benny Rubin, Phil Regan, Barton MacLane, Sharon Lynne, Akim Tamiroff, Helen Morgan, Patsy Kelly

'It has everything for the box office.'—*Variety*

The Godfather

US 1972 175m
Technicolor
Paramount / Alfran (Albert S. Ruddy)

When, after ruling for two generations, the Mafia's New York head dies of old age, his son takes over reluctantly but later learns how to kill.

A brilliantly-made film with all the fascination of a snake pit: a warm-hearted family saga except that the members are thieves and murderers. Cutting would help, but the duller conversational sections do heighten the cunningly judged moments of suspense and violence.

w Francis Ford Coppola, Mario Puzo, *novel* Mario Puzo *d* Francis Ford Coppola *ph* Gordon Willis *m* Nino Rota *pd* Dean Tavoularis

Marlon Brando (unintentionally comic in an absurd make-up), *Al Pacino*, Robert Duvall, James Caan, Richard Castellano, Diane Keaton, Talia Shire, Richard Conte, John Marley

'The immorality lies in his presentation of murderers as delightful family men—the criminal is the salt of the earth—and to our shame we rub it into the wounds of our Watergate-world morality and even ask for more.'—*Judith Crist, 1974*

'They have put pudding in Brando's cheeks and dirtied his teeth, he speaks hoarsely and moves stiffly, and these combined mechanics are hailed as great acting . . . Like star, like film, the keynote is inflation. *The Godfather* was made from a big bestseller, a lot of money was spent on it, and it runs over three hours. Therefore it's important.'—*Stanley Kauffmann*

AA: best picture; script; Marlon Brando
AAN: Francis Ford Coppola (as director); Al Pacino; Robert Duvall; James Caan

'The gospel according to today!'
Godspell

US 1973 102m TVC color
Columbia / Lansbury / Duncan / Beruh (Edgar Lansbury)

The Gospel according to St Matthew played out musically by hippies in the streets of New York.

Wild and woolly film version of the successful theatrical fantasy, surviving chiefly by virtue of its gleaming photography.

w David Greene, John Michael Tebelak, *play* John Michael Tebelak *d* David Greene *ph* Richard G. Heimann *m / ly* Stephen Schwarz

Victor Garber, David Haskell, Jerry Sroka, Lynne Thigpen, Robin Lamont

'A patch of terra incognita somewhere between *Sesame Street* and the gospel according to *Laugh-In*.'—*Bruce Williamson*

Going My Way

US 1944 126m bw
Paramount (Leo McCarey)

A young priest comes to a New York slum parish and after initial friction

charms the old pastor he is to
succeed.
Sentimental comedy which got away
with it wonderfully at the time,
largely through careful casting,
though it seems thin and obvious
now.

w Frank Butler, Frank Cavett, Leo
McCarey *d* Leo McCarey
ph Lionel Lindon *m* Robert
Emmett Dolan *songs Johnny
Burke, James Van Heusen, J. R.
Shannon*

Bing Crosby, Barry Fitzgerald, Rise
Stevens, Frank McHugh, James
Brown, Gene Lockhart, Jean
Heather, Porter Hall
 'I should not feel safe in
recommending it to anyone but a
simple-hearted sentimentalist with a
taste for light music.'—*Richard
Mallett, Punch*
 'The lessons, if I read them right,
are that leisureliness can be
excellent, that if you take a genuine
delight in character the universe is
opened to you, and perhaps above
all that a movie, like any other
genuine work of art, must be made
for love. But I am willing to bet that
the chief discernible result of *Going
My Way* will be an anxiety-ridden set
of vaudeville sketches about Pat and
Mike in cassocks.'—*James Agee*

† Father O'Malley reappeared in
The Bells of St Mary's and *Say One
for Me*.

AA: best picture; script; original
story (Leo McCarey); Leo McCarey
(direction); Bing Crosby; Barry
Fitzgerald; song, 'Swinging on a
Star' (*m* James Van Heusen,
ly Johnny Burke)
AAN: Lionel Lindon

Gold

GB 1974   124m
Technicolor   Panavision
Hemdale / Avton (Michael Kinger)
A South African mining engineer
falls for the boss's granddaughter
and exposes a conspiracy.
Old-fashioned thick ear with
spectacular underground sequences
and a rousing finale.

w Wilbur Smith, Stanley Price,
novel Goldmine by Wilbur Smith
d Peter Hunt *ph* Ousama Rawi
m Elmer Bernstein

Roger Moore, Susannah York, Ray
Milland, Bradford Dillman, John
Gielgud, Tony Beckley

AAN: song 'Wherever Love Takes
Me' (*m* Elmer Bernstein, *ly* Don
Black)

Gold Diggers of 1933

US 1933   96m   bw
Warner (Robert Lord)
Three Broadway chorus girls seek
rich husbands.
Cheerful, competent, well-cast;
numbers include 'My Forgotten
Man', 'We're in the Money' and
'Pettin' in the Park'.

w Erwin Gelsey, James Seymour,
David Boehm, Ben Markson
d Mervyn Le Roy *ch* Busby
Berkeley *songs* Harry Warren, Al
Dubin *ph* Sol Polito

Warren William, Joan Blondell,
Aline MacMahon, Ruby Keeler,
Dick Powell, Guy Kibbee, Ned
Sparks, Ginger Rogers, Clarence
Nordstrom
 'It sums up what is meant by the
phrase "pure thirties": electrically
wired chorus girls singing "In the
Shadows Let Me Come and Sing to
You" merge to form a big
illuminated violin.'—*New Yorker,
1979*
 'It is memorable chiefly because
Busby Berkeley created a mad
geometry of patterned chorines . . .
The innocent vulgarity of the big
numbers is charming and uproarious,
and aesthetically preferable to the
pretentious ballet finales of fifties
musicals like *An American in Paris*.
Even those of us who were children
at the time did not mistake *Gold
Diggers* for art—and certainly no
one took it for life.'—*Pauline Kael,
1968*

 'Your dream of perfect beauty
come true!'—*publicity*

The Gold Rush

US 1925   72m (sound
version 1942)   bw
Charles Chaplin
A lone prospector in the Yukon
becomes rich after various
adventures.
Essentially a succession of slowly but
carefully built visual gags. this is
Chaplin's finest example of comedy
drawn from utter privation: as such
it appealed vastly to the poor of the
world. As a clown. Chaplin himself
is near his best. though as usual
there is rather too much straining for
pathos.

w. d. p. m *Charles Chaplin*
ph Rollie Totheroh. Jack Wilson

Charles Chaplin, Georgia Hale.
Mack Swain. Tom Murray

The Golden Age of Comedy

US 1957   78m   bw
Robert Youngson
Productions
First of the scholarly compilations of
silent comedy which saved many
negatives from destruction, this is a
fast-paced general survey which
despite a facetious sound track does
provide a laugh a minute. It
particularly brought Laurel and
Hardy back into public notice, and
includes sections from *Two Tars* and
The Battle of the Century.

wd *Robert Youngson narrators*
Dweight Weist, Ward Wilson
m George Steiner

Stan Laurel, Oliver Hardy, Harry
Langdon, Ben Turpin, Will Rogers,
Billy Bevan, Charlie Chase, Andy
Clyde

Goldfinger

GB 1964   112m
Technicolor
UA/Eon (Harry Saltzman, Albert
R. Broccoli)
James Bond prevents an
international gold smuggler from
robbing Fort Knox.
Probably the liveliest and most
amusing of the Bond spy spoofs,
with a fairly taut plot between the
numerous highlights. The big budget
is well used.

w *Richard Maibaum. Paul Dehn.
novel* Ian Fleming d *Guy Hamilton
ph Ted Moore m John Barry
pd Ken Adam titles Robert
Brownjohn*

*Sean Connery. Honor Blackman.
Gert Frobe.* Harold Sakata. Shirley
Eaton. Bernard Lee. Lois Maxwell.
Desmond Llewellyn
'A dazzling object lesson in the
principle that nothing succeeds like
excess.'—*Penelope Gilliatt*
'A diverting comic strip for
grown-ups.'—*Judith Crist*

The Goldwyn Follies

US 1938   115m
Technicolor
Samuel Goldwyn
A Hollywood producer seeks the
average girl to test his scripts.
Goldwyn's failure to become
Ziegfeld, chiefly due to a lack of
humour in the script, still has a
soupçon of effective Hollywood
satire and some excellent numbers.

w Ben Hecht d George Marshall
ph Gregg Toland m Alfred
Newman ch George Balanchine
ad Richard Day

Kenny Baker, Vera Zorina, *the Ritz
Brothers, Adolphe Menjou*, Edgar
Bergen and Charlie McCarthy,
Helen Jepson, Phil Baker, Ella
Logan, Bobby Clark, Jerome
Cowan, Nydia Westman, Andrea
Leeds
'An advance glimpse at next
Sunday's amusement section from
any metropolitan
newspaper.'—*Variety*
'The bizarre in musical
pretentiousness.'—*Commonweal*
'Many features to suit all tastes
and not enough of them to suit
anybody's.'—*Time*

AAN: Alfred Newman

The Golem

Germany 1920   75m
approx   bw   silent
UFA
In 16th-century Prague a Jewish
Rabbi constructs a man of clay to
defend his people against a pogrom.
There were several versions of this

story (Germany 1913, sequel 1917; Czechoslovakia 1935 and 1951), but this is almost certainly the best, its splendid sets, performances and certain scenes all being clearly influential on later Hollywood films, especially *Frankenstein*.

w Paul Wegener, Henrik Galeen *d* Paul Wegener, Carl Boese *ph* Karl Freund, Guido Seeber *ad* Hans Poelzig

Paul Wegener, Albert Steinruck, Ernst Deutsch

Gone with the Wind
🎭🎭 US 1939   220m
✗ Technicolor
MGM / *David O. Selznick*
An egotistic Southern girl survives the Civil War but finally loses the only man she cares for.
The only film in history which could be profitably revived for forty years: 'still pure gold', said the *Daily Mirror* in 1975. Whole books have been written about it; its essential appeal is that of a romantic story with strong characters and an impeccable production. The widescreen version produced in the late sixties ruined its composition and colour, but it is to be hoped that the original negative still survives.

w Sidney Howard (and others), *novel* Margaret Mitchell *d* Victor Fleming (and George Cukor, Sam Wood) *ph* Ernest Haller, Ray Rennahan *m* Max Steiner *pd* William Cameron Menzies *ad* Lyle Wheeler

Clark Gable, Vivien Leigh, Olivia de Havilland, Leslie Howard, Thomas Mitchell, Barbara O'Neil, *Hattie McDaniel, Butterfly McQueen*, Victor Jory, Evelyn Keyes, Ann Rutherford, Laura Hope Crews, Harry Davenport, Jane Darwell, Ona Munson, Ward Bond.
'A major event in the history of the industry but only a minor event in motion picture art. There are moments when the two categories meet on good terms, but the long stretches between are filled with mere spectacular efficiency.'—*Franz Hoellering, The Nation*

'Shakespeare's *The Taming of the Shrew* seems to have got mixed up with one of the novels of Ethel M. Dell.'—*James Agate*
'Perhaps the key plantation movie.'—*Time Out, 1980*
'Forget it, Louis, no Civil War picture ever made a nickel.'—*Irving Thalberg to Louis B. Mayer, 1936*
† The best account of the film's making is in Gavin Lambert's 1975 book, *GWTW*.
†† In the early seventies a stage musical version toured the world; music by Harold Rome.

AA: best picture; Sidney Howard; Victor Fleming; Ernest Haller, Ray Rennahan; Lyle Wheeler; Vivien Leigh; Hattie McDaniel; Hal C. Kern and James E. Newcom (editors)
AAN: Max Steiner; Clark Gable; Olivia de Havilland

The Good Companions
🎭🎭 GB 1932   113m   bw
✗ Gaumont / Welsh-Pearson (T. A. Welsh, George Pearson)
Three ill-assorted people take to the road and in various capacities join the Dinky Doos pierrot troupe. Gallant, mini-budgeted version of Priestley's popular picaresque novel. A little faded now, it retains some of its vigour, and the performances please.

w W. P. Lipscomb, Angus Macphail, Ian Dalrymple *novel* J. B. Priestley *d* Victor Saville *ph* Bernard Knowles

Edmund Gwenn, Mary Glynne, John Gielgud, *Jessie Matthews*, Percy Parsons, A. W. Baskomb, Dennis Hoey, Richard Dolman, Frank Pettingell, Finlay Currie, *Max Miller*, Jack Hawkins, George Zucco

'To the memory of Irving Grant Thalberg we dedicate this picture—his last great achievement!'
The Good Earth
🎭🎭 US 1937   138m   bw
✗ MGM (*Irving Thalberg*)
A Chinese peasant grows rich but loses his beloved wife.

A massive, well-meaning and fondly remembered production which is nevertheless artificial, unconvincing and pretty undramatic in the second half. The star performances impress to begin with, then wear thin, but the final locust attack is as well done as it originally seemed. Historically valuable as a Hollywood prestige production of the thirties.

w Talbot Jennings, Tess Schlesinger, Claudine West, *play* Owen and Donald Davis, *novel* Pearl S. Buck d *Sidney Franklin* ph Karl Freund m Herbert Stothart *montage* Slavko Vorkapitch *ad* Cedric Gibbons

Paul Muni, Luise Rainer, Walter Connolly, Tilly Losch, Jessie Ralph, Charley Grapewin, Keye Luke, Harold Huber

'A true technical achievement with names enough to send it across. But it's not going to be easy to get the three-million-dollar investment back. And if it does come back it's going to take a long time.'—*Variety*

'Performances, direction and photography are of a uniform excellence, and have been fused perfectly into a dignified, beautiful, but soberly dramatic production.'—*New York Times*

'One of the superb visual adventures of the period.'—*John Baxter, 1968*

'Prestigious boredom, and it goes on for a very long time.'—*New Yorker, 1977*

AA: Karl Freund; Luise Rainer AAN: best picture; Sidney Franklin

The Good, the Bad and the Ugly
Italy 1966 180m
Techniscope
PEA (Alberto Grimaldi)
original title: *Il Buono, il Bruto, il Cattivo*
During the American Civil War, three men seek hidden loot. Intermittently lively, very violent, and interminably drawn out western with a number of rather hilarious stylistic touches.

w Age Scarpelli, Luciano Vincenzoni, Sergio Leone d Sergio Leone ph Tonino delli Colli m Ennio Morricone

Clint Eastwood, Eli Wallach, Lee Van Cleef

Goodbye Mr Chips
GB 1939 114m bw
MGM (Victor Saville)
The life of a shy schoolmaster from his first job to his death. Sentimental romance in MGM's best style, a long-standing favourite for its performance and humour; but the production seems slightly unsatisfactory these days.

w R. C. Sherriff, Claudine West, Eric Maschwitz, *novel* James Hilton d *Sam Wood* ph Frederick A. Young m Richard Addinsell

Robert Donat, Greer Garson, Paul Henreid, Lyn Harding, Austin Trevor, Terry Kilburn, John Mills, Milton Rosmer, Judith Furse

'Charming, quaintly sophisticated . . . more for the big situations than the smaller towns.'—*Variety*

'The whole picture has an assurance, bears a glow of popularity like the face of a successful candidate on election day. And it is wrong to despise popularity in the cinema.'—*Graham Greene*

'The picture has no difficulty in using two hours to retell a story that was scarcely above short story length. *Mr Chips* is worth its time.'—*New York Times*

'The novel became an American best seller when that old sentimentalist Alexander Woollcott touted it on the radio . . . the movie clogs the nose more than necessary.'—*Pauline Kael, 70s*

AA: Robert Donat
AAN: best picture; script; Sam Wood; Greer Garson

'This is Benjamin . . . he's a little worried about his future!'
The Graduate
US 1967 105m
Technicolor Panavision
UA/Embassy (Lawrence Turman)

A rich Californian ex-student is led into an affair with the wife of his father's friend, then falls in love with her daughter.

Richly reflecting the anything-goes mood of the late sixties, this lushly-filmed sex comedy opened a few new doors, looked ravishing, was well acted and had a popular music score, so that few people noticed that only the first half was any good.

w Calder Willingham, Buck Henry, *novel* Charles Webb *d* Mike Nichols *ph* Robert Surtees *songs* Paul Simon *singers* Simon and Garfunkel *m* Dave Grusin *pd* Richard Sylbert

Dustin Hoffman, Anne Bancroft, Katharine Ross, Murray Hamilton, William Daniels, Elizabeth Wilson

BENJAMIN: 'Mrs Robinson, if you don't mind my saying so, this conversation is getting a little strange.'

'Seeing *The Graduate* is a bit like having one's most brilliant friend to dinner, watching him become more witty and animated with every moment, and then becoming aware that what one may really be witnessing is the onset of a nervous breakdown.'—*Renata Adler*

'Yes, there are weaknesses . . . But in cinematic skill, in intent, in sheer connection with us, *The Graduate* is a milestone in American film history.'—*Stanley Kauffmann*

AA: Mike Nichols
AAN: best picture; script; Robert Surtees; Dustin Hoffman; Anne Bancroft; Katharine Ross

'The greatest cast in stage or screen history!'
Grand Hotel
US 1932   115m   bw
MGM (Irving Thalberg)
The lives of various hotel guests become intertwined and reach their climaxes.
It's a little faded now, but much of the magic still works in this first of the portmanteau movies; the production is opulent yet somehow

stiff, and the performances have survived with varying success.

w William A. Drake, *novel* Vicki Baum *d* Edmund Goulding *ph* William Daniels *ad* Cedric Gibbons

Greta Garbo, *John Barrymore,* Lionel Barrymore, Joan Crawford, Wallace Beery, Jean Hersholt, Lewis Stone

DOCTOR (Lewis Stone): 'Grand Hotel. Always the same. People come, people go. Nothing ever happens.'

GRUSINSKAYA (Greta Garbo): 'I want to be alone . . . I think I have never been so tired in my life.'

† Remade as *Weekend at the Waldorf.*
AA: best picture

La Grande Illusion
France 1937   117m   bw
RAC
During World War I, three captured French pilots have an uneasy relationship with their German commandant.
Celebrated mood piece with much to say about war and mankind; more precisely, it is impeccably acted and directed and has real tragic force.

w Jean Renoir, Charles Spaak *d* Jean Renoir *ph* Christian Matras, Claude Renoir, Bourgoin, Bourreaud *m* Joseph Kosma

Pierre Fresnay, Erich Von Stroheim, Jean Gabin, Julien Carette, Marcel Dalio, Gaston Modot, Jean Dasté, Dita Parlo

'Artistically masterful.'—*Variety*

'The story is true. It was told to me by my friends in the war . . . notably by Pinsard who flew fighter planes. I was in the reconnaissance squadron. He saved my life many times when the German fighters became too persistent. He himself was shot down seven times. His escapes are the basis for the story.'—*Jean Renoir*

'One of the true masterpieces of the screen.'—*Pauline Kael, 70s*

AAN: best picture

'The thousands who have read the book will know why WE WILL NOT SELL ANY CHILDREN TICKETS to see this picture!'

The Grapes of Wrath

US 1940 128m bw
TCF (Nunnally Johnson)

After the dust-bowl disaster of the thirties, Oklahoma farmers trek to California in the hope of a better life.

A superb film which could scarcely be improved upon. Though the ending is softened from the book, there was too much here for filmgoers to chew on. Acting, photography, direction combine to make this an unforgettable experience, a poem of a film.

w Nunnally Johnson, novel John Steinbeck d John Ford ph Gregg Toland m Alfred Newman

Henry Fonda, Jane Darwell, John Carradine, Charley Grapewin, Dorris Bowdon, Russell Simpson, Zeffie Tilbury, O. Z. Whitehead, John Qualen, Eddie Quillan, Grant Mitchell

TOM (Henry Fonda) reading grave marker: 'This here's William James Joad, died of a stroke, old, old man. His fokes bured him because they got no money to pay for funerls. Nobody kilt him. Just a stroke and he died.'

MA (Jane Darwell): 'Rich fellas come up, an' they die, an' their kids ain't no good, an' they die out. But we keep a-comin'. We're the people that live. Can't lick us. We'll go on forever, Pa, because we're the people.'

MA: 'Well, Pa, woman can change bettern a man. Man lives—well, in jerks. Baby born or somebody dies, that's a jerk. Gets a farm or loses one, an' that's a jerk. With a woman, it's all one flow, like a stream—little eddies, little waterfalls—but the river, it goes right on. Woman looks at it that way.'

'A genuinely great motion picture which makes one proud to have even a small share in the affairs of the cinema.'—Howard Barnes

'The most mature motion picture that has ever been made, in feeling, in purpose, and in the use of the medium.'—Otis Ferguson

'A sincere and searing indictment of man's cruel indifference to his fellows.'—Basil Wright

AA: John Ford; Jane Darwell
AAN: best picture; Nunnally Johnson; Henry Fonda

Grease

US 1978 110m
Metrocolor Panavision
Paramount / Robert Stigwood, Allan Carr

The path of true love in a fifties high school does not run smoothly.

Amiable 'period' musical for teenagers: a highly fashionable exploitation of the new star John Travolta, its commercialism was undeniable, and it carefully built in appeal to older age groups.

w Bronte Woodard, stage musical play Jim Jacobs, Warren Casey d Randal Kleiser ph Bill Butler pd Phil Jefries titles John Wilson

John Travolta, Olivia Newton-John, Stockard Channing, Eve Arden, Frankie Avalon, Joan Blondell, Edd Byrnes, Sid Caesar, Alice Ghostley, Sha Na Na, Jeff Conaway, Barry Pearl, Michael Tucci

'A bogus, clumsily jointed pastiche of late fifties high school musicals, studded with leftovers from West Side Story and Rebel Without A Cause.'—New Yorker

AAN: song, 'Hopelessly Devoted to You'

The Great Adventure

Sweden 1953 73m bw
Arne Sucksdorff

Two boys on a farm rescue an otter and keep it as a pet.

Superbly photographed wild life film featuring a variety of small animals.

w,d,ph,ed Arne Sucksdorff m Lars Erik Larsson

Anders Norberg, Kiell Sucksdorff,
Arne Sucksdorff

The Great Caruso

US 1950   109m
Technicolor
MGM (Joe Pasternak)
Semi-fictional biography of the
Italian tenor.
Dramatically flat but opulently
staged biopic, turned into a star
vehicle and a huge commercial
success.

w Sonya Levien, William Ludwig
d Richard Thorpe *ph* Joseph
Ruttenberg *md* Johnny Green,
Peter Herman Adler

Mario Lanza, Ann Blyth, Dorothy
Kirsten, Jarmila Novotna, Carl
Benton Reid, Eduard Franz,
Richard Hageman, Ludwig Donath,
Alan Napier

AAN: Johnny Green, Peter Herman
Adler

The Great Dictator

US 1940   129m   bw
Charles Chaplin
A Jewish barber is mistaken for
dictator Adenoid Hynkel.
Chaplin's satire on Hitler has a few
funny moments, but the rest is heavy
going, the production is
cheeseparing, and the final speech to
the world is a grave mistake.

wd Charles Chaplin *ph* Karl Struss,
Rollie Totheroh *md* Meredith
Willson *ad* J. Russell Spencer

Charles Chaplin, Paulette Goddard,
Jack Oakie (as Napaloni), Reginald
Gardiner, Henry Daniell, Billy
Gilbert, Maurice Moscovitch

'For this film he takes on more
than a mimed representation of
common humanity; he states, and
accepts, the responsibility of being
one of humanity's best and most
widely-known
representatives.'—*Basil Wright*
'The last impassioned speech
about peace and serenity still wrecks
everything that has gone before:
Chaplin mawkish can always
overrule Chaplin the innocent
mime.'—*New Yorker, 1978*

'You must go back to *Intolerance*
for another motion picture that is so
completely one man's personal
expression of his attitude on
something about which he feels
deeply and passionately.'—*James
Shelley Hamilton, National Board of
Review*
'No time for comedy? Yes, I say,
time for comedy. Time for Chaplin
comedy. No time ever for Chaplin to
preach as he does in those last six
minutes, no matter how deeply he
may feel what he wrote and says. He
is not a good preacher. Indeed, he is
frighteningly bad.'—*John O'Hara*
'Some moments actually work, but
they are very few and far
between.'—*Time Out, 1984*

AAN: best picture; Charles Chaplin
(as writer and actor); Meredith
Willson; Jack Oakie

The Great Escape

US 1963   173m   De Luxe
Panavision
UA/Mirisch/Alpha (John
Sturges)
Allied prisoners plan to escape from
a German prison camp.
Pretty good but overlong POW
adventure with a tragic ending.

w James Clavell, W. R. Burnett,
book Paul Brickhill *d* John Sturges
ph Daniel Fapp m Elmer Bernstein

James Garner, *Steve McQueen*,
Richard Attenborough, James
Donald, Charles Bronson, Donald
Pleasence, James Coburn, David
McCallum, Gordon Jackson, John
Leyton, Nigel Stock

Great Expectations

GB 1946   118m   bw
Rank/Cineguild (Anthony
Havelock-Allan)
A boy meets an escaped convict on
the Romney Marshes, with strange
consequences for both of them.
Despite the inevitable
simplifications, this is a superbly
pictorial rendering of a much-loved
novel, with all the famous characters
in safe hands and masterly
judgement in every department.

w Ronald Neame, David Lean, Kay Walsh, Cecil McGivern, Anthony Havelock-Allan *d* David Lean *ph* Guy Green *ad* John Bryan

John Mills, Bernard Miles, *Finlay Currie, Martita Hunt,* Valerie Hobson, *Jean Simmons,* Alec Guinness, Francis L. Sullivan, Anthony Wager, Ivor Barnard, Freda Jackson, Hay Petrie, O. B. Clarence, George Hayes, Torin Thatcher, Eileen Erskine

'The first big British film to have been made, a film that sweeps our cloistered virtues out into the open.'—*Richard Winnington*

'The best Dickens adaptation, and arguably David Lean's finest film.'—*NFT, 1969*

'It does for Dickens what *Henry V* did for Shakespeare. That is, it indicates a sound method for translating him from print to film . . . almost never less than graceful, tasteful and intelligent, and some of it better than that.'—*James Agee*

AA: Guy Green; John Bryan
AAN: best picture; script; David Lean (as director)

The Great Gatsby
⚜ US 1974 146m
✗ Eastmancolor
Paramount/Newdon (David Merrick)
Events leading to the death of a retired gangster and mysterious Long Island plutocrat.
Lavish production values and pleasing period sense but not much grip on the story or characters. Overlong footage is not made to seem shorter by snail's pace and dull performances.

w Francis Ford Coppola *d* Jack Clayton *ph* Douglas Slocombe *m* Nelson Riddle *pd* John Box

Robert Redford, Mia Farrow, Karen Black, Scott Wilson, *Sam Waterston,* Lois Chiles

'Pays its creator the regrettable tribute of erecting a mausoleum over his work.'—*Richard Combs*

'Leaves us more involved with

six-and-a-half-million dollars' worth of trappings than with human tragedy.'—*Judith Crist*

'A total failure of every requisite sensibility.'—*Stanley Kauffmann*

'Profoundly unfilmable: a poetic and ultimately pessimistic comment on the American dream is transformed by cinematic realism into pure prose.'—*Michael Billington, Illustrated London News*

AA: Nelson Riddle

'Sometimes there's a terrible penalty for telling the truth . . .'
The Great Lie
⚜ US 1941 107m bw
✗ Warner (Hal B. Wallis, Henry Blanke)
A determined girl loses the man she loves, believes him dead in a plane crash, and takes over the baby which his selfish wife does not want.
Absurd melodrama becomes top-flight entertainment with all concerned in cracking form and special attention on the two bitchy female leads, splendidly played. Classical music trimmings, too.

w Leonore Coffee, *novel* January Heights by Polan Banks *d* Edmund Goulding *ph* Tony Gaudio *m* Max Steiner

Bette Davis, Mary Astor, *George Brent,* Lucile Watson, Hattie McDaniel, Grant Mitchell, Jerome Cowan

AA: Mary Astor

'He'll give you the biggest heart sock, laugh shock you ever thrilled to!'
The Great McGinty
⚜ US 1940 83m bw
✗ Paramount
GB title: *Down Went McGinty*
A hobo and a crook have a hectic political career.
Lively comedy-drama which signalled the arrival as director of a new and stimulating Hollywood talent.

wd Preston Sturges *ph* William C. Mellor *m* Frederick Hollander

Brian Donlevy, *Akim Tamiroff*,
Muriel Angelus, Louis Jean Heydt,
Arthur Hoyt

PROLOGUE: 'This is the story of two
men who met in a banana republic.
One of them never did anything
dishonest in his life except for one
crazy minute. The other never did
anything honest in his life except for
one crazy minute. They both had to
leave the country.'

'This is his first directing job and
where has he been all our lives? He
has that sense of the incongruous
which makes some of the best
gaiety.'—*Otis Ferguson*

'The tough dialogue is matched by
short, snappy scenes; the picture
seems to have wasted no time, no
money.'—*Gilbert Seldes*

'A director as adroit and inventive
as any in the business . . . it starts
like a five-alarm fire and never
slackens pace for one moment until
its unexpected conclusion.'—*Pare
Lorentz*

'Sturges takes the success ethic
and throws it in the face of the
audience.'—*James Orsini*

'Capra with the gloves
off.'—*Raymond Durgnat*

AA: script

The Great Man

US 1956 92m bw
U-I (Aaron Rosenberg)
A memorial programme to a
much-loved TV personality turns
into an exposé.
Patchy melodrama with a *Citizen
Kane* framework; the best bits are
very effective.

w Jose Ferrer, Al Morgan, *novel* Al
Morgan *d* Jose Ferrer *ph* Harold
Lipstein *m* Herman Stein

Jose Ferrer, Dean Jagger, Keenan
Wynn, *Julie London*, Joanne
Gilbert, *Ed Wynn*, Jim Backus

'Its distinction is in its unwavering
tone—one of blunt and frequently
savage irony and cynicism.'—*MFB*

'The movie is almost over before
one realizes what a slick, fast sell it is
(resembling nothing so much as what
it is attacking).'—*Pauline Kael, 1968*

'The greatest comedy ever made!'
The Great Race

US 1965 163m
Technicolor Super
Panavision
Warner / Patricia / Jalem / Reynard
(Martin Jurow)
In 1908, the Great Leslie and
Professor Fate are leading
contenders in the first New York to
Paris car race.
Elaborate comedy spectacular with
many good moments, notably the
early disasters, a western saloon
brawl, and a custard pie fight.
Elsewhere, there is more evidence of
an oversize budget than of wit or
finesse, and the entire Prisoner of
Zenda spoof could have been
omitted. Excellent production detail
and general good humour.

w Arthur Ross *d* Blake Edwards
ph Russell Harlan *m* Henry
Mancini *pd* Fernando Carrere

Jack Lemmon, *Tony Curtis*, *Peter
Falk*, *Natalie Wood*, George
Macready, Ross Martin, Vivian
Vance, Dorothy Provine

AAN: Russell Harlan; song 'The
Sweetheart Tree' (*m* Henry Mancini,
ly Johnny Mercer)

'Miliza Korjus—rhymes with
gorgeous!'
The Great Waltz

US 1938 103m bw
MGM (Bernard Hyman)
Young Johann Strauss becomes
Vienna's waltz king.
Exhilarating old-fashioned studio-set
musical located in Hollywood's
endearing vision of Old Vienna,
assisted by streamlined production
and excellent cast. Musical schmaltz.

w Walter Reisch, Samuel
Hoffenstein, *story* Gottfried
Reinhardt *d* Julien Duvivier
ph Joseph Ruttenberg *m* Dmitri
Tiomkin

Fernand Gravet, Luise Rainer,
Miliza Korjus, Lionel Atwill, Hugh
Herbert, Herman Bing, Curt Bois
'Should click nicely, but in these
swingaroo days the waltz part may

slow down anticipated b.o.
enthusiasm.'—*Variety*

AA: Joseph Ruttenberg
AAN: Miliza Korjus

The Great Ziegfeld

US 1936 179m bw
MGM (Hunt Stromberg)

The growth and Broadway fame of
impresario Florenz Ziegfeld.
Mammoth biopic which despite a
few show-stopping numbers never
takes off dramatically and becomes
something of an endurance test;
interesting, however, as a
spectacular of its time.

w William Anthony McGuire
d Robert Z. Leonard *ph* Oliver T.
Marsh, Ray June, George Folsey
md Arthur Lange *ad* Cedric
Gibbons

William Powell, Luise Rainer (as
Anna Held), Myrna Loy (as Billie
Burke), Frank Morgan, Reginald
Owen, Nat Pendleton, Virginia
Bruce, *Ray Bolger*, Harriett Hoctor,
Ernest Cossart, *Fanny Brice*, Robert
Greig, Gilda Gray, Leon Errol,
Stanley Morner (Dennis Morgan)

'This huge inflated gas-blown
object bobs into the critical view as
irrelevantly as an airship advertising
somebody's toothpaste at a south
coast resort. It lasts three hours.
That is its only claim to special
attention.'—*Graham Greene*

'Everything should have been
tightened—not in the team job of
cutting those miles of negative, but
in boiling down the script, saving a
line here, combining two scenes into
one.'—*Otis Ferguson*

AA: best picture; Luise Rainer
AAN: William Anthony McGuire;
Robert Z. Leonard

The Greatest Show on Earth

US 1952 153m
Technicolor
Paramount/Cecil B. de Mille
(Henry Wilcoxon)

Various dramas come to a head
under the big top.

Moribund circus drama with bad
acting, stilted production, an
irrelevant train crash climax and a
few genuinely spectacular and
enjoyable moments.

w Frederic M. Frank, Theodore St
John, Frank Cavett, Barre Lyndon
d Cecil B. de Mille *ph* George
Barnes, Peverell Marley, Wallace
Kelley *m* Victor Young *ad* Hal
Pereira, Walter Tyler

Betty Hutton, Cornel Wilde, James
Stewart, Charlton Heston, Dorothy
Lamour, Gloria Grahame, Lyle
Bettger, Henry Wilcoxon, Emmett
Kelly, Lawrence Tierney, John
Kellogg, John Ringling North

AA: best picture
AAN: original story (Fredric M.
Frank, Theodore St John, Frank
Cavett); Cecil B. de Mille (as
director)

The Greatest Story Ever Told

US 1965 225m
Technicolor Ultra
Panavision 70
UA/George Stevens

Solemn spectacular with an
elephantine pace, shot in Utah
because allegedly it looked more like
Palestine than Palestine did. All
frightfully elegant and reverent, but
totally unmoving, partly because of
the fatal casting of stars in bit parts.
(John Wayne looks in merely to say
'Truly this man was the son of
God.')

w James Lee Barrett, George
Stevens, from various sources
d George Stevens *ph* William C.
Mellor, Loyal Griggs *m* Alfred
Newman *ad* Richard Day, William
Creber

Max Von Sydow, Dorothy McGuire,
Claude Rains, Jose Ferrer, David
McCallum, Charlton Heston, Sidney
Poitier, Donald Pleasence, Roddy
McDowall, Gary Raymond, Carroll
Baker, Pat Boone, Van Heflin, Sal
Mineo, Shelley Winters, Ed Wynn,
John Wayne, Telly Savalas, Angela
Lansbury, Joseph Schildkraut,
Victor Buono, Nehemiah Persoff

'George Stevens was once
described as a water buffalo of film

art. What this film more precisely suggests is a dinosaur.'—*MFB*

'God is unlucky in *The Greatest Story Ever Told*. His only begotten son turns out to be a bore . . . the photography is inspired mainly by Hallmark Cards . . . as the Hallelujah Chorus explodes around us stereophonically and stereotypically it becomes clear that Lazarus was not so much raised from the tomb as blasted out of it. As for pacing, the picture does not let you forget a single second of its four hours.'—*John Simon*

'No more than three minutes have elapsed before we suspect that Stevens' name and fame have been purchased by the Hallmark Greeting Card Company, and that what we are looking at is really a lengthy catalogue of greeting cards for 1965—for Those Who Care Enough to Send the Very Best.'—*Stanley Kauffmann*

'Who but an audience of diplomats could sit through this thing? As the picture ponderously unrolled it was mainly irritation that kept me awake.'—*Shana Alexander*, *Life*

'If the subject-matter weren't sacred, we would be responding to the picture in the most charitable way by laughing at it from start to finish.'—*Brendan Gill*, *New Yorker*

'A big windy bore.'—*Bruce Williamson*, *Playboy*

† The film was originally released at 4 hours 20 minutes. Subsequent versions were at 3 hours 58 minutes, 3 hours 17 minutes, 2 hours 27 minutes and 2 hours 7 minutes.

AAN: William C. Mellor, Loyal Griggs; Alfred Newman

Greed
US 1923   110m (24 fps)
bw   silent
Metro-Goldwyn (Erich Von Stroheim, Irving Thalberg)
An ex-miner dentist kills his avaricious wife. Later in Death Valley he also kills her lover, but is bound to him by handcuffs.

This much-discussed film is often cited as its director's greatest folly: the original version ran eight hours. Re-edited by June Mathis, it retains considerable power sequence by sequence, but is necessarily disjointed in development. However, it must be seen to be appreciated.

wd Erich Von Stroheim, *novel* McTeague by Frank Norris *ph* Ben Reynolds, William Daniels, Ernest B. Schoedsack *ad* Richard Day, Cedric Gibbons, Erich Von Stroheim

Gibson Gowland, Zasu Pitts, *Jean Hersholt*, Chester Conklin, Dale Fuller

'The end leaves one with an appalling sense of human waste, of futility, of the drabness and cruelty of lives stifled by genteel poverty. Every character in the film is overwhelmed by it.'—*Gavin Lambert*

'Von Stroheim is a genius—*Greed* established that beyond all doubt—but he is badly in need of a stopwatch.'—*Robert E. Sherwood*

† In 1972 Herman G. Weinberg published a complete screenplay with 400 stills.

†† The original length at the première is said to have been 420m.

'Their badge of honour was a green beret, and it said they had lived it all . . . the night jumps, the ambushes, the hand-to-hand combat, and the long nights of terror they filled with courage!'

The Green Berets
US 1968   141m
Technicolor   Panavision
Warner / Batjac (Michael Wayne)
After extensive training, two tough army detachments see service in Vietnam.
Overlong actioner criticized for unquestioningly accepting the Vietnam cause; in itself violent, exhausting and dull.

w James Lee Barrett, *novel* Robin Moore *d* John Wayne, Ray Kellogg *ph* Winton C. Hoch *m* Miklos Rozsa

John Wayne, David Janssen, Jim
Hutton, Aldo Ray, Raymond St
Jacques, Jack Soo, Bruce Cabot,
Patrick Wayne, Irene Tsu, Jason
Evers, Luke Askew

'Propaganda as crude as this can
only do damage to its
cause.'—*David Wilson*

'A film best handled from a
distance and with a pair of
tongs.'—*Penelope Gilliatt*

Green for Danger

GB 1946 93m bw
Rank/Individual (Frank
Launder, Sidney Gilliat)

A mysterious murderer strikes on
the operating table at a wartime
emergency hospital.

Classic comedy-thriller, with serious
detection balanced by excellent jokes
and performances, also by moments
of fright.

*w Sidney Gilliat, Claud Gurney,
novel* Christianna Brand *d Sidney
Gilliat ph* Wilkie Cooper *m* William
Alwyn

*Alastair Sim, Sally Gray, Rosamund
John, Trevor Howard, Leo Genn,
Megs Jenkins, Judy Campbell,*
Ronald Ward, Moore Marriott

'Slick, witty and consistently
entertaining.'—*Daily Telegraph*

'Launder and Gilliat have told an
exciting story excitingly.'—*Times*

The Green Pastures

US 1936 93m bw
Warner (Henry Blanke)

Old Testament stories as seen
through simple-minded negro eyes.

Though recently attacked as setting
back the cause of black
emancipation, this is a brilliantly
sympathetic and humorous film, very
cunningly adapted for the screen in a
series of dramatic scenes which make
the material work even better than it
did on the stage

w Marc Connelly, from his play and
stories by Roark Bradford
d William Keighley, *Marc Connelly
ph* Hal Mohr *m* Erich Wolfgang
Korngold

*Rex Ingram, Oscar Polk, Eddie
Anderson,* Frank Wilson, George
Reed

'I imagine God has a sense of
humour, and I imagine that He is
delighted with *The Green
Pastures.'—Don Herold*

'That disturbance around the
Music Hall yesterday was the noise
of shuffling queues in Sixth Avenue
and the sound of motion picture
critics dancing in the street.'—*Bosley
Crowther, New York Times*

'This is as good a religious play as
one is likely to get in this age from a
practised New York
writer.'—*Graham Greene*

Gregory's Girl

GB 1980 91m colour
Lake/NFFC/STV (Davina
Belling, Clive Parsons)

In a Scottish new town, a school
footballer becomes aware of sex.

Curiously diverting comedy peopled
by dreamers but handicapped by
impenetrable accents. An
unexpected world-wide success.

wd Bill Forsyth *ph* Michael Coulter
m Colin Tully

Gordon John Sinclair, Dee
Hepburn, Jake D'Arcy, Claire
Grogan

BFA: best script

Gremlins

US 1984 106m
Technicolor
Warner/Amblin (Michael Finnell)

Small furry creatures called mogwais
prove to be immensely prolific and
dangerous when wet.

Juvenile horror comic, a kind of
deliberate inversion of *E.T.* Slow to
start, and a little too knowingly
nasty, with variable special effects;
but a pretty hot commercial success.

w Chris Columbus *d* Joe Dante
(with Steven Spielberg as a
presumably involved producer)
ph John Hora *m* Jerry Goldsmith
gremlin designer Chris Walas
ed Tina Hirsch

Zach Galligan, Phoebe Cates, Hoyt

Axton, Polly Holliday, Keye Luke, Scott Brady, Edward Andrews

The Group

🎬🎬 US 1966 152m De Luxe
☓ UA/Famous Artists (Sidney Buchman)

The subsequent love lives of a group of girls who graduate from Vassar in 1933.

Patchy but generally fascinating series of interwoven sketches and character studies, with mainly tragic overtones; good attention to period detail and dazzling array of new talent.

w Sidney Buchman, novel Mary McCarthy d Sidney Lumet ph Boris Kaufman m Charles Gross pd Gene Callahan

Joanna Pettet, Candice Bergen, *Jessica Walter, Joan Hackett*, Elizabeth Hartman, Mary Robin-Redd, *Kathleen Widdoes*, Shirley Knight, Larry Hagman, *Hal Holbrook, Robert Emhardt*, Robert Mulligan, James Congdon, James Broderick

'Although it is a strange, inclusive, no-holds-barred movie that runs the gamut from scenes that are almost soap-operaish, to amusing scenes that are almost satire, to outrageously frank scenes that are almost voyeuristic, it is still greatly exhilarating while it provokes thought and pushes the viewer into examining his own conscience.'—*Philip T. Hartung, Commonweal*

Guess Who's Coming to Dinner

🎬 US 1967 112m
☓ Technicolor

Columbia/Stanley Kramer

A well-to-do San Francisco girl announces that she is going to marry a black man, and her parents find they are less broad-minded than they thought.

The problem picture that isn't really, since everyone is so nice and the prospective bridegroom is so eligible. It looks like a photographed play, but isn't based on one; the set

is unconvincing; but the acting is a dream.

w William Rose d Stanley Kramer ph Sam Leavitt md Frank de Vol pd Robert Clatworthy

Spencer Tracy, Katharine Hepburn, Katharine Houghton (Hepburn's niece), *Sidney Poitier*, Cecil Kellaway, Roy E. Glenn Snr, Beah Richards, Isabell Sanford, Virginia Christine

'Suddenly everybody's caught up in a kind of integrated drawing-room comedy, and unable to decide whether there's anything funny in it or not.'—*Ann Birstein, Vogue*

'A load of embarrassing rubbish. In the circumstances there is little that director Stanley Kramer can do but see that his camera plod from room to room and make the most of people sitting down and getting up again.'—*Penelope Mortimer*

'What Rose and Kramer have done is to create a number of elaborate Aunt Sallies, arrange them in attractive patterns, and dispose of them with the flick of a feather.'—*Basil Wright, 1972*

'Mendacious and sanctimonious drivel.'—*John Simon*

AA: William Rose; Katharine Hepburn
AAN: best picture; Stanley Kramer; Frank de Vol; Spencer Tracy; Cecil Kellaway; Beah Richards

The Guinea Pig

🎬🎬 GB 1948 97m bw
☓ Pilgrim (The Boultings)

US title: *The Outsider*

The first poor boy to win a scholarship to a famous public school has a hard time.

Enjoyable though unrealistic school drama with chief interest centring on the staff. A rude word ('kick up the arse') ensured its popularity.

w Bernard Miles, Warren Chetham Strode, from the latter's play d Roy Boulting ph Gilbert Taylor m John Wooldridge

Richard Attenborough, *Robert Flemyng, Cecil Trouncer*, Sheila Sim, Bernard Miles, Joan Hickson

Gulliver's Travels

🏹☺ US 1939 75m Technicolor
(Paramount) Max Fleischer

Animated cartoon version which
invents a Romeo-Juliet romance
between Lilliput and Blefuscu and
has the usual trouble with romantic
humans. At the time it represented a
genuine challenge to Disney, but has
not worn well in terms of pace or
inventiveness.
Fleischer made one more feature
cartoon, *Mr Bug Goes to Town*.

d Dave Fleischer m Victor Young
songs Ralph Rainger, Leo Robin

'Effective entertainment, but may
not reach the grosses of *Snow
White*.'—*Variety*

AAN: song 'Faithful Forever';
Victor Young

Gunfight at the OK Corral

🏹 US 1957 122m
Technicolor Vistavision
Paramount / Hal Wallis

Wyatt Earp and Doc Holliday defeat
the Clanton Gang.
Watchable, ambitious, but vaguely
disappointing super-western.

w Leon Uris d John Sturges
ph Charles B. Lang m Dmitri
Tiomkin

Burt Lancaster, *Kirk Douglas*, Jo
Van Fleet, Rhonda Fleming, John
Ireland, Frank Faylen, Kenneth
Tobey, Earl Holliman.

'Carefully and lavishly mounted,
but overlong and
overwrought.'—*John Cutts*

'His only friend was his gun—his
only refuge, a woman's heart!'
The Gunfighter

🏹 US 1950 84m bw
TCF (Nunnally Johnson)

A gunfighter fails to shake off his
past.
Downbeat, small-scale but very
careful adult western set in a
believable community.

w William Bowers, William Sellers
d Henry King ph Arthur Miller
m Alfred Newman

Gregory Peck, Helen Westcott,
Millard Mitchell, Jean Parker, Karl

Malden, Skip Homeier, Mae Marsh

'Preserves throughout a
respectable level of intelligence and
invention.'—*Lindsay Anderson*

'Not merely a good western, a
good film.'—*Richard Mallett, Punch*

'The movie is done in cold, quiet
tones of gray, and every object in
it—faces, clothing, a table, the
hero's heavy moustache—is given an
air of uncompromising authenticity,
suggesting those dim photographs of
the nineteenth-century
west . . .'—*Robert Warshow, The
Immediate Experience*

AAN: original story (William
Bowers)

'Thrills for a thousand movies
plundered for one mighty
show!'
'Romance aflame through
dangerous days and nights of
terror! In a land where anything
can happen—most of all to a
beautiful girl alone!'
Gunga Din

🏹 US 1939 117m bw
RKO (George Stevens)

Three cheerful army veterans meet
adventure on the North-West
Frontier.
Rousing period actioner with
comedy asides, one of the most
entertaining of its kind ever made.

w Joel Sayre, Fred Guiol, Ben
Hecht, Charles MacArthur,
poem Rudyard Kipling d George
Stevens ph Joseph H. August
m Alfred Newman ad Van Nest
Polglase

Gary Grant, *Victor McLaglen*,
Douglas Fairbanks Jnr, *Sam Jaffe*,
Eduardo Ciannelli, Joan Fontaine,
Montagu Love, Robert Coote, Cecil
Kellaway, Abner Biberman,
Lumsden Hare.

'One of the big money pictures
this year . . . will recoup plenty at
the box office window.'—*Variety*

'One of the most enjoyable
nonsense-adventure movies of all
time.'—*Pauline Kael, 1968*

'Bravura is the exact word for the
performances, and Stevens'

composition and cutting of the fight sequences is particularly stunning.'—*NFT, 1973*

The Guns of Navarone

GB 1961   157m
Technicolor   Cinemascope
Columbia / Carl Foreman (Cecil F. Ford)

In 1943 a sabotage team is sent to destroy two giant guns on a Turkish Island.

Ambitiously produced Boy's Own Paper heroics, with lots of noise and self-sacrifice; intermittently exciting but bogged down by philosophical chat.

w Carl Foreman, *novel* Alistair Maclean *d* J. Lee-Thompson *ph* Oswald Morris *m* Dmitri Tiomkin *ad* Geoffrey Drake

Gregory Peck, David Niven, Stanley Baker, Anthony Quinn, Anthony Quayle, James Darren, Gia Scala, James Robertson Justice, Richard Harris, Irene Papas, Bryan Forbes

  'A desperate imbalance: the moral arguments cut into the action without extending it.'—*Penelope Houston*

AAN: best picture; Carl Foreman; J. Lee-Thompson; Dmitri Tiomkin

'The girl who became the greatest show in show business!'

Gypsy

US 1962   149m
Technirama
Warner (Mervyn Le Roy)

The early days of stripteaser Gypsy Rose Lee, and the exploits of her ambitious mother.

A vaudeville musical that is nowhere near raucous enough, or brisk enough, for its subject, and is miscast into the bargain. The songs are great, but not here: Miss Russell is as boring as an electric drill in a role that should have been reserved for Ethel Merman.

w Leonard Spiegelgass, *book* Arthur Laurents *d* Mervyn Le Roy *m Jule Styne ly Stephen Sondheim ph* Harry Stradling *md* Frank Perkins *ad* John Beckman

Rosalind Russell, Natalie Wood, *Karl Malden*, James Milhollin

AAN: Harry Stradling; Frank Perkins

H

Hail the Conquering Hero
US 1944 101m bw
Paramount (Preston Sturges)

An army reject is accidentally thought a hero when he returns to his small-town home.

Skilfully orchestrated Preston Sturges romp, slightly marred by an overdose of sentiment but featuring his repertory of comic actors at full pitch.

wd Preston Sturges ph John Seitz m Werner Heymann

Eddie Bracken, William Demarest, Ella Raines, Franklin Pangborn, Elizabeth Patterson, Raymond Walburn, Alan Bridge, Georgia Caine, Freddie Steele, Jimmy Conlin, Torben Meyer

'Mob scenes, rough-houses and sharply serious passages are played for all the pantomime they are worth . . . one of the happiest, heartiest comedies in a twelvemonth.'—*Otis L. Guernsey Jnr*

'First rate entertainment, a pattern of film making, not to be missed.'—*Richard Mallett, Punch*

'The energy, the verbal density, the rush of Americana and the congestion seen periodically in *The Miracle of Morgan's Creek* stagger the senses in this newest film.'—*James Ursini*

'It tells a story so touching, so chock-full of human frailties and so rich in homely detail that it achieves a reality transcending the limitations of its familiar slapstick.'—*James Agee*

'He uses verbal as well as visual slapstick, and his comic timing is so quirkily effective that the dialogue keeps popping off like a string of firecrackers.'—*New Yorker, 1977*

AAN: Preston Sturges (as writer)

Hallelujah!
US 1929 106m bw
MGM (King Vidor)

A black cotton worker accidentally kills a man and decides to become a preacher.

Hollywood's unique black melodrama now seems stilted because of its early talkie technique, but at the time its picture of negro life had a freshness and truth which was not reached again for thirty years.

w Wanda Tuchock, King Vidor d King Vidor ph Gordon Avil md Eva Jessye

Daniel Haynes, Nina Mae McKinney, William Fountaine, Fannie Belle De Knight, Harry Gray

'The central theme became swamped by the forty or so singing sequences of folk songs, spirituals, baptism wails, love songs and blues.'—*Peter Noble, The Negro in Films*

AAN: King Vidor

Hallelujah, I'm a Bum
US 1933 80m bw
Lewis Milestone

GB titles: *Hallelujah I'm a Tramp; Lazy Bones*

The leader of a group of Central Park tramps smartens himself up for love of a lady who lost her memory. When she recovers it, he becomes a tramp again.

Curious whimsy expressed mainly in recitative, with embarrassing stretches relieved by moments of visual and verbal inspiration. Very typical of the Depression, with the tramps knowing best how life should be lived.

w S. N. Behrman, Ben Hecht d Lewis Milestone ph Lucien Andriot ad Richard Day rhymes/m/ly Richard Rodgers, Lorenz Hart

Al Jolson, *Harry Langdon*, Madge Evans, Frank Morgan, Chester Conklin

Songs: 'Hallelujah I'm a Bum'; 'You Are Too Beautiful'; 'I'll Do It Again'; 'What Do You Want with Money?'; 'I've Got to Get Back to New York'

'It must rise or fall by Al Jolson's rep . . . it won't bore, once in, but it's not a mass play picture.'—*Variety*

'Given a scene or two of high sentiment, he still has you wrapped round his little finger.'—*The Times, 1973*

Halloween
US 1978   91m
Metrocolor   Panavision
Falcon International (Irwin Yablans)

In a small Illinois town, a mad killer escapes from the asylum.
Single-minded shocker with virtually no plot, just a succession of bloody attacks in semi-darkness. Very well done if you like that kind of thing, though the final suggestion of the supernatural is rather baffling.

w John Carpenter, Debra Hill, *d* John Carpenter *ph* Dean Cundy *m* John Carpenter *pd* Tommy Wallace

Donald Pleasence, Jamie Lee Curtis, Nancy Loomis, P. J. Soles

'One of the cinema's most perfectly engineered devices for saying Boo!'—*Richard Combs, MFB*

Hamlet
GB 1948   142m   bw
Rank/Two Cities (Laurence Olivier)

Prince Hamlet takes too long making up his mind to revenge his father's death.
The play is sharply cut, then time is wasted having the camera prowl pointlessly along gloomy corridors . . . but much of the acting is fine, some scenes compel, and the production has a splendid brooding power.

w William Shakespeare *d* Laurence Olivier *ph* Desmond Dickinson *pd* Roger Furse *m* William Walton *ad* Carmen Dillon

Laurence Olivier, Eileen Herlie, Basil Sydney, Jean Simmons, Felix Aylmer, Norman Wooland, Terence Morgan, *Stanley Holloway,* Peter Cushing, Esmond Knight, Anthony Quayle, Harcourt Williams, John Laurie, Niall MacGinnis, Patrick Troughton

'Be you 9 or 90, a PhD or just plain Joe, *Hamlet* is the movie of the year.'—*Washington Times*

AA: best picture; Laurence Olivier (as actor)
AAN: Laurence Olivier (as director); William Walton; Jean Simmons

Hannah and her Sisters
US 1985   106m
Technicolor
Orion/Charles R. Joffe, Jack Rollins (Robert Greenhut)

Relationships intermingle for a New York family over a two-year period between Thanksgiving dinners.
Even though it has nowhere in particular to go, and certain scenes are over the top, this is a brilliantly assembled and thoroughly enjoyable mélange of fine acting and New Yorkish one-liners, with particularly sharp editing and a nostalgic music score.

w,d Woody Allen *ph* Carlo di Palma *m* popular and classical extracts *pd* Stuart Wurtzel *ed* Susan E. Morse

Woody Allen, Mia Farrow, Dianne Wiest, Michael Caine, Carrie Fisher, Barbara Hershey, Maureen O'Sullivan, Lloyd Nolan, Max von Sydow, Daniel Stern, Sam Waterston, Tony Roberts

'A loosely knit canvas of Manhattan interiors and exteriors.'—*Sight and Sound*
'One of Woody Allen's great films.'—*Variety*

The Happiest Days of Your Life

GB 1950   81m   bw
British Lion / Individual (Frank Launder)

A ministry mistake billets a girls' school on a boys' school.

Briskly handled version of a semi-classic post-war farce, with many familiar talents in excellent form.

w Frank Launder, John Dighton, *play* John Dighton   *d* Frank Launder   *ph* Stan Pavey   *m* Mischa Spoliansky

Alastair Sim, Margaret Rutherford, Joyce Grenfell, Richard Wattis, Edward Rigby, Guy Middleton, Muriel Aked, John Bentley, Bernadette O'Farrell

'Absolutely first rate fun.'—*Richard Mallett, Punch*

'Launder couldn't have knocked another laugh out of the situation if he'd used a hockey stick.'—*Sunday Express*

'The best mixed comedy pairing since Groucho Marx and Margaret Dumont.'—*Sunday Chronicle*

A Hard Day's Night

GB 1964   85m   bw
(UA) Proscenium (Walter Shenson)

Harassed by their manager and Paul's grandpa, the Beatles embark from Liverpool by train for a London TV show.

Comic fantasia with music; an enormous commercial success with the director trying every cinematic gag in the book, it led directly to all the kaleidoscopic swinging London spy thrillers and comedies of the later sixties, and so has a lot to answer for; but at the time it was a sweet breath of fresh air, and the Beatles even seemed willing and likeable.

w Alun Owen   *d* Richard Lester   *ph* Gilbert Taylor   *songs* The Beatles   *md* George Martin

The Beatles, Wilfrid Brambell, Norman Rossington, *Victor Spinetti*

'A fine conglomeration of madcap clowning . . . with such a dazzling use of camera that it tickles the intellect and electrifies the nerves.'—*Bosley Crowther*

'All technology was enlisted in the service of the gag, and a kind of nuclear gagmanship exploded.'—*John Simon*

AAN: Alun Owen; George Martin

Hard to Handle

US 1933   75m   bw
Warner (Robert Lord)

The success story of a cheerful public relations man.

Punchy star comedy with interesting sidelights on the social fads of the early thirties including marathon dancing, get-rich-quick schemes and grapefruit diets.

w Wilson Mizner, Robert Lord   *d* Mervyn Le Roy   *ph* Barney McGill

James Cagney, Ruth Donnelly, Mary Brian, Allen Jenkins, Claire Dodd

'Hokum this time instead of the realism that boosted him to stardom.'—*Variety*

'A violent, slangy, down-to-the-pavement affair which has many a mirthful moment.'—*Mordaunt Hall*

Harold Lloyd's World of Comedy

US 1962   97m   bw
Harold Lloyd

Generous clips from the comic climaxes of Lloyd's best silent and sound comedies including *Safety Last, The Freshman, Hot Water, Why Worry, Girl Shy, Professor Beware, Movie Crazy* and *Feet First.* As Lloyd's work lends itself well to extract, this can hardly fail to be a superb anthology capsuling the appeal of one of America's greatest silent comedians. The timing is just perfect.

w Walter Scharf   *commentary* Art Ross

Harvey

US 1950   104m   bw
U-I (John Beck)

A middle-aged drunk has an imaginary white rabbit as his friend, and his sister tries to have him certified.

An amiably batty play with splendid lines is here transferred virtually intact to the screen and survives superbly thanks to understanding by all concerned, though the star is as yet too young for a role which he later made his own.

w Mary Chase (with Oscar Brodney) from her play *d Henry Koster ph* William Daniels *m* Frank Skinner

James Stewart, Josephine Hull, Victoria Horne, Peggy Dow, Cecil Kellaway, Charles Drake, *Jesse White,* Nana Bryant, Wallace Ford

VETA LOUISE (Josephine Hull): 'Myrtle Mae, you have a lot to learn, and I hope you never learn it.'

ELWOOD (James Stewart): 'I've wrestled with reality for 35 years, and I'm happy, doctor. I finally won out over it.'

ELWOOD: 'Harvey and I have things to do . . . we sit in the bars . . . have a drink or two . . . and play the juke box. Very soon the faces of the other people turn towards me and they smile. They say: "We don't know your name, mister, but you're all right, all right." Harvey and I warm ourselves in these golden moments. We came as strangers—soon we have friends. They come over. They sit with us. They drink with us. They talk to us. They tell us about the great big terrible things they've done and the great big wonderful things they're going to do. Their hopes, their regrets. Their loves, their hates. All very large, because nobody ever brings anything small into a bar. Then I introduce them to Harvey, and he's bigger and grander than anything they can offer me. When they leave, they leave impressed. The same people seldom come back.'

ELWOOD (describing his first meeting with Harvey): 'I'd just helped Ed Hickey into a taxi. Ed had been mixing his drinks, and I

felt he needed conveying. I started to walk down the street when I heard a voice saying: "Good evening, Mr Dowd". I turned, and there was this big white rabbit leaning against a lamp-post. Well, I thought nothing of that! Because when you've lived in a town as long as I've lived in this one, you get used to the fact that everybody knows your name . . .'

AA: Josephine Hull
AAN: James Stewart

The Harvey Girls

US 1946   101m Technicolor
MGM (Arthur Freed)

A chain of 19th-century restaurants hires young ladies to go out west as waitresses.

Sprightly if overlong musical based on fact; a good example of an MGM middle-budget extravaganza.

w Edmund Beloin, Nathaniel Curtis *d* George Sidney *ph* George Folsey *md* Lennie Hayton *songs* Johnny Mercer, Harry Warren

Judy Garland, Ray Bolger, John Hodiak, Preston Foster, Virginia O'Brien, Angela Lansbury, Marjorie Main, Chill Wills, Kenny Baker, Selena Royle

'Anybody who did anything at all in America up to 1900 is liable to be made into a film by MGM.'—*Richard Winnington*

'An abundance of chromatic spectacle and an uncommonly good score.'—*New York Times*

'A perfect example of what Hollywood can do with its vast resources when it wants to be really showy.'—*New York Herald Tribune*

AA: song 'On the Atcheson, Topeka and the Santa Fe'
AAN: Lennie Hayton

Hatari!

US 1962   158m Technicolor
Paramount/Malabar (Howard Hawks)

International hunters in Tanganyika catch game to send to zoos.

Plotless adventure film with good animal sequences but no shape or suspense; a typical folly of its director, whose chief interest is seeing smart men and women in tough action. The elephants steal this overlong show.

w Leigh Brackett *d* Howard Hawks *ph Russell Harlan m Henry Mancini*

John Wayne, Elsa Martinelli, Red Buttons, Hardy Kruger

'Hawks was taking his friends and cast and crew on a trip he wanted to make personally, and the film is both the incidental excuse for and the record of that experience.'—*Joseph Gelmis, 1970*

AAN: Russell Harlan

Hawaii

US 1966   186m   De Luxe Panavision

UA/Mirisch (Lewis J. Rachmil)

In 1820 a pious Yale divinity student becomes a missionary to the Hawaiian islands.

Ambitious attempt to contrast naïve dogma with native innocence, ruined by badly handled sub-plots, storms, a childbirth sequence and other distractions, all fragments of an immense novel. Heavy going.

w Daniel Taradash, Dalton Trumbo, *novel* James A. Michener *d* George Roy Hill *ph* Russell Harlan *m* Elmer Bernstein *2nd unit* Richard Talmadge *pd* Cary Odell

Max Von Sydow, Julie Andrews, Richard Harris, *Jocelyn La Garde*, Carroll O'Connor, Torin Thatcher, Gene Hackman

'Consistently intelligent humanism gives it a certain stature among the wide screen spectacles.'—*Brenda Davies*

AAN: cinematography; Jocelyn La Garde

Hearts of the World

US 1918   80m (24 fps) bw   silent

Artcraft (David Wark Griffith)

Of various people involved in World War I, the patriotic and dutiful ones come out best.

Rather dim patriotic propaganda made by Griffith at the request of the British government and using a good deal of newsreel as well as reconstruction. The personal stories are on the predictable side.

wd David Wark Griffith *ph* Billy Bitzer *ed* James Smith

Lillian Gish, Dorothy Gish, Robert Harron, Josephine Crowell, Erich Von Stroheim, Noel Coward

'Here we have an art of pure emotion which can go beneath thought, beneath belief, beneath ideals, down to the brute fact of emotional psychology, and make a man or a woman who has hated war, all war, even this war, feel the surge of group emotion, group loyalty and group hate.'—*Kenneth MacGowan, The New Republic (1918)*

† For the screenplay credit Griffith used the pseudonym of Gaston de Tolignac

Heat and Dust

GB 1982   130m   colour Merchant Ivory Productions (Ismail Merchant)

A woman discovers India's past through her great-aunt's letters. Much praised by those who admire the work of this team, but found (as usual) mildly bewildering by others, this has at least a large enough budget to produce interest in its historically re-created backgrounds if not its complex plot structure.

w Ruth Prawer Jhabvala from her novel *d* James Ivory *ph* Walter Lassally *m* Richard Robbins

Julie Christie, Christopher Cazenove, Shashi Kapoor, Greta Scacchi, Nickolas Grace, Jennifer Kendal, Julian Glover, Susan Fleetwood

'A likeable patchwork of concepts and cameos.'—*Philip Strick, MFB*

BFA: screenplay

Heaven Can Wait
☻ US 1943   112m
Technicolor
TCF (Ernst Lubitsch)

On arrival in Hades, an elderly
playboy reports his peccadilloes to
Satan, who sends him Upstairs.

Charming period piece with fantasy
bookends; the essence of the piece is
its evocation of American society in
the nineties, and in its director's
waspish way with a funny scene.

*w Samson Raphaelson,
play* Birthday by Lazlo Bus-Fekete
d Ernst Lubitsch *ph* Edward
Cronjager *m* Alfred Newman
ad James Basevi, Leland Fuller

Don Ameche, Gene Tierney, *Laird
Cregar,* Charles Coburn, *Marjorie
Main,* Eugene Pallette, *Allyn Joslyn,*
Spring Byington, Signe Hasso, Louis
Calhern

'It was so good I half believed
Lubitsch could still do as well as he
ever did, given half a
chance.'—*James Agee*

AAN: best picture; Ernst Lubitsch;
Edward Cronjager

'What one loves about life are the
   things that fade . . .'
'The most talked-about film of the
   decade!'
'The only thing greater than their
   passion for America . . . was
   their passion for each other!'

Heaven's Gate
▒ US 1980   219m
Technicolor
UA / Michael Cimino

1890 Wyoming: established
cattlemen fight immigrants.

Totally incoherent, showy western
which was lambasted by the critics
and quickly withdrawn. A vital
turning point in Hollywood policy,
hopefully marking the last time a
whiz kid with one success behind
him is given a blank cheque to
indulge in self-abuse.

wd Michael Cimino *ph* Vilmos
Zsigmond *m* David Mansfield

Kris Kristofferson, Christopher
Walken, John Hurt, Sam Waterston,
Brad Dourif, Isabelle Huppert,
Joseph Cotten, Jeff Bridges

'The trade must marvel that
directors now have such power that
no one, in the endless months since
work on the picture began, was able
to impose some structure and
sense.'—*Variety*

'All too much and not
enough.'—*Sunday Times*

'A film which John Ford would
have brought in on time and on
budget with quite as much social,
critical and political comment—and
much more entertainment
value.'—*Margaret Hinxman, Daily
Mail*

'It fails so completely that you
might suspect Mr Cimino sold his
soul to the devil to obtain the success
of *The Deer Hunter*, and the devil
has just come around to
collect.'—*Vincent Canby, New York
Times*

Heimat
❀❀ West Germany 1984   924m
✗ part colour
Edgar Reitz / WDR / SFB
aka: *Homeland*

An epically conceived story of life in
a German village between 1919 and
1982.

Essentially a superior soap opera
with pretensions of grandeur, this
beautifully photographed serial has
moments of magic amid much that is
merely pretentious and unexplained.
Despite the symbolism and the irony
(a village idiot is ever present), an
eager if arty audience found that it
had much to say, though no one
could explain its lapses from colour
to black-and-white and back again.

w Edgar Reitz, Peter Steinbach
d Edgar Reitz *ph* Gernot Roll
m Nikos Mamangakis

Marita Breuer, Michael Lesch,
Dieter Schaad, Karin Kienzler, Eva
Maria Bayerswaltes, Rüdiger
Weigang, Karin Rasenach

Hell in the Pacific

US 1969 104m
Technicolor Panavision
Cinerama / Selmur (Reuben
Bercovitch)

During World War II, an American
pilot and a Japanese naval officer
who are stranded on the same tiny
Pacific island almost become friends.

Highly artificial and pretentious
allegorical two-parter which is
occasionally well acted and good to
look at.

w Alexander Jacobs, Eric Bercovici
d John Boorman *ph* Conrad Hall
m Lalo Schifrin

Lee Marvin, Toshiro Mifune

'No real reverberation and no real
excitement, intellectual or
physical.'—*Tom Milne*

Hello Dolly

US 1969 129m De Luxe
Todd-AO
TCF / Chenault (Ernest Lehman)

In 1890 New York, a widowed
matchmaker has designs on a
wealthy grain merchant.

Generally agreeable but overblown
musical based on a slight but much
worked-over farce, fatally
compromised by the miscasting of a
too-young star: Some exhilarating
moments.

w Ernest Lehman, *musical Jerry
Herman* (*m*/*ly*) and Michael Stewart
(*book*), from *Thornton Wilder's* play
The Matchmaker *d* Gene Kelly
ph Harry Stradling *md* Lennie
Hayton, Lionel Newman *pd* John
de Cuir *ch* Michael Kidd

Barbra Streisand, Walter Matthau,
*Michael Crawford, Marianne
McAndrew*, E. J. Peaker, Tommy
Tune, David Hurst

'The film leaves an oddly negative
impression; a good deal of synthetic
effervescence . . . but very little real
vitality.'—*David Wilson*

† Carol Channing, Ginger Rogers
and Betty Grable all fought to get
the title role.

AA: music direction; art direction;
set decoration
AAN: best picture; photography

Hell's Angels

US 1930 135m bw (some
scenes in colour)
Howard Hughes

Two Americans become fliers in
World War I.

Celebrated early talkie spectacular,
with zeppelin and flying sequences
that still thrill. The dialogue is
another matter, but all told this
expensive production, first planned
as a silent, is a milestone of cinema
history.

w Howard Estabrook, Harry Behn
d Howard Hughes *ph* Tony Gaudio,
Harry Perry, E. Burton Steene
m Hugo Reisenfeld

Ben Lyon, James Hall, Jean Harlow,
John Darrow, Lucien Prival

'That it will ever pay off for its
producer is doubtful . . . he's in so
deep it can't really matter to him
now. Minus blue nose interference,
it can't miss, but it's up to the brim
with sex.'—*Variety*

'It is not great, but it is as lavish as
an eight-ring circus, and when you
leave the theatre you will know you
have seen a movie and not a tinny
reproduction of a stage show.'—*Pare
Lorentz*

† The film was reissued in 1940 in a
96m version which has not survived.

AAN: Tony Gaudio, Harry Perry,
E. Burton Steene

Hellzapoppin

US 1942 84m bw
Universal / Mayfair (Glenn
Tryon, Alex Gottlieb)

Two incompetent comics make a
picture.

Zany modification of a smash
burlesque revue; the crazy jokes are
toned down and a romantic interest
is added (and tentatively sent up).
The result is patchy but often
hilarious, and the whole is a handy
consensus of forties humour and pop
music.

w Nat Perrin, Warren Wilson *d* H.
C. Potter *ph* Woody Bredell
md Charles Previn

Ole Olsen, Chic Johnson, Hugh

Herbert, Martha Raye, Mischa Auer, Robert Paige, Jane Frazee, Shemp Howard, Elisha Cook Jnr, Richard Lane

Helpmates
☺ US 1932   20m   bw

Stan helps Ollie clean up after a wild party while the wife was away. A brilliant succession of catastrophe gags in the stars' best tradition. Laurel and Hardy. Written by H. M. Walker; directed by James Parrott; for Hal Roach.

Henry V
☺☺ GB 1944   137m
Technicolor
Rank/Two Cities (Laurence Olivier)

Shakespeare's historical play is seen in performance at the Globe Theatre in 1603; as it develops, the scenery becomes more realistic.

Immensely stirring, experimental and almost wholly successful production of Shakespeare on film, sturdy both in its stylization and its command of more conventional cinematic resources for the battle.

w Laurence Olivier, Alan Dent, play William Shakespeare d Laurence Olivier ph Robert Krasker m William Walton ad Paul Sheriff

Laurence Olivier, Robert Newton, Leslie Banks, Esmond Knight, Renée Asherson, George Robey, Leo Genn, Ernest Thesiger, Ivy St Helier, Ralph Truman, Harcourt Williams, Max Adrian, Valentine Dyall, Felix Aylmer, John Laurie, Roy Emerton

'His production—it was his first time out as a director—is a triumph of colour, music, spectacle, and soaring heroic poetry, and, as actor, he brings lungs, exultation, and a bashful wit to the role.'—Pauline Kael, 70s

AAN: best picture; William Walton; Laurence Olivier (as actor)

Here Comes Mr Jordan
🎬 US 1941   93m   bw
Columbia (Everett Riskin)

A prizefighter who is also an amateur saxophonist crashes in his private plane and goes to heaven by mistake: he was supposed to survive and live another forty years. Unfortunately when he goes back for his body it has been cremated, so he has to find another one, recently deceased . . .

Weird heavenly fantasy which succeeded because of its novelty and because heaven in wartime was a comforting vision. As a movie taken on its own merits, it suffers from illogicalities, a miscast star and a wandering plot, but scene for scene there is enough firmness and control to make it memorable. It certainly had many imitations, including Angel on My Shoulder, Down to Earth, A Guy Named Joe, Heaven Only Knows, The Horn Blows at Midnight and That's the Spirit.

w Seton I. Miller, Sidney Buchman, play Halfway to Heaven by Harry Segall d Alexander Hall ph Joseph Walker m Frederick Hollander md Morris Stoloff

Robert Montgomery, Evelyn Keyes, Rita Johnson, Claude Rains, James Gleason, Edward Everett Horton, John Emery, Donald MacBride, Halliwell Hobbes, Don Costello

'There is something about this original so sweet-spirited and earnest that it transcends its plot devices and shines through its comedic asides to become a true morality play without once becoming either preachy or mawkish.'—Kit Parker catalogue, 1980

'Audiences loved this chunk of whimsy . . . the slickly hammy Rains gives Mr Jordan a sinister gloss, as if he were involved in some heavenly racket, like smuggling Chinese.'—Pauline Kael, 70s

† Remade 1978 as Heaven Can Wait.

AA: original story (Harry Segall); script
AAN: best picture; Seton I. Miller, Sidney Buchman; Alexander Hall; Joseph Walker; Robert Montgomery; James Gleason

'When the hands point up . . . the excitement starts!'

High Noon

US 1952 85m bw
Stanley Kramer

A marshal gets no help when he determines to defend his town against revengeful badmen.

A minor western with a soft-pedalled message for the world, this turned out to be a classic simply because it was well done, with every scene and performance clearly worked out. Cinematically it was pared to the bone, and the theme tune helped.

w Carl Foreman, *story* The Tin Star by John W. Cunningham *d* Fred Zinnemann *ph* Floyd Crosby *m* Dmitri Tiomkin *singer* Tex Ritter

Gary Cooper, Grace Kelly, Thomas Mitchell, Lloyd Bridges, Katy Jurado, Otto Kruger, Lon Chaney, Henry Morgan

'The western form is used for a sneak civics lesson.'—*Pauline Kael, 70s*

'Like nearly all the Kramer productions, this is a neat, well-finished and literate piece of work, though its limitations are more conventional than most.'—*Gavin Lambert*

'A western to challenge *Stagecoach* for the all-time championship.'—*Bosley Crowther*

'A series of crisp and purposeful scenes that interpret each other like the pins on a strategist's war map.'—*Robert L. Hatch*

'It is astonishing how much of the simple western story is told visually by rapid cross-cutting.'—*Films in Review*

'Few recent westerns have gotten so much tension and excitement into the classic struggle between good and evil.'—*Life*

AA: Dmitri Tiomkin; Gary Cooper; title song (*m* Dmitri Tiomkin, *ly* Ned Washington)

AAN: best picture; Carl Foreman; Fred Zinnemann

'The blazing mountain manhunt for Killer Mad-Dog Earle!'

High Sierra

US 1941 96m bw
Warner (Hal B. Wallis, Mark Hellinger)

An ex-con gangster plans one last heist in the Californian mountains, but is mortally wounded through his involvement with two women.

Rather dreary action melodrama which gave Bogart his first real star part (after George Raft turned it down). Remade 1955 as *I Died a Thousand Times*; also in 1949 as a western, *Colorado Territory*.

w John Huston, W. R. Burnett, *novel* W. R. Burnett *d* Raoul Walsh *ph* Tony Gaudio *m* Adolph Deutsch

Humphrey Bogart, Ida Lupino, Joan Leslie, Alan Curtis, Arthur Kennedy, Henry Hull, Henry Travers, Jerome Cowan

'The last swallow, perhaps, of the gangsters' summer.'—*William Whitebait*

'Like it or not, I'll be damned if you leave before the end, or go to sleep.'—*Otis Ferguson*

'As gangster pictures go, this one has everything—speed, excitement, suspense, and that ennobling suggestion of futility which makes for irony and poetry.'—*New York Times*

'They went up like men! They came down like animals!'

The Hill

GB 1965 122m bw
MGM / Seven Arts (Kenneth Hyman)

Prisoners rebel against the harsh discipline of a British military detention centre in North Africa during World War II.

Lurid melodrama which descends fairly quickly into black farce with a number of sweaty actors outshouting each other.

Enjoyable on this level when you can hear the dialogue through the poor sound recording.

w Ray Rigby, from his TV play
d Sidney Lumet *ph* Oswald Morris
m none

Sean Connery, Harry Andrews,
Michael Redgrave, Ian Bannen,
Alfred Lynch, *Ossie Davis*, Roy
Kinnear, Jack Watson, Ian Hendry

The Hindenburg
US 1975   125m
Technicolor   Panavision
Universal / Filmmakers (Robert
Wise)

In 1937, sabotage causes the airship
Hindenburg to crash on arrival at
New York.

An extremely uninteresting guess at
the cause of this famous disaster.
The plot and dialogue are leaden,
and such actors as have more than a
couple of lines look extremely glum.
The special effects, however, are fine
despite curious blue-rinse
photographic processing.

w Nelson Gidding, *novel* Michael M.
Mooney *d* Robert Wise *ph* Robert
Surtees *pd* Edward Carfagno
sp Albert Whitlock m David Shire

George C. Scott, Anne Bancroft,
Burgess Meredith, William
Atherton, Roy Thinnes, Gig Young,
Charles Durning, Robert Clary,
René Auberjonois

'The tackiest disaster movie yet—a
cheap and chaotic collage of painted
drops, wooden actors and
not-so-special effects that manages
to make one of this century's most
sensational real-life catastrophes
seem roughly as terrifying as a badly
stubbed toe.'—*Frank Rich*

AAN: Robert Surtees

Hiroshima Mon Amour
France / Japan 1959   91m
bw
Argos / Comei / Pathé / Daiei

A French actress working in
Hiroshima falls for a Japanese
architect and remembers her tragic
love for a German soldier during the
occupation.

Jumbled mixture of flashbacks and
flashforwards which can now be
recognized as typical of this director

and on its first appearance was
hailed as a work of art in an
innovative new style.

w Marguerite Duras *d Alain
Resnais ph* Sacha Vierny, Takahashi
Michio *m* Giovanni Fusco, Georges
Delerue

Emmanuele Riva, Eiji Okada

AAN: Marguerite Duras

His Girl Friday
US 1940   92m   bw
Columbia (Howard Hawks)

A remake of *The Front Page*, with
Hildy Johnson turned into a woman.
Frantic, hilarious black farce with all
participants at their best; possibly
the fastest comedy ever filmed, and
one of the funniest.

w Charles Lederer, play The Front
Page by Charles MacArthur, Ben
Hecht *d Howard Hawks ph* Joseph
Walker *m* Sydney Cutner
md Morris Stoloff

*Rosalind Russell, Cary Grant, Ralph
Bellamy*, Gene Lockhart, Porter
Hall, *Ernest Truex*, Cliff Edwards,
*Clarence Kolb, Roscoe Karns, Frank
Jenks*, Abner Biberman, Frank
Orth, John Qualen, Helen Mack,
Billy Gilbert, Alma Kruger

'The kind of terrific verbal
slam-bang that has vanished from
current film-making.'—*New Yorker,
1975*

'One of the fastest of all movies,
from line to line and from gag to
gag.'—*Manny Farber, 1971*

'Overlapping dialogue carries the
movie along at breakneck speed;
word gags take the place of the sight
gags of silent comedy, as this
vanished race of brittle, cynical,
childish people rush around on
corrupt errands.'—*Pauline Kael,
1968*

'The main trouble is that when
they made *The Front Page* the first
time, it stayed made.'—*Otis
Ferguson*

† The Rosalind Russell role had first
been turned down by Jean Arthur,
Ginger Rogers, Claudette Colbert
and Irene Dunne.

'More morphine for Herr Goering! The greatest gangster picture of all!'

'Did Hitler kill the one woman he loved? What was Hess to Hitler?'

The Hitler Gang

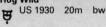 US 1944 101m bw
Paramount (B. G. De Sylva)

The rise to power of Hitler and his henchmen.

Though at the time it seemed rather like a serious cabaret turn, this fictionalization of historical fact has some good impersonations and dramatically effective scenes.

w Frances Goodrich, Albert Hackett *d* John Farrow *ph* Ernest Laszlo *m* David Buttolph

Robert Watson, Martin Kosleck (Goebbels), Victor Varconi (Hess), Luis Van Rooten (Himmler), Alexander Pope (Goering), Roman Bohnen, Ivan Triesault, Helene Thimig, Reinhold Schunzel, Sig Rumann, Alexander Granach

Hobson's Choice

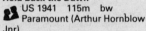 GB 1953 107m bw
British Lion / London (Norman Spencer)

In the 1890s a tyrannical Lancashire bootmaker is brought to heel by his plain-speaking daughter and her simple-minded husband.

Brilliantly played version of a famous working-class comedy, memorably set and photographed; one regrets only the slight decline of the predictable third act.

w Norman Spencer, Wynard Browne, *play* Harold Brighouse *d* David Lean *ph* Jack Hildyard *m* Malcolm Arnold *ad* Wilfrid Shingleton

Charles Laughton, *Brenda de Banzie*, *John Mills*, Richard Wattis, Helen Haye, Daphne Anderson, Prunella Scales

† Previously filmed in 1931 by Thomas Bentley for BIP from a screenplay by Frank Launder, with James Harcourt, Viola Lyel and Frank Pettingell.

Hog Wild

US 1930 20m bw

Stan helps Ollie to put a radio aerial on the roof of his house. Brilliantly sustained slapstick makes this one of the best star comedies of Laurel and Hardy. Written by H. M. Walker and Leo McCarey; directed by James Parrott; for Hal Roach.

'Master of love! He is to all women what each desires him to be!'

Hold Back the Dawn

US 1941 115m bw
Paramount (Arthur Hornblow Jnr)

A would-be immigrant into the US via Mexico marries a schoolteacher he does not love.

Surprisingly effective romantic melodrama with a nice style and some mordant lines in the script.

w Charles Brackett, Billy Wilder *d* Mitchell Leisen *ph* Leo Tover *m* Victor Young

Charles Boyer, Olivia de Havilland, Paulette Goddard, Victor Francen, Walter Abel, Curt Bois, Rosemary de Camp, Nestor Paiva, Mitchell Leisen

'All those years with all the others I closed my eyes and thought of you.'—*sample dialogue spoken by Paulette Goddard*

'It has all the vitamins for mass popular appeal.'—*Variety*

† The story is told by Boyer to Mitchell Leisen on a film set where he has just shot a scene from *I Wanted Wings*.

AAN: best picture; Charles Brackett, Billy Wilder; Leo Tover; Victor Young; Olivia de Havilland

'So daring—so tender—so human—so true—that everyone in love will want to see it!'

Holiday

US 1938 93m bw
Columbia (Everett Riskin)

GB titles: *Free to Live; Unconventional Linda*

A bright-minded rich girl steals her sister's fiancé, a struggling young lawyer.

Elegant and highly successful; still a
stage play on film, but subtly devised
to make the very most of the lines
and performances.

*w Donald Ogden Stewart d George
Cukor ph Franz Planer m Sidney
Cutner*

Katharine Hepburn, *Cary Grant*,
Doris Nolan, *Edward Everett
Horton*, *Ruth Donnelly*, *Lew Ayres*,
Henry Kolker, Binnie Barnes
  'Corking comedy . . . exhibitors
will pencil in some extra
days.'—*Variety*
  'The comedy is full of the best of
humour, edged with pathos never
allowed to drop into sentimentality.
It is played with the greatest
cheerfulness and a winning
skill.'—*Arthur Pollock, Brooklyn
Daily Eagle*
  'I suppose actually it is a neat and
sometimes elegant job, but under its
surface of too much brightness and
too many words it seems so deadly
bored and weary. Hell, save your
money and yawn at home.'—*Otis
Ferguson*
  'Played with the greatest
cheerfulness and a winning
skill.'—*Brooklyn Daily Eagle*

Holiday Inn
  US 1942   101m   bw
  Paramount (Mark Sandrich)
The joint proprietors of a roadhouse
hotel love the same girl.
Plain, simple-minded musical which
provided a peg for pleasant
performances and good numbers. It
hit the box office spot, especially as
it introduced 'White Christmas'.

*w Claude Binyon, Elmer Rice
d Mark Sandrich ph David Abel
m/ly Irving Berlin md Robert
Emmett Dolan*

Bing Crosby, Fred Astaire, Walter
Abel, Marjorie Reynolds, Virginia
Dale, Louise Beavers, Irving Bacon,
James Bell
  'The best musical drama of the
year.'—*New York Post*

† Marjorie Reynolds was dubbed by
Martha Mears.

AA: song 'White Christmas'
AAN: original story (Irving Berlin);
Robert Emmett Dolan

'It does for the motion picture
  what Alexander's Ragtime Band
  did for popular music!'
Hollywood Cavalcade
  US 1939   96m   Technicolor
  TCF (Harry Joe Brown)
The career of an old-time Hollywood
producer.
A lively first half with amusing
re-staging of early slapstick comedies
gives way depressingly to personal
melodrama, but there is enough
historical interest to preserve the
balance

*w Ernest Pascal d Irving
Cummings ph Allen M. Davey,
Ernest Palmer ad Richard Day,
Wiard B. Ihnen md Louis Silvers*

Don Ameche, Alice Faye, *J.
Edward Bromberg*, Alan Curtis,
Stuart Erwin, Jed Prouty, Buster
Keaton, Donald Meek, and the
original Keystone Kops
  'Surefire . . . should score heavily
in theatres of every type.'—*Variety*

† Alice Faye did not sing. The
Keystone Kops sequence was
directed by Mal St Clair. The
Ameche/Faye characters were
supposedly based on Mack Sennett
and Mabel Normand; Mack
Sennett's appearance under his own
name seemed to be an effort to
throw people off the scent.

The Hollywood Revue of 1929
  US 1929   116m
  part-Technicolor
MGM (Harry Rapf)
A variety show featuring most of
MGM's talent in slightly surprising
acts, this is something of a bore to sit
through but an archival must; and
just occasionally it boasts surprising
vitality.

*w Al Boasberg, Robert E. Hopkins
d Charles F. Reisner ph John
Arnold, Irving Ries, Maximillian
Fabian ch Sammy Lee
m/ly various*

Jack Benny, Buster Keaton, Joan Crawford, John Gilbert, Norma Shearer, Laurel and Hardy, Marion Davies, Marie Dressler, William Haines, Lionel Barrymore, Conrad Nagel, Bessie Love, Cliff Edwards, Nils Asther

AAN: best picture

Hombre

🐟 US 1967 111m De Luxe Panavision
TCF / Hombre Productions (Martin Ritt, Irving Ravetch)

Stagecoach passengers at the mercy of a robber are helped by a despised half-caste.

Slow but suspenseful western melodrama which works up to a couple of good climaxes but falls away in an unnecessary tragic ending.

w Irving Ravetch, Harriet Frank, novel Elmore Leonard d Martin Ritt ph James Wong Howe. m David Rose

Paul Newman, Diane Cilento, Fredric March, Richard Boone, Martin Balsam, Barbara Rush, Cameron Mitchell

'A fine array of quirkish characters . . . and some unusually literate dialogue.'—Tom Milne

'A scandalous record of low Marx at college—or life among the thirsty co-eds!'

Horse Feathers

😈 US 1932 69m bw Paramount (Herman J. Mankiewicz)

A college needs to win at football, and its corrupt new president knows just how to do it.

Possibly the Marxes' wildest yet most streamlined kaleidoscope of high jinks and irreverence, with at least one bright gag or line to the minute and lively musical interludes to boot. A classic of zany comedy.

w Bert Kalmar, Harry Ruby, S. J. Perelman, Will B. Johnstone d Norman Z. McLeod ph Ray June m / ly Bert Kalmar, Harry Ruby

Groucho, Chico, Harpo, Zeppo, Thelma Todd, Robert Greig

GROUCHO: 'You have the brain of a four-year-old child, and I'll bet he was glad to get rid of it.'

CHICO: 'There's a man outside with a big black moustache.'
GROUCHO: 'Tell him I've got one.'

GROUCHO (to Zeppo): 'You're a disgrace to our family name of Wagstaff, if such a thing is possible.'

GROUCHO: 'For years before my son
           was born
      I used to yell from night
           till morn
      Whatever it is—I'm
           against it!
      And I've been yelling
           since I first commenced
           it—I'm against it!'

'The current Marx comedy is the funniest talkie since the last Marx comedy, and the record it establishes is not likely to be disturbed until the next Marx comedy comes along. As for comparisons, I was too busy having a good time to make any.'—Philip K. Scheuer

The Hot Rock

😈 US 1972 105m De Luxe Panavision
TCF (Hal Landers, Bobby Roberts)
GB title: How to Steal a Diamond in Four Uneasy Lessons

Four crooks plan to rob the Brooklyn Museum of a priceless diamond.

Enjoyable variation on the caper theme, with relaxed comic performances and highly skilled technical back-up. It's refreshing to come across a film which hits its targets so precisely.

w William Goldman, novel Donald E. Westlake d Peter Yates ph Ed Brown m Quincy Jones

Robert Redford, George Segal, Zero Mostel, Paul Sand, Ron Leibman, Moses Gunn, William Redfield

'A funny, fast-paced, inventive and infinitely clever crime comedy, almost as if The French Connection had been remade as a piece of urban humour.'—*Michael Korda*

The Hound of the Baskervilles
US 1939 80m bw
(TCF) Gene Markey
Sherlock Holmes solves the mystery of a supernatural hound threatening the life of a Dartmoor baronet.
Basil Rathbone's first appearance as Sherlock Holmes is in a painstaking studio production which achieves good atmosphere and preserves the flavour if not the letter of the book but is let down by a curious lack of pace.

w Ernest Pascal, *novel* Arthur Conan Doyle *d* Sidney Lanfield *ph* Peverell Marley *m* Cyril Mockridge *ad* Thomas Little

Basil Rathbone, Nigel Bruce, Richard Greene, Wendy Barrie, Lionel Atwill, Morton Lowry, John Carradine, Barlowe Borland, Beryl Mercer, Ralph Forbes, E. E. Clive, Eily Malyon, Mary Gordon

'A startling mystery-chiller . . . will find many bookings on top spots of key duallers.'—*Variety*

'Lush dialogue, stagey sets and vintage supporting cast make it a delectable Hollywood period piece.'—*Judith Crist, 1980*

The House of Rothschild
US 1934 87m bw
(Technicolor sequence)
Twentieth Century (William Goetz, Raymond Griffith)
The chronicles of the famous banking family at the time of the Napoleonic Wars.
Lavish historical pageant with interesting scenes and performances.

w Nunnally Johnson, *play* George Hembert Westley *d* Alfred Werker *ph* Peverell Marley *m* Alfred Newman

George Arliss, Loretta Young, Boris Karloff, Robert Young, C. Aubrey Smith, Arthur Byron, Helen Westley, Reginald Owen, Florence Arliss, Alan Mowbray, Holmes Herbert

'A fine picture on all counts . . . one of those occasional 100% smashes which Hollywood achieves.'—*Variety*

'A good dramatic photoplay, finely presented, packed with ripe incident and quite beautiful photography.'—*C. A. Lejeune*

AAN: best picture

'The most astounding motion picture since motion pictures began! Man turned monster stalking show-world beauties! The ultimate dimension in terror!'
'You've never been scared until you've been scared in 3-D!'

House of Wax
US 1953 88m
Warnercolor 3-D
Warner (Brian Foy)
Mutilated in a fire at his wax museum, a demented sculptor arranges a supply of dead bodies to be covered in wax for exhibition at his new showplace.
Spirited remake of *The Mystery of the Wax Museum*; as a piece of screen narrative it leaves much to be desired, but the sudden shocks are well managed, perhaps because this is the first Grade-A 3-D film, packed with gimmicks irrelevant to the story and originally shown with stereophonic sound.

w Crane Wilbur *d* André de Toth *ph* Bert Glennon *m* David Buttolph

Vincent Price (whose horror career began here), Carolyn Jones, Paul Picerni, Phyllis Kirk, Frank Lovejoy

† The director could not see the 3-D effect, being blind in one eye.

The House on 92nd Street
US 1945 88m bw
TCF (Louis de Rochemont)
During World War II in New York, the FBI routs Nazi spies after the atomic bomb formula.
Highly influential documentary-style 'now it can be told' spy drama, which borrowed the feel of its producer's *March of Time* series and

applied them to a fairly true story set on genuine locations though with a modicum of fictional mystery and suspense.
Highly effective in its own right, it looked forward to *The Naked City* three years later; the later film unaccountably got most of the credit for taking Hollywood out into the open air.

w Barre Lyndon, Charles G. Booth, John Monks Jnr *d* Henry Hathaway *ph* Norbert Brodine *m* David Buttolph

William Eythe, Lloyd Nolan, Signe Hasso, *Leo G. Carroll*, Gene Lockhart, Lydia St Clair, Harry Bellaver

'Recommended entertainment for those who believe that naïve Americans are no match for wily Europeans in the spy trade, and for those who just like their movies to move.'—*Time*

'Imagine an issue of *The March of Time*. The hard agglomeration of fact; the road drill style; the voice. Prolong it to four times its usual length, throw in a fictional climax, and there you have *The House on 92nd Street*.'—*William Whitebait, New Statesman*

AA: original story (Charles G. Booth)

' "What are you? A man or a saint? I don't want him, I want you!" Her desire scorched both their lives with the vicious breath of scandal!'
How Green Was My Valley
US 1941 118m bw
TCF (Darryl F. Zanuck)
Memories of childhood in a Welsh mining village.
Prettified and unconvincing but dramatically very effective tearjerker in the style which lasted from Cukor's *David Copperfield* to *The Green Years*. High production values here add a touch of extra class, turning the result into a Hollywood milestone despite its intrinsic inadequacies.

w Philip Dunne, *novel* Richard Llewellyn *d* John Ford *ph* Arthur Miller *m* Alfred Newman

Walter Pidgeon, Maureen O'Hara, Roddy McDowall, Donald Crisp, Sara Allgood, Anna Lee, John Loder, Barry Fitzgerald, Patric Knowles, Morton Lowry, Arthur Shields, Frederic Worlock

'Perfection of cinematic narrative . . . pure visual action, pictures powerfully composed, dramatically photographed, smoothly and eloquently put together.'—*James Shelley Hamilton*

† The unseen narrator was Irving Pichel.

AA: best picture; John Ford; Arthur Miller; Donald Crisp
AAN: Philip Dunne; Alfred Newman; Sara Allgood

How the West Was Won
US 1962 162m Technicolor Cinerama
MGM/Cinerama (Bernard Smith)
Panoramic western following the daughter of a pioneering family from youth (1830) to old age, with several half-relevant stories along the way.
Muddled spectacular with splendid set-pieces but abysmal dullness in between, especially if not seen in three-strip Cinerama (the Cinemascope prints are muddy and still show the dividing lines). An all-star fairground show of its time.

w James R. Webb *d* Henry Hathaway (first half), John Ford (Civil War), George Marshall (train) *ph* William Daniels, Milton Krasner, Charles Lang Jnr, Joseph La Shelle *m* Alfred Newman *ad* George W. Davis, William Ferrari, Addison Hehr

Debbie Reynolds, Carroll Baker, Lee J. Cobb, Henry Fonda, Carolyn Jones, Karl Malden, Gregory Peck, George Peppard, Robert Preston, James Stewart, Eli Wallach, John Wayne, Richard Widmark, Brigid Bazlen, Walter Brennan, David Brian, Andy Devine, Raymond Massey, Agnes Moorehead, Henry Morgan, Thelma Ritter, Russ

Tamblyn, Spencer Tracy (narrator)
'That goddamned Cinerama . . .
do you know a waist shot is as close
as you could get with that
thing?'—*Henry Hathaway*

AA: James R. Webb
AAN: best picture; photography;
music

How to Marry a Millionaire

US 1953   96m   Technicolor
Cinemascope
TCF (Nunnally Johnson)

Three girls rent an expensive New
York apartment and set out to trap
millionaires.

Cinemascope's first attempt at
modern comedy was not quite as
disastrous as might have been
expected, largely because of the
expensiveness of everything and the
several stars still brightly twinkling,
but the handling of this variation on
the old *Golddiggers* theme, while
entirely amiable, is dramatically very
slack.

w Nunnally Johnson *d* Jean
Negulesco *ph* Joe MacDonald
md Alfred Newman *m* Cyril
Mockridge

*Lauren Bacall, Marilyn Monroe,
Betty Grable, William Powell,*
Cameron Mitchell, David Wayne,
Rory Calhoun, Alex D'Arcy, Fred
Clark

'Not only educational, but great
fun.'—*Star*

† The film has an eight-minute
pre-credits concert sequence, which
is pretty unnerving when it unspools
on TV.

How to Succeed in Business without Really Trying

US 1967   121m   De Luxe
Panavision
UA / Mirisch (David Swift)

A window cleaner cajoles his way to
the top of a New York company.
Cinematically uninventive but
otherwise brisk and glowing
adaptation of a sharp, slick
Broadway musical.

w David Swift, *musical book* Abe
Burrows, Jack Weinstock, Willie

Gilbert, *book* Shepherd Mead
d David Swift *ph* Burnett Guffey
m / ly Frank Loesser *ch* Dale
Moreda after Bob Fosse

*Robert Morse, Rudy Vallee, Michele
Lee,* Anthony Teague, Maureen
Arthur, Murray Matheson

'Shows how taste and talent can
succeed in bringing a stage musical
to the screen with its virtues
intact.'—*John Cutts*

Hud

US 1963   112m   bw
Panavision
Paramount / Salem / Dover (Martin
Ritt, Irving Ravetch)

Life is hard on a Texas ranch, and
the veteran owner is not helped by
his sexually arrogant ne'er-do-well
son, who is a bad influence on the
household.

Superbly set in an arid landscape, this
incisive character drama is extremely
well directed and acted but somehow
lacks the touch of greatness.

*w Irving Ravetch, Harriet Frank,
novel* Horseman Pass By by Larry
McMurty *d Martin Ritt ph James
Wong Howe m* Elmer Bernstein

*Paul Newman, Patricia Neal, Melvyn
Douglas,* Brandon de Wilde

AA: James Wong Howe; Patricia
Neal; Melvyn Douglas
AAN: script; Martin Ritt; Paul
Newman

Hue and Cry

GB 1946   82m   bw
Ealing (Henry Cornelius)

East End boys discover that their
favourite boys' paper is being used
by crooks to pass information.

The first 'Ealing comedy' uses vivid
London locations as background for
a sturdy comic plot with a climax in
which the criminals are rounded up
by thousands of boys swarming over
dockland.

*w T. E. B. Clarke d Charles
Crichton ph* Douglas Slocombe,
John Seaholme *m* Georges Auric

Alastair Sim, Jack Warner, Harry Fowler, Valerie White, Frederick Piper

'Refreshing, bloodtingling and disarming.'—*Richard Winnington*

The Human Comedy

US 1943 117m bw
MGM (Clarence Brown)

In a small town during the war, a telegram boy brings tragedy to others and is touched by it himself. Gooey, sentimental morale booster in the best MGM tradition, a variant on the Hardy family series but with all the pretensions of its author.

w Howard Estabrook, *novel* William Saroyan *d Clarence Brown ph* Harry Stradling *m* Herbert Stothart

Mickey Rooney, Frank Morgan, James Craig, Marsha Hunt, Jackie Jenkins, Fay Bainter, Ray Collins, Van Johnson, Donna Reed

Opening narration by Ray Collins: 'I am Matthew Macauley. I have been dead for two years. So much of me is still living that I know now the end is only the beginning. As I look down on my homeland of Ithaca, California, with its cactus, vineyards and orchards, I see that so much of me is still living there—in the places I've been, in the fields and streets and church and most of all in my home, where my hopes, my dreams, my ambitions still live in the daily life of my loved ones.'

'The dignity and simplicity of the ideas shade off into cheap pretentiousness.'—*Bosley Crowther*

'The best one can say of it . . . is that it tries on the whole to be "faithful" to Saroyan; not invariably a good idea.'—*James Agee*

'The Saroyan touch leaves nothing ordinary; the film is electric with the joy of life.'—*Time*

AA: original story
AAN: best picture; Clarence Brown; Harry Stradling; Mickey Rooney

The Hunchback of Notre Dame

US 1923 120m approx (24 fps)
bw silent
Universal

The deformed Notre Dame bellringer rescues a gypsy girl from the evil intentions of her guardian. Victorian gothic version with a riveting star performance.

w Percy Poore Sheehan, Edward T. Lowe Jnr, *novel* Notre Dame de Paris by Victor Hugo *d* Wallace Worsley *ph* Robert S. Newhard, Tony Kornman

Lon Chaney, Patsy Ruth Miller, Norman Kerry, Ernest Torrence, Gladys Brockwell, Kate Lester, Brandon Hurst, Tully Marshall

The Hunchback of Notre Dame

US 1939 117m bw
RKO (Pandro S. Berman)

This superb remake is one of the best examples of Hollywood expertise at work; art direction, set construction, costumes, camera, lighting and above all direction brilliantly support an irresistible story and bravura acting.

w Sonya Levien, Bruno Frank *d* William Dieterle *ph* Joseph H. August *m* Alfred Newman *ad* Van Nest Polglase

Charles Laughton, Cedric Hardwicke, Maureen O'Hara, Edmond O'Brien, Thomas Mitchell, Harry Davenport, Walter Hampden, Alan Marshal, George Zucco, Katherine Alexander, Fritz Leiber, Rod la Rocque

'A super thriller-chiller. Will roll up healthy grosses at the ticket windows.'—*Variety*

'Has seldom been bettered as an evocation of medieval life.'—*John Baxter, 1968*

'It exceeds in sheer magnificence any similar film in history. Sets are vast and rich in detail, crowds are immense, and camera uses of both are versatile, varied and veracious.'—*Motion Picture Herald*

† Other versions: *Esmeralda* (1906, French); *Notre Dame de Paris* (1911, French); *The Darling of Paris* (1917, US, with Theda Bara).

AAN: Alfred Newman

'Through miles of raging ocean he
    defied man's law!'
The Hurricane
  US 1937   110m   bw
  Samuel Goldwyn (Merritt
Hulburd)
The simple life on a South Pacific
island is disrupted, not only by a
vindictive governor but by a
typhoon.
Tolerable island melodrama with a
spectacular climax and a generally
good cast.

w Dudley Nichols, Oliver H. P.
Garrett, *novel* Charles Nordhof,
James Norman Hall   *d John Ford,
Stuart Heisler   ph Bert Glennon
m* Alfred Newman

Dorothy Lamour, Jon Hall, *C.
Aubrey Smith, Mary Astor,
Raymond Massey, Thomas Mitchell,*
John Carradine, Jerome Cowan

  'A big money picture . . . a
production masterpiece.'—*Variety*

† Remade in 1979.

AAN: Alfred Newman; Thomas
Mitchell

The Hustler
  US 1961   135m   bw
      Cinemascope
TCF / Robert Rossen

A pool room con man comes to grief
when he falls in love.
Downbeat melodrama with
brilliantly handled and atmospheric
pool table scenes; the love interest is
redundant.

w Robert Rossen, Sidney Carroll,
novel Walter Tevis   *d Robert
Rossen   ph Eugen Schufftan
m* Kenyon Hopkins

*Paul Newman, Jackie Gleason,
George C. Scott, Piper Laurie,
Myron McCormick,* Murray
Hamilton, Michael Constantine

  'There is an overall impression of
intense violence, and the air of
spiritual decadence has rarely been
conveyed so vividly.'—*David
Robinson*

  'The supreme classic of that great
American genre, the low-life
movie.'—*Observer*

AA: Eugen Schufftan
AAN: best picture; script; Robert
Rossen (as director); Paul Newman;
Jackie Gleason; George C. Scott;
Piper Laurie

I

'Six sticks of dynamite that
blasted his way to freedom . . .
and awoke America's
conscience!'

I Am a Fugitive from a Chain Gang

☆☆ US 1932 90m bw
Warner (Hal B. Wallis)

An innocent man is convicted and
after brutal treatment with the chain
gang becomes a vicious criminal on
the run.

Horrifying story in the
semi-documentary manner; a
milestone in Hollywood history and
still a fairly compelling piece of
shock entertainment.

*w Sheridan Gibney, Brown Holmes,
Robert E. Burns d Mervyn Le Roy
ph Sol Polito*

Paul Muni, Glenda Farrell, Helen
Vinson, Preston Foster, Allen
Jenkins, Edward J. Macnamara,
Berton Churchill, Edward Ellis

'A picture with guts . . .
everything about it is technically
100% . . . shy on romantic angles,
but should get nice money all
over.'—*Variety*

'To be enthusiastically
commended for its courage, artistic
sincerity, dramatic vigour, high
entertainment concept and social
message.'—*Wilton A. Barrett*

'I quarrel with the production not
because it is savage and horrible, but
because each step in an inevitable
tragedy is taken clumsily, and
because each character responsible
for the hero's doom is shown more
as a caricature than as a
person.'—*Pare Lorentz*

AAN: best picture; Paul Muni

'Crushed lips don't talk!'
I Confess

US 1953 94m bw
Warner / Alfred Hitchcock

A priest hears the confession of a
murderer and cannot divulge it to

the police even though he is himself
suspected.

Hitchcock is always worth watching,
and although this old chestnut gives
him very restricted scope he imbues
the story with a strong feeling for its
setting (Quebec) and an
overpowering sense of doom.

*w George Tabori, William
Archbald, play Paul Anthelme
d Alfred Hitchcock ph Robert
Burks m Dmitri Tiomkin*

Montgomery Clift, Anne Baxter,
Brian Aherne, Karl Malden, Dolly
Haas, O. E. Hasse

'Whatever its shortcomings, it has
the professional concentration of
effect, the narrative control, of a
story teller who can still make most
of his rivals look like
amateurs.'—*MFB*

I Know Where I'm Going

GB 1945 91m bw
GFD / The Archers (Michael
Powell, Emeric Pressburger)

A determined girl travels to the
Hebrides to marry a wealthy old
man, but is stranded on Mull and
marries a young naval officer
instead.

A strange assembling of attractive
but disparate elements: romance,
comedy, bleak scenery, a trained
hawk and a dangerous whirlpool. At
the time it seemed to represent the
Elizabethan age of the British
cinema, and remains entertaining for
its parts though a bit of a puzzle as a
whole

*wd Michael Powell, Emeric
Pressburger ph Erwin Hillier,
Wendy Hiller, Roger Livesey,
Pamela Brown, Nancy Price, Finlay
Currie, John Laurie, George
Carney, Walter Hudd*

'Continuously fresh and
interesting, intelligently written and
played, and full of beautiful
photography.'—*Richard Mallett,
Punch*

'The sensitive photography and
the intelligent if not very imaginative
use of sound do more than enough
to make eloquent the influence of
place on people; and the whole thing
is undertaken with taste and
modesty.'—*James Agee*

'She knows all about love
potions . . . and lovely motions!'
I Married a Witch
US 1942   82m   bw
(UA) Cinema Guild / René
Clair
A Salem witch and her sorcerer
father come back to haunt the
descendant of the Puritan who had
them burned.
Delightful romantic comedy fantasy
which shows all concerned at the top
of their form. Hollywood
moonshine, impeccably distilled.

w Robert Pirosh, Marc Connelly,
novel The Passionate Witch by
Thorne Smith *d René Clair ph* Ted
Tetzlaff *m* Roy Webb

*Fredric March, Veronica Lake, Cecil
Kellaway, Robert Benchley*, Susan
Hayward, Elizabeth Patterson,
Robert Warwick
'A delightful sense of oddity and
enchantment.'—*New York World
Telegram*

AAN: Roy Webb

I See a Dark Stranger
GB 1945   112m   bw
GFD / Individual (Frank
Launder, Sidney Gilliat)
US title: *The Adventuress*
An Irish colleen who hates the
English comes to England to spy for
the Germans but falls in love with a
young English officer.
Slipshod plotting does not quite
destroy the jolly atmosphere of this
comedy-thriller which has the cheek
to take an IRA member as its
heroine. Good fun, very well staged.

*w Frank Launder, Sidney Gilliat,
Wolfgang Wilhelm d* Frank
Launder *ph* Wilkie Cooper
m William Alwyn

Deborah Kerr, Trevor Howard,
Raymond Huntley, Norman Shelley,
Michael Howard, Brenda Bruce,
Liam Redmond, Brefni O'Rouke
'It is the cinematic equivalent of
Irish blarney which inspires most of
this picture.'—*MFB*
'There is some intelligence, grace
and fun here, but essentially this
seems to me a supercilious drama, as
if it had been made by bright young
men who had decided to package
and toss a bone to the
groundlings.'—*James Agee*

I Wake Up Screaming
US 1941   79m   bw
TCF (Milton Sperling)
GB and alternative title: *Hot Spot*
A model is murdered and her sister
joins forces with the chief suspect to
find the real killer.
Moody thriller with plenty going for
it including one memorable
performance.

w Dwight Taylor, *novel* Steve
Fisher *d H. Bruce Humberstone
ph* Edward Cronjager *m* Cyril
Mockridge

Betty Grable, Victor Mature, Carole
Landis, *Laird Cregar*, William
Gargan, Alan Mowbray, Allyn
Joslyn, Elisha Cook Jnr
† Remade as *Vicki.*

I Want to Live
US 1958   120m   bw
(UA) Walter Wanger
A vagrant prostitute is executed in
the gas chamber despite growing
doubt as to her guilt.
Sober, harrowing treatment of the
Barbara Graham case, uneasily
adapted to provide a star role amid
the tirade against capital
punishment.

w Nelson Gidding, Don
Mankiewicz *d* Robert Wise
ph Lionel Lindon *m* John Mandel

Susan Hayward, Simon Oakland,
Virginia Vincent, Theodore Bikel,
Wesley Lau, Philip Coolidge
'An inconclusive amalgam of
variously unexplored
themes.'—*Peter John Dyer*

AA: Susan Hayward
AAN: Nelson Gidding, Don
Mankiewicz; Robert Wise; Lionel
Lindon

I Was a Male War Bride

US 1949 105m bw
TCF (Sol C. Siegel)
GB title: *You Can't Sleep Here*
A WAC in Europe marries a French
officer and can't get him home.
High-spirited farce against realistic
backgrounds of war-torn Europe,
which scarcely accord with Cary
Grant's pretending to be a
Frenchman (and later a
Frenchwoman). Funny, though.

w Charles Lederer, Hagar Wilde,
Leonard Spiegelgass *d* Howard
Hawks *ph* Norbert Brodine,
Osmond Borradaile *m* Cyril
Mockridge *md* Lionel Newman

Cary Grant, *Ann Sheridan*, Marion
Marshall, Randy Stuart
  'It is excellent light entertainment
but it is not likely to appeal to the
prudish and some discretion should
be exercised in booking it.'—*CEA
Film Report*

Ice Cold in Alex

GB 1958 132m bw
ABP (W. A. Whittaker)
US title: *Desert Attack*
In 1942 Libya, the commander of a
motor ambulance gets his vehicle
and passengers to safety despite the
hazards of minefields and a German
spy.
Engrossing desert adventure with
plenty of suspense sequences
borrowed from *The Wages of Fear*;
long, but very well presented.

w T. J. Morrison, Christopher
Landon *d* J. Lee-Thompson
ph Gilbert Taylor *m* Leighton Lucas

John Mills, Sylvia Sims, Anthony
Quayle, Harry Andrews

Idiot's Delight

US 1939 105m bw
MGM (Hunt Stromberg)
At the outbreak of World War II, in
a hotel on the Swiss border, a hoofer
with an all-girl troupe meets an old
flame masquerading as a Russian
countess.
Interesting but quite unsuccessful
film version of a highly artificial play
which had been carried off superbly

by the Lunts but was now somewhat
less well cast, though it did represent
an early Hollywood challenge to
Hitler. The flagwaving in fact made
it more than a little boring.

w Robert E. Sherwood, from his
play *d* Clarence Brown *ph* William
Daniels *m* Herbert Stothart

Clark Gable, Norma Shearer,
Edward Arnold, Charles Coburn,
Burgess Meredith, Joseph
Schildkraut, Laura Hope Crews,
Skeets Gallagher, Pat Patterson,
Fritz Feld
  'Exceptionally entertaining
comedy, a b.o. sock.'—*Variety*
  'The fun and excitement are still
there, however filtered it may
be.'—*Film Daily*
  'The mood of the whole thing is
forced and cheap—the coming world
war staged by Maurice
Chevalier.'—*Otis Ferguson*
  'Exactly the same pseudo-qualities
as *The Petrified Forest*: a moral
prentiousness, a kind of cellophaned
intellectuality.'—*Graham Greene*

If . . .

GB 1968 111m
Eastmancolor
Paramount/Memorial (Lindsay
Anderson, Michael Medwin)
Discontent at a boys' public school
breaks out into rebellion.
Allegorical treatment of school life
with much fashionable emphasis on
obscure narrative, clever cutting,
variety of pace, even an
unaccountable changing from colour
to monochrome and vice versa.
Intelligence is clearly at work, but it
seems to have suffered from
undigested gobs of Pinter, and the
film as a whole makes no discernible
point.

w David Sherwin *d* Lindsay
Anderson *ph* Miroslav Ondricek
m Marc Wilkinson *pd* Jocelyn
Herbert

Malcolm McDowell, David Wood,
Richard Warwick, Robert Swann,
Christine Noonan, Peter Jeffrey,
Arthur Lowe, Anthony Nicholls
  'The school . . . is the perfect
metaphor for the established system

all but a few of us continue to
accept.'—*David Wilson*

'It's something like the Writing on
the Wall.'—*Lindsay Anderson*

'Combines a cold and queasy view
of youth with a romantic view of
violence.'—*New Yorker*

If I Had a Million

US 1932 88m bw
Paramount (Benjamin Glazer,
Louis D. Lighton)

Various people each receive a
million dollars from an eccentric who
wants to test their reactions.
Interesting, dated multi-part comedy
drama remembered chiefly for the
brief sequence in which Laughton
blows a raspberry to his boss and
Fields chases road hogs. As an
entertainment it's patchy, lacking an
overall style.

w Claude Binyon, Whitney Bolton,
Malcolm Stuart Boylan, John Bright,
Sidney Buchman, Lester Cole,
Isabel Dawn, Boyce DeGaw, Walter
de Leon, Oliver H. P. Garrett,
Harvey Gates, Grover-Jones, Ernst
Lubitsch, Lawton Mackaill, Joseph
L. Mankiewicz, William Slavens
McNutt, Seton I. Miller, Tiffany
Thayer, *story* Robert D. Andrews
d Ernst Lubitsch, Norman Taurog,
Stephen Roberts, Norman Z.
McLeod, James Cruze, William A.
Seiter, H. Bruce Humberstone

W. C. Fields, *Charles Laughton*,
May Robson, Richard Bennett,
Alison Skipworth, Gary Cooper,
Wynne Gibson, George Raft, Jack
Oakie, Frances Dee, Charles
Ruggles, Mary Boland, Roscoe
Karns, Gene Raymond, Lucien
Littlefield

'Not uninteresting, but spotty in
retrospect . . . the cinematic
porridge is naturally replete with a
diversity of seasonings.'—*Variety*

'It develops an obvious idea in an
obvious way.'—*Time*

'Both living a secret—each afraid
to tell!'

I'll Be Seeing You

US 1944 85m bw
David O. Selznick (Dore
Schary)

A lady convict at home on parole for
Christmas meets and falls for a
shell-shocked soldier.
Schmaltzy, middle-American
romantic drama with some nicely
handled moments and plenty of
talent on hand. In the Hollywood
mainstream.

w Marion Parsonnet, *novel* Charles
Martin *d William Dieterle ph* Tony
Gaudio *m* Daniele Amfitheatrof

Ginger Rogers, *Joseph Cotten*,
Shirley Temple, Spring Byington,
Tom Tully, Chill Wills

'A sentimental, improbable
picture, but unexpectedly rewarding
in detail.'—*Richard Mallett*, *Punch*

I'm All Right Jack

GB 1959 104m bw
British Lion / Charter (Roy
Boulting)

A world-innocent graduate takes a
job in industry; by starting at the
bottom he provokes a national
strike.
Satirical farce which manages to hit
most of its widespread targets and
finds corruption in high, low and
middle places. A not inaccurate
picture of aspects of British life in
the fifties, and a presage of the satire
boom to come with *Beyond the
Fringe* and *That Was the Week That
Was*.

w Frank Harvey, *John Boulting*,
novel Private Life by *Alan Hackney*
d John Boulting *ph* Max Greene
m Ken Hare

Ian Carmichael, *Peter Sellers*, Irene
Handl, Richard Attenborough,
Terry-Thomas, Dennis Price,
Margaret Rutherford, Liz Fraser,
John Le Mesurier, Sam Kydd

'Just a sensitive gal who climbed
the ladder of success . . . wrong
by wrong! A story about a gal
who lost her reputation—and
never missed it!'

I'm No Angel

US 1933 88m bw
Paramount (William Le
Baron)

A carnival dancer gets off a murder
charge, moves into society and sues
a man for breach of promise.

The star's most successful vehicle, credited with saving the fortunes of Paramount remains a highly diverting side show with almost a laugh a minute. Released before the Legion of Decency was formed, it also contains some of Mae's fruitiest lines.

w *Mae West* d Wesley Ruggles ph Leo Tover *songs* Harvey Brooks (m), Gladys Dubois (ly)

Mae West, Edward Arnold, Cary Grant, Gregory Ratoff, Ralf Harolde, Kent Taylor, Gertrude Michael

'The most freewheeling of all Mae's screen vehicles, and the most satisfying of the lot.'—*James Robert Parish*

'A quality of balance and proportion which only the finest films attain.'—*Views and Reviews*

Imitation of Life

US 1934 109m bw
Universal

A woman becomes rich through the pancake recipe of her black servant, but the latter has a tragic life because her daughter passes for white.
Monumentally efficient tearjerker, generally well done.

w William Hurlbut, *novel* Fannie Hurst d John Stahl ph Merritt Gerstad m Heinz Roemheld

Claudette Colbert, Warren William, *Louise Beavers*, Ned Sparks, Rochelle Hudson, Fredi Washington, Alan Hale, Henry Armetta

'Grim and harsh stuff . . . its reception in the south cannot be judged or guessed by a northerner.'—*Variety*

'Classic, compulsively watchable rags-to-riches-and-heartbreak weeper.'—*New Yorker,* 1977

AAN: best picture

The Importance of Being Earnest

GB 1952 95m Technicolor
Rank / Javelin / Two cities
(Teddy Baird)

Two wealthy and eligible bachelors of the nineties have problems with their marriage prospects.
Disappointly stagey rendering (when compared, say, with *Occupe-toi d'Amélie*) of Britain's most wondrously witty lighter-than-air comedy of manners. As a record of a theatrical performance, however, it is valuable

w Anthony Asquith, *play* Oscar Wilde d Anthony Asquith ph Desmond Dickinson m Benjamin Frankel ad Carmen Dillon

Michael Redgrave, Michael Denison, Edith Evans, Margaret Rutherford, Joan Greenwood, Miles Malleson, Dorothy Tutin, Walter Hudd

'A more positive decision on style should have been taken. A film of this kind must be either an adaptation or a piece of filmed theatre. This one, being partially both, is not wholly either.'—*Gavin Lambert*

In Old Chicago

US 1937 115m bw
TCF (Kenneth MacGowan)

Events leading up to the great Chicago fire include a torrid romance between a gambler and a café singer.
Spectacular melodrama which with its two-million-dollar budget was a deliberate attempt to outdo *San Francisco*, and only failed because the cast was less interesting. A splendid studio super-production.

w Lamar Trotti, Sonya Levien, *novel* We the O'Learys by Niven Busch d Henry King, ph Peverell Marley m Louis Silvers sp H. Bruce Humberstone, Daniel B. Clark, Fred Sersen, Louis J. Witte ad William Darling

Tyrone Power, Alice Faye, Don Ameche, *Alice Brady*, Andy Devine, Brian Donlevy, Phyllis Brooks, Tom Brown, Sidney Blackmer, Berton Churchill, Paul Hurst, Rondo Hatton, Eddie Collins

'Sock spectacle film . . . an elaborate and liberally budgeted entertainment.'—*Variety*

**WITH COMPLIMENTS
OF
⬡TDK.**

TDK HAS THE TAPE
FOR ALL YOUR EQUIPMENT NEEDS

DYNAMIC CASSETTE LOW NOISE HIGH OUTPUT
NORMAL BIAS 120µs EQ

IEC I / TYPE I NORMAL POSITION

D90

ACOUSTIC DYNAMIC CASSETTE SUPER LOW NOISE HIGH OUTPUT
NORMAL BIAS 120µs EQ

IEC I / TYPE I NORMAL POSITION

AD90

NORMAL POSITION

D ☆ Britain's most popular audio cassette.
☆ Reliable performance low noise ferric tape.
☆ Ideal for budget personal and portable stereo players.
☆ Available in 46, 60, 90 & 120 minute tape lengths.

NORMAL POSITION

AD ☆ Excellent performance super ferric tape with wide dynamic range and very low tape hiss.
☆ Ideal for quality portable equipment and in-car hi-fi.
☆ Available in 46, 60, 90 & 120 minute tape lengths.

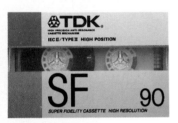

CHROME POSITION

SF ☆ TDK's excellent budget priced chrome position cassette.
☆ Suitable for use in a wide range of quality audio machines.
☆ Available in 46, 60 & 90 minute tape lengths.

CHROME POSITION

SA ☆ A TDK worldwide favourite.
☆ Super Avilyn cassette which gives high output levels and very low tape noise.
☆ Available in 46, 54, 60, 80 & 90 minute tape lengths.

CHROME POSITION

SA-X ☆ High performance Type II chrome position audio cassette.
☆ Extremely clear distortion free sound.
☆ Ideally suited for recording from a digital source.
☆ Available in 60 & 90 minute tape lengths.

THE SPECIALISTS IN SOUND AND VISION.

For further information on TDK audio or video tapes, please write to: Customer Service Department,
TDK UK Ltd., 44 Wellesley Road, Croydon CR0 9XW or telephone: 01-680 0023 for an information pack.

NEW FROM TDK

SCREEN GREATS

The high quality video tape and reference point for all video enthusiasts. Available in two and three hour tape lengths.

E-HG (EXTRA HIGH GRADE TAPE)

A must for video buffs everywhere. The E-HG Extra High Grade tape has been specifically designed for recording and storing valuable material. It is a top performance tape that gives superbly sharp pictures and vividly clear sound even in the long play mode. For quality reproduction of quality materials – use TDK E-HG.

A COMPREHENSIVE INDEXING SYSTEM FOR FAST IDENTIFICATION

Inside the pack you will find removable self-adhesive labels for use in easy identification of your favourite recordings. They will help you to safely catalogue your very own collection. All you need to do is affix them to the index cards provided. e.g.

ROMANCE   MUSICALS

SPECIAL SEE-THROUGH CASE FOR EASY VIDEO IDENTIFICATION

The Screen Greats video cassette sleeve is specially designed to allow quick and easy identification of your recordings using the index cards provided.

⊛TDK.
DON'T MISS IT. TDK IT.

AA: Alice Brady
AAN: best picture; Niven Busch
(original story); Louis Silvers

'A thousand thrills . . . and Hayley
Mills'
In Search of the Castaways
  👑 GB 1961   100m
    Technicolor
Walt Disney (Hugh Attwooll)
With the aid of an eccentric
professor, three children seek their
lost explorer father in some
geographically fantastic regions of
South America.
Engaging Victorian fantasy which
starts realistically but builds up to
sequences in the manner of *The
Wizard of Oz* and concludes in
Treasure Island vein. Jaunty juvenile
fare.

w Lowell S. Hawley, *novel* Captain
Grant's Children by Jules Verne
d Robert Stevenson *ph* Paul
Beeson *m* William Alwyn
ad Michael Stringer

Maurice Chevalier, Hayley Mills,
George Sanders, Wilfrid Hyde
White, *Wilfrid Brambell*

In the Heat of the Night
  🎯 US 1967   109m   De Luxe
  UA/Mirisch (Walter Mirisch)
In a small southern town, the
bigoted and bombastic sheriff on a
murder hunt grudgingly accepts the
help of a black detective.
Overrated policier in which the
personality clash is amusing (and was
timely) but the murder puzzle is a
complete throwaway.

w Sterling Sillphant *d* Norman
Jewison *ph* Haskell Wexler
m Quincy Jones

Sidney Poitier, Rod Steiger, Warren
Oates, Quentin Dean, William
Schallert
  'A very nice film and a very good
film and yes, I think it's good to see
a black man and a white man
working together . . . but it's not
going to take the tension out of New
York City; it's not going to stop the
riots in Chicago.'—*Rod Steiger*
† Poitier subsequently starred in a
couple of very inferior sequels, *They*

Call Me Mister Tibbs and *The
Organization.*

AA: best picture; Sterling Silliphant;
Rod Steiger
AAN: Norman Jewison

'No one is as good as Bette when
she's bad!'
In This Our Life
  👥 US 1942   101m   bw
   ❌ Warner (David Lewis)
A neurotic girl steals her sister's
husband, leaves him in the lurch,
dominates her hapless family and is
killed while on the run from the
police.
Splendid star melodrama with good
supporting acting and background
detail.

w Howard Koch, *novel* Ellen
Glasgow *d* John Huston *ph* Ernest
Haller *m* Max Steiner

Bette Davis, Charles Coburn, Olivia
de Havilland, Frank Craven, George
Brent, Dennis Morgan, Billie Burke,
Hattie McDaniel, Lee Patrick,
Walter Huston (uncredited)

In Which We Serve
  🎖 GB 1942   114m   bw
  Rank/Two Cities (Noel
Coward)
Survivors from a torpedoed
destroyer recall their life at sea and
on leave.
Dated but splendid flagwaver; an
archetypal British war film of almost
limitless propaganda value.

w Noel Coward *d* Noel Coward,
David Lean ph Ronald Neame
m Noel Coward

Noel Coward, Bernard Miles, *John
Mills,* Richard Attenborough, *Celia
Johnson,* Kay Walsh, Joyce Carey,
Michael Wilding, Penelope Dudley
Ward, Kathleen Harrison, Philip
Friend, George Carney, Geoffrey
Hibbert, James Donald
  COMMANDER (Noel Coward): 'The
Torrin has been in one scrap after
another, but even when we've had
men killed, the majority survived
and brought the old ship back. Now
she lies in 1500 fathoms and with her
more than half our shipmates. If
they had to die, what a grand way to

go! And now they lie all together with the ship we loved, and they're in very good company. We've lost her, but they're still with her. There may be less than half the *Torrin* left, but I feel that we'll all take up the battle with even stronger heart. Each of us knows twice as much about fighting, and each of us has twice as good a reason to fight. You will all be sent to replace men who've been killed in other ships, and the next time you're in action, remember the *Torrin*! I should like to add that there isn't one of you that I wouldn't be proud and honoured to serve with again.'

'One of the screen's proudest achievements at any time and in any country.'—*Newsweek*

'Never at any time has there been a reconstruction of human experience which could touch the savage grandeur and compassion of this production.'—*Howard Barnes, New York Herald Tribune*

† The story and the Coward character were based on the experiences of Louis Mountbatten, whose ship, HMS *Kelly*, was sunk under him.

AAN: best picture; Noel Coward (as writer)

'The hero is back!'
Indiana Jones and the Temple of Doom
US 1984   118m   Rank/De Luxe   Panavision
Paramount/Lucasfilm (Robert Watts)
A prequel to *Raiders of the Lost Ark*: Jones in 1935 finds the sacred Sankara stone.
Slow-starting adventure romp with much ingenuity and too much brutality and horror. In the US it caused the creation of a new censor certificate: PG(13).

w Willard Huyck, Gloria Katz, *story* George Lucas *d* Steven Spielberg *ph* Douglas Slocombe, Allan Daviau *m* John Williams *pd* Elliot Scott

Harrison Ford, Kate Capshaw, Ke Huy Kwan, Philip Stone

'One of the most sheerly pleasurable physical comedies ever made.'—*Pauline Kael, New Yorker*

'A two-hour series of none too carefully linked chase sequences . . . sitting on the edge of your seat gives you a sore bum but also a numb brain.'—*Guardian*

AAN: music

'How dare he make love to me—and not be a married man!'
Indiscreet
GB 1958   100m   Technicolor
Grandon (Stanley Donen)
An American diplomat in London falls in love with an actress but protects himself by saying he is married.
Affairs among the ultra rich, amusing when played by these stars but with imperfect production values which the alarmingly thin plot allows one too much time to consider.

w Norman Krasna, from his play Kind Sir *d* Stanley Donen *ph* Frederick A. Young *m* Richard Bennett, Ken Jones

Cary Grant, Ingrid Bergman, Phyllis Calvert, Cecil Parker, David Kossoff, Megs Jenkins

'One is often on the point of being bored, but one never is, quite.'—*Richard Roud*

'A film to which you would not hesitate to take your jeweller, your architect, your home decorator, your dressmaker and your domestic staff.'—*Alexander Walker*

The Informer
US 1935   91m   bw
RKO (Cliff Reid)
An IRA leader is betrayed by a simple-minded hanger-on who wants money to emigrate; he is hounded by fellow rebels and his own conscience.
A tedious plot is turned into brilliant cinema by full-blooded acting and a highly stylized yet brilliantly

effective *mise en scène* which never attempts reality.

w Dudley Nichols, *novel* Liam O'Flaherty *d* John Ford *ph* Joseph H. August *m* Max Steiner *ad* Van Nest Polglase

Victor McLaglen, Heather Angel, Margot Grahame, Una O'Connor, Wallace Ford, Preston Foster, J. M. Kerrigan, Joe Sawyer, Donald Meek

'A tough subject, a sure critic's picture, but dubious box office.'—*Variety*

'As impressive as *Scarface*, or anything in the whole powerful literature redolent of fog and grime and dreariness which the Germans gave to the Americans.'—*Bardèche and Brasillach*

'Among the best five pictures since the coming of sound.'—*Baltimore Sun*

† An early British sound version was made in 1929 by Arthur Robison for BIP, with Lars Hansen and Lya de Putti.

AA: Dudley Nichols; John Ford; Max Steiner; Victor McLaglen
AAN: best picture

Inherit the Wind

US 1960   127m   bw
UA/Lomitas (Stanley Kramer)

A fictionalized account of the 1925 Scopes 'monkey trial', when a schoolmaster was accused of teaching the theory of evolution. Splendid theatrics with fine performances, marred by boring subplots but enhanced by a realistic portrait of a sweltering southern town.

w Nathan E. Douglas, Harold Jacob Smith, *play* Jerome Lawrence, Robert E. Lee *d* Stanley Kramer *ph* Ernest Laszlo *m* Ernest Gold

Spencer Tracy, Fredric March, Florence Eldridge, Gene Kelly, Dick York, Donna Anderson, Harry Morgan, Elliott Reid, Claude Akins

AAN: script; Ernest Laszlo; Spencer Tracy

The Inn of the Sixth Happiness

GB 1958   158m   De Luxe
Cinemascope
TCF (Mark Robson)

An English servant girl becomes a missionary and spends many arduous years in China.
Romanticized biopic of Gladys Aylward, with lots of children, a happy ending, and everyone sensationally miscast. Somehow it all works, even North Wales standing in for China.

w Isobel Lennart, *book* The Small Woman by Alan Burgess *d* Mark Robson *ph* Frederick A. Young *m* Malcolm Arnold

Ingrid Bergman, Curt Jurgens, Robert Donat, Athene Seyler, Ronald Squire, Richard Wattis, Moultrie Kelsall

AAN: Mark Robson

'Wild longings . . . fierce desires he could not name . . . for an interlude of stolen love! To one woman he gave his memories—to another he gave his dreams!'

Intermezzo

US 1939   69m   bw
David O. Selznick
GB title: *Escape to Happiness*

A renowned, married violinist has an affair with his musical protégée. Archetypal cinema love story, Hollywoodized from a Swedish original but quite perfect in its brief, sentimental way.

w George O'Neil, *original scenario* Gosta Stevens, Gustav Molander *d* Gregory Ratoff *ph* Gregg Toland *m* Robert Henning, Heinz Provost *m* (*score*) Lou Forbes

Leslie Howard, *Ingrid Bergman*, John Halliday, Edna Best, Cecil Kellaway

† William Wyler is said to have assisted in the direction.

AAN: Lou Forbes

Intolerance

US 1916   115m approx (24 fps)   bw   silent
D. W. Griffith

Four stories—including Belshazzar's feast and the massacre of St Bartholomew—of intolerance through the ages are intercut and linked by the image of a mother and her baby: 'out of the cradle, endlessly rocking.'

A massive enterprise of which audiences at the time and after were quite intolerant. Hard to take in parts, it rises to a fine climax as all the stories come to a head, including a modern one with a race between a car and train, and has been called 'the only film fugue'. At the time, by far the most expensive film ever made.

wd D. W. Griffith ph Billy Bitzer
Mae Marsh, Lillian Gish, Constance Talmadge, Robert Harron, Elmo Lincoln, Eugene Pallette

'A mad, brilliant, silly extravaganza. Perhaps the greatest movie ever made. In it one can see the source of most of the major traditions of the screen: the methods of Eisenstein and Von Stroheim, the Germans and the Scandinavians, and, when it's bad, de Mille.'—*New Yorker, 1980*

Intruder in the Dust

US 1949   87m   bw
MGM (Clarence Brown)

In a southern town, a boy and an old lady solve a mystery and prevent a black man from being lynched. Excellent character drama which also offers vivid local colour, a murder puzzle and social comment. A semi-classic.

w Ben Maddow, novel William Faulkner d Clarence Brown ph Robert Surtees m Adolph Deutsch

Juano Hernandez, Elizabeth Patterson, David Brian, Claude Jarman Jnr, *Porter Hall*, Will Geer

'It is surely the years of range and experience which have given him a control of the medium so calm, sure and—apparently—easy that he can make a complex story seem simple and straightforward.'—*Pauline Kael*

'A really good movie that is also and incidentally the first honestly worked out "racial" film I have seen.'—*Richard Winnington*

'An example of gripping film craftsmanship.'—*News of the World*

'The world as they knew it was slipping away from them. Time was running out for the human race. And there was nothing to hold on to—except each other!'
Invasion of the Body Snatchers

US 1956   80m   bw   Superscope
Allied Artists / Walter Wanger

A small American town is imperceptibly taken over by an alien force.

Persuasive, thoroughly satisfying, low-budget science fiction, put across with subtlety and intelligence in every department

w Daniel Mainwaring, novel Jack Finney d Don Siegel ph Ellsworth Fredericks m Carmen Dragon

Kevin McCarthy, Dana Wynter, Larry Gates, King Donovan, Carolyn Jones, Virginia Christine, Sam Peckinpah

'Even the moon is frightened of me—frightened to death!'
The Invisible Man

US 1933   71m   bw
Universal (Carl Laemmle Jnr)

A scientist discovers a means of making himself invisible, but in the process becomes a megalomaniac. Superb blend of eccentric character comedy, melodrama and trick photography in a Hollywood English setting; remarkably faithful to the spirit of the book. It made a star of Claude Rains in his first film, even though he is seen for only a couple of seconds.

w R. C. Sherriff, Philip Wylie, novel H. G. Wells d James Whale ph Arthur Edeson sp John P. Fulton m W. Frank Harling

Claude Rains, Gloria Stuart, William Harrigan, Henry Travers, E. E.

Clive, *Una O'Connor*, Forrester Harvey, Dudley Digges, Holmes Herbert

GRIFFIN (Claude Rains): 'We'll start with a few murders. Big men, little men—just to show we make no distinction.'

'Well made and full of intentional and unintentional laughs. Should do well.'—*Variety*

'Taken either as a technical exercise or as a sometimes profoundly moving retelling of the Frankenstein fable, it is one of the most rewarding of recent films.'—*William Troy*

† Sequels, successively less interesting, were *The Invisible Man Returns* (1940), *Invisible Woman* (1941), *Invisible Agent* (1942), *The Invisible Man's Revenge* (1944) and *Abbott and Costello Meet the Invisible Man* (1951). A TV series with an anonymous hero was made by ATV in 1955; a Universal one with David McCallum followed in 1975, and was restructured as *The Gemini Man* in 1976.

†† Boris Karloff had been first choice for the role, but he turned it down.

Invitation to the Dance
GB 1954 92m Technicolor MGM (Arthur Freed)

Three stories in dance and mime. Unsuccessful ballet film which closed its star's great period and virtually ended the heyday of the Hollywood musical. The simple fact emerged that European ballet styles were not Kelly's forte; yet there was much to enjoy in *Circus*, *Ring around the Rosy* and *The Magic Lamp*.

w, ch, d Gene Kelly ph Frederick A. Young, m Jacques Ibert, André Previn, Rimsky-Korsakov ad Alfred Junge
Gene Kelly, Igor Youskevitch, Tommy Rall, Belita, Tamara Toumanova

'Out of the dark fantastic madness of his science he created her—the panther woman—throbbing to the hot flush of new-found love!'

Island of Lost Souls
US 1932 74m bw Paramount

On a remote South Sea island, mad Dr Moreau transforms animals into humans by vivisection.
Unchilling but interesting thriller with a rolling-eyed star performance.

w Waldemar Young, Philip Wylie, *story* The Island of Dr Moreau by H. G. Wells d Erle C. Kenton ph Karl Struss

Charles Laughton, Bela Lugosi, Richard Arlen, Kathleen Burke, Leila Hyams

It Always Rains on Sunday
GB 1947 92m bw Ealing (Henry Cornelius)

An escaped convict takes refuge in his married mistress's house in East London.
Influential slumland melodrama, now dated—the stuff of every other television play—but at the time electrifyingly vivid and very well done.

w Angus Macphail, *Robert Hamer*, *Henry Cornelius*, *novel* Arthur La Bern d Robert Hamer ph Douglas Slocombe m Georges Auric

Googie Withers, John McCallum, Jack Warner, Edward Chapman, Susan Shaw, Sidney Tafler

'Let me pay it the simplest of compliments and say that it has the persuasiveness of an exciting story professionally told.'—*Sunday Times*

It Came from Outer Space
US 1953 80m bw 3-D U-I (William Alland)

A young astronomer sees a space ship land in the Arizona desert and tracks down the occupants who can adopt human appearance at will.
Quite bright science fiction, the first to use this theme of borrowing bodies and the first to utilize the western desert locations. 3-D adds a shock moment or two.

w Harry Essex, *story* Ray Bradbury *d Jack Arnold ph* Clifford Stine *m* Herman Stein *md* Joseph Gershenson

Richard Carlson, Barbara Rush, Charles Drake, Kathleen Hughes

'A solid piece of eerie entertainment, replete with wild screams and bug-eyed monsters guaranteed to send scared customers out of this world.'—*Hollywood Reporter*

'Desert was Arnold's favourite location, and he used it consistently to create a sense of strangeness and menace otherwise much restricted by his budgets.'—*Time Out, 1982*

It Happened One Night
US 1934 105m bw
Columbia (Frank Capra)
A runaway heiress falls in love with the reporter who is chasing her across America.
Highly successful and influential romantic comedy, the first to use buses and motels as background and still come up sparkling; it remains superlative in patches, but overall has a faded, dated air.

w Robert Riskin, *story* Night Bus by Samuel Hopkins Adams *d Frank Capra ph* Joseph Walker *md* Louis Silvers

Clark Gable, *Claudette Colbert*, Walter Connolly, Roscoe Karns, Alan Hale, Ward Bond, Jameson Thomas, Arthur Hoyt

'A laughing hit that will mean important coin.'—*Variety*

'It will be a long day before we see so little made into so much.'—*Otis Ferguson*

'Something to revive your faith in a medium which could belong among the great arts.'—*Robert Forsythe*

'We may look askance at Capra's sententious notions about the miserable rich and the happy poor, but there's no doubting the chord he struck in depression audiences.'—*Time Out, 1980*

'It made audiences happy in a way that only a few films in each era do. In the mid-30s, the Colbert and Gable of this film became Americans' idealized view of themselves—breezy, likeable, sexy, gallant, and maybe just a little harebrained. It was the *Annie Hall* of its day—before the invention of anxiety.'—*Pauline Kael, 70s*

† Remade 1956 (badly) as *You Can't Run away From It*.

†† Robert Montgomery was the first choice for the Gable role, but he refused it because he had been on a bus in *Fugitive Lovers*. The Colbert role was first offered to Myrna Loy, Margaret Sullavan and Constance Bennett. Colbert was lured by a 40,000-dollar fee.

'One of the most entertaining films that has ever been offered to the public.'—*Observer*

AA: best picture; Robert Riskin; Frank Capra; Clark Gable; Claudette Colbert

It Happened Tomorrow
US 1944 84m bw
(UA) Arnold Pressburger
A reporter meets an old man with the power to show him tomorrow's newspaper headlines, so that he always gets scoops—including his own death . . .
Engaging fantasy, flawlessly made and quietly very entertaining.

w Dudley Nichols, *René Clair d René Clair ph* Archie Stout *m* Robert Stolz

Dick Powell, Linda Darnell, Jack Oakie, *John Philliber*, Edgar Kennedy, Ed Brophy, George Cleveland, Sig Rumann

'Students of cinematic style will find many shrewdly polished bits to admire and enjoy.'—*James Agee*

'Diverting escapist entertainment for all audiences.'—*Variety*

AAN: Robert Stolz

It Should Happen to You
US 1954 87m bw
Columbia (Fred Kohlmar)
A slightly daffy New York model with an urge to be famous rents a huge billboard and puts her name on it.

Likeable comedy which starts brightly and slowly falls apart, disappointing considering the credentials of the talents involved and the satiric possibilities of the plot.

w Ruth Gordon, Garson Kanin *d* George Cukor *ph* Charles Lang *m* Frederick Hollander

Judy Holliday, Jack Lemmon, Peter Lawford, Michael O'Shea

It Started with Eve
US 1941   93m   bw
Universal (Joe Pasternak)
A dying millionaire wants to see his grandson engaged, so a waitress obliges for an hour . . . but the old man recovers.
Charming comedy which was probably the star's best film; remade as *I'd Rather be Rich*.

w Norman Krasna, Leo Townsend *d* Henry Koster *ph* Rudolph Maté *md* Charles Previn, Hans Salter

Deanna Durbin, Charles Laughton, Robert Cummings, Margaret Tallichet, Guy Kibbee, Walter Catlett, Catherine Doucet
'The perfect 8 to 80 picture.'—*Variety*

AAN: Charles Previn, Hans Salter

An Italian Straw Hat
France 1927   74m (24 fps)
bw   silent
Albatross
original title: *Un Chapeau de Paille d'Italie*
The hero is prevented from getting to a wedding when his horse chews up a lady's straw hat and her escort demands that it be replaced.
Lively but gentle comedy of errors, a stage farce expanded for the screen and filled with visual gags. A very influential and still amusing piece.

wd René Clair, *play* Eugène Labiche *ph* Maurice Desfassiaux, Nicholas Roudakoff *ad* Lazare Meerson

Albert Préjean, Olga Tschekowa, Marise Maia, Alice Tissot
'The very springtime of screen comedy.'—*Tatler*

'One of the funniest films ever made.'—*Tribune*, 1945
'Still one of the funniest films in the world.'—*Sunday Times* 1948

It's a Mad Mad Mad Mad World
US 1963   192m
Technicolor   Ultra
Panavision 70
UA / Stanley Kramer
An assortment of people including a frustrated cop are overcome by greed when they hear of buried loot. Three hours of frantic chasing and violent slapstick is too much even when done on this scale and with this cast, but one must observe that scene for scene it is extremely well done and most of the players are in unusually good form though they all outstay their welcome and are upstaged by the stunt men.

w William and Tania Rose *d* Stanley Kramer *ph* Ernest Laszlo *m* Ernest Gold *stunts* Carey Loftin *titles* Saul Bass

Spencer Tracy, Jimmy Durante, *Milton Berle*, Sid Caesar, Ethel Merman, Buddy Hackett, Mickey Rooney, Dick Shawn, *Phil Silvers*, *Terry-Thomas*, Jonathan Winters, Edie Adams, Dorothy Provine, Eddie Anderson, Jim Backus, William Demarest, Peter Falk, Paul Ford, Leo Gorcey, Ben Blue, Edward Everett Horton, Buster Keaton, Joe E.Brown, Carl Reiner, the Three Stooges, Zasu Pitts, Sterling Holloway, Jack Benny, Jerry Lewis
'To watch on a Cinerama screen in full colour a small army of actors inflict mayhem on each other with cars, planes, explosives and other devices for more than three hours with stereophonic sound effects is simply too much for the human eye and ear to respond to, let alone the funny bone.'—*Dwight MacDonald*

AAN: Ernest Laszlo; Ernest Gold; title song (*m* Ernest Gold, *ly* Mack David)

It's a Wonderful Life

US 1946 129m bw
RKO/Liberty Films (Frank Capra)

A man is prevented from committing suicide by an elderly angel, who takes him back through his life to show him what good he has done. Superbly assembled small-town comedy drama in a fantasy framework; arguably Capra's best and most typical work.

w *Frances Goodrich*, Albert Hackett, *Frank Capra d Frank Capra ph Joseph Walker, Joseph Biroc m* Dmitri Tiomkin

James Stewart, Henry Travers, Donna Reed, Lionel Barrymore, Thomas Mitchell, Beulah Bondi, Frank Faylen, Ward Bond, Gloria Grahame, H. B. Warner, Frank Albertson, Samuel S. Hinds, Mary Treen

CLARENCE (Henry Travers): 'Everytime you hear a bell ring, it means that some angel's just got his wings.'

'One of the most efficient sentimental pieces since *A Christmas Carol.'—James Agee*

'The most brilliantly made motion picture of the 1940s, so assured, so dazzling in its use of screen narrative.'—*Charles Higham*

'In its own icky, bittersweet way, it's terribly effective.'—*New Yorker, 1977*

AAN: best picture; Frank Capra; James Stewart

It's in the Bag

US 1945 87m bw
(UA) Mahattan Productions
GB title: *The Fifth Chair*

The owner of a flea circus seeks a legacy hidden in one of five chairs which have been sold to a variety of people.

Patchily amusing, star-studded comedy which was also filmed as *Keep Your Seats Please* and *The Twelve Chairs*. Full enjoyment requires some knowledge of American radio characters.

w Jay Dratler, Alma Reville
d Richard Wallace ph Russell Metty m Werner Heymann

Fred Allen, Binnie Barnes, *Jack Benny*, Robert Benchley, Don Ameche, Victor Moore, Rudy Vallee, William Bendix, Jerry Colonna

'An untidy piece that doesn't make the most of itself but is full of fun.'—*Richard Mallett, Punch*

Ivan the Terrible

USSR 1942–6 100m (part one), 88m (part two) bw (some Agfacolor in part two)
Mosfilm
original title: *Ivan Groznyi*

The life of a 16th-century tsar.

A heavy-going film overflowing with grim, gloomy and superbly composed images: the plot is by the way, and part two (also known as *The Boyars' Plot*) is not up to the standard of part one, in which the coronation sequence alone is a masterpeice of cinema.

wd, ed Sergei Eisenstein
ph Edouard Tissé (exteriors), Andrei Moskvin (interiors) m Sergei Prokoviev ad Isaac Shpinel, L. Naumova

Nikolai Cherkassov, Ludmilla Tselikovskaya, Serafima Birman

'A visual opera, with all of opera's proper disregard of prose-level reality . . . an extraordinarily bold experiment, fascinating and beautiful to look at.'—*James Agee*

J

'A love story every woman would die a thousand deaths to live!'

Jane Eyre

US 1943 96m bw
TCF (William Goetz)

In Victorian times, a harshly treated orphan girl becomes governess in a mysterious Yorkshire mansion with a brooding master.

Sharply paced, reasonably faithful and superbly staged Hollywood version of Charlotte Brontë's archetypal romantic novel which stimulated so many imitations, including *Rebecca*.

w Aldous Huxley, Robert Stevenson, John Houseman d Robert Stevenson ph George Barnes m Bernard Herrmann sp Fred Sersen ad Wiard B. Ihnen, James Basevi

Joan Fontaine, Orson Welles, Margaret O'Brien, Henry Daniell, John Sutton, Agnes Moorehead, Elizabeth Taylor, Peggy Ann Garner, Sara Allgood, Aubrey Mather, Hillary Brooke, Edith Barrett, Ethel Griffies, Barbara Everest, John Abbott

'A careful and tame production, a sadly vanilla-flavoured Joan Fontaine, and Orson Welles treating himself to road operatic sculpturings of body, cloak and diction, his eyes glinting in the Rembrandt gloom, at every chance, like side orders of jelly.'—*James Agee*

'The essentials are still there; and the non-essentials, such as the gloom, the shadows, the ground mist, the rain and the storms, have been expanded and redoubled and magnified to fill up the gaps.'—*Richard Mallett, Punch*

Jason and the Argonauts

GB 1963 104m
Technicolor
Columbia/Charles H. Schneer

With help and hindrance from the gods, Jason voyages in search of the Golden Fleece and meets all kinds of monsters.

Rambling semi-classic mythological fantasy which keeps its tongue firmly in its cheek and provides a framework for some splendid stop-frame animation.

w Jan Read, Beverly Cross d Don Chaffey ph Wilkie Cooper m Bernard Herrmann sp Ray Harryhausen

Todd Armstrong, Honor Blackman, Niall MacGinnis, Andrew Faulds, Nancy Kovack

Jaws

US 1975 125m
Technicolor Panavision
Universal/Zanuck–Brown
(William S. Gilmore Jnr)

A man-eating shark causes havoc off the Long Island coast.

In the exploitation-hungry seventies this film took more money than any other. In itself, despite genuinely suspenseful and frightening sequences, it is a slackly narrated and sometimes flatly handled thriller with an over-abundance of dialogue and, when it finally appears, a pretty unconvincing monster.

w Peter Benchley, Carl Gottlieb, novel Peter Benchley d Steven Spielberg ph Bill Butler m John Williams

Robert Shaw, Roy Scheider, Richard Dreyfuss, Lorraine Gary, Murray Hamilton, Carl Gottlieb

'A mind-numbing repast for sense-sated gluttons. Shark stew for the stupefied.'—*William S. Pechter*

'The opening sequences have few parallels in modern cinema; like the shower scene in *Psycho* they will haunt a whole generation.'—*Les Keyser, Hollywood in the Seventies*

AA: John Williams
AAN: best picture

'New songs and old favourites sung by Mr Jolson during the action of the story on the Vitaphone!'

The Jazz Singer
US 1927 89m bw
Warner

A cantor's son makes it big in show business.

Archetypal Jewish weepie which became of absorbing interest as the first talkie film (songs and a few fragments of speech) and in its way, surprisingly, is not half bad.

w Alfred A. Cohn, *play* Samson Raphaelson *d* Alan Crosland *ph* Hal Mohr
Al Jolson, May McAvoy, Warner Oland, Eugenie Besserer, Otto Lederer

'A beautiful period piece, extravagantly sentimental . . . yet entirely compelling in its own conviction.'—*NFT, 1969*

'*The Jazz Singer* definitely establishes the fact that talking pictures are imminent. Everyone in Hollywood can rise up and declare that they are not, and it will not alter the fact. If I were an actor with a squeaky voice I would worry.'—*Welford Beaton, The Film Spectator.*

AAN: Alfred A. Cohn

Jesse James
US 1938 106m
Technicolor
TCF (Nunnally Johnson)

After the Civil War, two brothers take to train robbing when railroad employees harass their family.

The life of an outlaw turns into family entertainment when Hollywood bathes it in sentiment, soft colour, family background and warm humour. It works dangerously well, and the action sequences are splendid.

w Nunnally Johnson d Henry King ph George Barnes md Louis Silvers ad William Darling, George Dudley

Tyrone Power, Henry Fonda, Nancy Kelly, Jane Darwell, Randolph Scott, Henry Hull, Slim

Summerville, Brian Donlevy, J. Edward Bromberg, John Carradine, Donald Meek

'Sock outdoors meller, vigorous and intensely dramatic in its unfolding . . . box office smacko.'—*Variety*

'An authentic American panorama.'—*New York Times*

† Sequel 1940: *The Return of Frank James.*

Remake 1957: *The True Story of Jesse James.*

Jeux Interdits
France 1952 84m bw
Robert Dorfmann (Paul Joly)
aka: *Forbidden Games; The Secret Game*

In 1940, the little daughter of refugee parents sees her parents killed, and takes refuge with a peasant family, the small son of which helps her bury her dead puppy. They make a game of building a cemetery, which leads to a village feud . . .

Poignant anti-war tract which seemed a masterpiece at the time and is full of marvellous moments, but no longer holds up as a whole.

w Jean Aurenche, Pierre Bost, novel François Boyer *d René Clément ph* Robert Juliard *m* Narciso Yepes

Brigitte Fossey, Georges Poujouly, Amédée, Laurence Badie, Jacques Marin, Suzanne Courtal, Lucien Hubert

'A truly imposing achievement of blending several seemingly unrelated elements into a totally meaningful whole.'—*John Simon, 1967*

AA: best foreign film

AAN: François Boyer (original story)

Jezebel
US 1938 104m bw
Warner (Henry Blanke)

Before the Civil War, a southern belle stirs up trouble among the menfolk by her wilfulness and spite, but atones when a plague strikes.

Superb star melodrama, tossed to her in compensation for losing *Gone with the Wind*, and dealt with in high style by all concerned.

w Clements Ripley, Abem Finkel, John Huston, *play* Owen Davis Snr *d* William Wyler *ph* Ernest Haller *m* Max Steiner

Bette Davis, Henry Fonda, George Brent, Margaret Lindsay, Fay Bainter, Richard Cromwell, Donald Crisp, Henry O'Neill, John Litel, Spring Byington, Eddie Anderson, Gordon Oliver, Irving Pichel

'Good femme film, assured of okay results.'—*Variety*

'Its excellences come from many sources—good plotting and writing, a director and photographer who know how to make the thing flow along with dramatic pictorial effect, and a cast that makes its story a record of living people.'—*James Shelley Hamilton, National Board of Review*

'Without the zing Davis gave it, it would have looked very mossy indeed.'—*Pauline Kael, 1968*

AA: Bette Davis; Fay Bainter
AAN: best picture; Ernest Haller; Max Steiner

'There was temptation in her helpless silence—and then torment!'
Johnny Belinda
US 1948   103m   bw
Warner (Jerry Wald)
In a remote fishing community, a deaf mute girl is raped and the sympathetic local doctor is suspected of being the father of her baby. Melodrama of the old school which in 1948 seemed oddly to mark a new permissiveness and made a big star of Jane Wyman; the production and locations were also persuasive.

w Irmgard Von Cube, Allen Vincent, *play* Elmer Harris *d* Jean Negulesco *ph* Ted McCord *m* Max Steiner *md* Leo F. Forbstein

Jane Wyman, Lew Ayres, Charles Bickford, Agnes Moorehead, Stephen McNally, Jan Sterling, Rosalind Ivan, Mabel Paige

'Hollywood has tried something dangerously different here, and succeeded in making a powerful and sensitive job of it.'—*Observer*

'An atmosphere in which the hokey, tearjerking elements are used for more than mere pathos—an example of technique over subject matter.'—*Pauline Kael, 70s*

AA: Jane Wyman
AAN: best picture; script; Jean Negulesco; Ted McCord; Max Steiner; Lew Ayres; Charles Bickford; Agnes Moorehead

The Jolson Story
US 1946   129m
Technicolor
Columbia (Sidney Skolsky)
Asa Yoelson, son of a cantor, becomes Al Jolson, the great entertainer of the twenties; but showbiz success brings marital difficulties.
Whitewashed biopic in impeccable Hollywood style, with everything working shamelessly right, a new star in the leading role, perfect if unambitious production values, and a deluge of the best songs ever written.

w Stephen Longstreet *d* Alfred E. Green, *Joseph H. Lewis ph* Joseph Walker *md* Morris Stoloff

Larry Parks (using Jolson's own voice), *William Demarest, Evelyn Keyes, Ludwig Donath, Tamara Shayne*, Bill Goodwin, *Scotty Beckett*, John Alexander
'I have nothing in the world against this picture except that at least half of it seemed to me enormously tiresome.'—*James Agee*

AA: Morris Stoloff
AAN: Joseph Walker; Larry Parks; William Demarest

Jour de Fête
France 1948   87m   bw
Francinex (Fred Orain)
A village postman sees a film about the efficiency of the American postal service and decides to smarten himself up.
First, and some say best, of Tati's comedy vehicles: two-thirds superb

local colour, one-third hilarious slapstick.

w Jacques Tati, Henri Marquet d Jacques Tati ph Jacques Mercanton *m* Jean Yatove

Jacques Tati, Guy Decomble, Paul Fankeur, Santa Relli

'You could watch it with a bout of toothache and it would make you laugh.'—*Daily Express*

† A reissue version had colour items hand-painted in each frame, and proved quite effective.

Le Jour Se Lève
France 1939 95m bw
Sigma
aka: *Daybreak*

A murderer is besieged by police in his attic room, remembers his past through the night, and shoots himself.

A model of French poetic realism, and a much-praised film which was almost destroyed when it was bought for an American remake (*The Long Night*).

w Jacques Viot, Jacques Prévert d Marcel Carné ph Curt Courant, Philippe Agostini, André Bac *m Maurice Jaubert ad Alexander Trauner*

Jean Gabin, Jules Berry, Arletty, Jacqueline Laurent

'The man walks about his room, moves a few things, lies on his bed, looks out of the window, chain-smokes . . . and one is genuinely interested in him all the time (remembering afterwards that there exist directors who contrive to be boring even when they use fifteen characters in a motor car chase crackling with revolver shots).'—*Richard Mallett, Punch*

Journey into Fear
US 1942 71m bw
RKO (Orson Welles)

A munitions expert finds himself in danger from assassins in Istanbul, and has to be smuggled home.

Highly enjoyable impressionist melodrama supervised by Orson Welles and full of his touches and excesses.

w Joseph Cotten, Orson Welles, novel Eric Ambler d Norman Foster (and *Orson Welles*) *ph* Karl Struss *m* Constantin Bakaleinikoff

Joseph Cotten, Dolores del Rio, Jack Moss, Orson Welles, Ruth Warrick, Agnes Moorehead

'Brilliant atmosphere, the nightmare of pursuit, eccentric encounters on the way, and when the shock comes it leaps at eye and ear.'—*William Whitebait*

† A 1976 remake, much heralded, was for obscure legal reasons hardly seen. Directed by Daniel Mann for New World, it starred Zero Mostel, Shelley Winters, Stanley Holloway, Vincent Price, Donald Pleasence, Sam Waterston, Joseph Wiseman, Scott Marlowe and Yvette Mimieux.

Journey to the Center of the Earth
US 1959 132m De Luxe
Cinemascope
TCF (Charles Brackett)

An Edinburgh professor and assorted colleagues follow an explorer's trail down an extinct Icelandic volcano to the earth's centre.

Enjoyable hokum which gets more and more fantastic but only occasionally misses its footing; it ends splendidly with the team being catapulted out of Stromboli on a tide of lava.

w Walter Reisch, Charles Brackett, novel Jules Verne *d Henry Levin ph* Leo Tover *m Bernard Hevmann ad* Lyle R. Wheeler, Franz Bachelin, Herman A. Blumenthal

James Mason, Arlene Dahl, Pat Boone, Peter Ronson, Diane Baker, Thayer David

'The attraction of a Jules Verne fantasy . . . There is about the whole film a good-natured enjoyment of its own excesses.'—*Penelope Houston*

Journey's End

🎞 GB-US 1930   120m   bw
Gainsborough / Welsh-
Pearson / Tiffany-Stahl (George
Pearson)

France 1917: personal tensions
mount as men die in the trenches.
Primitive early sound version (made
in Hollywood because of better
equipment) of a justly celebrated
play first performed a year earlier.
Cinematically uninteresting, with
acting generally over the top, but it
kept Whale and Clive in Hollywood
where they shortly collaborated on
Frankenstein.

w Joseph Moncure March, Gareth
Gundrey, *play R. C. Sherriff*
d James Whale *ph* Benjamin Kline

Colin Clive, Ian MacLaren, David
Manners, Billy Bevan, Anthony
Bushell, Robert Adair

'No crystal gazing required to
forecast a big measure of
success.'—*Variety*

'It has been transferred to the
screen with the greatest possible tact
and discretion.'—*James Agate*

'Hollywood has produced its first
sex-appeal-less film. Mr George
Pearson is to be congratulated on his
restraint.'—*Punch*

'Almost painfully English . . . I
cannot believe that the strangulated
emotions which resulted can have
meant much to audiences outside the
English-speaking world.'—*Basil
Wright, 1972*

'See it now! Remember it always!'
'A story so momentous it required
six Academy Award stars and a
cast of 1,186 players!'

Juarez

✂🎞 US 1939   132m   bw
Warner (Hal B. Wallis, Henry
Blanke)

A revolutionary leader causes the
downfall of Emperor Maximilian of
Mexico.
Spectacular historical drama with
many fine moments which do not
quite coalesce into a dramatic whole,
chiefly owing to the lack of a single
viewpoint.

w John Huston, Wolfgang
Reinhardt, Aeneas Mackenzie
d William Dieterle ph Tony Gaudio
m Erich Wolfgang Korngold

Brian Aherne, Bette Davis, Paul
Muni, Claude Rains, John Garfield,
Donald Crisp, Gale Sondegaard,
Joseph Calleia, Gilbert Roland,
Henry O'Neill, Pedro de Cordoba,
Montagu Love, Harry Davenport

'With such potent box office
values, its success at theatres seems
assured.'—*Variety*

'A million dollars' worth of
ballroom sets, regimentals, gauze
shots and whiskers.'—*Otis Ferguson*

'Dramatically by far the most
effective of Warners' biographical
films of the thirties.'—*Graham
Greene*

'Muni's big-star solemn
righteousness is like a dose of
medicine.'—*New Yorker, 1977*

† Based vaguely on two novels: *The
Phantom Crown* by Bertita Harding,
and *Maximilian and Carlotta* by
Franz Werfel.
†† According to Brian Aherne the
film was to have been called *The
Phantom Crown*, but Muni's
contract enabled him to insist that
the name of his character should
appear in the title.

AAN: Brian Aherne

'The things you'll see and the
things you'll feel are the things
that will be part of you as long
as you live!'

Judgment at Nuremberg

🏆🎞 US 1961   190m   bw
UA / Roxlom (Stanley Kramer)

A fictionalized version of the 1948
trial of the Nazi leaders for crimes
against humanity.
Interminable, heavy-going dramatic
documentary expanded from a
succinct TV play into a courtroom
marathon with philosophical asides.
All good stuff, but too much of it.

w Abby Mann, from his play
d Stanley Kramer ph Ernest Laszlo
m Ernest Gold pd Rudolph Sternad

Spencer Tracy, Marlene Dietrich,
Burt Lancaster, Richard Widmark,

Maximilian Schell, Judy Garland, Montgomery Clift, William Shatner, Edward Binns, Werner Klemperer, Torben Meyer, Alan Baxter, Ray Teal

'Some believe that by tackling such themes Kramer earns at least partial remission from criticism. How much? 20 per cent off for effort?'—*Stanley Kauffmann*

† Burt Lancaster replaced Laurence Olivier, who was originally cast.

AA: Abby Mann; Maximilian Schell
AAN: best picture; Stanley Kramer; Ernest Laszlo; Spencer Tracy; Judy Garland; Montgomery Clift

Jules et Jim

France 1962   105m   bw
Franscope
Films du Carrosse / SEDIF (Marcel Berbert)
Before World War I, in Paris, a girl alternates between a French and a German student, and after the war they meet again to form a constantly shifting triangle.
The plot bores before the end, but the treatment is consistently interesting and the acting almost equally so.

François Truffaut, Jean Gruault, novel Henri-Pierre Roche
d François Truffaut *ph* Raoul Coutard *m* Georges Delerue

Oskar Werner, Jeanne Moreau, Henri Serre

'The sense is of a director intoxicated with the pleasure of making films.'—*Penelope Houston, MFB*

'A story of turmoil, of courage, of love!'
Julia

US 1977   117m
Technicolor
TCF (Julien Derode)
Lillian Hellman reflects on the fortunes of her friend Julia, filled with enthusiasm for European causes and finally killed by the Nazis.
Thoughtful, elegant patchwork of thirties memories, a vehicle for actors and a subtle, self-effacing director.

w Alvin Sargent, *book* Pentimento by Lillian Hellman *d* Fred Zinnemann *ph* Douglas Slocombe *m* Georges Delerue *ph* Carmen Dillon, Gene Callahan, Willy Holt

Jane Fonda, Vanessa Redgrave, Jason Robards Jnr, Maximilian Schell, Hal Holbrook, Rosemary Murphy, Cathleen Nesbitt, Maurice Denham

'After a while it becomes apparent that Zinnemann and Sargent are trafficking in too many quotations and flashbacks because they can't find the core of the material.'—*Pauline Kael*

AA: script; Vanessa Redgrave; Jason Robards Jnr
AAN: best picture; Fred Zinnemann; Douglas Slocombe; Georges Delerue; Jane Fonda; Maximilian Schell

'Greater than *Ivanhoe!*'
Julius Caesar

US 1953   121m   bw
MGM (John Houseman)
Cassius and Brutus lead the conspirators who murder Caesar, but are themselves routed by Mark Antony.
Straightforward, rather leaden presentation of Shakespeare's play, lit by effective moments in the acting, but the sudden change from talk to battle is not smoothed over.

wd Joseph L. Mankiewicz *ph* Joseph Ruttenberg *m* Miklos Rozsa *ad* Cedric Gibbons, Edward Carfagno

John Gielgud, James Mason, Marlon Brando, Greer Garson, Deborah Kerr, Louis Calhern, Edmond O'Brien, George Macready, Michael Pate, John Hoyt, Alan Napier

'Thrill to ruthless men and their goddess-like women in a sin-swept age!'—*publicity*
'Thrill to traitors and heroes, killings and conspiracies, passions and violence in Rome's most exciting age!'—*publicity*

AAN: best picture; Joseph Ruttenberg; Miklos Rozsa; Marlon Brando

'Men staked their lives for just one
    look at the thrilling beauty of
    this tiger woman!'
The Jungle Princess

US 1936   84m   bw
    Paramount (E. Lloyd
Sheldon)

A British hunter is injured on a
tropical island and rescued by a
native girl and her animal retinue.
Dorothy Lamour's first film role cast
her as the female Tarzan she was to
play (in a sarong, of course) a dozen
times again. This is strictly a
programmer, but after its success it
was all done again, rather better, as
Her Jungle Love.

w Cyril Hume, Gerald Geraghty,
Gouverneur Morris   *d* William
Thiele   *ph* Harry Fischbeck
md Boris Morros

Dorothy Lamour, *Ray Milland*,
Akim Tamiroff, Lynne Overman,
Molly Lamont, Hugh Buckler

'Fairly palatable entertainment
most of the way.'—*Variety*

'Poor Mr Lynne Overman is
expected to lend humorous relief to
a film already richly
comic.'—*Graham Greene*

† On this trip the tiger was Liamu
and the chimp Bogo.

K

Kagemusha
Japan 1980 179m
Eastmancolor
TCF / Toho (Akira Kurosawa)
aka: *The Double; Shadow Warrior*
On the death of a clan chief his place
is taken by the lookalike hired to
overlook battlefields while the chief
is really busy elsewhere.
Fascinating Japanese epic centring
on stately ritual and court intrigue,
with the occasional battle for
spectacular action; one of the
director's most impressive works.

*w Akira Kurosawa, Masato Ide
d Akira Kurosawa ph Kazuo
Miyagawa, Asaiachi Nakai
m Shinichiro Ikebe*

Tatsura Nakadai, Tsutomu
Yamazaki, Kenichi Hagiwara

AAN: best foreign film; art direction
BFA: direction; costume design

Kameradschaft
Germany 1931 92m bw
Nerofilm
aka: *Comradeship*
On the Franco-German border
French miners are imprisoned below
ground and Germans burrow to free
them.
Salutary message film with good
dramatic pointing.

*w Laszlo Vajda, Karl Otten, Peter
Martin Lampel d G. W. Pabst
ph Fritz Arno Wagner, Robert
Baberski*

Ernst Busch, Alexander Granach,
Fritz Kampers, Gustav Puttjer

'A storm of fear and fury in the
sizzling Florida keys!'
Key Largo
US 1948 101m bw
Warner (Jerry Wald)
A returning war veteran fights
gangsters on the Florida keys.
Moody melodrama on similar lines
to *To Have and Have Not*: it sums
up the post-war mood of despair,
allows several good acting
performances, and builds up to a
pretty good action climax.

*w Richard Brooks, John Huston,
play Maxwell Anderson d John
Huston ph Karl Freund m Max
Steiner*

*Humphrey Bogart, Lauren Bacall,
Claire Trevor, Edward G. Robinson,
Lionel Barrymore,* Thomas Gomez,
Marc Lawrence

'It's a confidently directed,
handsomely shot movie, and the cast
go at it as if the nonsense about
gangsters and human dignity were
high drama.'—*New Yorker, 1977*

'A completely empty, synthetic
work.'—*Gavin Lambert*

AA: Claire Trevor

The Kid
US 1921 52m approx (24
fps) bw silent
First National / Charles Chaplin
A tramp brings up an abandoned
baby, and later loses him to his
mother; but there is a happy ending.
Sentimental comedy set in the slums.
The comedy is very sparingly laid
on, but the effect of the whole is
much less painful than the synopsis
would suggest, the production is
comparatively smooth, the child
actor is sensational, and the film
contains much of the quintessential
Chaplin.

*wd Charles Chaplin ph Rollie
Totheroh*

*Charles Chaplin, Jackie Coogan,
Edna Purviance*

The Killers
US 1946 105m bw
U-I (Mark Hellinger)
TV title: *A Man Alone*
In a small sleazy town a gangster
waits for two assassins to kill him,
and we later find out why.

Elaborate tale of cross and
double-cross, stunningly executed.

w Anthony Veiller, story Ernest
Hemingway *d* Robert Siodmak
ph Elwood Bredell *m* Miklos Rozsa

Burt Lancaster, Edmond O'Brien,
Ava Gardner, Albert Dekker, Sam
Levene, John Miljan, Virginia
Christine, Vince Barnett, Charles D.
Brown, Donald MacBride, Phil
Brown, Charles McGraw, William
Conrad

'About one tenth is Hemingway's,
the rest is Universal-International's.'
—Richard Winnington

'Seldom does a melodrama
maintain the high tension that
distinguishes this one.'*—Variety*

'There is nothing unique or even
valuable about the picture, but
energy combined with attention to
form and detail doesn't turn up
every day; neither does good
entertainment.'*—James Agee*

† John Huston contributed to the
script but is not credited.

AAN: Anthony Veiller; Robert
Siodmak; Miklos Rozsa

The Killing Fields
    GB 1984   141m   colour
    Goldcrest/Enigma (*David
Puttnam*)
An American journalist is engulfed
in the horror of Cambodia, and his
native adviser disappears and is
thought to be dead.
Brilliantly filmed, but probably too
strong for a commercial audience to
stomach, this true adventure tosses
one into the horror of modern war
and leaves one reeling despite its
comparatively happy ending.

w Bruce Robinson, from the article
'The Death and Life of Dith Pran'
by Sidney Schanberg *d* Roland
Joffe *ph* Chris Menges *m* Mike
Oldfield *pd* Roy Walker *ed* Jim
Clark

Sam Waterston (as Sidney
Schanberg), *Haing S. Ngor* (as Dith
Pran), John Malkovitch, Julian
Sands, Craig T. Nelson

AA: Haing S. Ngor (supporting
actor), photography, editing
AAN: best picture, Sam Waterston,
adapted screenplay
BFA: best picture, adapted
screenplay, Haing S. Ngor
(supporting actor)

Kind Hearts and Coronets
    GB 1949   106m   bw
    Ealing (Michael Relph)
An impecunious heir eliminates
eight D'Ascoynes who stand
between him and the family fortune.
Witty, genteel black comedy well set
in the stately Edwardian era and
quite deserving of its reputation for
wit and style; yet the effect is
curiously muffled and several
opportunities missed.

*w Robert Hamer, John Dighton,
novel* Noblesse Oblige by Roy
Horniman *d* Robert Hamer
ph Douglas Slocombe

Dennis Price, Alec Guinness (in
eight roles), *Valerie Hobson, Joan
Greenwood*, Miles Malleson, Arthur
Lowe

'A brilliant misfire for the reason
that its plentiful wit is literary and
practically never pictorial.'*—Richard
Winnington*

'Enlivened with cynicism, loaded
with dramatic irony and shot through
with a suspicion of social
satire.'*—Daily Telegraph*

'A film which can be seen and
seen again with undiminished
pleasure.'*—Basil Wright, 1972*

A Kind of Loving
    GB 1962   112m   bw
    Anglo-Amalgamated/
Waterhall/Vic Films (Joe Janni)
A young north country draughtsman
is forced into marriage, has to live
with his dragon-like mother in law,
and finally sorts out a relationship
with his unhappy wife.
Blunt melodrama with strong kinship
to *Saturday Night and Sunday
Morning*, strikingly directed and
photographed amid urban grime and
suburban conformity.

w Keith Waterhouse, Willis Hall, novel Stan Barstow d John Schlesinger ph Denys Coop m Ron Grainer

Alan Bates, June Ritchie, Thora Hird, Bert Palmer, Gwen Nelson

'You will be shocked by this highly moral film only if you are shocked by life.'—*Evening News*

King Kong

US 1933 100m bw
RKO (Merian C. Cooper)

A film producer on safari brings back a giant ape which terrorizes New York.

The greatest monster movie of all, a miracle of trick work and suspense, with some of the most memorable moments in film history.

w James Creelman, Ruth Rose, story Edgar Wallace d Merian C. Cooper, Ernest Schoedsack ph Edward Linden, Verne Walker, J. O. Taylor sound effects Murray Spivak chief technician Willis J. O'Brien m Max Steiner

Robert Armstrong, Fay Wray, Bruce Cabot, Frank Reicher

CARL DENHAM (Robert Armstrong): 'It wasn't the airplanes. It was beauty killed the beast.'

'If properly handled, should gather good grosses in a walk . . . and may open up a new medium for scaring babies via the screen.'—*Variety*

'Just amusing nonsense punctuated by such reflections as why, if the natives wanted to keep the monster on the other side of the wall, they should have built a door big enough to let him through.'—*James Agate*

AAN: photography

King of Jazz

US 1930 101m
Technicolor
Universal (Carl Laemmle Jnr)
Musical revue.

Stylish, spectacular, revelatory early musical: a treasure trove.

devised/d John Murray Anderson w Harry Ruskin, Charles

MacArthur *pd* Hal Mohr, Ray Rennahan, Jerome Ash *ad Herman Rose*

Paul Whiteman and his orchestra, John Boles, Bing Crosby (with the Rhythm Boys), Laura la Plante, Glenn Tryon, Slim Summerville, Walter Brennan

Songs: 'Happy Feet'; 'A Bench in the Park'; 'My Bridal Veil'; 'Song of the Dawn'; 'I Like to Do Things for You'; 'Music Has Charms'; 'My Lover'; 'It Happened in Monterey'; 'Ragamuffin Romeo'; 'So the Bluebirds and the Blackbirds Got Together'

'A box office picture anywhere for one week.'—*Variety*

'Under a master director and the reverent genius of great players, the story of Christ has taken human form and greater understanding!'

'Dramatic magnificence, spectacular splendour, riotous joy, tigerish rage, undying love, terrifying tempests, appalling earthquakes!'

King of Kings

US 1927 155m approx
(24 fps) (various versions)
bw silent
(Pathé) Cecil B. de Mille

The life of Jesus, seen more or less from the viewpoint of Mary Magdalene.

A patchy but frequently moving and pictorially effective work, ranging from the sublime (the first view of Jesus as a blind man regains his sight) to the ridiculous ('Harness my zebras, gift of the Nubian king!' says Mary Magdalene in a sub-title).

w Jeanie Macpherson d Cecil B. de Mille ph J. Peverell Marley

H. B. Warner, Jacqueline Logan, Joseph Schildkraut (Judas), Ernest Torrence (Peter), Victor Varconi (Pilate), Dorothy Cumming (Mary, mother of Jesus), Rudolph Schildkraut (Caiaphas)

'The most impressive of all motion

pictures.'—*Mordaunt Hall, New York Times*

'A picture which will tend to standardize the world's conception of the New Testament . . . de Mille has one of the best business minds in pictures and making *King of Kings* was the most brilliant stroke of his successful business career.'—*Welford Beaton, The Film Spectator*

'Even Hell had to have a monarch!'
King Rat
🐀 US 1965   134m   bw
Columbia/Coleytown (James Woolf)
In Singapore's Changi Gaol during World War II an American corporal lives more comfortably than the other prisoners by shabby dealings with the camp guards.
Overlong but generally gripping character melodrama—'not a story of escape but a story of survival'.

wd Bryan Forbes, *novel* James Clavell *ph* Burnett Guffey *m* John Barry

George Segal, Tom Courtenay, John Mills, James Fox, Denholm Elliott, Todd Armstrong, Patrick O'Neal, James Donald, Alan Webb, Leonard Rossiter, Geoffrey Bayldon

AAN: Burnett Guffey

'The town they talk of in whispers!'
King's Row
🐾 US 1941   127m   bw
Warner (David Lewis)
In a small American town during the early years of the century, three children grow up into a world of cruelty and madness.
Superb Hollywood melodrama, a Peyton Place with great visual strength, haunting music and a wholly absorbing if incredible plot.

w Casey Robinson, *novel* Henry Bellamann *d* Sam Wood *ph* James Wong Howe *m* Erich Wolfgang Korngold *pd* William Cameron Menzies

Ann Sheridan, Robert Cummings, Ronald Reagan, *Claude Rains*, Betty Field, Charles Coburn, Nancy Coleman, *Maria Ouspenskaya*, Harry Davenport, Judith Anderson, Karen Verne

DRAKE (Ronald Reagan): 'Where's the rest of me?'

'Half masterpiece and half junk.'—*James Agate*

'Out of the hushed strangeness of these lives, and out of the shadows that hid their shame, filmdom has fashioned a drama most unusual, most touching and most wonderful!'—*publicity*

'Tranquilly accepting many varieties of psychopathic behaviour as the simple facts of life, this film has its own kind of sentimental glow, yet the melodramatic incidents are surprisingly compelling.'—*New Yorker, 1982*

'One of the great melodramas, a veritable Mount Rushmore of physical and emotional cripples.'—*Time Out, 1981*

AAN: best picture; Sam Wood; James Wong Howe

Kipps
♀ GB 1941   112m   bw
TCF (Edward Black)
US title: *The Remarkable Mr Kipps*
In 1906, a draper's assistant comes into money and tries to crash society.
Charming, unassuming film of a well-loved novel, later musicalized as *Half a Sixpence*.

w Sidney Gilliat, *novel* H. G. Wells *d* Carol Reed *ph* Arthur Crabtree *m* Charles Williams

Michael Redgrave, Phyllis Calvert, Diana Wynyard, *Arthur Riscoe*, Max Adrian, Helen Haye, Michael Wilding, Lloyd Pearson, Edward Rigby, Hermione Baddeley, Frank Pettingell, Beatrice Varley, Kathleen Harrison, Felix Aylmer

'It has the old fashioned charm of wax roses under a glass bell.'—*New York Times*

'I don't care what you do to me,
  Mike—just do it fast!'
Kiss Me Deadly
  US 1955   105m   bw
  UA/Parklane (Robert Aldrich)
By helping a girl who is nevertheless
murdered, Mike Hammer prevents
crooks from stealing a case of
radio-active material.
Curiously arty and excruciatingly
boring private eye thriller, a ripe
piece of cinematic cheese full of tilt
shots and symbols: even the titles
read from down to up.

w A. I. Bezzerides d Robert
Aldrich ph Ernest Laszlo m Frank
de Vol

Ralph Meeker, Albert Dekker,
Cloris Leachman, Paul Stewart,
Juano Hernandez, Wesley Addy,
Maxene Cooper
   'This meeting of "art" and pulp
literature is, to say the least,
curious.'—*Monthly Film Bulletin*

'She had all London on a
  MARRY-go-round!'
Kitty
  US 1945   103m   bw
  Paramount (Karl Tunberg)
In 18th-century London, an
aristocrat makes a duchess of a
guttersnipe.
Well-detailed period *Pygmalion*
which works much better than one
would expect.

w Darrell Ware, Karl Tunberg,
novel Rosamund Marshall
d *Mitchell Leisen ph Daniel L.
Fapp m Victor Young*
*Paulette Goddard, Ray Milland,
Cecil Kellaway, Constance Collier,
Reginald Owen*, Patric Knowles,
Dennis Hoey, Sara Allgood, Eric
Blore, Gordon Richards, Michael
Dyne
   'Enough sex, wit and urbane
cynicism to make one forget a
footling ending.'—*Peter John Dyer,
MFB*
   'It is excellently cast, delightfully
acted, and the rather sordid story is
told with subtlety and skill.'—*Picture
Show*

'The most glamorous study of
unrelieved sordidness that the screen
has presented.'—*Motion Picture
Herald*

'The most daring novel ever
  written by a man about a
  woman!'
Kitty Foyle
  US 1940   108m   bw
  RKO (Harry E. Edgington,
David Hempstead)
A white-collar girl has a troubled
love life.
Solid entertainment of its time,
especially aimed at ambitious young
ladies.

w Dalton Trumbo, Donald Ogden
Stewart, *novel* Christopher Morley
d Sam Wood ph Robert de Grasse
m Roy Webb
Ginger Rogers, Dennis Morgan,
James Craig, *Eduardo Ciannelli*,
Ernest Cossart, Gladys Cooper,
Mary Treen

AA: Ginger Rogers
AAN: best picture; Dalton Trumbo,
Donald Ogden Stewart; Sam Wood

Klute
  US 1971   114m
  Technicolor   Panavision
Warner (Alan J. Pakula)
A policeman leaves the force to
investigate the disappearance of a
research scientist, and takes up with
a call girl who is involved.
Excellent adult thriller with attention
to detail and emphasis on character.

w Andy K. Lewis, Dave Lewis
d Alan J. Pakula ph Gordon Willis
m Michael Small

Jane Fonda, Donald Sutherland,
Charles Cioffi, Roy Scheider, Rita
Gam

AA: Jane Fonda
AAN: Andy K. Lewis, Dave Lewis

The Knack
  GB 1965   84m   bw
  UA/Woodfall (Oscar
Lewenstein)
A sex-starved young teacher lets one
room of his house to a successful

womanizer, another to an innocent
girl from the north.
An excuse for an anarchic series of
visual gags, a kaleidoscope of
swinging London in which anything
goes. Brilliantly done in the style of
A Hard Day's Night.

w Charles Wood, *play* Ann Jellicoe
d Richard Lester *ph* David Watkin
m John Barry

*Michael Crawford, Ray Brooks, Rita
Tushingham*, Donal Donnelly

Knight without Armour
GB 1937   107m   bw
London Films (Alexander
Korda)
During the Russian Revolution of
1917, a widowed countess is helped
to safety by a British translator.
Underrated romantic adventure with
big production values and some
splendid moments.

w Lajos Biro, Arthur Wimperis,
Frances Marion, *novel* James Hilton
ph Harry Stradling *d* Jacques
Feyder *m* Miklos Rozsa

Robert Donat, Marlene Dietrich,
Irene Vanbrugh, Herbert Lomas,
Austin Trevor, Basil Gill, David
Tree, John Clements, Lawrence
Hanray

'Another feather in the cap of
Alexander Korda for his series of
artistic film productions. There is
relatively little to find fault with and
much to praise.'—*Variety*

'A first class thriller, beautifully
directed, with spare and convincing
dialogue and a nearly watertight
scenario.'—*Graham Greene*

'There are three sides to this love
story!'
Kramer versus Kramer
US 1979   105m
Technicolor
Columbia/Stanley Jaffe (Richard
C. Fischoff)
A divorced advertising executive
gets temporary custody of his
seven-year-old son.
New-fashioned tearjerker, as slick as
a colour supplement and catnip to
the emotion-starved masses.

wd Robert Benton, *novel* Avery
Corman *ph* Nestor Almendros
md Erma E. Levin *pd* Paul Sylbert

Dustin Hoffman, Justin Henry,
Meryl Streep, Jane Alexander,
Howard Duff

'Pastel colours, a cute kid and a
good script made this one of the
most undeserved successes of the
year: wall-to-wall sentiment.'—*Time
Out*

AA: best picture; Robert Benton (as
director); Dustin Hoffman; Meryl
Streep; screen play adapted from
another medium
AAN: Justin Henry

L

Lady and the Tramp
US 1955 76m
Technicolor Cinemascope
Walt Disney (Erdmann Penner)
A pedigree spaniel falls foul of two
Siamese cats and has a romantic
adventure with a mongrel who helps
her.
Pleasant cartoon feature in Disney's
cutest and most anthropomorphic
vein.

d Hamilton Luske, Clyde Geronomi,
Wilfred Jackson m Oliver Wallace

The Lady Eve
US 1941 97m bw
Paramount (Paul Jones)
A lady cardsharper and her father
are outsmarted on a transatlantic
liner by a millionaire simpleton; she
plans an elaborate revenge.
Hectic romantic farce, the first to
show its director's penchant for
mixing up sexual innuendo, funny
men and pratfalls. There are
moments when the pace drops, but
in general it's scintillating
entertainment, especially after
viewing its weak remake *The Birds
and the Bees*.

wd Preston Sturges, play Monckton
Hoffe ph Victor Milner m Leo
Shuken, Charles Bradshaw
*Barbara Stanwyck, Henry Fonda,
Charles Coburn, Eugène Pallette,*
William Demarest, Eric Blore,
Melville Cooper, Martha O'Driscoll,
Janet Beecher, Robert Greig, Luis
Alberni, Jimmy Conlin
   'The whole theme, with all its
variations of keys, is played to one
end, to get laughs, and at several
different levels it gets
them.'—*National Board of Review*
   'Preston Sturges, they tell me, is
known in Hollywood as "the
streamlined Lubitsch". This needn't
put you off, because if he goes on

producing films as lively as this one
he will one day come to be known as
Preston Sturges.—*William Whitebait*
   'This time Preston Sturges has
wrapped you up another package
that is neither very big nor very
flashy, but the best fun in
months.'—*Otis Ferguson*
   'A mixture of visual and verbal
slapstick, of high artifice and
pratfalls . . . it represents the dizzy
high point of Sturges' writing.'—*New
Yorker, 1977*
   'The brightest sort of nonsense, on
which Preston Sturges' signature is
written large. The result has a
sustained comic flavour and an
individual treatment that are rarely
found in Hollywood's antic
concoctions.'—*New York Herald
Tribune*
   'A more charming or distinguished
gem of nonsense has not occurred
since *It Happened One Night*.'—*New
York Times*

AAN: Monckton Hoffe (original
story)

Lady for a Day
US 1933 95m bw
Columbia
Gangsters help an old apple seller to
pose as a rich woman when her
daughter visits.
Splendid sentimental comedy full of
cinematic resource; the best
translation of Runyon to the screen.

w Robert Riskin, story Madame La
Gimp by Damon Runyon d Frank
Capra ph Joseph Walker
May Robson, Warren William, Guy
Kibbee, Glenda Farrell, Ned Sparks,
Jean Parker, Walter Connolly, Nat
Pendleton
   'Exceptionally adroit direction and
scenario . . . sell it with plenty of
adjectives as it will please
everybody.'—*Variety*

AAN: best picture; Robert Riskin;
Frank Capra; May Robson

The Lady from Shanghai

US 1948 87m bw
Columbia (Richard Wilson,
William Castle)

A seaman becomes involved in the
maritime wanderings of a crippled
lawyer and his homicidal frustrated
wife.

Absurd, unintelligible, plainly much
cut and rearranged, this thriller was
obviously left too much in Welles'
hands and then just as unfairly taken
out of them; but whole sequences of
sheer brilliance remain, notably the
final shoot-out in the hall of mirrors.

wd Orson Welles, novel If I Die
Before I Wake by Sherwood King
ph Charles Lawton Jnr *m* Heinz
Roemheld

Orson Welles, Rita Hayworth,
Everett Sloane, Glenn Anders, Ted
de Corsia, Erskine Sanford, Gus
Schilling

  'The slurred social conscience of
the hero leads him to some murky
philosophizing, all of which with
many individualities of diction clog
the issue and the sound track.
Sub-titles, I fear, would have
helped.'—*Richard Winnington*

'The minx in mink with a yen for
men!'

Lady in the Dark

US 1944 100m
Technicolor

Paramount (Richard Blumenthal)

The editress of a fashion magazine is
torn between three men, has
worrying dreams, and takes herself
to a psychoanalyst.

Lush, stylish and frequently amusing
version of a Broadway musical,
lacking most of the songs; despite its
faults, an excellent example of studio
spectacle and a very typical forties
romantic comedy.

w Frances Goodrich, Albert
Hackett, *play* Moss Hart *d* Mitchell
Leisen *ph* Ray Rennahan *m* Kurt
Weill *ly* Ira Gershwin *md* Robert
Emmett Dolan *sp* Gordon Jennings
ad Hans Dreier

Ginger Rogers, Warner Baxter, Ray

Milland, Jon Hall, *Mischa Auer*,
Mary Phillips, Barry Sullivan

† The film was completed in 1942
but held up because of overstock.

†† Paramount chief Buddy de Sylva
is credited with ruining the film by
cutting the theme song, 'My Ship',
which is the key to the
psychoanalysis.

AAN: Ray Rennahan; Robert
Emmett Dolan

Lady Killer

US 1933 76m bw
Warner (Henry Blanke)

A cinema usher turns to crime, flees
to Hollywood, and becomes a movie
star.

Hectic slam-bang action comedy
with melodramatic moments. Great
fun.

w Ben Markson, *novel* The Finger
Man by Rosalind Keating Shaffer
d Roy del Ruth *ph* Tony Gaudio
md Leo F. Forbstein

James Cagney, Mae Clarke, Leslie
Fenton, Margaret Lindsay, Henry
O'Neill, Willard Robertson,
Raymond Hatton, Russell Hopton

  'An all-time high in roughneck
character work even for this
rough-and-tumble star.'—*Variety*

  'A kind of résumé of everything
he has done to date in the
movies.'—*New York Evening Post*

  'Sprightly, more or less daring,
thoroughly entertaining.'—*New
York World Telegram*

The Lady Vanishes

GB 1938 97m bw
Gaumont

British / Gainsborough (Edward
Black)

En route back to England by train
from Switzerland, an old lady
disappears and two young people
investigate.

The disappearing lady trick
brilliantly refurbished by Hitchcock
and his screenwriters, who even get
away with a horrid model shot at the
beginning. Superb, suspenseful,
brilliantly funny, meticulously
detailed entertainment.

w *Sidney Gilliat, Frank Launder,*
novel The Wheel Spins by Ethel
Lina White d *Alfred Hitchcock*
ph Jack Cox *md* Louis Levy

Margaret Lockwood, Michael
Redgrave, Dame May Whitty, Paul
Lukas, Basil Radford, Naunton
Wayne, Catherine Lacey, Cecil
Parker, Linden Travers, Googie
Withers, *Mary Clare,* Philip Leaver

'If it were not so brilliant a
melodrama, we should class it as a
brilliant comedy.'—*Frank S. Nugent*

'No one can study the deceptive
effortlessness with which one thing
leads to another without learning
where the true beauty of this
medium is to be mined.'—*Otis*
Ferguson

'Directed with such skill and
velocity that it has come to represent
the very quintessence of screen
suspense.'—*Pauline Kael, 70s*

† Hitchcock was actually second
choice as director. The production
was ready to roll as *Lost Lady,*
directed by Roy William Neill, with
Charters and Caldicott already in
place, when Neill became
unavailable and Hitch stepped in.

Lassie Come Home

US 1943 88m Technicolor
MGM (Samuel Marx)
A poor family is forced to sell its
beloved dog, but she makes a
remarkable journey to return to
them.
First of the Lassie films and certainly
the best: an old-fashioned
heartwarmer.

w Hugo Butler, *novel* Eric Knight
d Fred M. Wilcox *ph* Leonard
Smith *m* Daniele Amfitheatrof

Roddy McDowall, Elizabeth Taylor,
Donald Crisp, Edmund Gwenn,
Dame May Whitty, Nigel Bruce,
Elsa Lanchester, J. Pat O'Malley

'The late Eric Knight wrote this
immortal essay in
Doggery-Woggery. MGM finished it
off.'—*Richard Winnington*

AAN: Leonard Smith

The Last Detail

US 1973 104m Metrocolor
Columbia / Acrobat
Persky–Bright (Gerald Ayres)
Two hardened naval petty officers
escort a young recruit, sentenced for
thieving, from Virginia to a New
Hampshire jail, and give him a wild
last night.
Foul-mouthed weekend odyssey,
with a few well-observed moments
for non-prudes. Technically the
epitome of Hollywood's most
irritating seventies fashion, with
fuzzy sound recording, dim
against-the-light photography, and a
general determination to show up
the ugliness of everything around us.

w Robert Towne, *novel* Darryl
Ponicsan d Hal Ashby *ph* Michael
Chapman *m* Johnny Mandel

Jack Nicholson, Otis Young, Randy
Quaid, Clifton James, Carol Kane

'Visually it is relentlessly
lower-depths gloomy, and the
material, though often very funny, is
programmed to wrench your
heart.'—*New Yorker*

AAN: Robert Towne; Jack
Nicholson; Randy Quaid

The Last Flight

US 1931 80m bw
Warner
In 1919, four veteran American fliers
stay on in Paris in the hope of
calming their shattered physical and
emotional states.
Fascinatingly offhand study on
post-war cynicism and the faint hope
of a better world, beautifully written
and directed in a manner more
effective than *The Sun Also Rises*.

w *John Monk Saunders,* from his
novel Single Lady d *William*
Dieterle *ph* Sid Hickox

Richard Barthelmess, Helen
Chandler, David Manners, John
Mack Brown, *Elliott Nugent,* Walter
Byron

'If the crowd can understand that
girl character in this picture the film
is an undoubted grosser.'—*Variety*

'A narrative as tight and spare as a
Racine tragedy . . . unique in

Hollywood of that time in its persistent, calculated understatement.'—*Tom Milne, 1975*

† In magazine form the story was known as 'Nikki and her War Birds'.

The Last Hurrah
US 1958   125m   bw
Columbia (John Ford)
The political boss of a New England town fights his last campaign. Enjoyable if disjointed melodrama, an old man's film crammed with cameo performances from familiar faces: important as one of Hollywood's great sentimental reunions.

w Frank Nugent, novel Edwin O'Connor *d John Ford ph* Charles Lawton Jnr

Spencer Tracy, Jeffrey Hunter, Dianne Foster, *Pat O'Brien, Basil Rathbone, Edward Brophy, Donald Crisp, James Gleason, John Carradine, Ricardo Cortez, Wallace Ford, Frank McHugh,* Frank Albertson, Anna Lee, Jane Darwell, Willis Bouchey, Basil Ruysdael

† A TV version was subsequently made with Carroll O'Connor.

The Last Laugh
Germany 1924   73m approx
(24 fps)   bw   silent
UFA
original title: *Der Letzte Mann*
The old doorman of a luxury hotel is given the job of lavatory attendant but comes into a fortune and gets his revenge.
Ironic anecdote made important by its virtual abandonment of dialogue and whole-hearted adoption of the camera eye technique which gives some thrilling dramatic effects.

w Carl Mayer d F. W. Murnau ph Karl Freund

Emil Jannings, Max Hiller, Maly Delschaft, Hans Unterkirchen

  'A marvellous picture—marvellous in its simplicity, its economy of effect, its expressiveness, and its dramatic power.'—*Life*

† A German remake of 1955 had Hans Albers in the lead and was of no interest.

The Last Picture Show
US 1971   118m   bw
Columbia / LPS / BDS
(Stephen J. Friedman)
Teenage affairs in a small Texas town in 1951, ending with the hero's embarkation for Korea and the closing of the tatty cinema. Penetrating nostalgia with over-emphasis on sex; the detail is the attraction.

w Larry McMurty, Peter Bogdanovich *d Peter Bogdanovich ph* Robert Surtees *m* original recordings *pd* Polly Platt

Timothy Bottoms, Jeff Bridges, Cybill Shepherd, *Ben Johnson, Cloris Leachman,* Ellen Burstyn
  'The most important work by a young American director since *Citizen Kane.*'—*Paul D. Zimmerman*
  'So many things in it are so good that I wish I liked it more.'—*Stanley Kauffmann*

AA: Ben Johnson; Cloris Leachman
AAN: best picture; script; Peter Bogdanovich (as director); Robert Surtees; Jeff Bridges; Ellen Burstyn

Last Year in Marienbad
France / Italy 1961   94m
bw   Dyaliscope
Terra / Tamara / Cormoran / Precitel / Como / Argos / Cinetel / Silver / Cineriz (Raymond Froment)
In a vast old-fashioned hotel, a man meets a woman who may or may not have had an affair with him the previous year in Marienbad—or was it Frederiksbad?
A dreamy, elegant film which presents a puzzle with no solution. It has its attractions for film buffs and cryptogram addicts, but is not for anyone who simply wants to be told a story.

w Alain Robbe-Grillet d Alain Resnais ph Sacha Vierny *m* Francis Seyrig *ad* Jacques Saulnier

Delphine Seyrig, Giorgio Albertazzi, Sacha Pitoeff

'Elaborate, ponderous and meaningless.'—*Newsweek*

'Clearly the film's creators know exactly what they want to do and have done it with complete success. Whether one responds to the result is entirely a matter of temperament.'—*John Russell Taylor, MFB*

AAN: Alain Robbe-Grillet

Laughter in Paradise

GB 1951 93m bw
ABPC (*Mario Zampi*)

An eccentric leaves in his will a fortune for each of his relations providing they will perform certain embarrassing or criminal acts. A funny idea gets half-hearted treatment, but the good bits are hilarious.

w Michael Pertwee, Jack Davies *d* Mario Zampi *ph* William McLeod *m* Stanley Black

Alastair Sim, *Joyce Grenfell*, Hugh Griffith, Fay Compton, John Laurie, George Cole, Guy Middleton, Ronald Adam, Leslie Dwyer, A. E. Matthews, Beatrice Campbell

† Remade 1972 as *Some Will, Some Won't*.

Laura

US 1944 85m bw
TCF (Otto Preminger)

A beautiful girl is murdered . . . or is she? A cynical detective investigates.

A quiet, streamlined little murder mystery that brought a new adult approach to the genre and heralded the mature *film noir* of the later forties. A small cast responds perfectly to a classically spare script, and in Clifton Webb a new star is born.

w Jay Dratler, Samuel Hoffenstein, Betty Reinhardt, *novel* Vera Caspary *d* Otto Preminger *ph* Joseph La Shelle *m* David Raksin

Dana Andrews, *Clifton Webb*, Gene

Tierney, Judith Anderson, *Vincent Price*, Dorothy Adams, James Flavin

WALDO LYDECKER (Clifton Webb): 'Its lavish, but I call it home.'

WALDO: 'I shall never forget the weekend Laura died. A silver sun burned through the sky like a huge magnifying glass. It was the hottest Sunday in my recollection. I felt as if I were the only human being left in New York . . . I had just begun Laura's story when another of those detectives came to see me. I had him wait.'

WALDO: 'In my case, self-absorption is completely justified. I have never discovered any other subject quite so worthy of my attention.'

'Everybody's favourite chic murder mystery.'—*New Yorker, 1977*

† Rouben Mamoulian directed some scenes before handing over to Preminger.

AA: Joseph La Shelle
AAN: script; Otto Preminger; Clifton Webb

The Lavender Hill Mob

GB 1951 78m bw
Ealing (Michael Truman)

A timid bank clerk conceives and executes a bullion robbery. Superbly characterized and inventively detailed comedy, one of the best ever made at Ealing or in Britain.

w T. E. B. Clarke *d* Charles Crichton *ph* Douglas Slocombe *m* Georges Auric

Alec Guinness, *Stanley Holloway*, Sidney James, Alfie Bass, Marjorie Fielding, Edie Martin, John Gregson, Gibb McLaughlin

'Amusing situations and dialogue are well paced and sustained throughout: the climax is delightful.'—*MFB*

AA: T. E. B. Clarke
AAN: Alec Guinness

Lawrence of Arabia

GB 1962   221m
Technicolor   Super
Panavision 70
Columbia / Horizon (Sam Spiegel)

An adventurer's life with the Arabs,
told in flashbacks after his accidental
death in the thirties.

Sprawling epic which manages after
four hours to give no insight
whatever into the complexities of
character of this mysterious historic
figure, but is often spectacularly
beautiful and exciting along the way.

*w Robert Bolt d David Lean
ph Frederick A. Young m Maurice
Jarre pd John Box ad John Stoll*

*Peter O'Toole, Omar Sharif, Arthur
Kennedy,* Jack Hawkins, Donald
Wolfit, Claude Rains, Anthony
Quayle, *Alec Guinness,* Anthony
Quinn, Jose Ferrer, Michel Ray, Zia
Mohyeddin

'Grandeur of conception is not up
to grandeur of setting.'—*Penelope
Houston*

'Lean has managed to market
epics as serious entertainment rather
than as the spectacles they
are.'—*Time Out, 1980*

† Albert Finney turned down the
role before O'Toole was offered it.

AA: best picture; David Lean;
Frederick A. Young; Maurice Jarre
AAN: Robert Bolt; Peter O'Toole;
Omar Sharif

The League of Gentlemen

GB 1960   112m   bw
Rank / Allied Film Makers
(Michael Relph)

An ex-army officer recruits
high-class misfits with guilty secrets
to help him in a bank robbery.

Delightfully handled comedy
adventure, from the days (alas)
when crime did not pay; a lighter
ending would have made it a classic.

*w Bryan Forbes, novel John Boland
d Basil Dearden ph Arthur
Ibbetson m Phiip Green*

Jack Hawkins, Richard
Attenborough, *Roger Livesey, Nigel
Patrick,* Bryan Forbes, Kieron

Moore, Terence Alexander, *Norman
Bird,* Robert Coote, Melissa
Stribling, Nanette Newman, Gerald
Harper, Patrick Wymark, David
Lodge, Doris Hare, Lydia Sherwood

The Leopard

US / Italy 1963   205m
Technirama
TCF / Titanus / SNPC / GPC
(Goffredo Lombardo)
original title: *Il Gattopardo*

The family life of an Italian
nobleman at the time of Garibaldi.

Elaborate, complex family saga,
painted like an old master with great
care and attention to detail, but with
not much chance outside Italy of
delivering its original dramatic force.
Visconti had asked for Lancaster, so
TCF picked up the international
release but couldn't make head or
tail of it commercially; they even
ruined its high quality by releasing a
dubbed, shortened version in
Cinemascope and De Luxe colour of
poor standard.

*wd Luchino Visconti,
novel Giuseppe de Lampedusa
ph Giuseppe Rotunno m Nino Rota
ad Mario Garbuglia*

Burt Lancaster, Claudia Cardinale,
Alain Delon, Paolo Stoppa, Serge
Reggiani, Leslie French

Let George Do It

GB 1940   82m   bw
Ealing (Basil Dearden)

A ukelele player accidentally goes to
Bergen instead of Blackpool and is
mistaken for a spy.

Generally thought to be the best
George Formby vehicle, with plenty
of pace, good situations and catchy
tunes.

*w John Dighton, Austin Melford,
Angus MacPhail, Basil Dearden
d Marcel Varnel ph Gordon Dines,
Ronald Neame*

George Formby, Phyllis Calvert,
Garry Marsh, Romney Brent,
Bernard Lee, Coral Browne, Torin
Thatcher, Hal Gordon

'With all my heart, I still love the man I killed!'

The Letter

US 1940 95m bw
Warner (Robert Lord)

A rubber plantation owner's wife kills a man in what seems to have been self-defence; but a letter from her proves it to have been a crime of passion, and becomes an instrument of blackmail.

Excellent performances and presentation make this the closest approximation on film to reading a Maugham story of the Far East, though censorship forced the addition of an infuriating moral ending.

w Howard Koch, story W. Somerset Maugham d William Wyler ph Tony Gaudio m Max Steiner

Bette Davis, Herbert Marshall, James Stephenson, Sen Yung, Frieda Inescort, Gale Sondergaard, Bruce Lester, Tetsu Komai

'The writing is taut and spare throughout . . . the unravelling of Maugham's story is masterly and the presentaiton visual and cinematic . . . the audience at the trade show did not move a finger.'—James Agate

† Herbert Marshall played the lover in the first version and the husband in the second.

AAN: best picture; William Wyler; Tony Gaudio; Max Steiner; Bette Davis; James Stephenson

'The story that will live . . . as long as there is love!'

Letter from an Unknown Woman

US 1948 89m bw
Universal / Rampart (John Houseman)

A woman wastes her life in unrequited love for a rakish pianist. Superior 'woman's picture' which gave its director his best chance in America to re-create his beloved Vienna of long ago. Hollywood production magic at its best.

w Howard Koch, novel Stefan Zweig d Max Ophuls ph Franz

Planer m Daniele Amfitheatrof ad Alexander Golitzen

Joan Fontaine, Louis Jourdan, Mady Christians, Art Smith, Marcel Journet

'A film full of snow, sleigh bells, lights gleaming in ornamental gardens and trysts at night.'—Charles Higham, 1972

'It is fascinating to watch the sure deft means by which Ophuls sidetracks seemingly inevitable clichés and holds on to a shadowy, tender mood, half buried in the past. Here is a fragile filmic charm that is not often or easily accomplished.'—Richard Winnington

'Film narrative of a most skilled order.'—William Whitebait

'Probably the toniest "woman's picture" ever made.'—Pauline Kael, 70s

'A peek into the other woman's male!'

A Letter to Three Wives

US 1949 102m bw
TCF (Sol C. Siegel)

Three wives on a picnic receive word from a friend that she has run off with one of their husbands. Amusing short-story compendium which seemed more revelatory at the time than it does now, and paved the way for its writer-director's heyday.

wd Joseph L. Mankiewicz, novel John Klempner ph Arthur Miller m Alfred Newman

Jeanne Crain, Ann Sothern, Linda Darnell, Jeffrey Lynn, Kirk Douglas, Paul Douglas, Barbara Lawrence, Connie Gilchrist, Florence Bates, Hobart Cavanaugh, and the voice of Celeste Holm

'A mere shadow of those acid Hollywood comedies of the thirties . . . over-written and under-directed . . . but it has a supply of ironies and makes a certain alkaline comment on present-day American customs and manners.'—Richard Winnington

'Replete with sharp dialogue. He aims barbed darts at the country's favourite institutions, and makes them socre with telling effect.'—*Variety*

AA: Joseph L. Mankiewicz (as writer); Joseph L. Mankiewicz (as director)
AAN: best picture

Libeled Lady
♉ US 1936 98m bw
MGM (Lawrence Weingarten)
An heiress sues a newspaper, and the editor hires a friend to compromise her.
Lively four-star romantic comedy which sums up its era as well as any.

w Maurine Watkins, Howard Emmett Rogers, George Oppenheimer d Jack Conway ph Norbert Brodine m William Axt

Jean Harlow, Myrna Loy, Spencer Tracy, William Powell, Walter Connolly, Charley Grapewin, Cora Witherspoon, E. E. Clive, Charles Trowbridge
  'Handsomely mounted and produced, lavishly costumed, cleverly written and artfully directed, *Libeled Lady* is entirely worthy of the noble comedians who head its cast.'—*Bland Johaneson, New York Daily Mirror*

† Remade as *Easy to Wed*; central situation borrowed for *Man's Favorite Sport.*

AAN: best picture

The Life and Death of Colonel Blimp
♉ GB 1943   163m
Technicolor
GFD / Archers (Michael Powell, Emeric Pressburger)
US title: *Colonel Blimp*
A British soldier survives three wars and falls in love with three women. Not the Blimp of the cartoon strip, but a sympathetic figure in a warm, consistently interesting if idiosyncratic love story against a background of war. The Archers as usual provide a sympathetic German lead (friend of the hero); quite a coup in wartime.

wd Michael Powell, Emeric Pressburger ph Jack Cardiff m Allan Gray ad Alfred Junge

Roger Livesey, Anton Walbrook, Deborah Kerr, Roland Culver, James McKechnie, Albert Lieven, Arthur Wontner, A. E. Matthews, David Hutcheson, Ursula Jeans, John Laurie, Harry Welchman
  'There is nothing brilliant about the picture, but it is perceptive, witty and sweet-tempered.'—*James Agee*
  'No one else has so well captured English romanticism banked down beneath emotional reticence.'—*Time Out, 1985*

'He plucked from the gutter a faded rose and made an immortal masterpiece!'
The Life of Emile Zola
♉ US 1937 116m bw
Warner (Henry Blanke)
The French writer intervenes in the case of Alfred Dreyfus, condemned unjustly to Devil's Island.
The box office success of this solidly-carpentered piece of Hollywood history was compounded in equal parts of star power and the sheer novelty of having such a thing turn up at the local Odeon.

w Norman Reilly Raine story Heinz Herald and Geza Herczeg d William Dieterle ph Tony Gaudio m Max Steiner ad Anton Grot

Paul Muni, Joseph Schildkraut, Gale Sondergaard, Gloria Holden, Donald Crisp, Erin O'Brien Moore, John Litel, Henry O'Neill, Morris Carnovsky, Ralph Morgan, Louis Calhern, Robert Barrat, Vladimir Sokoloff, Harry Davenport, Robert Warwick, Walter Kingsford
  'Destined to box office approval of the most substantial character. It is finely made and merits high rating as cinema art and significant recognition as major showmanship.'—*Variety*
  'Along with *Louis Pasteur*, it ought to start a new category—the Warner crusading films, costume division.'—*Otis Ferguson*

'A grave story told with great dignity and superbly played and produced.'—*Pare Lorentz*

'One of the fine ones which begin as a film and end as an experience.'—*John Grierson*

'Rich, dignified, honest and strong, it is at once the finest historical film ever made and the greatest screen biography.'—*New York Times*

AA: best picture; script; Joseph Schildkraut

AAN: original story; William Dieterle; Max Steiner; Paul Muni

Lifeboat

US 1944 96m bw
TCF (Kenneth MacGowan)
Survivors from a torpedoed passenger ship include the U-Boat commander responsible.
Propaganda gimmick melodrama interesting for the casting and for Hitchcock's response to the challenge of filming in one cramped set.

w Jo Swerling, *story* John Steinbeck *d* Alfred Hitchcock *ph* Glen MacWilliams *m* Hugo Friedhofer

Tallulah Bankhead, *Walter Slezak*, Henry Hull, John Hodiak, Canada Lee, William Bendix, Mary Anderson, Heather Angel, Hume Cronyn

'The initial idea—a derelict boat and its passengers as microcosm—is itself so artificial that . . . it sets the whole pride and brain too sharply to work on a tour de force for its own sake.'—*James Agee*

AAN: John Steinbeck; Alfred Hitchcock; Glen MacWilliams

Limelight

US 1952 144m bw
Charles Chaplin
A broken-down music hall comedian is stimulated by a young ballerina to a final hour of triumph.
Sentimental drama in a highly theatrical London East End setting. In other hands it would be very hokey, but Chaplin's best qualities, as well as his worst, are in evidence,

and in a way the film sums up his own career.

w,d,m Charles Chaplin *ph* Karl Struss *ad* Eugene Lourié *photographic consultant* Rollie Totheroh

Charles Chaplin, *Claire Bloom*, *Buster Keaton*, Sydney Chaplin, Nigel Bruce, Norman Lloyd

'From the first reel it is clear that he now wants to talk, that he *loves* to talk . . . where a development in the story line might easily be conveyed by a small visual effect, he prefers to make a speech about it . . . it is a disturbing rejection of the nature of the medium itself.'—*Walter Kerr*

'Surely the richest hunk of self-gratification since Huck and Tom attended their own funeral.'—*New Yorker, 1982.*

'His exhortations about life, courage, consciousness and "truth" are set in a self-pitying, self-glorifying story.'—*Pauline Kael, 70s*

AA: Charles Chaplin (for music)

The Lion in Winter

GB 1968 134m
Eastmancolor Panavision
Avco Embassy / Haworth (Martin Poll)
Henry II and Eleanor of Aquitaine celebrate Christmas together and have a family row.
An acting feast for two principals and assorted supports, a talking marathon in which not all the talk is good, a smart comedy with sudden lapses into melodrama; stimulating in parts but all rather tiresome by the end, especially as there is not much medieval splendour.

w James Goldman, from his play *d* Anthony Harvey *ph* Douglas Slocombe *m* John Barry

Katharine Hepburn, *Peter O'Toole*, Jane Merrow, John Castle, Anthony Hopkins, Nigel Terry, Timothy Dalton

'He is not writing a factual movie about the Plantagenets but an interpretation in which he combines their language and ours.'—*Philip T. Hartung*

AA: James Goldman; John Barry; Katharine Hepburn
AAN; best picture; Anthony Harvey; Peter O'Toole

The List of Adrian Messenger
US 1963   98m   bw
U-I / Joel (Edward Lewis)

An intelligence officer traps a mass murderer with a penchant for disguise.

Old-fashioned mystery thriller, as though Holmes and Watson were combating a modern Moriarty (and a rough-hewn production). The whole thing is camped up like an end-of-term treat, and as a further gimmick four guest stars allegedly appear under heavy disguise in cameo parts.

w Anthony Veiller, *novel* Philip MacDonald   d John Huston   ph Joe MacDonald   m Jerry Goldsmith

George C. Scott, *Kirk Douglas*, *Clive Brook*, Dana Wynter, Jacques Roux, Walter Tony Huston, Herbert Marshall, Bernard Archard, Gladys Cooper; and Robert Mitchum, Frank Sinatra, Burt Lancaster, Tony Curtis

'A leisurely, underplayed thriller with some good performances and a gimmick which turns it into a guessing contest.'—*L.A. Times*

Little Caesar
US 1930   77m   bw
Warner

The rise and fall of a vicious gangster.

Its central character clearly modelled on Al Capone, this also has historical interest as vanguard of a spate of noisy gangster films. The star was forever identified with his role, and the film, though technically dated, moves fast enough to maintain interest over fifty years later.

w Francis Faragoh, Robert E. Lee, *novel* W. R. Burnett   d Mervyn Le

Roy   *ph* Tony Gaudio   *m* Erno Rapee

Edward G. Robinson, Douglas Fairbanks Jnr, Glenda Farrell, William Collier Jnr, Ralph Ince, George E. Stone, Thomas Jackson, Stanley Fields, Sidney Blackmer

'It has irony and grim humour and a real sense of excitement and its significance does not get in the way of the melodrama.'—*Richard Dana Skinner*

'One of the best gangster talkers yet turned out . . . a swell picture.'—*Variety*

AAN: Francis Faragoh, Robert E. Lee

The Little Foxes
US 1941   116m   bw
Samuel Goldwyn

A family of schemers in post-Civil war days will stop at nothing to outwit each other.

Superb film of a brilliant play; excellent to look at and listen to, with a compelling narrative line and memorable characters.

w Lillian Hellman, from her play   d William Wyler   ph Gregg Toland   m Meredith Willson

Bette Davis, *Herbert Marshall*, *Teresa Wright*, Richard Carlson, *Charles Dingle*, *Dan Duryea*, *Carl Benton Reid*, *Patricia Collinge*, Jessica Grayson, Russell Hicks

HORACE GIDDENS (Herbert Marshall): 'Maybe it's easy for the dying to be honest. I'm sick of you, sick of this house, sick of my unhappy life with you. I'm sick of your brothers and their dirty tricks to make a dime. There must be better ways of getting rich than building sweatshops and pounding the bones of the town to make dividends for you to spend. You'll wreck the town, you and your brothers. You'll wreck the country, you and your kind, if they let you. But not me, I'll die my own way, and I'll do it without making the world any worse. I leave that to you.'

'One of the really beautiful jobs in the whole range of movie making.'—*Otis Ferguson*

'No one knows better than Wyler when to shift the camera's point of view, when to cut, or how to relate the characters in one shot to those in the next . . . you never have to wonder where you are in a Wyler picture.'—*Arthur Knight*

AAN: best picture; Lillian Hellman; William Wyler; Meredith Wilson; Bette Davis; Teresa Wright; Patricia Collinge

Little Miss Marker

US 1934   80m   bw
Paramount (B. P. Schulberg)
GB title: *The Girl in Pawn*
A cynical racetrack gambler is forced to adopt a little girl, who not only softens him but saves him from his enemies.
The twin appeals of Temple (a new hot property) and Runyon made this a big hit of its time.

w William R. Lipman, Sam Hellman, Gladys Lehman, *story* Damon Runyon *d* Alexander Hall *ph* Alfred Gilks *songs* Leo Robin, Ralph Rainger

Shirley Temple, Adolphe Menjou, Dorothy Dell, Charles Bickford, Lynne Overman, Frank McGlynn Snr, Willie Best

'A good response to that element which claims there is nothing good in pictures. Clean, funny, with thrills and heart appeal all nicely blended.'—*Variety*

'No one can deny that the infant was a trouper: she delivers her lines with a killer instinct.'—*Pauline Kael, 70s*

† Remade as *Sorrowful Jones.*

The Little Princess

US 1939   93m   Technicolor
TCF (Gene Markey)
In Victorian London a little girl is left at a harsh school when her father goes abroad.
One of the child star's plushest vehicles, a charming early colour

film complete with dream sequence and happy ending.

w Ethel Hill, Walter Ferris, *novel* Frances Hodgson Burnett *d* Walter Lang *ph* Arthur Miller, *William Skall md* Louis Silvers

Shirley Temple, Richard Greene, Anita Louise, Ian Hunter, Cesar Romero, Arthur Treacher, Mary Nash, Sybil Jason, Miles Mander, Marcia Mae Jones, Beryl Mercer, E. E. Clive

'They leap from the book and live!'

Little Women

US 1933   115m   bw
RKO (David O. Selznick, Merian C. Cooper, Kenneth MacGowan)
The growing up of four sisters in pre-Civil War America.
Charming 'big picture' of its day, with excellent production and performances.

w Sarah Y. Mason, Victor Heerman, *novel* Louisa May Alcott *d George Cukor ph* Henry Gerrard *m* Max Steiner

Katharine Hepburn, Paul Lukas, Joan Bennett, Frances Dee, Jean Parker, *Spring Byington,* Edna May Oliver, Douglass Montgomery, Henry Stephenson, Samuel S. Hinds, John Lodge, Nydia Westman

'If to put a book on the screen with all the effectiveness that sympathy and good taste and careful artifice can devise is to make a fine motion picture, then *Little Women* is a fine picture.'—*James Shelley Hamilton*

'One of the most satisfactory pictures I have ever seen.'—*E. V. Lucas, Punch*

'A reminder that emotions and vitality and truth can be evoked from lavender and lace as well as from machine guns and precision dances.'—*Thornton Delehanty, New York Post*

AA: script
AAN: best picture; George Cukor

'1750 to 1! Always outnumbered!
Never outfought!'

Lives of a Bengal Lancer
US 1934   119m   bw
Paramount (Louis D. Lighton)
Adventures on the North-West
Frontier.
British army heroics are here taken
rather solemnly, but the film is
efficient and fondly remembered.

w Waldemar Young, John F.
Balderston, Achmed Abdullah,
Grover Jones, William Slavens
McNut, book Francis Yeats-Brown
d Henry Hathaway ph Charles
Lang m Milan Roder

Gary Cooper, Franchot Tone,
Richard Cromwell, Sir Guy
Standing, C. Aubrey Smith, Monte
Blue, Kathleen Burke, Colin Tapley,
Douglass Dumbrille, Akim
Tamiroff, Noble Johnson
  'The best army picture every
made.'—Daily Telegraph

AAN: best picture; script; Henry
Hathaway

The Living Desert
US 1953   72m   Technicolor
Walt Disney (James Algar)
A light-hearted documentary
showing the animals and insects
which live in American desert areas.
The aim is entertainment and Disney
is not above faking, i.e. the famous
sequence in which scorpions appear
to do a square dance, but on its level
the thing is brilliantly done.

w James Algar, Winston Hibler, Ted
Sears d James Algar ph N. Paul
Kenworthy Jnr, Robert H. Grandall
m Paul Smith special processes Ub
Iwerks
  'The film has the same cosy
anthropomorphism as a Disney
cartoon and its facetious
commentary and vulgar music score
are typical of others in the
series.'—Georges Sadoul

† The other 'True Life Adventures'
were: Seal Island 49 (3 reels), Beaver
Valley 50 (3 reels), Nature's Half
Acre 51 (3 reels), Water Birds 52 (3

reels), Prowlers of the Everglades 53
(3 reels), The Vanishing Prairie 54,
The African Lion 55, Secrets of Life
56, White Wilderness 58, Jungle Cat
60.

The Lodger
GB 1926   84m approx (24
fps)   bw   silent
Gainsborough (Michael Balcon)
Subtitle: A Story of the London
Fog
A modern version of the novel about
a stranger who is (in this case)
wrongly thought to be Jack the
Ripper.
The first true Hitchcock film, full of
his familiar dramatic visual touches.
Oddly enough it was followed by
three years during which he seemed
to forget them.

w Eliot Stannard, Alfred Hitchcock,
novel Mrs Belloc Lowndes d Alfred
Hitchcock ph Baron Ventimiglia
ed Ivor Montagu
Ivor Novello, June, Marie Ault,
Arthur Chesney, Malcolm Keen
  'It was the first time I exercised
my style . . . you might almost say it
was my first picture.'—Alfred
Hitchcock, 1966

Lola Montes
France/Germany 1955
140m   Eastmancolor
Cinemascope
Gamma/Florida/Oska
The life of the famous courtesan and
her romance with the King of
Bavaria, told in diverting fragments
by a circus ringmaster.
An elaborate, expensive and trickily
presented historical charade which
confused the public and bankrupted
its production company; but the
various shorter versions released
didn't help.

w Max Ophuls, Annette Wademant,
Franz Geiger, novel Cécil
Saint-Laurent d Max
Ophuls ph Christian Matras
m Georges Auric ad Jean
d'Aubonne, Willy Schatz.
Martine Carol, Anton Walbrook,

Peter Ustinov, Ivan Desny, Oskar Werner, Will Quadflieg

'If you want to know what form can really do for content, rush along.'—*Derek Malcolm, The Guardian, 1978*

Lolita

GB 1962 152m bw
MGM / Seven
Arts / AA / Anya / Transworld
(James B. Harris)

A middle-aged lecturer falls for a 14-year-old girl and marries her mother to be near her.

Fitfully amusing but slightly plotted and very lengthy screen version of a sensational novel in which the heroine is only twelve, which makes a difference. The flashback introduction and various comic asides are pretentious and alienating.

w Vladimir Nabokov, from his novel *d* Stanley Kubrick
ph Oswald Morris *m* Nelson Riddle

James Mason, Shelley Winters, Sue Lyon, Peter Sellers

'The director's heart is apparently elsewhere. Consequently, we face the problem without the passion, the badness without the beauty, the agony without the ecstasy.'—*Andrew Sarris*

'A diluted *Blue Angel* with a teenage temptress instead of a tart.'—*Stanley Kauffmann*

'So clumsily structured that you begin to wonder whether what was shot and then cut out, whether the beginning was intended to be the end; and it is edited in so dilatory a fashion that after the first hour, almost every scene seems to go on too long.'—*Pauline Kael*

† Before Mason was cast, Noel Coward and Laurence Olivier were sought for the role of Humbert Humbert.

AAN: Vladimir Nabokov

'The love of woman in their eyes—the salt of the sea in their blood!'

The Long Voyage Home

US 1940 104m bw
Walter Wanger

Merchant seamen on shore leave get drunk, philosophize and have adventures.

Stagey-looking but dramatically interesting amalgam of four one-act plays by Eugene O'Neill, with talent abounding.

w Dudley Nichols *d John Ford*
ph Gregg Toland *m* Richard Hageman

John Wayne, Thomas Mitchell, Ian Hunter, Ward Bond, Barry Fitzgerald, Wilfrid Lawson, *Mildred Natwick,* John Qualen, Arthur Shields, Joe Sawyer

'One of the finest of all movies that deal with life at sea.'—*Pauline Kael, 70s*

AAN: best picture; Dudley Nichols; Gregg Toland, Richard Hageman

The Longest Day

US 1962 169m bw
Cinemascope
TCF (*Darryl F. Zanuck, Elmo Williams*)

A multi-faceted account of the landings in Normandy in June 1944. Extraordinarily noisy war spectacular, enjoyable as a violent entertainment once one has caught all the threads, but emotionally unaffecting because every part is played by a star.

w Cornelius Ryan, Romain Gary, James Jones, David Pursall, Jack Seddon, *book* Cornelius Ryan
d Andrew Marton, Ken Annakin, Bernhard Wicki *ph* Henri Persin, Walter Wottitz, Pierre Levent, Jean Bourgoin *m* Maurice Jarre, Paul Anka

John Wayne, Robert Mitchum, Henry Fonda, Robert Ryan, Rod Steiger, Robert Wagner, Paul Anka, Fabian, Tommy Sands, Richard Beymer, Mel Ferrer, Jeffrey Hunter, Sal Mineo, Roddy McDowall, Stuart Whitman, Steve Forrest, Eddie Albert, Edmond O'Brien, Red Buttons, Tom Tryon, Alexander Knox, Ray Danton, Ron Randell, Richard Burton, Donald Houston, Kenneth More, Peter Lawford, Richard Todd, Leo Genn, John

Gregson, Sean Connery, Michael Medwin, Leslie Phillips, Irina Demich, Bourvil, Jean-Louis Barrault, Christian Marquand, Arletty, Curt Jurgens, Paul Hartmann, Gert Frobe, Wolfgang Preiss, Peter Van Eyck, Christopher Lee, Eugene Deckers, Richard Wattis

AA: photography
AAN: best picture

Lord Jim
🎭 GB 1964   154m
🏹 Technicolor   Super Panavision
Columbia / Keep (René Dupont)
Adventures of a sailor who prowls the Far East looking for truth; he helps enslaved natives, is raped by a tribal chief, and finally sacrifices his life.
Lush and very boring farrago of miscellaneous incident, with a central character about whose fate no one can care. However, an expensive production must have its points of interest, and the belated introduction of a gentleman villain gives a little edge.

wd Richard Brooks, *novel* Joseph Conrad *ph* Frederick A. Young *m* Bromislau Kaper *pd* Geoffrey Drake

Peter O'Toole, *James Mason*, Eli Wallach, Paul Lukas, Jack Hawkins, Daliah Lavi, Curt Jurgens, Akim Tamiroff

Lost Horizon
🎬 US 1937   130m (released at 118m)   bw
Columbia (Frank Capra)
Escaping from an Indian revolution, four people are kidnapped by plane and taken to an idyllic civilization in a Tibetan valley, where the weather is always kind and men are not only gentle to each other but live to a very advanced age.
Much re-cut romantic adventure which leaves out some of the emphasis of a favourite Utopian novel but stands up pretty well on its own, at least as a supreme example

of Hollywood moonshine, with perfect casting, direction and music. If the design has a touch of Ziegfeld, that's Hollywood.

w Robert Riskin, *novel James Hilton*
d Frank Capra *ph* Joseph Walker
m Dmitri Tiomkin *ad* Stephen Goosson

Ronald Colman, H. B. Warner, Thomas Mitchell, Edward Everett Horton, Sam Jaffe, Isabel Jewell, Jane Wyatt, Margo, John Howard
   'One of the most impressive of all thirties films, a splendid fantasy which physically and emotionally, lets out all the stops.'—*John Baxter, 1968*
   'One is reminded of a British critic's comment on *Mary of Scotland,* the "inaccuracies must have involved tremendous research".'—*Robert Stebbins*
   'The best film I've seen for ages, but will somebody please tell me how they got the grand piano along a footpath on which only one person can walk at a time with rope and pickaxe and with a sheer drop of three thousand feet or so?'—*James Agate*
   'If the long dull ethical sequences had been cut to the bone there would have been plenty of room for the real story: the shock of western crudity and injustice on a man returned from a more gentle and beautiful way of life.'—*Graham Greene*

† A 1943 reissue trimmed down the negative still further, to 109 minutes; but in 1979 the American Film Institute began to restore a print of the original length and this has now been shown widely.

AAN: best picture; Dmitri Tiomkin; H. B. Warner

Lost in a Harem
😺 US 1944   89m   bw
MGM (George Haight)
Two travelling entertainers in the Middle East get mixed up with a conniving sultan, who hypnotizes them.
Lively, well-staged romp which

shows the comedians at their best and uses astute borrowings from burlesque, pantomime, and Hollywood traditions of fantasy and running jokes.

w Harry Ruskin, John Grant, Harry Crane d Charles Reisner ph Lester White m David Snell

Bud Abbott, Lou Costello, Douglass Dumbrille, Marilyn Maxwell, John Conte, Jimmy Dorsey and his Orchestra

'Boiling passions in the burning sands!'
The Lost Patrol
US 1934 74m bw
RKO (Cliff Reid)

A small British army group is lost in the Mesopotamian desert under Arab attack.

Much-copied adventure story of a small patrol under attack (compare *Sahara, Bataan* and *The Last of the Comanches* for a start). The original now seems pretty starchy but retains moments of power.

w Dudley Nichols, story Patrol by Philip MacDonald d John Ford ph Harold Wenstrom m Max Steiner

Victor McLaglen, Boris Karloff, Wallace Ford, Reginald Denny, J. M. Kerrigan, Billy Bevan, Alan Hale

'Although the running time is long, there's nothing draggy about it.'—*Variety*

† A silent British version was released in 1929, written and directed by Walter Summers for British Instructional, with Cyril McLaglen, Sam Wilkinson and Terence Collier.

AAN: Max Steiner

'Shot at only by cameras—yet falling in flames!'
The Lost Squadron
US 1932 79m bw
RKO (David O. Selznick)

World War I pilots find work stunting for a movie studio.

Unusual comedy-drama with several points of interest.

w Herman J. Mankiewicz, Wallace Smith d George Archainbaud ph Leo Tover, Edward Cronjager m Max Steiner

Richard Dix, Mary Astor, Erich Von Stroheim, Joel McCrea, Dorothy Jordan, Hugh Herbert, Robert Armstrong

'A pretty good show . . . whether it will get back what it cost is something else again.'—*Variety*

'From the best-seller that was talked about in whispers!'
'The picture that dares to bare a man's soul!'
The Lost Weekend
US 1945 101m bw
Paramount (*Charles Brackett*)

Two days in the life of a young dipsomaniac writer.

Startlingly original on its release, this stark little drama keeps its power, especially in the scenes on New York streets and in a dipso ward. It could scarcely have been more effectively filmed.

w Charles Brackett, Billy Wilder, novel Charles Jackson d Billy Wilder ph John F. Seitz m Miklos Rozsa

Ray Milland, Jane Wyman, Philip Terry, Howard da Silva, Frank Faylen

DON BIRNAM (Ray Milland): 'It shrinks my liver, doesn't it, Nat? It pickles my kidneys, yeah. But what does it do to my mind? It tosses the sandbags overboard so the balloon can soar. Suddenly I'm above the ordinary. I'm competent, supremely competent. I'm walking a tightrope over Niagara Falls. I'm one of the great ones. I'm Michelangelo, moulding the beard of Moses. I'm Van Gough, painting the pure sunlight. I'm Horowitz, playing the Emperor Concerto. I'm John Barrymore before the movies got him by the throat. I'm Jesse James and his two brothers—all three of 'em. I'm W. Shakespeare. And out there it's not Third Avenue any longer—it's the Nile, Nat, the

Nile—and down it moves the barge of Cleopatra.'

'A reminder of what celluloid is capable of achieving when used by a good director.'—*Spectator*

'I undershtand that liquor interesh; innerish; intereshtsh are rather worried about thish film. Thatsh tough.'—*James Agee*

'Most to be admired are its impressions of bare dreadful truth: the real crowds in the real streets as the hero-victim lugs his typewriter to the pawnshop, the trains screaming overhead, the awful night as he makes his escape from the alcoholics' ward.'—*Dilys Powell*

'A distinguished film, rich in cinematic ingenuity.'—*The Times*

AA: best picture; script; Billy Wilder (as director); Ray Milland
AAN: John F. Seitz; Miklos Rozsa

Love Affair

US 1939 89m bw
RKO (Leo McCarey)

On a transatlantic crossing, a European man of the world meets a New York girl, but their romance is flawed by misunderstanding and physical accident.

The essence of Hollywood romance, and one of the most fondly remembered films of the thirties, perhaps because of the easy comedy sense of the first half.

w Delmer Daves, Donald Ogden Stewart, *story* Mildred Cram, Leo McCarey d Leo McCarey ph Rudolph Maté

Charles Boyer, Irene Dunne, Maria Ouspenskaya, Lee Bowman, Astrid Allwyn, Maurice Moscovitch

'Production is of grade A quality . . . its b.o. chances look good.'—*Variety*

'Those excited over the mastery of form already achieved in pictures, will like to follow this demonstration of the qualities of technique and imagination the films must always have and keep on recruiting to their service . . . Clichés of situation and attitude are lifted almost beyond

recognition by a morning freshness of eye for each small thing around.'—*Otis Ferguson*

'McCarey brought off one of the most difficult things you can attempt with film. He created a mood, rather than a story; he kept it alive by expert interpolations; he provided comedy when he needed comedy and poignancy when he needed substance; and he did it with the minimum of effort.'—*Pare Lorentz*

† Remade as *An Affair to Remember*.

AAN: best picture; original story; Irene Dunne; Maria Ouspenskaya; song 'Wishing' (*m/ly* Buddy de Sylva)

The Love Goddesses

US 1965 87m bw
Paramount/Walter Reade/Sterling

A light-hearted account of female sexuality on the Hollywood screen. Sharp-eyed compilation film which is worth a dozen books on the subject.

pd Saul J. Turell, Graeme Ferguson m Percy Faith *narrator* Carl King

'A compilation of shrapnel from old sex-bomb movies, full of deliciously improbable moments.'—*Newsweek*

† Clips include *Blonde Venus*, *Morocco*, *True Heart Susie*, *Cleopatra* (1934), *Intolerance*, *The Cheat*, *The Sheik*, *Blood and Sand*, *The Sorrows of Satan*, *The Loves of Sunya*, *Diary of a Lost Girl*, *Ecstasy*, *L'Atlantide*, *Peter the Tramp*, *Cabin in the Cotton*, *Platinum Blonde*, *Gold Diggers of 1933*, *No Man of Her Own*, *Professional Sweetheart*, *Love Me Tonight*, *I'm No Angel*, *Baby Face*, *They Won't Forget*, *College Swing*, *Her Jungle Love*, *Gilda*, *A Place in the Sun*, *Some Like it Hot*.

Love Me Tonight

US 1932 104m bw
Paramount (Rouben Mamoulian)

A Parisian tailor accidentally moves into the aristocracy.

The most fluently cinematic comedy musical ever made, with sounds and words, lyrics and music, deftly blended into a compulsively and consistently laughable mosaic of sophisticated nonsense; one better than the best of Lubitsch and Clair.

w Samuel Hoffenstein, Waldemar Young, George Marion Jnr, play Tailor in the Château by Leopold Marchand and Paul Armont *d Rouben Mamoulian ph Victor Milner songs Rodgers and Hart*

Maurice Chevalier, Jeanette MacDonald, Charles Butterworth, Charles Ruggles, Myrna Loy, C. Aubrey Smith, Elizabeth Patterson, Ethel Griffies, Blanche Frederici, Robert Greig

'A musical frolic, whimsical in its aim and delicately carried out in its pattern.'—*Variety*

'Gay, charming, witty, it is everything that the Lubitsch musicals should have been but never were.' *John Baxter, 1968*

'With the aid of a pleasant story, a good musician, a talented cast and about a million dollars, he has done what someone in Hollywood should have done long ago—he has illustrated a musical score.'—*Pare Lorentz*

'It has that infectious spontaneity which distinguishes the American musical at its best.'—*Peter Cowie, 1970*

'A rich amalgam of filmic invention, witty decoration and wonderful songs.'—*NFT, 1974*

'What a picture! First you have Chevalier, and last you have Chevalier!'—*Photoplay*

Love on the Dole

GB 1941 100m bw
British National (John Baxter)
Life among unemployed cotton workers in industrial Lancashire between the wars.
Vividly characterized, old-fashioned social melodrama, well made on a low budget; a rare problem picture for Britain at this time.

w Walter Greenwood, Barbara K. Emery, Rollo Gamble, novel Walter Greenwood d John Baxter m Richard Addinsell

Deborah Kerr, Clifford Evans, *George Carney*, Joyce Howard, Frank Cellier, Geoffrey Hibbert, *Mary Merrall*, Maire O'Neill, *Marjorie Rhodes*, A. Bromley Davenport, Marie Ault, Iris Vandeleur, Kenneth Griffith

The Love Parade

US 1929 112m bw
Paramount (Ernst Lubitsch)
The prince of Sylvania marries.
Primitive sound operetta set among the idle European rich, with clear but faded instances of the Lubitsch touch.

w Ernest Vajda, Guy Bolton, play The Prince Consort by Leon Xanrof and Jules Chancel *d Ernst Lubitsch ph Victor Milner songs* Victor Schertzinger, Clifford Grey

Maurice Chevalier, Jeanette MacDonald, Lupino Lane, Lillian Roth, Edgar Norton, Lionel Belmore, Eugene Pallette

'The first truly cinematic screen musical in America.'—*Theodore Huff*

AAN: best picture, Ernst Lubitsch; Victor Milner; Maurice Chevalier

Love Story

US 1970 100m Movielab
Paramount (David Golden)
Two students marry; she dies.
A barrage of ripe old Hollywood clichés spiced with new-fangled bad language. In the circumstances, well enough made, and certainly astonishingly popular.

w Erich Segal, from his novelette d Arthur Hiller ph Dick Kratina m Bach, Mozart, Handel *md* Francis Lai

Ali MacGraw, Ryan O'Neal, Ray Milland, John Marley

'Camille with bullshit.'—*Alexander Walker*

AAN: best picture; Erich Segal;
Arthur Hiller; Francis Lai; Ali
MacGraw; Ryan O'Neal; John
Marley

The Loved One
🎭 US 1965 118m bw
MGM/Filmways (Neil Hartley)
A young English poet in California
gets a job at a very select burial
ground.
A pointed satire on the American
way of death has been allowed to get
out of hand, with writer and actors
alike laying it on too thick; but there
are pleasantly waspish moments in a
movie advertised as 'the motion
picture with something to offend
everybody'.

w Terry Southern, Christopher
Isherwood, *novel* Evelyn Waugh
d Tony Richardson *ph* Haskell
Wexler *m* John Addison
pd Rouben Ter-Arutunian

Robert Morse, John Gielgud, Rod
Steiger, *Liberace*, Anjanette Comer,
Jonathan Winters, Dana Andrews,
Milton Berle, James Coburn, Tab
Hunter, Margaret Leighton, Roddy
McDowall, Robert Morley, Lionel
Stander
'Even a chaotic satire like this is
cleansing, and it's embarrassing to
pan even a bad movie that comes out
against God, mother and
country.'—*Pauline Kael, 1968*
'A spineless farrago of collegiate
gags.'—*Stanley Kauffmann*
'A sinking ship that makes it to
port because everyone on board is
too giddy to panic.'—*New Yorker,
1978*

Lovers and Other Strangers
🎭 US 1969 104m Metrocolor
ABC/David Susskind
After living together for eighteen
months, Susan and Mike decide to
get married, and find their parents
have sex problems of their own.
Wise, witty and well acted sex farce,
with many actors making the most of
ample chances under firm directorial
control.

w Renée Taylor, Joseph Bologna,
David Zelag Goodman *d* Cy
Howard *ph* Andrw Laszlo *m* Fred
Karlin

*Gig Young, Anne Jackson, Richard
Castellano*, Bonnie Bedelia, Michael
Brandon, *Beatrice Arthur*, Robert
Dishy, Harry Guardino, Diane
Keaton, Cloris Leachman. Anne
Meara, *Marian Hailey*
'An extremely engaging
comedy.'—*Gillian Hartnoll*

AA: song 'For All We Know'
(*m* Fred Karlin, *ly* Robb Wilson,
Arthur James)
AAN: script; Richard Castellano

Lucky Jim
🎭 GB 1957 95m bw
British Lion/Charter (Roy
Boulting)
At a provincial university, an
accident-prone junior lecturer has a
disastrous weekend with his girl
friend and his professor.
Quite funny in its own right, this is a
vulgarization of a famous comic
novel which got its effects more
subtly, with more sense of place,
time and character.

w Jeffrey Dell, Patrick Campbell,
novel Kingsley Amis *d* John
Boulting *ph* Max Greene *m* John
Addison

*Ian Carmichael, Hugh Griffith,
Terry-Thomas*, Sharon Acker, Jean
Anderson, Maureen Connell, Clive
Morton, John Welsh, Reginald
Beckwith, Kenneth Griffith
'An almost endless ripple of
comfortable laughter.'—*News
Chronicle*

Lust for Life
🎭🎭 US 1956 122m
ˣ Metrocolor Cinemascope
MGM (John Houseman)
The life of Vincent Van Gogh.
Fairly absorbing, not inaccurate, but
somehow uninspiring biopic,
probably marred by poor colour and
wide screen; despite good work all

round, it simply doesn't fall into a classic category.

w Norman Corwin, *book* Irving Stone *d* Vincente Minnelli *ph* F. A. Young, Russell Harlan *m* Miklos Rosza *ad* Cedric Gibbons, Hans Peters, Preston Ames

Kirk Douglas, Anthony Quinn (as Gauguin), James Donald, Pamela Brown, Everett Sloane, Niall MacGinnis, Noel Purcell, Henry Daniell, Lionel Jeffries, Madge Kennedy, Jill Bennett, Laurence Naismith

'Two hours of quite shattering and exciting entertainment.'—*Alan Dent, Illustrated London News*

AA: Anthony Quinn
AAN: Norman Corwin; Kirk Douglas

M

M

Germany 1931　118m　bw
Nero Film (Seymour Nebenzal)

A psychopathic murderer of children evades the police but is caught by the city's criminals who find his activities getting them a bad name. An unmistakable classic whose oddities are hardly worth criticizing, this is part social melodrama and part satire, but entirely unforgettable, with most of its sequences brilliantly staged.

w Thea Von Harbou, Paul Falkenberg, Adolf Jansen, Karl Vash d Fritz Lang ph Fritz Arno Wagner m Adolf Jansen ad Karl Vollbrecht, Emil Hasler

Peter Lorre, Otto Wernicke, Gustav Grundgens

'Visual excitement, pace, brilliance of surface and feeling for detail.'—*New Yorker, 1977*

† Of Lang's later work, *Fury* comes closest to the feeling and style of *M*.

Mad Love

US 1935　83m　bw
MGM (John Considine Jnr)
GB title: *The Hands of Orlac*

A pianist loses his hands in an accident; a mad surgeon, in love with the pianist's wife, grafts on the hands of a murderer.
Absurd Grand Guignol done with great style which somehow does not communicate itself in viewer interest, only in cold admiration.

w Guy Endore, P. J. Wolfson, John Balderston, novel The Hands of Orlac by Maurice Renard d Karl Freund ph Chester Lyons, Gregg Toland m Dmitri Tiomkin

Colin Clive, Peter Lorre, Frances Drake, Ted Healy, Edward Brophy, Isabel Jewell, Sara Haden

'The results in screen potency are disappointing . . . will probably do fair biz.'—*Variety*

The Magic Box

GB 1951　118m
Technicolor
Festival Films (Ronald Neame)

The life of William Friese-Greene, a British cinema pioneer who died in poverty.
A joint British film industry venture to celebrate the Festival of Britain, this rather downbeat and uneventful story takes on the nature of a pageant or a series of charades, with well-known people appearing to no good purpose. But it means well.

w Eric Ambler d John Boulting ph Jack Cardiff m William Alwyn pd John Bryan

Robert Donat, Margaret Johnson, Maria Schell, John Howard Davies, Renée Asherson, Richard Attenborough, Robert Beatty, Michael Denison, Leo Genn, Marius Goring, Joyce Grenfell, Robertson Hare, Kathleen Harrison, Jack Hulbert, Stanley Holloway, Glynis Johns, Mervyn Johns, Barry Jones, Miles Malleson, Muir Mathieson, A. E. Matthews, John McCallum, Bernard Miles, Laurence Olivier, Cecil Parker, Eric Portman, Dennis Price, Michael Redgrave, Margaret Rutherford, Ronald Shiner, Sybil Thorndike, David Tomlinson, Cecil Trouncer, Peter Ustinov, Kay Walsh, Emlyn Williams, Harcourt Williams, Googie Withers

'An honest and often a very moving film.'—*Daily Express*

'Patriotic, sentimental, overlong and faintly embarrassing.'—*Time Out, 1984*

'Real life screened more daringly than it's ever been before!'

The Magnificent Ambersons

US 1942　88m　bw
RKO (Orson Welles)

A proud family loses its wealth and its control of the neighbourhood, and its youngest male member gets his come-uppance.

Fascinating period drama told in brilliant cinematic snippets; owing to studio interference the last reels are weak, but the whole is a treat for connoisseurs, and a delight in its fast-moving control of cinematic narrative.

wd Orson Welles, *novel* Booth Tarkington *ph* Stanley Cortez *m* Bernard Herrmann *ad* Mark-Lee Kirr

Joseph Cotten, Dolores Costello, Agnes Moorehead, Tim Holt, Anne Baxter, Ray Collins, Richard Bennett, Erskine Sanford, Donald Dillaway

NARRATOR (Welles): 'And now Major Amberson was engaged in the profoundest thinking of his life, and he realized that everything which had worried him or delighted him during his lifetime—all his buying and building and trading and banking—that it was all a trifle and a waste beside what concerned him now, for the Major knew now that he had to plan how to enter an unknown country where he was not even sure of being recognized as an Amberson.'

NARRATOR: 'Something had happened. A thing which years ago had been the eagerest hope of many, many good citizens of the town. And now it had come at last: George Amberson Minafer had got his come-uppance. He got it three times filled and running over. But those who had so longed for it were not there to see it, and they never knew it. Those who were still living had forgotten all about it and all about him.'

'Rich in ideas that many will want to copy, combined in the service of a story that few will care to imitate.'—*C. A. Lejeune*

'Nearly every scene is played with a casual perfection which could only come from endless painstaking planning and rehearsals, and from a wonderful sense of timing.'—*Basil Wright, 1972*

'Even in this truncated form it's amazing and memorable.'—*Pauline Kael, 70s*

† Previously filmed in 1925 as *Pampered Youth.*

†† The credits are all at the end and all spoken, ending with: 'I wrote and directed the picture. My name is Orson Welles.'

AAN: best picture; Stanley Cortez; Agnes Moorehead

Magnificent Obsession
US 1954   108m
Technicolor
Universal (*Ross Hunter*)
The playboy who is half-responsible for the death of a woman's husband and for her own blindness becomes a surgeon and cures her. Sent Ross Hunter to the commercial heights as a remaker of thirties weepies. This one worked best.

w Robert Blees *d* Douglas Sirk *ph* Russell Metty *m* Frank Skinner

Jane Wyman, Rock Hudson, Agnes Moorehead, Barbara Rush, Otto Kruger, Gregg Palmer, Paul Cavanagh, Sara Shane

AAN: Jane Wyman

'They were seven—and they fought like seven hundred!'
The Magnificent Seven
US 1960   138m   De Luxe
Panavision
UA / Mirisch–Alpha (John Sturges)
A Mexican village hires seven American gunmen for protection against bandits.
Popular western based on the Japanese *Seven Samurai*; good action scenes, but the rest is verbose and often pretentious.

w William Roberts *d* John Sturges *ph* Charles Lang Jnr *m* Elmer Bernstein

Yul Brynner, Steve McQueen, Robert Vaughn, James Coburn, Charles Bronson, Horst Buchholz, Eli Wallach, Brad Dexter, Vladimir Sokoloff, Rosenda Monteros

AAN: Elmer Bernstein

Major Barbara

GB 1941   121m   bw
Gabriel Pascal

The daughter of an armaments millionaire joins the Salvation Army but resigns when it accepts her father's donation.

Stagey but compulsive version of a play in which the author takes typical side swipes at anything and everything within reach, allowing for some gorgeous acting (and overacting) by an impeccable cast.

w Anatole de Grunwald, Gabriel Pascal, *play* Bernard Shaw
d Gabriel Pascal, Harold French, David Lean   *ph* Ronald Neame
m William Walton   *ed* Charles Friend *costumes* Cecil Beaton
ad Vincent Korda, John Bryan

Wendy Hiller, *Rex Harrison*, *Robert Morley*, *Robert Newton*, *Marie Lohr*, Emlyn Williams, Sybil Thorndike, Deborah Kerr, David Tree, Felix Aylmer, Penelope Dudley Ward, Walter Hudd, Marie Ault, Donald Calthrop

'Shaw's ebullience provides an unslackening fount of energy . . . his all-star cast of characters are outspoken as no one else is in films except the Marx Brothers.'—*William Whitebait*

'Grandpa moves in! Daughter moves out! And the riot starts!'

Make Way for Tomorrow

US 1937   94m   bw
Paramount (Leo McCarey)

An elderly couple are in financial difficulty and have to be parted because their children will not help. Sentimental drama which had a devastating effect at the time but now seems oversimplified and exaggerated.

w Vina Delmar, *novel* The Years Are So Long by Josephine Lawrence   *d* Leo McCarey
ph William C. Mellor   *m* George Antheil

Victor Moore, *Beulah Bondi*, Thomas Mitchell, Fay Bainter, Porter Hall, Barbara Read, Maurice Moscovitch, Elizabeth Risdon, Gene Lockhart

'Needs special exploitation: even so, business is apt to be spotty where played solo.'—*Variety*

'The most brilliantly directed and acted film of the year.'—*John Grierson*

'A sense of misery and inhumanity is left vibrating in the nerves.'—*Graham Greene*

'A guy without a conscience! A dame without a heart!'
'He's as fast on the draw as he is in the drawing room!'

The Maltese Falcon

US 1941   101m   bw
Warner (Henry Blanke)

After the death of his partner, private eye Sam Spade is dragged into a quest for a priceless statuette. A remake which shows the difference between excellence and brilliance; here every nuance is subtly stressed, and the cast is perfection.

wd John Huston   *ph* Arthur Edeson
m Adolph Deutsch

Humphrey Bogart, *Mary Astor*, *Sidney Greenstreet*, *Elisha Cook Jnr*, *Barton MacLane*, *Lee Patrick*, *Peter Lorre*, Gladys George, *Ward Bond*, *Jerome Cowan*

GUTMAN (Sidney Greenstreet): 'I distrust a close-mouthed man. He generally picks the wrong time to talk and says the wrong things. Talking's something you can't do judiciously, unless you keep in practice. Now, sir, we'll talk if you like. I'll tell you right out, I'm a man who likes talking to a man who likes to talk.'

SPADE (Humphrey Bogart) to Cairo (Peter Lorre): 'When you're slapped, you'll take it and like it!'

SPADE to Brigid (Mary Astor): 'Don't be too sure I'm as crooked as I'm supposed to be.'

GUTMAN: 'I distrust a man who says when. If he's got to be careful not to drink too much, it's because he's not to be trusted when he does.'

'The first crime melodrama with finish, speed and bang to come along in what seems like ages.'—*Otis Ferguson*

'A work of entertainment that is yet so skilfully constructed that after many years and many viewings, it has the same brittle explosiveness—and some of the same surprise—that it had in 1941.'—*Pauline Kael, 1968*

'The trick which Mr Huston has pulled is a combination of American ruggedness with the suavity of the English crime school—a blend of mind and muscle—plus a slight touch of pathos.'—*Bosley Crowther, New York Times*

'Admirable photography of the sort in which black and white gives full value to every detail, every flicker of panic.'—*Francis Wyndham*

AAN: best picture; John Huston (as writer); Sidney Greenstreet

A Man and a Woman

France 1966   102m
Eastmancolor
Les Films 13
aka: *Un Homme et une Femme*
A racing driver and a script girl, both of whose spouses are dead, meet while visiting their children, and an affair leads to marriage. Slight romantic drama so tricked out with smart images that it looks like a series of expensive commercials. A great box office success, but its director never again succeeded in this vein which he made his own.

w Claude Lelouch, Pierre Uytterhoven *d* Claude Lelouch *ph* Claude Lelouch *m* Francis Lai
Anouk Aimée, Jean-Louis Trintignant

'When in doubt, Lelouch's motto seems to be, use a colour filter or insert lyrical shots of dogs and horses; when in real doubt, use both.'—*Tom Milne, MFB*

'A slick item with all the Hollywood ingredients.'—*John Simon*

AA: Claude Lelouch, Pierre Uytterhoven
AAN: Claude Lelouch (as director); Anouk Aimée

The Man Between

GB 1953   101m   bw
British Lion / London Films (Carold Reed)
Ivo Kern operates successfully as a West Berlin racketeer; love causes a softening of his attitudes and leads to his death.
Imitation *Third Man* with an uninteresting mystery and a solemn ending. Good acting and production can't save it.

w Harry Kurnitz *d* Carol Reed
ph Desmond Dickinson *m* John Addison *ad* André Andreiev

James Mason, Hildegarde Neff, Claire Bloom, Geoffrey Toone, Ernst Schroeder

'Reed's love of photogenic corruption, his technical finesse, and his feeling for atmospheric intrigue almost make something really good out of a synthetic script.'—*Variety*

'A cold-hearted film about people with cold feet.'—*Daily Express*

A Man for All Seasons

GB 1966   120m
Technicolor
Columbia / Highland (Fred Zinnemann)
Sir Thomas More opposes Henry VIII's divorce, and events lead inexorably to his execution.
Irreproachable film version of a play which has had its narrative tricks removed but stands up remarkably well. Acting, direction, sets, locations and costumes all have precisely the right touch.

w Robert Bolt, from his play *d* Fred Zinnemann *ph* Ted Moore
m Georges Delerue *pd* John Box

Paul Scofield, Wendy Hiller, Susannah York, Robert Shaw, Orson Welles, Leo McKern, Nigel Davenport, John Hurt, Corin Redgrave, Cyril Luckham, Jack Gwyllim

† Reports indicate that Charlton Heston badly wanted the role of Sir Thomas More. He finally played it in a 1988 TV version.

AA: best picture; Robert Bolt; Fred
Zinnemann; Ted Moore; Paul
Scofield
AAN: Wendy Hiller; Robert Shaw

The Man from Laramie
　US 1955　104m
　Technicolor　Cinemascope
Columbia (William Goetz)
A wandering cowman seeks revenge
on those who killed his brother.
Grade A western with new-fangled
touches of brutality touching off the
wide screen spectacle.

w Philip Yordan, Frank Burt
d *Anthony Mann* ph Charles Lang
Jnr m George Duning md Morris
Stoloff

James Stewart, Arthur Kennedy,
Donald Crisp, Cathy O'Donnell,
Alex Nicol, Aline MacMahon,
Wallace Ford, Jack Elam

Man Hunt
　US 1941　98m　bw
　TCF (Kenneth MacGowan)
A big game hunter misses a shot at
Hitler and is chased back to England
by the Gestapo.
Despite hilariously inaccurate
English backgrounds, this is perhaps
its director's most vivid Hollywood
thriller, though watered down in
tone from the original novel.

w Dudley Nichols, *novel* Rogue
Male by Geoffrey Household
d *Fritz Lang* ph Arthur Miller
m Alfred Newman

Walter Pidgeon, Joan Bennett,
George Sanders, John Carradine,
Roddy McDowall, Ludwig Stossel,
Heather Thatcher, Frederick
Worlock

'A tense and intriguing thriller
that is both propaganda and exciting
entertainment.'—*Paul M. Jensen,
1969*

'In its manipulation of these dark
and intent forces on a checkerboard,
it manages to take your breath
away.'—*Otis Ferguson*

† Remade for TV in 1976 as *Rogue
Male*

The Man In Grey
　GB 1943　116m　bw
　GFD / Gainsborough (Edward
Black)
In Regency times, an aristocratic
girl's love for her less fortunate
friend is repaid by jealousy,
treachery and murder.
Rather dully performed flashback
costume melodrama which caught
the public imagination in the middle
of a dreary world war, especially as
its evil leading characters were
played by stars who rapidly went
right to the top. The several
imitations which followed, including
The Wicked Lady, *Jassy* and *Hungry
Hill*, became known as the
Gainsborough school.

w Margaret Kennedy, Leslie Arliss,
Doreen Montgomery, *novel* Lady
Eleanor Smith d Leslie Arliss
ph Arthur Crabtree m Cedric
Mallabey ad Walter Murton

James Mason, *Margaret Lockwood*,
Phyllis Calvert, *Stewart Granger*,
Helen Haye, Nora Swinburne,
Raymond Lovell, Martita Hunt

'All the time-tested materials:
gypsy fortune-teller; scowling,
black-browed villain; gushy diary
kept by a doe-eyed girl who munches
candied violets; fire-breathing
adventuress who dotes on discord
and low-cut gowns . . .'—*Time*

The Man in the Iron Mask
　US 1939　110m　bw
　Edward Small
King Louis XIV keeps his twin
brother prisoner.
Exhilarating swashbuckler based on
a classic novel, with a complex plot,
good acting and the three
musketeers in full cry.

w George Bruce, *novel* Alexandre
Dumas d James Whale ph Robert
Planck m Lucien Moraweck

Louis Hayward, *Warren William* (as
D'Artagnan), Alan Hale, Bert
Roach, Miles Mander, Joan
Bennett, *Joseph Schildkraut*, Walter
Kingsford, Marion Martin, Montagu
Love, Albert Dekker

'Substantial entertainment for general appeal and satisfaction.'—*Variety*

'A sort of combination of *The Prisoner of Zenda* and *The Three Musketeers*, with a few wild west chases thrown in . . . not unentertaining.'—*Richard Mallett, Punch*

† Remade 1976 as a TV movie with Richard Chamberlain, and 1978 as *The Fifth Musketeer*.

AAN: Lucien Moraweck

The Man in the White Suit

☺ GB 1951 81m bw
Ealing (Sidney Cole)

A scientist produces a fabric that never gets dirty and never wears out. Unions and management are equally aghast.

Brilliant satirical comedy played as farce and put together with meticulous cinematic counterpoint, so that every moment counts and all concerned give of their very best.

w Roger Macdougall, John Dighton, Alexander Mackendrick d Alexander Mackendrick ph Douglas Slocombe m Benjamin Frankel

Alec Guinness, Joan Greenwood, Cecil Parker, Vida Hope, *Ernest Thesiger*, Michael Gough, Howard Marion Crawford, Miles Malleson, *George Benson, Edie Martin*

'The combination of an ingenious idea, a bright, funny and imaginative script, skilful playing and perceptive brisk direction has resulted once more in a really satisfying Ealing comedy.'—*Richard Mallett, Punch*

AAN: script

'Who were the women who twisted his life and love—gutting the flame of his incredible genius?'

Man of a Thousand Faces

👓👓 US 1957 122m bw
✕ Cinemascope
U-I (Robert Arthur)

The rise to fame of silent screen character actor Lon Chaney.

Moderately commendable biopic with a strong sense of period Hollywood, an excellent star performance, but too much sudsy emoting about deaf mute parents and an ungrateful wife.

w R. Wright Campbell, Ivan Goff, Ben Roberts d Joseph Pevney ph Russell Metty m Frank Skinner ad Alexander Golitzen

James Cagney, Dorothy Malone, Robert Evans (as Irving Thalberg), Roger Smith, *Marjorie Rambeau*, Jane Greer, Jim Backus

'The script and conception are so maudlin and degrading that Cagney's high dedication becomes somewhat oppressive.'—*Pauline Kael, 70s*

AAN: script

The Man Who Came to Dinner

☺ US 1941 112m bw
Warner (Jack Saper, Jerry Wald)

An acid-tongued radio celebrity breaks his hip while on a lecture tour, and terrorizes the inhabitants of the suburban home where he must stay for several weeks.

Delightfully malicious caricature of Alexander Woolcott which, though virtually confined to one set, moves so fast that one barely notices the lack of cinematic variety, and certainly provides more than a laugh a minute, especially for those old enough to understand all the references.

w Julius J. and Philip G. Epstein, play George S. Kaufman, Moss Hart d William Keighley ph Tony Gaudio m Frederick Hollander

Monty Woolley, Bette Davis, Ann Sheridan, *Jimmy Durante* (spoofing Harpo Marx), *Reginald Gardiner* (spoofing Noel Coward), Richard Travis, *Billie Burke*, Grant Mitchell, *Ruth Vivian, Mary Wickes*, George Barbier, Elisabeth Fraser

WHITESIDE (Monty Woolley) to his nurse, who won't let him eat chocolates: 'I had an aunt who ate a box of chocolates every day of her life. She lived to be a hundred and two, and when she had been dead three days, she looked healthier than you do now!'

NURSE (Mary Wickes): 'I am not only walking out on this case, Mr Whiteside, I am leaving the nursing profession, I became a nurse because all my life, ever since I was a little girl, I was filled with the idea of serving a suffering humanity. After one month with you, Mr Whiteside, I am going to work in a munitions factory. From now on, anything I can do to help exterminate the human race will fill me with the greatest of pleasure. If Florence Nightingale had ever nursed YOU, Mr Whiteside, she would have married Jack the Ripper instead of founding the Red Cross!'

WHITESIDE (introducing his secretary): 'This ageing debutante, Mr Jefferson, I retain in my employ only because she is the sole support of her two-headed brother.'

BANJO (Jimmy Durante): 'Did you ever get the feeling that you wanted to stay, and still get the feeling that you wanted to go?'

BEVERLY CARLTON (Reginald Gardiner impersonating Noel Coward): 'Don't tell me how you are, Sherry, I want none of the tiresome details. I've very little time, and so the conversation will be entirely about me, and I shall love it. Shall I tell you how I glittered through the South Seas like a silver scimitar, or would you rather hear how I finished a three-act play with one hand and made love to a maharaja's daughter with the other?'

The Man Who Could Work Miracles

GB 1936 82m bw
London (Alexander Korda)
A city clerk discovers he has the power to work miracles (given him by sportive gods) and nearly causes the end of the earth.
Slow-moving but rather pleasing variation on a simple theme.

w Lajos Biro, *story* H. G. Wells
d Lothar Mendes *ph* Harold

Rosson *m* Mischa Spoliansky
Roland Young, Ralph Richardson, Ernest Thesiger, Edward Chapman, Joan Gardner, Sophie Stewart, Robert Cochrane, George Zucco, Lawrence Hanray, George Sanders

'Supposedly a comedy. A weakling: little draw power on this side.'—*Variety*

'Sometimes fake poetry, sometimes unsuccessful comedy, sometimes farce, sometimes sociological discussion, without a spark of creative talent or a trace of film ability.'—*Graham Greene*

The Man Who Knew Too Much

GB 1934 84m bw
GFD/Gaumont British (Ivor Montagu)
A child is kidnapped by spies to ensure her father's silence, but he springs into action.
Splendid early Hitchcock which after a faded start moves into memorable sequences involving a dentist, an East End mission and the Albert Hall. All very stagey by today's standards, but much more fun than the expensive remake.

w A. R. Rawlinson, Charles Bennett, D. B. Wyndham Lewis, Edwin Greenwood, Emlyn Williams
d Alfred Hitchcock *ph* Curt Courant *m* Arthur Benjamin
Leslie Banks, Edna Best, *Peter Lorre*, Nova Pilbeam, Frank Vosper, Hugh Wakefield, Pierre Fresnay

'A natural and easy production that runs smoothly and has the hallmark of sincerity.'—*Variety*

'The film's mainstay is its refined sense of the incongruous.'—*Peter John Dyer, 1964*

'The strangest story in the annals of naval espionage!'
The Man Who Never Was

GB 1955 102m De Luxe Cinemascope
TCF/André Hakim
In 1943, the British secret service confuses the Germans by dropping a dead man into the sea with false documents.

Mainly enjoyable true life war story marred by an emotional romantic sub-plot with a double twist but helped by an equally fictitious spy hunt which cheers up the last half hour.

w Nigel Balchin, *book* Ewen Montagu *d* Ronald Neame *ph* Oswald Morris *m* Alan Rawsthorne

Clifton Webb, Robert Flemyng, Gloria Grahame, *Stephen Boyd,* Laurence Naismith, Josephine Griffin

The Man Who Shot Liberty Valance

US 1962   122m   bw
Paramount / John Ford (Willis Goldbeck)

A tenderfoot becomes a hero for shooting a bad man, but the shot was really fired by his friend and protector.

Clumsy, obvious western with the director over-indulging himself but providing some good scenes in comedy vein.

w James Warner Bellah, Willis Goldbeck *d* John Ford *ph* William H. Clothier *m* Cyril Mockridge

James Stewart, John Wayne, Vera Miles, Lee Marvin, Edmond O'Brien, Andy Devine, Jeanette Nolan, John Qualen, Ken Murray, Woody Strode, Lee Van Cleef, Strother Martin, John Carradine

'Like Queen Victoria, John Wayne has become lovable because he stayed in the saddle into a new era.'—*Judith Crist*

'A heavy-spirited piece of nostalgia.'—*Pauline Kael, 1975*

'A film whose fascination lies less in what it is itself than in what it reveals about the art of its maker.'—*William S. Pechter*

The Man Who Would Be King

US 1975   129m   colour
Panavision
Columbia / Allied Artists / Persky-Bright / Devon (John Foreman)

In India in the 1880s, two adventurers find themselves accepted as kings by a remote tribe, but greed betrays them.

After an ingratiating start this ambitious fable becomes more predictable, and comedy gives way to unpleasantness. Despite its sporadic high quality, one does not remember it with enthusiasm.

w John Huston, Gladys Hill, *story* Rudyard Kipling *d* John Huston *ph* Oswald Morris *m* Maurice Jarre *pd* Alexander Trauner

Sean Connery, Michael Caine, Christopher Plummer (as Kipling), Saeed Jaffrey, Jack May, Shakira Caine

AAN: script

The Manchurian Candidate

US 1962   126m   bw
UA / MC (Howard W. Koch)

A Korean war 'hero' comes back a brainwashed zombie triggered to kill a liberal politician, his control being his own monstrously ambitious mother.

Insanely plotted but brilliantly handled spy thriller, a mixture of Hitchcock, Welles and *All the King's Men.*

w George Axelrod, *novel* Richard Condon *d* John Frankenheimer *ph* Lionel Lindon *m* David Amram *pd* Richard Sylbert

Frank Sinatra, Laurence Harvey, Janet Leigh, James Gregory, Angela Lansbury, Henry Silva, John McGiver

'The unAmerican film of the year.'—*Penelope Houston*

'An intelligent, funny, superbly written, beautifully played, and brilliantly directed study of the all-embracing fantasy in everyday social, emotional and political existence.'—*Philip Strick, 1973*

'Although it's a thriller, it may be the most sophisticated political satire ever to come out of Hollywood.'—*Pauline Kael, 70s*

AAN: Angela Lansbury

'She'll find a home in every heart!
  She'll reach the heart of every
  home!'

Mandy

GB 1952 93m bw
Ealing (Leslie Norman)

US title: *The Crash of Silence*

A little girl, born deaf, is sent to a
special school.

Carefully wrought and very
sympathetic little semi-documentary
film in which all the adults underplay
in concession to a new child star who
alas did not last long at the top.

w Nigel Balchin, Jack Whittingham,
novel This Day Is Ours by Hilda
Lewis *d Alexander Mackendrick*
ph Douglas Slocombe *m* William
Alwyn

Jack Hawkins, Terence Morgan,
Phyllis Calvert, *Mandy Miller*,
Godfrey Tearle, Dorothy Alison

Manhattan

US 1979 96m bw
Panavision

UA / Jack Rollins / Charles H. Joffe

Episodes in the sex life of a TV
comedy writer with an obsession
about New York.

As close to a summation of Woody
Allen's views and *oeuvre* as anybody
needs; some smart jabs about the
lives we lead are sometimes bogged
down in earnestness and half-comic
despair.

w Woody Allen, Marshall Brickman
d Woody Allen *ph* Gordon Willis
md Tom Pierson

Woody Allen, Diane Keaton, Meryl
Streep, Mariel Hemingway, Michael
Murphy

'Given that the identity of his films
has increasingly been determined by
his compulsion to talk about the
things he finds important, but also by
his fear of having them come out as
anything but a joke, it is not
surprising that he has scarcely been
able to decide on a form for his
"art": from the anything-for-a-laugh
skittering of his early films, to the
broad parodies and pastiches of his
middle period, to the recent

confessional/psychoanalytical
mode.'—*Richard Combs, MFB*

'A masterpiece that has become a
film for the ages by not seeking to be
a film of the moment.'—*Andrew
Sarris*

Manhattan Melodrama

US 1934 93m bw
MGM (David O. Selznick)

Two slum boys grow up friends, one
as district attorney and the other as a
gangster.

Archetypal American situation
drama, with the bad guy inevitably
indulging in self-sacrifice at the end.
An all-star cast makes it palatable in
this case, though the film is
inevitably dated.

w Oliver H. P. Garrett, Joseph L.
Mankiewicz, *story* Arthur Caesar
d W. S. Van Dyke *ph* James Wong
Howe

William Powell, Clark Gable, Myrna
Loy, Leo Carrillo, Nat Pendleton,
George Sidney, Isabel Jewell,
Thomas E. Jackson

'Action meller of the big town . . .
replete with punchy, popularly-
appealing ingredients.'—*Variety*

† *Manhattan Melodrama* gained
some irrelevant fame as the movie
John Dillinger was watching when he
was cornered and shot.

AA: Arthur Caesar

Marathon Man

US 1976 126m Metrocolor
Paramount (Robert Evans,
Sidney Beckerman)

A vicious Nazi returns from Uruguay
to New York in search of diamonds
which had been kept for him by his
now-dead brother, and is outwitted
by the young brother of an
American agent he has killed.
Complex mystery thriller which
seems to have things to mutter about
freedom and McCarthyism and
Nazism, but finally settles down to
being a simple shocker with a
nick-of-time climax. The
presentation is dazzling.

w William Goldman, from his novel
d John Schlesinger ph Conrad Hall
m Michael Small *pd* Richard
MacDonald

Dustin Hoffman, *Laurence Olivier*,
Roy Scheider, William Devane,
Marthe Keller, Fritz Weaver, Marc
Lawrence

'A film of such rich texture and
density in its construction, so
fascinatingly complex in its
unfolding, so engrossing in its
personalities, and so powerful in its
performance and pace that the
seduction of the senses has physical
force.'—*Judith Crist, Saturday
Review*

'Fashionably violent . . . distinctly
self-conscious . . . conventionally
moralistic . . . and absolutely devoid
of resonance.'—*Tom Milne, MFB*

'If at the film's end, you have
followed the series of double and
triple crosses, braved the torture
scenes, and still don't know what it
was about, you're bound to have
company.'—*Paul Coleman, Film
Information*

'A Jewish revenge
fantasy.'—*Pauline Kael*

'He has made a most elegant,
bizarre, rococo melodrama out of
material which, when you think
about it, makes hardly any sense at
all.'—*Vincent Canby, New York
Times*

AAN: Laurence Olivier

Margie

US 1946   94m   Technicolor
TCF (Walter Morosco)
A married woman reminisces about
her college days, when she married
the French teacher despite her
tendency to lose her bloomers at the
most embarrassing moments.
Wholly pleasing nostalgia, very
smartly and brightly handled.

w F. Hugh Herbert, *stories* Ruth
McKinney, Richard Bransten
d Henry King ph Charles Clarke
md Alfred Newman

Jeanne Crain, Glenn Langan, *Alan
Young*, Lynn Bari, Barbara
Lawrence, Conrad Janis, Esther
Dale

Marie Antoinette

US 1938   160m   bw
MGM (Hunt Stromberg)
The last days of the French court
before the revolution.
Too slow by half, and so glamorized
and fictionalized as to lack all
interest, this long delayed
production stands only as an
example of MGM's expensive
prestige movies of the thirties.

w Claudine West, Donald Ogden
Stewart, Ernest Vajda *d* W. S. Van
Dyke *ph* William Daniels *montage*
Slavko Vorkapitch *m* Herbert
Stothart *ad* Cedric Gibbons

Norma Shearer, Tyrone Power, John
Barrymore, Robert Morley, Gladys
George, Anita Louise, Joseph
Schildkraut, Henry Stephenson,
Reginald Gardiner, Peter Bull,
Albert Dekker, Cora Witherspoon,
Barnett Parker, Joseph Calleia,
Henry Kolker, George Zucco,
Henry Daniell, Harry Davenport,
Barry Fitzgerald, Mae Busch,
Robert Barrat

'Produced on a scale of
incomparable splendour and
extravagance, it approaches real
greatness as cinematic historical
literature.'—*Variety*

'A resplendent bore.'—*New
Yorker, 1977*

AAN: Herbert Stothart; Norma
Shearer; Robert Morley

Marius

France 1931   125m   bw
Marcel Pagnol / Paramount
The son of a Marseilles waterfront
café owner gives up his sweetheart to
go to sea.
Celebrated character drama which
succeeds through the realism and
vitality of its people and their
dialogue.

w Marcel Pagnol, from his play
d Alexander Korda *ph* Ted Pahle
m Francis Grammon

Raimu, *Pierre Fresnay*, Charpin,
Orane Demazis

† Two sequels with the same players
and from the same pen made this a
famous trilogy. In *Fanny* (1932,

128m, *d* Marc Allégret) the heroine
marries an old widower to give her
baby a father. In *César* (1936, 117m,
d Marcel Pagnol) Marius comes back
twenty years later and is reunited
with his family

†† *Port of Seven Seas* (MGM 1938)
was a hammy and stagey Hollywood
compression of the trilogy.

The Mark of Zorro

US 1940   94m   bw
TCF (Raymond Griffith)
After being educated in Spain,
Diego de Vega returns to California
and finds the country enslaved and
his father half-corrupted by tyrants.
Disguising himself as a masked
bandit, he leads the country to expel
the usurpers.
Splendid adventure stuff for boys of
all ages, an amalgam of *The Scarlet
Pimpernel* and *Robin Hood* to which
in this version the director adds an
overwhelming pictorial sense which
makes it stand out as the finest of all.

w John Tainton Foote, Garrett Fort,
Bess Meredyth   *d Rouben
Mamoulian   ph Arthur Miller
m Alfred Newman   ad* Richard Day,
Joseph C. Wright

*Tyrone Power, Basil Rathbone, J.
Edward Bromberg*, Linda Darnell,
Eugene Pallette, Montagu Love,
Janet Beecher, Robert Lowery

AAN: Alfred Newman

Marty

US 1955   91m   bw
UA/Hecht–Hill–Lancaster
(Harold Hecht)
A 34-year-old Bronx butcher fears
he will never get a girl because he is
unattractive, but at a Saturday night
dance he meets a girl with similar
fears. Unfortunately she is not
Italian . . .
The first of the filmed teleplays
which in the mid-fifties seemed like a
breath of spring to Hollywood (they
were cheap) and also brought in a
new wave of talent. This is one of
the best, its new naturalistic dialogue
falling happily on the ear; but it has
been so frequently imitated since

that its revolutionary appearance is
hard to imagine.

w Paddy Chayevsky, from his play
*d Delbert Mann   ph Joseph La
Shelle   m* Roy Webb

*Ernest Borgnine, Betsy Blair, Esther
Minciotti, Joe Mantell*, Karen Steele,
Jerry Paris
    'Something rare in the American
cinema today: a subtle, ironic and
compassionate study of ordinary
human relationships.'—*Gavin
Lambert*

AA: best picture; Paddy Chayevsky;
Delbert Mann; Ernest Borgnine
AAN: Joseph La Shelle; Betsy Blair;
Joe Mantell

Mary Poppins

US 1964   139m
Technicolor
Walt Disney (Bill Walsh)
In Edwardian London a magical
nanny teaches two slightly naughty
children to make life enjoyable for
themselves and others.
Sporadically a very pleasant and
effective entertainment for children
of all ages, with plenty of brightness
and charm including magic tricks,
the mixing of live with cartoon
adventures, and just plain fun. It
suffers, however, from a wandering
narrative in the second half (when
Miss Poppins scarcely appears) and
from Mr Van Dyke's really
lamentable attempt at Cockney.

w Bill Walsh, Don da Gradi, *novel*
P. L. Travers   *d* Robert Stevenson
ph Edward Colman   *m/ly Richard
M. and Robert B. Sherman   pd* Tony
Walton   *sp Eustace Lycett, Peter
Ellenshaw, Robert A. Mattey*

Julie Andrews, David Tomlinson,
Glynis Johns, Dick Van Dyke,
Reginald Owen, Ed Wynn, Matthew
Garber, Karen Dotrice, Hermione
Baddeley, Elsa Lanchester, Arthur
Treacher, Jane Darwell

AA: Richard M. and Robert B.
Sherman; Julie Andrews; song
'Chim Chim Cheree'
AAN: best picture; script; Robert
Stevenson; Edward Colman

M*A*S*H

US 1970 116m De Luxe
Panavision
TCF / Aspen (Ingo Preminger,
Leon Ericksen)

Surgeons at a mobile hospital in
Korea spend what spare time they
have chasing women and bucking
authority.

Savage comedy of man's rebellion in
the face of death, alternating sex
farce with gory operation scenes;
hailed as the great anti-everything
film, and certainly very funny for
those who can take it. It led to a
television series which for once did
not disgrace its original.

w Ring Lardner Jnr, *novel* Richard
Hooker *d* Robert Altman
ph Harold E. Stine *m* Johnny
Mandel

Donald Sutherland, Elliott Gould,
Tom Skerritt, Sally Kellerman,
Robert Duvall, Jo Ann Pflug, René
Auberjonois, Gary Burghof

'Bloody funny. A hyper-acute
wiretap on mankind's death
wish.'—*Joseph Morgenstern*

'The laughter is blood-soaked and
the comedy cloaks a bitter and
terrible truth.'—*Judith Crist*

'A foul-mouthed, raucous,
anti-establishment comedy,
combining gallows humour, sexual
slapstick and outrageous
satire.'—*Les Keyser, Hollywood in
the Seventies*

AA: Ring Lardner Jnr
AAN: best picture; Robert Altman;
Sally Kellerman

The Mask of Dimitrios

US 1944 99m bw
Warner (Henry Blanke)

A timid Dutch novelist is drawn into
a Middle-Eastern intrigue with
money at the centre of it.

Generally successful international
intriguer, moodily shot in evocative
sets, and remarkable for its time in
that the story is not distorted to fit
romantic stars: character actors bear
the entire burden.

w Frank Gruber, *novel* Eric Ambler
d Jean Negulesco *ph* Arthur
Edeson *m* Adolph Deutsch

*Peter Lorre, Sidney Greenstreet,
Zachary Scott, Faye Emerson, Victor
Francen, Steven Geray, Florence
Bates, Eduardo Ciannelli, Kurt Katch,
John Abbott, Monte Blue*

'The picture has more mood than
excitement.'—*Pauline Kael, 70s*

A Matter of Life and Death

GB 1946 104m
Technicolor
GFD / Archers (Michael Powell,
Emeric Pressburger
US title: *Stairway to Heaven*

A pilot with brain damage after
bailing out is torn between this world
and the next, but an operation puts
things to rights.

Outrageous fantasy which seemed
more in keeping after the huge death
toll of a world war, and in any case
learned the Hollywood lesson of
eating its cake and still having it, the
supernatural elements being capable
of explanation. A mammoth
technical job in the heavenly
sequences, it deserves full marks for
its sheer arrogance, wit, style and
film flair.

wd Michael Powell, Emeric
Pressburger *ph* Jack Cardiff
m Allan Gray *pd* Hein Heckroth

*David Niven, Roger Livesey, Kim
Hunter, Marius Goring, Raymond
Massey, Abraham Sofaer*

'Powell and Pressburger seem to
have reached their heaven at last
. . . an illimitable Wembley stadium,
surrounded by tinkly music and
mists, from which all men of insight,
if they were ever careless enough to
get there, would quickly blaspheme
their way out.'—*Richard Winnington*

'A dazzling mesh of visionary
satire, post-war politics and the
mystical side of English
romanticism.'—*Tony Rayns, Time
Out, 1979*

'Beautifully written, beautifully
acted, beautifully executed . . . you
would think such formidable merits

would add up to quite a film—and darned if they don't.'—*Time Out*

'This film, whether or not you find its philosophy half-baked, is downright good cinema, doing things that couldn't be done in any other medium'—*Tribune*

'It compelled attention and created emotion.'—*Basil Wright, 1972*

Maytime

US 1937   132m   bw (sepia sequence)
MGM (Hunt Stromberg)
An opera star falls in love with a penniless singer but her jealous impresario shoots him.
Lush romantic musical which turns gradually into melodrama and ends in a ghostly reunion for the lovers. If that's what you like, it could scarcely be better done.

w Noel Langley, *operetta* Rida Johnson Young   *d* Robert Z. Leonard   *ph* Oliver T. Marsh   *m* Sigmund Romberg   *md* Herbert Stothart

Jeanette MacDonald, Nelson Eddy, John Barrymore, Herman Bing, Lynne Carver, Rafaela Ottiano, Paul Porcasi, Sig Rumann
'Click operetta . . . cinch for the foreign market also.'—*Variety*
'Enjoyable for more than camp reasons . . . the atmosphere of thwarted passion is compelling.'—*Pauline Kael, 70s*

† Shooting had begun in colour with Frank Morgan in Bing's part and Paul Lukas in Barrymore's; this footage, directed by Edmund Goulding, was abandoned on Irving Thalberg's death.

AAN: Herbert Stothart

Meet John Doe

US 1941   123m   bw
Liberty Films (Frank Capra)
A tramp is hired to embody the common man in a phony political drive, and almost commits suicide. Vividly staged but over-sentimental Capra extravaganza with high spots outnumbering low.

w Robert Riskin   *d* Frank Capra   *ph* George Barnes   *m* Dmitri Tiomkin

Gary Cooper, *Barbara Stanwyck*, Edward Arnold, Walter Brennan, James Gleason, Spring Byington, Gene Lockhart, Rod la Rocque, Irving Bacon, Regis Toomey, Ann Doran, Warren Hymer, Andrew Tombes
'Capra is as skilled as ever in keeping things moving along briskly and dramatically.'—*National Board of Review*
'The meanings were so distorted that the original authors sued . . . It starts out in the confident Capra manner, but with a darker tone; by the end, you feel puzzled and cheated.'—*Pauline Kael, 70s*

AAN: original story (Richard Connell, Robert Presnell)

Meet Me in St Louis

US 1944   113m   Technicolor
MGM (Arthur Freed)
Scenes in the life of an affectionate family at the turn of the century. Patchy but generally highly agreeable musical nostalgia with an effective sense of the passing years and seasons.

w Irving Brecher, Fred F. Finklehoffe, *novel* Sally Benson   *d* Vincente Minnelli   *ph* George Folsey   *md* Georgie Stoll

Judy Garland, Margaret O'Brien, Tom Drake, Leon Ames, Mary Astor, Lucille Bremer, June Lockhart, *Harry Davenport*, Marjorie Main, Joan Carroll, Hugh Marlowe, Robert Sully, Chill Wills
'A family group framed in velvet and tinsel . . . it has everything a romantic musical should have.'—*Dilys Powell, 1955*

AAN: script; George Folsey; Georgie Stoll; song 'The Trolley Song' (*m/ly* Ralph Blane, Hugh Martin)

'A completely new experience between men and women!'

The Men

US 1950 85m bw
Stanley Kramer

reissue title: *Battle Stripe*

Paraplegic war veterans are prepared for civilian life; the fiancée of one of them helps overcome his problems. Vivid semi-documentary melodrama, at the time rather shocking in its no-holds-barred treatment of sexual problems.

w Carl Foreman d Fred Zinnemann ph Robert de Grasse m Dmitri Tiomkin

Marlon Brando, Teresa Wright, Everett Sloane, Jack Webb, Howard St John

'Don't be misled into feeling that to see this film is merely a duty; it is, simply, an experience worth having.'—*Richard Mallett, Punch*

AAN: Carl Foreman

'Surrender to the happy seduction of Ernst Lubitsch's most glorious picture holiday!'

The Merry Widow

US 1934 99m bw
MGM

A bankrupt king orders a nobleman to woo a wealthy American widow. Patchy, but sometimes sparkling version.

w Samson Raphaelson, Ernest Vajda d Ernst Lubitsch ph Oliver T. Marsh m Franz Lehar

Maurice Chevalier, Jeanette MacDonald, Edward Everett Horton, Una Merkel, George Barbier, Donald Meek, Sterling Holloway, Shirley Ross

'Fine all-around job and an entertainment natural.'—*Variety*

'It is Lubitsch; it is also Hollywood; it is the cream of the American bourgeois film. It is a charlotte russe.'—*Peter Ellis, New Masses*

Metropolis

Germany 1926 120m approx (24 fps) bw silent
UFA (Erich Pommer)

In the year 2000, the workers in a modernistic city live underground and unrest is quelled by the persuasion of a saintly girl, Maria; but a mad inventor creates an evil Maria to incite them to revolt. Always somewhat overlong, and certainly heavy-going in places, this futuristic fantasy not only has many brilliant sequences which created genuine excitement and terror, but it inspired a great many Hollywood clichés to come, notably the Frankenstein theme. The BBC's version of the seventies, with an electronic music sound track, is the most satisfactory.

w Thea Von Harbou d Fritz Lang ph Karl Freund, Günther Rittau sp Eugen Schufftan ad Otto Hunte, Erich Kettelhut, Karl Vollbrecht

Brigitte Helm, Alfred Abel, Gustav Fröhlich, Rudolf Klein-Rogge, Fritz Rasp

'It goes too far and always gets away with it.'—*New Yorker, 1978*

'A wonderful, stupefying folly.'—*New Yorker, 1982*

† In 1984 Giorgio Moroder put out his own new version, with tinted sequences and a re-edited running time of 83 minutes. It was received with a mixture of distaste, respect and caution.

Midnight

US 1939 95m bw
Paramount (Arthur Hornblow Jnr)

A girl stranded in Paris is hired by an aristocrat to seduce the gigolo paying unwelcome attention to his wife.

Sparkling sophisticated comedy which barely flags until a slightly disappointing ending; all the talents involved are in excellent form.

w Billy Wilder, Charles Brackett, story Edwin Justus Mayer, Franz Schultz d Mitchell Leisen ph Charles Lang m Frederick Hollander

Claudette Colbert, Don Ameche, *John Barrymore,* Francis Lederer,

Mary Astor, Elaine Barrie, Hedda Hopper, Rex O'Malley

'Leisen's masterpiece, one of the best comedies of the thirties.'—*John Baxter, 1968*

'One of the authentic delights of the thirties.'—*New Yorker, 1976*

'It has the elements of an American *La Règle du Jeu*.'—*John Gillett*

'Just about the best light comedy ever caught by the camera.'—*Motion Picture Daily*

'To tell you the truth, I ain't a real cowboy. But I'm one helluva stud!'

Midnight Cowboy

US 1969   113m   De Luxe
UA / Jerome Hellman

A slightly dim-witted Texan comes to New York to offer his services as a stud for rich ladies, but spends a hard winter helping a tubercular con man.

Life in the New York gutter, brilliantly if not too accurately observed by a master showman with no heart.

w Waldo Salt, *novel* James Leo Herlihy   *d* John Schlesinger *ph* Adam Holender *md* John Barry *pd* John Robert Lloyd

Jon Voight, Dustin Hoffman, Brenda Vaccaro, Sylvia Miles, John McGiver

'If only Schlesinger's directorial self-discipline had matched his luminous sense of scene and his extraordinary skill in handling actors, this would have been a far more considerable film.'—*Arthur Schlesinger Jnr (no relation)*

'A great deal besides cleverness, a great deal of good feeling and perception and purposeful dexterity.'—*Stanley Kauffmann*

AA: best picture; Waldo Salt; John Schlesinger
AAN: Dustin Hoffman; Jon Voight; Sylvia Miles

Midnight Express

GB 1978   121m
Eastmancolor
Columbia / Casablanca (Alan Marshall, David Puttnam)

Tribulations of an American student arrested in Turkey for carrying hashish.

Misleadingly-titled wallow in prison atrocities, extremely well made but certainly not entertaining and with little discernible point.

w Oliver Stone, *memoir* Billy Hayes *d* Alan Parker *ph* Michael Seresin *m* Giorgio Moroder

Brad Davis, Randy Quaid, John Hurt, Irene Miracle, Bo Hopkins

'One of the ugliest sado-masochistic trips, with heavy homosexual overtones, that our thoroughly nasty movie age has yet produced.'—*Richard Schickel, Time*

'The film details all [the horrors] so relentlessly on one screaming note that it is rather like being hit in the gut until you no longer feel a thing.'—*Derek Malcolm, The Guardian*

'Muted squalor with a disco beat in the background, all packaged as social protest.'—*New Yorker, 1982*

AA: script; music
AAN: best picture; Alan Parker; John Hurt

'Three centuries in the making!'

A Midsummer Night's Dream

US 1935   133m   bw
Warner (Max Reinhardt)

Two pairs of lovers sort out their problems with fairy help at midnight in the woods of Athens.

Shakespeare's play is treated with remarkable respect in this super-glamorous Hollywood adaptation based on the Broadway production by Max Reinhardt. Much of it comes off, and visually it's a treat.

w Charles Kenyon, Mary McCall Jnr, *play* William Shakespeare *d* Max Reinhardt, William Dieterle *ph* Hal Mohr, Fred Jackman, Byron Haskin, H. F. Koenekamp

*m Mendelssohn md Erich Wolfgang
Korngold ch Bronislawa Nijinska
ad Anton Grot*

James Cagney, Dick Powell, Jean
Muir, Ross Alexander, Olivia de
Havilland, Joe E. Brown, Hugh
Herbert, Arthur Treacher, Frank
McHugh, Otis Harlan, Dewey
Robinson, *Victor Jory*, Verree
Teasdale, *Mickey Rooney*, Anita
Louise, Grant Mitchell, Ian Hunter,
Hobart Cavanaugh

'General b.o. chances could be
improved by judicious pruning and
appreciative selling . . . a fine
prestige picture not only for Warners
but for the industry as a
whole.'—*Variety*

'You must see it if you want to be
in a position to argue about the
future of the film!'—*Picturegoer*

'The publicity push behind the film
is tremendous—it is going to be a
success or everyone at Warner
Brothers is going to get
fired.'—*Robert Forsythe*

'Its assurance as a work of film
technique is undoubted.'—*John
Baxter, 1968*

'Its worst contradiction lies in the
way Warners first ordered up a
whole batch of foreign and
high-sounding names to handle
music, dances, general
production—and then turned around
and handed them empty vessels for
actors.'—*Otis Ferguson*

AA: photography
AAN: best picture

'The kind of woman most men
    want . . . and shouldn't have!'
Mildred Pierce
    US 1945   113m   bw
    Warner (Jerry Wald)
A dowdy housewife breaks with her
husband, becomes the owner
(through hard work) of a restaurant
chain, and survives a murder case
before true love comes her way.
A woman's picture par excellence,
glossily and moodily photographed,
with a star suffering in luxury on
behalf of the most ungrateful
daughter of all time.

*w Ranald MacDougall, Catherine
Turney, novel James M. Cain
d Michael Curtiz ph Ernest Haller
m Max Steiner ad Anton Grot*

Joan Crawford, Jack Carson,
Zachary Scott, *Eve Arden, Ann
Blyth*, Bruce Bennett, George
Tobias, Lee Patrick, Moroni Olsen

'Constant, lambent, virulent
attention to money and its effects,
and more authentic suggestions of
sex than one hopes to see in
American films.'—*James Agee*

AA: Joan Crawford
AAN: best picture; script; Ernest
Haller; Eve Arden; Ann Blyth

Le Million
    France 1931   89m   bw
    Tobis (Frank Clifford)
An artist and an ingratiating crook
search Paris for a lost lottery ticket.
With its delicate touch, perfect sense
of comedy timing and infectious use
of recitative and song, this is superb
screen entertainment using most of
the medium's resources.

wd René Clair, musical comedy
Georges Berr, M. Guillemaud
*ph Georges Périnal m Georges Van
Parys, Armand Bernard, Philippe
Parès ad Lazare Meerson*

Annabella, René Lefèvre, *Paul
Olivier*, Louis Allibert, Vanda
Gréville, Raymond Cordy

'A good musical farce that ought
to do well everywhere . . . it has
speed, laughs, splendid photography
and a good cast.'—*Variety*

'René Clair at his exquisite best;
no one else has ever been able to
make a comedy move with such
delicate inevitability.'—*New Yorker,
1978*

† The style of this film was
developed and expanded in
Hollywood by Lubitsch in *One Hour
with You* and by Mamoulian in *Love
Me Tonight*.

Millions Like Us
    GB 1943   103m   bw
    GFD / Gainsborough (Edward
Black)

The tribulations of a family in wartime, especially of the meek daughter who goes into war work and marries an airman, who is killed. Fragmentary but reasonably accurate picture of the Home Front during World War II; a little more humour would not have been out of place, but as propaganda it proved an effective weapon.

wd Frank Launder, Sidney Gilliat ph Jack Cox *md* Louis Levy

Patricia Roc, Gordon Jackson, Moore Marriott, Eric Portman, Anne Crawford, Basil Radford, Naunton Wayne, Joy Shelton, Megs Jenkins

'There is an unsentimental warmheartedness which I hope we shall cling to and extend in filmed representations of the British scene.'—*Richard Winnington*

† The only picture Launder and Gilliat directed side by side on the floor.

Mine Own Executioner

GB 1947   108m   bw
London Films

A lay psychiatrist undertakes the care of a mentally disturbed war veteran, but fails to prevent him from murdering his wife.

When this film first appeared it seemed like the first adult drama featuring sophisticated people to emerge from a British studio. Time and television have blunted its impact, but it remains a well-told suspense melodrama with memorable characters.

w Nigel Balchin, from his novel d Anthony Kimmins ph Wilkie Cooper *m* Benjamin Frankel

Burgess Meredith, Kieron Moore, Dulcie Gray, Barbara White, Christine Norden

'The first psychoanalytical film that a grown-up can sit through without squirming.'—*Richard Winnington*

'His secret meant death to one man if he didn't talk . . . to countless thousands if he did!'

Ministry of Fear

US 1944   85m   bw
Paramount (Seton I. Miller)

During World War II in England, a man just out of a mental hospital wins a cake at a village fair and finds himself caught up in bewildering intrigues.

Little to do with the novel, but a watchable, well-detailed little thriller on Hitchcock lines, once you forgive the usual phoney Hollywood England.

w Seton I. Miller, *novel* Graham Greene *d Fritz Lang ph* Henry Sharp *m* Victor Young

Ray Milland, Marjorie Reynolds, Carl Esmond, Hillary Brooke, Dan Duryea, Percy Waram, Alan Napier, Erskine Sanford

'A crisp and efficiently made thriller with no pretension to intellectual content.'—*Paul Jensen*

The Miracle of Morgan's Creek

US 1943   99m   bw
Paramount (Preston Sturges)

Chaos results when a stuttering hayseed tries to help a girl accidentally pregnant by a soldier she met hazily at a dance.

Weird and wonderful one-man assault on the Hays Office and sundry other American institutions such as motherhood and politics; an indescribable, tasteless, roaringly funny mêlée, as unexpected at the time as it was effective, like a kick in the pants to all other film comedies.

wd Preston Sturges ph John Seitz *m* Leo Shuken, Charles Bradshaw

Betty Hutton, Eddie Bracken, William Demarest, Diana Lynn, Porter Hall, Akim Tamiroff, Brian Donlevy, Alan Bridge

OFFICER KOCKENLOCKER (William Demarest): 'Daughters. They're a mess no matter how you look at 'em. A headache till they get married—*if* they get married—and after that they get worse . . . Either they leave their husbands and come back with four kids and move into your guest room or the husband loses his job and the whole caboodle comes back. Or else they're so homely that you can't get rid of them at all and they sit around like Spanish moss and shame you into an early grave.'

EMILY KOCKENLOCKER (Diana Lynn): 'If you don't mind my mentioning it, father, I think you have a mind like a swamp.'

'Like taking a nun on a roller coaster.'—*James Agee*

'This film moves in a fantastic and irreverent whirl of slapstick, nonsense, farce, sentiment, satire, romance, melodrama—is there any ingredient of dramatic entertainment except maybe tragedy and grand opera that hasn't been tossed into it?'—*National Board of Review*

'Bad taste or no bad taste, I thoroughly enjoyed it.'—*Richard Mallett, Punch*

AAN: Preston Sturges (as writer)

Miracle on 34th Street

US 1947 94m bw
TCF (William Perlberg)
GB title: *The Big Heart*
A department store Santa Claus claims to be the real thing.
Mainly charming comedy fantasy which quickly became an American classic but does suffer from a few dull romantic stretches.

wd George Seaton, *story* Valentine Davies *ph* Charles Clarke, Lloyd Ahern *m* Cyril Mockridge

Edmund Gwenn, Maureen O'Hara, John Payne, Natalie Wood, Gene Lockhart, Porter Hall, William Frawley, Jerome Cowan, Thelma Ritter

'Altogether wholesome, stimulating and enjoyable.'—*Motion Picture Herald*

AA: George Seaton (as writer); Valentine Davies; Edmund Gwenn
AAN: best picture

Mirage

US 1965 109m bw
U-I (Harry Keller)
During a New York power blackout, an executive falls to his death from a skyscraper and a cost accountant loses his memory.
Striking puzzler, rather slowly developed but generally effective and with a strong sense of place and timing.

w Peter Stone, *novel* Walter Ericson *d* Edward Dmytryk *ph* Joe MacDonald *m* Quincy Jones

Gregory Peck, Diane Baker, Walter Abel, *Walter Matthau*, Leif Erickson, Kevin McCarthy

'Worthy of Hitchcock at his vintage best.'—*Daily Express*

Les Misérables

US 1935 109m bw
Twentieth Century (Darryl F. Zanuck)
Unjustly convicted and sentenced to years in the galleys, Jean Valjean emerges to build up his life again but is hounded by a cruel and relentless police officer.
Solid, telling, intelligent version of a much-filmed classic novel; in adaptation and performance it is hard to see how this film could be bettered.

w W. P. Lipscomb, *novel* Victor Hugo *d* Richard Boleslawski *ph* Gregg Toland *m* Alfred Newman

Fredric March, Charles Laughton, Cedric Hardwicke, Rochelle Hudson, Frances Drake, John Beal, Jessie Ralph, Florence Eldridge

'Brilliant filmization, sure fire for heavy money.'—*Variety*

'Unbelievably thrilling in all the departments of its manufacture . . . a memorable experience in the cinema.'—*New York Times*

'A superlative effort, a thrilling, powerful, poignant picture.'—*New York Evening Post*

'Deserving of rank among the cinema's finest achievements.'—*New York World Telegram*

† Other versions of the story: 1909, 1913 (French); 1917 (William Farnum); 1923 (French: Gabriel Gabrio); 1929 as *The Bishop's Candlesticks* (Walter Huston); 1934 (French: Harry Baur); 1946 (Italian: Gino Cervi); 1952; 1956 (French: Jean Gabin); 1978 (British: Richard Jordan).

AAN: best picture; Gregg Toland

Mission to Moscow

US 1943 112m bw
Warner (Robert Buckner)

The Russian career of US Ambassador Joseph E. Davies. Stodgy but fascinating wartime propaganda piece viewing the Russians as warm-hearted allies; in the later days of the McCarthy witch hunt, Jack L. Warner regretted he had ever allowed it to be made.

w Howard Koch, *book* Joseph E. Davies *d* Michael Curtiz *ph* Bert Glennon *m* Max Steiner

Walter Huston, Ann Harding, Oscar Homolka, George Tobias, Gene Lockhart, Eleanor Parker, Richard Travis, Helmut Dantine, Victor Francen, Henry Daniell, Barbara Everest, Dudley Field Malone, Roman Bohnen, Maria Palmer, Moroni Olsen, Minor Watson.

'A mishmash: of Stalinism with New Dealism with Hollywoodism with opportunism with shaky experimentalism with mesmerism with onanism, all mosaicked into a remarkable portrait of what the makers of the film think the Soviet Union is like—a great glad two-million-dollar bowl of canned borscht, eminently approvable by the Institute of Good Housekeeping.'—*James Agee*

Mr Blandings Builds His Dream House

US 1948 84m bw
RKO (Norman Panama, Melvin Frank)

A New York advertising man longs to live in the Connecticut countryside, but finds the way to rural satisfaction is hard.

It hasn't the lightness and brightness of the book, but this is a fun film for the middle-aged who like to watch three agreeable stars doing their thing.

w Norman Panama, Melvin Frank, *novel* Eric Hodgkin *d* H. C. Potter *ph* James Wong Howe *m* Leigh Harline *md* Constantin Bakaleinikoff

Cary Grant, *Myrna Loy*, *Melvyn Douglas*, *Reginald Denny*, Louise Beavers, Ian Wolfe, Harry Shannon, Nestor Paiva, Jason Robards

'A bulls-eye for middle-class middlebrows.'—*James Agee*

'I loved it. That was really a pleasure to make.'—*H. C. Potter, 1973*

Mr Deeds Goes to Town

US 1936 118m bw
Columbia (Frank Capra)

A small-town poet inherits a vast fortune and sets New York on its heels by his honesty.

What once was fresh and charming now seems rather laboured in spots, and the production is parsimonious indeed, but the courtroom scene still works, and the good intentions conquer all.

w Robert Riskin, *story* Opera Hat by Clarence Budington Kelland *d* Frank Capra *ph* Joseph Walker *m* Adolph Deutsch *md* Howard Jackson

Gary Cooper, *Jean Arthur*, Raymond Walburn, Lionel Stander, Walter Catlett, George Bancroft, Douglass Dumbrille, H. B. Warner, Ruth Donnelly, *Margaret Seddon*, *Margaret McWade*

'I have an uneasy feeling he's on his way out. He's started to make pictures about themes instead of people.'—*Alistair Cooke*

'Everywhere the picture goes, from the endearing to the absurd, the accompanying business is carried through with perfect zip and relish.'—*Otis Ferguson*

'A comedy quite unmatched on the screen.'—*Graham Greene*

'The film culminates in a courtroom sequence that introduced the word "pixilated" to just about every American home, and set people to examining each other's casual scribbles or sketches—their "doddles".'—*Pauline Kael, 70s*

AA: Frank Capra
AAN: best picture; Robert Riskin; Gary Cooper

Mr Skeffington

US 1944 127m bw
Warner (Julius J. and Philip G. Epstein)

A selfish beauty finally turns to her discarded dull husband; when he is blind, he doesn't mind her faded looks.

Long, patchily made, but thoroughly enjoyable star melodrama.

w Julius J. and Philip G. Epstein, *novel* 'Elizabeth' *d* Vincent Sherman *ph* Ernest Haller *m* Franz Waxman

Bette Davis, Claude Rains, Walter Abel, Richard Waring, George Coulouris, John Alexander, Jerome Cowan

'An endless woman's page dissertation on What To Do When Beauty Fades.'—*James Agee*

'To call the film a good one would be to exaggerate; but entertaining and interesting, I insist, it is.'—*Richard Mallett, Punch*

AAN: Bette Davis; Claude Rains

'Stirring—in the seeing!
Precious—in the remembering!'

Mr Smith Goes to Washington

US 1939 130m bw
Columbia (Frank Capra)

Washington's youngest senator exposes corruption in high places, almost at the cost of his own career. Archetypal high-flying Capra vehicle, with the little man coming out top as he seldom does in life. Supreme gloss hides the corn, helter-skelter direction keeps one watching, and all concerned give memorable performances. A cinema classic.

w Sidney Buchman, story Lewis R. Foster *d Frank Capra ph Joseph Walker m Dmitri Tiomkin montage Slavko Vorkapich*

James Stewart, Claude Rains, Jean Arthur, Thomas Mitchell, Edward Arnold, Guy Kibbee, Eugene Pallette, Beulah Bondi, *Harry Carey*, H. B. Warner, Astrid Allwyn, Ruth Donnelly, Charles Lane, Porter Hall

SMITH (James Stewart): 'I wouldn't give you two cents for all your fancy rules if, behind them, they didn't have a little bit of plain, ordinary kindness—and a little looking out for the other fella, too.'

'Timely and absorbing drama presented in best Capra craftsmanship.'—*Variety*

'More fun, even, than the Senate itself . . . not merely a brilliant jest, but a stirring and even inspiring testament to liberty and freedom.'—*Frank S. Nugent, New York Times*

'It says all the things about America that have been crying out to be said again—and says them beautifully.'—*Los Angeles Times*

'The great American picture.'—*Billboard*

'I feel that to show this film in foreign countries will do inestimable harm to American prestige all over the world.'—*Joseph P. Kennedy, then American ambassador to Great Britain*

'A totally compelling piece of movie-making, upholding the virtues of traditional American ideals.'—*NFT, 1973*

'Very good, beautifully done and extremely entertaining; long, but worth the time it takes.'—*Richard Mallett, Punch*

'More of the heartfelt than is good for the stomach.'—*New Yorker, 1977*

AA: Lewis R. Foster
AAN: best picture; Sidney Buchman; Frank Capra; Dmitri Tiomkin; James Stewart; Claude Rains; Harry Carey

Mrs Miniver

US 1942   134m   bw
MGM (Sidney Franklin)

An English housewife survives
World War II.

This is the rose-strewn English
village, Hollywood variety, but when
released it proved a beacon of
morale despite its false sentiment,
absurd rural types and melodramatic
situations. It is therefore beyond
criticism, except that some of the
people involved should have known
better.

w Arthur Wimperis, George
Froeschel, James Hilton, Claudine
West, *novel* Jan Struther *d* William
Wyler *ph* Joseph Ruttenberg
m Herbert Stothart

Greer Garson, Walter Pidgeon,
Teresa Wright, Richard Ney, Dame
May Whitty, Henry Travers,
Reginald Owen, Henry Wilcoxon,
Helmut Dantine, Rhys Williams,
Aubrey Mather

VICAR (Henry Wilcoxon) preaching
final sermon in bombed church: .
'This is not only a war of soldiers in
uniforms. It is a war of the
people—of all the people—and it
must be fought not only on the
battlefield but in the cities and in the
villages, in the factories and on the
farms, in the home and in the heart
of every man, woman and child who
loves freedom. Well, we have buried
our dead, but we shall not forget
them. Instead, they will inspire us
with an unbreakable determination
to free ourselves and those who
come after us from the tyranny and
terror that threaten to strike us
down. This is the people's war. It is
our war. We are the fighters. Fight
it, then. Fight it with all that is in us.
And may God defend the right.'
  'That almost impossible feat, a
war picture that photographs the
inner meaning, instead of the
outward realism of World War
II.'—*Time*

AA: best picture; script; William
Wyler; Joseph Ruttenberg; Greer
Garson; Teresa Wright
AAN: Walter Pidgeon; Dame May
Whitty; Henry Travers

Moby Dick

GB 1956   116m
Technicolor
Warner/Moulin (John Huston)

A whaling skipper is determined to
harpoon the white whale which
robbed him of a leg.

Pretentious period adventure, rather
too obsessed with symbolism and
certainly too slowly developed, but
full of interesting detail which almost
outweighs the central miscasting.

w Ray Bradbury, John Huston,
novel Herman Melville *d* John
Huston *ph Oswald Morris m* Philip
Stainton

Gregory Peck, Richard Basehart,
Friedrich Ledebur, Leo Genn,
Orson Welles, James Robertson
Justice, Harry Andrews, Bernard
Miles, Noel Purcell, Edric Connor,
Joseph Tomelty, Mervyn Johns
  'Interesting more often than
exciting.'—*Variety*

'You'll never laugh as long and as
   loud again as long as you live!
   The laughs come so fast and so
   furious you'll wish it would end
   before you collapse!'

Modern Times

US 1936   87m   bw
Charles Chaplin

An assembly-line worker goes
berserk but can't get another job.
Silent star comedy produced in the
middle of the sound period; flashes
of genius alternate with sentimental
sequences and jokes without punch.

wd/m Charles Chaplin *ph* Rollie
Totheroh, Ira Morgan

Charles Chaplin, Paulette Goddard,
Henry Bergman, Chester Conklin,
Tiny Sandford
  'A natural for the world market
. . . box office with a capital
B.'—*Variety*
  'A feature picture made out of
several one- and two-reel shorts,
proposed titles being *The Shop, The
Jailbird, The Singing Waiter.*'—*Otis
Ferguson*

Mona Lisa

GB 1986 104m
Technicolor
HandMade / Palace (Stephen Woolley, Patrick Cassavetti)

An ex-con becomes chauffeur for a prostitute and becomes involved in the kinkier areas of the vice trade. Only this actor could make a hit of this unsavoury yarn, with its highlights of sex and violence. But he did.

w Neil Jordan, David Leland d Neil Jordan ph Roger Pratt m Michael Kamen pd Jamie Leonard ed Lesley Walker

Bob Hoskins, Cathy Tyson, Michael Caine

'The 1931 nut crop is ready!'
Monkey Business

US 1931 81m bw
Paramount (Herman J. Mankiewicz)

Four ship's stowaways crash a society party and catch a few crooks. The shipboard part of this extravaganza is one of the best stretches of Marxian lunacy, but after the Chevalier impersonations it runs out of steam. Who's grumbling?

w S. J. Perelman, Will B. Johnstone, Arthur Sheekman d Norman Z. McLeod ph Arthur L. Todd

Groucho, Chico, Harpo, Zeppo, Thelma Todd, Rockcliffe Fellowes, Ruth Hall, Harry Woods

'Surefire for laughs despite working along familiar lines . . . picture has started off by doing sweeping business all over, and no reason why it shouldn't continue to tickle wherever it plays.'—Variety

Monsieur Hulot's Holiday

France 1953 91m bw
Cady / Discina (Fred Orain)
original title: Les Vacances de Monsieur Hulot

An accident-prone bachelor arrives at a seaside resort and unwittingly causes havoc for himself and everyone else.

Despite lame endings to some of the jokes, this is a film to set the whole world laughing, Hulot himself being an unforgettable character and some of the timing magnificent. One feels that it could very nearly happen.

w Jacques Tati, Henri Marquet d Jacques Tati ph Jacques Mercanton, Jean Mouselle m Alain Romans

Jacques Tati, Nathalie Pascaud, Michèle Rolla, Valentine Camax

'The casual, amateurish air of his films clearly adds to their appeal: it also appears to explain their defects.'—Penelope Houston, MFB

'It had me laughing out loud with more enjoyment than any other comedy film this year.'—Daily Express

AAN: script.

'Makes Ben-Hur look like an epic!'
Monty Python and the Holy Grail

GB 1975 90m Technicolor
EMI / Python (Monty) Pictures / Michael White (Mark Forstater)

King Arthur and his knights seek the Holy Grail.

Hellzapoppin-like series of linked sketches on a medieval theme; some slow bits, but often uproariously funny and with a remarkable visual sense of the middle ages.

w Graham Chapman, John Cleese, Terry Gilliam, Eric Idle, Michael Palin d Terry Gilliam, Terry Jones ph Terry Bedford animation Terry Gilliam m Neil Innes pd Roy Smith

Graham Chapman, John Cleese, Terry Gilliam, Eric Idle, Michael Palin

'The team's visual buffooneries and verbal rigmaroles are piled on top of each other with no attention to judicious timing or structure, and a form which began as a jaunty assault on the well-made revue sketch and an ingenious misuse of television's fragmented style of presentation, threatens to become as unyielding and unfruitful as the conventions it originally attacked.'—Geoff Brown

The Moon and Sixpence

US 1943   85m   bw (colour sequence)
Albert Lewin / David L. Loew
(Stanley Kramer)

A stockbroker leaves his wife and family, spends some selfish years painting in Paris and finally dies of leprosy on a South Sea island.
Pleasantly literary adaptation of an elegant novel based on the life of Gauguin; a little stodgy in presentation now, but much of it still pleases.

w Albert Lewin, *novel* W. Somerset Maugham *d* Albert Lewin *ph* John Seitz *m* Dmitri Tiomkin

George Sanders, Herbert Marshall (as Maugham), *Steve Geray*, Doris Dudley, Elena Verdugo, Florence Bates, Heather Thatcher, Eric Blore, Albert Basserman

'An admirable film until the end, when it lapses into Technicolor and techni-pathos.'—*James Agate*

AAN: Dmitri Tiomkin

The Moon is Blue

US 1953   99m   bw
Otto Preminger

A spry young girl balances the attractions of a middle-aged lover against her young one.
Paper-thin comedy partly set on top of the Empire State Building (and thereafter in a dowdy set); mildly amusing in spots, it gained notoriety, and a Production Code ban, by its use of such naughty words as 'virgin' and 'mistress'.

w F. Hugh Herbert, from his play *d* Otto Preminger *ph* Ernest Laszlo *m* Herschel Burke Gilbert

Maggie McNamara, David Niven, William Holden, Tom Tully, Dawn Addams

PATTY (Maggie McNamara): 'Men are usually bored with virgins. I'm so glad you're not . . . Have you a mistress?'

DONALD: 'Don't you think it's better for a girl to be preoccupied with sex than occupied with it?'

'It adds nothing to the art of cinema and certainly does not deserve the attention it will get for flouting the Production Code.'—*Philip T. Hartung*

† The film was made simultaneously in German, as *Die Jungfrau auf dem Dach*, with Hardy Kruger, Johanna Matz and Johannes Heesters.

AAN: Maggie McNamara; title song (*m* Herschel Burke Gilbert, *ly* Sylvia Fine)

The Moon is Down

US 1943   90m   bw
TCF (Nunnally Johnson)

A Norwegian village resists the Nazis.
Sombre, talkative, intelligent little drama, the best of the resistance films, shot on the set of *How Green Was My Valley* (with snow covering).

w *Nunnally Johnson, novel* John Steinbeck *d* Irving Pichel *ph* Arthur Miller *m* Alfred Newman

Henry Travers, Cedric Hardwicke, Lee J. Cobb, Dorris Bowden, Margaret Wycherly, Peter Van Eyck, John Banner

'This may well be a true picture of Norway and its people. But it fails to strike fire, to generate passion. It leaves one feeling rather proud but also sad.'—*Bosley Crowther*

The More the Merrier

US 1943   104m   bw
Columbia (George Stevens)

In crowded Washington during World War II, a girl allows two men to share her apartment and falls in love with the younger one.
Thoroughly amusing romantic comedy with bright lines and situations; remade less effectively as *Walk Don't Run*.

w Robert Russell, Frank Ross, Richard Flournoy, Lewis R. Foster *d* George Stevens *ph* Ted Tetzlaff *m* Leigh Harline *md* Morris Stoloff

Jean Arthur, Joel McCrea, Charles Coburn, Richard Gaines, Bruce Bennett

'The gayest comedy that has come from Hollywood in a long time. It has no more substance than a watermelon, but is equally delectable.'—*Howard Barnes*

'Farce, like melodrama, offers very special chances for accurate observation, but here accuracy is avoided ten times to one in favour of the easy burlesque or the easier idealization which drops the bottom out of farce. Every good moment frazzles or drowns.'—*James Agee*

AA: Charles Coburn
AAN: best picture; script; original story (Frank Ross, Robert Russell); George Stevens; Jean Arthur

Morgan—A Suitable Case for Treatment

GB 1966 97m bw
British Lion/Quintra (Leon Clore)

A young woman determines to leave her talented but half-mad artist husband, who has a fixation on gorillas and behaves in a generally uncivilized manner.
Archetypal sixties marital fantasy, an extension of *Look Back in Anger* in the mood of swinging London. As tiresome as it is funny—but it *is* funny.

w David Mercer, from his play
d Karel Reisz ph Larry Pizer, *Gerry Turpin m Johnny Dankworth*

Vanessa Redgrave, *David Warner*, Robert Stephens, Irene Handl, Newton Blick, Nan Munro

'Poor Morgan: victim of a satire that doesn't bite, lost in a technical confusion of means and ends, and emerging like an identikit photograph, all bits and pieces and no recognizable face.'—*Penelope Houston*

'The first underground movie made above ground.'—*John Simon*
'I think *Morgan* is so appealing to college students because it shares their self-view: they accept this mess of cute infantilism and obsessions and aberrations without expecting the writer and director to resolve it

and without themselves feeling a necessity to sort it out.'—*Pauline Kael*

AAN: Vanessa Redgrave

Morning Departure

GB 1950 102m bw
Rank/Jay Lewis (Leslie Parkyn)
US title: *Operation Disaster*

Twelve men are caught in a trapped submarine, and only eight can escape.
Archetypal stiff-upper-lip service tragedy, which moves from briskness to a slow funereal ending.

*w William Fairchild, play Kenneth Woolard d Roy Baker
ph Desmond Dickinson*

John Mills, Richard Attenborough, Nigel Patrick, Lana Morris, Peter Hammond, Helen Cherry, James Hayter, Andrew Crawford, George Cole, Michael Brennan, Wylie Watson, Bernard Lee, Kenneth More

'Revealing the amazing things a woman will do for love!'

Morocco

US 1930 97m bw
Paramount (Louis D. Lighton)

A cabaret singer arrives in Morocco and continues her wicked career by enslaving all the men in sight; but true love reaches her at last.
The star's first American film reveals her quintessence, and although wildly dated in subject matter remains a perversely enjoyable entertainment.

w Jules Furthman, novel Amy Jolly by Benno Vigny d Josef Von Sternberg ph Lee Garmes m Karl Hajos

Marlene Dietrich, Gary Cooper, Adolphe Menjou, Ullrich Haupt, Juliette Compton, Francis McDonald

'Lightweight story with good direction . . . needs plenty of exploitation to do over average.'—*Variety*

'A definite step forward in the art of motion pictures.'—*National Board of Review*

'A cinematic pattern brilliant, profuse, subtle, and at almost every turn inventive.'—*Wilton A. Barrett*

'Enchantingly silly, full of soulful grand passions, drifting cigarette smoke, and perhaps a few too many pictorial shots of the Foreign Legion marching this way and that.'—*New Yorker, 1979*

AAN: Josef Von Sternberg; Lee Garmes; Marlene Dietrich

The Mortal Storm
US 1940   100m   bw
MGM (Sidney Franklin)
A German family in the thirties is split by Nazism.
Solid anti-Nazi melodrama typical of the period before America entered the war; good performances outweigh unconvincing studio sets.

w Claudine West, George Froeschel, Andersen Ellis, *novel* Phyllis Bottome *d* Frank Borzage *ph* William Daniels *m* Edward Kane

Margaret Sullavan, Robert Young, James Stewart, Frank Morgan, Robert Stack, Bonita Granville, Irene Rich, Maria Ouspenskaya

'The love story of today with the popular stars of *The Shop Around the Corner*!'—*publicity*

† The film caused Goebbels to ban the showing of MGM pictures in all German territories.

The Most Dangerous Game
US 1932   63m   bw
(RKO) Merian C. Cooper
GB title: *The Hounds of Zaroff*
A mad hunter lures guests on to his island so that he can hunt them down like animals.
Dated but splendidly shivery melodrama with moments of horror and mystery and a splendidly photographed chase sequence. Much imitated in curious ways, and not only by direct remakes such as *A Game of Death* and *Run for the Sun*.

w James Creelman, *story* Richard Connell *d* Ernest B. Schoedsack, Irving Pichel *ph* Henry Gerrard *m* Max Steiner

Leslie Banks, Joel McCrea, Fay Wray, Robert Armstrong, Noble Johnson
'Futile stab at horror film classification, ineffective as entertainment and minus cast names to compensate.'—*Variety*

Mother
USSR 1926   90m approx (24 fps)   bw   silent
Mezhrabpom–Russ
original title: *Mat*
A mother incriminates her strike-breaking son, but realizes her error.
Propagandist social melodrama which is also brilliantly conceived and edited, with sequences matching those of Eisenstein.

w N. Zarkhi, V. I. Pudovkin, *novel* Maxim Gorky *d* V. I. Pudovkin *ph* A. Golovnia

Vera Baranovskaya, Nikolai Batalov

† Other versions appeared in 1920 and (*d* Mark Donskoi) 1955.

Moulin Rouge
GB 1952   119m
Technicolor
Romulus (Jack Clayton)
Fictional biopic of Toulouse Lautrec. The dramatic emphasis is on the love affairs of the dwarfish artist, but the film's real interest is in its evocation of 19th-century Montmartre, and especially in the first twenty-minute can can sequence. Nothing later can stand up to the exhilaration of this, and the film slowly slides into boredom.

w John Huston, Anthony Veiller, *novel* Pierre La Mure *d* John Huston *ph* Oswald Morris *m* Georges Auric *ad* Paul Sheriff

Jose Ferrer, Zsa Zsa Gabor, Katherine Kath, Colette Marchand

AAN: best picture; John Huston (as director); Jose Ferrer; Colette Marchand

The Mudlark

GB 1950 98m bw
TCF (Nunnally Johnson)

A scruffy boy from the docks breaks into Windsor Castle to see Queen Victoria and ends her fifteen years of seclusion.

A pleasant whimsical legend which could have done without the romantic interest, but which despite an air of unreality provides warm-hearted, well-upholstered entertainment for family audiences.

w *Nunnally Johnson*, *novel* Theodore Bonnet d *Jean Negulesco* ph *Georges Périnal* m William Alwyn ad C. P. Norman

Alec Guinness, Irene Dunne, *Andrew Ray*, Anthony Steel, Constance Smith, *Finlay Currie*, *Edward Rigby*

'It comes to life!'
'A love story that lived for three
   thousand years!'

The Mummy

US 1932 72m bw
Universal (Stanley Bergerman)

An Egyptian mummy comes back to life and covets a young girl.

Strange dreamlike horror film with only fleeting frissons but plenty of narrative interest despite the silliest of stories and some fairly stilted acting.

w *John I. Balderston* d *Karl Freund* ph *Charles Stumar*

Boris Karloff, Zita Johann, David Manners, Arthur Byron, Edward Van Sloan

'Should show profit despite fairy tale theme.'—*Variety*

'It beggars description . . . one of the most unusual talkies ever produced.'—*New York Times*

'Editing very much in the Germanic style, magnificent lighting and a superb performance from Karloff make this a fantasy almost without equal.'—*John Baxter, 1968*

† The star was billed simply as 'Karloff the uncanny'.

'A bloody funny movie!'
Murder by Death

US 1976 94m Metrocolor
Columbia / Ray Stark

Several (fictional) detectives are invited to stay at the home of a wealthy recluse, and mystery and murder follow.

Sometimes thin but generally likeable spoof of a longstanding genre; the stars seize their opportunities avidly, and the film does not outstay its welcome.

w *Neil Simon* d Robert Moore ph David M. Walsh m Dave Grusin pd Stephen Grimes

Peter Falk, Alec Guinness, Peter Sellers, Truman Capote, Estelle Winwood, Elsa Lanchester, Eileen Brennan, James Coco, David Niven, Maggie Smith, Nancy Walker

'Plenty of scene-stealing actors but not many scenes worth stealing.'—*Michael Billington*, *Illustrated London News*

'Polished performances fail to compensate for a vacuous and frustratingly tortuous plot.'—*Sight and Sound*

'It seems to me that if you haven't watched the real Thin Man and the real Bogie in the real *Maltese Falcon* you won't see the joke; and if you have watched them, the joke is not good enough.'—*Dilys Powell*, *Sunday Times*

Murder on the Orient Express

GB 1974 131m
Technicolor

EMI / GW Films (John Brabourne, Richard Goodwin)

In the early thirties, Hercule Poirot solves a murder on a snowbound train.

Reasonably elegant but disappointingly slackly-handled version of a classic mystery novel. Finney overacts and his all-star support is distracting, while as soon as the train chugs into its snowdrift the film stops moving too, without even a dramatic 'curtain'.

w *Paul Dehn*, *novel* Agatha Christie d Sidney Lumet ph Geoffrey

Unsworth *m* Richard Rodney
Bennett *pd* Tony Walton

Albert Finney, *Ingrid Bergman*,
Lauren Bacall, Wendy Hiller, Sean
Connery, Vanessa Redgrave,
Michael York, Martin Balsam,
Richard Widmark, Jacqueline
Bisset, Jean-Pierre Cassel, Rachel
Roberts, George Coulouris, *John
Gielgud*, Anthony Perkins, Colin
Blakely, Jeremy Lloyd, Denis
Quilley

'Audiences appear to be so hungry
for this type of entertainment that
maybe it hardly matters that it isn't
very good.'—*Judith Crist*

AA: Ingrid Bergman
AAN: Paul Dehn; Geoffrey
Unsworth; Richard Rodney Bennett;
Albert Finney

The Music Man
US 1962   151m
Technirama
Warner (Morton da Costa)

A confidence trickster persuades a
small-town council to start a boys'
band, with himself as the agent for
all the expenses.

Reasonably cinematic, thoroughly
invigorating transference to the
screen of a hit Broadway musical.
Splendid period 'feel', standout
performances, slight sag in second
half.

w Marion Hargrove, *book* Meredith
Wilson *d* Morton da Costa
ph Robert Burks *md* Ray Heindorf
ch Onna White *songs* Meredith
Wilson

Robert Preston, Shirley Jones,
Buddy Hackett, *Hermione Gingold*,
Pert Kelton, Paul Ford

'This is one of those triumphs that
only a veteran performer can have;
Preston's years of experience and his
love of performing come together
joyously.'—*Pauline Kael*

AA: Ray Heindorf
AAN: best picture

'They'll take this town by storm
. . . fighting, laughing, loving,
breaking every law of the seven
seas!'

Mutiny on the Bounty
US 1935   135m   bw
MGM (Irving Thalberg, Albert
Lewin)

An 18th-century British naval vessel
sets off for South America but
during a mutiny the captain is cast
adrift and the mutineers settle in the
Pitcairn Islands.

A still-entertaining adventure film
which seemed at the time like the
pinnacle of Hollywood's
achievement but can now be seen to
be slackly told, with wholesale
pre-release editing very evident.
Individual scenes and performances
are however refreshingly well
handled.

w Talbot Jennings, Jules Furthman,
Carey Wilson, *book* Charles
Nordhoff, James Hall *d Frank
Lloyd ph* Arthur Edeson
m Herbert Stothart

Charles Laughton, *Clark Gable*,
Franchot Tone, Movita, Dudley
Digges, Henry Stephenson, Donald
Crisp, Eddie Quillan, Francis Lister,
Spring Byington, Ian Wolfe

BLIGH (Charles Laughton):
'Casting me adrift 3,500 miles from a
port of call! You're sending me to
my doom, eh? Well, you're wrong,
Christian. I'll take this boat, as she
floats, to England if I must. I'll live
to see you—all of you—hanging
from the highest yardarm in the
British fleet . . .'

'Nothing to stand in the way of a
box office dynamite rating.'—*Variety*

'Incidents are made vivid in terms
of the medium—the swish and pistol
crack of the lash, the sweating lean
bodies, the terrible labour, and the
ominous judgment from the
quarterdeck.'—*Otis Ferguson*

AA: best picture
AAN: script; Frank Lloyd; Herbert
Stothart; Charles Laughton; Clark
Gable; Franchot Tone (whose role
was originally to have been played
by Robert Montgomery)

'She was everything the west
   was—young, fiery, exciting!'
My Darling Clementine
   US 1946 98m bw
   TCF (Samuel G. Engel)
Wyatt Earp cleans up Tombstone
and wipes out the Clanton gang at
the OK corral.
Archetypal western mood piece, full
of nostalgia for times gone by and
crackling with memorable scenes and
characterizations.

w Samuel G. Engel, Winston Miller,
book Wyatt Earp, Frontier Marshal
by Stuart N. Lake *d* John Ford
ph Joe MacDonald *m* Cyril
Mockridge

*Henry Fonda, Victor Mature, Walter
Brennan*, Linda Darnell, Cathy
Downs, Tim Holt, Ward Bond, *Alan
Mowbray*, John Ireland, Jane
Darwell
   'Every scene, every shot is the
product of a keen and sensitive
eye.'—*Bosley Crowther*
   'Considerable care has gone to its
period reconstruction, but the view
is a poetic one.'—*Lindsay Anderson*

My Fair Lady
   US 1964 175m
   Technicolor   Super Panavision
70
CBS/Warner (Jack L. Warner)
Musical version of *Pygmalion*, about
a flower girl trained by an arrogant
elocutionist to pass as a lady.
Careful, cold transcription of a stage
success; cinematically quite
uninventive when compared with
Pygmalion itself, but a pretty good
entertainment.

w Alan Jay Lerner, *play* Pygmalion
by Bernard Shaw *d* George Cukor
ph Harry Stradling *m* Frederick
Loewe *ch* Hermes Pan *ad* Gene
Allen *costumes* Cecil Beaton

Rex Harrison, Audrey Hepburn,
Stanley Holloway, Wilfrid Hyde
White, Gladys Cooper, Jeremy
Brett, Theodore Bikel, Isobel
Elsom, Mona Washbourne, Walter
Burke
   'The property has been not so
much adapted as elegantly
embalmed.'—*Andrew Sarris*

AA: best picture; George Cukor;
Harry Stradling; Rex Harrison
AAN: Alan Jay Lerner; Stanley
Holloway; Gladys Cooper

My Favorite Blonde
   US 1942 78m bw
   Paramount (Paul Jones)
A burlesque comic travelling by train
helps a lady in distress and lives to
regret it.
Smartly paced spy comedy thriller,
one of its star's best vehicles.

w Don Hartman, Frank Butler,
Melvin Frank, Norman Panama
d Sidney Lanfield ph William
Mellor m David Buttolph

Bob Hope, Madeleine Carroll, Gale
Sondergaard, George Zucco, Lionel
Royce, Walter Kingsford, Victor
Varconi

'The funniest, fastest honeymoon
   ever screened!'
My Favorite Wife
   US 1940 88m bw
   RKO (Leo McCarey)
A lady explorer returns after several
shipwrecked years to find that her
husband has married again.
A well-worn situation gets its
brightest treatment in this light star
vehicle.

w Sam and Bella Spewack, Leo
McCarey d Garson Kanin
ph Rudolph Maté m Roy Webb
Cary Grant, Irene Dunne, Randolph
Scott, Gail Patrick, Ann Shoemaker,
Donald MacBride
   'One of those comedies with a
glow on it.'—*Otis Ferguson*
† Other variations: *Too Many
Husbands, Our Wife, Three for the
Show, Move Over Darling.*

AAN: script; Roy Webb

My Girl Tisa
   US 1948 95m bw
   United States Pictures (Milton
Sperling)
An immigrant girl in New York in
the nineties falls for an aspiring
politician, is threatened with
deportation but saved by the
intervention of Theodore Roosevelt.

Charming period fairy tale with excellent background detail and attractive performances.

w Allen Boretz, *play* Lucille S. Prumbs, Sara B. Smith *d Elliott Nugent ph* Ernest Haller *m* Max Steiner

Lilli Palmer, Sam Wanamaker, Alan Hale, Stella Adler, Akim Tamiroff

My Learned Friend

GB 1943 76m bw
Ealing (Robert Hamer)

A shady lawyer is last on a mad ex-convict's murder list of those who helped get him convicted.

Madcap black farce, plot-packed and generally hilarious; the star's last vehicle, but one of his best, with superbly timed sequences during a pantomime and on the face of Big Ben.

w John Dighton, Angus Macphail d Basil Dearden, Will Hay ph Wilkie Cooper *m* Ernest Irving

Will Hay, Claude Hulbert, Mervyn Johns, Ernest Thesiger, Charles Victor, Lloyd Pearson, Maudie Edwards, G. H. Mulcaster, Gibb McLaughlin

My Man Godfrey

US 1936 90m bw
Universal (Gregory La Cava)

A zany millionaire family invite a tramp to be their butler and find he is richer than they are.

Archetypal Depression concept which is also one of the best of the thirties crazy sophisticated comedies, though its pacing today seems somewhat unsure.

w Morrie Ryskind, Eric Hatch, Gregory La Cava d Gregory La Cava ph Ted Tetzlaff *m* Charles Previn

Carole Lombard, William Powell, Alice Brady, Mischa Auer, Eugene Pallette, Gail Patrick, Alan Mowbray, Jean Dixon

AAN: best picture; script; Gregory La Cava (as director); Carole Lombard; William Powell; Alice Brady; Mischa Auer

'Images of wax that throbbed with human passion. Almost woman! What did they lack?

Mystery of the Wax Museum

US 1933 77m Technicolor
Warner (Henry Blanke)

A sculptor disfigured in a fire builds a wax museum by covering live victims in wax.

Archetypal horror material is augmented by a sub-plot about drug-running and an authoritative example of the wisecracking reporter school of the early thirties. The film is also notable for its highly satisfactory use of two-colour Technicolor and for its splendid art direction. Remade 1953 as *House of Wax*.

w Don Mullally, Carl Erickson, play Charles S. Belden *d Michael Curtiz ph Ray Rennahan ad Anton Grot*

Lionel Atwill, Fay Wray, *Glenda Farrell*, Frank McHugh, Gavin Gordon, Allen Vincent, Edwin Maxwell

ATWILL: 'I offer you immortality, my child. Think of it: in a thousand years you shall be as lovely as you are now!'

'Would have been certain of better gate support a year ago. Recognizing this, the Technicolor and hyper-weirdness were apparently mandatory studio precautions to offset the element of belated arrival.'—*Variety*

'Marvellously grisly chiller.'—*Judith Crist, 1977*

'Its most telling details are its horrific ones. The fire at the beginning, with lifelike figures melting into grisly ooze; night time in the city morgue, with a dead body suddenly popping up as a side effect of embalming fluid; chases through shadows as the ghoulish sculptor collects bodies for his exhibit; and the shock when Atwill's homemade wax face crumbles to the floor and exposes the hidden demon.'—*Tom Shales, The American Film Heritage, 1972*

N

The Naked City

US 1948 96m bw
Universal (Mark Hellinger)

New York police track down a killer.
Highly influential documentary
thriller which, shot on location in
New York's teeming streets, claimed
to be giving an impression of city
life; actually its real mission was to
tell an ordinary murder tale with an
impressive accumulation of detail
and humour. The narrator's last
words became a cliché: 'There are
eight million stories in the naked
city. This has been one of them.'

w *Malvin Wald*, *Albert Maltz*
d *Jules Dassin* ph *William Daniels*
m *Frank Skinner*, *Miklos Rozsa*
md *Milton Schwarzwald*

Barry Fitzgerald, *Don Taylor*,
Howard Duff, Dorothy Hart, Ted de
Corsia, Adelaide Klein

AA: William Daniels

AAN: original story (Malvin Wald)

The Narrow Margin

US 1950 70m bw
RKO (Stanley Rubin)

Police try to guard a prosecution
witness on a train from Chicago to
Los Angeles.
Tight little thriller which takes every
advantage of its train setting. What
the trade used to call a sleeper, it
gave more satisfaction than many a
top feature.

w *Earl Felton* d *Richard Fleischer*
ph *George E. Diskant*

Charles McGraw, *Marie Windsor*,
Jacqueline White, Queenie Leonard
'A taut, breathlessly fast and
highly suspenseful "sleeper" par
excellence.'—*Time Out*, 1986

AAN: original story (Martin
Goldsmith, Jack Leonard)

'The damnedest thing you ever
saw!'

Nashville

US 1975 161m
Metrocolor Panavision
Paramount / ABC (Robert Altman)

A political campaign in Nashville
organizes a mammoth pop concert to
gain support.
Kaleidoscopic, fragmented,
multi-storied musical melodrama, a
mammoth movie which can be a
bore or an inspiration according to
taste. Certainly many exciting
moments pass by, but the length is
self-defeating.

w Joan Tewkesbury d Robert
Altman ph Paul Lohmann
md Richard Baskin

Geraldine Chaplin, David Arkin,
Barbara Baxley, Ned Beatty, Karen
Black, Keith Carradine, Henry
Gibson, Keenan Wynn, Lily Tomlin,
Ronee Blakley
'A gigantic parody . . . crammed
with samples taken from every level
of Nashville society, revealed in
affectionate detail bordering on
caricature in a manner that would
surely delight Norman
Rockwell.'—*Philip Strick*
'Wildly over-praised Altman, with
all the defects we once looked on as
marks of healthy ambitiousness:
terrible construction, messy editing,
leering jokes at its own characters,
unending pomposity.'—*Time Out*,
1980

AA: song 'I'm Easy' (m/ly Keith
Carradine)
AAN: best picture; Robert Altman;
Lily Tomlin; Ronee Blakley

Naughty Marietta

US 1935 106m bw
MGM (Hunt Stromberg)

A French princess goes to America
and falls in love with an Indian
scout.

Period operetta which set the seal of success on the MacDonald-Eddy team. In itself, dated but quite pleasing for those who like the genre.

w John Lee Mahin, Frances Goodrich, Albert Hackett, *operetta* Rida Johnson Young *d* W. S. Van Dyke *ph* William Daniels *m* Victor Herbert *ad* Cedric Gibbons

Jeanette MacDonald, Nelson Eddy, Frank Morgan, Elsa Lanchester, Douglass Dumbrille, Joseph Cawthorn, Cecelia Parker, Walter Kingsford

'Slow-moving operetta which singing must sustain.'—*Variety*

'When these two profiles come together to sing Ah Sweet Mystery of Life, it's beyond camp, it's in a realm of its own.'—*Judith Crist, 1977*

AAN: best picture

The Navigator

US 1924   63m approx (24 fps)   bw   silent
Metro-Goldwyn / Buster Keaton (Joseph M. Schenck)
A millionaire and his girl are the only people on a transatlantic liner marooned in mid-ocean.
A succession of hilarious sight gags: the star in top form

w Jean Havez, Clyde Bruckman, J. A. Mitchell *d* Buster Keaton, Donald Crisp *ph* Elgin Lessley, Byron Houck

Buster Keaton, Kathryn McGuire

'Studded with hilarious moments and a hundred and one adroit gags.'—*Photoplay*

'Television will never be the same!'

'Prepare yourself for a perfectly outrageous motion picture!'

Network

US 1976   121m
Metrocolor   Panavision
MGM / UA (Howard Gottfried, Fred Caruso)
A network news commentator begins to say what he thinks about the world and becomes a new

messiah to the people and an embarrassment to his sponsors. Overheated satire which in between its undoubted high points becomes noisy and tiresome, not helped by fuzzy photography. Its very existence in a commercial system, however, is as remarkable as its box-office success.

w Paddy Chayevsky *d* Sidney Lumet *ph* Owen Roizman *m* Elliot Lawrence

Peter Finch, William Holden, Faye Dunaway, Robert Duvall, Wesley Addy, Ned Beatty, Beatrice Straight, John Carpenter

HOWARD BEALE (Peter Finch) on live television: 'I don't know what to do about the depression and the inflation and the Russians and the crime in the streets. All I know is that first you've got to get mad. You've got to say: "I'm a human being, god damn it, my life has some value!" So I want you to get up now. I want all of you to get up out of your chairs. I want you to get up right now and go to the window, open it and stick your head out and yell "I'm mad as hell, and I'm not going to take this any more!"'

Ditto: 'Ladies and gentlemen, I would like at this moment to announce that I will be retiring from this programme in two weeks' time because of poor ratings. Since this show was the only thing I had going for me in my life, I have decided to kill myself. I'm going to blow my brains out right on this programme a week from today.'

MAX SCHUMACHER (William Holden): 'You're television incarnate, Diana, indifferent to suffering, insensitive to joy. All of life is reduced to the common rubble of banality. War, murder, death—all the same to you as bottles of beer, and the daily business of life is a corrupt comedy. You even shatter the sensations of time and space into split seconds and instant replays. You're madness, Diana.'

'The cast of this messianic farce take turns yelling at us soulless masses.'—*New Yorker*

'Too much of this film has the hectoring stridency of tabloid headlines.'—*Michael Billington, Illustrated London News*

† The theme was taken up a year later in the shortlived TV series *W.E.B.*

AA: Paddy Chayevsky; Peter Finch; Faye Dunaway; Beatrice Straight
AAN: best picture; Sidney Lumet; Owen Roizman; William Holden; Ned Beatty

Never Give a Sucker an Even Break

US 1941   70m   bw
Universal
GB title: *What a Man*

W. C. Fields dives off an aeroplane into the lap of a young woman who has never seen a man; she falls in love with him.
Stupefyingly inept in its scripting and pacing, this comedy is often irresistibly funny because of the anti-everything personality of its writer-star. No one else could have got away with it, or would have been likely to try.

w John T. Neville, Prescott Chaplin, *story* Otis Criblecoblis (W. C. Fields)   *d* Edward Cline   *ph* Charles Van Enger   *m* Frank Skinner

W. C. Fields, Gloria Jean, Leon Errol, Butch and Buddy, Franklin Pangborn, Anne Nagel, Mona Barrie, Ann Miller, Margaret Dumont

'A beautifully timed exhibition of mock pomposity, puzzled ineffectualness, subtle understatement and true-blue nonchalance.'—*James Agee*

The Next of Kin

GB 1942   102m   bw
Ealing (S. C. Balcon)

Careless talk causes loss of life in a commando raid.
A propaganda instructional film which was made so entertainingly that it achieved commercial success and remains an excellent example of how to make a bitter pill palatable.

w Thorold Dickinson, Basil Bartlett,

Angus Macphail, John Dighton   *d* Thorold Dickinson   *ph* Ernest Palmer   *m* William Walton

Mervyn Johns, Nova Pilbeam, Stephen Murray, Reginald Tate, Basil Radford, Naunton Wayne, Geoffrey Hibbert, Philip Friend, Mary Clare, Basil Sydney

'The detail everywhere is curious and surprising, with something of the fascination of a Simenon crime being unravelled.'—*William Whitebait*

'A raging torrent of emotion that even nature can't control!'

Niagara

US 1952   89m   Technicolor
TCF (Charles Brackett)

While visiting Niagara Falls, a faithless wife is plotting to murder her husband, but he turns the tables.
Excellent suspenser with breathtaking locations; in the best Hitchcock class though slightly marred by the emphasis on Monroe's wiggly walk (it was her first big part).

w Charles Brackett, Walter Reisch, Richard Breen   *d* Henry Hathaway   *ph* Joe MacDonald   *m* Sol Kaplan

Joseph Cotten, Jean Peters, *Marilyn Monroe*, Don Wilson, Casey Adams

'The story is most imaginatively treated, the production values are excellent.'—*CEA Film Report*

'Seen from any angle, the Falls and Miss Monroe leave little to be desired.'—*New York Times*

'It would have turned out a much better picture if James Mason had played the husband as I wanted. He has that intensity, that neurotic edge. He was all set to do it, but his daughter Portland said she was sick of seeing him die in his pictures.'
—*Henry Hathaway*

'This isn't a good movie but it's compellingly tawdry and nasty . . . the only movie that explored the mean, unsavoury potential of Marilyn Monroe's cuddly, infantile perversity.'—*Pauline Kael, 70s*

Nicholas Nickleby

GB 1947   108m   bw
Ealing (John Croydon)

The adventures of a Victorian schoolmaster, deprived of his rightful fortune, who joins a band of travelling entertainers.

Quite tasteful and expert but too light-handed potted version of Dickens, which suffered by comparison with the David Lean versions.

w John Dighton, *novel* Charles Dickens *d* Alberto Cavalcanti *ph* Gordon Dines *m* Lord Berners

Derek Bond, *Cedric Hardwicke, Alfred Drayton. Sybil Thorndike,* Stanley Holloway, James Hayter, Sally Ann Howes, Jill Balcon, Cyril Fletcher, Fay Compton

'Here's richness! Not all the novel, perhaps, but enough to make a film full of the Dickens spirit.'—*Star*

The Niebelungen

Germany 1924   bw   silent
Decla-Bioscop (Erich Pommer)

Part One: 'Siegfried': 115m approx (24 fps)
Part Two: 'Kriemheld's Revenge': 125m approx (24 fps)

Siegfried kills a dragon and marries a princess of Burgundy but the fierce queen Brunhilde arranges his death. His widow marries Attila the Hun and they massacre the Burgundians. Stately, warlike legends are transformed into a slow, chilling, awe-inspiring sequence of films, the décor being of special interest. The films were conceived as a tribute to the German nation, and were among Hitler's favourites.

w Thea Von Harbou   *d Fritz Lang* *ph* Carl Hoffmann, Gunther Rittau *ad* Otto Hunte, Karl Volbrecht, Erich Kettelhut

Paul Richter, Marguerite Schön, Theodor Loos, Hannah Ralph, Rudolph Klein-Rogge

A Night at the Opera

US 1935   96m   bw
MGM (Irving Thalberg)

Three zanies first wreck, then help an opera company.

Certainly among the best of the Marxian extravaganzas, and the first to give them a big production to play with as well as musical interludes by other than themselves for a change of pace. The mix plays beautifully

w George S. Kaufman, Morrie Ryskind   d Sam Wood   ph Merritt Gerstad *md* Herbert Stothart

Groucho, Chico, Harpo (Zeppo absented himself from here on), *Margaret Dumont,* Kitty Carlisle, Allan Jones, Walter Woolf King, *Sig Rumann*

'Corking comedy with the brothers at par and biz chances excellent . . . songs in a Marx picture are generally at a disadvantage because they're more or less interruptions, the customers awaiting the next laugh.'—*Variety*

A Night in Casablanca

US 1946   85m   bw
David L. Loew

Three zanies rout Nazi refugees in a North African hotel.

The last authentic Marxian extravaganza; it starts uncertainly, builds to a fine sustained frenzy, then peters out in some overstretched airplane acrobatics.

w Joseph Fields, Roland Kibbee, Frank Tashlin   *d* Archie Mayo *ph* James Van Trees   *m* Werner Janssen *pd* Duncan Cramer

Groucho, Chico, Harpo, Sig Rumann, Lisette Verea, Charles Drake, Lois Collier, Dan Seymour

KORNBLOW (Groucho Marx): 'I don't mind being killed, but I resent hearing it from a character whose head comes to a point.'

KORNBLOW: 'From now on the essence of this hotel will be speed. If a customer asks you for a three-minute egg, give it to him in two minutes. If he asks you for a two-minute egg, give it to him in one minute. If he asks you for a one-minute egg, give him the chicken and let him work it out for himself.'

BEATRICE (Lisette Verea): 'My name's Beatrice Ryner. I stop at the hotel.'

KORNBLOW: 'My name's Ronald Kornblow. I stop at nothing.'

'It is beside the main point to add that it isn't one of their best movies; for the worst they might ever make would be better worth seeing than most other things I can think of.'—*James Agee*

Night Mail

GB 1936 24m bw
GPO Film Unit (John Grierson)

A 'film poem' showing the journey of the mail train from London to Glasgow.
One of the best and most influential of British documentaries: despite a few absurdities, it remains a pleasure to watch.

wd Basil Wright, Harry Watt ph J. Jones, H. E. Fowle m Benjamin Britten poem W. H. Auden sound arrangements Alberto Cavalcanti

Night of the Demon

GB 1957 87m bw
Columbia/Sabre (Frank Bevis)

US title: *Curse of the Demon*
An occultist despatches his enemies by raising a giant medieval devil.
Despite dim work from the leads, this supernatural thriller is intelligently scripted and achieves several frightening and memorable sequences in the best Hitchcock manner

w Charles Bennett, Hal E. Chester, story Casting the Runes by M. R. James d Jacques Tourneur ph Ted Scaife m Clifton Parker ad Ken Adam

Dana Andrews, Peggy Cummins, *Niall MacGinnis, Athene Seyler,* Brian Wilde, Maurice Denham, Ewan Roberts, Liam Redmond, Reginald Beckwith

The Night of the Generals

GB 1967 148m
Technicolor Panavision
Columbia/Horizon/Filmsonor (Sam Spiegel)

A German intelligence agent tracks down a psychopathic Nazi general who started killing prostitutes in Warsaw during World War I.
A curiously bumpy narrative which is neither mystery nor character study but does provide a few effective sequences and impressive performances. The big budget seems well spent.

w Joseph Kessel, Paul Dehn, novel Hans Helmut Hirst d Anatole Litvak ph Henri Decaë m Maurice Jarre pd Alexander Trauner

Peter O'Toole, *Omar Sharif, Tom Courtenay,* Donald Pleasence, Joanna Pettet, *Philippe Noiret,* Charles Gray, Coral Brown, John Gregson, Harry Andrews, Nigel Stock, Christopher Plummer, Juliette Greco

'The "who" is obvious from the first and the "dunnit" interminable.'—*Judith Crist, 1973*

'Lurid and vivid, if nothing else.'—*Robert Windeler*

'The scenes! The story! The stars! But above all—the suspense!

The Night of the Hunter

US 1955 93m bw
UA/Paul Gregory

A psychopathic preacher goes on the trial of hidden money, the secret of which is held by two children.
Weird, manic fantasy in which evil finally comes to grief against the forces of sweetness and light (the children, an old lady, water, animals). Although the narrative does not flow smoothly there are splendidly imaginative moments, and no other film has ever quite achieved its texture.

w James Agee, novel Davis Grubb d Charles Laughton ph Stanley Cortez m Walter Schumann

Robert Mitchum, Shelley Winters, Lillian Gish, Don Beddoe, Evelyn Varden, Peter Graves, James Gleason

PREACHER (Robert Mitchum): 'Lord, you sure knew what you was doing when you brung me to this very cell at this very time. A man

6666

with ten thousand dollars hid somewhere, and a widder in the makin'.'

'One of the most frightening movies ever made.'—*Pauline Kael, 1968*

'A genuinely sinister work, full of shocks and over-emphatic sound effects, camera angles and shadowy lighting.'—*NFT, 1973*

'One of the most daring, eloquent and personal films to have come from America in a long time.'—*Derek Prouse*

The Night of the Iguana
US 1964   125m   bw
MGM / Seven Arts (Ray Stark)
A disbarred clergyman becomes a travel courier in Mexico and is sexually desired by a teenage nymphomaniac, a middle-aged hotel owner and a frustrated itinerant artist.
The author is most tolerable when poking fun at his own types, and this is a sharp, funny picture with a touch of poetry.

w Anthony Veiller, *play Tennessee Williams d John Huston ph Gabriel Figueroa m* Benjamin Frankel *ad* Stephen Grimes

Richard Burton, Deborah Kerr, Ava Gardner, Sue Lyon, *Grayson Hall, Cyril Delevanti*

'One man . . . three women . . . one night!'—*publicity*

'Whatever poetry it had seems to have leaked out.'—*New Yorker, 1982*

AAN: Gabriel Figueroa; Grayson Hall

A Night to Remember
GB 1958   123m   bw
Rank (William Macquitty)
The story of the 1912 sea disaster when the *Titanic* struck an iceberg. A major film enterprise featuring hundreds of cameos, none discernibly more important than the other. On this account the film seems alternately stiff and flabby as narrative, but there is much to enjoy and admire along the way, though

the sense of awe is dissipated by the final model shots.

w Eric Ambler, book Walter Lord *d* Roy Baker *ph* Geoffrey Unsworth *m* William Alwyn

Kenneth More, Honor Blackman, Michael Goodliffe, David McCallum, George Rose, Anthony Bushell, Ralph Michael, John Cairney, Kenneth Griffith, Frank Lawton, Michael Bryant.

'A worthy, long-drawn-out documentary, with noticeably more honesty about human nature than most films, but little shape or style.'—*Kenneth Cavender*

Night Train to Munich
GB 1940   93m   bw
TCF (Edward Black)
aka: *Gestapo; Night Train*
A British agent poses as a Nazi in order to rescue a Czech inventor. First-rate comedy suspenser obviously inspired by the success of *The Lady Vanishes* and providing much the same measure of thrills

w Frank Launder, Sidney Gilliat, novel Report on a Fugitive by Gordon Wellesley *d* Carol Reed *ph* Otto Kanturek *m* Charles Williams *md* Louis Levy

Margaret Lockwood, *Rex Harrison, Basil Radford, Naunton Wayne*, Paul Henreid, Keneth Kent, Felix Aylmer, Roland Culver, *Eliot Makeham, Raymond Huntley*, Wyndham Goldie

'A very nice triumph of skill and maturity in films, and thus a pleasure to have.'—*Otis Ferguson*

AAN: Gordon Wellesley

'The picture that kids the commissars!'
'Garbo laughs!'
'Don't pronounce it—see it!'
Ninotchka
US 1939   110m   bw
MGM (Ernst Lubitsch)
A Paris playboy falls for a communist emissary sent to sell some crown jewels.

Sparkling comedy on a theme which has been frequently explored; delicate pointing and hilarious character comedy sustain this version perfectly until the last half hour, when it certainly sags; but it remains a favourite Hollywood example of this genre.

w Charles Brackett, Billy Wilder, Walter Reisch, story Melchior Lengyel *d* Ernst Lubitsch *ph* William Daniels *m* Werner Heymann

Greta Garbo, Melvyn Douglas, Sig Rumann, Alexander Granach, Felix Bressart, Ina Claire, Bela Lugosi

PROLOGUE: This picture takes place in Paris in those wonderful days when a siren was a brunette and not an alarm—and if a Frenchman turned out the light it was not on account of an air raid!

NINOTCHKA (Greta Garbo): 'I must have a complete report of your negotiations and a detailed expense account.'

BULJANOFF (Felix Bressart): 'No, non, Ninotchka. Don't ask for it. There is an old Turkish proverb that says, if something smells bad, why put your nose in it?'

NINOTCHKA: 'And there is an old Russian saying, the cat who has cream on his whiskers had better find good excuses.'

NINOTCHKA: 'The last mass trials were a great success. There are going to be fewer but better Russians.'

'High calibre entertainment for adult audiences, and a top attraction for the key de-luxers.'—*Variety*

'The Lubitsch style, in which much was made of subtleties—glances, finger movements, raised eyebrows—has disappeared. Instead we have a hard, brightly lit, cynical comedy with the wisecrack completely in control.'—*John Baxter, 1968*

† William Powell and Robert Montgomery were formerly considered for the Melvyn Douglas role.

AAN: best picture; script; story; Greta Garbo

'Turn back, I tell you! Any minute may be too late!'
No Highway
GB 1951 98m bw
US title: *No Highway in the Sky*

During a transatlantic flight, a boffin works out that the plane's tail is about to fall off from metal fatigue. The central premise of this adaptation from a popular novel is fascinating, but the romantic asides are a distraction and the characters cardboard; the film still entertains through sheer professionalism.

w R. C. Sherriff, Oscar Millard, Alec Coppel, novel Nevil Shute *d* Henry Koster *ph* Georges Périnal

James Stewart, Marlene Dietrich, Glynis Johns, Jack Hawkins, Janette Scott, Elizabeth Allan, Kenneth More, Niall MacGinnis, Ronald Squire

North by Northwest
US 1959 136m Technicolor Vistavision
MGM (Alfred Hitchcock)

A businessman is mistaken for a spy, and enemy agents then try to kill him because he knows too much. Delightful chase comedy-thriller with a touch of sex, a kind of compendium of its director's best work, with memories of *The 39 Steps, Saboteur* and *Foreign Correspondent* among others.

w Ernest Lehman d Alfred Hitchcock ph Robert Burks m Bernard Herrmann

Cary Grant, Eva Marie Saint, James Mason, Leo G. Carroll, Martin Landau, Jessie Royce Landis, Adam Williams

'It is only when you adopt the basic premise that Cary Grant could not possibly come to harm that the tongue in Hitchcock's cheek becomes plainly visible.'—*Hollis Alpert, Saturday Review*

AAN: Ernest Lehman

Northwest Frontier
GB 1959   129m
Eastmancolor   Cinemascope
Rank/Marcel Hellman
US title: *Flame Over India*
In 1905 an English officer during a
rebellion escorts a young Hindu
prince on a dangerous train journey.
Thoroughly enjoyable Boys' Own
Paper adventure story with excellent
set pieces and a spot-the-villain
mystery.

w *Robin Estridge* d *J.
Lee-Thompson* ph *Geoffrey
Unsworth* m *Mischa Spoliansky*

Kenneth More, Lauren Bacall,
Herbert Lom, Ursula Jeans, Wilfrid
Hyde White, I. S. Johar, Eugene
Deckers, Ian Hunter
  '*Northwest Frontier* seems to have
borrowed its eccentric engine from
The General, its hazardous
expedition from *Stagecoach* and its
background of tribal violence from
The Drum.'—*Penelope Houston*

'Ten stars! Two love stories! One
  thousand thrills!'
Northwest Mounted Police
US 1940   125m
Technicolor
Paramount (Cecil B. de Mille)
A Texas Ranger seeks a fugitive in
Canada. Typical big-scale action
concoction de de Mille, but in this
case none of it's very memorable and
the detail is poor.

w *Alan Le May, Jesse Lasky Jnr, C.
Gardner Sullivan* d *Cecil B. de
Mille* ph *Victor Milner, Howard
Greene* m *Victor Young*

Gary Cooper, Paulette Goddard,
Madeleine Carroll, Preston Foster,
Robert Preston, George Bancroft,
Lynne Overman, Akim Tamiroff,
Walter Hampden, Lon Chaney Jnr,
Montagu Love, George E. Stone
  'Two hours of colour, killing,
kindness and magnificent
country.'—*Otis Ferguson*
  'A movie in the grand style. God's
own biggest trees and mountains for
prop and backdrop; staunch courage
and lofty aims among the good

people; cunning and teachery lurking
within the sinister forces; the
ominous note of doom finally stifled
by the fortitude of noble
men.'—*Time*

AAN: Victor Milner, Howard
Greene; Victor Young

**Northwest Passage
(Part One, Rogers' Rangers)**
US 1940   126m
Technicolor
MGM (Hunt Stromberg)
Colonial rangers fight it out with
hostile Indians.
Part Two was never made, but no
one seemed to mind that the
characters in Part One never got
round to seeking the titular sea
route. The adventures depicted had
the feel of historical actuality, and
the star was well cast.

w *Lawrence Stallings, Talbot
Jennings, novel* Kenneth Roberts
d *King Vidor* ph *Sidney Wagner,
William V. Skall* m *Herbert
Stothart*

Spencer Tracy, Robert Young, Ruth
Hussey, Walter Brennan, Nat
Pendleton, Robert Barrat, Lumsden
Hare, Donald MacBride
  'Half men, half demons, warriors
such as the world has never
known . . . they lived with death and
danger for the women who hungered
for their love!'—*publicity*

AAN: Sidney Wagner, William V.
Skall

Nothing Sacred
US 1937   77m   Technicolor
David O. Selznick
A girl thought to be dying of a rare
disease is built up by the press into a
national heroine; but the diagnosis
was wrong.
Hollywood's most bitter and
hilarious satire, with crazy comedy
elements and superb wisecracks; a
historical monument of screen
comedy, though its freshness at the
time can't now be recaptured.

w *Ben Hecht, story* Letter to the

Editor by James H. Street
d William Wellman ph W. Howard
Greene m Oscar Levant

*Carole Lombard, Fredric March,
Walter Connolly*, Charles Winninger,
Sig Rumann, Frank Fay, Maxie
Rosenbloom, Margaret Hamilton,
Hedda Hopper, Monty Woolley,
Hattie McDaniel, Olin Howland,
John Qualen

DOCTOR (Charles Winninger): 'I'll
tell you briefly what I think of
newspapermen. The hand of God,
reaching down into the mire,
couldn't elevate one of them to the
depths of degradation.'

EDITOR (Walter Connolly): 'I am
sitting here, Mr Cook, toying with
the idea of cutting out your heart
and stuffing it—like an olive!'

'Hit comedy . . . will be one of the
big grossers of the year.'—*Variety*

'Because it does hold up a mirror,
even though a distorting mirror, to a
very real world of ballyhoo and
cheap sensationalism, the pleasure to
be obtained from it is something
more than the usual mulish
guffaw.'—*Spectator*

† Refashioned in 1953 as a stage
musical, *Hazel Flagg*, with music by
Jule Styne; this in turn became a
Martin and Lewis comedy *Living It
Up* (Jerry Lewis in the Carole
Lombard part).

Notorious
US 1946   101m   bw
RKO (Alfred Hitchcock)
In Rio, a notorious lady marries a
Nazi renegade to help the US
government but finds herself falling
in love with her contact.
Superb romantic suspenser
containing some of Hitchcock's best
work.

*w Ben Hecht d Alfred Hitchcock
ph Ted Tetzlaff m Roy Webb*

*Cary Grant, Ingrid Bergman, Claude
Rains,* Louis Calhern, Leopoldine
Konstantin, Reinhold Schunzel

'Velvet smooth in dramatic action,
sharp and sure in its characters, and

heavily charged with the intensity of
warm emotional appeal.'—*Bosley
Crowther*

'The suspense is terrific.'—*New
Yorker, 1976*

'A film in the supercharged
American idiom which made
Casablanca popular.'—*Hermione
Rich Isaacs, Theatre Arts*

AAN: Ben Hecht; Claude Rains

Now Voyager
US 1942   117m   bw
Warner (Hal B. Wallis)
A dowdy frustrated spinster takes
the psychiatric cure and embarks on
a doomed love affair.
A basically soggy script still gets by,
and how, through the romantic
magic of its stars, who were all at
their best; and suffering in mink
went over very big in wartime.

*w Casey Robinson, novel Olive
Higgins Prouty d Irving Rapper
ph Sol Polito m Max Steiner*

*Bette Davis, Claude Rains, Paul
Henreid,* Gladys Cooper, John
Loder, Bonita Granville, Ilka Chase,
Lee Patrick, Charles Drake,
Franklin Pangborn

CHARLOTTE (Bette Davis): 'Oh,
Jerry, don't let's ask for the moon.
We have the stars!'

'If it were better, it might not
work at all. This way, it's a crummy
classic.'—*New Yorker, 1977*

AA: Max Steiner
AAN: Bette Davis; Gladys Cooper

'Filmed in Belgium, Italy,
Africa . . . and mostly in the
conscience of a beautiful young
girl!'

The Nun's Story
US 1959   151m
Technicolor
Warner (Henry Blanke)
A Belgian girl joins a strict order,
endures hardship in the Congo, and
finally returns to ordinary life.
The fascinating early sequences of
convent routine are more interesting
than the African adventures, but this

is a careful, composed and impressive film with little Hollywood exaggeration.

w *Robert Anderson, book Kathryn C. Hulme d Fred Zinnemann ph Franz Planer m Franz Waxman*

Audrey Hepburn, Peter Finch, Edith Evans, Peggy Ashcroft, Dean Jagger, Mildred Dunnock, Patricia Collinge, Beatrice Straight

'A major directorial achievement . . . the best study of the religious life ever made in the American cinema.'—*Albert Johnson, Film Quarterly*

AAN: best picture; Robert Anderson; Fred Zinnemann; Franz Planer; Franz Waxman; Audrey Hepburn

O

Objective Burma

US 1944   142m   bw
Warner (Jerry Wald)

Exploits of an American platoon in the Burma campaign.

Overlong but vivid war actioner which caused a diplomatic incident by failing to mention the British contribution.

w Ranald MacDougall, Lester Cole, Alvah Bessie d Raoul Walsh ph James Wong Howe m Franz Waxman

Errol Flynn, James Brown, William Prince, George Tobias, Henry Hull, Warner Anderson, John Alwin

'At the rate Errol Flynn and co. knock off the Japanese, it may make you wonder why the war need outlast next weekend.'—*Time*

'I am amazed that Warner Brothers ever made it, or having made it failed to think again and smother it.'—*Reynolds News*

† The film was not released in Britain until 1982, and then with an apologetic prologue.

AAN: original story (Alvah Bessie); Franz Waxman

Occupe-Toi d'Amélie

France 1949   95m   bw
Lux (Louis Wipf)

aka: *Keep an Eye on Amelia*

A Parisian cocotte agrees to go through a mock marriage ceremony with her lover's best friend to fool his uncle: but the ceremony turns out to be real.

Hilarious and superbly stylized adaptation of a period boulevard farce: the play starts in a theatre, showing the audience, but gradually cinema technique takes over.

Acting, timing and editing are all impeccable, and the production stands as a model of how such things should be done.

w Jean Aurenche, Pierre Bost, play Georges Feydeau d Claude Autant-Lara ph André Bac m René Cloërc

Danielle Darrieux, Jean Desailly, Bourvil, Carette, Grégoire Aslan

'Even those who do not respond to the artificialities of French vaudeville will admire the ingenuity and elegance of treatment.'—*Gavin Lambert, MFB*

'Most people, I think, could see it with considerable enjoyment even twice on the same evening.'—*Richard Mallett, Punch*

The Odd Couple

US 1968   105m
Technicolor   Panavision
Paramount (Howard W. Koch)

A fussy divorce-shocked newswriter moves in with his sloppy sportscaster friend, and they get on each other's nerves.

Straight filming of a funny play which sometimes seems lost on the wide screen, but the performances are fine.

w Neil Simon, from his play d Gene Saks ph Robert B. Hauser m Neal Hefti

Jack Lemmon, Walter Matthau, John Fiedler, Herb Edelman, David Sheiner, Larry Haines, Monica Evans, Carole Sheely, Iris Adrian

OSCAR (Walter Matthau): 'I can't take it anymore, Felix. I'm crackin' up. Everything you do irritates me. And when you're not here, the things I know you're gonna do when you come in irritate me. You leave me little notes on my pillow. I told you 158 times I cannot stand little notes on my pillow. "We are all out of cornflakes, F.U." It took me three hours to figure out that F.U. was Felix Ungar. It's not your fault, Felix. It's a rotten combination, that's all.'

AAN: Neil Simon

Odd Man Out
GB 1946   115m   bw
GFD / Two Cities (Carol Reed)
US title: *Gang War*
An IRA gunman, wounded and on
the run in Belfast, is helped and
hindered by a variety of people.
Superbly crafted but rather empty
dramatic charade, visually and
emotionally memorable but with
nothing whatever to say.

w F. L. Green, R. C. Sherriff,
novel F. L. Green *d* Carol Reed
ph Robert Krasker *m* William
Alwyn

*James Mason, Robert Newton,
Kathleen Ryan,* F. J. McCormick,
Cyril Cusack, Robert Beatty, Fay
Compton, Dan O'Herlihy, Denis
O'Dea, Maureen Delany, Joseph
Tomelty, William Hartnell

'The story seems to ramify too
much, to go on too long, and at its
unluckiest to go arty. Yet detail by
detail *Odd Man Out* is made with
great skill and imaginativeness and
with a depth of ardour that is very
rare.'—*James Agee*
'Quite simply the most imaginative
film yet produced in England,
comparable with *Quai des Brumes*
and *Le Jour se Lève.*'—*William
Whitebait, New Statesman*

The Odessa File
GB 1974   129m
Eastmancolor   Panavision
Columbia / Domino / Oceanic
(John Woolf)
In 1963, a young German reporter
tracks down a gang of neo-Nazis.
Elaborate but uninvolving suspenser
with several excellent cliffhanging
sequences and a let-down climax.

w Kenneth Ross, George Markstein,
novel Frederick Forsyth *d* Ronald
Neame *ph* Oswald Morris
m Andrew Lloyd Webber *pd* Rolf
Zeherbauer

Jon Voight, Maria Schell,
Maximilian Schell, Mary Tamm,
Derek Jacobi, Peter Jeffrey, *Noel
Willman*

'As resistible a parcel of sedative
entertainment as ever induced
narcolepsy in a healthy
man.'—*Benny Green, Punch*

Odette
GB 1950   123m   bw
Herbert Wilcox
A Frenchwoman with an English
husband spies for the French
resistance, is caught and tortured.
Deglamorized true life spy story with
emotional moments let down by
generally uninspired handling, also
by the too-well-known image of its
star, who however gives a
remarkable performance.

w Warren Chetham Strode,
book Jerrard Tickell *d* Herbert
Wilcox *ph* Max Greene *m* Anthony
Collins

Anna Neagle, Trevor Howard, Peter
Ustinov, Marius Goring
'As a work of art, pretty flat . . .
though innumerable people will find
it moving and impressive, they will
have done the work
themselves.'—*Richard Mallett,
Punch*

I'm decent, I tell ya! Nobody's got
the right to call me names!'
'The picture Hollywood said could
never be made!'
Of Mice and Men
US 1939   107m   bw
Hal Roach (Lewis Milestone)
An itinerant worker looks after his
mentally retarded cousin, a giant
who doesn't know his own strength.
A strange and unexpected tragedy
which has strength and is very
persuasively made but seems
somehow unnecessary.

w Eugene Solow, *novel* John
Steinbeck *d Lewis Milestone*
ph Norbert Brodine m Aaron
Copland

*Burgess Meredith, Lon Chaney Jnr,
Betty Field,* Charles Bickford,
Roman Bohnen, Bob Steele, Noah
Beery Jnr

AAN: best picture; Aaron Copland

'It's an almighty laugh!'
Oh, God!
US 1977 104m
Technicolor
Warner (Jerry Weintraub)
A bewildered supermarket manager is enlisted by God to prove to the world that it can only work if people try.
Overlong but generally amiable reversion to the supernatural farces of the forties: its success seems to show that people again need this kind of comfort.

w Larry Gelbart, *novel* Avery Corman *d* Carl Reiner *ph* Victor Kemper *m* Jack Elliott

George Burns, John Denver, Ralph Bellamy, Donald Pleasence, Teri Garr, William Daniels, Barnard Hughes, Paul Sorvino, Barry Sullivan, Dinah Shore, Jeff Corey, David Ogden Stiers

'Undeniably funny and almost impossible to dislike.'—*Tom Milne, MFB*

'Basically a single-joke movie: George Burns is God in a football cap.'—*Pauline Kael, New Yorker*

AAN: Larry Gelbart

Oh Mr Porter
GB 1937 84m bw
GFD/Gainsborough (Edward Black)
The stationmaster of an Irish halt catches gun-runners posing as ghosts.
Marvellous star comedy showing this trio of comedians at their best, and especially Hay as the seedy incompetent. The plot is borrowed from *The Ghost Train*, but each line and gag brings its own inventiveness. A delight of character comedy and cinematic narrative.

w Marriott Edgar, *Val Guest*, *J. O. C. Orton*, *story* Frank Launder *d* Marcel Varnel *ph* Arthur Crabtree *md* Louis Levy

Will Hay, Moore Marriott, Graham Moffatt, Dave O'Toole, Dennis Wyndham

'That rare phenomenon: a film comedy without a dud scene.'—*Peter Barnes, 1964*

'Behind it lie the gusty uplands of the British music hall tradition, whose rich soil the British film industry is at last beginning to exploit.'—*Basil Wright*

Oh What a Lovely War
GB 1969 144m
Technicolor Panavision
Paramount/Accord (Brian Duffy, Richard Attenborough)
A fantasia with music on World War I.
A brave all-star attempt which comes off only in patches; the pier apparatus from the stage show really doesn't translate, the piece only works well when it becomes cinematic, as in the recruiting song and the final track-back from the graves. But there are many pleasures, as well as yawns, along the way.

w Len Deighton, *stage show* Joan Littlewood, Charles Chilton *d* Richard Attenborough *ph* Gerry Turpin *m* various *md* Alfred Ralston *pd* Don Ashton

Ralph Richardson, Meriel Forbes, John Gielgud, Kenneth More, John Clements, Paul Daneman, Joe Melia, Jack Hawkins, John Mills, Maggie Smith, Michael Redgrave, Laurence Olivier, Susannah York, Dirk Bogarde, Phyllis Calvert, Vanessa Redgrave

'This musical lampoon is meant to stir your sentiments, evoke nostalgia, and make you react to the obscenity of battles and bloodshed, and apparently it does all that for some people.'—*New Yorker, 1977*

'A naïve, sentimental, populist affair, using many (too many) clever devices yet making the same old simplistic statements.'—*John Simon*

'An overlong and rarely cinematic musical satire that ladles its anti-war message on by the bucketload.'—*Time Out, 1984*

'A picture straight from the heart of America!'

Oklahoma!

⚡ US 1955 143m
Technicolor Todd-AO
Magna / Rodgers and Hammerstein (Arthur Hornblow Jnr)

A cowboy wins his girl despite the intervention of a sinister hired hand. Much of the appeal of the musical was in its simple timeworn story and stylized sets; the film makes the first merely boring and the latter are replaced by standard scenery, not even of Oklahoma. The result is efficient rather than startling or memorable.

w Sonya Levien, William Ludwig, '*book*' Oscar Hammerstein, *play* Green Grow the Rushes by Lynn Riggs *d* Fred Zinnemann *ph* Robert Surtees *songs* Richard Rodgers, Oscar Hammerstein II *m* Robert Russell Bennett, Jay Blackton, Adolph Deutsch *pd* Oliver Smith

Gordon Macrae, Shirley Jones, Rod Steiger, Gloria Grahame, Charlotte Greenwood, Gene Nelson, Eddie Albert

AA: music score
AAN: Robert Surtees; Robert Russell Bennett, Jay Blackton, Adolph Deutsch

The Old Dark House

🕯 US 1932 71m bw
Universal (Carl Laemmle Jnr)

Stranded travellers take refuge in the house of a family of eccentrics. Marvellous horror comedy filled with superb grotesques and memorable lines, closely based on a Priestley novel but omitting the more thoughtful moments. A stylist's and connoisseur's treat.

w Benn W. Levy, R. C. Sherriff, *novel* Benighted by J. B. Priestley *d* James Whale *ph* Arthur Edeson *ad* Charles D. Hall

Melvyn Douglas, Charles Laughton, Raymond Massey, Boris Karloff, Ernest Thesiger, Eva Moore, Gloria Stuart, Lilian Bond, Brember Wills, John Dudgeon (Elspeth Dudgeon)

'Somewhat inane, it's a cinch for trick ballyhooing. Better for the nabes than the big keys.'—*Variety*

'An unbridled camp fantasy directed with great wit.'—*Charles Higham*

'Each threat as it appears is revealed to be burlap and poster paint . . . despite storm, attempted rape and a remarkable final chase, the film is basically a confidence trick worked with cynical humour by a brilliant technician.'—*John Baxter, 1968*

'Basically a *jeu d'esprit* in which comedy of manners is edged into tragedy of horrors, the film never puts a foot wrong.'—*Tom Milne, MFB, 1978*

The Old Maid

👯 US 1939 95m bw
Warner (Henry Blanke)

When her suitor is killed in the Civil War, an unmarried mother lets her childless cousin bring up her daughter as her own.

A 'woman's picture' par excellence, given no-holds-barred treatment by all concerned but a little lacking in surprise.

w Casey Robinson, *play* Zoe Akins, *novel* Edith Wharton *d* Edmund Goulding *ph* Tony Gaudio *m* Max Steiner *md* Leo F. Forbstein

Bette Davis, Miriam Hopkins, George Brent, Jane Bryan, Donald Crisp, Louise Fazenda, Henry Stephenson, Jerome Cowan, William Lundigan, Rand Brooks

'Stagey, sombre and generally confusing fare. Must aim for the femme trade chiefly.'—*Variety*

'It is better than average and sticks heroically to its problem, forsaking all delights and filling a whole laundry bag with wet and twisted handkerchiefs.'—*Otis Ferguson*

'The picture isn't bad, but it trudges along and never becomes exciting.'—*New Yorker, 1977*

'Much much more than a
musical!'

Oliver!

GB 1968   146m
Technicolor   Panavision 70
Columbia / Warwick / Romulus
(John Woolf)

A musical version of *Oliver Twist*.
The last, perhaps, of the splendid
film musicals which have priced
themselves out of existence; it drags
a little in spots but on the whole it
does credit both to the show and the
original novel, though eclipsed in
style by David Lean's straight
version.

w Vernon Harris, *play* Lionel Bart,
*novel Charles Dickens d Carol
Reed ph Oswald Morris m Lionel
Bart md John Green pd John Box
ch Onna White*

Ron Moody, Oliver Reed, Harry
Secombe, *Mark Lester*, Shani Wallis,
Jack Wild, Hugh Griffith, Joseph
O'Conor, Leonard Rossiter, Hylda
Baker, Peggy Mount, Megs Jenkins

'Only time will tell if it is a great
film but it is certainly a great
experience.'—*Joseph Morgenstern*

'There is a heightened discrepancy
between the romping jollity with
which everyone goes about his
business and the actual business
being gone about . . . such narrative
elements as the exploitation of child
labour, pimping, abduction,
prostitution and murder combine to
make *Oliver!* the most non-U subject
ever to receive a U certificate.'—*Jan
Dawson*

AA: best picture; Carol Reed; John
Green
AAN: Vernon Harris; Oswald
Morris; Ron Moody; Jack Wild

Oliver Twist

GB 1948   116m   bw
GFD / Cineguild (Ronald
Neame)

A foundling falls among thieves but
is rescued by a benevolent old
gentleman.
Simplified, brilliantly cinematic
version of a voluminous Victorian

novel, beautiful to look at and
memorably played, with every scene
achieving the perfect maximum
impact.

*w David Lean, Stanley Haynes,
novel Charles Dickens d David
Lean ph Guy Green m Arnold
Bax pd John Bryan*

*Alec Guinness, Robert Newton,
Francis L. Sullivan, John Howard
Davies, Kay Walsh, Anthony
Newley, Henry Stephenson, Mary
Clare, Gibb McLaughlin, Diana
Dors*

'A thoroughly expert piece of
movie entertainment.'—*Richard
Winnington*

Olympische Spiele

Germany 1936   Part 1,
118m; Part 2, 107m   bw
Leni Riefenstahl

An account of the Berlin Olympic
Games.
This magnificent film is in no sense a
mere reporting of an event. Camera
movement, photography and editing
combine with music to make it an
experience truly Olympian,
especially in the introductory
symbolic sequence suggesting the
birth of the games. It was also,
dangerously, a hymn to Nazi
strength.

*d,ed Leni Riefenstahl
assistant Walter Ruttman ph Hans
Ertl, Walter Franz and 42 others
m Herbert Windt*

'Here is the camera doing superbly
what only the camera can do:
refashioning the rhythms of the
visible; of the moment seen.'—*Dilys
Powell*

'Good morning. You are one day
closer to the end of the world!'

The Omen

US 1976   111m   De Luxe
Panavision
TCF (Harvey Bernhard)

The adopted child of an ambassador
to Great Britain shows unnerving
signs of being diabolically inspired.
Commercially successful variation on
The Exorcist, quite professionally

assembled and more enjoyable as entertainment than its predecessor.

w David Seltzer *d Richard Donner ph* Gil Taylor *m* Jerry Goldsmith

Gregory Peck, Lee Remick, David Warner, Billie Whitelaw, Leo McKern, Harvey Stevens, Patrick Troughton, Anthony Nicholls, Martin Benson

'A cut above the rest in that it has an ingenious premise, a teasingly labyrinthine development, a neat sting in its tail, and enough confidence in its own absurdities to carry them off.'—*David Robinson, The Times*

'Dreadfully silly . . . its horrors are not horrible, its terrors are not terrifying, its violence is ludicrous.'—*New York Times*

'More laughs than an average comedy.'—*Judith Crist*

'I did it strictly for the money.'—*David Seltzer*

† Gregory Peck inherited his role from Charlton Heston, who turned it down.

AA: Jerry Goldsmith
AAN: song '*Ave Satani*'

'Growing up isn't easy at any age.'
On Golden Pond
US 1981   109m   colour
ITC/IPC (Bruce Gilbert)

An 80-year-old, his wife and his daughter spend a holiday at their New England lakeside cottage.
A film remarkable not so much for what it is—a well-acted, decent screen presentation of a rather waffling and sentimental play—as for the fact that in the sophisticated eighties enough people paid to see it to make it a box office record breaker. This was mainly due to affection for its star, whose last film it was, but also to an American desire for a reversion to the old values of warmth and humanity after the sex and violence which the screen had lately been offering.

w Ernest Thompson, from his play *d* Mark Rydell *ph* Peter R. Norman *m* Dave Grusin

Henry Fonda, Katharine Hepburn, Jane Fonda, Doug McKeon, Dabney Coleman

'Moments of truth survive some cloying contrivance; Rydell directs on bended knees.'—*Sight and Sound*

'Two of Hollywood's best-loved veterans deserve a far better swansong than this sticky confection.'—*Time Out*

'The kind of uplifting twaddle that traffics heavily in rather basic symbols: the gold light on the pond stands for the sunset of life, and so on.'—*Pauline Kael, New Yorker*

AA: Ernest Thompson; Henry Fonda; Katharine Hepburn
AAN: Mark Rydell; editing (Robert L. Wolfe); Dave Grusin; Jane Fonda
BFA: best actress (Katharine Hepburn)

On the Avenue
US 1937   89m   bw
TCF (Gene Markey)

An heiress rages because she is being satirized in a revue, but later falls in love with the star.
Bright musical which keeps moving and uses its talents wisely.

w Gene Markey, William Conselman *d* Roy del Ruth

ph Lucien Andriot *m/ly* Irving Berlin *ch* Seymour Felix

Dick Powell, Madeleine Carroll, The Ritz Brothers, George Barbier, Alice Faye, Walter Catlett, Joan Davis, E. E. Clive

Songs include 'He Ain't Got Rhythm'; 'The Girl on the Police Gazette'; 'This Year's Kisses'; 'I've Got My Love to Keep Me Warm'. The title song was dropped before release

'An amusing revue, with a pleasant score and a disarming informality in its production to lure us into liking it.'—*New York Times*

† Revamped as *Let's Make Love.*

On the Beach

US 1959 134m bw
United Artists / Stanley
Kramer

When most of the world has been devastated by atomic waste, an American atomic submarine sets out to investigate.

Gloomy prophecy which works well in spasms but is generally too content to chat rather than imagine. A solid prestige job nevertheless.

w John Paxton, James Lee Barrett, *novel* Nevil Shute *d* Stanley *Kramer* *ph* Giuseppe Rotunno, *Daniel Fapp* *m* Ernest Gold *pd* Rudolph Sternad

Gregory Peck, Ava Gardner, *Fred Astaire*, Anthony Perkins, Donna Anderson, John Tate, Lola Brooks

'Its humanism is clearly of the order that seeks the support of a clamorous music score. The characters remain little more than spokesmen for timid ideas and Salvation Army slogans, their emotions hired from a Hollywood prop room; which is all pretty disturbing in a film about nothing less than the end of the world.'—*Robert Vas*

AAN: Ernest Gold

On the Town

US 1949 98m Technicolor
MGM (*Arthur Freed*)

Three sailors enjoy twenty-four hours' leave in New York.

Most of this brash location musical counts as among the best things ever to come out of Hollywood; the serious ballet towards the end tends to kill it, but it contains much to be grateful for.

w Betty Comden, *Adolph Green*, *ballet* Fancy Free by Leonard Bernstein *d/ch* Gene Kelly, *Stanley Donen* *ph* Harold Rosson *md* Lennie Hayton, Roger Edens *songs* various

Gene Kelly, Frank Sinatra, Jules Munshin, Vera-Ellen, Betty Garrett, Ann Miller, Tom Dugan, Florence Bates, Alice Pearce

'A film that will be enjoyed more than twice.'—*Lindsay Anderson*

'So exuberant that it threatens at moments to bounce right off the screen.'—*Time*

'The speed, the vitality, the flashing colour and design, the tricks of timing by which motion is fitted to music, the wit and invention and superlative technical accomplishment make it a really exhilarating experience.'—*Richard Mallett, Punch*

AA: Lennie Hayton, Roger Edens

On the Waterfront

US 1954 108m bw
Columbia / Sam Spiegel

After the death of his brother, a young stevedore breaks the hold of a waterfront gang boss.

Intense, broody dockside thriller with 'method' performances; very powerful of its kind, and much imitated.

w Budd Schulberg, from his novel *d* Elia Kazan *ph* Boris Kaufman *m* Leonard Bernstein *ad* Richard Day

Marlon Brando, Eva Marie Saint, *Lee J. Cobb*, Rod Steiger, Karl Malden, Pat Henning, Leif Erickson, James Westerfield, John Hamilton.

'An uncommonly powerful, exciting and imaginative use of the screen by gifted professionals.'—*New York Times*

'A medley of items from the Warner gangland pictures of the thirties, brought up to date.'—*Steven Sondheim, Films in Review*

† Sample dialogue: 'Charlie, oh Charlie, you don't understand. I coulda had class. I coulda been a contender.'

AA: best picture; Budd Schulberg; Elia Kazan; Boris Kaufman; Richard Day; Marlon Brando; Eva Marie Saint
AAN: Leonard Bernstein; Lee J. Cobb; Rod Steiger; Karl Malden

One Flew over the Cuckoo's Nest
🎭 US 1975   134m   De Luxe
✗ UA / Fantasy Films (Paul
Zaentz, Michael Douglas)
A cheerful immoralist imprisoned
for rape is transferred for
observation to a state mental
hospital.
Wildly and unexpectedly commercial
film of a project which had lain
dormant for fourteen years, this
amusing and horrifying film
conveniently sums up
anti-government attitudes as well as
make love not war and all that. It's
certainly impossible to ignore.

w Laurence Hauben, Bo Goldman,
novel Ken Kesey *d* Milos Forman
ph Haskell Wexler *m* Jack Nitzche
pd Paul Sylbert

Jack Nicholson, Louise Fletcher,
William Redfield, Will Sampson,
Brad Dourif, Christopher Lloyd
  'Lacks the excitement of movie
art, but the story and the acting
make the film emotionally
powerful.'—*New Yorker*

AA: best picture; script; Milos
Forman; Jack Nicholson; Louise
Fletcher
AAN: Haskell Wexler; Jack
Nitzche; Brad Dourif

'Gayest screen event of the year!'
One Hour with You
😈 US 1932   84m   bw
  Paramount (*Ernst Lubitsch*)
The affairs of a philandering Parisian
doctor.
Superbly handled comedy of
manners in Lubitsch's most inventive
form, handled by a most capable
cast. Unique entertainment of a kind
which is, alas, no more.

w Samson Raphaelson, play Only a
Dream by Lothar Schmidt *d George
Cukor, Ernst Lubitsch ph* Victor
Milner *m* Oscar Straus, *Richard
Whiting ly Leo Robin ad* Hans
Dreier

*Maurice Chevalier, Jeanette
MacDonald, Genevieve Tobin,
Roland Young,* Charles Ruggles,
George Barbier

'Sure fire if frothy screen fare,
cinch b.o. at all times.'—*Variety*
  'A brand new form of musical
entertainment . . . he has mixed
verse, spoken and sung, a smart and
satiric musical background, asides to
the audience, and sophisticated
dialogue, as well as lilting and
delightful songs . . . The result is
something so delightful that it places
the circle of golden leaves jauntily
upon the knowing head of
Hollywood's most original
director.'—*Philadelphia Inquirer*

† A remake of Lubitsch's silent
success *The Marriage Circle.*

AAN: best picture

One Hundred and One Dalmatians
🐕 US 1961   79m   Technicolor
  Walt Disney
The dogs of London help save
puppies which are being stolen for
their skins by a cruel villainess.
Disney's last really splendid feature
cartoon, with the old flexible style
cleverly modernized and plenty of
invention and detail in the story line.
The London backgrounds are
especially nicely judged.

w Bill Peet, *novel* Dodie Smith
d Wolfgang Reitherman, Hamilton
S. Luske, Clyde Geronimi

One Hundred Men and a Girl
🎵 US 1937   84m   bw
  Universal (*Joe Pasternak*)
A young girl persuades a great
conductor to form an orchestra of
unemployed musicians.
Delightful and funny musical fable,
an instance of the Pasternak formula
of sweetness and light at its richest
and best.

*w Bruce Manning, Charles Kenyon,
Hans Kraly d* Henry Koster
ph Joseph Valentine *m* Charles
Previn *songs* various

*Deanna Durbin, Adolphe Menjou,
Leopold Stokowski, Alice Brady,
Mischa Auer, Eugene Pallette,* Billy
Gilbert, Alma Kruger, Jed Prouty,
Frank Jenks, Christian Rub

'Smash hit for all the family . . . something new in entertainment.' —*Variety*

'Apart from its value as entertainment, which is considerable, it reveals the cinema at its sunny-sided best.'—*New York Times.*

'An original story put over with considerable skill.'—*Monthly Film Bulletin*

AA: Charles Previn
AAN: best picture; original story (Hans Kraly)

The One That Got Away
GB 1957   111m   bw
Rank (Julian Wintle)

A German flier, Franz Von Werra, is captured and sent to various British prisoner-of-war camps, from all of which he escapes.
True-life biopic, developed in a number of suspense and action sequences, all very well done.

w Howard Clewes, *book* Kendal Burt, James Leasor *d* Roy Baker *ph* Eric Cross *m* Hubert Clifford

Hardy Kruger, Michael Goodliffe, Colin Gordon, *Alec McCowen*

One, Two, Three
US 1961   115m   bw
Panavision
United Artists / Mirisch / Pyramid (Billy Wilder)

An executive in West Berlin is trying to sell Coca Cola to the Russians while preventing his boss's daughter from marrying a communist.
Back to *Ninotchka* territory, but this time the tone is that of a wild farce which achieves fine momentum in stretches but also flags a lot in between, teetering the while on the edge of taste.

w Billy Wilder, I. A. L. Diamond, *play* Ferenc Molnar *d* Billy Wilder *ph* Daniel Fapp *m* André Previn

James Cagney, Horst Buchholz, Arlene Francis, Pamela Tiffin, Lilo Pulver, Howard St John, Leon Askin

'A sometimes bewildered, often wonderfully funny exercise in nonstop nuttiness.'—*Time*

'This first-class featherweight farce is a serious achievement.'—*Stanley Kauffmann*

AAN: Daniel Fapp

Romance as glorious as the towering Andes!'
Only Angels Have Wings
US 1939   121m   bw
Columbia (Howard Hawks)

Tension creeps into the relationships of the men who fly cargo planes over the Andes when a stranded showgirl sets her cap at the boss.
For an action film this is really too restricted by talk and cramped studio sets, and its theme was more entertainingly explored in *Red Dust*. Still, it couldn't be more typical of the Howard Hawks film world, where men are men and women have to be as tough as they are.

w Jules Furthman, *story* Howard Hawks *d* Howard Hawks *ph* Joseph Walker, Elmer Dyer *m* Dmitri Tiomkin *md* Morris Stoloff

Cary Grant, Jean Arthur, Rita Hayworth, Richard Barthelmess, Thomas Mitchell, Sig Rumann, Victor Kilian, John Carroll, Allyn Joslyn

'All these people did the best they could with what they were given—but look at it.'—*Otis Ferguson*

Only Two Can Play
GB 1962   106m   bw
British Lion / Vale (Launder and Gilliat)

A much married assistant librarian in a Welsh town has an abortive affair with a councillor's wife.
Well characterized and generally diverting 'realistic' comedy which slows up a bit towards the end but contains many memorable sequences and provides its star's last good character performance.

w Bryan Forbes, novel That
Uncertain Feeling by *Kingsley Amis*
d Sidney Gilliat ph John Wilcox
m Richard Rodney Bennett
ad Albert Witherick

*Peter Sellers, Mai Zetterling, Virginia
Maskell,* Richard Attenborough,
Raymond Huntley, John Le
Mesurier, *Kenneth Griffith*

Open City
Italy 1945   101m   bw
Minerva
original title: *Roma, Città Aperta*
Italian underground workers defy
the Nazis in Rome towards the end
of the war.
A vivid newsreel quality is achieved
by this nerve-stretching melodrama
in which all the background detail is
as real as care could make it.

w Sergio Amidei, Federico Fellini
d Roberto Rossellini *ph* Ubaldo
Arata *m* Renzo Rossellini

Aldo Fabrizzi, *Anna Magnani,*
Marcello Pagliero, Maria Michi

AAN: script

Orchestra Wives
US 1942   97m   bw
TCF (William Le Baron)
A small town girl marries the
trumpet player of a travelling swing
band.
Fresh and lively musical of its
period, full of first-class music and
amusing backstage backbiting.

w Karl Tunberg, Darrell Ware
d Archie Mayo *ph* Lucien Ballard
md Alfred Newman

Ann Rutherford, George
Montgomery, Lynn Bari, *Glenn
Miller and his Orchestra,* Carole
Landis, Jackie Gleason, Cesar
Romero
'A natural for any theatre that
hasn't got an ironclad rule against
jive.'—*Hollywood Reporter*

AAN: song 'I've Got a Girl in
Kalamazoo' (*m* Harry Warren,
ly Mack Gordon)

'Everything is in its proper
place—except the past!'
Ordinary People
US 1980   124m
Technicolor
Paramount/Wildwood (Ronald L.
Schwary)
The eldest son of a well-heeled
American family is drowned, and the
survivors take stock and indulge in
recriminations.
An actor's piece which on that level
succeeds very well, and accurately
pins down a certain species of
modern American family.

w Alvin Sargent, novel Judith Guest
d Robert Redford *ph* John Bailey
m Marvin Hamlisch

Donald Sutherland, *Mary Tyler
Moore, Timothy Hutton,* Judd
Hirsch, Elizabeth McGovern, M.
Emmet Walsh
'This is an academic exercise in
catharsis: it's earnest, it means to
improve people, and it lasts a
lifetime.'—*New Yorker*

AA: best film; Alvin Sargent;
Robert Redford; Timothy Hutton
AAN: Mary Tyler Moore; Judd
Hirsch (supporting actor)

Orphée
France 1949   112m   bw
André Paulvé 1/Films du
Palais Royal
Death, represented by a princess,
falls in love with Orpheus, a poet,
and helps him when he goes into hell
in pursuit of his dead love.
Fascinating poetic fantasy which may
have been finally unintelligible but
was filled to overflowing with
memorable scenes and cinematic
tricks, from the entry to the
hereafter through a mirror to
intercepted code messages such as
'L'oiseau compte avec ses doigts'.
The closest the cinema has got to
poetry.

wd Jean Cocteau, from his play
ph Nicolas Hayer *m* Georges Auric
ad Jean d'Eaubonne

Jean Marais, François Périer, Maria

Casarès, Marie Déa, Edouard
Dermithe, Juliette Greco
  'It is a drama of the visible and the
invisible . . . I interwove many
myths. Death condemns herself in
order to help the man she is duty
bound to destroy. The man is saved
but Death dies: it is the myth of
immortality.'—*Jean Cocteau*

† See the sequel *Le Testament
d'Orphée.*

†† The film was dedicated to its
designer Christian Bérard (1902–49).

Our Hospitality
  US 1923 70m approx (24
fps) bw silent
Metro / Buster Keaton (Joseph M.
Schenck)
Around 1850, a southerner returns
home to claim his bride and finds
himself in the middle of a blood
feud.
Charming rather than hilarious star
comedy with a splendid ancient train
and at least one incredible stunt by
the star.

w Jean Havez, Joseph Mitchell,
Clyde Bruckman *d* Buster Keaton,
Jack Blystone *ph* Elgin Lessley,
Gordon Jennings

Buster Keaton, Natalie Talmadge,
Joe Keaton, Buster Keaton Jnr
  'A novelty mélange of dramatics,
low comedy, laughs and thrills . . .
one of the best comedies ever
produced.'—*Variety*

Our Man In Havana
  GB 1959 112m bw
  Cinemascope
Columbia / Kingsmead (Carol
Reed)
A British vacuum cleaner salesman
in Havana allows himself to be
recruited as a spy, and wishes he
hadn't.
The wry flavour of the novel does
not really translate to the screen,
and especially not to the wide
screen, but a few lines and
characters offer compensation.

w Graham Greene, from his novel
d Carol Reed *ph* Oswald Morris

m Hermanos Deniz Cuban Rhythm
Band

Alec Guinness, *Noel Coward*, Burl
Ives, Maureen O'Hara, Ernie
Kovacs, *Ralph Richardson*, Jo
Morrow, Paul Rogers, Grégoire
Aslan, Duncan Macrae
  'The main weakness is the absence
of economic, expressive cutting and
visual flow. As a result . . . stretches
of dialogue become tedious to
watch; and the essential awareness
of the writer's shifting tensions yields
disappointingly to the easier
mannerisms of any conventional
comedy-thriller.'—*Peter John Dyer*

'The story of a love affair that
  lasted a lifetime!'
Our Town
  US 1940 90m bw
  Principal Artists / Sol Lesser
Birth, life and death in a small New
Hampshire community.
One of the main points of the play,
the absence of scenery, is abandoned
in this screen version, and the
graveyard scene has to be presented
as a dream, but the film retains the
narrator and manages to make
points of its own while absorbing the
endearing qualities which made the
play a classic.

w Thornton Wilder, Frank Craven,
Harry Chantlee, *play* Thornton
Wilder *d Sam Wood ph* Bert
Glennon *m* Aaron Copland
pd William Cameron Menzies

Frank Craven, William Holden,
Martha Scott, Thomas Mitchell, *Fay
Bainter*, Guy Kibbee, Beulah Bondi,
Stuart Erwin
  'You can nearly smell things
cooking, and feel the night
air.'—*Otis Ferguson*

AAN: best picture; Aaron Copland;
Martha Scott

Out of Africa
  US / GB 1985 150m Rank
  colour
Universal / Sydney Pollack
In 1914 Karen Blixen arrives in
Africa for a marriage of convenience

with a German baron who ignores
her; a white hunter remedies the
situation.
Heavy going but critically lauded
transcription of a semi-classic which
ambles along for an extremely long
time without really getting
anywhere.

w Kurt Luedtke, from writings of
'Isak Dinesen' (Karen Blixen)
d Sydney Pollack *ph* David Watkin
m John Barry *pd* Stephen Grimes

Meryl Streep, Robert Redford,
Klaus Maria Brandauer, Michael
Kitchen, Michael Gough
  'It's a long way to go for a
downbeat ending.'—*Variety*
  'The film purrs pleasantly along
like one of its own big cats.'—*Sight
and Sound*

AA: best picture; photography;
music; art direction
AAN: Meryl Streep; direction;
Klaus Maria Brandauer (supporting
actor); adapted screenplay

'You're no good and neither am I.
  We deserve each other!'
Out of the Past
🐆 US 1947 97m bw
    RKO (Warren Duff)
GB title: *Build My Gallows High*
A private detective is hired by a
hoodlum to find his homicidal girl
friend; he does, and falls in love with
her.
Moody *film noir* with Hollywood
imitating French models; plenty of
snarling and a death-strewn climax.

w Geoffrey Homes, from his novel
Build My Gallows High *d Jacques
Tourneur ph* Nicholas Musuraca
m Roy Webb

*Robert Mitchum, Jane Greer, Kirk
Douglas,* Rhonda Fleming, Richard
Webb, Steve Brodie, Virginia
Huston, Dickie Moore
  'Is this not an outcrop of the
national masochism induced by a
quite aimless, newly industrialized
society proceeding rapidly on its way
to nowhere?'—*Richard Winnington*

  'Mitchum is so sleepily
self-confident with the women that
when he slopes into clinches you
expect him to snore in their
faces.'—*James Agee*

'Even her love was primitive!'
An Outcast of the Islands
🎭 GB 1951 102m bw
 ✕ London Films (Carol Reed)
A shiftless trader finds a secret Far
Eastern trading post where he can be
happy—but even here he becomes
an outcast.
An interesting but not wholly
successful attempt to dramatize a
complex character study. It looks
great and is well acted.

w William Fairchild, *novel* Joseph
Conrad *d* Carol Reed *ph John
Wilcox m* Brian Easdale

Trevor Howard, Ralph Richardson,
Kerima, Robert Morley, Wendy
Hiller, George Coulouris, Frederick
Valk, Wilfrid Hyde White, Betty
Ann Davies
  'The script is so overwhelmed by
the narrative itself that the
characters and relationships fail to
crystallize . . . while the handling is
often intelligent, ingenious, and has
its effective moments, no real
conception emerges.'—*Gavin
Lambert*
  'Its sordidness is not veneered by
the usual lyricism of
Hollywood.'—*London Evening
News*
  'The most powerful film ever
made in this country.'—*Observer*

The Ox-Bow Incident
🐎 US 1943 75m bw
    TCF (Lamar Trotti)
GB title: *Strange Incident*
A cowboy is unable to prevent three
wandering travellers being unjustly
lynched for murder.
Stark lynch law parable, beautifully
made but very depressing.

w Lamar Trotti, *novel* Walter Van
Tilburg Clark *d* William Wellman
ph Arthur Miller m Cyril Mockridge

Henry Fonda, Henry Morgan, Jane Darwell, Anthony Quinn, Dana Andrews, Mary Beth Hughes, William Eythe, Harry Davenport, *Frank Conroy*

'Realism that is as sharp and cold as a knife.'—*Frank S. Nugent, New York Times*

'Very firm, respectable, and sympathetic; but I still think it suffers from *rigor artis*.'—*James Agee*

AAN: best picture

P

Padre Padrone

Italy 1977 113m
Eastmancolor
Radiotelevisione Italia (Tonino
Paoletti)
aka: *Father and Master*

The author recounts how he grew up
with a violent and tyrannical father.

A vivid chunk of autobiography with
food for thought on several levels,
and a clever piece of film-making to
boot.

*wd Paolo Taviani, Vittorio Taviani,
book Gavino Ledda ph Mario
Masini md Egisto Macchi*

Omero Antonutti, Saverio Marconi,
Marcella Michelangeli

'Ben and pardner shared
everything—even their wife!'

Paint Your Wagon

US 1969 164m
Technicolor Panavision 70
Paramount / Alan Jay Lerner (Tom
Shaw)

During the California Gold Rush,
two prospectors set up a Mormon
menage with the same wife.

Good-looking but uncinematic and
monumentally long version of an old
musical with a new plot and not
much dancing. There are minor
pleasures, but it really shouldn't
have been allowed.

*w Paddy Chayevsky, musical
play Alan Jay Lerner, Frederick
Loewe d Joshua Logan ph William
A. Fraker md Nelson Riddle
pd John Truscott*

Lee Marvin, Clint Eastwood, Jean
Seberg, Harve Presnell, Ray
Walston

'One of those big movies in which
the themes are undersized and the
elements are juggled around until
nothing fits together right and even
the good bits of the original show

you started with are shot to
hell.'—*Pauline Kael*

AAN: Nelson Riddle

The Pajama Game

US 1957 101m
Warnercolor
Warner / George Abbott

Workers in a pajama factory demand
a pay rise, but their lady negotiator
falls for the new boss.

Brilliantly conceived musical on an
unlikely subject, effectively
concealing its Broadway origins and
becoming an expert, fast-moving,
hard-hitting piece of modern musical
cinema.

*w George Abbott, Richard Bissell,
book Seven and a Half Cents by
Richard Bissell d Stanley Donen,
ph Harry Stradling songs Richard
Adler, Jerry Ross ch Bob Fosse*

Doris Day, John Raitt, *Eddie Foy
Jnr*, Reta Shaw, Carol Haney

The Paleface

US 1948 91m Technicolor
Paramount (Robert L. Welch)

Calamity Jane undertakes an
undercover mission against
desperadoes, and marries a timid
dentist as a cover.

Splendid wagon train comedy
western with the stars in excellent
form. Sequel, *Son of Paleface*;
remake, *The Shakiest Gun in the
West* (1968).

*w Edmund Hartman, Frank Tashlin
d Norman Z. McLeod ph Ray
Rennahan m Victor Young*

Bob Hope, Jane Russell, Robert
Armstrong, Iris Adrian, Robert
Watson, Jack Searle, Joe Vitale,
Clem Bevans, Charles Trowbridge

AA: song 'Buttons and Bows'
(*m* Jay Livingston, *ly* Ray Evans)

The Palm Beach Story

👁 US 1942 88m bw
Paramount (Paul Jones)

The wife of a penurious engineer takes off for Florida to set her sights on a millionaire.

Flighty comedy, inconsequential in itself, but decorated with scenes, characters and zany touches typical of its creator, here at his most brilliant if uncontrolled.

wd Preston Sturges *ph* Victor Milner *m* Victor Young

Claudette Colbert, Joel McCrea, Rudy Vallee, Mary Astor, Sig Arno, Robert Warwick, Torben Meyer, Jimmy Conlin, William Demarest, Jack Norton, Robert Greig, Roscoe Ates, Chester Conklin, Franklin Pangborn, Alan Bridge, *Robert Dudley*

HACKENSACKER (Rudy Vallee): 'That's one of the tragedies of this life, that the men most in need of a beating up are always enormous.'

WEENIE KING (Robert Dudley): 'Anyway, I'd be too old for you. Cold are the hands of time that creep along relentlessly, destroying slowly but without pity that which yesterday was young. Alone, our memories resist this disintegration and grow more lovely with the passing years. That's hard to say with false teeth.'

'Surprises and delights as though nothing of the kind had been known before . . . farce and tenderness are combined without a fault.'—*William Whitebait*

'Minus even a hint of the war . . . packed with delightful absurdities.'—*Variety*

Paper Moon

👁 US 1973 103m bw
Paramount/Saticoy (Peter Bogdanovich)

In the American midwest in the thirties, a bible salesman and a plain little girl make a great con team.

Unusual but overrated comedy, imperfectly adapted from a very funny book, with careful but disappointing period sense and photography. A lot more style and gloss was required.

w Alvin Sargent, *novel* Addie Pray by *Joe David Brown* *d* Peter Bogdanovich *ph* Laszlo Kovacs *m* popular songs and recordings

Ryan O'Neal, Tatum O'Neal, Madeleine Kahn, John Hillerman

'I've rarely seen a film that looked so unlike what it was about.'—*Stanley Kauffmann*

'At its best the film is only mildly amusing, and I'm not sure I could recall a few undeniable highlights if pressed on the point.'—*Gary Arnold*

'Bogdanovich once again deploys the armoury of nostalgia with relentless cunning to evoke the threadbare side of American life forty years ago . . . one of those rare movies which engages at least two of the senses.'—*Benny Green, Punch*

'It is so enjoyable, so funny, so touching that I couldn't care less about its morals.'—*Daily Telegraph*

AA: Tatum O'Neal
AAN: Alvin Sargent; Madeleine Kahn

Les Parents Terribles

👁 France 1948 98m bw
Sirius

Life with a family in which the children are as neurotic as the parents.

Alternately hilarious and tragic, this is a fascinating two-set piece of filmed theatre, with every performance a pleasure.

wd Jean Cocteau, from his play *ph* Michel Kelber *m* Georges Auric *ad* Christian Bérard, Guy de Gastyne

Jean Marais, Yvonne de Bray, Gabrielle Dorziat, Marcel André, Josette Day

† In 1953 a curious and unsatisfactory British version was made by Charles Frank under the title *Intimate Relations*, with Marian Spencer, Russell Enoch, Ruth Dunning, Harold Warrender and Elsy Albiin.

Paris, Texas

West Germany / France
1984   148m   colour
Road Movies / Argos (Don Guest,
Anatole Dauman)

After separating from his wife a man
goes missing and is later found in the
small town where he was born.

Long, enigmatic but generally
fascinating puzzle-without-a-solution
about people who never find what
they want.

w Sam Shepard d Wim Wenders
ph Robby Müller m Ry Cooder

Harry Dean Stanton, Dean
Stockwell, Aurore Clement, Hunter
Carson, Nastassja Kinski, Bernhard
Wicki

† NB: Filmed in English.
BFA: best director

Une Partie de Campagne

France 1936   40m   bw
Pantheon / Pierre
Braunberger
aka: A Day in the Country

Around 1880, a Parisian tradesman
and his family picnic one Sunday in
the country, and one of the
daughters falls in love.

An unfinished film which was much
admired for its local colour, like an
impressionist picture come to life.

wd Jean Renoir, story Guy de
Maupassant ph Claude Renoir,
Jean Bourgoin m Joseph Kosma

Sylvie Bataille, Georges Darnoul,
Jane Marken, Paul Temps

A Passage to India

GB 1984   163m
Technicolor
EMI / John Brabourne-Richard
Goodwin / HBO / John
Heyman / Edward Sands

An English girl in India accuses a
native of rape.

Another film about India under the
Raj seems somewhat redundant after
The Jewel in the Crown, Gandhi and
The Far Pavilions, but at least under
David Lean's direction this is
intelligent and good to look at.

w, d, ed David Lean, novel E. M.

Forster ph Ernest Day m Maurice
Jarre pd John Box

Judy Davis, Alec Guinness, Victor
Bannerjee, Peggy Ashcroft, James
Fox, Nigel Havers, Richard Wilson,
Antonia Pemberton, Michael
Culver, Art Malik

AA: Peggy Ashcroft (supporting
actress); music
AAN: best picture; direction; Judy
Davis; adapted screenplay;
photography; editing; art direction
BFA: Peggy Ashcroft

The Passionate Friends

GB 1948   91m   bw
GFD / Cineguild (Eric Ambler)
US title: One Woman's Story

A woman marries an older man,
then meets again her young lover.

A simple and obvious dramatic
situation is tricked out with
flashbacks and the inimitable high
style of its director to make a
satisfying entertainment.

w Eric Ambler, novel H. G. Wells
d David Lean ph Guy Green
m Richard Addinsell

Ann Todd, Trevor Howard, Claude
Rains, Betty Ann Davies, Isabel
Dean, Arthur Howard, Wilfrid Hyde
White

'Mr Lean plants his clues with the
certainty of a master of the detective
story, and heightens their effect with
a sure handling of camera and sound
track.'—The Times

Passport to Pimlico

GB 1949   84m   bw
Ealing (E. V. H. Emmett)

Part of a London district is
discovered to belong to Burgundy,
and the inhabitants find themselves
free of rationing restrictions.

A cleverly detailed little comedy
which inaugurated the best period of
Ealing, its preoccupation with
suburban man and his foibles. Not
exactly satire, but great fun, and
kindly with it.

w T. E. B. Clarke d Henry
Cornelius ph Lionel Banes
m Georges Auric

Stanley Holloway, *Margaret Rutherford*, Basil Radford, Naunton Wayne, Hermione Baddeley, John Slater, Paul Dupuis, Jane Hylton, Raymond Huntley, Betty Warren, Barbara Murray, Sidney Tafler

† The film was based on a genuine news item. The Canadian government presented to the Netherlands the room in which Princess Juliana was to bear a child.
AAN: T. E. B. Clarke

Paths of Glory

US 1957   86m   bw
UA/Bryna (James B. Harris)

In 1916 in the French trenches, three soldiers are courtmartialled for cowardice.

Incisive melodrama chiefly depicting the corruption and incompetence of the high command; the plight of the soldiers is less interesting. The trench scenes are the most vivid ever made, and the rest is shot in genuine castles, with resultant difficulties of lighting and recording; the overall result is an overpowering piece of cinema.

w Stanley Kubrick, Calder Willingham, Jim Thompson, *novel* Humphrey Cobb *d Stanley Kubrick ph* Georg Krause *m* Gerald Fried

Kirk Douglas, Adolphe Menjou, George Macready, Wayne Morris, Richard Anderson, Ralph Meeker, Timothy Carey

  'A bitter and biting tale, told with stunning point and nerve-racking intensity.'—*Judith Crist*
  'Beautifully performed, staged, photographed, cut and scored.'—*Colin Young*

'Nobody ever won a war by dying for his country. He won it by making the other poor dumb bastard die for his country!'

Patton

US 1970   171m   DeLuxe
Dimension 150
TCF (Frank McCarthy)
GB title: *Patton—Lust for Glory*

World War II adventures of an aggressive American general.

Brilliantly handled wartime character study which is also a spectacle and tries too hard to have it both ways, but as a piece of film-making is hard to beat.

w Francis Ford Coppola, Edmund H. North *d Franklin Schaffner ph* Fred Koenekamp *m Jerry Goldsmith*

George C. Scott, Karl Malden, Michael Bates, Stephen Young, Michael Strong, Frank Latimore

  'Here is an actor so totally immersed in his part that he almost makes you believe he is the man himself.'—*John Gillett*

AA: best picture; script; Franklin Schaffner; George C. Scott
AAN: Fred Koenekamp; Jerry Goldsmith

Pépé le Moko

France 1936   90m   bw
Paris Film

A Parisian gangster lives in the Algerian casbah where the police can't get at him; but love causes him to emerge and be shot.

Romantic melodrama modelled on the American gangster film but with a decided poetic quality of its own: the Americans promptly paid it the compliment of remaking it as the not-too-bad *Algiers*.

w Henri Jeanson, Roger d'Ashelbe, *novel* Roger d'Ashelbe (Henri la Barthe) *d* Julien Duvivier *ph* Jules Kruger *m* Vincent Scotto *ad* Jacques Krauss

Jean Gabin, Mireille Balin, Gabriel Gabrio, Lucas Gridoux

  'One of the most compelling of all French films.'—*New Yorker, 1977*
  'Perhaps there have been pictures as exciting on the thriller level . . . but I cannot remember one which has succeeded so admirably in raising the thriller to a poetic level.'—*Graham Greene*

Perfect Strangers

GB 1945   102m   bw
MGM / London Films
(Alexander Korda)

US title: *Vacation from Marriage*

A downtrodden clerk and his dowdy
wife go to war, and come back
unrecognizably improved.
Pleasant comedy with good actors;
but the turnabout of two such
caricatures really strains credibility.

w Clemence Dane, Anthony
Pelissier *d* Alexander Korda
ph Georges Périnal *m* Clifton
Robert Donat, Deborah Kerr,
Glynis Johns, Ann Todd, Roland
Culver, Elliot Mason, Eliot
Makeham, Brefni O'Rourke,
Edward Rigby

'War is supposed to be the
catalyst, the sportsman's bracer; and
the film's chief weakness is its failure
to show the briefly exalted couple
sinking back, uncontrollably, under
their peacetime stone.'—*James Agee*

AA: original story (Clemence Dane)

Peter Pan

US 1953   76m   Technicolor
Walt Disney

Three London children are taken
into fairyland by a magic flying boy
who cannot grow up.
Solidly crafted cartoon version of a
famous children's play; not Disney's
best work, but still miles ahead of
the competition.

supervisor Ben Sharpsteen
d Wilfred Jackson, Clyde Geronomi,
Hamilton Luske

The Petrified Forest

US 1936   83m   bw
Warner (Henry Blanke)

Travellers at a way station in the
Arizona desert are held up by
gangsters.
Rather faded melodrama (it always
was), which is important to
Hollywood for introducing such
well-used figures as the poet idealist
hero and the gangster anti-hero, and
for giving Bogart his first meaty role.
Otherwise, the settings are artificial,

the acting theatrical, the
development predictable and the
dialogue pretentious.

w Charles Kenyon, Delmer Daves,
play Robert E. Sherwood *d* Archie
Mayo *ph* Sol Polito *md* Leo F.

Forbstein

Leslie Howard, Bette Davis,
Humphrey Bogart, Genevieve
Tobin, Dick Foran, Joe Sawyer,
Porter Hall, Charley Grapewin

ALAN SQUIER (Leslie Howard): 'Let
there be killing. All this evening I've
had a feeling of destiny closing in.'

JACKIE (Joe Sawyer): 'Now, just
behave yourself and nobody'll get
hurt. This is Duke Mantee, the
world-famous killer, and he's
hungry.'

'Marquee draft should offset the
philosophic meanderings which
minimize appeal.'—*Variety*

'Drama slackens under the weight
of Mr Sherwood's rather half-baked
philosophy.'—*Alistair Cooke*

'There is good dramatic material
here, but Mr Sherwood doesn't see
his play as certain things happening,
but as ideas being expressed,
"significant" cosmic ideas . . . Life
itself, which crept in during the
opening scene, embarrassed perhaps
at hearing itself so explicitly
discussed, crept out again, leaving us
only with the symbols, the too
pasteboard desert, the stunted
cardboard studio trees.'—*Graham
Greene*

† Remade as *Escape in the Desert.*

'Everybody in this town hides
   behind plain wrappers!'

Peyton Place

US 1957   157m   De Luxe
Cinemascope
TCF (Jerry Wald)

Sex, frustration and violence ferment
under the placid surface of a small
New England town.
Well-made film of what was at the
time a scandalous bestseller, one of
the first to reveal those nasty secrets
of 'ordinary people'.

w John Michael Hayes, *novel* Grace
Metalious *d* Mark Robson
ph William Mellor *m* Franz
Waxman

Lana Turner, Arthur Kennedy,
Hope Lange, Lee Philips, Lloyd
Noland, Diane Varsi, Russ
Tamblyn, Terry Moore, Barry Coe,
David Nelson, Betty Field, Mildred
Dunnock, Leon Ames, Lorne
Greene

AAN: best picture; John Michael
Hayes; Mark Robson; William
Mellor; Lana Turner; Arthur
Kennedy; Hope Lange; Diane Varsi;
Russ Tamblyn

Phantom Lady
US 1944 87m bw
Universal (Joan Harrison)
A man is accused of murder and his
only alibi is a mysterious lady he met
in a bar.
Odd little thriller which doesn't
really hold together but is made for
the most part with great style.

w Bernard C. Shoenfeld,
novel William Irish *d* Robert
Siodmak *ph* Woody Bredell
m Hans Salter

Franchot Tone, Alan Baxter, Ella
Raines, Elisha Cook Jnr, Fay Helm,
Andrew Tombes

Phantom of the Opera
US 1925 94m (24 fps) bw
(Technicolor sequence)
silent
Universal
A disfigured man in a mask abducts
the prima donna of the Paris Opera
House to his lair in the sewers
below.
Patchy but often splendid piece of
Grand Guignol which not only
provided its star with a famous role
but was notable for its magnificent
visual style.

w Raymond Shrock, Elliot Clawson,
novel Gaston Leroux *d* Rupert
Julian *ph* Charles Van Enger, *Virgil
Miller ad* Dan Hall

Lon Chaney, Mary Philbin, Norman
Kerry, Gibson Gowland

† In 1930 an 89m talkie version was
issued, with approximately 35%
dialogue which had been recorded
by the surviving actors, and some
new footage.

The Phantom of the Opera
US 1943 92m Technicolor
Universal (George Waggner)
This version is more decorous and
gentlemanly, with much attention
paid to the music, but it certainly has
its moments.

w Erich Taylor, Samuel
Hoffenstein, *d* Arthur Lubin
ph Hal Mohr, W. Howard Greene
m Edward Ward *ad John B.
Goodman, Alexander Golitzen*

Claude Rains, Nelson Eddy,
Susanna Foster, Edgar Barrier, Leo
Carrillo, J. Edward Bromberg, Jane
Farrar, Hume Cronyn
'A grand and gaudy
entertainment.'—*Manchester
Guardian*

AA: Hal Mohr, W. Howard Greene;
John B. Goodman, Alexander
Golitzen

'Uncle Leo's bedtime story for you
older tots! The things they do
among the playful rich—oh
boy!'
The Philadelphia Story
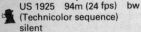
US 1940 112m bw
MGM (Joseph L. Mankiewicz)
A stuffy heiress, about to be married
for the second time, turns human
and returns gratefully to number
one.
Hollywood's most wise and sparkling
comedy, with a script which is even
an improvement on the original play.
Cukor's direction is so discreet you
can hardly sense it, and all the
performances are just perfect.

w Donald Ogden Stewart,
*play Philip Barry d George Cukor
ph* Joseph Ruttenberg *m Franz
Waxman ad* Cedric Gibbons

*Katharine Hepburn, Cary Grant,
James Stewart, Ruth Hussey, Roland
Young, John Halliday, Mary Nash,
Virginia Weidler, John Howard,
Henry Daniell*

'There are just not enough superlatives sufficiently to appreciate this show.'—*Hollywood Reporter*

'An exceptionally bright job of screenplay writing . . . Though films like this do little to advance the art of motion pictures, they may help to convince some of the more discerning among cultural slugabeds that when movies want to turn their hand to anything, they can turn it.'—*Otis Ferguson*

† Cary Grant donated his salary to war relief.

AA: Donald Ogden Stewart; James Stewart

AAN: best picture; George Cukor; Katharine Hepburn; Ruth Hussey

---

'A town—a stranger—and the things he does to its people! Especially its women!'

Picnic
US 1956 113m Technicolor Cinemascope
Columbia (Fred Kohlmar)
A brawny wanderer causes sexual havoc one summer in a small American town.
Seminal melodrama setting new directions for Hollywood and illustrating the side of life the Hardy family never showed. Generally quite compulsive despite some overacting.

w Daniel Taradash, *play William Inge d* Joshua Logan *ph* James Wong Howe *m* George Duning *pd* Joe Mielziner *ad* William Flannery

William Holden, Kim Novak, Rosalind Russell, *Susan Strasberg*, Arthur O'Connell, Cliff Robertson, Betty Field, Verna Felton, Reta Shaw

'Mr Logan's idea of an outing in the corn country includes a choir of at least a hundred voices, a camera so alert that it can pick up the significance of the reflection of a Japanese lantern in a pool (futility, wistfulness, the general transience of life, as I get it) and a sound track let loose in the most formidable music

I've heard in my time at the movies.'—*New Yorker*

AAN: best picture; Joshua Logan; George Duning; Arthur O'Connell

---

The Picture of Dorian Gray
US 1945 110m bw
(Technicolor inserts)
MGM (Pandro S. Berman)
A Victorian gentleman keeps in the attic a picture of himself, which shows his age and depravity while he stays eternally young.
Elegant variation on *Dr Jekyll and Mr Hyde*, presented in portentous style which suits the subject admirably.

wd Albert Lewin, *novel* Oscar Wilde *ph* Harry Stradling *m* Herbert Stothart

George Sanders, *Hurd Hatfield*, Donna Reed, Angela Lansbury, Peter Lawford

SIR HENRY (George Sanders): 'If I could get back my youth, I'd do anything in the world—except get up early, take exercise or be respectable.'

SIR HENRY: 'I apologize for the intelligence of my remarks, Sir Thomas, I had forgotten that you were a Member of Parliament.'

DORIAN (Hurd Hatfield): 'If only the picture could change and I could be always what I am now. For that, I would give anything. Yes, there's nothing in the whole world I wouldn't give. I'd give my soul for that.'

'Respectful, earnest, and, I'm afraid, dead.'—*James Agee*

'Loving and practised hands have really improved Wilde's original, cutting down the epigrammatic flow . . . and rooting out all the preciousness which gets in the way of the melodrama.'—*Richard Winnington*

AA: Harry Stradling
AAN: Angela Lansbury

The Pink Panther

☺ US 1963 113m
Technirama
UA/Mirisch (Martin Jurow)

An incompetent *surêté* inspector is in
Switzerland on the trail of a jewel
thief called The Phantom.

Sporadically engaging mixture of
pratfalls, Raffles, and Monsieur
Hulot, all dressed to kill and quite
palatable for the uncritical. Inspector
Clouseau later became a cartoon
character and also provoked five
sequels: *A Shot in the Dark*,
Inspector Clouseau, *The Return of
the Pink Panther*, *The Pink Panther
Strikes Again* and *The Revenge of the
Pink Panther*, plus two issued after
the star's death.

w Maurice Richlin, Blake Edwards
d Blake Edwards *ph* Philip
Lathrop *m* Henry Mancini
ad Fernando Carrere *animation* De
Patie-Freleng

David Niven, Peter Sellers,
Capucine, Claudia Cardinale,
Robert Wagner, Brenda de Banzie,
Colin Gordon

AAN: Henry Mancini

'Out of a dream world into yours!'
Pinocchio

🎬 US 1940 77m Technicolor
Walt Disney

The blue fairy breathes life into a
puppet, which has to prove itself
before it can turn into a real boy.

Charming, fascinating, superbly
organized and streamlined cartoon
feature without a single second of
boredom.

supervisors Ben Sharpsteen,
Hamilton Luske *m/ly* Leigh
Harline, Ned Washington, Paul J.
Smith

'A film of amazing detail and
brilliant conception.'—*Leonard
Maltin*

'A work that gives you almost
every possible kind of pleasure to be
got from a motion
picture.'—*Richard Mallett, Punch*

'The limits of the animated
cartoon have been blown so wide
open that some of the original
wonder of pictures has been
restored.'—*Otis Ferguson*

AA: Leigh Harline (*m*); song 'When
You Wish Upon a Star' (*m* Leigh
Harline, *ly* Ned Washington)

A Place in the Sun

🎭 US 1951 122m bw
Paramount/George Stevens

A poor young man, offered the
chance of a rich wife, allows himself
to be convicted and executed for the
accidental death of his former
fiancée.

Overblown, overlong and
over-praised melodrama from a
monumental novel of social guilt;
sometimes visually striking, this
version alters the stresses of the plot
and leaves no time for sociological
detail. A film so clearly intended as
a masterpiece could hardly fail to be
boring.

w Michael Wilson, Harry Brown,
novel An American tragedy by
Theodore Dreiser *d* George Stevens
ph William C. Mellor *m* Franz
Waxman *ad* Hans Dreier, Walter
Tyler

Montgomery Clift, Elizabeth Taylor,
Shelley Winters, Anne Revere,
Keefe Brasselle, Fred Clark,
Raymond Burr, Frieda Inescort,
Shepperd Strudwick, Kathryn
Givney, Walter Sande

'An almost incredibly painstaking
work . . . mannered enough for a
very fancy Gothic murder mystery.
This version gives the story a
modern setting, but the town is an
arrangement of symbols of wealth,
glamour and power versus symbols
of poor, drab helplessness—an
arrangement far more suitable to the
thirties than to the fifties.'—*Pauline
Kael*

AA: script; George Stevens; William
C. Mellor; Franz Waxman
AAN: best picture; Montgomery
Clift; Shelley Winters

'Grandest love story ever told!'
The Plainsman

🪶 US 1936 113m bw
Paramount/Cecil B. de Mille

The life of Wild Bill Hickok and his
friends Buffalo Bill and Calamity
Jane.

Standard big-scale thirties western;
narrative lumpy, characters
idealized, spectacle impressive,
technical credits high.

w Waldemar Young, Lynn Riggs,
Harold Lamb   *d* Cecil B. de Mille
ph Victor Milner, George Robinson
m George Antheil   *md* Boris Morros

Gary Cooper, James Ellison, Jean
Arthur, Charles Bickford, Helen
Burgess, Porter Hall, Paul Harvey,
Victor Varconi

'It should do all right for business,
ranging from big to good, possibly
irregular in spots.'—*Variety*

'Certainly the finest western since
The Virginian; perhaps the finest
western in the history of the
film.'—*Graham Greene*

† The story was remade as a TV
movie in 1966, with Don Murray

'Somewhere in the universe, there
     must be something better than
     man!'

Planet of the Apes
      US 1968   119m   De Luxe
     Panavision
TCF/Apjac (Mort Abrahams)
Astronauts caught in a time warp
land on a planet which turns out to
be Earth in the distant future, when
men have become beasts and the
apes have taken over.

Stylish, thoughtful science fiction
which starts and finishes splendidly
but suffers from a sag in the middle.
The ape make-up is great.

w Michael Wilson, Rod Serling,
novel Monkey Planet by Pierre
Boulle   *d* Franklin Schaffner
ph Leon Shamroy   *m* Jerry
Goldsmith

Charlton Heston, Roddy McDowall,
Kim Hunter, Maurice Evans, James
Whitmore, James Daly, Linda
Harrison

'One of the most telling science
fiction films to date.'—*Tom Milne*

† Sequels, in roughly descending
order of interest, were BENEATH

THE PLANT OF THE APES
(1969), ESCAPE FROM THE
PLANET OF THE APES (1970),
CONQUEST OF THE PLANET
OF THE APES (1972) and
BATTLE FOR THE PLANET OF
THE APES (1973). A TV series
followed in 1974, and a cartoon
series in 1975.

AAN: Jerry Goldsmith

'It knows what scares you!'
Poltergeist
      US 1982   114m
     Metrocolor   Panavision
MGM/SLM (Steven Spielberg)
Suburban life is disrupted when
through her TV set a young girl
releases unpleasant forces from the
cemetery over which the modern
estate was built.

Skilful but dramatically thin and
sometimes rather nasty horror movie
in which the producer's hand seems
often to have controlled the
director's. Misjudgement must be
the reason that it was not the huge
success intended.

w Steven Spielberg, Michael Grais,
Mark Victor   *d* Tobe Hooper   *ph*
Matthew F. Leonetti   *m* Jerry
Goldsmith   *ed* Michael Kahn

Jobeth Williams, Craig T. Nelson,
Beatrice Straight, Dominique
Dunne, Oliver Robbins

AAN: music, visual effects (Richard
Edlund, Michael Wood, Bruce
Nicholson)

Portrait of Jennie
      US 1948   86m   bw (tinted
     sequence)
David O. Selznick
GB title: *Jennie*
A penniless artist meets a strange
girl who seems to age each time he
sees her; they fall in love and he
discovers that she has long been
dead, though she finally comes to
life once more during a sea storm
like the one in which she perished.
A splendid example of the higher
Hollywood lunacy: a silly story with
pretensions about life and death and

time and art, presented with superb persuasiveness by a first-class team of actors and technicians.

w Peter Berneis, Paul Osborn, Leonard Bernovici, *novel* Robert Nathan *d* William Dieterle *ph* Joseph August *m* Dmitri Tiomkin, after Debussy

Jennifer Jones, Joseph Cotten, Ethel Barrymore, David Wayne, Lillian Gish, Henry Hull, Florence Bates

PROLOGUE: Since time began man has looked into the awesome reaches of infinity and asked the eternal questions: What is time? What is life? What is space? What is death? Through a hundred civilizations, philosophers and scientists have come together with answers, but the bewilderment remains . . . Science tells us that nothing ever dies but only changes, that time itself does not pass but curves around us, and that the past and the future are together at our side for ever. Out of the shadows of knowledge, and out of a painting that hung on a museum wall, comes our story, the truth of which lies not on our screen but in your hearts.

JENNIE'S SONG:

'Where I come from,
    nobody knows . . .
And where I'm going,
    everything goes . . .
The wind blows,
The sea flows . . .
And nobody knows . . .'

EBEN (Joseph Cotten): 'I want you, not dreams of you.'

JENNIE (Jennifer Jones): 'There is no life, my darling, until you love and have been loved. And then there is no death.'

'Easily the Selznick masterpiece, rich in superb performances, tasteful direction and superb photography.'—*Motion Picture Herald*

'One of the most exquisite fantasy films ever made . . . a milieu rich in visual and aural imagery . . . a sensuous evocation of time and timelessness.'—*Cinefantastique*

'Though the story may not make

sense, the pyrotechnics, joined to the dumbfounded silliness, keep one watching.'—*New Yorker 1976*

AAN: Joseph August

The Poseidon Adventure

US 1972   117m   De Luxe Panavision

TCF / Kent (Irwin Allen)

A luxury liner is capsized, and trapped passengers have to find their way to freedom via an upside down world.

Tedious disaster movie which caught the public fancy and started a cycle. Spectacular moments, cardboard characters, flashes of imagination.

w Stirling Silliphant, Wendell Mayes, *novel* Paul Gallico *ph* Harold Stine *d* Ronald Neame *m* John Williams *pd* William Creber

Gene Hackman, Ernest Borgnine, Shelley Winters, Red Buttons, Carol Lynley, Leslie Nielson, Arthur O'Connell, Pamela Sue Martin, Roddy McDowall, Eric Shea, Jack Albertson, Stella Stevens

'The script is the only cataclysm in this waterlogged *Grand Hotel*.'—*New Yorker*

AA: song 'The Morning After (*m/ly* Al Kasha, Joel Hirschhorn)
AAN: Harold Stine; John Williams; Shelley Winters

'Five charming sisters on the gayest merriest manhunt that ever snared a bewildered bachelor! Girls! take a lesson from these husband hunters!'

Pride and Prejudice

US 1940   116m   bw

MGM (Hunt Stromberg)

An opinionated young lady of the early 19th century wins herself a rich husband she had at first despised for his pride.

A pretty respectable version of Jane Austen's splendid romantic comedy, with a generally excellent cast; full of pleasurable moments.

w Aldous Huxley, Jane Murfin,

play Helen Jerome, *novel Jane
Austen d* Robert Z. Leonard
ph Karl Freund *m* Herbert Stothart

*Laurence Olivier, Greer Garson,
Edmund Gwenn, Mary Boland,
Melville Cooper, Edna May Oliver,*
Karen Morley, Frieda Inescort,
Bruce Lester, Edward Ashley, Ann
Rutherford, Maureen O'Sullivan, E.
E. Clive, Heather Angel, Marsha
Hunt

'The most deliciously pert comedy
of old manners, the most crisp and
crackling satire in costume that we
can remember ever having seen on
the screen.'—*Bosley Crowther*

'Animated and bouncing, the
movie is more Dickens that Austen;
once one adjusts to this, it's a happy
and carefree viewing
experience.'—*New Yorker, 1980*

The Prisoner of Shark Island
US 1936 95m bw
TCF (Darryl F. Zanuck)
The story of the doctor who treated
the assassin of President Lincoln.
Well-mounted historical semi-fiction
with excellent detail.

w Nunnally Johnson d John Ford
ph Bert Glennon *md* Louis Silvers

Warner Baxter, Gloria Stuart, Joyce
Kay, Claude Gillingwater, Douglas
Wood, Harry Carey, Paul Fix, John
Carradine

'Strong film fare for men; will
have to be sold for femme
appeal.'—*Variety*

The Prisoner of Zenda
US 1937 101m bw
David O. Selznick
An Englishman on holiday in
Ruritania finds himself helping to
defeat a rebel plot by impersonating
the kidnapped king at his
coronation.
A splendid schoolboy adventure
story is perfectly transferred to the
screen in this exhilarating
swashbuckler, one of the most
entertaining films to come out of
Hollywood.

w John Balderston, Wells Root,
Donald Ogden Stewart,
novel Anthony Hope *d* John
Cromwell *ph* James Wong Howe
m Alfred Newman

*Ronald Colman, Douglas Fairbanks
Jnr,* Madeleine Carroll, David
Niven, Raymond Massey, Mary
Astor, *C. Aubrey Smith,* Byron
Foulger, Montagu Love

'The most pleasing film that has
come along in ages.'—*New York
Times*

AAN: Alfred Newman

'The things I do for England!'
The Private Life of Henry VIII
GB 1933 97m bw
London Films (*Alexander
Korda*)
How Henry beheaded his second
wife and acquired four more.
This never was a perfect film, but
certain scenes are very funny and its
sheer sauciness established the
possibility of British films making
money abroad, as well as starting
several star careers. It now looks
very dated and even amateurish in
parts.

*w Lajos Biro, Arthur Wimperis
d* Alexander Korda *ph* Georges
Périnal *m* Kurt Schroeder

Charles Laughton, Elsa Lanchester,
Robert Donat, Merle Oberon,
Binnie Barnes, Franklin Dyall, Miles
Mander, Wendy Barrie, Claud
Allister, Everly Gregg

'Among the best anywhere and by
far the top British picture . . .
figures a sock entry, especially for
the best houses.'—*Variety*

AA: Charles Laughton
AAN: best picture

The Private Life of Sherlock Holmes
GB 1970 125m De Luxe
Panavision
UA/Phalanx/Mirisch/Sir Nigel
(Billy Wilder)
A secret Watson manuscript reveals
cases in which Sherlock Holmes
became involved with women.

What started as four stories is reduced to two, one brightly satirical and the other no more than a careful and discreet recreation, with the occasional jocular aside, of the flavour of the stories themselves. A very civilized and pleasing entertainment except for the hurried rounding-off which is a let-down.

w Billy Wilder, I. A. L. Diamond d Billy Wilder *ph* Christopher Challis *m* Miklos Rozsa *ad Alexander Trauner*

Robert Stephens, Colin Blakely, Genevieve Page, Clive Revill, Christopher Lee, Catherine Lacey, Stanley Holloway

'Affectionately conceived and flawlessly executed.'—*NFT*, *1974*
'Wilder's least embittered film, and by far his most moving. Great.'—*Time Out, 1984*

The Private Lives of Elizabeth and Essex

US 1939   106m Technicolor
Warner (Robert Lord)
reissue title: *Elizabeth the Queen*
Elizabeth I falls in love with the Earl of Essex, but events turn him into a rebel and she has to order his execution.
Unhistorical history given the grand treatment; a Hollywood picture book, not quite satisfying dramatically despite all the effort.

w Norman Reilly Raine, Aeneas Mackenzie, play Elizabeth the Queen by Maxwell Anderson *d* Michael Curtiz *ph* Sol Polito *m* Erich Wolfgang Korngold

Bette Davis, Errol Flynn, Olivia de Havilland, Donald Crisp, Vincent Price, Alan Hale, Henry Stephenson, Henry Daniell, Leo G. Carroll, Nanette Fabray, Robert Warwick, John Sutton

'Solid box office material, with fine grosses and holdovers indicated . . . in all technical departments, picture has received topnotch investiture.'—*Variety*
'A rather stately, rigorously posed and artistically technicolored production.'—*Frank S. Nugent*
AAN: Sol Polito; Erich Wolfgang Korngold

Private's Progress

GB 1956   97m   bw
British Lion / Charter (Roy Boulting)
An extremely innocent young national serviceman is taught a few army dodges and becomes a dupe for jewel thieves.
Celebrated army farce with satirical pretensions; when released it had something to make everyone in Britain laugh.

w Frank Harvey, John Boulting, novel Alan Hackney *d John Boulting ph* Eric Cross *m* John Addison

Ian Carmichael, Terry-Thomas, Richard Attenborough, *Dennis Price,* Peter Jones, William Hartnell, Thorley Walters, Ian Bannen, Jill Adams, Victor Maddern, Kenneth Griffith, Miles Malleson, *John Le Mesurier*

The Prize

US 1963   135m
Metrocolor   Panavision
MGM / Roxbury (Pandro S. Berman)
In Stockholm during the Nobel Prize awards, a drunken American author stumbles on a spy plot. Whatever the original novel is like, the film is a Hitchcock pastiche which works better than most Hitchcocks: suspenseful, well characterized, fast moving and funny from beginning to end.

w Ernest Lehman, novel Irving Wallace *d Mark Robson ph* William Daniels *m* Jerry Goldsmith

Paul Newman, Elke Sommer, *Edward G. Robinson,* Diane Baker, Kevin McCarthy, *Leo G. Carroll,* Micheline Presle

The Professionals

US 1966   123m
Technicolor   Panavision
Columbia / Pax (Richard Brooks)

Skilled soldiers of fortune are hired by a millionaire rancher to get back his kidnapped wife.

Strong-flavoured star western with good suspense sequences.

wd Richard Brooks, *novel* A Mule for the Marquesa by Frank O'Rourke *ph* Conrad Hall *m* Maurice Jarre

Burt Lancaster, Lee Marvin, Robert Ryan, Jack Palance, Ralph Bellamy, Claudia Cardinale, Woody Strode

'After the *Lord Jim* excursion, it is good to see Brooks back on his own professional form, filming the tight, laconic sort of adventure which usually seems to bring out the best in Hollywood veterans.'—*Penelope Houston*

'It has the expertise of a cold old whore with practised hands and no thoughts of love.'—*Pauline Kael, 1968*

AAN: Richard Brooks (as writer and as director); Conrad Hall

'The screen's master of suspense moves his camera into the icy blackness of the unexplained!'
'Don't give away the ending—it's the only one we have!'

Psycho

US 1960   109m   bw
Shamley / Alfred Hitchcock

At a lonely motel vicious murders take place and are attributed to the manic mother of the young owner.

Curious shocker devised by Hitchcock as a tease and received by most critics as an unpleasant horror piece in which the main scene, the shower stabbing, was allegedly directed not by Hitchcock but by Saul Bass. After enormous commercial success it achieved classic status over the years; despite effective moments of fright, it has a childish plot and script, and its interest is that of a tremendously successful confidence trick, made for very little money by a TV crew.

w Joseph Stefano, *novel* Robert Bloch *d* Alfred Hitchcock (and *Saul Bass*) *ph* John L. Russell *m* Bernard Herrmann

Anthony Perkins, Vera Miles, John Gavin, Janet Leigh, John McIntire, Martin Balsam, Simon Oakland

'Probably the most visual, most cinematic picture he has ever made.'—*Peter Bogdanovich*

'I think the film is a reflection of a most unpleasant mind, a mean, sly, sadistic little mind.'—*Dwight MacDonald*

† When asked by the press what he used for the blood in the bath, Mr Hitchcock said: 'Chocolate sauce'.

†† This is the whole text of Hitchcock's trailer, in which he audaciously wandered round the sets and practically gave away the entire plot:

Here we have a quiet little motel, tucked away off the main highway, and as you see perfectly harmless looking, whereas it has now become known as the scene of a crime . . . This motel also has an adjunct, an old house which is, if I may say so, a little more sinister looking. And in this house the most dire, horrible events took place. I think we can go inside because the place is up for sale—though I don't know who would buy it now.

In that window in the second floor, the one in front, that's where the woman was first seen. Let's go inside. You see, even in daylight this place looks a bit sinister. It was at the top of these stairs that the second murder took place. She came out of that door there and met the victim at the top. Of course in a flash there was the knife, and in no time the victim tumbled and fell with a horrible crash . . . I think the back broke immediately it hit the floor. It's difficult to describe the way . . . the twisting of the . . . I won't dwell on it.

Come upstairs. Of course the victim, or should I say victims, hadn't any idea of the kind of people they'd be confronted with in this house. Especially the woman. She was the weirdest and the most . . . well, let's go into her bedroom.

Here's the woman's room, still beautifully preserved. And the imprint of her body on the bed where she used to lie. I think some of her clothes are still in the wardrobe. (He looks, and shakes his head.) Bathroom.

This was the son's room but we won't go in there because his favourite spot was the little parlour behind the office in the motel. Let's go down there. This young man . . . you have to feel sorry for him. After all, being dominated by an almost maniacal woman was enough to . . . well, let's go in. I suppose you'd call this his hideaway. His hobby was taxidermy. A crow here, an owl there. An important scene took place in this room. There was a private supper there. By the way, this picture has great significance because . . . let's go along into cabin number one. I want to show you something there.

All tidied up. The bathroom. Oh, they've cleaned all this up now. Big difference. You should have seen the blood. The whole place was . . . well, it's too horrible to describe. Dreadful. And I tell you, a very important clue was found here. (Shows toilet.) Down there. Well the murderer, you see, crept in here very slowly—of course, the shower was on, there was no sound, and . . . MUSIC WELLS UP FIERCELY, SHOWER CURTAIN SWISHES ACROSS, BLACKOUT. Voice: THE PICTURE YOU MUST SEE FROM THE BEGINNING—OR NOT AT ALL.

AAN: Alfred Hitchcock; John L. Russell; Janet Leigh

'Drama that hurls a mighty challenge to all humanity!'
The Public Enemy
US 1931   84m   bw
Warner
GB title: *Enemies of the Public*
Two slum boys begin as bootleggers, get too big for their boots, and wind up dead.

Although it doesn't flow as a narrative, this early gangster film still has vivid and startling scenes and was most influential in the development of the urban American crime film.

w Harvey Thew, Kubec Glasmon, John Bright *d* William Wellman *ph* Dev Jennings *m* David Mendoza
James Cagney, Edward Woods, Jean Harlow, Joan Blondell, Beryl Mercer, Donald Cook, Mae Clarke, Leslie Fenton

'Roughest, most powerful and best gang picture to date. So strong as to be repulsive in some aspects, plus a revolting climax. No strong cast names but a lot of merit.'—*Variety*

'The real power of *The Public Enemy* lies in its vigorous and brutal assault on the nerves and in the stunning acting of James Cagney.'—*James Shelley Hamilton*

'A postscript said that the producers wanted to "depict honestly an environment that exists today in certain strata of American life, rather than glorify the hoodlum or the criminal". The film had a different effect: Cagney was playful and dynamic, and so much more appealing than the characters opposed to him that audiences rooted for him in spite of themselves.'—*Martin Quigley Jnr, 1970*

AAN: Kubec Glasmon, John Bright

The Pumpkin Eater
GB 1964   118m   bw
Columbia / Romulus (James Woolf)
A compulsive mother (of eight children) finds her third marriage rocking when she gets evidence of her husband's affairs.
Brilliantly made if basically rather irritating kaleidoscope of vivid scenes about silly people, all quite recognizable as sixties Londoners; very well acted.

w Harold Pinter, *novel* Penelope Mortimer *d* Jack Clayton *ph* Oswald Morris, Georges Delerue

Anne Bancroft, Peter Finch, James Mason, Maggie Smith, Cedric Hardwicke, Richard Johnson, Eric Porter

'There never was a film so rawly memorable.'—*Evening Standard*

'It is solid, serious, intelligent, stylish. It is also, for the most part, quite dead.'—*The Times*

'It plays like a house afire.'—*Time*

AAN: Anne Bancroft

Pygmalion

🐱 GB 1938　96m　bw
Gabriel Pascal

A professor of phonetics takes a bet that he can turn a Cockney flower seller in six months into a lady who can pass as a duchess.

Perfectly splendid Shavian comedy of bad manners, extremely well filmed and containing memorable lines and performances; subsequently turned into the musical *My Fair Lady*. One of the most heartening and adult British films of the thirties.

w Anatole de Grunwald, W. P. Lipscomb, Cecil Lewis, Ian Dalrymple, *play Bernard Shaw* *d Anthony Asquith, Leslie Howard* *ph* Harry Stradling *m Arthur Honegger*

Leslie Howard, Wendy Hiller, Wilfrid Lawson, Scott Sunderland, Marie Lohr, David Tree, Esmé Percy, Everley Gregg, Jean Caddell

HIGGINS (Leslie Howard): 'Yes, you squashed cabbage leaf, you disgrace to the noble architecture of these columns, you incarnate insult to the English language, I can pass you off as the Queen of Sheba.'

HIGGINS: 'Where the devil are my slippers, Eliza?'

'Ought to have big potentialities in the US, with some cutting . . . An introductory title briefly gives the source of the play, which was Shakespeare's *Pygmalion*.'(!)—*Variety*

'An exhibition of real movie-making—of a sound score woven in and out of tense scenes, creating mood and tempo and characterization.'—*Pare Lorentz*

'Every possible care has been taken in the presentation of what may well prove to have a significant effect on future British film production, for it is live, human entertainment, flawlessly presented and making an obvious appeal to all kinds of audiences.'—*The Cinema*

AAN: best picture; script; Bernard Shaw; Leslie Howard; Wendy Hiller

Q

Q Planes

GB 1939 82m bw
Harefield / London Films
(Irving Asher, Alexander Korda)
US title: *Clouds over Europe*
A secret ray helps spies to steal test aircraft during proving flights.
Lively comedy thriller distinguished by a droll leading performance.

w Ian Dalrymple, Brock Williams, Jack Whittingham, Arthur Wimperis *d Tim Whelan ph* Harry Stradling *md* Muir Mathieson

Ralph Richardson, Laurence Olivier, Valerie Hobson, George Merritt, George Curzon, Gus McNaughton, David Tree

Quai des Brumes

France 1938 89m bw
Rabinovitch
US title: *Port of Shadows*
An army deserter rescues a girl from crooks but is killed before they can escape.
Artificial, set-bound, but at the time wholly persuasive melodrama which became one of the archetypal French films of the thirties, its doomed lovers syndrome not being picked up by Hollywood until after World War II.

w Jacques Prévert, *novel* Pierre MacOrlan *d* Marcel Carné *ph* Eugen Schüfftan *m* Maurice Jaubert *ad* Alexander Trauner

Jean Gabin, Michèle Morgan, Michel Simon, Pierre Brasseur

'Unity of space, time and action give the film a classical finish.'—*Georges Sadoul*

† The plot was in fact almost identical with that of *Pépé le Moko*. The romantic pessimism of these films, plus *Le Jour Se Lève*, so suited the mood of France that Vichy officials later said: 'If we have lost the war it is because of *Quai des Brumes*.'

Quartet

GB 1948 120m bw
GFD / Gainsborough
(Anthony Darnborough)
Four stories introduced by the author.
This entertaining production began the compendium fashion (*Full House, Phone Call from a Stranger*, etc) and is fondly remembered, though all the stories had softened endings and the middle two did not work very well as drama.
Subsequent Maugham compilations were *Trio* and *Encore*.

w R. C. Sherriff, *stories* W. Somerset Maugham *m* John Greenwood

THE FACTS OF LIFE *d* Ralph Smart *ph* Ray Elton

Basil Radford, Naunton Wayne, Mai Zetterling, Jack Watling, James Robertson Justice

THE ALIEN CORN *d* Harold French *ph* Ray Elton

Dirk Bogarde, Françoise Rosay, Raymond Lovell, Honor Blackman, Irene Browne

THE KITE *d* Arthur Crabtree *ph* Ray Elton

George Cole, Hermione Baddeley, Susan Shaw, Mervyn Johns, Bernard Lee

THE COLONEL'S LADY *d* Ken Annakin *ph* Reg Wyer

Cecil Parker, Linden Travers, Nora Swinburne, Ernest Thesiger, Felix Aylmer, Henry Edwards, Wilfrid Hyde White

Quatermass and the Pit

GB 1967 97m Technicolor
Hammer / Anthony Nelson Keys
US title: *Five Million Years to Earth*
Prehistoric skulls are unearthed during London Underground excavations, and a weird and deadly force makes itself felt.

The third film of a Quatermass serial is the most ambitious, and in many ways inventive and enjoyable, yet spoiled by the very fertility of the author's imagination: the concepts are simply too intellectual to be easily followed in what should be a visual thriller. The climax, in which the devil rears over London and is 'earthed', is satisfactorily harrowing.

w *Nigel Kneale*, from his TV serial d *Roy Ward Baker* ph *Arthur Grant* m *Tristam Cary*

Andrew Keir, James Donald, Barbara Shelley, Julian Glover, Duncan Lamont, Edwin Richfield, Peter Copley

Queen Christina
US 1933   101m   bw
MGM (Walter Wanger)
The queen of 17th-century Sweden, distressed at the thought of a political marriage, goes wandering through her country in men's clothes and falls in love with the new Spanish ambassador.
The star vehicle par excellence, superb to look at and one of its star's most fondly remembered films. Historically it's nonsense, but put across with great style.

w *Salka Viertel, H. M. Harwood, S. N. Behrman d Rouben Mamoulian ph William Daniels m Herbert Stothart*

Greta Garbo, John Gilbert, Ian Keith, Lewis Stone, C. Aubrey Smith, Reginald Owen, Elizabeth Young

ANTONIO (John Gilbert): 'It's all a question of climate. You cannot serenade a woman in a snowstorm. All the graces in the art of love—elaborate approaches that will make the game of love amusing—can only be practised in those countries that quiver in the heat of the sun.'

CHRISTINA (Greta Garbo): 'I have been memorizing this room. In the future, in my memory, I shall live a great deal in this room.'

'The shortcomings such as they are, are so far overshadowed by the potency of the premier satellite, the sterling support the Mamoulian montage and the Behrman crisp dialogue that they're relatively unimportant; for Christina is cinch b.o.'—*Variety*

'Garbo, as enchanting as ever, is still enveloped by her unfathomable mystery.'—*Photoplay*

'An unending series of exceptional scenes.'—*Modern Screen*

† The leading male role was announced in turn for Leslie Howard, Franchot Tone, Nils Asther, Bruce Cabot and Laurence Olivier; Garbo turned them all down.

The Queen of Spades
GB 1948   96m   bw
ABP/World Screen Plays (Anatole de Grunwald)
A Russian officer tries to wrest from an ancient countess the secret of winning at cards, in return for which he has sold his soul to the devil; but she dies of fright and haunts him. Disappointingly slow-moving but splendidly atmospheric recreation of an old Russian story with all the decorative stops out; the chills when they come are quite frightening, the style is impressionist and the acting suitably extravagant.

w *Rodney Ackland, Arthur Boys, novel Alexander Pushkin d Thorold Dickinson ph Otto Heller m Georges Auric ad Oliver Messel*
Anton Walbrook, *Edith Evans*, Ronald Howard, Yvonne Mitchell, Mary Jerrold

'The photography is adventurous, the cutting imaginative and the sets startling.'—*Evening Standard*

'It is fine to come across such distinguished filmcraft.'—*Evening News*

The Quiet Man
US 1952   129m   Technicolor
Republic/Argosy (John Ford, Merian C. Cooper)
An Irish village version of *The Taming of the Shrew*, the tamer being an ex-boxer retired to the land of his fathers and in need of a wife.

Archetypal John Ford comedy, as Irish as can be, with everything but leprechauns and the Blarney Stone on hand. Despite some poor sets the film has a gay swing to it, much brawling vigour and broad comedy, while the actors all give their roistering best.

w Frank Nugent, story Maurice Walsh d John Ford ph Winton C. Hoch, Archie Stout m Victor Young

John Wayne, Maureen O'Hara, Barry Fitzgerald, Victor McLaglen, Ward Bond, Mildred Natwick, Francis Ford, Arthur Shields, Eileen Crowe, Sean McClory, Jack McGowran

'Ford's art and artifice . . . are employed to reveal a way of life—stable, rooted, honourable, purposeful in nature's way, and thereby rhythmic. Everyone is an individual, yet everyone and everything has a place.'—Henry Hart, Films in Review

AA: John Ford; Winton C. Hoch, Archie Stout

AAN: best picture; Frank Nugent; Victor McLaglen

Quiet Wedding

GB 1940   80m   bw
Paramount / Conqueror (Paul Soskin)
Middle-class wedding preparations are complicated by family guests. A semi-classic British stage comedy is admirably filmed with a splendid cast.

w Terence Rattigan, Anatole de Grunwald, play Esther McCracken d Anthony Asquith

Margaret Lockwood, Derek Farr, A. E. Matthews, Marjorie Fielding, Athene Seyler, Peggy Ashcroft, Margaretta Scott, Frank Cellier, Roland Culver, Jean Cadell, David Tomlinson, Bernard Miles

'A completely unpretentious and charming film, the components of which are as delicately balanced as the mechanism of a watch.'—New York Times

'No subtelty of glance, movement or dialogue has been missed, no possible highlight omitted.'—Monthly Film Bulletin

† Production was halted five times when bombs fell on the studio.

†† Remade as Happy is The Bride.

Quo Vadis

US 1951   171m
Technicolor
MGM (Sam Zimbalist)
A Roman commander under Nero falls in love with a Christian girl and jealous Poppea has them both thrown to the lions. Spectacular but stagey and heavy-handed Hollywood version of a much-filmed colossus which shares much of its plot line with The Sign of the Cross. Three hours of solemn tedium with flashes of vigorous acting and a few set pieces to take the eye; but the sermonizing does not take away the bad taste of the emphasis on physical brutality.

w John Lee Mahin, S. N. Behrman, Sonya Levien d Mervyn Le Roy ph Robert Surtees, William V. Skall m Miklos Rozsa ad Cedric Gibbons, Edward Carfagno, William Horning

Robert Taylor, Deborah Kerr, Peter Ustinov, Leo Genn, Patricia Laffan, Finlay Currie, Abraham Sofaer, Marina Berti, Buddy Baer, Felix Aylmer, Nora Swinburne, Ralph Truman, Norman Wooland

'In making this film, MGM feel privileged to add something of permanent value to the cultural treasure house of mankind . . .'—publicity

'Ancient Rome is going to the dogs, Robert Taylor is going to the lions, and Peter Ustinov is going crazy!'—publicity

AAN: best picture; Robert Surtees, William V. Skall; Miklos Rozsa; Peter Ustinov; Leo Genn

R

Raiders of the Lost Ark
US 1981   115m
Metrocolor   Panavision
Paramount/Lucasfilm (Frank
Marshall)

In the thirties, an American
archaeologist and explorer beats the
Nazis to a priceless artifact, the
magical box containing fragments of
the stones on which God wrote his
laws.

Commercially very successful, this
attempted wrap-up of the Saturday
morning serials of two generations
ago spends a great deal of money
and expertise on frightening us
rather than exciting us; in Dolby
sound the experience is horrendous.
Second time round, one can better
enjoy the ingenious detail of the
hero's exploits and ignore the
insistence on unpleasantness; still,
there are boring bits in between, and
the story doesn't make a lot of sense.

w Lawrence Kasdan d Steven
Spielberg ph Douglas Slocombe
pd Norman Reynolds m John
Williams

Harrison Ford, Karen Allen, Ronald
Lacey, Paul Freeman, John
Rhys-Davies, Denholm Elliott

'Both de trop and not
enough.'—Sight and Sound

'Children may well enjoy its
simple-mindedness, untroubled by
the fact that it looks so shoddy and
so uninventive.'—Observer

'Kinesthetically, the film gets to
you, but there's no exhilaration, and
no surge of feeling at the
end.'—Pauline Kael, New Yorker

† Tom Selleck was the first choice
for the lead, but was tied up with his
TV series Magnum.

AA: editing (Michael Kahn); visual
effects
AAN: best picture; Steven
Spielberg; Douglas Slocombe; John
Williams
BFA: Norman Reynolds

The Railway Children
GB 1970   108m
Technicolor
EMI (Robert Lynn)

Three Edwardian children and their
mother move into Yorkshire when
their father is imprisoned as a spy,
and have adventures on the railway
line while helping to prove his
innocence.

Fresh and agreeable family film with
many pleasing touches to
compensate for its meandering plot.

wd Lionel Jeffries, novel E. Nesbit
ph Arthur Ibbetson m Johnny
Douglas

Dinah Sheridan, William Mervyn,
Jenny Agutter, Bernard Cribbins,
Iain Cuthbertson, Gary Warren,
Sally Thomsett

The Rains Came
US 1939   103m   bw
TCF (Harry Joe Brown)

High-class parasites in India during
the Raj redeem themselves when a
flood disaster strikes.

Wholly absorbing disaster
spectacular in which the
characterization and personal plot
development are at least as
interesting as the spectacle, and all
are encased in a glowingly
professional production.

w Philip Dunne, Julien Josephson,
novel Louis Bromfield d Clarence
Brown ph Arthur Miller m Alfred
Newman sp Fred Sersen

Myrna Loy, George Brent, Tyrone
Power, Brenda Joyce, Maria
Ouspenskaya, Joseph Schildkraut,
H. B. Warner, Nigel Bruce, Mary
Nash, Jane Darwell, Marjorie
Rambeau, Henry Travers

'A big box-office picture with the
advantage of a new locale.'—Variety

'It would be difficult to improve on the direction, the outbreak of the monsoon, a curtain billowing in the breeze, a lamp casting the shadow of lattice work against white silk, servants scattering for cover . . .'—*Charles Higham, 1972*

'Slick Hollywood film-making at its professional best.'—*Channel 4, 1982*

† Myrna Loy was third choice after Dietrich and Lamarr; Brent second choice after Ronald Colman.

AAN: Alfred Newman

The Rake's Progress

GB 1945   123m   bw
GFD/Individual (Frank Launder, Sidney Gilliat)
US title: *Notorious Gentleman*

The career of a cheerful ne'er-do-well playboy of the thirties. The road to ruin played for light comedy, with silly endpapers in which, quite out of character, the rake becomes a war hero. Generally good production, witty script.

w Frank Launder, Sidney Gilliat, *story* Val Valentine *d* Sidney Gilliat *ph* Wilkie Cooper *m* William Alwyn *pd* David Rawnsley

Rex Harrison, Lilli Palmer, Margaret Johnston, Godfrey Tearle, Griffith Jones, Guy Middleton, Jean Kent, Marie Lohr, Garry Marsh, David Horne, Alan Wheatley

† In the American version Harrison crowned the Martyr's Memorial not with a chamber pot but with a top hat.

Ran

Japan 1985   161m   colour
Herald-Ace/Nippon-Herald/Greenwich (Masato Hara, Serge Silberman)

A Japanese version of *King Lear*, with three sons instead of three daughters.

Predictable bloodshed and tremendous style are evident in this oriental epic from a master hand at the age of 75.

w Akiro Kurosawa, Hideo Oguni, Masato Ide *d Akiro Kurosawa ph Takao Saito m* Toru Takemitsu

Tatsuya Nakadai, Satoshi Terao, Jinpachi Nezu, Daisuke Ryu

'Prepare to be astonished . . . a towering achievement in any language.'—*People*

AAN: direction, photography, art direction

Random Harvest

US 1942   126m   bw
MGM (Sidney Franklin)

A shell-shocked officer in the 1914–18 war escapes from an asylum, marries a music hall singer and is idyllically happy until a shock makes him remember that he is the head of a noble family. His wife, whom he does not now remember, dutifully becomes his secretary and years later another shock brings memory and happiness back.

A silly enough story works remarkably well in this rather splendid, no holds barred, roses round the door romance in Hollywood's best style with incomparable stars. A triumph of the Peg's Paper syndrome, and hugely enjoyable because it is done so enthusiastically.

w Claudine West, George Froeschel, Arthur Wimperis, *novel* James Hilton *d* Mervyn Le Roy *ph* Joseph Ruttenberg *m* Herbert Stothart

Ronald Colman, Greer Garson, Susan Peters, Philip Dorn, Reginald Owen, Henry Travers, Margaret Wycherly, Bramwell Fletcher, Arthur Margetson

'I would like to recommend this film to those who can stay interested in Ronald Colman's amnesia for two hours and who could with pleasure eat a bowl of Yardley's shaving soap for breakfast.'—*James Agee*

'A strangely empty film . . . its characters are creatures of fortune, not partisans in determining their own fates.'—*Bosley Crowther, New York Times*

'It is cast with pearly players in

every part. Its pedigreed plot is savoured with just the right mixture of ups and downs, ecstasy and well-bred anguish, implausibility and psyche. And it moves towards its climax with the measured tread and nicely timed emotional bumps of a Hearst Cosmopolitan serial. It is perhaps the clearest example of the year of how a studio possessing lion's shares of movie-making capital and ingratiating talent can mate these two to synthesize a magnificent neuter, which will predictably bring in vast box office returns with which to produce more neuters.'—*John McManus, PM*

AAN: best picture; script; Mervyn Le Roy; Herbert Stothart; Ronald Colman; Susan Peters

Rashomon

Japan 1951   83m   bw
Daiei
aka: *In the Woods*

In medieval Japan, four people have different versions of a violent incident when a bandit attacks a nobleman in the forest.
Indescribably vivid in itself, and genuinely strange (one of the versions is told by a ghost), *Rashomon* reintroduced Japanese films to the world market and was remade (badly) in Hollywood as *The Outrage*.

wd Akira Kurosawa, *story* Inside a Bush by Ryunosuke Akutagawa *ph* Kazuo Matsuyama *m* Takashi Matsuyama

Toshiro Mifune, Machiko Kyo, Masayuki Mori, Takashi Shimura
'A masterpiece, and a revelation.'—*Gavin Lambert, MFB*

AA: best foreign film

'Man against terrifying monster—in the most spectacular underwater scenes ever filmed!'
Reap the Wild Wind
US 1942   124m
Technicolor
Paramount / Cecil B. de Mille
Seafaring salvage engineers fight

over a southern belle.
Georgia-set period adventure; intended as another *Gone with the Wind*, it simply doesn't have the necessary, but on its level it entertains solidly, climaxing with the famous giant squid fight.

w Alan le May, Jesse Lasky Jnr *d* Cecil B. de Mille *ph* Victor Milner, Dewey Wrigley, William V. Skall *m* Victor Young *ad* Hans Dreier, Roland Anderson

Ray Milland, John Wayne, *Paulette Goddard*, Raymond Massey, Robert Preston, Lynne Overman, Susan Hayward, Charles Bickford, Walter Hampden, Louise Beavers, Martha O'Driscoll, Hedda Hopper
'The essence of all his experience, the apogee of all his art, and as jamful a motion picture as has ever played two hours upon a screen.'—*Howard Barnes, New York Herald Tribune*

† The underwater scenes were filmed in the Santa Monica Pan Pacific Marine Museum, which had a pool 100 feet long and 50 feet wide. The 50-foot giant squid was operated by a 24-button electronic keyboard.

AAN: photography

Rear Window
US 1954   112m
Technicolor
Alfred Hitchcock

A news photographer, confined to his room by a broken leg, sees a murder committed in a room on the other side of the court.
Artificial but fairly gripping suspenser of an unusual kind; with such restricted settings, all depends on the script and the acting, and they generally come up trumps.

w John Michael Hayes, *novel* Cornell Woolrich *d* Alfred Hitchcock *ph* Robert Burks *m* Franz Waxman

James Stewart, Grace Kelly, Raymond Burr, Judith Evelyn, Wendell Corey, Thelma Ritter

AAN: John Michael Hayes; Alfred Hitchcock; Robert Burks

Rebecca

🎬 US 1940 130m bw
🎬 David O. Selznick

The naïve young second wife of a
Cornish landowner is haunted by the
image of his glamorous first wife
Rebecca.

The supreme Hollywood
entertainment package, set in Monte
Carlo and Cornwall, with generous
helpings of romance, comedy,
suspense, melodrama and mystery,
all indulged in by strongly-drawn
characters, and directed by the new
English wizard for the glossiest
producer in town, from a novel
which sold millions of copies. It
really couldn't miss, and it didn't.

*w Robert E. Sherwood, Joan
Harrison, novel Daphne du Maurier
d Alfred Hitchcock ph George
Barnes m Franz Waxman*

*Laurence Olivier, Joan Fontaine,
George Sanders, Judith Anderson,
Nigel Bruce, Gladys Cooper,
Florence Bates, Reginald Denny, C.
Aubrey Smith, Melville Cooper, Leo
G. Carroll, Leonard Carey*

NARRATOR: 'Last night I dreamed I
went to Manderley again . . .'

FAVELL (George Sanders) to Mrs
De Winter: 'I say, marriage with
Max is not exactly a bed of roses, is
it?'

MRS DANVERS (Judith Anderson):
'You're overwrought, madam. I've
opened a window for you. A little air
will do you good. Why don't you go?
Why don't you leave Manderley? He
doesn't need you. He's got his
memories. He doesn't love you—he
wants to be alone again with *her*.
You've nothing to stay for. You've
nothing to live for, have you, really?
Look down there. It's easy, isn't it?
Why don't you? Go on, go on, don't
be afraid . . .

MAXIM (Laurence Olivier): 'You
thought I loved Rebecca? You
thought that? I hated her. Oh, I was
carried away by her—enchanted by
her, as everyone was—and when I
was married, I was told I was the
luckiest man in the world. She was

so lovely, so accomplished, so
amusing. "She's got the three things
that really matter in a wife,"
everyone said, "breeding, brains and
beauty." And I believed them
completely. But I never had a
moment's happiness with her. She
was incapable of love, or tenderness,
or decency.'

'A carefully considered trying out
of the superior technical resources
now at Hitchcock's
disposal.'—*George Perry, 1965*

'Hitchcock fans will have to put up
with a surprising lack of the
characteristic Hitchcock
improvisations in the way of salty
minor personages and humorous
interludes, and satisfy themselves
with a masterly exhibition of the
Hitchcock skill in creating suspense
and shock with his action and his
camera.'—*National Board of Review*

AA: best picture; George Barnes
AAN: script; Alfred Hitchcock;
Franz Waxman; Laurence Olivier;
Joan Fontaine; Judith Anderson

The Red Badge of Courage

🎬 US 1951 69m bw
🎬 MGM (Gottfried Reinhardt)

A youth called up during the Civil
War gets his first taste of battle.
Fresh, poetic, but dramatically
unsatisfactory filming of a classic
American novel. The story of its
production is fascinatingly told in
Picture, a book by Lillian Ross.

*wd John Huston, novel Stephen
Crane ph Harold Rosson
m Bronislau Kaper*

*Audie Murphy, Bill Mauldin,
Douglas Dick, Royal Dano, John
Dierkes, Andy Devine, Arthur
Hunnicutt*

The Red Balloon

🎬 France 1955 34m
🎬 Technicolor

A lonely boy finds a balloon which
becomes his constant companion and
finally lifts him to the skies.
Absorbing and quite perfectly timed
fantasy, one of the great film shorts.

With Pascal Lamorisse; written and
directed by *Albert Lamorisse*;
photographed by *Edmond Sechan*;
music by *Maurice Le Roux*; for Films
Montsouris

'He treated her rough—and she
  loved it!'
Red Dust
☻ US 1932   86m   bw
   MGM (Hunt Stromberg)
On a rubber plantation in
Indo-China, the overseer is pursued
by his engineer's bride but himself
falls for a stranded prostitute.
Vigorous romantic melodrama with
echoes of *Rain*; remade as *Congo
Maisie* (1940) and *Mogambo* (1954).

w John Lee Mahin, *play* Wilson
Collison   *d* Victor Fleming
ph Harold Rosson

Clark Gable, *Jean Harlow*, Mary
Astor, Gene Raymond, Donald
Crisp, Tully Marshall, Forrester
Harvey

  'Lots of pash, sex and undress . . .
an exhib's delight and a cinch for
fancy takings. Done so expertly it
almost overcomes the basic script
shortcomings.'—*Variety*
  'Gable and Harlow have full play
for their curiously similar sort of
good-natured toughness.'—*Time*

† The Gable role was first
announced for John Gilbert.

†† Scenes showing the shooting of
Red Dust are included in *Bombshell*.

The Red Shoes
GB 1948   136m
Technicolor
GFD / The Archers (*Michael
Powell, Emeric Pressburger*)
A girl student becomes a great ballet
star but commits suicide when torn
between love and her career.
Never was a better film made from
such a penny plain story so
unpersuasively written and
performed; the splendour of the
production is in the intimate view it
gives of life backstage in the ballet
world with its larger-than-life
characters. The ballet excerpts are
very fine, and the colour discreet;

the whole film is charged with
excitement.

wd Michael Powell, *Emeric
Pressburger* *ph* Jack Cardiff
m Brian Easdale *pd* Hein Heckroth

Anton Walbrook, *Moira Shearer*,
Marius Goring, Robert Helpmann,
Albert Basserman, Frederick
Ashton, Leonide Massine, Ludmilla
Tcherina, Esmond Knight

  'In texture, like nothing the
British cinema has ever seen.'—*Time
Out, 1981*

AA: Brian Easdale
AAN: best picture; original story
(Michael Powell, Emeric
Pressburger)

'Not since *Gone with the Wind*
has there been a great romantic
epic like it!'
Reds
US 1981   196m
Technicolor
Paramount (Warren Beatty)
The last years of John Reed, an
American writer who after stormy
romantic vicissitudes goes with his
wife to Russia and writes *Ten Days
That Shook the World*.
Interminably long but full of quality,
this immensely detailed work was a
most unlikely project to succeed in
the eighties, but its very strangeness
enabled it to break even.

w Warren Beatty, Trevor Griffiths
d Warren Beatty *ph* Vittorio
Storaro *m* Stephen Sondheim
pd Richard Sylbert

Warren Beatty, Diane Keaton,
Edward Herrman, Jerzy Kosincki,
Jack Nicholson, Maureen Stapleton,
Paul Sorvino

AA: Warren Beatty (as director);
Vittorio Storaro; Maureen Stapleton
(supporting actress)
AAN: best picture; screenplay;
editing (Dede Allen, Craig McKay);
Warren Beatty (as actor); Diane
Keaton; Jack Nicholson
BFA: best supporting actor (Jack
Nicholson); best supporting actress
(Maureen Stapleton)

La Règle du Jeu

France 1939   113m   bw
La Nouvelle Edition Française
(Claude Renoir)
aka: *The Rules of the Game*

A count organizes a weekend
shooting party which results in
complex love intrigues among
servants as well as masters.
Celebrated satirical comedy with a
uniquely bleak outlook.

w Jean Renoir, Carl Koch *d* Jean
Renoir *ph* Jean Bachelet, Alain
Renoir *m* Joseph Kosma, Roger
Desormières *ad* Eugène Lourié,
Max Douy

Marcel Dalio, Nora Gregor, Jean
Renoir, Mila Parély, Julien Carette,
Gaston Modot, Roland Toutain

'It is a question of panache, of
preserving a casual indifference to
the workings of fate.'—*The Times*

'How brilliantly Renoir focuses
the confusion! The rather fusty
luxury of the chateau, the constant
mindless slaughter of wild animals,
the minuets of adultery and
seduction, the gavottes of mutual
hatred or mistrust . . .'—*Basil
Wright, 1972*

† The film was originally banned as
indicting the corruption of France,
and during the war the negative was
destroyed during an air raid; but
eventually a full version was pieced
together from various materials.

Rembrandt

GB 1936   85m   bw
London Films (Alexander
Korda)
Episodes in the life of the
17th-century painter.
Austerely comic, gently tragic
character piece, superbly staged and
photographed, with a great
performance at its centre.

w Lajos Biro, June Head, Carl
Zuckmayer *d* Alexander Korda
ph Georges Périnal, Richard Angst
m Geoffrey Toye

Charles Laughton, Elsa Lanchester,
Gertrude Lawrence, Edward
Chapman, Walter Hudd, Roger
Livesey, Herbert Lomas, Allan
Jeayes, Sam Livesey, Raymond
Huntley, John Clements

'Never exciting, and only partly
believable . . . a feature film without
a story plot.'—*Variety*

'Amazingly full of that light which
the great master of painting subdued
to his supreme purpose.'—*James
Agate*

'The film is ruined by lack of story
and continuity: it has no drive. Like
The Private Life of Henry the Eighth
it is a series of unrelated
tableaux.'—*Graham Greene*

Remember Last Night?

US 1936   80m   bw
Universal
Socialites with hangovers find that
murder was committed during their
party.
Ingenious but overlong mixture of
styles: farce, *Thin Man* comedy,
murder mystery, satire, fantasy.
Very well worth looking at.

w Harry Clark, Dan Totheroh,
Doris Malloy, *novel* The Hangover
Murders by Adam Hobhouse
d James Whale *ph* Joseph
Valentine *m* Franz Waxman

Robert Young, Edward Arnold,
Arthur Treacher, Constance
Cummings, Robert Armstrong, Sally
Eilers, Reginald Denny, Ed Brophy,
Jack La Rue, Gustav Von
Seyffertitz, Gregory Ratoff

'It will be hard to sell because it is
hard to understand . . . the basic
story can scarcely be followed, while
the superficial gloss of phoney
sophistication neither fits a narrative
in which four murders and two
suicides are recorded, nor carries
conviction of itself.'—*Variety*

'Parodying the detective thriller in
a dazzling cascade of gags, this
brilliant divertissement eventually
takes off into pure surrealism.'
—*Tom Milne, MFB, 1974*

Repulsion

GB 1965   105m   bw
Compton / Tekli (Gene
Gutowski)
A Belgian manicurist in London is

driven by pressures into neurotic
withdrawal; terrified above all by
sex, she locks herself up in her
gloomy flat and murders her
boyfriend and landlord when they
try to approach her.
Weird, unmotivated but undeniably
effective Grand Guignol in the form
of a case history; little dialogue,
which is just as well as the director at
that time clearly had no ear for the
language.

w Roman Polanski, Gerard Brach
d Roman Polanski ph Gilbert
Taylor m Chico Hamilton

Catherine Deneuve, Ian Hendry,
John Fraser, Patrick Wymark,
Yvonne Furneaux

'An unashamedly ugly film, but as
a lynx-eyed view of a crumbling
mind it is a masterpiece of the
macabre.'—Daily Mail

Rhapsody in Blue

US 1945 139m bw
Warner (Jesse L. Lasky)
The life story of composer George
Gershwin.
No more trustworthy on factual
matters than other Hollywood
biopics of its era, this rather glum
saga at least presented the music and
the performers to excellent
advantage.

w Howard Koch, Elliot Paul
d Irving Rapper ph Sol Polito
md Ray Heindorf, Max Steiner
ch Le Roy Prinz ad Anton Grot,
John Hughes

Robert Alda, Joan Leslie, Alexis
Smith, Charles Coburn, Julie
Bishop, Albert Basserman, Oscar
Levant, Herbert Rudley, Rosemary
de Camp, Morris Carnovsky, Al
Jolson, Paul Whiteman, George
White, Hazel Scott

'With no story at all, this two-hour
concert of Gershwin music would be
well worth the price of
admission.'—Daily Mail

AAN: Ray Heindorf, Max Steiner

Richard III

GB 1955 161m
Technicolor Vistavision
London Films (Laurence Olivier)
Shakespeare's play about Richard
Crookback, his seizure of the throne
and his defeat at Bosworth.
Theatrical but highly satisfying
filming of a splendidly melodramatic
view of history. Interesting but not
fussy camera movement, delightful
sets (followed by a disappointingly
'realistic' battle) and superb
performances.

w William Shakespeare (adapted by
Laurence Olivier, Alan Dent, with
additions) d Laurence Olivier
ph Otto Heller, Roger Furse
m William Walton ad Carmen
Dillon

Laurence Olivier, Claire Bloom,
Ralph Richardson, Cedric
Hardwicke, Stanley Baker, Alec
Clunes, John Gielgud, Mary
Kerridge, Pamela Brown, Michael
Gough, Norman Wooland, Helen
Haye, Patrick Troughton, Clive
Morton, Andrew Cruickshank

'Wherever the play was
loose-jointed or ill-fitting. Sir
Laurence has been its tinker and its
tailor, but never once its
butcher.'—Paul Dehn, News
Chronicle

AAN: Laurence Olivier

Rififi

France 1955 116m bw
Indus/Pathé/Prima
original title: Du Rififi chez les
Hommes
After an elaborate raid on a
jewellery store, thieves fall out and
the caper ends in bloodshed.
A film with much to answer for, in
the form of hundreds of imitations
showing either detailed accounts of
robberies (Topkapi, Gambit) or
gloomy looks at the private lives of
criminals. At the time it seemed
crisp and exciting, and the 25-minute
silent robbery sequence is quite
something.

w René Wheeler, Jules Dassin, Auguste le Breton, *novel* Auguste le Breton *d* Jules Dassin *ph* Philippe Agostini *m* Georges Auric

Jean Servais, Carl Mohner, Robert Manuel, Marie Sabouret, Perlo Vita (Jules Dassin)

† Several 'sequels' were made using the word *rififi* (criminal argot for 'trouble') in the title, but in plot terms they were entirely unrelated.

Rio Bravo

US 1959   141m
Technicolor
Warner / Armada (Howard Hawks)
A wandering cowboy and a drunken sheriff hold a town against outlaws. Cheerfully overlong and slow-moving western in which everybody, including the director, does his thing. All very watchable for those with time to spare, but more a series of revue sketches than an epic.

w Jules Furthman, Leigh Brackett *d* Howard Hawks *ph* Russell Harlan *m* Dmitri Tiomkin

John Wayne, *Dean Martin*, Ricky Nelson, Angie Dickinson, Walter Brennan, Ward Bond, John Russell, Pedro Gonzalez Gonzalez, Claude Akins, Harry Carey Jnr, Bob Steele

† More or less remade in 1966 as *El Dorado* and in 1970 as *Rio Lobo*.

The Road Back

US 1937   105m   bw
Universal (James Whale)
After World War I, German soldiers go home to problems and disillusion. A major work, intended as a sequel to *All Quiet on the Western Front*. Despite impressive sequences, it doesn't quite reach inspiring heights.

w R. C. Sherriff, Charles Kenyon, *novel* Erich Maria Remarque *d* James Whale *ph* John Mescall, *George Robinson* *m* Dmitri Tiomkin *ad* Charles D. Hall

Richard Cromwell, John King, Slim Summerville, Andy Devine, Barbara Read, Louise Fazenda, Noah Beery Jnr, Lionel Atwill, John Emery,

Etienne Giradot, Spring Byington, Laura Hope Crews

'Big and frequently effective, but a let-down in toto . . . does not compare with *All Quiet* in quality or power.'—*Variety*

'They call it an all-star cast and that means there isn't a single player of any distinction to be picked out of the herd. . . . It might be funny if it wasn't horrifying. This is America seeing the world in its own image.'—*Graham Greene*

† The film is said to have been extensively reshot after protests from the German consul in Los Angeles. No 35mm negative now exists, as it reverted to Remarque and was lost.

'The land of the free gone wild! The heyday of the hotcha! The shock-crammed days G-men took ten whole years to lick!'

The Roaring Twenties

US 1939   106m   bw
Warner (Hal B. Wallis)
A World War I veteran returns to New York, innocently becomes involved in bootlegging, builds up an empire and dies in a gang war. Among the last of the Warner gangster cycle, this was perhaps the best production of them all, despite the familiar plot line: stars and studio were in cracking form.

w Jerry Wald, Richard Macaulay, Robert Rossen, *story* Mark Hellinger *d* Raoul Walsh, *Anatole Litvak* *ph* Ernest Haller *m* Heinz Roemheld

James Cagney, Humphrey Bogart, Priscilla Lane, Jeffrey Lynn, Gladys George, Frank McHugh, Paul Kelly, Elizabeth Risdon

† The James Cagney character was based on Larry Fay, who was Texas Guinan's partner, and Gladys George is clearly Guinan herself.

'The miracle story of all time!'

The Robe

US 1953   135m
Technicolor   Cinemascope
TCF (Frank Ross)
Followers and opponents of Jesus

are affected by the robe handed down by him at his crucifixion. The first film in Cinemascope was, surprisingly, a biblical bestseller, but the crowded Roman sets hid most of the flaws in the process. The film itself was competent and unsurprising in the well-tried *Sign of the Cross* manner.

w Philip Dunne, *novel* Lloyd C. Douglas *d* Henry Koster *ph* Leon Shamroy *m* Alfred Newman

Richard Burton, Jean Simmons, Michael Rennie, *Victor Mature*, Jay Robinson, Torin Thatcher, Dean Jagger, Richard Boone, Betta St John, Jeff Morrow, Ernest Thesiger, Dawn Addams

† Power was originally cast in the Burton role, and Burt Lancaster in Mature's.

AAN: best picture; Leon Shamroy; Richard Burton

Robin Hood

US 1922 127m approx (24 fps) bw silent
Douglas Fairbanks
Robin Hood combats Prince John and the Sheriff of Nottingham. An elaborate version of the legend which featured some of Hollywood's most celebrated sets and allowed the star to perform a selection of exhilarating stunts.

w Douglas Fairbanks *d* Allan Dwan *ph* Arthur Edeson *ad* Wilfrid Buckland, Irvin J. Martin,

Douglas Fairbanks, Wallace Beery, Alan Hale, Enid Bennett

'The high water mark of film production. It did not grow from the bankroll, it grew from the mind.'—*R. E. Sherwood*

'A story book picture, as gorgeous and glamorous a thing in innumerable scenes as the screen has yet shown . . . thrilling entertainment for the whole family group.'—*National Board of Review*

Rocco and his Brothers

Italy / France 1960   180m bw
Titanus / Les Films Marceau (Goffredo Lombardo)
A peasant family moves into Milan, and each of its five brothers has his problems.
Massive portmanteau of realistic stories, a bit hard to take despite its undoubted brilliance.

w Luchino Visconti, Suso Cecchi D'Amico, Vasco Pratolini *d* Luchino Visconti *ph* Giuseppe Rotunno *m* Nino Rota

Alain Delon, Renato Salvatori, Annie Giradot, Katina Paxinou, Roger Hanin, Paolo Stoppa, Suzy Delair, Claudia Cardinale

'His whole life was a million-to-one shot!'

Rocky

US 1976   119m
Technicolor
UA / Chartoff-Winkler (Gene Kirkwood)
A slightly dimwitted Philadelphia boxer makes good.
Pleasantly old-fashioned comedy-drama with rather unattractive characters in the modern manner. Despite the freshness, on the whole *Marty* is still preferable.

w Sylvester Stallone *d* John G. Avildsen *ph* James Crabe *m* Bill Conti

Sylvester Stallone, Burgess Meredith, Talia Shire, Burt Young, Carl Weathers, Thayer David

AA: best picture; John G. Avildsen
AAN: Sylvester Stallone (as writer); song 'Gotta Fly Now' (*m* Bill Conti, *ly* Carol Connors, Ayn Robbins); Sylvester Stallone (as actor); Burgess Meredith; Talia Shire; Burt Young

Roman Holiday

US 1953   118m   bw
Paramount (William Wyler)
A princess on an official visit to Rome slips away incognito and falls in love with a newspaperman.

Wispy, charming, old-fashioned
romantic comedy shot in Rome and
a little obsessed by the locations; one
feels that a studio base would have
resulted in firmer control of the
elements. The stars, however, made
it memorable.

w Ian McLellan Hunter, John
Dighton *d William Wyler* *ph* Franz
Planer, Henri Alekan *m* Georges
Auric

Gregory Peck, Audrey Hepburn,
Eddie Albert, Hartley Power,
Harcourt Williams

'While Capra, or in a different
way Lubitsch, could have made
something wholly enjoyable from it,
it would seem that Wyler's technique
is now too ponderously inflexible for
such lightweight material.'—*MFB*

AA: original story (Ian McLellan
Hunter); Audrey Hepburn
AAN: best picture; script; William
Wyler; photography; Eddie Albert

Roman Scandals
US 1933 93m bw
Samuel Goldwyn
A troubled young man dreams
himself back in ancient Rome.
Musical farce which is not only
pretty entertaining on its own
account but remains interesting for a
number of reasons; as its star's best
vehicle, for its Depression bookends,
as a spoof on *The Sign of the Cross*
and the inspiration of scores of other
comedies in which the heroes
dreamed themselves back into other
times. Note also the musical
numbers, the chariot race finale, and
the rare appearance of Ruth Etting.

w William Anthony McGuire,
George Oppenheimer, Arthur
Sheekman, Nat Perrin, *story* George
S. Kaufman, Robert E. Sherwood
d Frank Tuttle *chariot
sequence* Ralph Cedar *ph* Gregg
Toland *m* Alfred Newman
ch Busby Berkeley *songs* various

Eddie Cantor, Gloria Stuart, Ruth
Etting, Edward Arnold, Alan
Mowbray, Verree Teasdale

'An extraordinary rigmarole

containing everything from chariot
races to a torch song.'—*Time*

Rome Express
GB 1932 94m bw
Gaumont (Michael Balcon)
Thieves and blackmail victims are
among the passengers on an express
train.
Just a little faded now as sheer
entertainment, this remains the
prototype train thriller from which
*The Lady Vanishes, Murder on the
Orient Express* and a hundred others
are all borrowed; it also spawned
myriad movies in which strangers are
thrown together in dangerous
situations. Technically it still works
very well, though the script needs
modernizing.

w Clifford Grey, Sidney Gilliat,
Frank Vosper, Ralph Stock
d Walter Forde *ph* Gunther Krampf

Conrad Veidt, Gordon Harker,
Esther Ralston, Joan Barry, Harold
Huth, Cedric Hardwicke, Donald
Calthrop, Hugh Williams, Finlay
Currie, Frank Vosper, Muriel Aked,
Eliot Makeham

'A first class craftsman's
job.'—*Basil Wright*

'Technically, and in a sense
intellectually speaking, this film puts
Forde into Class A1.'—*Cinema
Quarterly*

HARKER: 'Discretion is the better
part of Wagons Lits.'

† Remade 1948 as *Sleeping Car to
Trieste.*

La Ronde
France 1950 100m bw
Sacha Gordine
In 1900 Vienna, an elegant compère
shows that love is a merry-go-round:
prostitute meets soldier meets
housemaid meets master meets
married woman meets husband
meets midinette meets poet meets
actress meets officer meets prostitute
meets soldier . . .
Superb stylized comedy with a fine
cast, subtle jokes, rich decor and
fluent direction; not to mention a
haunting theme tune.

w Jacques Natanson, Max Ophuls, *novel* Arthur Schnitzler *d Max Ophuls ph* Christian Matras *m* Oscar Straus

Anton Walbrook, Simone Signoret, Serge Reggiani, Simone Simon, Daniel Gélin, Danielle Darrieux, Fernand Gravey, Odette Joyeux, Jean-Louis Barrault, Isa Miranda, Gérard Philippe

'One of the most civilized films to have come from Europe in a long time.'—*Gavin Lambert, MFB*

'A film that drags on and on by what seems like geometric progression.'—*John Simon, 1968*

AAN: script

Room at the Top
GB 1958   117m   bw
Remus (John and James Woolf)

An ambitious young clerk causes the death of his real love but manages to marry into a rich family.

Claimed as the first British film to take sex seriously, and the first to show the industrial north as it really was, this melodrama actually cheats on both counts but scene for scene is vivid and entertaining despite a weak central performance.

w Neil Paterson, *novel* John Braine *d* Jack Clayton *ph* Freddie Francis *m* Mario Nascimbene

Laurence Harvey, *Simone Signoret*, Heather Sears, Donald Wolfit, Ambrosine Philpotts, Donald Houston, Raymond Huntley, John Westbrook, Allan Cuthbertson, Hermione Baddeley, Mary Peach

'A drama of human drives and torments told with maturity and precision.'—*Stanley Kauffmann*

AA: Neil Paterson; Simone Signoret
AAN: best picture; Jack Clayton; Laurence Harvey; Hermione Baddeley

A Room with a View
GB 1985   115m   colour
Merchant Ivory / Goldcrest

An innocent Edwardian girl travelling in Italy has her eyes opened to real life and romance.

Competent, unexciting equivalent of a television classic mini-series which so perfectly filled a need as to become a runaway commercial success.

w Ruth Prawer Jhabvala *novel* E. M. Forster *d* James Ivory *ph* Tony Pierce-Roberts *m* Richard Robbins *pd* Gianna Quaranta, Brian Ackland-Snow *ed* Humphrey Dixon

Maggie Smith, Denholm Elliott, Helena Bonham Carter, Julian Sands, Daniel Day Lewis, Simon Callow, Judi Dench, Rosemary Leach, Rupert Graves

'Quality-starved filmgoers will welcome it.'—*Variety*

'Song by song . . . scene by scene
. . . the thrill grows greater!'
Rose of Washington Square
US 1939   86m   bw
TCF (Nunnally Johnson)

Tribulations of a Broadway singer in love with a worthless husband.

Revamping of the Fanny Brice story; smartly done, but the material interpolated for Jolson is what makes the film notable.

w Nunnally Johnson *d* Gregory Ratoff *ph* Karl Freund *m* Louis Silvers *songs* various

Alice Faye, Tyrone Power, *Al Jolson, Hobart Cavanaugh*, William Frawley, Joyce Compton, Louis Prima and his band

'This is Jolson's picture . . . the rest is also-ran.'—*Variety*

'Jolson's singing is something for the memory book.'—*New York Times*

† Fanny Brice sued TCF for 75,000 dollars for invasion of privacy; the defendants settled.

'The low down story of a high
class gal!'
Roxie Hart
US 1942   72m   bw
TCF (Nunnally Johnson)

A twenties showgirl confesses for the sake of publicity to a murder of which she is innocent.

Crowded Chicago burlesque which

now seems less funny than it did but is full of smart moments.

w Nunnally Johnson, play Chicago by Maurine Watkins *d William Wellman ph* Leon Shamroy *m* Alfred Newman

Ginger Rogers, George Montgomery, *Adolphe Menjou,* Lynne Overman, Nigel Bruce, Spring Byington, Sara Allgood, William Frawley

DEDICATION: To all the beautiful women in the world who have shot their husbands full of holes out of pique.

'A masterpiece of form, of ensemble acting, of powerhouse comedy and scripting.'—*NFT, 1974*

† The play was also filmed in 1927 under its original title, with Phyllis Haver.

'Five comedy stars in a five-star comedy!'
Ruggles of Red Gap
US 1935   90m   bw
Paramount (Arthur Hornblow Jnr)

A British butler has a startling effect on the family of an American rancher who takes him out west.
A famous comedy which seemed hilarious at the time but can now be seen as mostly composed of flat spots; the performances however are worth remembering.

w Walter de Leon, Harlan Thompson, Humphrey Pearson, *novel* Harry Leon Wilson *d* Leo McCarey *ph* Alfred Gilks

Charles Laughton, Mary Boland, Charles Ruggles, Zasu Pitts, Roland Young, Leila Hyams, James Burke, Maude Eburne, Lucien Littlefield

'Plenty of marquee strength, and dynamite on the inside. An A1 comedy.'—*Variety*
'A sane, witty, moving and quite

unusual picture of Anglo-American relations.'—*C. A. Lejeune*
'The most heart-warming comedy of the season . . . there is about it a sympathetic and even a patriotic quality which is touching.'—*Literary Digest*
'The archetypal film they don't make any more, partly because comedy has now grown too raucous to favour the quiet drollery of players like Charlie Ruggles and Mary Boland, partly because even McCarey himself had trouble after the thirties, separating sentiment from sentimentality.'—*Time Out, 1980*

† Remade as *Fancy Pants.*

AAN: best picture

Ryan's Daughter
GB 1970   206m
Metrocolor   Panavision 70
MGM / Faraway (Anthony Havelock-Allan)

1916 Ireland: a village schoolmaster's wife falls for a British officer.
A modestly effective pastoral romantic melodrama, stretched on the rack of its director's meticulous film-making technique and unnecessarily big budget. A beautiful, impressive, well-staged and well-acted film, but not really four hours' worth of drama.

w Robert Bolt *d David Lean ph Frederick A. Young m* Maurice Jarre *pd* Stephen Grimes (who created an entire village)

Sarah Miles, Robert Mitchum, Chris Jones, John Mills, Trevor Howard, Leo McKern

'Instead of looking like the money it cost to make, the film feels like the time it took to shoot.'—*Alexander Walker*
'Gush made respectable by millions of dollars tastefully wasted.'—*Pauline Kael*

AA: Frederick A. Young; John Mills
AAN: Sarah Miles

S

Sabotage
GB 1936 76m bw
Gaumont British (Michael Balcon, Ivor Montagu)
US title: *A Woman Alone*
The proprietor of a small London cinema is a dangerous foreign agent.
Unattractively plotted but fascinatingly detailed Hitchcock suspenser with famous sequences and a splendidly brooding melodramatic atmosphere.

w Charles Bennett, Ian Hay, Helen Simpson, E. V. H. Emmett, *novel* The Secret Agent by Joseph Conrad *d Alfred Hitchcock* *ph* Bernard Knowles *md* Louis Levy

Oscar Homolka, Sylvia Sidney, John Loder, Desmond Tester, Joyce Barbour, Matthew Boulton

'Tightly packed, economical, full of invention and detail.'—*NFT, 1961*

Saboteur
US 1942 108m bw
Universal (Frank Lloyd, Jack H. Skirball)
A war worker unjustly suspected of sabotage flees across the country and unmasks a spy ring.
Flawed Hitchcock action thriller, generally unsatisfactory in plot and pace but with splendid sequences at a ball, in Radio City Music Hall, and atop the Statue of Liberty.

w Peter Viertel, Joan Harrison, Dorothy Parker, *story* Alfred Hitchcock *d Alfred Hitchcock* *ph* Joseph Valentine *m* Frank Skinner *md* Charles Previn

Robert Cummings, Priscilla Lane, Otto Kruger, Alan Baxter, Alma Kruger, *Norman Lloyd*

'It throws itself forward so rapidly that it allows slight opportunity for looking back.'—*New York Times*
'The drama of a nation stirred to action, of a people's growing realization of themselves and their responsibilities.'—*Motion Picture Herald*

† Hitchcock wanted for the three leading roles Gary Cooper, Barbara Stanwyck and Harry Carey, but all refused or were unavailable.

Safety Last
US 1923 70m (24 fps) bw silent
Harold Lloyd
A small-town boy goes to the big city and to impress his girl friend enters a contest to climb a skyscraper.
Marvellous star comedy which set a new standard not only in sight gags but in the comedy-thrill stunts which become Lloyd's stock-in-trade.

w Harold Lloyd, Sam Taylor, Tim Whelan, Hal Roach *d* Sam Taylor, Fred Newmeyer *ph* Walter Lundin

Harold Lloyd, Mildred Davis, Noah Young

'She fell in love with the toughest guy on the toughest street in the world!'

San Francisco
US 1936 117m bw
MGM (John Emerson, Bernard Hyman)
The loves and career problems of a Barbary Coast saloon proprietor climax in the 1906 earthquake.
Incisive, star-packed, superbly-handled melodrama which weaves in every kind of appeal and for a finale has some of the best special effects ever conceived.

w Anita Loos, *story* Robert Hopkins *d* W. S. Van Dyke *ph* Oliver T. Marsh *m* Edward Ward *md* Herbert Stothart *montage* John Hoffman *title song* Bronislau Kaper

Clark Gable, Spencer Tracy, Jeanette MacDonald, Jack Holt, Jessie Ralph,

Ted Healy, Shirley Ross, Al Shean, Harold Huber

'Prodigally generous and completely satisfying.'—*Frank S. Nugent*

AAN: best picture; Robert Hopkins; W. S. Van Dyke; Spencer Tracy

'My name is Stryker. Sgt John M. Stryker. You're gonna be my squad!'
Sands of Iwo Jima
US 1949 109m bw
Republic (Edmund Grainger)
During World War II in the Pacific, a tough sergeant of marines moulds raw recruits into fighting men but is himself shot by a sniper.
Celebrated star war comic, still quite hypnotic in its flagwaving way.

w Harry Brown, James Edward Grant *d* Allan Dwan *ph* Reggie Lanning *m* Victor Young

John Wayne, John Agar, Adele Mara, Forest Tucker, Arthur Franz, Julie Bishop, Richard Jaeckel

'The battle sequences are terrifyingly real . . . but the personal dramatics make up a compendium of war-picture clichés.'—*Variety*

'Say what you like about the sentimental flavour of war pictures such as this, there's no denying they keep you in your seat.'—*Richard Mallett, Punch*

AAN: Harry Brown (original story); John Wayne

Saturday Night and Sunday Morning
GB 1960 89m bw
Bryanston/Woodfall (Harry Salzman, Tony Richardson)
A Nottingham factory worker is dissatisfied with his lot, gets into trouble through an affair with a married woman, but finally settles for convention.
Startling when it emerged, this raw working-class melodrama, with its sharp detail and strong comedy asides, delighted the mass audience chiefly because of its strong central character thumbing his nose at

authority. Matching the mood of the times, and displaying a new attitude to sex, it transformed British cinema and was much imitated.

w Alan Sillitoe, from his novel *d* Karel Reisz *ph* Freddie Francis *m* Johnny Dankworth

Albert Finney, Shirley Anne Field, *Rachel Roberts*, Bryan Pringle, Norman Rossington, Hylda Baker

'Here is a chance for our own new wave.'—*Evening Standard*

† Warwickshire never showed the film because the producers refused to delete two love scenes. David Kingsley of British Lion said: 'We are not prepared to agree that a film of outstanding importance and merit should be re-edited by the Mrs Grundys of the Warwickshire County Council. It is fortunate for the world that Warwickshire's greatest and often bawdy son, William Shakespeare, was not subject in his day to the restrictions of prim and petty officialdom.'

Saturday Night Fever
US 1978 119m Movielab Paramount/Robert Stigwood (Milt Felsen)
Italian roughnecks in Brooklyn live for their Saturday night disco dancing, and one of them falls in love with a girl who makes him realize there are better things in life.
Foul-mouthed, fast-paced slice of life which plays like an updated version of *Marty* except that all the characters seem to have crawled from under stones. The slick direction, fast editing and exciting dance numbers do something to take away the sour taste.

w Norman Wexler, *story* Nik Cohn *d* John Badham *ph* Ralf D. Bode *songs* Barry, Robin and Maurice Gibb (and others), performed by the Bee Gees *ed* David Rawlins *pd* Charles Bailey

John Travolta, Karen Lynn Gorney, Barry Miller, Joseph Cali, Paul Pape, Bruce Ornstein

'A stylish piece of contemporary

anthropology, an urban safari into darkest America, a field study of the mystery cults among the young braves and squaws growing up in North Brooklyn.'—*Alan Brien, Sunday Times*

AAN: John Travolta

'I am not allowed to love. But I will love you if that is your desire!'

Sayonara

US 1957 147m
Technirama
Goetz Pictures-Pennebaker
(William Goetz)

An American air force major in Tokyo after the war falls in love with a Japanese actress.

A lush travelogue interrupted by two romances, one tragic and one happy. A great success at the time, though mainly of interest to Americans; now vaguely dated.

w Paul Osborn, *novel* James A. Michener *d* Joshua Logan *ph* Ellsworth Fredericks *m* Franz Waxman *ad* Ted Haworth

Marlon Brando, Miyoshi Umeki, Miiko Taka, Red Buttons, Ricardo Montalban, Patricia Owens, Kent Smith, Martha Scott, James Garner

AA: Miyoshi Umeki; Red Buttons
AAN: best picture; Paul Osborn; Joshua Logan; Ellsworth Fredericks; Marlon Brando

---

Scaramouche

US 1952 115m
Technicolor
MGM (Carey Wilson)

A young man disguises himself as an actor to avenge the death of his friend at the hands of a wicked marquis.

Cheerful swashbuckler set in French revolutionary times, first filmed in the twenties with Ramon Novarro. MGM costume production at somewhere near its best.

w Ronald Millar, George Froeschel, *novel* Rafael Sabatini *d* George Sidney *ph* Charles Rosher *m* Victor Young *ad* Cedric Gibbons, Hans Peters

Stewart Granger, Mel Ferrer, Eleanor Parker, Janet Leigh, Henry Wilcoxon, Nina Foch, Lewis Stone, Robert Coote, Richard Anderson

† The sword fight, at 6½ minutes, is credited with being the longest in cinema history.

'I'm going to run the whole works. There's only one law: do it first, do it yourself, and keep doing it!'

Scarface

US 1932 99m bw
Howard Hughes
aka: *The Shame of a Nation*

The life and death of a Chicago gangster of the twenties.

Obviously modelled on Al Capone, with an incestuous sister thrown in, this was perhaps the most vivid film of the gangster cycle, and its revelling in its own sins was not obscured by the subtitle, *The Shame of a Nation*.

w Ben Hecht, Seton I. Miller, John Lee Mahin, W. R. Burnett, Fred Pasley, *novel* Armitage Trail
d Howard Hawks *ph* Lee Garmes, L. W. O'Connell *m* Adolph Tandler, Gus Arnheim

Paul Muni, Ann Dvorak, George Raft, Boris Karloff, Osgood Perkins, Karen Morley, C. Henry Gordon, Vince Barnett, Henry Armetta, Edwin Maxwell.

'Presumably the last of the gangster films, on a promise, it is going to make people sorry that there won't be any more. Should draw wherever it can play.'—*Variety*

'More brutal, more cruel, more wholesale than any of its predecessors.'—*James Shelley Hamilton*

'Because it was so close to the actual events, it possesses a kind of newsreel quality which cannot be recaptured or imitated. It vibrates with the impact of things that were real and deeply felt.'—*National Film Theatre programme, 1961*

† On original release added scenes showed Tony tried, convicted and hanged, though since Muni is never seen, it appears that they were an

afterthought made when he was not
available.

The Scarlet Claw
US 1944 74m bw
Universal (Roy William Neill)

Grisly revenge murders take place in
the fog-bound Canadian village of
Le Mort Rouge.

Possibly the best of the modernized
Sherlock Holmes series, with a plot
hastily borrowed from *The Hound of
the Baskervilles*.

w Edmund L. Hartmann, Roy
William Neill d Roy William Neill
ph George Robinson md Paul
Sawtell

Basil Rathbone, Nigel Bruce, Miles
Mander, Gerald Hamer, Paul
Cavanagh, Kay Harding, Arthur
Hohl

> Based on a private diary of
> Catherine the Great!'
> 'The screen's reigning beauty in a
> wild pageant of barbaric
> splendour!'

The Scarlet Empress
US 1934 109m bw
Paramount

A fantasia on the love life of
Catherine the Great.

A marvellous, overwhelming,
dramatically insubstantial but
pictorially brilliant homage to a star;
not to everyone's taste, but a film to
remember.

w Manuel Komroff d Josef Von
Sternberg ph Bert Glennon md W.
Franke Harling, John M. Leipold,
Milan Roder ad Hans Dreier, Peter
Balbusch, Richard Kollorsz
costumes Travis Banton

Marlene Dietrich, John Lodge, Sam
Jaffe, Louise Dresser, C. Aubrey
Smith, Gavin Gordon, Jameson
Thomas

> 'She's photographed behind veils
> and fishnets, while dwarfs slither
> about and bells ring and everybody
> tries to look degenerate.'—*New
> Yorker, 1975*
> 'A ponderous, strangely beautiful,
> lengthy and frequently wearying
> production.'—*Mordaunt Hall, New
> York Times*

The Scarlet Pimpernel
GB 1934 98m bw
London Films (Alexander
Korda)

In the early days of the French
revolution, an apparently foppish
Englishman leads a daring band in
rescuing aristocrats from the
guillotine.

First-class period adventure with a
splendid and much imitated plot,
strong characters, humour and a
richly detailed historical background.

w Robert E. Sherwood, Sam
Berman, Arthur Wimperis, Lajos
Biro, novel Baroness Orczy
d Harold Young ph Harold Rosson
m Arthur Benjamin

Leslie Howard, Merle Oberon,
Raymond Massey, Nigel Bruce,
Bramwell Fletcher, Anthony
Bushell, Joan Gardner, Walter Rilla

> 'Excellent British import that will
> do business.'—*Variety*
> 'One of the most romantic and
> durable of all swashbucklers.'—*New
> Yorker, 1976*
> 'A triumph for the British film
> world.'—*Sunday Times*

† The story was remade as *The
Elusive Pimpernel* and in 1982 in a
TV version starring Anthony
Andrews. See also *The Return of the
Scarlet Pimpernel*.

> 'I've been wanting to laugh in
> your face ever since I met you.
> You're old and ugly and I'm sick
> of you—sick, sick, sick!'

Scarlet Street
US 1945 103m bw
(Universal) Walter Wanger
(Fritz Lang)

A prostitute is murdered by her
client and her pimp is executed for
the crime.

Daring but rather gloomy
Hollywood melodrama, the first in
which a crime went unpunished
(though the culprit was shown
suffering remorse). Interesting and
heavily Teutonic, but as
entertainment not a patch on the
similar but lighter *The Woman in the
Window*, which the same team had
made a year previously.

w Dudley Nichols, *play* La Chienne by George de La fouchardière (filmed by Jean Renoir in 1932) *d* Fritz Lang *ph* Milton Krasner *m* Hans Salter *ad* Alexander Golitzen

Edward G. Robinson, Joan Bennett, Dan Duryea, Jess Barker, Margaret Lindsay, Rosalind Ivan, Samuel S. Hinds, Arthur Loft

'The director unerringly chooses the right sound and image to assault the spectator's sensibilities.'—*C. A. Lejeune*

Scott of the Antarctic
GB 1948   111m
Technicolor
Ealing (Sidney Cole)

After long preparation, Captain Scott sets off on his ill-fated 1912 expedition to the South Pole.

The stiff-upper-lip saga par excellence; inevitable knowledge of the end makes it pretty downbeat, and the actors can only be sincere; but the snowscapes, most of them artificial, are fine.

w Ivor Montagu, Walter Meade, Mary Hayley Bell *d* Charles Frend *ph* Geoffrey Unsworth, Jack Cardiff, Osmond Borradaile *m* Ralph Vaughan Williams

John Mills, James Robertson Justice, Derek Bond, Harold Warrender, Reginald Beckwith, Kenneth More, James McKechnie, John Gregson

The Scoundrel
US 1935   74m   bw
Paramount (Ben Hecht, Charles MacArthur)

A famous writer dies; his ghost comes back to find the meaning of love.

Unique thirties supernatural melodrama with barbs of dated wit despatched by a splendid cast. Nonsense, but great nonsense.

wd Ben Hecht, Charles MacArthur *ph* Lee Garmes *m* George Antheil

Noel Coward, *Alexander Woolcott*, Julie Haydon, Stanley Ridges, Eduardo Ciannelli

'Good Hotel Algonquin literati stuff, but not for the Automat trade.'—*Variety*

'An unmistakable whiff from a gossip column world which tries hard to split the difference between an epigram and a wisecrack.'—*William Whitebait*

'Practically flawless drama. It's arty, but if this is art, let us have more of it.'—*Photoplay*

'An impudent work . . . but there are brains in it, and observation, and even a kind of stunted poetry.'—*Observer*

† Helen Hayes and Edna Ferber made cameo appearances.

AA: original story
AAN: script

The Sea Hawk
US 1940   122m   bw
Warner (Hal B. Wallis, Henry Blanke)

Elizabeth I encourages one of her most able captains to acts of piracy against the Spanish.

Wobbly-plotted but stirring and exciting seafaring actioner, with splendid battle and duel scenes.

w Seton I. Miller, Howard Koch *d* Michael Curtiz *ph* Sol Polito *m* Erich Wolfgang Korngold *ad* Anton Grot

Errol Flynn, Flora Robson, Brenda Marshall, *Henry Daniell*, Claude Rains, Donald Crisp, Alan Hale, Una O'Connor, James Stephenson, Gilbert Roland, William Lundigan

'Endless episodes of court intrigue tend to diminish the effect of the epic sweep of the high seas dramatics.'—*Variety*

AAN: Erich Wolfgang Korngold

The Sea Wolf
US 1941   90m   bw
Warner (Henry Blanke)

Survivors of a ferry crash in San Francisco Bay are picked up by a psychopathic freighter captain who keeps them captive.

Much filmed action suspenser which in this version looks great but overdoes the talk.

w Robert Rossen, *novel* Jack London *d* Michael Curtiz *ph* Sol Polito *m* Erich Wolfgang Korngold

Edward G. Robinson, Alexander Knox, Ida Lupino, John Garfield, Gene Lockhart, Barry Fitzgerald, Stanley Ridges, David Bruce, Howard da Silva

'A Germanic, powerful work almost devoid of compromise.'—*Charles Higham, 1972*

† Other versions appeared in 1913, with Hobart Bosworth; in 1920, with Noah Beery; in 1925, with Ralph Ince; in 1930, with Milton Sills; in 1950 (as *Barricade*, turned into a western) with Raymond Massey; in 1958 (as *Wolf Larsen*), with Barry Sullivan; and in 1975 (Italian), as *Wolf of the Seven Seas*, with Chuck Connors.

The Searchers
US 1956   119m
Technicolor   Vistavision
Warner / C. V. Whitney (Merian C. Cooper)

A Confederate war veteran tracks down the Indians who have slaughtered his brother and sister-in-law and carried off their daughter.

Desultory, easy-going, good-looking western in typical Ford style; a bit more solemn than usual.

w Frank S. Nugent, *novel* Alan le May *d* John Ford *ph* Winton C. Hoch *m* Max Steiner

John Wayne, Jeffrey Hunter, Natalie Wood, Vera Miles, Ward Bond, John Qualen, Henry Brandon, Antonio Moreno

'You can read a lot into it, but it isn't very enjoyable.'—*Pauline Kael 70s*

The Secret Life of Walter Mitty
US 1947   110m
Technicolor
Samuel Goldwyn

A mother's boy dreams of derring-do, and eventually life catches up with fiction.

This pleasantly remembered star comedy, though it never had much to do with Thurber, can now be seen to have missed most of its opportunities, though the nice moments do tend to compensate

w Ken Englund, Everett Freeman, *story* James Thurber *d* Norman Z. McLeod *ph* Lee Garmes *m* David Raksin

Danny Kaye, Virginia Mayo, Boris Karloff, Florence Bates, Fay Bainter, Thurston Hall, Ann Rutherford, Gordon Jones, Reginald Denny

Sergeant York
US 1941   134m   bw
Warner (Jesse L. Lasky)

The story of a gentle hillbilly farmer who became a hero of World War I. Standard real-life fiction given the big treatment; a key Hollywood film of its time in several ways.

w Aben Finkel, Harry Chandler, Howard Koch, John Huston *d* Howard Hawks *ph* Arthur Edeson *m* Max Steiner

Gary Cooper, Joan Leslie, Walter Brennan, George Tobias, David Bruce, Stanley Ridges, Margaret Wycherly, Dickie Moore, Ward Bond

'I hardly think the effect is any different from that of a parade, with colours and a band; it is stirring and it is too long; there are too many holdups and too many people out of step, and your residue of opinion on the matter is that it will be nice to get home and get your shoes off.'—*Otis Ferguson*

'It has all the flavour of true Americana, the blunt and homely humour of backwoodsmen and the raw integrity peculiar to simple folk.'—*Bosley Crowther, New York Times*

AA: Gary Cooper
AAN: best picture; script; Howard Hawks; Sol Polito; Max Steiner; Walter Brennan; Margaret Wycherly

The Servant
GB 1963   116m   bw
Elstree / Springbok (Joseph Losey, Norman Priggen)

A rich, ineffectual young man is gradually debased and overruled by his sinister manservant and his sexy 'sister'.

Acclaimed in many quarters on its first release, this downbeat melodrama now seems rather naïve and long drawn out; its surface gloss is undeniable, but the final orgy is more risible than satanic.

w Harold Pinter, *novel* Robin Maugham *d* Joseph Losey *ph* Douglas Slocombe *m* Johnny Dankworth

Dirk Bogarde, *James Fox*, *Sarah Miles*, Wendy Craig, Catherine Lacey, Richard Vernon

'Moodily suggestive, well acted, but petering out into a trickle of repetitious unmeaningful nastiness.'—*John Simon*

The Set Up
US 1949 72m bw
RKO (Richard Goldstone)

An ageing boxer refuses to pull his last fight, and is beaten up by gangsters.

One of the most brilliant little *film noirs* of the late forties; thoroughly studio-bound, yet evoking a brilliant feeling for time and place. Photography, direction, editing, acting are all of a piece

w Art Cohn, *poem* Joseph Moncure March *d* Robert Wise *ph* Milton Krasner *md* Constantin Bakaleinikoff

Robert Ryan, Audrey Totter, George Tobias, Alan Baxter, Wallace Ford

'I now pronounce you—men and wives!'

Seven Brides for Seven Brothers
US 1954 104m Anscocolor Cinemascope
MGM (Jack Cummings)

In the old west, seven hard-working brothers decide they need wives, and carry off young women from the villages around.

Disappointingly studio-bound western musical, distinguished by an excellent score and some brilliant

dancing, notably the barn-raising sequence.

w Frances Goodrich, Albert Hackett, *story* Sobbin' Women by Stephen Vincent Benet *d* Stanley Donen *ph* George Folsey *ch* Michael Kidd *songs* Johnny Mercer, Gene de Paul *m* Adolph Deutsch, Saul Chaplin

Howard Keel, *Jane Powell*, *Jeff Richards*, *Russ Tamblyn*, *Tommy Rall*, *Howard Petrie*, *Marc Platt*, *Jacques d'Amboise*, *Matt Mattox*

AA: Adolph Deutsch, Saul Chaplin
AAN: best picture; script; George Folsey

Seven Days in May
US 1964 120m bw
Seven Arts / Joel / John Frankenheimer (Edward Lewis)

An American general's aide discovers that his boss intends a military takeover because he considers the President's pacifism traitorous. Absorbing political mystery drama marred only by the unnecessary introduction of a female character. Stimulating entertainment.

w Rod Sterling, *novel* Fletcher Knebel, Charles W. Bailey II *d* John Frankenheimer *ph* Ellsworth Fredericks *m* Jerry Goldsmith

Kirk Douglas, Burt Lancaster, Fredric March, Ava Gardner, Martin Balsam, *Edmond O'Brien*, George Macready, John Houseman

'A political thriller which grips from start to finish.'—*Penelope Houston*

'In the best tradition of the suspense thriller, with the ultimate thrill our awareness of its actual potential.'—*Judith Crist*

AAN: Edmond O'Brien

Seven Days to Noon
GB 1950 94m bw
London Films (The Boulting Brothers)

A professor engaged on atomic research threatens to blow up London unless his work is brought to an end.

Persuasively understated suspense

piece which was subsequently much copied, so that it now seems rather obvious.

w Frank Harvey, Roy Boulting, Paul Dehn, James Bernard d John Boulting ph Gilbert Taylor m John Addison

Barry Jones, Olive Sloane, André Morell, Joan Hickson, Sheila Manahan, Hugh Cross, Ronald Adam, Marie Ney

'A first rate thriller that does not pretend to a serious message, but yet will leave a query in the mind.'—*Richard Winnington*

'A film of great tension and excitement with a climax that is reached after breathless suspense.'—*Star*

AA: script

Seven Samurai

Japan 1954   155m   bw
Toho (Shojiro Motoki)
original title: *Shichi-nin no Samurai*

16th-century villagers hire samurai to defend their property against an annual raid by bandits.
Superbly strange, vivid and violent medieval adventure which later served as the basis for the western *The Magnificent Seven*.

w Akira Kurosawa, Shinobu Hashimoto, Hideo Oguni d Akira Kurosawa ph Asaichi Nakai m Fumio Hayasaka

Toshiro Mifune, Takashi Shimura, Kuninori Kodo

'It is as sheer narrative, rich in imagery, incisiveness and sharp observation, that it makes its strongest impact . . . It provides a fascinating display of talent, and places its director in the forefront of creative film-makers of his generation.'—*Gavin Lambert, Sight and Sound*

'This, on the surface, is a work of relentless, unmitigated action, as epic as any film ever made, and, again on the surface, sheer entertainment. Yet it is also an unquestionable triumph of art.'—*John Simon*

The Seventh Cross

US 1944   112m   bw
MGM (Pandro S. Berman)
Seven Germans escape from a concentration camp, and the Nazis threaten to execute them all. Just one escapes.
Impressive melodrama, brilliantly limiting its escape/suspense story to studio sets. Old-style Hollywood production at its best; but a rather obviously contrived story.

w Helen Deutsch, novel Anna Seghers d Fred Zinnemann ph Karl Freund m Roy Webb ad Cedric Gibbons, Leonid Vasian

Spencer Tracy, Signe Hasso, Hume Cronyn, Jessica Tandy, Agnes Moorehead, Felix Bressart, George Macready, George Zucco

AAN: Hume Cronyn

The Seventh Seal

Sweden 1957   95m   bw
Svensk Filmindustri (Allan Ekelund)
original title: *Det Sjunde Inseglet*
Death comes for a knight, who challenges him to a game of chess while he tries to show illustrations of goodness in mankind: but Death takes them all away in the end.
A modestly budgeted minor classic which, because of its international success and its famous shots, is seldom analysed in detail. In fact its storyline is meandering and apparently pointless, and it is kept going by its splendid cinematic feel and its atmosphere is that of a dark world irrationally sustained by religion.

wd Ingmar Bergman ph Gunnar Fischer m Erik Nordgren

Max Von Sydow, Bengt Ekerot, Gunnar Bjornstrand, Nils Poppe, Bibi Andersson, Gunnel Lindblom

'The most extraordinary mixture of beauty and lust and cruelty, Odin-worship and Christian faith, darkness and light.'—*Alan Dent, Illustrated London News*

The Seventh Veil

GB 1945   94m   bw
Theatrecraft / Sydney
Box / Ortus

A concert pianist is romantically torn
between her psychiatrist, her
guardian, and two other fellows.

A splendid modern melodrama in
the tradition of *Jane Eyre* and
Rebecca; it set the seal of
moviegoing approval on psychiatry,
classical music, and James Mason,
and it is the most utter tosh.

*w Muriel and Sydney Box
d Compton Bennett ph Reg Wyer
m Benjamin Frankel*

*James Mason, Ann Todd, Herbert
Lom*, Albert Lieven, Hugh
McDermott, Yvonne Owen, David
Horne, Manning Whiley

'An example of the intelligent,
medium-priced picture made with
great technical polish which has
represented for Hollywood the
middle path between the vulgar and
the highbrow,'—*Spectator*

'A popular film that does not
discard taste and
atmosphere.'—*Daily Mail*

'A rich, portentous mixture of
Beethoven, Chopin, Kitsch and
Freud.'—*Pauline Kael, 1968*

'An odd, artificial, best sellerish
kind of story, with reminiscences of
Trilby and *Jane Eyre* and all their
imitations down to
Rebecca.'—*Richard Mallett, Punch*

'Maybe, with a few veils stripped
away, all of us have a fantasist inside
who gobbles up this sadomasochistic
sundae.'—*Pauline Kael, 70s*

AA: script

Shadow of a Doubt

US 1943   108m   bw
Universal (Jack H. Skirball)

A favourite uncle comes to visit his
family in a small Californian town.
He is actually on the run from
police, who know him as the Merry
Widow murderer.

Hitchcock's quietest film is
memorable chiefly for its depiction
of small-town life; but the script is
well written and keeps the suspense
moving slowly but surely.

*w Thornton Wilder, Sally Benson,
Alma Reville, story* Gordon
McDonell *d Alfred Hitchcock
ph* Joe Valentine *m* Dmitri Tiomkin

Joseph Cotten, Teresa Wright,
Hume Cronyn, Macdonald Carey,
Patricia Collinge, Henry Travers,
Wallace Ford

'Some clever observation of
rabbity white-collar life which, in
spite of a specious sweetness, is the
best since *It's a Gift*.'—*James Agee*

† Remade in 1959 as *Step Down to
Terror*, with Charles Drake.

AAN: original story

Shane

US 1953   118m
Technicolor
Paramount (George Stevens, Ivan
Moffat)

A mysterious stranger helps a family
of homesteaders.

Archetypal family western, but much
slower and statelier than most, as
though to emphasize its own quality,
which is evident anyway.

w A. B. Guthrie Jnr, novel Jack
Schaefer *d George Stevens
ph* Loyal Griggs *m* Victor Young

Alan Ladd, Jean Arthur, Van
Heflin, *Jack Palance*, Brandon de
Wilde, Ben Johnson, Edgar
Buchanan, Emile Meyer, Elisha
Cook Jnr, John Dierkes

'A kind of dramatic documentary
of the pioneer days of the
west.'—*MFB*

'Westerns are better when they're
not too self-importantly
self-conscious.'—*New Yorker, 1975*

'Stevens managed to infuse a new
vitality, a new sense of realism into
the time-worn story through the
strength and freshness of his
visuals.'—Arthur Knight

AA: Loyal Griggs
AAN: best picture; A. B. Guthrie
Jnr; George Stevens; Jack Palance;
Brandon de Wilde

Shanghai Express

US 1932   84m   bw
Paramount

A British officer and his old flame meet on a train which is waylaid by Chinese bandits.

Superbly pictorial melodrama which set the pattern for innumerable train movies to come, though none matched its deft visual quality and few sketched in their characters so neatly. Plot and dialogue are silent style, but refreshingly so.

w Jules Furthman *d* Josef Von Sternberg *ph* Lee Garmes *m* W. Franke Harling *ad* Hans Dreier

Marlene Dietrich, Clive Brook, Warner Oland, Anna May Wong, Eugene Pallette, Lawrence Grant, Louise Closser Hale, Gustav Von Seyffertitz

LILY (Marlene Dietrich): 'It took more than one man to change my name to Shanghai Lily.'

'Good programme picture bolstered by the Dietrich name . . . Excellent camerawork overcomes really hoke melodramatic story.'—*Variety*

'A limited numbers of characters, all meticulously etched, highly atmospheric sets and innumerable striking photographic compositions.'—*Curtis Harrington, 1964*

AA: Lee Garmes
AAN: best picture; Josef Von Sternberg

She Done Him Wrong

US 1933   68m   bw
Paramount (William le Baron)
A lady saloon keeper of the Gay Nineties falls for the undercover cop who is after her.

As near undiluted Mae West as Hollywood ever came: fast, funny, melodramatic and pretty sexy; also a very atmospheric and well-made movie.

w Mae West, from her play Diamond Lil (with help on the scenario from Harry Thew, John Bright) *d* Lowell Sherman *ph* Charles Lang *songs* Ralph Rainger

Mae West, Cary Grant, Owen Moore, Gilbert Roland, Noah Beery, David Landau, Rafaela Ottiano, Rochelle Hudson, Dewey Robinson

'Only alternative to a strong drawing cast nowadays, if a picture wants business, is strong entertainment. This one has neither.'—*Variety*

AAN: best picture

She Wore a Yellow Ribbon

US 1949   103m
Technicolor
RKO / Argosy (John Ford, Merian C. Cooper)
Problems of a cavalry officer about to retire.

Fragmentary but very enjoyable western with all Ford ingredients served piping hot.

w Frank Nugent, Laurence Stallings, *story* James Warner Bellah *d* John Ford *ph* Winton C. Hoch *m* Richard Hageman

John Wayne, Joanne Dru, John Agar, Ben Johnson, Harry Carey Jnr, Victor McLaglen, Mildred Natwick, George O'Brien, Arthur Shields

AA: Winton C. Hoch

The Sheik

US 1921   73m (24 fps)
bw   silent
Famous Players-Lasky / George Melford
An English heiress falls for a desert chieftain.

Archetypal romantic tosh which set the seal on Valentino's superstardom

w Monte M. Katterjohn, *novel* E. M. Hull *d* George Melford *ph* William Marshall

Rudolph Valentino, Agnes Ayres, Adolphe Menjou, Walter Long, Lucien Littlefield

'A photoplay of tempestuous love between a madcap English beauty and a bronzed Arab chief!'—*publicity*

† *Son of the Sheik*, released in 1926, was even more popular.

Ship of Fools
✤✤ US 1965   150m   bw
✗ Columbia/Stanley Kramer
In 1933 a German liner leaves Vera
Cruz for Bremerhaven with a mixed
bag of passengers.
Ambitious, serious, quite fascinating
slice-of-life shipboard
multi-melodrama. Capable
mounting, memorable performances
and a bravura finale erase memories
of padding and symbolic pretensions

w *Abby Mann, novel* Katherine
Anne Porter *d Stanley Kramer*
ph Ernest Laszlo m Ernest Gold

*Vivien Leigh, Simone Signoret,
Oskar Werner, Heinz Ruhmann,*
Jose Ferrer, Lee Marvin, Elizabeth
Ashley, *Michael Dunn*, George
Segal, Jose Greco, Charles Korvin,
Alf Kjellin, Werner Klemperer,
John Wengraf, Lilia Skala, Karen
Verne

GLOCKEN (Michael Dunn): 'My
name is Karl Glocken, and this is a
ship of fools. I'm a fool. You'll meet
more fools as we go along. This tub
is packed with them. Emancipated
ladies and ballplayers. Lovers. Dog
lovers. Ladies of joy. Tolerant Jews,
Dwarfs. All kinds. And who
knows—if you look closely enough,
you may even find yourself on
board!'

'When you're not being hit over
the head with the symbolism, you're
being punched in the stomach by
would-be inventive camera work
while the music score unremittingly
fills your nostrils with acrid
exhalations.'—*John Simon*

'There is such wealth of reflection
upon the human condition, so subtle
an orchestration of the elements of
love and hate, that it is not fair to
tag this with the label of any other
film.'—*New York Times*

AA: Ernest Laszlo
AAN: best picture; Abby Mann;
Simone Signoret; Oskar Werner;
Michael Dunn

The Shoes of the Fisherman
✤✤ US 1968   157m
✗ Metrocolor   Panavision
MGM (George Englund)
After twenty years as a political
prisoner, a Russian bishop becomes
Pope.
Predigested but heavy-going
picturization of a bestseller; big
budget, big stars, big hopes. In fact a
commercial dud, with plenty of
superficial interest but more
dramatic contrivance than religious
feeling.

w John Patrick, James Kennaway,
novel Morris West *d Michael
Anderson ph Erwin Hiller m* Alex
North *ad Edward Carfagno, George
W. Davis*

Anthony Quinn, David Janssen,
Laurence Olivier, Oskar Werner,
John Gielgud, Barbara Jefford, Leo
McKern, Vittorio de Sica, Clive
Revill, Paul Rogers

'A splendidly decorated curate's
egg'—*MFB*

AAN: Alex North

The Shop around the Corner
♉ US 1940   97m   bw
MGM (Ernst Lubitsch)
In a Budapest shop, the new
floorwalker and a girl who dislikes
him find they are pen pals.
Pleasant period romantic comedy
which holds no surprises but is
presented with great style.

w *Samson Raphaelson,
play* Nikolaus Laszlo *d Ernst
Lubitsch ph* William Daniels
m Werner Heymann

James Stewart, Margaret Sullavan,
Frank Morgan, Joseph Schildkraut,
Sara Haden, *Felix Bressart*, William
Tracy

'It's not pretentious but it's a
beautiful job of picture-making, and
the people who did it seem to have
enjoyed doing it just as much as their
audiences will enjoy seeing
it.'—*James Shelley Hamilton*

'An agreeably bittersweet example
of light entertainment.'—*Charles
Higham, 1972*

'One of the most beautifully acted
and paced romantic comedies ever

made in this country.'—*New Yorker*, 1978

† Remade as *In The Good Old Summertime*.

Show Business

US 1944 92m bw
RKO (Eddie Cantor)

The careers of four friends in vaudeville.

Lively low-budget period musical which probably presents the best picture of what old-time vaudeville was really like; a lot of fun when the plot doesn't get in the way.

w Joseph Quillan, Dorothy Bennett *d* Edwin L. Marin *ph* Robert de Grasse, Vernon L. Walker *m* George Duning *md* Constantin Bakaleinikoff *ch* Nick Castle

Eddie Cantor, Joan Davis, George Murphy, Constance Moore, Don Douglas, Nancy Kelly

'Bits of archaic vaudeville which give off a moderately pleasant smell of peanuts and cigar smoke.'—*James Agee*

Showboat

US 1936 110m bw
Universal (Carl Laemmle Jnr)

Lives and loves of the personnel on an old-time Mississippi showboat. Great style and excellent performances but there are longueurs in the middle.

w Oscar Hammerstein II, from his book for the Broadway musical from Edna Ferber's novel *d* James Whale *ph* John Mescall *m* Jerome Kern *ly* Oscar Hammerstein II

Irene Dunne, Allan Jones, Helen Morgan, Paul Robeson, Charles Winninger, Hattie McDaniel, Donald Cook, Sammy White

'For three quarters of its length good entertainment; sentimental, literary, but oddly appealing.'—*Graham Greene*

'A picture which will proudly lead all the entertainments the world has ever seen!'

The Sign of the Cross

US 1932 123m bw
Paramount (Cecil B. de Mille)

In the days of Nero, a Roman officer is converted to Christianity.

A heavily theatrical play becomes one of de Mille's most impressive films, the genuine horror of the arena mingling with the debauched humour of the court. A wartime prologue added in 1943 prolongs the film without improving it.

w Waldemar Young, Sidney Buchman, *play* Wilson Barrett *d* Cecil B. de Mille *ph* Karl Struss *m* Rudolph Kopp

Fredric March, Elissa Landi, *Charles Laughton, Claudette Colbert*, Ian Keith, Harry Beresford, Arthur Hohl, Nat Pendleton

'A beautiful film to watch . . . a triumph of popular art.'—*Charles Higham, 1972*

'However contemptible one may find de Mille's moralizing it is impossible not to be impressed by *The Sign of the Cross*.'—*John Baxter, 1968*

'De Mille's bang-them-on-the-head-with-wild-orgies-and-imperilled-virginity style is at its ripest.'—*New Yorker, 1976*

'Preposterous, but the laughter dies on the lips.'—*NFT, 1974*

'This slice of "history" has it all: Laughton's implicitly gay Nero fiddling away while an impressive miniature set burns, Colbert bathing up to her nipples in asses' milk, Christians and other unfortunates thrown to a fearsome menagerie, much suggestive slinking about in Mitchell Leisen's costumes, much general debauchery teetering between the sadistic and the erotic. Not for people with scruples.'—*Geoff Brown, Time Out, 1980*

AAN: Karl Struss

Since You Went Away

US 1944 172m bw
David O. Selznick

When hubby is away at the war, his wife and family adopt stiff upper lips.

Elaborate flagwaving investigation of the well-heeled American home front in World War II, with everyone brimming with goodwill and not a dry eye in the place. Absolutely superbly done, if it must be done at all, and a symposium of Hollywood values and techniques of the time.

w David O. Selznick, *book* Margaret Buell Wilder *d* John Cromwell *ph* Stanley Cortez, Lee Garmes *m* Max Steiner *pd* William L. pereira

Claudette Colbert, Joseph Cotton, Jennifer Jones, Shirley Temple, Agnes Moorehead, Monty Woolley, Lionel Barrymore, Guy Madison, Robert Walker, Hattie McDaniel, Craig Stevens, Keenan Wynn, Albert Basserman, Nazimova, Lloyd Corrigan

PREFACE: 'This is the story of the unconquerable fortress—the American home, 1943.'

'A deft, valid blend of showmanship, humour, and yard-wide Americanism.'—*James Agee*

'The whole litany of that middle-class synthetic emotionalism, meticulously annotated over a decade by tough and sentimental experts, has been procured for us.'—*Richard Winnington*

'A rather large dose of choking sentiment.'—*Bosley Crowther*

'It is not an average US reality. It is an average US dream.'—*Time*

'Selznick wrote the script himself, intending his story to be moving and simple, along epic lines; the result is pedestrian in a peculiarly grandiose manner.'—*Pauline Kael, 70s*

AA: Max Steiner
AAN: best picture; Stanley Cortez; Claudette Colbert; Jennifer Jones; Monty Woolley

Sing As We Go

GB 1934   80m   bw
ATP (Basil Dean)

An unemployed millgirl gets various holiday jobs in Blackpool.
A splendid, pawky star vehicle which is also the best picture we have of industrial Lancashire in the thirties. Great fun.

w J. B. Priestley, *Gordon Wellesley* *d* Basil Dean

Gracie Fields, John Loder, *Frank Pettingell*, Dorothy Hyson, Stanley Holloway

'We have an industrial north that is bigger than Gracie Fields running around a Blackpool fun fair.'—*C. A. Lejeune*

The Singing Fool

US 1928   110m   bw
Warner

A successful singer goes on the skids when his small son dies.
Early talkie musical, a sensation because of its star's personality, but a pretty maudlin piece of drama.

w C. Graham Baker, *play* Leslie S. Barrows *d* Lloyd Bacon *ph* Byron Haskin *songs* Lew Brown, Ray Henderson, B. G. De Sylva

Al Jolson, Davey Lee, Betty Bronson, Josephine Dunn, Arthur Housman

'Obvious and tedious as the climax is, when the black-faced comedian stands before the camera and sings "Sonny Boy" you know the man is greater, somehow, than the situation, the story or the movie.'—*Pare Lorentz*

Singin' in the Rain

US 1952   102m
Technicolor
MGM (Arthur Freed)

When talkies are invented, the reputation of one female star shrivels while another grows.
Brilliant comic musical, the best picture by far of Hollywood in transition, with the catchiest tunes, the liveliest choreography, the most engaging performances and the most hilarious jokes of any musical

w Adolph Green, *Betty Comden* *d/ch* Gene Kelly, Stanley Donen *ph* Harold Rosson *m* Nacio Herb Brown *md* Lennie Hayton *ly* Arthur Freed

*Gene Kelly, Donald O'Connor,
Debbie Reynolds, Millard Mitchell,
Jean Hagen*, Rita Moreno, Cyd
Charisse, *Douglas Fowley*

'Perhaps the most enjoyable of all
movie musicals.'—*New Yorker, 1975*

AAN: Lennie Hayton; Jean Hagen

'Personal! Powerful! Human!
Heroic!'

Sink the Bismarck

GB 1960 97m bw
Cinemascope
TCF / John Brabourne

In 1941, Britain's director of naval
operations arranges the trapping and
sinking of Germany's greatest
battleship.

Tight little personal drama which
would have been better on a
standard screen, as its ships are
plainly models and much of the
footage stretched-out newsreel.
Nevertheless, a good example of the
stiff-upper-lip school.

w Edmund H. North *d* Lewis
Gilbert *ph* Christopher Challis
m Clifton Parker *md* Muir
Mathieson

Kenneth More, Dana Wynter, Karel
Stepanek, Carl Mohner, Laurence
Naismith, Geoffrey Keen, Michael
Hordern, Maurice Denham, Esmond
Knight

Sitting Pretty

US 1948 84m bw
TCF (Samuel G. Engel)

A young couple acquire a most
unusual male baby sitter, a
self-styled genuis who sets the
neighbourhood on its ears by writing
a novel about it.

Out of the blue, a very funny
comedy which entrenched Clifton
Webb as one of Hollywood's great
characters and led to two sequels,
Mr Belvedere Goes to College and
Mr Belvedere Rings the Bell.

w F. Hugh Herbert, *novel* Belvedere
by Gwen Davenport *d* Walter Lang
ph Norbert Brodine *m* Alfred
Newman

Clifton Webb, Robert Young,

Maureen O'Hara, *Richard Haydn*,
Louise Allbritton, Ed Begley, Randy
Stuart, Larry Olsen

AAN: Clifton Webb

Sixty Glorious Years

GB 1938 95m Technicolor
Imperator (Herbert Wilcox)
US title: *Queen of Destiny*

Scenes from the life of Queen
Victoria.

A stately pageant apparently
composed of material which couldn't
be fitted into the previous year's
black-and-white success *Victoria the
Great*. Fascinating, though the
camerawork is not very nimble.

w Robert Vansittart, Miles
Malleson, Charles de Grandcourt
d Herbert Wilcox *ph* Frederick A.
Young

Anna Neagle, Anton Walbrook, C.
Aubrey Smith, Walter Rilla, Charles
Carson, Felix Aylmer, Lewis Casson

'One of the most artistic and
expensive films made in
England.'—*Variety*

† The two films were edited together
in 1943 to make a new selection
called *Queen Victoria*, and in the
process the original negatives were
accidentally destroyed, so that both
films now have to be printed from
unattractive dupes.

'Think of the crime . . . then go
one step further . . . If it was
murder, where's the body? If it
was for a woman, which
woman? If it's only a game, why
the blood?

Sleuth

GB 1972 139m colour
Palomar (Morton Gottlieb)

A successful thriller writer invents a
murder plot which rebounds on
himself.

Well-acted version of a highly
successful piece of stage trickery;
despite hard work all round it seems
much less clever and arresting on the
screen, and the tricks do show.

w Anthony Shaffer, from his play

d Joseph L. Mankiewicz *ph* Oswald
Morris *m* John Addison

Laurence Olivier, Michael Caine

AAN: Joseph L. Mankiewicz; John
Addison; Laurence Olivier; Michael
Caine

A Slight Case of Murder
🐱 US 1938 85m bw
Warner (Sam Bischoff)
When a beer baron tries to go
legitimate his colleagues attempt to
kill him, but end up shooting each
other.
Amusing black farce, remade to less
effect as *Stop, You're Killing Me.*

w Earl Baldwin, Joseph Schrank,
play Damon Runyon, Howard
Lindsay *d* Lloyd Bacon *ph* Sid
Hickox *m* M. K. Jerome, Jack
Scholl

Edward G. Robinson, Jane Bryan,
Willard Parker, *Ruth Donnelly*,
Allen Jenkins, John Litel, Harold
Huber, Edward Brophy, Bobby
Jordan

'Nothing funnier has been
produced by Hollywood for a long
time . . . a mirthful and hilarious
whimsy.'—*Variety*

'The complications crazily mount,
sentiment never raises its ugly head,
a long nose is made at violence and
death.'—*Graham Greene*

The Small Back Room
🐱🐱 GB 1949 106m bw
London Films / The Archers
US title: *Hour of Glory*
A bomb expert with a lame foot and
a drink problem risks his life
dismantling a booby bomb and
returns to his long-suffering girl
friend.
Rather gloomy suspense thriller with
ineffective personal aspects but
well-made location sequences and a
fascinating background of boffins at
work in post-war London.

wd Michael Powell, *Emeric
Pressburger, novel* Nigel Balchin
ph Christopher Challis *m* Brian
Easdale

David Farrar, Kathleen Byron, Jack
Hawkins, Leslie Banks, Robert
Morley, Cyril Cusack

Smiles of a Summer Night
🐱 Sweden 1955 105m bw
Svensk Filmindustri
original title: *Sommarnattens
Leende*
A country lawyer meets again a
touring actress who was once his
mistress, and accepts an invitation
for him and his young wife to stay at
her mother's country home for a
weekend.
Comedy of high period manners with
an admirable detached viewpoint
and elegant trappings. It later
formed the basis of Stephen
Sondheim's *A Little Night Music*, a
stage musical which was later filmed.

wd Ingmar Bergman *ph* Gunnar
Fischer *m* Erik Nordgren

Gunnar Bjornstrand, Eva Dahlbeck,
Ulla Jacobsson, Harriet Andersson,
Margit Carlquist, Naima Wifstrand,
Jarl Kulle

The Snake Pit
🐱🐱 US 1948 108m bw
TCF (Anatole Litvak, Robert
Bassler)
A girl becomes mentally deranged
and has horrifying experiences in an
institution.
A headline-hitting film which made a
stirring plea for more sympathetic
treatment of mental illness. Very
well made, and arrestingly acted, but
somehow nobody's favourite movie.

w Frank Partos, Millen Brand,
novel Mary Jane Ward *d* Anatole
Litvak *ph* Leo Tover *m* Alfred
Newman

Olivia de Havilland, Leo Genn,
Mark Stevens, Celeste Holm, Glenn
Langan, Leif Erickson, Beulah
Bondi, Lee Patrick, Natalie Schaefer
'A film of superficial veracity that
requires a bigger man than Litvak; a
good film with bad things.'—*Herman
G. Weinberg*

† The British censor insisted on a
foreword explaining that everyone in

the film was an actor and that conditions in British mental hospitals were unlike those depicted.

AAN: best picture; script; Anatole Litvak; Alfred Newman; Olivia de Havilland

Snow White and the Seven Dwarfs

US 1937 82m Technicolor
Walt Disney

Disney's first feature cartoon, a mammoth enterprise which no one in the business thought would work. The romantic leads were wishy-washy but the splendid songs and the marvellous comic and villainous characters turned the film into a world-wide box office bombshell which is almost as fresh today as when it was made.

w Ted Sears, Otto Englander, Earl Hurd, Dorothy Ann Blank, Richard Creedon, Dick Richard, Merrill de Maris, Webb Smith, from the fairy tale by the brothers Grimm *supervising director* David Hand *m* Frank Churchill, Leigh Harline, Paul Smith *songs* Larry Morey, *Frank Churchill*

'The first full-length animated feature, the turning point in Disney's career, a milestone in film history, and a great film.'—*Leonard Maltin*

'Sustained fantasy, the animated cartoon grown up.'—*Otis Ferguson*

AAN: Frank Churchill, Leigh Harline, Paul Smith

'Out of one masterpiece, another has been created!'

The Snows of Kilimanjaro

US 1952 117m
Technicolor
TCF (Darryl F. Zanuck)

A hunter lies wounded in Africa and while waiting for help looks back over his life and loves.

Hollywood version of a portable Hemingway, with reminiscences of several novels stirred into a lush and sprawling mix of action and romance, open spaces and smart salons. A big popular star film of its time, despite constricted and unconvincing characters.

w Casey Robinson, *story* Ernest Hemingway *d* Henry King *ph* Leon Shamroy *m* Bernard Herrmann

Gregory Peck, Susan Hayward, Ava Gardner, Hildegard Neff, Leo G. Carroll, Torin Thatcher, Marcel Dalio

'A naïve kind of success story with a conventional boy-meets-lots-of-girls plot.'—*Karel Reisz*

'The succinct and vivid qualities associated with Hemingway are rarely evoked, and what has been substituted is for the most part meandering, pretentious and more or less maudlin romance.'—*Newsweek*

AAN: Leon Shamroy

Some Like It Hot

US 1959 122m bw
UA / Mirisch (Billy Wilder)

Two unemployed musicians accidentally witness the St Valentine's Day Massacre and flee to Miami disguised as girl musicians. Overstretched but sporadically very funny comedy which constantly flogs its central idea to death and then recovers with a smart line or situation. It has in any case become a milestone of film comedy.

w Billy Wilder, I. A. L. Diamond *d* Billy Wilder *ph* Charles Lang Jnr *m* Adolph Deutsch

Jack Lemmon, Tony Curtis, Marilyn Monroe, Joe E. Brown, George Raft, Pat O'Brien, Nehemiah Persoff, George E. Stone, Joan Shawlee

'Hectic slapstick, smartass movie pardies, sexist stereotyping, crass one-liners, and bad taste galore.' *Time Out, 1984*

AAN: script; Billy Wilder (as director); Charles Lang Jnr; Jack Lemmon

'The black shadows of the past
  bred this half-man,
  half-demon!'
Son of Frankenstein
🎬 US 1939 99m bw
  Universal (Rowland V. Lee)
The old baron's son comes home and
starts to dabble, with the help of a
broken-necked and vindictive
shepherd.
Handsomely mounted sequel to
Bride of Frankenstein and the last of
the classic trio. The monster is less
interesting, but there are plenty of
other diversions, including the
splendid if impractical sets.

*w Willis Cooper d Rowland V. Lee
ph George Robinson m Frank
Skinner ad Jack Otterson*

*Basil Rathbone, Boris Karloff, Bela
Lugosi, Lionel Atwill*, Josephine
Hutchinson, Donnie Dunagan,
Emma Dunn, *Edgar Norton*,
Lawrence Grant
  'Rather strong material for the top
keys, picture will still garner plenty
of bookings in the secondary first
runs along the main stem.'—*Variety*

  'The slickness of production gives
a kind of refinement to the horrific
moments and a subtlety to the
suspense.'—*Film Weekly*

'We're going to see Jennifer
  Jones again in . . .'
The Song of Bernadette
🎬 US 1943 156m bw
  TCF (William Perlberg)
A peasant girl has a vision of the
Virgin Mary at what becomes the
shrine of Lourdes.
Hollywood religiosity at its most
commercial; but behind the lapses of
taste and truth is an excellent
production which was phenomenally
popular and created a new star.

*w George Seaton, novel Franz
Werfel d Henry King ph Arthur
Miller m Alfred Newman ad James
Basevi, William Darling*

Jennifer Jones, William Eythe,
Charles Bickford, Vincent Price, Lee
J. Cobb, Gladys Cooper, Anne
Revere, Roman Bohnen, Patricia
Morison, Aubrey Mather, Charles

Dingle, Mary Anderson, Edith
Barrett, Sig Rumann

PROLOGUE: 'For those who believe
in God, no explanation is necessary.
For those who do not believe in
God, no explanation is possible.

  'A tamed and pretty image, highly
varnished, sensitively lighted, and
exhibited behind immaculate glass,
the window at once of a shrine and
of a box office.'—*James Agee*

  'It contains much to conciliate
even the crustiest and most
prejudiced objector.'—*Richard
Mallett, Punch*

AA: Arthur Miller; Alfred Newman;
Jennifer Jones
AAN: best picture; George Seaton;
Henry King; Charles Bickford;
Gladys Cooper; Anne Revere

A Song to Remember
🎬 US 1944 113m
  Technicolor
Columbia (Louis F. Edelman)
The life and death of Chopin and his
liaison with George Sand.
Hilarious classical musical biopic
which was unexpectedly popular and
provoked a flood of similar pieces.
As a production, not at all bad, but
the script . . .

*w Sidney Buchman d Charles
Vidor ph Tony Gaudio md Miklos
Rozsa, Morris Stoloff piano José
Iturbi ad Lionel Banks, Van Nest
Polglase*

Cornel Wilde, Merle Oberon, Paul
Muni, Stephen Bekassy, Nina Foch,
George Coulouris, Sig Arno,
Howard Freeman, George Macready
  'It is the business of Hollywood to
shape the truth into box-office
contours.'—*Richard Winnington*

  'This glorious picture is a major
event in film history.'—*Hollywood
Reporter*

  'As infuriating and funny a
misrepresentation of an artist's life
and work as I have seen.'—*James
Agee*

AAN: original story (Ernest
Marischka); Tony Gaudio; Miklos
Rozsa, Morris Stoloff; Cornel Wilde

'The first experiences of a young man in the mysteries of woman!'

Sons and Lovers

GB 1960   103m   bw
Cinemascope

TCF / Company of Artists / Jerry Wald

A Nottingham miner's son learns about life and love.

Well produced and generally absorbing, if unsurprising treatment of a famous novel.

w Gavin Lambert, T. E. B. Clarke, novel D. H. Lawrence *d Jack Cardiff ph Freddie Francis m* Mario Nascimbene

Dean Stockwell, Trevor Howard, Wendy Hiller, Mary Ure, Heather Sears, William Lucas, Donald Pleasence, Ernest Thesiger

'An album of decent Edwardian snapshots.'—*Peter John Dyer*

'A rare, remarkable and courageous film.'—*Daily Herald*

AA: Freddie Francis

AAN: best picture; script; Jack Cardiff; Trevor Howard; Mary Ure

Sons of the Desert

US 1934   68m   bw
Hal Roach

GB title: *Fraternally Yours*

Stan and Ollie want to go to a Chicago convention, but kid their wives that they are going on a cruise for health reasons.

Archetypal Laurel and Hardy comedy, unsurpassed for gags, pacing and sympathetic characterization.

w Frank Craven, Byron Morgan d William A. Seiter ph Kenneth Peach

Stan Laurel, Oliver Hardy, Charlie Chase, Mae Busch, Dorothy Christie

The Sound Barrier

GB 1952   118m   bw
London Films (David Lean)

US title: *Breaking the Sound Barrier*

An aircraft manufacturer takes risks with the lives of his family and friends to prove that the sound barrier can be broken.

Riveting, then topical, melodrama with splendid air sequences; a bit upper crust, but with well-drawn characters.

w Terence Rattigan d David Lean ph Jack Hildyard m Malcolm Arnold

Ralph Richardson, Nigel Patrick, Ann Todd, John Justin, Dinah Sheridan, Joseph Tomelty, Denholm Elliott

'The most exciting film about the air that has ever been produced anywhere.'—*Daily Express*

'A peacetime film as exciting as any wartime one.'—*Sunday Dispatch*

AAN: Terence Rattigan

The Sound of Music

US 1965   172m   De Luxe
Todd-AO

TCF / Argyle (Robert Wise)

In 1938 Austria, a trainee nun becomes governess to the Trapp family, falls in love with the widower father, and helps them all escape from the Nazis.

Slightly muted, very handsome version of an enjoyably old-fashioned stage musical with splendid tunes.

w Ernest Lehman, book Howard Lindsay, Russel Crouse *d Robert Wise ph Ted McCord m/ly Richard Rodgers, Oscar Hammerstein II md Irwin Kostal pd Boris Leven*

Julie Andrews, Christopher Plummer, Richard Haydn, Eleanor Parker, *Peggy Wood,* Anna Lee, Marni Nixon

' . . . sufficient warning to those allergic to singing nuns and sweetly innocent children.'—*John Gillett*

AA: best picture; Robert Wise; Irwin Kostal

AAN: Ted McCord; Julie Andrews; Peggy Wood

South Pacific

US 1958   170m
Technicolor   Todd-AO

Magna / S. P. Enterprises (Buddy Adler)

In 1943 an American navy nurse on a South Pacific island falls in love with a middle-aged French planter who becomes a war hero.
Overlong, solidly produced film of the musical stage hit, with great locations, action climaxes and lush photography (also a regrettable tendency to use alarming colour filters for dramatic emphasis).

w Paul Osborn, Richard Rodgers, Oscar Hammerstein II, Joshua Logan, *stories* Tales of the South Pacific by James A. Michener
d Joshua Logan *ph* Leon Shamroy *m/ly* Richard Rodgers, Oscar Hammerstein II *md* Alfred Newman, Ken Darby *ch* Le Roy Prinz

Mitzi Gaynor, Rossano Brazzi, Ray Walston, John Kerr, France Nuyen, Juanita Hall

AAN: Leon Shamroy; Alfred Newman, Ken Darby

South Riding
GB 1937 91m bw
London Films (Alexander Korda, Victor Saville)
A schoolmistress in a quiet Yorkshire dale exposes crooked councillors and falls for the depressed local squire.
Dated but engrossing multi-drama from a famous novel; a good compact piece of film-making

w Ian Dalrymple, Donald Bull, *novel* Winifred Holtby *d* Victor Saville *ph* Harry Stradling *m* Richard Addinsell

Ralph Richardson, *Edna Best*, Edmund Gwenn, Ann Todd, Glynis Johns, John Clements, Marie Lohr, Milton Rosmer, Edward Lexy
'Another artistic Korda film . . . lacking in a story of popular appeal.'—*Variety*
'A convincing and dramatic picture of English provincial life.'—*Film Weekly*

'She was his woman! And he was her man! That's all they had to fight with—against the world, the flesh, and the devil!'
The Southerner
US 1945 91m bw
(UA) David Loew, Robert Hakim
Problems of penniless farmers in the deep south.
Impressive, highly pictorial outdoor drama, more poetic than *The Grapes of Wrath* and lacking the acting strength.

wd Jean Renoir, *novel* Hold Autumn in Your Hand by George Sessions Perry *ph* Lucien Andriot *m* Werner Janssen

Zachary Scott, Betty Field, *Beulah Bondi*, J. Carrol Naish, Percy Kilbride, Blanche Yurka, Norman Lloyd
'I cannot imagine anybody failing to be spellbound by this first successful essay in Franco-American screen collaboration.'—*Richard Winnington*
'You can smell the earth as the plough turns it up; you can sense the winter and the rain and the sunshine.'—*C. A. Lejeune*

† Some sources state that the script was by William Faulkner.

AAN: Jean Renoir (as director); Werner Janssen

Spartacus
US 1960 196m Super Technirama 70
U-I/Bryna (Edward Lewis)
The slaves of ancient Rome revolt and are quashed.
Long, well-made, downbeat epic with deeper than usual characterization and several bravura sequences.

w Dalton Trumbo, *novel* Howard Fast *d* Stanley Kubrick *ph* Russell Metty *m* Alex North *pd* Alexander Golitzen

Kirk Douglas, Laurence Olivier, Charles Laughton, Tony Curtis, Jean Simmons, Peter Ustinov, John Gavin, Nina Foch, Herbert Lom,

John Ireland, John Dall, Charles
McGraw, Woody Strode

'Everything is depicted with a lack
of imagination that is truly
Marxian.'—*Anne Grayson*

'A lot of first-rate professionals
have pooled their abilities to make a
first-rate circus.'—*Stanley
Kauffmann*

'One comes away feeling rather
revolted and not at all
ennobled.'—*Alan Dent, Illustrated
London News*

AA: Russell Metty; Peter Ustinov
AAN: Alex North

Spellbound
US 1945 111m bw
David O. Selznick

The new head of a mental institution
is an impostor and an amnesiac; a
staff member falls in love with him
and helps him recall the fate of the
real Dr Edwardes.

Enthralling and rather infuriating
psychological mystery; the Hitchcock
touches are splendid, and the stars
shine magically, but the plot could
have stood a little more attention.

w Ben Hecht, Angus MacPhail,
novel The House of Dr Edwardes
by Francis Beeding *d Alfred
Hitchcock ph George Barnes dream
sequence Salvador Dali m Miklos
Rozsa ad James Basevi*

*Ingrid Bergman, Gregory Peck, Leo
G. Carroll, Michael Chekhov,*
Rhonda Fleming, John Emery,
Norman Lloyd, Steve Geray

'Just about as much of the id as
could be safely displayed in a
Bergdorf Goodman
window.'—*James Agee*

'Glossily produced and wildly
improbable.'—*George Perry, 1965*

'Bergman's apple-cheeked
sincerity has rarely been so out of
place as in this confection whipped
up by jaded chefs.'—*New Yorker,
1976*

AA: Miklos Rozsa
AAN: best picture; Alfred
Hitchcock; George Barnes; Michael
Chekhov

The Spiral Staircase
US 1945 83m bw
RKO (Dore Schary)

A small town in 1906 New England
is terrorized by a psychopathic killer
of deformed girls.

Archetypal old dark house thriller,
superbly detailed and set during a
most convincing thunderstorm. Even
though the identity of the villain is
pretty obvious, this is a superior
Hollywood product.

w Mel Dinelli, *novel* Some Must
Watch by Ethel Lina White
d Robert Siodmak ph Nicholas
Musuraca m Roy Webb ad Albert
S. D'Agostino, Jack Okey

Dorothy McGuire, George Brent,
Kent Smith, Ethel Barrymore, Rhys
Williams, Rhonda Fleming, Gordon
Oliver, Sara Allgood, James Bell

'A nice, cosy and well-sustained
atmosphere of horror.'—*C. A.
Lejeune*

AAN: Ethel Barrymore

Spring in Park Lane
GB 1948 92m bw
British Lion/Herbert Wilcox

A diamond merchant's niece falls for
a footman who just happens to be an
impoverished lord in disguise.

Flimsy but highly successful romantic
comedy which managed to get its
balance right and is still pretty
entertaining, much more so than its
sequel *Maytime in Mayfair*.

w Nicholas Phipps, *play* Come Out
of the Kitchen by Alice Duer Miller
d Herbert Wilcox ph Max Greene
m Robert Farnon

*Anna Neagle, Michael Wilding, Tom
Walls, Nicholas Phipps,* Peter
Graves, Marjorie Fielding, *Nigel
Patrick, Lana Morris*

'A never-failing dream of Olde
Mayfaire and its eternally funny
butlers and maids, its disguised lords
and ladies.'—*Richard Winnington*

'A gag comedy which absolutely
sparkles.'—*Picture Show*

'The best comedy any British
studio has produced for more years
than I care to remember.'—*News of
the World*

The Spy Who Came in from the Cold

GB 1966   112m   bw
Paramount/Salem (Martin Ritt)

A British master spy is offered a chance to get even with his East German opponent by being apparently sacked, disillusioned, and open for recruitment.

The old undercover yarn with trimmings of such sixties malaises as death wish, anti-establishmentism and racial problems. As a yarn, quite gripping till it gets too downbeat, but very harshly photographed.

w Paul Dehn, Guy Trosper, *novel* John Le Carré *d* Martin Ritt *ph* Oswald Morris *m* Sol Kaplan *pd* Tambi Larsen

Richard Burton, Claire Bloom, *Oskar Werner*, Peter Van Eyck, Sam Wanamaker, Rupert Davies, George Voskovec, Cyril Cusack, Michael Hordern, Robert Hardy, Bernard Lee, Beatrix Lehmann

AAN: Richard Burton

Stage Door

US 1937   93m   bw
RKO (Pandro S. Berman)

Life in a New York theatrical boarding house for girls.
Melodramatic, sharply comedic, always fascinating slice of stagey life from a Broadway hit; the performances alone make it worth preserving.

w Morrie Ryskind, Anthony Veiller, *play* Edna Ferber, George S. Kaufman *d* Gregory La Cava *ph* Robert de Grasse *m* Roy Webb *ad* Van Nest Polglase

Katharine Hepburn, Ginger Rogers, Adolphe Menjou, Gail Patrick, Constance Collier, Andrea Leeds, Lucille Ball, Samuel S. Hinds, Jack Carson, Franklin Pangborn, Eve Arden

'It is a long time since we have seen so much feminine talent so deftly handled.'—*Otis Ferguson*

'Zest and pace and photographic eloquence.'—*Frank S. Nugent, New York Times*

'A rare example of a film substantially improving on a stage original and a remarkably satisfying film on all levels.'—*NFT, 1973*

'One of the flashiest, most entertaining comedies of the 30s, even with its tremolos and touches of heartbreak.'—*Pauline Kael, 70s*

AAN: best picture; script; Gregory La Cava; Andrea Leeds

Stagecoach

US 1939   99m   bw
(UA) Walter Wanger

Various western characters board a stagecoach in danger from an Indian war party.
What looked like a minor western, with a plot borrowed from Maupassant's *Boule de suif*, became a classic by virtue of the firm characterization, restrained writing, exciting climax and the scenery of Monument Valley. Whatever the reasons, it damn well works.

w Dudley Nichols, *story* Stage to Lordsburg by Ernest Haycox *d* John Ford *ph* Bert Glennon, Ray Binger *m* Richard Hageman, W. Frank Harling, John Leopold, Leo Shuken, Louis Gruenberg *md* Boris Morros

Claire Trevor, John Wayne, Thomas Mitchell, George Bancroft, Andy Devine, Berton Churchill, Louise Platt, John Carradine, Donald Meek, Tim Holt, Chris-Pin Martin

'It displays potentialities that can easily drive it through as one of the surprise big grossers of the year.'—*Variety*

'The basic western, a template for everything that followed.'—*John Baxter, 1968*

'Grand Hotel on wheels.'—*New Yorker, 1975*

'A motion picture that sings a song of camera.'—*Frank S. Nugent, New York Times*

AA: music; Thomas Mitchell
AAN: best picture; John Ford; Bert Glennon; Ray Binger

Stalag 17

US 1953   120m   bw
Paramount (Billy Wilder)

Comedy and tragedy for American servicemen in a Nazi prisoner-of-war camp.

High jinks, violence and mystery in a sharply calculated mixture; an atmosphere quite different from the understated British films on the subject.

w Billy Wilder, Edwin Blum, *play* Donald Bevan, Edmund Trzinski *d* Billy Wilder *ph* Ernest Laszlo *m* Franz Waxman

William Holden, Don Taylor, Otto Preminger, *Robert Strauss*, Harvey Lembeck, Richard Erdman, Peter Graves, Neville Grand, Sig Rumann

'A facility for continuous rapid-fire action which alternately brings forth the laughs and tingles the spine.'—*Otis L. Guernsey Jnr*

'Raucous and tense, heartless and sentimental, always fast-paced, it has already been assigned by critics to places on their lists of the year's ten best movies.'—*Life*

AA: William Holden
AAN: Billy Wilder (as director), Robert Strauss

Star!

🎖 US 1968   194m   De Luxe Todd-AO

TCF / Robert Wise (Saul Chaplin)

Revue artist Gertrude Lawrence rises from poverty to international stardom and a measure of happiness.

Elephantiasis finally ruins this patient, detached, generally likeable recreation of a past theatrical era. In the old Hollywood style, it would probably have been even better on a smaller budget; but alas the star would still have been ill at ease with the drunken termagant scenes.

w William Fairchild *d* Robert Wise *ph* Ernest Laszlo *md* Lennie Hayton *ch* Michael Kidd *pd* Boris Leven

Julie Andrews, Richard Crenna, Michael Craig, *Daniel Massey* (as Noel Coward), John Collin, Robert Reed, Bruce Forsyth, Beryl Reid, Jenny Agutter

† Short version: *Those Were the Happy Days*.

AAN: Ernest Laszlo; Lennie Hayton; title song (*m* James Van Heusen, *ly* Sammy Cahn); Daniel Massey

A Star Is Born

🎭 US 1937   111m
   Technicolor

David O. Selznick

A young actress meets Hollywood success and marries a famous leading man, whose star wanes as hers shine brighter.

Abrasive romantic melodrama which is also the most accurate study of Hollywood ever put on film.

w Dorothy Parker, Alan Campbell, Robert Carson, *story* William A. Wellman, based partly on *What Price Hollywood* (1932) *d* William A. Wellman *ph* W. Howard Greene *m* Max Steiner

Janet Gaynor, Fredric March, *Adolphe Menjou, Lionel Stander*, Andy Devine, May Robson, Owen Moore, Franklin Pangborn

'One of those rare ones which everyone will want to see and talk about . . . disproves the tradition that good pictures can't be made with a Hollywood background.'—*Variety*

'Good entertainment by any standards.'—*Frank S. Nugent, New York Times*

'A peculiar sort of masochistic self-congratulatory Hollywood orgy.'—*New Yorker, 1975*

The first colour job that gets close to what colour must eventually come to: it keeps the thing in its place, underlining the mood and situation of the story rather than dimming everything else out in an iridescent razzle-dazzle.'—*Otis Ferguson*

AA: original story; W. Howard Greene
AAN: best picture; script; William A. Wellman; Janet Gaynor; Fredric March

Star Spangled Rhythm

🎖 US 1942   99m   bw
   Paramount (Joseph Sistrom)

The doorman of Paramount Studios pretends to his sailor son that he is a big producer.

Frenetic farce involving most of the talent on Paramount's payroll and culminating in an 'impromptu' show staged for the navy. A good lighthearted glimpse of wartime Hollywood.

w Harry Tugend *d* George Marshall *ph* Leo Tover, Theodor Sparkuhl *md* Robert Emmett Dolan *songs* Johnny Mercer, Harold Arlen

Betty Hutton, Eddie Bracken, *Victor Moore*, *Walter Abel*, Anne Revere, Cass Daley, Gil Lamb, Macdonald Carey, Bob Hope, Bing Crosby, Paulette Goddard, Veronica Lake, Dorothy Lamour, Vera Zorina, Fred MacMurray, Ray Milland, Lynne Overman, Franchot Tone, Dick Powell, *Walter Dare Wahl and Co*, *Cecil B. de Mille*, *Preston Sturges*, Alan Ladd, Rochester, Katherine Dunham, Susan Hayward

AAN: Robert Emmett Dolan; song 'Black Magic' (*m* Harold Arlen, *ly* Johnny Mercer)

Star Wars

US 1977 121m
Technicolor Panavision
TCF/Lucasfilm (Gary Kurtz)

A rebel princess in a distant galaxy escapes, and with the help of her robots and a young farmer overcomes the threatening forces of evil.

Flash Gordon rides again, but with timing so impeccably right that the movie became a phenomenon and one of the top grossers of all time. In view of the hullaballoo, some disappointment may be felt with the actual experience of watching it . . . but it's certainly good harmless fun, put together with style and imagination

wd George Lucas *ph* Gilbert Taylor *m* John Williams *pd* John Barry *sp* many and various

Mark Hamill, Harrison Ford, Carrie Fisher, Peter Cushing, Alec Guinness, Anthony Daniels (See

Threepio), Kenny Baker (Artoo Detoo), Dave Prowse (Darth Vader)

'A great work of popular art, fully deserving the riches it has reaped.'—*Time*

'Acting in this movie I felt like a raisin in a giant fruit salad. And I didn't even know who the coconuts or the canteloups were.'—*Mark Hamill*

'He intended his film, Lucas confesses, for a generation growing up without fairy tales. His target audience was fourteen years and younger . . . It was a celebration, a social affair, a collective dream, and people came again and again, dragging their friends and families with them.'—*Les Keyser, Hollywood in the Seventies*

'The loudness, the smash and grab editing and the relentless pacing drive every idea from your head, and even if you've been entertained you may feel cheated of some dimension—a sense of wonder, perhaps.'—*New Yorker, 1982*

'Heartless fireworks ignited by a permanently retarded director with too much clout and cash.'—*Time Out, 1984*

AA: John Williams
AAN: best picture; script; direction; Alec Guinness

The Stars Look Down

GB 1939 110m bw
Grafton (Isadore Goldschmidt)

The son of a coal miner struggles to become an MP.

Economically but well made social drama from a popular novel, with good pace and backgrounds.

w J. B. Williams, A. J. Cronin, *novel* A. J. Cronin *d* Carol Reed *ph* Max Greene *m* Hans May

Michael Redgrave, Margaret Lockwood, Edward Rigby, Emlyn Williams, Nancy Price, Allan Jeayes, Cecil Parker, Linden Travers

'Dr Cronin's mining novel has produced a very good film—I doubt whether in England we have ever produced a better.'—*Graham Greene*

State Fair

  US 1933 98m bw
Fox (Winfield Sheehan)

Dad wants his prize pig to win at the fair, but the younger members of his family have romance in mind.

Archetypal family film, much remade but never quite so pleasantly performed.

w Paul Green, Sonya Levien, *novel* Phil Stong *d* Henry King *ph* Hal Mohr *md* Louis de Francesco

Will Rogers, Janet Gaynor, Lew Ayres, Sally Eilers, Norman Foster, Louise Dresser, Frank Craven, Victor Jory, Hobart Cavanaugh

'A pungent, good-humoured motion picture.'—*Pare Lorentz*

'Vigour, freshness and sympathy abound in its admittedly idealized fantasy treatment of small-town life.'—*Charles Higham, 1972*

AAN: best picture; script

State of the Union

  US 1948 110m bw
(MGM) Liberty Films (Frank Capra)

GB title: *The World and His Wife*

An estranged wife rejoins her husband when he is running for president.

Brilliantly scripted political comedy which unfortunately goes soft at the end but offers stimulating entertainment most of the way.

w Anthony Veiller, Myles Connelly, *play* Howard Lindsay, *Russel Crouse d Frank Capra ph* George J. Folsey *m* Victor Young

Spencer Tracy, Katharine Hepburn, Adolphe Menjou, Van Johnson, Angela Lansbury, Lewis Stone, Howard Smith, Raymond Walburn, Charles Dingle

'A triumphant film, marked all over by Frank Capra's artistry.'—*Howard Barnes*

Stella Dallas

  US 1937 106m bw
Samuel Goldwyn

An uncouth woman loses both husband and daughter.

Fashionable remake with excellent talent; 1937 audiences came to sneer and stayed to weep.

w Victor Heerman, Sara Y. Mason *d King Vidor ph* Rudolph Maté *m* Alfred Newman

Barbara Stanwyck, John Boles, Anne Shirley, Barbara O'Neil, Alan Hale, Marjorie Main, Tim Holt

'A tear-jerker of A ranking. There are things about the story that will not appeal to some men, but no one will be annoyed or offended by it. And the wallop is inescapably there for femmes.'—*Variety*

† Goldwyn's premier choices for the lead were Ruth Chatterton and Gladys George.

AAN: Barbara Stanwyck; Anne Shirley

'All it takes is a little confidence!'
The Sting

  US 1973 129m
Technicolor

Universal / Richard Zanuck, David Brown (Tony Bill, Michael S. Phillips)

In twenties Chicago, two con men stage an elaborate revenge on a big-time gangster who caused the death of a friend.

Bright, likeable, but overlong, unconvincingly studio-set and casually developed comedy suspenser cashing in on star charisma but riding to enormous success chiefly on its tinkly music and the general lack of simple entertainment.

w David S. Ward *d George Roy Hill ph* Robert Surtees *m Scott Joplin* (arranged by Marvin Hamlisch) *ad* Henry Bumstead

Paul Newman, *Robert Redford,* Robert Shaw, Charles Durning, Ray Walston, Eileen Brennan

'A visually claustrophobic, mechanically plotted movie that's meant to be a roguishly charming entertainment.'—*New Yorker*

'It demonstrates what can happen when a gifted young screenwriter has

the good fortune to fall among
professionals his second time
out.'—*Judith Crist*

'A testament to the value of blue
eyes and bright smiles.'—*Les
Keyser, Hollywood in the Seventies*

AA: best picture; David S. Ward;
George Roy Hill; Marvin Hamlisch
AAN: Robert Surtees; Robert
Redford

Stormy Weather
US 1943 77m bw
TCF (Irving Mills)
A backstage success story lightly
based on the career of Bill
Robinson.
Virtually a high-speed revue with
all-black talent, and what talent! The
production is pretty slick too.

w Frederick Jackson, Ted Koehler
d Andrew Stone *ph* Leon Shamroy,
Fred Sersen *md* Benny Carter
ch Clarence Robinson

*Bill Robinson, Lena Horne, Fats
Waller, Ada Brown, Cab Calloway,*
Katherine Dunham and her
Dancers, Eddie Anderson, Flournoy
Miller, *The Nicholas Brothers,*
Dooley Wilson

'A first-rate show, a spirited
divertissement . . . a joy to the
ear.'—*New York Times*

The Story of GI Joe
US 1945 108m bw
(UA) Lester Cowan (David
Hall)
aka: *War Correspondent*
Journalist Ernie Pyle follows fighting
men into the Italian campaign.
Slow, convincing, sympathetic war
film with good script and
performances; not by any means the
usual action saga.

w Leopold Atlas, Guy Endore,
Philip Stevenson, *book Ernie Pyle*
d William A. Wellman *ph* Russell
Metty *m* Ann Ronell, Louis
Applebaum

Burgess Meredith, Robert Mitchum,
Freddie Steele, Wally Cassell,
Jimmy Lloyd, Jack Reilly

'It is humorous, poignant and
tragic, an earnestly human reflection
of a stern life and the dignity of
man.'—*Thomas M. Pryor*

'A tragic and eternal work of
art.'—*James Agee*

'One of the best films of the
war.'—*Richard Mallett, Punch*

AAN: script; music score; song
'Linda' (*m/ly* Ann Ronell); Robert
Mitchum

The Story of Louis Pasteur
US 1936 85m bw
Warner (Henry Blanke)
How the eminent 19th-century
French scientist overcomes obstacles
in finding cures for various diseases.
Adequate biopic which caused a
sensation and started a trend; some
of the others were better but this was
the first example of Hollywood
bringing schoolbook history to box
office life.

w Sheridan Gibney, Pierre Collins
d William Dieterle *ph* Tony Gaudio
m Bernhard Kaun, Heinz Roemheld

Paul Muni, Josephine Hutchinson,
Anita Louise, Donald Woods, Fritz
Leiber, Henry O'Neill, Porter Hall,
Akim Tamiroff, Walter Kingsford

'Probably limited b.o. but a
creditable prestige picture.'—*Variety*

'What should be vital and
arresting has been made hollow and
dull . . . we are tendered something
that is bright and stagey for
something out of life.'—*Otis
Ferguson*

'More exciting than any gangster
melodrama.'—*C. A. Lejeune*

AA: script; Paul Muni
AAN: best picture

'A woman suspected! A woman
  desired! A woman possessed!
'The film in which you hear the
  characters think!'

Strange Interlude
US 1932 110m bw
MGM (Irving Thalberg)
GB title: *Strange Interval*
Problems of an unfulfilled wife and
her lover.
Surprising film version of a very
heavy modern classic, complete with

asides to the audience; very dated now, but a small milestone in Hollywood's development

w Bess Meredyth, C. Gardner Sullivan, *play* Eugene O'Neill d Robert Z. Leonard *ph* Lee Garmes

Norma Shearer, Clark Gable, May Robson, Alexander Kirkland, Ralph Morgan, Robert Young, Maureen O'Sullivan, Henry B. Walthall

'Chiefly a reserved seat attraction, dubious for general release appeal.'—*Variety*

'A cinematic novelty to be seen by discerning audiences.'—*Film Weekly*

'More exciting than a thousand "action" movies.'—*Pare Lorentz*

'Fate drew them together and only murder can part them!'
'Whisper her name!'
The Strange Love of Martha Ivers
US 1946 116m bw
Paramount/Hal B. Wallis
A murderous child becomes a wealthy woman with a spineless lawyer husband; the melodrama starts when an ex-boy friend returns to town.
Irresistible star melodrama which leaves no stone unturned; compulsive entertainment of the old school

w Robert Rossen d Lewis Milestone *ph* Victor Milner m Miklos Rozsa

Barbara Stanwyck, Van Heflin, Kirk Douglas, Lizabeth Scott, Judith Anderson, Roman Bohnen

AAN: original story (Jack Patrick)

A Streetcar Named Desire
US 1951 122m bw
Charles K. Feldman/Elia Kazan
A repressed southern widow is raped and driven mad by her brutal brother-in-law.
Reasonably successful, decorative picture from a highly theatrical but influential play; unreal sets and atmospheric photography vaguely Sternbergian.

w Tennessee Williams, from his play d Elia Kazan *ph* Harry Stradling m Alex North *ad* Richard Day

Vivien Leigh, Marlon Brando, Kim Hunter, Karl Malden

AA: Vivien Leigh; Kim Hunter; Karl Malden
AAN: best picture; Tennessee Williams; Elia Kazan; Harry Stradling; Alex North; Marlon Brando

'There's no speed limit and no brake when Sullivan travels with Veronica Lake!'
Sullivan's Travels
US 1941 90m bw
Paramount (Paul Jones)
A Hollywood director tires of comedy and goes out to find real life. Marvellously sustained tragi-comedy which ranges from pratfalls to the chain gang and never loses its grip or balance.

wd Preston Sturges *ph* John Seitz m Leo Shuken

Joel McCrea, Veronica Lake, Robert Warwick, William Demarest, Franklin Pangborn, Porter Hall, Byron Foulger, Eric Blore, Robert Greig, Torben Meyer, *Jimmy Conlin*, Margaret Hayes
DEDICATION: 'To all the funny men and clowns who have made people laugh.'

'A brilliant fantasy in two keys—slapstick farce and the tragedy of human misery.'—*James Agee*

'The most witty and knowing spoof of Hollywood movie-making of all time.'—*Film Society Review*

'A deftly sardonic apologia for Hollywood make-believe.'—*New York Times*

'Reflecting to perfection the mood of wartime Hollywood, it danced on the grave of thirties social cinema.'—*Eileen Bowser, 1969*

The Sun Also Rises
US 1957 129m
Eastmancolor Cinemascope
TCF (Darryl F. Zanuck)
In Paris after World War I an impotent journalist meets a

nymphomaniac lady of title, and they and their odd group of friends have various saddening adventures around Europe.

Not a bad attempt to film a difficult novel, though Cinemascope doesn't help and the last half hour becomes turgid. *The Last Flight* conveyed the same atmosphere rather more sharply.

w Peter Viertel, *novel* Ernest Hemingway *d* Henry King *ph* Leo Tover *m* Hugo Friedhofer

Tyrone Power, Ava Gardner, *Errol Flynn*, Eddie Albert, Mel Ferrer, Robert Evans, Juliette Greco, Gregory Ratoff, Marcel Dalio, Henry Daniell

Sunrise

<a>👥</a> US 1927   97m (24 fps)
<a>✗</a>   bw   silent
Fox
A villager in love with a city woman tries to kill his wife but then repents and spends a happy day with her. Lyrical melodrama, superbly handled: generally considered among the finest Hollywood productions of the twenties.

w Carl Meyer, *novel* A Trip to Tilsit by Hermann Sudermann *d* F. W. Murnau *ph* Karl Struss, Charles Rosher *m* (sound version) Hugo Riesenfeld

Janet Gaynor, George O'Brien, Margaret Livingston

OPENING TITLE: 'This story of a man and his wife is of nowhere and everywhere, you might hear it anywhere and at any time.'

'It is filled with intense feeling and in it is embodied an underlying subtlety . . . exotic in many ways for it is a mixture of Russian gloom and Berlin brightness.'—*Mordaunt Hall, New York Times*

'Not since the earliest, simplest moving pictures, when locomotives, fire engines and crowds in streets were transposed to the screen artlessly and endearingly, when the entranced eye was rushed through tunnels and over precipices on runaway trains. has there been such

joy in motion as under Murnau's direction.'—*Louise Bogan, The New Republic*

'The story is told in a flowing, lyrical German manner that is extraordinarily sensual, yet perhaps too self-conscious, too fable-like, for American audiences.'—*Pauline Kael, 70s*

AA: Karl Struss, Charles Rosher; Janet Gaynor

'It happened in Hollywood . . . a love story . . . a drama real and ruthless, tender and terrifying!'
Sunset Boulevard
<a>👥</a> US 1950   110m   bw
<a>✗</a>   Paramount (Charles Brackett)
A luckless Hollywood scriptwriter goes to live with a wealthy older woman, a slightly dotty and extremely possessive relic of the silent screen.

Incisive melodrama with marvellous moments but a tendency to overstay its welcome; the first reels are certainly the best, though the last scene is worth waiting for and the malicious observation throughout is a treat

w Charles Brackett, Billy Wilder, D. M. Marshman Jnr *d* Billy Wilder *ph* John F. Seitz *m* Franz Waxman

Gloria Swanson, William Holden, Erich Von Stroheim, Fred Clark, Nancy Olson, Jack Webb, Lloyd Gough, Cecil B. de Mille, H. B. Warner, Anna Q. Nilsson, Buster Keaton, Hedda Hopper

'That rare blend of pungent writing, expert acting, masterly direction and unobtrusively artistic photography which quickly casts a spell over an audience and holds it enthralled to a shattering climax.'—*New York Times* (T.M.P.)

'Miss Swanson's performance takes her at one bound into the class of Boris Karloff and Tod Slaughter.'—*Richard Mallett, Punch*

'A weird, fascinating motion picture about an art form which, new as it is, is already haunted by ghosts.'—*Otis L. Guernsey Jnr, New York Herald Tribune*

AA: script; Franz Waxman
AAN: best picture; Billy Wilder (as
director); John F. Seitz; Gloria
Swanson; William Holden; Erich
Von Stroheim; Nancy Olson

'For the price of a movie, you'll
    feel like a million!'
The Sunshine Boys
    US 1975 111m Metrocolor
    MGM / Rastar (Ray Stark)
Two feuding old vaudeville
comedians come together for a
television spot, and ruin it.
Over-extended sketch in which one
main role is beautifully underplayed,
the other hammed up, and the
production lacks any kind of style.
The one-liners are good, though.

w Neil Simon, from his play
d Herbert Ross *ph* David M.
Walsh *md* Harry V. Lojewski

Walter Matthau, *George Burns*,
Richard Benjamin, Carol Arthur

'It's just shouting, when it needs to
be beautifully timed routines.'—*New
Yorker*
   'They feud with ill-matched
resources, and the movie's visual
delights vanish with the title
sequence.'—*Sight and Sound*

† George Burns stepped in when
Jack Benny became ill and died.

AA: George Burns
AAN: Neil Simon; Walter Matthau

'You'll believe a man can fly!'
Superman
    US / GB 1978 142m
    colour Panavision
Warner / Alexander Salkind (Pierre
Spengler)
A baby saved from the planet
Krypton when it explodes grows up
as a newspaperman and uses his
tremendous powers to fight evil and
support the American way.
Long, lugubrious and only patchily
entertaining version of the famous
comic strip, with far too many
irrelevant preliminaries and a
misguided sense of its own
importance.

w Mario Puzo, David Newman,
Robert Benton, Leslie Newman
d Richard Donner *ph* Geoffrey
Unsworth *m* John Williams
pd John Barry *sp* various

Christopher Reeve, Marlon Brando,
Margot Kidder, Jackie Cooper,
Glenn Ford, Phyllis Thaxter, Trevor
Howard, Gene Hackman, Ned
Beatty, Susannah York, Valerie
Perrine

'Though one of the two or three
most expensive movies made to
date, it's cheesy-looking, and the
plotting is so hit or miss that the
story never seems to get started; the
special effects are far from wizardly
and the editing often seems hurried
and jerky just at the crucial
points.'—*New Yorker*
   'It gives the impression of having
been made in panic—in fear that
style or too much imagination might
endanger its approach to the
literal-minded.'—*Pauline Kael, New
Yorker*
   'The epitome of supersell.'—*Les
Keyser, Hollywood in the Seventies*

† Reprehensible records were set by
Brando getting three million dollars
for a ten-minute performance (and
then suing for a share of the gross);
and by the incredible 7½-minute
credit roll at the end.

†† Tiny roles were played by Noel
Neill, who was Lois Lane in the TV
series, and by Kirk Alyn, who was
Superman in two serials.

AAN: John Williams

Suspicion
    US 1941 99m bw
    RKO (Alfred Hitchcock)
A sedate young girl marries a
playboy, and comes to suspect that
he is trying to murder her.
Rather artificial and stiff Hitchcock
suspenser, further marred by an
ending suddenly switched to please
the front office. Full of the
interesting touches one would
expect.

w Samson Raphaelson, Alma
Reville, Joan Harrison, *novel* Before

the Fact by Francis Iles *d Alfred
Hitchcock ph Harry Stradling
m Franz Waxman*

Joan Fontaine, Cary Grant, Nigel
Bruce, Cedric Hardwicke, May
Whitty, Isabel Jeans, Heather
Angel, Leo G. Carroll

'The fact that Hitchcock throws in
a happy end during the last five
minutes, like a conjuror explaining
his tricks, seems to me a pity; but it
spoils the film only in retrospect, and
we have already had our
thrills.'—*William Whitebait, New
Statesman*

AA: Joan Fontaine

AAN: best picture; Franz Waxman

'This is the story of J.J.—but not
  the way he wants it told!'
Sweet Smell of Success
❀❀ US 1957 96m bw
  ✗ UA/Norma/Curtleigh
(James Hill)

A crooked press agent helps a
megalomaniac New York columnist
break up his sister's marriage.
Moody, brilliant, Wellesian
melodrama put together with great
artificial style; the plot matters less
than the photographic detail and the
skilful manipulation of decadent
characters, bigger than life-size

*w Clifford Odets, Ernest Lehman
d Alexander Mackendrick ph James
Wong Howe m Elmer Bernstein
ad Edward Carrere*

Burt Lancaster, *Tony Curtis*, Martin
Milner, Sam Levene, Susan
Harrison, Barbara Nichols, *Emile
Meyer*

'A sweet slice of perversity, a
study of dollar and power
worship.'—*Pauline Kael*

T

Take Me Out to the Ball Game

US 1949 93m Technicolor
MGM (Arthur Freed)
GB title: *Everybody's Cheering*
A woman takes over a baseball team and the players are antagonistic.
Lively, likeable nineties comedy musical which served as a trial run for *On the Town* and in its own right is a fast-moving, funny, tuneful delight with no pretensions.

w Harry Tugend, George Wells *d* Busby Berkeley *ph* George Folsey *md* Adolph Deutsch *songs* Betty Comden, Adolph Green, Roger Edens

Gene Kelly, Frank Sinatra, Esther Williams, *Betty Garrett*, Jules Munshin, Edward Arnold, Richard Lane, Tom Dugan

'His love challenged the flames of revolution!'

A Tale of Two Cities

US 1935 121m bw
MGM (David O. Selznick)
A British lawyer sacrifices himself to save another man from the guillotine.
Richly detailed version of the classic melodrama, with production values counting more than the acting.

w W. P. Lipscomb, S. N. Behrman, *novel* Charles Dickens *d* Jack Conway *ph* Oliver T. Marsh *m* Herbert Stothart

Ronald Colman, Elizabeth Allan, Basil Rathbone, Edna May Oliver, Blanche Yurka, Reginald Owen, Henry B. Walthall, Donald Woods, Walter Catlett, H. B. Warner, Claude Gillingwater, Fritz Leiber

'A screen classic . . . technically it is about as flawless as possible . . . it has been made with respectful and loving care.'—*Variety*

'A prodigiously stirring production . . . for more than two hours it crowds the screen with beauty and excitement.'—*New York Times*

† Originally prepared at Warners for Leslie Howard.

AAN: best picture

The Tales of Hoffman

GB 1951 127m
Technicolor
British Lion / London / Michael Powell, Emeric Pressburger
The poet Hoffman, in three adventures, seeks the eternal woman and is beset by eternal evil.
Overwhelming combination of opera, ballet, and rich production design, an indigestible hodgepodge with flashes of superior talent.

wd Michael Powell, Emeric Pressburger *ph* Christopher Challis *m* Jacques Offenbach *pd* Hein Heckroth

Robert Rounseville, Robert Helpmann, Pamela Brown, Moira Shearer, Frederick Ashton, Leonide Massine, Ludmilla Tcherina, Ann Ayars, Mogens Wieth; music conducted by Sir Thomas Beecham with the Royal Philharmonic Orchestra

'The most spectacular failure yet achieved by Powell and Pressburger, who seem increasingly to dissipate their gifts in a welter of aimless ingenuity.'—*Gavin Lambert*

'An art director's picnic: I marvelled without being enthralled.'—*Richard Mallett, Punch*

'Enchanting, a labour of love.'—*Sunday Telegraph*

'It echoes the peak of the Victorian spirit.'—*Time*

Tales of Manhattan

US 1942 118m bw
TCF (Boris Morros, Sam Spiegel)
Separate stories of a tail coat, which passes from owner to owner.

The stories are all rather disappointing in their different veins, but production standards are high and a few of the stars shine. A sequence starring W. C. Fields was deleted before release.

w Ben Hecht, Ferenc Molnar, Donald Ogden Stewart, Samuel Hoffenstein, Alan Campbell, Ladislas Fodor, Laslo Vadnay, Laszlo Gorog, Lamar Trotti, Henry Blankfort *d* Julien Duvivier *ph* Joseph Walker *m* Sol Kaplan

Charles Boyer, Rita Hayworth, Thomas Mitchell, Eugene Pallette; Ginger Rogers, Henry Fonda, Cesar Romero, Gail Patrick, Roland Young; *Charles Laughton*, Elsa Lanchester, Victor Francen, Christian Rub; *Edward G. Robinson*, George Sanders, James Gleason, Harry Davenport; Paul Robeson, Ethel Waters, Eddie Anderson

† Duvivier was clearly chosen to make this film because of his success with the similar *Carnet de Bal*; he and Boyer went on to make the less successful *Flesh and Fantasy* on similar lines.

The Talk of the Town
US 1942   118m   bw
Columbia (George Stevens, Fred Guiol)
A girl loves both a suspected murderer and the lawyer who defends him.
Unusual mixture of comedy and drama, delightfully handled by three sympathetic stars.

w Irwin Shaw, Sidney Buchman d George Stevens ph Ted Tetzlaff *m* Frederick Hollander

Ronald Colman, Cary Grant, Jean Arthur, Edgar Buchanan, Glenda Farrell, Charles Dingle, Emma Dunn, Rex Ingram
  'A rip-roaring, knock-down-and-drag-out comedy about civil liberties.'—*John T. McManus*
  'Well tuned and witty, at its best when it sticks to the middle ground

between farce and melodrama. The chief fault of the script is its excessive length and the fact that a standard lynching mob climax is followed by a prolonged anti-climax.'—*Newsweek*
  'I can't take my lynching so lightly, even in a screwball. Still, I am all for this kind of comedy and for players like Arthur and Grant, who can mug more amusingly the most scriptwriters can write.'—*Manny Farber*
  'Did the authors think they were writing a Shavian comedy of ideas? The ideas are garbled and silly, but the people are so pleasant that the picture manages to be quite amiable and high-spirited.'—*Pauline Kael, 70s*

† Two endings were filmed: the eventual choice of mate for Miss Arthur was determined by audience reaction at previews.

AAN: best picture; original story (Sidney Harmon); script; Ted Tetzhaff; Frederick Hollander

A Taste of Honey
GB 1961   100m   bw
British Lion/ Bryanston/Woodfall (Tony Richardson)
Adventures of a pregnant Salford teenager, her sluttish mother, black lover and homosexual friend.
Fascinating offbeat comedy drama with memorable characters and sharply etched backgrounds.

w Shelagh Delaney, Tony Richardson, *play* Shelagh Delaney *d* Tony Richardson *ph* Walter Lassally *m* John Addison

Rita Tushingham, Dora Bryan, Murray Melvin, Robert Stephens, Paul Danquah
  'Tart and lively around the edges and bitter at the core.'—*Peter John Dyer*
  'Rich, full work, directed with an unerring sense of rightness.'—*New Yorker*

'The mightiest dramatic spectacle of all the ages!'

The Ten Commandments

🎭🎭 US 1923   150m approx (24 fps)   part Technicolor
silent
Paramount / Famous
Players-Lasky (Cecil B. de Mille)

Moses leads the Israelites into the promised land in modern San Francisco; a story of two brothers shows the power of prayer and truth. The two halves in fact are totally disconnected; but this is a de Mille spectacular and therefore beyond reproach, while as a Hollywood milestone it cannot be denied a place in the Hall of Fame.

w Jeanie MacPherson *d* Cecil B. de Mille *ph* Bert Glennon and others (*colour*, Ray Renahan)

Theodore Roberts, Richard Dix, Rod la Rocque, Edythe Chapman, Leatrice Joy, Nita Naldi

'It will last as long as the film on which it is recorded.'—*James R. Quirk, Photoplay*

The Ten Commandments

🎭🎭 US 1956   219m
Technicolor   Vistavision
Paramount / Cecil B. de Mille
(Henry Wilcoxon)

The life of Moses and his leading of the Israelites to the Promised Land. Popular but incredibly stilted and verbose bible-in-pictures spectacle. A very long haul along a monotonous route, with the director at his pedestrian worst.

w Aeneas Mackenzie, Jesse L. Lasky Jnr, Jack Gariss, Frederic M. Frank *d* Cecil B. de Mille *ph* Loyal Griggs *m* Elmer Bernstein

Charlton Heston, Yul Brynner, Edward G. Robinson, Anne Baxter, Nina Foch, Yvonne de Carlo, John Derek, H. B. Warner, Henry Wilcoxon, Judith Anderson, John Carradine, Douglass Dumbrille, Cedric Hardwicke, Martha Scott, Vincent Price, Debra Paget

'De Mille not only moulds religion into a set pattern of Hollywood conventions; he has also become an expert at making entertainment out of it.'—*Gordon Gow, Films and Filming*

'The result of all these stupendous efforts? Something roughly comparable to an eight-foot chorus girl—pretty well put together, but much too big and much too flashy . . . What de Mille has really done is to throw sex and sand into the moviegoers' eyes for almost twice as long as anyone else has ever dared to.'—*Time*

'What a story it tells! What majesty it encompasses! What loves it unveils! What drama it unfolds!'—*publicity*

AAN: best picture; Loyal Griggs

Terms of Endearment

🎭🎭 US 1983   132m   Metrocolor
Paramount (James L. Brooks)

An eccentric widow fends off suitors while interfering with her daughter's marriage; but all is forgiven when the daughter dies.

This shapeless film is little more than an excuse for actors and writer to show off, which they do to great excess; but parts of it are entertaining enough and it certainly impressed the Academy Award committee.

w,d James L. Brooks, *novel* Larry McMurtry *ph* Andrzej Bartkowiak *m* Michael Gore *pd* Polly Platt

Shirley Maclaine, Jack Nicholson, Debra Winger, Danny DeVito, Jeff Daniels, John Lithgow

'An outsize sitcom and a crassly constructed slice of anti-feminism that contrives to rub liberal amounts of soap in the viewer's eyes.'—*Sight and Sound*

AA: best picture; Shirley Maclaine; Jack Nicholson; direction; adaptation
AAN: John Lithgow; editing (Richard Marks); Michael Gore; art direction; Debra Winger

Thank Your Lucky Stars

🎬 US 1943   127m   bw
Warner (Mark Hellinger)

Eddie Cantor and his double get involved in planning a patriotic show.

All-star wartime musical with some unexpected turns and a generally funny script.

w Norman Panama, Melvin Frank, James V. Kern d David Butler ph Arthur Edeson md Leo F. Forbstein ch Le Roy Prinz songs Frank Loesser, Arthur Schwartz

Eddie Cantor, Dennis Morgan, Joan Leslie, Edward Everett Horton, S. Z. Sakall, Humphrey Bogart, Jack Carson, *Bette Davis,* Olivia de Havilland, *Errol Flynn,* John Garfield, Alan Hale, Ida Lupino, *Ann Sheridan,* Dinah Shore, George Tobias, Spike Jones and his City Slickers, Willie Best, Hattie McDaniel

'The loudest and most vulgar of the current musicals, it is also the most fun, if you are amused when show people kid their own idiom.'—*James Agee*

'An all-star show with the conspicuous flavour of amateur night at the studio.'—*New York Times*

'Everyone had a good time making it.'—*Motion Picture Herald*

AAN: song 'They're Either Too Young or Too Old'

That Hamilton Woman
US 1941   128m   bw
London Films (Alexander Korda)
GB title: *Lady Hamilton*
The affair of Lord Nelson and Emma Hamilton.
Bowdlerized version of a famous misalliance; coldly made but quite effective scene by scene, with notable performances.

w Walter Reisch, R. C. Sherriff d Alexander Korda ph Rudolph Maté m Miklos Rozsa

Laurence Olivier, Vivien Leigh, Gladys Cooper, Alan Mowbray, Sara Allgood, Henry Wilcoxon, Halliwell Hobbes

AAN: Rudolph Maté

'Boy! do we need it now!'
That's Entertainment
US 1974   137m
Metrocolor   70mm (blown up) / scope
MGM (Daniel Melnick, Jack Haley Jnr)
Fred Astaire, Gene Kelly, Elizabeth Taylor, James Stewart, Bing Crosby, Liza Minnelli, Donald O'Connor, Debbie Reynolds, Mickey Rooney and Frank Sinatra introduce highlights from MGM's musical past.
A slapdash compilation which was generally very big at the box office and obviously has fascinating sequences, though the narration is sloppily sentimental and the later wide-screen sequences let down the rest.

wd Jack Haley Jnr ph various m various

principal stars as above plus Judy Garland, Esther Williams, Eleanor Powell, Clark Gable, Ray Bolger

'While many ponder the future of MGM, none can deny that it has one hell of a past.'—*Variety*

'It is particularly gratifying to get the key sequences from certain movies without having to sit through a fatuous storyline.'—*Michael Billington, Illustrated London News*

'No other film in town offers such a harvest of undiluted joy.'—*Sunday Express*

That's Entertainment Part Two
US 1976   133m
Metrocolor   70mm (blown up) / scope
MGM (Saul Chaplin, Daniel Melnick)
More of the above, introduced by Fred Astaire and Gene Kelly, with comedy and drama sequences as well as musical.

d Gene Kelly titles Saul Bass ph various principal stars as above plus Jeanette MacDonald, Nelson Eddy, the Marx Brothers, Laurel and Hardy, Jack Buchanan, Judy Garland, Ann Miller, Mickey Rooney, Oscar Levant, Louis Armstrong, etc.

'Kill one and two others take its place! Don't turn your back or you're doomed! And don't tell anyone what Them are!'

Them!

US 1954   94m   bw
Warner (David Weisbart)

Atomic bomb radiation causes giant ants to breed in the New Mexico desert.

Among the first, and certainly the best, of the post-atomic monster animal cycle, this durable thriller starts with several eerie desert sequences and builds up to a shattering climax in the Los Angeles sewers. A general air of understatement helps a lot.

w Ted Sherdeman, *story* George Worthing Yates   *d Gordon Douglas* *ph* Sid Hickox   *m* Bronislau Kaper

Edmund Gwenn, James Whitmore, Joan Weldon, James Arness, Onslow Stevens

'I asked the editor: How does it look? And he said: Fine. I said: Does it look honest? He said: As honest as twelve foot ants can look.'—*Gordon Douglas*

They Died with Their Boots On

US 1941   140m   bw
Warner (Robert Fellows)

The life of General Custer and his death at Little Big Horn.

It seems it all happened because of an evil cadet who finished up selling guns to the Indians. Oh, well! The first half is romantic comedy, the second steels itself for the inevitable tragic outcome, but it's all expertly mounted and played in the best old Hollywood style.

w Wally Kline, Aeneas Mackenzie *d Raoul Walsh   ph* Bert Glennon *m* Max Steiner

Errol Flynn, Olivia de Havilland, Arthur Kennedy, Charles Grapewin, Anthony Quinn, Sidney Greenstreet, Gene Lockhart, Stanley Ridges, John Litel, Walter Hampden, Regis Toomey, Hattie McDaniel

'Talk and die! Until now their lips were frozen with fear!'

They Won't Forget

US 1937   94m   bw
Warner (Mervyn Le Roy)

The murder of a girl in a southern town leads to a lynching.

Finely detailed social drama, a classic of American realism; harrowing to watch.

w Robert Rossen, *Aben Kandel*, *novel* Death in the Deep South by Ward Greene   *d Mervyn Le Roy* *ph* Arthur Edeson, Warren Lynch *m* Adolph Deutsch   *md* Leo F. Forbstein

Claude Rains, Gloria Dickson, Edward Norris, Otto Kruger, Allyn Joslyn, Linda Perry, Elisha Cook Jnr, Lana Turner, Cy Kendall, Elizabeth Risdon

'Not only an honest picture, but an example of real movie-making.'—*Pare Lorentz*

The Thief of Bagdad

US 1924   approx 135m (24 fps)   bw   silent
Douglas Fairbanks

In old Bagdad, a thief uses magic to outwit the evil Caliph.

Celebrated silent version of the old fable, its camera tricks a little timeworn now but nevertheless maintaining the air of a true classic by virtue of its leading performance and driving narrative energy.

w Lotta Woods, Douglas Fairbanks *d* Raoul Walsh   *ph* Arthur Edeson *m* Mortimer Wilson   *ad* William Cameron Menzies

Douglas Fairbanks, Snitz Edwards, Charles Belcher, Anna May Wong, Julanne Johnston, Etta Lee, Brandon Hurst, Sojin

'An entrancing picture, wholesome and compelling, deliberate and beautiful, a feat of motion picture art which has never been equalled.'—*New York Times*

'Here is magic. Here is beauty. Here is the answer to cynics who give the motion picture no place in the family of the arts . . . a work of rare genius.'—*James Quirk, Photoplay*

The Thief of Bagdad
🏔 GB 1940   109m
Technicolor
London Films (Alexander Korda)
A boy thief helps a deposed king thwart an evil usurper.
Marvellous blend of magic, action and music, the only film to catch on celluloid the overpowering atmosphere of the Arabian Nights.

w Miles Malleson, Lajos Biro d Michael Powell, Ludwig Berger, Tim Whelan ph Georges Périnal, Osmond Borradaile m Miklos Rozsa sp Lawrence Butler

Conrad Veidt, Sabu, John Justin, June Duprez, Morton Selten, Miles Malleson, Rex Ingram, Mary Morris

ABU (Sabu): 'I'm Abu the thief, son of Abu the thief, grandson of Abu the thief, most unfortunate of ten sons with a hunger that yearns day and night . . .'

AGED KING (Morton Selten): 'This is the Land of Legend, where everything is possible when seen through the eyes of youth.'

'The true stuff of fairy tale.'—*Basil Wright*

'Both spectacular and highly inventive.'—*NFT, 1969*

'Magical, highly entertaining, and now revalued by Hollywood moguls Lucas and Coppola.'—*Time Out, 1980*

AA: Georges Périnal, Osmond Borradaile
AAN: Miklos Rozsa

'A laugh tops every thrilling moment!'
The Thin Man
🏆 US 1934   93m   bw
MGM (Hunt Stromberg)
In New York over Christmas, a tipsy detective with his wife and dog solves the murder of an eccentric inventor.
Fast-moving, alternately comic and suspenseful mystery drama

developed in brief scenes and fast wipes. It set a sparkling comedy career for two stars previously known for heavy drama, it was frequently imitated, and it showed a wisecracking, affectionate married relationship almost for the first time.

w Frances Goodrich, Albert Hackett, novel Dashiell Hammett d W. S. Van Dyke ph James Wong Howe m William Axt

William Powell, Myrna Loy, Maureen O'Sullivan, Nat Pendleton, Minna Gombell, Edward Ellis, Porter Hall, Henry Wadsworth, William Henry, Harold Huber, Cesar Romero, Edward Brophy

'A strange mixture of excitement, quips and hard-boiled sentiment . . . full of the special touches that can come from nowhere but the studio, that really make the feet a movie walks on.'—*Otis Ferguson*

† Sequels, on the whole of descending merit, included the following, all made at MGM with the same star duo: 1936: *After the Thin Man* (110m). 1939: *Another Thin Man* (102m). 1941: *Shadow of the Thin Man* (97m). 1944: *The Thin Man Goes Home* (100m). 1947: *Song of the Thin Man* (86m).

AAN: best picture; script; W. S. Van Dyke; William Powell

The Thing
🦅 US 1951   87m   bw
RKO/Winchester (Howard Hawks)
GB title: *The Thing from Another World*
A US scientific expedition in the Arctic is menaced by a ferocious being they inadvertently thaw out from a spaceship.
Curiously drab suspense shocker mainly set in corridors, with insufficient surprises to sustain its length. It does, however, contain the first space monster on film, and is quite nimbly made, though it fails to use the central gimmick from its original story.

w Charles Lederer, story Who Goes

There by J. W. Campbell Jnr
d Christian Nyby (with mysterious help, either Hawks or Orson Welles) *ph* Russell Harlan
m Dmitri Tiomkin

Robert Cornthwaite, Kenneth Tobey, Margaret Sheridan, Bill Self, Dewey Martin, James Arness (as the thing)

LAST SPEECH OF FILM: 'I bring you warning—to every one of you listening to the sound of my voice. Tell the world, tell this to everyone wherever they are: watch the skies, watch everywhere, keep looking—watch the skies!'

'There seems little point in creating a monster of such original characteristics if he is to be allowed only to prowl about the North Pole, waiting to be destroyed by the superior ingenuity of the US Air Force.'—*Penelope Houston*

'A monster movie with pace, humour and a collection of beautifully timed jabs of pure horror.'—*NFT, 1967*

Things to Come

GB 1936 113m bw
London Films (Alexander Korda)
War in 1940 is followed by plague, rebellion, a new glass-based society, and the first rocketship to the moon. Fascinating, chilling and dynamically well-staged vignettes tracing mankind's future. Bits of the script and acting may be wobbly, but the sets and music are magnificent, the first part of the prophecy chillingly accurate, and the whole mammoth undertaking almost unique in film history.

w H. G. Wells, from his book The Shape of Things to Come
d/pd William Cameron Menzies ph Georges Périnal m Arthur Bliss sp Harry Zech, Ned Mann ad Vincent Korda

Raymond Massey, Edward Chapman, Ralph Richardson, Margaretta Scott, Cedric Hardwicke, Sophie Stewart, Derrick de Marney, John Clements

CABAL (Raymond Massey): 'It is this or that—all the universe or nothing. Which shall it be, Passworthy? Which shall it be?'

THEOTOCOPULOS (Cedric Hardwicke): 'What is this progress? What is the good of all this progress onward and onward? We demand a halt. We demand a rest . . . an end to progress! Make an end to this progress now! Let this be the last day of the scientific age!'

'Successful in every department except emotionally. For heart interest Mr Wells hands you an electric switch . . . It's too bad present-day film distribution isn't on a Wells 2040 basis, when the negative cost could be retrieved by button pushing. It's going to be harder than that. It's going to be almost impossible.'—*Variety*

'An amazingly ingenious technical accomplishment, even if it does hold out small hope for our race . . . the existence pictured is as joyless as a squeezed grapefruit.'—*Don Herold*

'A leviathan among films . . . a stupendous spectacle, an overwhelming, Dorean, Jules Vernesque, elaborated *Metropolis*, staggering to eye, mind and spirit, the like of which has never been seen and never will be seen again.'—*The Sunday Times*

The Third Man

GB 1949 100m bw
British Lion / London Films / David O. Selznick / Alexander Korda (Carol Reed)
An unintelligent but tenacious writer of westerns arrives in post-war Vienna to join his old friend Harry Lime, who seems to have met with an accident . . . or has he?
Totally memorable and irresistible romantic thriller. Stylish from the first to the last, with inimitable backgrounds of zither music and war-torn buildings pointing up a then-topical black market story full of cynical characters but not without humour. Hitchcock with feeling, if you like.

w *Graham Greene* d *Carol Reed*
ph *Robert Krasker* m *Anton Karas*

*Joseph Cotten, Trevor Howard,
Alida Valli, Orson Welles, Bernard
Lee, Wilfrid Hyde White,* Ernst
Deutsch, Siegfried Breuer, Erich
Ponto, Paul Hoerbiger

HARRY LIME (Orson Welles): 'Look
down there. Would you really feel
any pity if one of those dots stopped
moving for ever? If I offered you
twenty thousand pounds for every
dot that stopped, would you really,
old man, tell me to keep my money,
or would you calculate how many
dots you could afford to spare? Free
of income tax, old man, free of
income tax. It's the only way to save
money nowadays.'

LIME: 'In Italy for thirty years
under the Borgias they had warfare,
terror, murder and bloodshed, but
they produced Michelangelo,
Leonardo da Vinci and the
Renaissance. In Switzerland, they
had brotherly love; they had five
hundred years of democracy and
peace—and what did that produce?
The cuckoo clock.'

'Sensitive and humane and
dedicated, [Reed] would seem to be
enclosed from life with no specially
strong feelings about the stories that
come his way other than that they
should be something he can perfect
and polish with a craftsman's
love.'—*Richard Winnington*

'Crammed with cinematic plums
which could do the early Hitchcock
proud.'—*Time*

AA: Robert Krasker
AAN: Carol Reed

The Thirty-Nine Steps
GB 1935   81m   bw
Gaumont British (Ivor
Montagu)
A spy is murdered; the man who has
befriended her is suspected, but
eludes the police until a chase across
Scotland produces the real villains.
Marvellous comedy thriller with
most of the gimmicks found not only

in Hitchcock's later work but in
anyone else's who has tried the same
vein. It has little to do with the
original novel, and barely sets foot
outside the studio, but it makes
every second count, and is
unparalleled in its use of timing,
atmosphere and comedy relief.

w *Charles Bennett, Alma Reville,
novel* John Buchan d *Alfred
Hitchcock ph Bernard Knowles
m* Hubert Bath, Jack Beaver
md Louis Levy

Robert Donat, Madeleine Carroll,
Godfrey Tearle, Lucie Mannheim,
Peggy Ashcroft, John Laurie, *Wylie
Watson, Helen Haye,* Frank Cellier

'A narrative of the unexpected—a
humorous, exciting, dramatic,
entertaining, pictorial, vivid and
novel tale told with a fine sense of
character and a keen grasp of the
cinematic idea.'—*Sydney W. Carroll*

'A miracle of speed and
light.'—*Otis Ferguson*

'Such is the zest of the Hitchcock
plot that the original point of the
title was totally forgotten, and half a
line had to be added at the end by
way of explanation.'—*George Perry,
1965*

Thirty Seconds over Tokyo
US 1944   138m   bw
MGM (Sam Zimbalist)
How the first American attack on
Japan was planned.
Sturdy World War II action
flagwaver, with Tracy guesting as
Colonel Dolittle.

w *Dalton Trumbo* d *Mervyn Le
Roy ph* Harold Rosson, Robert
Surtees m Herbert Stothart

Spencer Tracy, Van Johnson,
Robert Walker, Phyllis Thaxter, Tim
Murdock, Don Defore, Robert
Mitchum

'All of the production involving
planes and technical action is so fine
that the film has the tough and literal
quality of an air force
documentary.'—*Bosley Crowther,
New York Times*

'A big studio, big scale film, free
of artistic pretensions, it is

transformed by its not very imaginative but very dogged sincerity into something forceful, simple and thoroughly sympathetic.'—*James Agee*

AAN: Harold Rosson, Robert Surtees

This Gun for Hire

US 1942 81m bw
Paramount (Richard M. Blumenthal)

A professional killer becomes involved in a fifth columnist plot.

Efficient Americanization of one of its author's more sombre entertainments. The melodrama has an authentic edge and strangeness to it, and it established the star images of both Ladd and Lake, as well as being oddly downbeat for a Hollywood product of this jingoistic time.

w Albert Maltz, W. R. Burnett, *novel* A Gun for Sale by *Graham Greene d* Frank Tuttle *ph* John Seitz *m* David Buttolph

Alan Ladd, Veronica Lake, Robert Preston, *Laird Cregar*, Tully Marshall, Mikhail Rasumny, Marc Lawrence

This Happy Breed

GB 1944 114m
Technicolor
GFD / Two Cities / Cineguild (Noel Coward, Anthony Havelock-Allan)

Life between the wars for a London suburban family.

Coward's domestic epic is unconvincingly written and largely miscast, but sheer professionalism gets it through, and the decor is historically interesting.

w David Lean, Ronald Neame, Anthony Havelock-Allan, *play* Noel Coward *d* David Lean *ph* Ronald Neame

Robert Newton, Celia Johnson, Stanley Holloway, John Mills, Kay Walsh, Amy Veness, Alison Leggatt

'Nearly two hours of the pleasure of recognition, which does not come

very far up the scale of aesthetic values.'—*Richard Mallett, Punch*

This Is the Army

US 1943 121m
Technicolor
Warner (Jack L. Warner, Hal B. Wallis)

Army recruits put on a musical revue.

Mammoth musical flagwaver.

w Casey Robinson, Claude Binyon *d* Michael Curtiz *ph* Bert Glennon, Sol Polito *songs* Irving Berlin *m* Ray Heindorf

George Murphy, Joan Leslie, Irving Berlin, George Tobias, Alan Hale, Charles Butterworth, Rosemary de Camp, Dolores Costello, Una Merkel, Stanley Ridges, Ruth Donnelly, Kate Smith, Frances Langford, Gertrude Niesen, Ronald Reagan, Joe Louis

AA: Ray Heindorf

The Thomas Crown Affair

US 1968 102m De Luxe
Panavision
UA / Mirisch / Simkoe / Solar (Norman Jewison)

A bored property tycoon masterminds a bank robbery and is chased by a glamorous insurance investigator.

Not so much a movie as an animated colour supplement, this glossy entertainment makes style its prime virtue, plays cute tricks with multiple images and has a famous sexy chess game, but is not above being boring for the rest of the way.

w Alan R. Trustman *d* Norman Jewison *ph* Haskell Wexler *m* Michel Legrand *ad* Robert Boyle

Steve McQueen, Faye Dunaway, Paul Burke, Jack Weston, Yaphet Kotto

'Jewison and Wexler seem to have gone slightly berserk, piling up tricks and mannerisms until the film itself sinks out of sight, forlorn and forgotten.'—*Tom Milne*

'A glimmering, empty film reminiscent of an *haute couture*

model—stunning on the surface, concave and undernourished beneath.'—*Stefan Kanter*

AA: song 'The Windmills of Your Mind' (*m* Michel Legrand, *ly* Alan and Marilyn Bergman)
AAN: Michel Legrand

Thoroughly Modern Millie
US 1967   138m
Technicolor
Universal (Ross Hunter)

In the twenties, a young girl comes to New York, becomes thoroughly modern, falls for her boss, and has various adventures unmasking a white slave racket centring on a Chinese laundry.

Initially most agreeable but subsequently very patchy spoof of twenties fads and films, including a Harold Lloyd thrill sequence which just doesn't work and a comedy performance from Beatrice Lillie which does. Tunes and performances are alike variable.

w Richard Morris *d* George Roy Hill *ph* Russell Metty *ad* Alexander Golitzen, George Webb *m* Elmer Bernstein *md* André Previn, Joseph Gershenson *ch* Joe Layton *songs* various

Julie Andrews, Mary Tyler Moore, *John Gavin*, James Fox, Carol Channing, *Beatrice Lillie*, Jack Soo, Pat Morita, Anthony Dexter

'What a nice 65-minute movie is buried therein!'—*Judith Crist*

AA: Elmer Bernstein
AAN: André Previn, Joseph Gershenson; title song (*m* James Van Heusen, *ly* Sammy Cahn); Carol Channing

Those Magnificent Men in Their Flying Machines, or How I Flew from London to Paris in 25 hours and 11 Minutes
GB 1965   133m
Technicolor   Todd-AO
TCF (Stan Marguilies, Jack Davies)

In 1910, a newspaper owner sponsors a London to Paris air race. Long-winded, generally agreeable

knockabout comedy with plenty to look at but far too few jokes to sustain it.

w Jack Davies, Ken Annakin *d* Ken Annakin *ph* Christopher Challis *m* Ron Goodwin *pd* Tom Morahan

Sarah Miles, Stuart Whitman, Robert Morley, Eric Sykes, Terry-Thomas, James Fox, Alberto Sordi, Gert Frobe, Jean-Pierre Cassel, Karl Michael Vogler, Irina Demich, Benny Hill, Flora Robson, Sam Wanamaker, Red Skelton, Fred Emney, Cicely Courtneidge, Gordon Jackson, John Le Mesurier, Tony Hancock, William Rushton

'There is many a likely gag, but none that survives the second or third reprise. It could have been a good bit funnier by being shorter: the winning time is 25 hours 11 minutes, and by observing some kind of neo-Aristotelian unity the film seems to last exactly as long.'—*John Simon*

AAN: script

The Three Caballeros
US 1945   70m   Technicolor
Walt Disney (Norman Ferguson)

A programme of shorts about South America, linked by Donald Duck as a tourist.

Rapid-fire mélange of fragments supporting the good neighbour policy, following the shorter *Saludos Amigos* of 1943. The kaleidoscopic sequences and the combination of live action with cartoon remain of absorbing interest.

w various *d* various *m* Edward Plumb, Paul J. Smith, Charles Wolcott

† Stories include Pablo the Penguin, Little Gauchito, a Mexican sequence and some adventures with Joe Carioca.

AAN: Edward Plumb, Paul J. Smith, Charles Wolcott

Three Coins in the Fountain

⚑ US 1954 102m De Luxe
Cinemascope
TCF (Sol C. Siegel)

Three American girls find romance
in Rome.

An enormous box office hit, the
pattern of which was frequently
repeated against various
backgrounds; it was actually remade
in Madrid as *The Pleasure Seekers*.
In itself a thin entertainment, but the
title song carried it.

w John Patrick, *novel* John H.
Secondari d Jean Negulesco
ph Milton Krasner m Victor Young
song Jule Styne, *Sammy Cahn*

Clifton Webb, Dorothy McGuire,
Louis Jourdan, Jean Peters, Rossano
Brazzi, Maggie McNamara, Howard
St John, Kathryn Givney, Cathleen
Nesbitt

AA: Milton Krasner; title song
AAN: best picture

'Out of the inferno of war came
  three men and a woman—to
  live their lives, to strive for
  happiness, to seek love!'
Three Comrades

🎭 US 1938 98m bw
✗ MGM (Joseph L. Mankiewicz)

In twenties Germany, three friends
find life hard but derive some joy
from their love for a high-spirited
girl who is dying of tuberculosis.

Despairing romance becomes a
sentimental tearjerker with all the
stops out; immaculately produced
and very appealing to the masses,
but prevented by censorship from
being the intended indictment of
Nazi Germany. The final scene in
which the two surviving comrades
are joined in the churchyard by their
ghostly friends still packs a wallop.

w F. Scott Fitzgerald, Edward A.
Paramore, *novel* Erich Maria
Remarque d Frank Borzage
ph Joseph Ruttenberg m Franz
Waxman

Margaret Sullavan, Robert Taylor,
Robert Young, Franchot Tone, Guy
Kibbee, Lionel Atwill, Henry Hull,
Charley Grapewin

'Just what Frank Borzage is trying
to prove is very difficult to fathom
. . . there must have been some
reason for making this picture, but it
certainly isn't in the name of
entertainment.'—*Variety*

'A remarkably high combination
of talents has made it all very
impressive and moving—good
writing, a good man at the camera,
good actors, and presiding over them
a good director . . . such
unforgettable bits as the pursuit of
the boy who shot Gottfried, a
glimpse from under the muffling
blanket of the girl's stricken face, the
startling downswoop of the camera's
eye upon the girl getting up from
bed to remove the burden of her
illness from those who love her.
These are high moments in a film full
of beauty.'—*National Board of
Review*

'A love story, beautifully told and
consummately acted, but so
drenched in hopelessness and heavy
with the aroma of death, of wasted
youth in a world of foggy shapes and
nameless menaces, that its beauty
and strength are often clouded and
betrayed.'—*Time*

AAN: Margaret Sullavan

'His code name is Condor. In the
  next twenty-four hours
  everyone he trusts will try to kill
  him.'
Three Days of the Condor

⚑ US 1975 118m
Technicolor Panavision
Paramount / Dino de
Laurentiis / Wildwood (Stanley
Schneider)

An innocent researcher for a branch
of the CIA finds himself marked for
death by assassins employed by
another branch.

Entertaining New York-based
thriller which shamelessly follows
most of the twists of *The 39 Steps*. It
is just possible to follow its
complexities, and the dialogue is
smart.

w Lorenzo Semple Jnr, David
Rayfiel, *novel* Six Days of the

Condor by James Grady *d Sydney
Pollack ph Owen Roizman m Dave
Grusin*

Robert Redford, Faye Dunaway,
Cliff Robertson, Max Von Sydow,
John Houseman, Walter McGinn

The Three Musketeers

US 1948 125m
Technicolor
MGM (Pandro S. Berman)
High-spirited version of the famous
story, with duels and fights presented
like musical numbers. Its vigour and
inventiveness is a pleasure to behold.

*w Robert Ardrey d George Sidney
ph Robert Planck m Herbert
Stothart*

Gene Kelly, Lana Turner, June
Allyson, Frank Morgan, Van Heflin,
Angela Lansbury, Vincent Price,
Keenan Wynn, John Sutton, Gig
Young, Robert Coote, Reginald
Owen, Ian Keith, Patricia Medina

'A heavy, rough-housing mess. As
Lady de Winter, Lana Turner
sounds like a drive-in waitress
exchanging quips with hotrodders,
and as Richelieu, Vincent Price
might be an especially crooked used
car dealer. Angela Lansbury wears
the crown of France as though she
had won it at a county fair.'—*New
Yorker, 1980*

AAN: Robert Planck

The Three Musketeers (The
Queen's Diamonds)

Panama 1973 107m
Technicolor
Film Trust (Alex Salkind)
Jokey version with realistic blood;
despite very lively highlights it
wastes most of its high production
cost by not giving its plot a chance;
but money was saved by issuing the
second half separately as *The Four
Musketeers* (*The Revenge of Milady*).
The latter section was less attractive.

*w George MacDonald Fraser
d Richard Lester ph David Watkin
m Michel Legrand pd Brian Eatwell*

Michael York, Oliver Reed, Richard

Chamberlain, Frank Finlay, Raquel
Welch, Geraldine Chaplin, Spike
Milligan, Faye Dunaway, Charlton
Heston, Christopher Lee,
Jean-Pierre Cassel

'It's one dragged-out forced laugh.
No sweep, no romance, no
convincing chivalric tradition to
mock.'—*Stanley Kauffmann*

Three Smart Girls

US 1936 86m bw
Universal (Joe Pasternak)
Three sisters bring their parents back
together.
Pleasant, efficient family film which
made a world star of Deanna Durbin

*w Adele Comandini, Austin Parker
d Henry Koster ph Joseph
Valentine md Charles Previn*

Deanna Durbin, Barbara Read, Nan
Grey, Charles Winninger, Binnie
Barnes, Ray Milland, Alice Brady,
Mischa Auer, Ernest Cossart,
Hobart Cavanaugh
'Surefire entertainment for any and
all types of audiences. It also has
that rare quality of making an
audience feel better for having seen
it.'—*Variety*

'Idiotically tuned in to happiness,
but it isn't boring.'—*New Yorker,
1978*

'Clever, intelligent and witty, this
delightful bit of entertainment has a
genuineness which is rare.'
—*Photoplay*

† Remade as *Three Daring
Daughters.*

AAN: best picture; script

3.10 to Yuma

US 1957 92m bw
Columbia (David Heilwell)
A sheriff has to get his prisoner on
to a train despite the threatening
presence of the prisoner's outlaw
friends.
Tense, well-directed but rather talky
low-budget western: excellent
performances and atmosphere flesh
out an unconvincing physical
situation.

w Halsted Welles *d Delmer Daves*
ph Charles Lawton Jnr m George
Duning
Glenn Ford, *Van Heflin*, Felicia
Farr, Leora Dana, Henry Jones,
Richard Jaeckel, Robert Emhardt
   'A vivid, tense and intelligent
story about probable people,
enhanced by economical writing and
supremely efficient direction and
playing.'—*Guardian*

Thunder Rock

GB 1942 112m bw
Charter Films (John Boulting)
A journalist disgusted with the world
of the thirties retires to a lighthouse
on Lake Michigan and is haunted by
the ghosts of immigrants drowned a
century before.
Subtle adaptation of an impressive
and topical anti-isolationist play,
very well acted and presented.

w Jeffrey Dell, Bernard Miles, *play
Robert Ardrey d* Roy Boulting
ph Mutz Greenbaum (Max Greene)
m Hans May
Michael Redgrave, *Lilli Palmer*,
Barbara Mullen, *James Mason*,
Frederick Valk, *Frederick Cooper*,
Finlay Currie, *Sybilla Binder*
   'Boldly imaginative in theme and
treatment.'—*Sunday Express*
   'More interesting technically than
anything since *Citizen
Kane*.'—*Manchester Guardian*
   'If I thought it wouldn't keep too
many people away, I'd call it a work
of art.'—*Daily Express*
   'What a stimulus to thought it is,
this good, brave, outspoken,
unfettered picture.'—*Observer*

Till the Clouds Roll By

US 1946 137m
Technicolor
MGM (Arthur Freed)
The life and times of composer
Jerome Kern.

Better-than-average biopic with
better-than-average tunes and stars.

w Myles Connolly, Jean Holloway
d Richard Whorf *ph* Harry
Stradling, George J. Folsey
md Lennie Hayton

Robert Walker, Judy Garland,
Lucille Bremer, Van Heflin, Mary
Nash, Dinah Shore, Van Johnson,
June Allyson, Tony Martin, Kathryn
Grayson, *Lena Horne*, *Frank
Sinatra*, *Virginia O'Brien*
   'A little like sitting down to a soda
fountain de luxe special of
maple walnut on vanilla on burnt
almond on strawberry on butter
pecan on coffee on raspberry
sherbert on tutti frutti with hot
fudge, butterscotch, marshmallow,
filberts, pistachios, shredded
pineapple, and rainbow sprills on
top, go double on the whipped
cream.'—*James Agee*

Tin Pan Alley

US 1940 95m bw
TCF (Kenneth MacGowan)
During World War I and after, two
dancing girls love the same
composer.
Archetypal musical, full of
Broadway clichés, razzmatazz and
zip. Remade 1950 as *I'll Get By*, not
to such peppy effect.

w Robert Ellis, Helen Logan
*d Walter Lang ph Leon Shamroy
ch Seymour Felix* songs Mack
Gordon, Harry Warren *m* Alfred
Newman
Alice Faye, *Betty Grable*, *John
Payne*, *Jack Oakie*, Allen Jenkins,
Esther Ralston, The Nicholas
Brothers, John Loder, Elisha Cook
Jnr

AA: Alfred Newman

The Titfield Thunderbolt

GB 1952 84m Technicolor
Ealing (Michael Truman)
When a branch railway line is
threatened with closure, the villagers
take it over as a private concern.
Undervalued on its release in the
wake of other Ealing comedies, this
now seems among the best of them
as well as an immaculate colour
production showing the England that
is no more; the script has pace, the
whole thing is brightly polished and
the action works up to a fine
climactic frenzy.

*w T. E. B. Clarke d Charles
Crichton ph Douglas Slocombe
m Georges Auric*

Stanley Holloway, George Relph,
John Gregson, Godfrey Tearle, *Edie
Martin*, Naunton Wayne, Gabrielle
Brune, Hugh Griffith, Sidney James,
Jack McGowran, Ewan Roberts,
Reginald Beckwith

To Be or Not to Be
♉ US 1942 99m bw
(Alexander Korda) Ernst
Lubitsch
Warsaw actors get involved in an
underground plot and an
impersonation of invading Nazis,
including Hitler.
Marvellous free-wheeling
entertainment which starts as drama
and descends through romantic
comedy and suspense into farce;
accused of bad taste at the time, but
now seen as an outstanding example
of Hollywood moonshine, kept
alight through sheer talent and
expertise.

w Edwin Justus Mayer, story Ernst
Lubitsch, Melchior Lengyel *d Ernst
Lubitsch ph Rudolph Maté
m Werner Heymann ad Vincent
Korda*

Jack Benny, Carole Lombard,
Robert Stack, *Stanley Ridges, Felix
Bressart, Lionel Atwill, Sig Rumann,
Tom Dugan*, Charles Halton

TURA in disguise (Jack Benny):
'That great, great Polish actor
Joseph Tura—you must have heard
of him.'

ERHARDT (Sig Rumann): 'Ah, yes
. . . what he did to Shakespeare, we
are now doing to Poland!'

'The comedy is hilarious, even
when it is hysterically
thrilling.'—*Commonweal*
'As effective an example of comic
propaganda as *The Great Dictator*
and far better directed.'—*Charles
Higham, 1972*
'Based on an indiscretion, but
undoubtedly a work of art.'—*James
Agee*
'In any other medium it would be
acknowledged as a classic to rank

with *The Alchemist* or *A Modest
Proposal.'*—*Peter Barnes*
'Lubitsch's comic genius and
corrosive wit are displayed at every
turn.'—*John Baxter*
'The actual business at hand . . . is
nothing less than providing a good
time at the expense of Nazi myth
. . . Lubitsch distinguishes the film's
zanier moments with his customary
mastery of sly humour and
innuendo, and when the story calls
for outright melodrama he is more
than equal to the
occasion.'—*Newsweek*
AAN: Werner Heymann

To Have and Have Not
♉♉ US 1945 100m bw
Warner (Howard Hawks)
An American charter boat captain in
Martinique gets involved with Nazis.
Fairly routinely made studio
adventure notable for first pairing of
Bogart and Bacall, as an imitation of
Casablanca, and for its consistent
though not outstanding
entertainment value. Remade later
as *The Breaking Point* and *The Gun
Runners*, and not dissimilar from
Key Largo.

*w Jules Furthman, William Faulkner,
novel* Ernest Hemingway *d Howard
Hawks ph Sid Hickox m* Franz
Waxman (uncredited) *md* Leo F.
Forbstein

Humphrey Bogart, Lauren Bacall,
Walter Brennan, Hoagy Carmichael,
Dolores Moran, Sheldon Leonard,
Dan Seymour, Marcel Dalio
'Remarkable for the ingenuity and
industry with which the original story
and the individualities of Ernest
Hemingway have been rendered
down into Hollywood
basic.'—*Richard Winnington*
'Sunlight on the lattice, sex in the
corridors, a new pianist at the café,
pistol shots, the fat sureté man
coming round after dark.'—*William
Whitebait*

Tobacco Road
♉♉ US 1941 84m bw
TCF (Jack Kirkland, Harry H.
Oshrin)

Poor whites in Georgia are turned off their land.

This bowdlerized version of a sensational book and play has superbly orchestrated farcical scenes separated by delightfully pictorial quieter moments: it isn't what was intended, but in its own way it's quite marvellous.

w Nunnally Johnson, novel Erskine Caldwell, *play* Jack Kirkland *d John Ford ph* Arthur Miller *m* David Buttolph

Charley Grapewin, Elizabeth Patterson, Dana Andrews, Gene Tierney, *Marjorie Rambeau*, Ward Bond, William Tracy, Zeffie Tilbury, Slim Summerville, Grant Mitchell, Russell Simpson, Spencer Charters

'The whole world loves him!'
Tom Jones
⚔ GB 1963 129m
🐿 Eastmancolor
UA / Woodfall (Tony Richardson)
In 18th-century England a foundling is brought up by the squire and marries his daughter after many adventures.

Fantasia on Old England, at some distance from the original novel, with the director trying every possible jokey approach against a meticulously realistic physical background. Despite trade fears, the *Hellzapoppin* style made it an astonishing box office success (the sex helped), though it quickly lost its freshness and was much imitated.

w John Osborne, *novel* Henry Fielding *d* Tony Richardson *ph* Walter Lassally, *Manny Wynn m* John Addison *pd* Ralph Brinton

Albert Finney, Susannah York, Hugh Griffith, Edith Evans, Joan Greenwood, Diane Cilento, George Devine, Joyce Redman, David Warner, Wilfrid Lawson, Freda Jackson, Rachel Kempson
'Uncertainty, nervousness, muddled method . . . desperation is writ large over it.'—*Stanley Kauffmann*
'Much of the time it looks like a home movie, made with sporadic

talent by a group with more enthusiasm than discipline.'—*Tom Milne*
'It is as though the camera had become a method actor: there are times when you wish you could buy, as on certain juke boxes, five minutes' silence . . . Obviously a film which elicits such lyric ejaculations from the reviewers cannot be all good.'—*John Simon*

† The narrator was Michael MacLiammoir.

AA: best picture; John Osborne; Tony Richardson; John Addison
AAN: Albert Finney; Hugh Griffith; Edith Evans; Diane Cilento; Joyce Redman

Tootsie
☻ US 1982 116m colour
Columbia / Mirage / Punch (Sydney Pollack)
An out-of-work actor pretends to be a woman in order to get a job in a soap opera.

As with *Genevieve* and *Whisky Galore*, an unlikely comedy subject makes an instant classic. It's all in the handling.

w Larry Gelbart, Murray Shisgal, story Don McGuire *d* Sydney Pollack *ph* Owen Roizman *m* Dave Grusin *pd* Peter Larkin *ed* Frederick and William Steinkamp

Dustin Hoffman, Jessica Lange, Teri Garr, Dabney Coleman, Charles Durning, Sydney Pollack, George Gaynes

AA: Jessica Lange
AAN: best picture; Dustin Hoffman; Teri Garr; Sydney Pollack as director; original screenplay; cinematography; editing; song, 'It Might Be You'; sound
BFA: Dustin Hoffman

Top Hat
🎞 US 1935 100m bw
RKO (Pandro S. Berman)
The path of true love is roughened by mistaken identities.

Marvellous Astaire-Rogers musical, with a more or less realistic London supplanted by a totally artificial

Venice, and show stopping numbers
in a style which is no more separated
by amusing plot complications lightly
handled by a team of deft *farceurs*.

*w Dwight Taylor, Allan Scott
d Mark Sandrich ph David Abel,
Vernon Walker m/ly Irving Berlin
ch Hermes Pan ad Van Nest
Polglase, Carroll Clark*

*Fred Astaire, Ginger Rogers, Edward
Everett Horton, Helen Broderick,
Eric Blore, Erik Rhodes*

'The theatres will hold their own
world series with this one. It can't
miss.'—*Variety*

'In 25 years *Top Hat* has lost
nothing of its gaiety and
charm.'—*Dilys Powell, 1960*

AAN: best picture; song 'Cheek to
Cheek'

Topper

US 1937   96m   bw
(MGM) Hal Roach (Milton H.
Bren)

A stuffy banker is haunted by the
ghosts of his sophisticated friends the
Kirbys, who are visible only to him.
Influential supernatural farce, still
pretty funny and deftly acted though
a shade slow to g going.

*w Jack Jevne, Eric Hatch, Eddie
Moran, novel The Jovial Ghosts by
Thorne Smith d Norman Z.
McLeod ph Norbert Brodine
md Arthur Morton*

*Cary Grant, Constance Bennett,
Roland Young, Billie Burke, Alan
Mowbray, Eugene Pallette, Arthur
Lake, Hedda Hopper*

'How substantial the fan support
will be is difficult to anticipate . . .
None of the other films of similar
theme aroused more than mild
enthusiasm among a small group
who patronize the arty theatres and
talk about pictures in terms of art
expression . . . Effort to excuse the
story's absurdities on the theory that
the intent is farce comedy does not
entirely excuse the production from
severe rebuke. Fact also that the
living dead are always facetious may
be shocking to sensibilities. Some of
the situations and dialogue offend
conventional good taste.'—*Variety*

AAN: Roland Young

Topper Returns

US 1941   87m   bw
Hal Roach

A girl ghost helps Topper solve her
own murder.
Spirited supernatural farce which
spoofs murder mysteries, spooky
houses, frightened servants, dumb
cops, etc, in a pacy, accomplished
and generally delightful manner.

*w Jonathan Latimer, Gordon
Douglas, with additional dialogue by
Paul Gerard Smith d Roy del Ruth
ph Norbert Brodine m Werner
Heyman*

*Roland Young, Joan Blondell, Eddie
Anderson, Carole Landis, Dennis
O'Keefe, H. B. Warner, Billie
Burke, Donald McBride, Rafaela
Ottiano*

Tora! Tora! Tora!

US 1970   144m   De Luxe
Panavision
TCF (Elmo Williams)
A reconstruction from both sides of
the events leading up to Pearl
Harbor.
Immense, largely studio-bound,
calcified war spectacle with much
fidelity to the record but no villains
and no hero, therefore no drama and
no suspense.

*w Larry Forrester, Hideo Oguni,
Ryuzo Kikushima d Richard
Fleischer, Ray Kellogg, Toshio
Masuda, Kinji Fukasaku ph Charles
F. Wheeler and Japanese crews
m Jerry Goldsmith sp L. B. Abbott,
Art Cruickshank*

Martin Balsam, Joseph Cotten,
James Whitmore, Jason Robards,
Edward Andrews, Leon Ames,
George Macready, Soh Yamamura,
Takahiro Tamura

'One of the least stirring and least
photogenic historical epics ever
perpetrated on the screen.'—*Gary
Arnold*

AAN: Charles F. Wheeler

Torn Curtain

US 1966   119m
Technicolor
Universal / Alfred Hitchcock

A defector who is really a double
agent is embarrassed when his girl
friend follows him into East
Germany.

Patchy Hitchcock with some
mechanically effective suspense
sequences, efforts at something new,
a few miscalculations, some evidence
of carelessness and a little enjoyable
repetition of old situations.

w Brian Moore, *d Alfred
Hitchcock ph* John F. Warren
m John Addison

Paul Newman, Julie Andrews,
Wolfgang Kieling, Ludwig Donath,
Lila Kedrova, Hans-Joerg Felmy,
Tamara Toumanova

‘The pace is plodding and the
actors stranded by their director's
customary lack of concern with
performance.’—*Time Out*, *1984*

‘They had the perfect love affair.
Until they fell in love!’

A Touch of Class

GB 1973   106m
Technicolor   Panavision
Avco / Brut / Gordon Films (Melvin
Frank)

A married American businessman in
London has a hectic affair with a
dress designer.

Amiable and very physical sex farce
with hilarious highlights and a few
longueurs between; the playing
keeps it above water.

w Melvin Frank, Jack Rose
d Melvin Frank *ph* Austin
Dempster *m* John Cameron

Glenda Jackson, *George Segal*, Paul
Sorvino, Hildegarde Neil

‘Machine-tooled junk.’—*William
S. Pechter*

AA: Glenda Jackson
AAN: best picture; script; John
Cameron; song, ‘All That Love
Went to Waste’ (*m* George Barrie,
ly Sammy Cahn)

‘One tiny spark becomes a night
of towering suspense!’

The Towering Inferno

US 1974   165m   De Luxe
Panavision
TCF / Warner (Irwin Allen)

The world's tallest building is
destroyed by fire on the night of its
inauguration.

Showmanlike but relentlessly padded
disaster spectacular, worth seeing for
its cast of stars, its sheer
old-fashioned expertise, and its
special effects.

w Stirling Silliphant, *novels* The
Tower by Richard Martin Stern, The
Glass Inferno by Thomas M. Scortia,
Frank M. Robinson *d John
Guillermin, Irwin Allen ph* Fred
Koenekamp, Joseph Biroc *m* John
Williams *sp* Bill Abott *pd* William
Creber

Paul Newman, Steve McQueen,
William Holden, Faye Dunaway,
Fred Astaire, Susan Blakely,
Richard Chamberlain, Robert
Vaughn, Jennifer Jones, O. J.
Simpson, Robert Wagner

‘Several generations of blue-eyed
charmers act their roles as if each
were under a separate bell
jar.’—*Verina Glaessner*

‘Each scene of someone horribly
in flames is presented as a feat for
the audience's delectation.’—*New
Yorker*

‘The combination of Grade A
spectacle and B-picture characters
induces a feeling of sideline
detachment.’—*Michael Billington,
Illustrated London News*

AA: photography; song ‘We May
Never Love Like This Again’ (*m / ly*
Al Kasha, Joel Hirschhorn)
AAN: best picture; John Williams;
Fred Astaire

A Town like Alice

GB 1956   117m   bw
Rank / Vic Films (Joseph
Janni)

US title: *The Rape of Malaya*

Life among women prisoners of the
Japanese in Malaya, especially one
who is finally reunited with her
Australian lover.

Genteelly harrowing war film, formlessly adapted from the first part of a popular novel; a big commercial success of its day.

w W. P. Lipscomb, Richard Mason, *novel* Nevil Shute *d* Jack Lee *ph* Geoffrey Unsworth *m* Matyas Seiber

Virginia McKenna, Peter Finch, Takagi, Marie Lohr, Maureen Swanson, Jean Anderson, Renée Houston, Nora Nicholson

Trading Places
US 1983 116m
Technicolor
Paramount/Landis-Folsey (Aaron Russo)

Two rich men arrange a wager on the effects of environment over heredity, and arrange for a con man and a stockbroker to change places. Surprisingly witty comedy, which while not aspiring to great heights, and marred by a few excesses, brought a refreshing breath of air to a declining genre.

w Timothy Harris, Herschel Weingrod *d* John Landis *ph* Robert Paynter *m* Elmer Bernstein *pd* Gene Rudolf

Dan Aykroyd, Eddie Murphy, *Ralph Bellamy, Don Ameche, Denholm Elliott*, Jamie Lee Curtis, Kristin Holby

'Proof positive that the genuine American populist comedy can still attract attention.'—*John Pym, MFB*

BFA: Jamie Lee Curtis, Denholm Elliott

Trapeze
US 1956 105m De Luxe
Cinemascope
UA/Hecht–Lancaster (James Hill)

A circus partnership almost breaks up when a voluptuous third member is engaged.
Concentrated, intense melodrama filmed almost entirely within a French winter circus and giving a very effective feel, almost a smell, of the life therein. Despite great skill in the making, however, the length is too great for a wisp of plot that goes back to *The Three Maxims* and doubtless beyond.

w James R. Webb *d* Carol Reed *ph* Robert Krasker *m* Malcolm Arnold

Burt Lancaster, Tony Curtis, Gina Lollobrigida, Thomas Gomez, Johnny Puleo, Katy Jurado, Sidney James

† This version was supposedly adapted from a Max Catto novel, *The Killing Frost*, but in 1932 Harmonie of Germany issued a film with the title *Trapeze* and a remarkably similar story. It had a scenario by Alfred Machard and was directed by E. A. Dupont. The Anna Neagle film *The Three Maxims* was also very similar, but that was supposedly an original by Herman Mankiewicz.

Treasure Island
US 1934 105m bw
MGM (Hunt Stromberg)

An old pirate map leads to a long sea voyage, a mutiny, and buried treasure.
Nicely mounted Hollywood version of a classic adventure story, a little slow in development but meticulously produced.

w John Lee Mahin, *novel* Robert Louis Stevenson *d* Victor Fleming *ph* Ray June, Clyde de Vinna, Harold Rosson *m* Herbert Stothart

Wallace Beery, Jackie Cooper, Lewis Stone, *Lionel Barrymore*, Otto Kruger, Douglass Dumbrille, Nigel Bruce, Chic Sale

'While much of it entrances, the whole is somewhat tiring.'—*Variety*

'The first three-quarters is so lively and well established in its mood as to make the whole quite worth going to.'—*Otis Ferguson*

'Greed, gold and gunplay on a Mexican mountain of malice!'
'The nearer they got to their treasure the further they got from the law!'

The Treasure of the Sierra Madre
US 1948 126m bw
Warner (Henry Blanke)

Three gold prospectors come to grief through greed.
Well-acted but partly miscast action

fable on the oldest theme in the world; rather tedious and studio-bound for a film with such a high reputation.

wd John Huston, *novel* B. Traven *ph* Ted McCord *m* Max Steiner *md* Leo F. Forbstein

Humphrey Bogart, *Walter Huston*, Tim Holt, Alfonso Bedoya, John Huston, Bruce Bennett, Barton MacLane

'This bitter fable is told with cinematic integrity and considerable skill.'—*Henry Hart*

'The faces of the men, in close-up or in a group, achieve a kind of formal pattern and always dominate the screen.'—*Peter Ericsson*

'One of the very few movies made since 1927 which I am sure will stand up in the memory and esteem of qualified people alongside the best of the silent movies.'—*James Agee*

AA: John Huston (as writer and director); Walter Huston
AAN: best picture

A Tree Grows in Brooklyn

US 1945 128m bw
TCF (Louis D. Lighton)

Life for an Irish family with a drunken father in New York's teeming slums at the turn of the century.

A superbly-detailed studio production of the type they don't make any more: a family drama with interest for everybody.

w Tess Slesinger, Frank Davis, *novel* Betty Smith *d* Elia Kazan *ph* Leon Shamroy *m* Alfred Newman

Peggy Ann Garner, James Dunn, Dorothy McGuire, Joan Blondell, Lloyd Nolan, Ted Donaldson, James Gleason, Ruth Nelson, John Alexander, Adeline de Walt Reynolds, Charles Halton

'He tells a maximum amount of story with a minimum of film. Little touches of humour and human understanding crop up throughout.'—*Frank Ward NBR*

'An artistically satisfying and emotionally quickening tearjerker.'—*Kine Weekly*

'Its drabness is softened by a glow of love and hope.'—*Picture Show*

AA: James Dunn
AAN: script

Triumph of the Will

Germany 1936 120m bw
Leni Riefenstahl / Nazi Party

The official record of the Nazi party congress held at Nuremberg in 1934.

A devastatingly brilliant piece of film-making—right from the opening sequence of Hitler descending from the skies, his plane shadowed against the clouds. The rally scenes are a terrifying example of the camera's power of propaganda. After World War II it was banned for many years because of general fears that it might inspire a new Nazi party.

d, ed Leni Riefenstahl ph Sepp Allgeier and 36 assistants *m* Herbert Windt

Trouble in Paradise

US 1932 86m bw
Paramount (Ernst Lubitsch)

Jewel thieves insinuate themselves into the household of a rich Parisienne, and one falls in love with her.

A masterpiece of light comedy, with sparkling dialogue, innuendo, great performances and masterly cinematic narrative. For connoisseurs, it can't be faulted, and is the masterpiece of American sophisticated cinema.

w Samson Raphaelson, *Grover Jones*, play The Honest Finder by Laszlo Aladar *d* Ernst Lubitsch *ph* Victor Milner *m* W. Franke Harling

Herbert Marshall, Miriam Hopkins, Kay Francis, Edward Everett Horton, Charles Ruggles, C. Aubrey Smith, Robert Greig, Leonid Kinskey

'Swell title, poor picture. Better for the class houses than the subsequents.'—*Variety*

'One of the gossamer creations of Lubitsch's narrative art . . . it would be impossible in this brief notice to describe the innumerable touches of

wit and of narrative skill with which
it is unfolded.'—*Alexander Bakshy*

'A shimmering, engaging piece of
work . . . in virtually every scene a
lively imagination shines
forth.'—*New York Times*

'An almost continuous musical
background pointed up and
commented on the action. The
settings were the last word in
modernistic design.'—*Theodor Huff,
1948*

The True Glory

GB / US 1945   90m   bw
Ministry of
Information / Office of War
Information
The last year of the war, retold by
edited newsreels: D-Day to the Fall
of Berlin.
A magnificent piece of reportage,
worth a dozen fiction films in its
exhilarating Shakespearean fervour,
though the poetic commentary does
occasionally go over the top. One of
the finest of all compilations.

*w Eric Maschwitz, Arthur Macrae,
Jenny Nicholson, Gerald Kersh, Guy
Trosper d Carol Reed, Garson
Kanin research Peter Cusick
m William Alwyn*

'Dwarfs all the fiction pictures of
the year.'—*Richard Mallett, Punch*
'Bold, welcome but inadequate
use of blank verse; much more
successful use of many bits of
individualized vernacular narration,
unusually free of falseness. Very
jab-paced, energetic cutting;
intelligent selection of shots, of
which several hundred are
magnificent.'—*James Agee*
'An inspiring recital of human
endeavour which all the world will
want to see.'—*The Cinema*

True Grit

US 1969   128m
Technicolor
Paramount / Hal B. Wallis (Paul
Nathan)
In the old west, a young girl wanting
to avenge her murdered father seeks
the aid of a hard-drinking old
marshal.

Disappointingly slow-moving and
uninventive semi-spoof western with
a roistering performance from a
veteran star, who won a sentimental
Oscar for daring to look fat and old.

*w Marguerite Roberts, novel Charles
Portis d Henry Hathaway
ph Lucien Ballard m Elmer
Bernstein*

John Wayne, Kim Darby, Glen
Campbell, Dennis Hopper, Jeremy
Slate, Robert Duvall, Strother
Martin, Jeff Corey

'Readers may remember it as a
book about a girl, but it's a film
about John Wayne.'—*Stanley
Kauffmann*

'There is a slight consistent
heightening or lowering into
absurdity, but there is also a strong
feeling for the unvarnished
preposterousness of everyday
existence.'—*John Simon*

† *Rooster Cogburn* featured more
adventures of the Wayne character,
who also showed up on TV in 1978
in the guise of Warren Oates

AA: John Wayne
AAN: title song (*m* Elmer
Bernstein, *ly* Don Black)

Tumbleweeds

US 1925   80m (24 fps)
bw   silent
United Artists / William S. Hart
A wandering cowboy helps a family
of settlers.
The same plot as *Shane* works
wonders in the last film of William S.
Hart, which has the apparently
authentic flavour of the old west.

*w C. Gardner Sullivan, story Hal G.
Evarts d King Baggott ph Joseph
August*

William S. Hart, Barbara Bedford,
Lucien Littlefield, Monte Collins

† Reissued in 1939 with an added
eight-minute introduction by Hart,
showing how the west has changed.

The Tunnel

GB 1935   94m   bw
Gaumont (Michael Balcon)
US title: *Transatlantic Tunnel*

Crooked finances mar the completion of an undersea tunnel to America.

A rare example of British science fiction from this period, though the film was in fact first made in German and French versions, the latter with Jean Gabin

w Curt Siodmak, L. DuGarde Peach, Clemence Dane, *novel* Bernard Kellerman *d* Maurice Elvey *ph* Gunther Krampf *m* Louis Levy

Richard Dix, Leslie Banks, Madge Evans, Helen Vinson, C. Aubrey Smith, George Arliss, Walter Huston, Basil Sydney, Jimmy Hanley

Twelve Angry Men

US 1957 95m bw (UA) Orion–Nova (Henry Fonda, Reginald Rose)

A murder case jury about to vote guilty is convinced otherwise by one doubting member.

Though unconvincing in detail, this is a brilliantly tight character melodrama which is never less than absorbing to experience. Acting and direction are superlatively right, and the film was important in helping to establish television talents in Hollywood.

w Reginald Rose, from his play *d* Sidney Lumet *ph* Boris Kaufman *m* Kenyon Hopkins

Henry Fonda, Lee J. Cobb, E. G. Marshall, Jack Warden, Ed Begley, Martin Balsam, John Fiedler, Jack Klugman, George Voskovec, Robert Webber, Edward Binns, Joseph Sweeney

AAN: best picture; Reginald Rose; Sidney Lumet

'A story of twelve men as their women never knew them!'

Twelve O'Clock High

US 1949 132m bw TCF (Darryl F. Zanuck)

During World War II, the commander of a US bomber unit in Britain begins to crack under the strain.

Absorbing character drama, justifiably a big box office success of its day, later revived as a TV series. All production values are excellent.

w Sy Bartlett, Beirne Lay Jnr *d* Henry King *ph* Leon Shamroy *m* Alfred Newman

Gregory Peck, Hugh Marlowe, Gary Merrill, Millard Mitchell, Dean Jagger, Robert Arthur, Paul Stewart, John Kellogg

'The best war film since the fighting stopped.'—*Daily Mirror*

'Integrity all the way down the line.'—*New York Times*

AA: Dean Jagger
AAN: best picture; Gregory Peck

Twentieth Century

US 1934 91m bw Columbia (Howard Hawks)

A temperamental Broadway producer trains an untutored actress, but when a star she proves a match for him.

Though slightly lacking in pace, this is a marvellously sharp and memorable theatrical burlesque, and the second half, set on the train of the title, reaches highly agreeable peaks of insanity.

w Ben Hecht, Charles MacArthur, *play* Napoleon of Broadway by Charles Bruce Millholland *d* Howard Hawks *ph* Joseph August

John Barrymore, *Carole Lombard*, Roscoe Karns, Walter Connolly, Ralph Forbes, *Etienne Girardot*, Charles Lane, Edgar Kennedy

'Probably too smart for general consumption . . . a long shot for grosses outside the large cities that boast a cosmopolitan clientele.'—*Variety*

'Notable as the first comedy in which sexually attractive, sophisticated stars indulged in their own slapstick instead of delegating it to their inferiors.'—*Andrew Sarris, 1963*

'In the role of Jaffe John Barrymore fits as wholly and smoothly as a banana in a skin.'—*Otis Feguson*

Twenty Thousand Leagues under the Sea

✗ US 1954 122m
Technicolor Cinemascope
Walt Disney

Victorian scientists at sea are wrecked and captured by the mysterious captain of a futuristic submarine.

Pretty full-blooded adaptation of a famous yarn, with strong performances and convincing art and trick work.

w Earl Felton, *novel Jules Verne
d Richard Fleischer ph* Franz Planer, Franz Lehy, Ralph Hammeras, Till Gabbani *m* Paul Smith *ad John Meehan*

Kirk Douglas, James Mason, Paul Lukas, Peter Lorre, Robert J. Wilke, Carlton Young, Ted de Corsia

2001: A Space Odyssey

GB 1968 141m
Metrocolor Panavision
MGM / Stanley Kubrick (Victor Lyndon)

From ape to modern space scientist, mankind has striven to reach the unattainable.

A lengthy montage of brilliant model work and obscure symbolism, this curiosity slowly gathered commercial momentum and came to be cherished by longhairs who used it as a trip without LSD.

w Stanley Kubrick, Arthur C. Clarke, *story* The Sentinel by Arthur C. Clarke *d* Stanley Kubrick
*ph Geoffrey Unsworth, John Alcott
m* various classics *pd Tony Masters, Harry Lange, Ernie Archer ad* John Hoesli

Gary Lockwood, Keir Dullea, William Sylvester, Leonard Rossiter, Robert Beatty, Daniel Richter

'Somewhere between hypnotic and immensely boring.'—*Renata Adler*

'Morally pretentious, intellectually obscure and inordinately long . . . intensely exciting visually, with that peculiar artistic power which comes from obsession . . . a film out of control, an infuriating combination of exactitude on small points and incoherence on large ones.'—*Arthur Schlesinger Jnr*

'The satire throughout is tepid and half-hearted, and tends to look like unintended stupidity.'—*John Simon*

AAN: script; Stanley Kubrick

U

Ugetsu Monogatari

Japan 1953 94m bw
Daiei (Masaichi Nagata)

During a 16th-century civil war two potters find a way of profiteering, but their ambitions bring disaster on their families.

Unique mixture of action, comedy and the supernatural, with strong, believable characters participating and a delightfully delicate touch in script and direction. On its first release it began to figure in many best ten lists, but quickly seemed to fade from public approbation.

w Matsutaro Kawaguchi, from 17th-century collection by Akinara Ueda, Tales of a Pale and Mysterious Moon after the Rain *d* Kenji Mizoguchi *ph* Kazuo Miyagawa *m* Fumio Hayasaka

Masayuki Mori, Machiko Kyo, Sakae Ozawa, Mitsuko Mito

Ulysses

Italy 1954 103m
Technicolor
Lux Film / Ponti-de Laurentiis (Fernando Cinquini)

Ulysses and his crew sail under the curse of Cassandra, and encounter Circe, the sirens and the cyclops.

Peripatetic adventure yarn not too far after Homer; narrative style uncertain but highlights good.

w Franco Brusati, Mario Camerini, Ennio de Concini, Hugh Gray, Ben Hecht, Ivo Perelli, Irwin Shaw, *poem* The Odyssey by Homer *d* Mario Camerini *ph* Harold Rosson *m* Alessandro Cicognini

Kirk Douglas, Silvana Mangano, Anthony Quinn, Rosanna Podesta

'Plunging over the falls—lashed at the stake—trapped by savages in the mightiest love-spectacle de Mille ever filmed!'

Unconquered

US 1947 146m
Technicolor
Paramount / Cecil B. de Mille

An 18th-century English convict girl is deported to the American colonies and suffers various adventures before marrying a Virginia militiaman.

Cardboard epic, expensive and noisy but totally unpersuasive despite cannon, arrows, fire and dynamite.

w Charles Bennett, Frederic M. Frank, Jesse Lasky Jnr, *novel* Neil H. Swanson *d* Cecil B. de Mille *ph* Ray Rennahan *m* Victor Young

Paulette Goddard, Gary Cooper, Boris Karloff, Howard da Silva, Cecil Kellaway, Ward Bond, Katherine de Mille, Henry Wilcoxon, C. Aubrey Smith, Victor Varconi, Virginia Grey, Porter Hall, Mike Mazurki

'De Mille bangs the drum as loudly as ever but his sideshow has gone cold on us.'—*Richard Winnington*

'A five-million dollar celebration of Gary Cooper's virility, Paulette Goddard's femininity, and the American frontier spirit.'—*Time*

'I bought this woman for my own . . . and I'll kill the man who touches her!'—*publicity*

'Love as burning as Sahara's sands!'

Under Two Flags

US 1936 111m bw
TCF (Raymond Griffith)

A dashing French Foreign Legionnaire is helped by a café girl. Despite a highly predictable plot (cf *Destry Rides Again*) this was a solidly-produced epic with a nice deployment of star talent.

w W. P. Lipscomb, Walter Ferris, novel 'Ouida' *d* Frank Lloyd *ph* Ernest Palmer *m* Louis Silvers

Ronald Colman, Claudette Colbert, Rosalind Russell, Victor McLaglen, J. Edward Bromberg, Nigel Bruce, Herbert Mundin, Gregory Ratoff, C. Henry Gordon, John Carradine, Onslow Stevens

'How Ouida would have loved the abandon of this picture, the thirty-two thousand rounds of ammunition shot off into the Arizona desert, the cast of more than ten thousand, the five thousand pounds which insured the stars against camel bites . . . and, in the words of the programme, a fort two hundred feet square, an Arabian oasis with eight full-sized buildings, a forest of transplanted date palms, two Arabian cities, a horse market and a smaller fort.'—*Graham Greene*

Unfaithfully Yours

US 1948 105m bw
TCF (Preston Sturges)

An orchestral conductor believes his wife is unfaithful, and while conducting a concert thinks of three different ways of dealing with the situation.

A not entirely happy mixture of romance, farce, melodrama and wit, but in general a pretty entertaining concoction and the last major film of its talented writer-director.

wd Preston Sturges ph Victor Milner *m* Alfred Newman

Rex Harrison, Linda Darnell, Barbara Lawrence, Rudy Vallee, Kurt Kreuger, Lionel Stander, *Edgar Kennedy*, *Al Bridge*, Julius Tannen, Torben Meyer, Robert Greig

'Harrison discovers more ways of tripping over a telephone cable than one can count, and his efforts to falsify evidence through a recalcitrant tape recorder are as funny as anything thought up by

Clair in *A Nous La Liberté* or by Chaplin in *Modern Times*.'—*Basil Wright, 1972*

† The Rex Harrison character is named Sir Alfred de Carter and is meant to be Sir Thomas Beecham. (In America the equivalent of Beecham's Pills is Carter's Little Liver Pills.)

†† The pieces of music played are as follows:
For murder: the Semiramide Overture by Rossini
For surrender: the Venusberg music from *Tannhäuser*, by Wagner
For Russian roulette: Francesca da Rimini by Tchaikovsky

The Unforgiven

US 1960 125m
Technicolor Panavision
UA / James
Productions / Hecht–Hill–Lancaster
(James Hill)

A rancher's daughter is suspected of being an Indian orphan, and violence results.

Good-looking, expensive but muddled racist western, hard to enjoy.

w Ben Maddow, *novel* Alan le May *d* John Huston *ph* Franz Planer *m* Dmitri Tiomkin

Burt Lancaster, Audrey Hepburn, Audie Murphy, Lillian Gish, Charles Bickford, Doug McClure, John Saxon, Joseph Wiseman, Albert Salmi

'How much strain can a director's reputation take? Of late, John Huston seems to have been trying to find out. I think he has carried the experiment too far with *The Unforgiven* . . . a work of profound phoniness, part adult western, part that *Oklahoma!* kind of folksy Americana.'—*Dwight MacDonald*

'Ludicrous . . . a hodgepodge of crudely stitched sententiousness and lame story-conference inspirations.'—*Stanley Kauffmann*

'A love haunted by nameless evil
which fought to live in their
hearts!'

The Uninvited

US 1944　98m　bw
Paramount (Charles Brackett)

A girl returns to her family house
and is haunted by her mother's
spirit, which seems to be evil.
One of the cinema's few genuine
ghost stories, and a good one,
though encased in a rather stiff
production; it works up to a fine
pitch of frenzy.

w *Dodie Smith*, *novel* Uneasy
Freehold by Dorothy Macardle
d *Lewis Allen*　ph *Charles Lang*
m *Victor Young*

Ray Milland, Ruth Hussey, *Gail
Russell*, Donald Crisp, Cornelia Otis
Skinner, Dorothy Stickney, Barbara
Everest, Alan Napier

'It will hold audiences glued to
their seats.'—*Variety*

'It sets out to give you the
shivers—and will do so, if you're
readily disposed.'—*New York Times*

'I experienced thirty-five first class
jolts, not to mention a well
calculated texture of minor
frissons.'—*Nation*

'Still manages to ice the blood
with its implied horrors . . . you can
almost smell the ghostly
mimosa.'—*Peter John Dyer, 1966*

'A superior and satisfying
shocker.'—*Newsweek*

† British critics of the time
congratulated the director on not
showing the ghosts: in fact the visible
manifestations had been cut by the
British censor.

AAN: Charles Lang

Union Pacific

US 1939　133m　bw
Paramount / Cecil B. de Mille

Indians and others cause problems
for the railroad builders.
Standard big-scale western climaxing
in a spectacular wreck; not exactly
exciting, but very watchable.

w Walter de Leon, C. Gardner
Sullivan, Jesse Lasky Jnr　d *Cecil B.
de Mille*　ph Victor Milner, Dewey
Wrigley　m John Leipold, Sigmund
Krumgold　ad Hans Dreier, Roland
Anderson

Barbara Stanwyck, Joel McCrea,
Akim Tamiroff, Robert Preston,
Lynne Overman, Brian Donlevy,
Robert Barrat, Anthony Quinn,
Stanley Ridges, Henry Kolker,
Evelyn Keyes, Regis Toomey

'A socko spectacular, surefire for
big grosses right down the
line.'—*Variety*

'This latest de Mille epic contains
all the excelsior qualities we expect
of his work—that sense of a
Salvationist drum beating round the
next corner—but it is never as funny
as *The Crusades* and he has lost his
touch with crowds.'—*Graham
Greene*

'Excitement is the dominant
emotion, with swift succession of
contrasting materials and episodes,
grim and gay, often furious,
sometimes funny. The narrative and
action take hold at the start and
never let go.'—*Motion Picture
Herald*

'The largest conglomeration of
thrills and cold-blooded murder
since Pauline was in
peril.'—*Brooklyn Daily Eagle*

'A movie in the old tradition,
melodramatic and breathtaking and
altogether wonderful.'—*Photoplay*

† De Mille's last picture in black and
white.

V

Valley of the Dolls

🕶 US 1967 123m De Luxe
✘ Panavision
TCF/Red Lion (David Weisbart)

An innocent young actress is corrupted by Broadway and Hollywood, and takes to drugs.

Cliché-ridden but good-looking road-to-ruin melodrama from a bitchy bestseller; production values high, but the whole thing goes over the top at the end.

w Helen Deutsch, Dorothy Kingsley, *novel* Jacqueline Susann
d Mark Robson *ph* William H. Daniels *m* André Previn *md* John Williams *ad* Jack Martin Smith, Richard Day

Barbara Parkins, Patty Duke, Susan Hayward, Paul Burke, Sharon Tate, Martin Milner, Tony Scotti, Charles Drake, Alex Davion, Lee Grant, Robert H. Harris

'What kind of pills do you take to sit through a film like this?'—*The Golden Turkey Awards*

'A skilfully deceptive imitation of a real drama . . . on a closer look the characters turn out to be images that have almost nothing to do with people.'—*Christian Science Monitor*

'One of the most stupefyingly clumsy films ever made by alleged professionals.'—*Joseph Morgenstern, Newsweek*

† Judy Garland was originally slated to play the Susan Hayward part

AAN: John Williams

Vampyr

🦇 Germany/France 1931 83m bw
Tobis Klangfilm/Carl Dreyer
US title: *Castle of Doom*
aka: *The Strange Adventure of David Gray*

A young man staying in a remote inn suspects that he is surrounded by vampires and has a dream of his own death.

Vague, misty, virtually plotless but occasionally frightening and always interesting to look at, this semi-professional film long since joined the list of minor classics for two scenes: the hero dreaming of his own death and the villain finally buried by flour in a mill.

w Christen Jul, Carl Dreyer, *story* 'Carmilla' by Sheridan Le Fanu
d Carl Dreyer *ph* Rudolph Maté, Louis Née *m* Wolfgang Zeller

Julian West, Sybille Schmitz, Maurice Schutz, Jan Hieronimko

'It makes our contemporary, explicit Draculas look like advertisements for false teeth.'—*Sunday Times, 1976*

'It is intensely a film of hints, of eerie non sequiturs, of barely perceivable yet striking images . . . evil wafts off the screen like a smell of bad breath.'—*New Statesman, 1976*

'Imagine we are sitting in an ordinary room. Suddenly we are told there is a corpse behind the door. In an instant, the room is completely altered; everything in it has taken another look; the light, the atmosphere have changed, though they are physically the same. This is because *we* have changed, and the objects are as *we* perceive them. That is the effect I meant to get in my film.'—*Carl Dreyer*

Vera Cruz

🗡 US 1953 94m
Technicolor Superscope
UA/Hecht-Lancaster (James Hill)

Adventurers in 1860 Mexico become involved in a plot against Emperor Maximilian.

Terse, lively western melodrama with unusual locations and comedy and suspense touches. Great outdoor entertainment.

w Roland Kibbee, James R. Webb, Borden Chase d Robert Aldrich ph Ernest Laszlo m Hugo Friedhofer

Gary Cooper, Burt Lancaster, Denise Darcel, Cesar Romero, George Macready, Sarita Montiel, Ernest Borgnine, Morris Ankrum, Charles Bronson

Vertigo

US 1958   128m
Technicolor   Vistavision
(Paramount) Alfred Hitchcock
A detective with a fear of heights is drawn into a complex plot in which a girl he loves apparently falls to her death. Then he meets her double . . .
Double identity thriller which doesn't really hang together but has many sequences in Hitchcock's best style despite central miscasting.

w Alec Coppel, Samuel Taylor, novel D'entre les Morts by Pierre Boileau, Thomas Narcejac d Alfred Hitchcock ph Robert Burks m Bernard Herrmann

James Stewart, Kim Novak, Barbara Bel Geddes, Tom Helmore, Henry Jones

'Fear is the oxygen of blackmail. If Barrett was paying, others are. Find me one!'

Victim

GB 1961   100m   bw
Rank / Allied Film
Makers / Parkway (Michael Relph)
A barrister with homosexual inclinations tracks down a blackmailer despite the risk to his own reputation.
A plea for a change in the law is very smartly wrapped up as a murder mystery which allows all aspects to be aired, and the London locations are vivid.

w Janet Green, John McCormick d Basil Dearden ph Otto Heller m Philip Green

Dirk Bogarde, Sylvia Syms, John Barrie, Norman Bird, Peter McEnery, Anthony Nicholls, Dennis Price, Charles Lloyd Pack, Derren Nesbitt, John Cairney, Hilton Edwards, Peter Copley, Donald Churchill, Nigel Stock
   'Ingenious, moralistic, and moderately amusing.'—*Pauline Kael, 70s*

Victoria the Great

GB 1937   112m   bw
(Technicolor sequence)
British Lion / Imperator / Herbert Wilcox
Episodes in the life of Queen Victoria.
A decent film with all the British virtues, and a milestone in the cinema of its time. Script and performances are excellent; production sometimes falters a little.

w Robert Vansittart, Miles Malleson, plays Victoria Regina by Laurence Housman d Herbert Wilcox ph F. A. Young, William V. Skall m Anthony Collins

Anna Neagle, Anton Walbrook, H. B. Warner, Walter Rilla, Mary Morris, C. V. France, Charles Carson, Felix Aylmer, Derrick de Marney
   'The effect of the final colour reel is to make the picture look like something enamelled on pottery and labelled "A Present from Blackpool".'—*James Agate*

The Victors

GB 1963   175m   bw
Panavision
Columbia / Open Road (Carl Foreman)
World War II adventures of an American infantry platoon.
Patchy compendium with moral too heavily stressed but plenty of impressive scenes and performances along the way. The mixture of realism and irony, though, doesn't really mix.

w Carl Foreman, novel The Human Kind by Alexander Baron d Carl Foreman ph Christopher Challis m Sol Kaplan

George Peppard, George Hamilton, Albert Finney, Melina Mercouri, Eli

Wallach, Vince Edwards, Rosanna
Schiaffino, James Mitchum, *Jeanne
Moreau*, Elke Sommer, Senta
Berger, Peter Fonda, Michael Callan
  'Doggerel epic.'—*John Coleman*
  'War has revealed Mr Foreman as
a pompous bore.'—*John Simon*
  'Having made a point through an
image it continually feels the need to
state it all over again by way of
dialogue.'—*Penelope Houston*

Victory through Air Power
US 1943 65m Technicolor
Walt Disney
The history of aviation and the
theories of Major Alexander de
Seversky.
What was thought by many to be
propaganda was in fact a
demonstration of Disney's own
fascination with the theories of a
controversial figure. The cartoon
segments are put together with the
studio's accustomed brilliance.

w various *d* H. C. Potter (live
action), various *m* Edward J.
Plumb, Paul J. Smith, Oliver J.
Wallace

AAN: Edward J. Plumb, Paul J.
Smith, Oliver J. Wallace

The Vikings
US 1958 116m
Technirama
UA/KD Productions (Jerry
Bresler)
Two Viking half-brothers quarrel
over the throne of Northumbria.
Slightly unpleasant and brutal but
extremely well-staged and
good-looking epic in which you can
almost feel the harsh climate. Fine
colour, strong performances, natural
settings, vivid action, and all
production values as they should be.

w Calder Willingham, *novel* The
Viking by Edison Marshall
d Richard Fleischer *ph* Jack Cardiff
m Mario Nascimbene credit
titles United Productions of America
narrator Orson Welles

Kirk Douglas, *Tony Curtis*, Ernest
Borgnine, Janet Leigh, Alexander

Knox, Frank Thring, James Donald,
Maxine Audley, Eileen Way

The VIPs
GB 1963 119m
Metrocolor Panavision
MGM (Anatole de Grunwald)
Passengers at London Airport are
delayed by fog and spend the night
at a hotel.
Multi-story compendium cunningly
designed to exploit the real-life
Burton–Taylor romance. In itself,
competent rather than stimulating.

w Terence Rattigan *d* Anthony
Asquith *ph* Jack Hildyard
m Miklos Rozsa

Richard Burton, Elizabeth Taylor,
Maggie Smith, Rod Taylor, *Margaret
Rutherford*, Louis Jourdan, Elsa
Martinelli, Orson Welles, Linda
Christian, Dennis Price, Richard
Wattis, David Frost, Robert Coote,
Joan Benham, Michael Hordern,
Lance Percival, Martin Miller
  'If Mr Rattigan's Aunt Edna still
goes to the pictures she should like
his latest offering, especially if she
has a good lunch first.'—*Brenda
Davies*

AA: Margaret Rutherford

'1001 nights of glorious romantic
adventure!'
Viva Villa
US 1934 110m bw
MGM (David O. Selznick)
The career of a Mexican rebel.
Gutsy action drama with some
smoothing over of fact in the name
of entertainment. A big, highly
competent production of its year.

w Ben Hecht *d* Jack Conway
ph James Wong Howe, Charles G.
Clarke *m* Herbert Stothart

Wallace Beery, Fay Wray, Leo
Carrillo, Donald Cook, Stuart
Erwin, George E. Stone, Joseph
Schildkraut, Henry B. Walthall,
Katherine de Mille
  'Glorified western . . . strong b.o.
fodder, handicapped a bit perhaps
by its abnormal masculine
appeal.'—*Variety*

'A strange poem of violence.'—*John Baxter, 1968*

'A glorified horse opera . . . the spectator's excitement is incited by the purely physical impact of the furious riding and war sequences, by the frequent sadism, and by the lively musical score.'—*Irving Lerner*

AAN: best picture; script

Von Ryan's Express

US 1965   117m   De Luxe Cinemascope
TCF (Saul David)

In an Italian POW camp during World War II, an unpopular American captain leads English prisoners in a train escape.

Exhilarating action thriller with slow spots atoned for by nail-biting finale, though the downbeat curtain mars the general effect.

w Wendell Mayes, Joseph Landon, *novel* Davis Westheimer *d* Mark Robson *ph* William H. Daniels, Harold Lipstein *m* Jerry Goldsmith

Frank Sinatra, Trevor Howard, Sergio Fantoni, Edward Mulhare, Brad Dexter, John Leyton, Wolfgang Preiss, James Brolin, Adolfo Celi, Rafaela Cara

Voyage of the Damned

GB 1976   155m
Eastmancolor
ITC / Associated General (Robert Fryer)

In 1939, a ship leaves Hamburg for Cuba with Jewish refugees; but Cuba won't take them.

High-minded, expensive, but poorly devised rehash of *Ship of Fools*, with too many stars in cameos and not enough central plot.

w Steve Shagan, David Butler, *book* Gordon Thomas, Max Morgan-Witts *d* Stuart Rosenberg *ph* Billy Williams *m* Lalo Schifrin

Faye Dunaway, Max Von Sydow, Oskar Werner, Malcolm McDowell, James Mason, Orson Welles, Katharine Ross, Ben Gazzara, Lee Grant, Sam Wanamaker, Julie Harris, Helmut Griem, Luther Adler, Wendy Hiller, Nehemiah Persoff, Maria Schell, Fernando Rey, Donald Houston, Jose Ferrer, Denholm Elliott, Janet Suzman

'Not a single moment carries any conviction.'—*New Yorker*

'The movie stays surprisingly distanced and impersonal, like a panning shot that moves too quickly for all the details to register.'—*Charles Champlin, Los Angeles Times*

'With a story that is true (or thereabouts), tragic in its detail and implications, and about which it is impossible to take a neutral attitude, you feel an absolute bounder unless you give it the thumbs up.'—*Barry Took, Punch*

AAN: script; Lalo Schifrin; Lee Grant

W

The Wages of Fear

France / Italy 1953   140m
bw
Filmsonor / CICC / Vera
original title: *Le Salaire de la Peur*

The manager of a Central American oilfield offers big money to drivers who will take nitro-glycerine into the jungle to put out an oil well fire.

After too extended an introduction to the less than admirable characters, this fascinating film resolves itself into a suspense shocker with one craftily managed bad moment after another.

wd Henri-Georges Clouzot, *novel* Georges Arnaud *ph* Armand Thirard *m* Georges Auric

Yves Montand, Folco Lulli, Peter Van Eyck, *Charles Vanel*, Vera Clouzot, William Tubbs

'As skilful as, in its preoccupation with violence and its unrelieved pessimism, it is unlikeable.'—*Penelope Houston, Sight and Sound*

'It has some claim to be the greatest suspense thriller of all time; it is the suspense not of mystery but of Damocles' sword.'—*Basil Wright, 1972*

Wagonmaster

US 1950   86m   bw
RKO / Argosy (John Ford, Merian C. Cooper)

Adventures of a Mormon wagon train journeying towards Utah in 1879.

Low-key Ford western, essentially a collection of incidents, fondly and enjoyably presented.

w Frank Nugent, Patrick Ford
d John Ford *ph* Bert Glennon
m Richard Hageman

Ben Johnson, Joanne Dru, Harry Carey Jnr, Ward Bond, Charles Kemper, Alan Mowbray, Jane Darwell, Russell Simpson

'The feel of the period, the poetry of space and of endeavour, is splendidly communicated.'—*Lindsay Anderson*

'What emerges at the end is nothing less than a view of life itself, the view of a poet.'—*Patrick Gibbs, 1965*

A Walk in the Sun

US 1946   117m   bw
Lewis Milestone Productions

The exploits of a single army patrol during the Salerno landings of 1943, on one vital morning.

Vivid war film in a minor key, superbly disciplined and keenly acted.

w Robert Rossen *novel* Harry Brown *d* Lewis Milestone
ph Russell Harlan *m* Fredric Efrem Rich

Dana Andrews, Richard Conte, Sterling Holloway, John Ireland, George Tyne, Herbert Rudley, Richard Benedict, Norman Lloyd, Lloyd Bridges, Huntz Hall

'Concerned with the individual rather than the battlefield, the film is finely perceptive, exciting, and very moving.'—*Penelope Houston*

'A swiftly overpowering piece of work.'—*Bosley Crowther*

'A notable war film, if not the most notable war film to come from America.'—*Richard Winnington*

'After nearly two hours one is sorry when it ends.'—*Richard Mallett, Punch*

War and Peace

US / Italy 1956   208m
Technicolor   Vistavision
Carlo Ponti / Dino de Laurentiis

A Russian family's adventures at the time of Napoleon's invasion.

Despite miscasting and heavy

dubbing, the pictorial parts of this précis of a gargantuan novel are powerful and exciting enough; the human side drags a little.

w Bridget Boland, Robert Westerby, King Vidor, Mario Camerini, Ennio de Concini, Ivo Perelli, *novel* Leo Tolstoy *d King Vidor* (battle scenes), *Mario Soldati ph Jack Cardiff* (battle scenes), *Aldo Tonti m* Nino Rota *ad Mario Chiari*

Audrey Hepburn, Henry Fonda, Mel Ferrer, *Herbert Lom*, John Mills, Oscar Homolka, Wilfrid Lawson, Vittorio Gassman, Anita Ekberg, Helmut Dantine, Milly Vitale, Barry Jones

'The film has no more warmth than pictures in an art gallery.'— *Philip T. Hartung*

AAN: King Vidor; Jack Cardiff

War and Peace

USSR 1967 507m Sovcolor 'Scope 70mm Mosfilm

An immensely long Russian version with some of the most magnificently spectacular battle scenes ever filmed. A treat for the eyes throughout, and perhaps less taxing than reading the novel, which it follows punctiliously.

w Sergei Bondarchuk, Vasili Solovyov *d Sergei Bondarchuk ph Anatoli Petritsky m* Vyacheslav Ovchinnikov

Lyudmila Savelyeva, Sergei Bondarchuk, Vyacheslav Tikhonov

† The film was five years in production and cost between 50 and 70 million dollars.

AA: best foreign film

The War Wagon

US 1967 99m Technicolor Panavision Universal / Batjac (Marvin Schwartz)

Two cowboys and an Indian plan to ambush the gold wagon of a crooked mining contractor.

Exhilarating but simply-plotted action western with strong comedy elements and a cast of old reliables.

w Clair Huffaker, from his novel Badman *d Burt Kennedy ph* William H. Clothier *m* Dmitri Tiomkin

John Wayne, *Kirk Douglas*, Howard Keel, Robert Walker, Keenan Wynn, Bruce Cabot, Gene Evans, Bruce Dern

'It all works splendidly.'—*MFB*

Waterloo Bridge

US 1940 103m bw MGM (Sidney Franklin)

An army officer marries a ballerina; when he is reported missing his family ignore her and she sinks into prostitution.

Lush, all-stops-out remake of the 1931 film.

w S. N. Behrman, Hans Rameau, George Froeschel *d* Mervyn Le Roy *ph Joseph Ruttenberg m* Herbert Stothart

Vivien Leigh, Robert Taylor, Lucile Watson, Virginia Field, Maria Ouspenskaya, C. Aubrey Smith, Steffi Duna

'The director uses candlelight and rain more effectively than he does the actors.'—*New Yorker, 1977*

AAN: Joseph Ruttenberg; Herbert Stothart

Waxworks

Germany 1924 62m approx (24 fps) bw silent Neptun-Film original title: *Das Wachsfigurenkabinett*

A young poet in a fairground waxwork museum concocts stories about Haroun al Raschid, Ivan the Terrible and Jack the Ripper.

The form later became familiar in such horror films as *Torture Garden* and *Tales from the Crypt*, but here the emphasis is not on horror but on grotesquerie, and indeed the idea is somewhat more entertaining than the rather plodding execution.

w Henrik Galeen *d* Paul Leni *ph* Helmar Lerski *ad* Paul Leni, Ernst Stern, Alfred Junge

William Dieterle, Emil Jannings,
Conrad Veidt, Werner Krauss

The Way Ahead
🎬 GB 1944   115m   bw
🎬 GFD / Two Cities (John Sutro,
Norman Walker)
US title: *Immortal Battalion*
Adventures of a platoon of raw
recruits during World War II.
Memorable semi-documentary
originally intended as a training film;
the warm humour of the early
scenes, however, never leads quite
naturally into the final action and
tragedy.

w Eric Ambler, Peter Ustinov
d Carol Reed *ph* Guy Green
m William Alwyn

*David Niven, Stanley Holloway,
Raymond Huntley, William Hartnell,
James Donald, John Laurie, Leslie
Dwyer, Hugh Burden, Jimmy
Hanley, Renée Asherson, Penelope
Dudley Ward, Reginald Tate, Leo
Genn, Mary Jerrold, Peter Ustinov*

Way Down East
🎬 US 1920   110m approx (24
🎬 fps)   bw with colour
sequence   silent
D. W. Griffith
A country girl is seduced; her baby
dies; her shame is revealed; but a
kindly farmer rescues her from
drowning and marries her.
Old-fashioned tearjerker impeccably
mounted and very typical of its
director in its sentimental mood. The
ice floe sequence is famous for its
excitement and realism.

w Anthony Paul Kelly, Joseph R.
Grismer, D. W. Griffith, *play* Lottie
Blair Parker *d D. W. Griffith*
ph Billy Bitzer, Henrik Sortov

Lillian Gish, Richard Barthelmess,
Lowell Sherman, Creighton Hale
  'Griffith took a creaking, dated
stage melodrama and turned it into a
melodramatic epic.'—*Pauline Kael,
70s*

Way Out West
🎬 US 1937   66m   bw
🎬 Hal Roach (Stan Laurel)

Laurel and Hardy come to
Brushwood Gulch to deliver the
deed to a gold mine.
Seven reels of perfect joy, with the
comedians at their very best in
brilliantly-timed routines, plus two
song numbers as a bonus.

w Jack Jevne, Charles Rogers, James
Parrott, Felix Adler *d* James Horne
ph Art Lloyd, Walter Lundin
m Marvin Hatley

*Stan Laurel, Oliver Hardy, James
Finlayson, Sharon Lynne*, Rosina
Lawrence
  'Thin returns indicated . . . for
added feature on duallers.'—*Variety*
  'Not only one of their most perfect
films, it ranks with the best screen
comedy anywhere.'—*David
Robinson, 1962*
  'The film is leisurely in the best
sense; you adjust to a different
rhythm and come out feeling relaxed
as if you'd had a vacation.'—*New
Yorker, 1980*

AAN: Marvin Hatley

The Way to the Stars
🎬 GB 1945   109m   bw
🎬 Two Cities (Anatole de
Grunwald)
US title: *Johnny in the Clouds*
World War II as seen by the guests
at a small hotel near an airfield.
Generally delightful comedy drama
suffused with tragic atmosphere but
with very few flying shots, one of the
few films which instantly bring back
the atmosphere of the war in Britain
for anyone who was involved.

w Terence Rattigan, Anatole de
Grunwald / *poem* John Pudney
d Anthony Asquith *ph* Derrick
Williams *m* Nicholas Brodszky

*John Mills, Rosamund John, Michael
Redgrave, Douglass Montgomery,
Basil Radford, Stanley Holloway,
Joyce Carey, Renée Asherson, Felix
Aylmer, Bonar Colleano, Trevor
Howard, Jean Simmons*
  'Not for a long time have I seen a
film so satisfying, so memorable, or
so successful in evoking the precise
mood and atmosphere of the recent
past.'—*Richard Mallett, Punch*

'Humour, humanity, and not a sign of mawkishness . . . a classic opening sequence, with the camera wandering through an abandoned air base, peering in at each detail in the nissen huts, the sleeping quarters, the canteens, noting all the time a procession of objects each of which will have its own special significance in the action of the film.'—*Basil Wright, 1972*

'Everything seemed so important then—even love!'
The Way We Were
US 1973 118m
Eastmancolor Panavision
Columbia / Rastar (Ray Stark)
The romance and marriage of an upper-crust young novelist and a Jewish bluestocking girl, from college to Hollywood in the thirties, forties and fifties.
Instant nostalgia for Americans, some fun and a lot of boredom for everybody is provided by this very patchy star vehicle which makes a particular mess of the McCarthy witch hunt sequence but has undeniable moments of vitality.

w Arthur Laurents, from his novel *d* Sydney Pollack *ph* Harry Stradling Jnr *m* Marvin Hamlisch

Barbra Streisand, *Robert Redford*, Patrick O'Neal, Viveca Lindfors, Bradford Dillman, Lois Chiles, Allyn Ann McLerie, Herb Edelman, Murray Hamilton
'Not one moment of the picture is anything but garbage under the gravy of false honesty.'—*Stanley Kauffmann*
'A real curate's egg of a movie, composed of so many disparate parts as to put you in mind of Leacock's knight, who got on his horse and rode off furiously in all directions.'—*Benny Green, Punch*

AA: Marvin Hamlisch; title song (*m* Marvin Hamlisch, *ly* Alan and Marilyn Bergman)
AAN: Harry Stradling Jnr; Barbra Streisand

Went the Day Well?
GB 1942 92m bw
Ealing (S. C. Balcon)
US title: *Forty-eight Hours*
Villagers resist when German paratroopers invade an English village and the squire proves to be a quisling.
Could-it-happen melodrama which made excellent wartime propaganda; generally well staged.

w Angus MacPhail, John Dighton, Diana Morgan, *story* Graham Greene *d* Alberto Cavalcanti *ph* Willie Cooper *m* William Walton

Leslie Banks, Elizabeth Allen, Frank Lawton, Basil Sydney, Valerie Taylor, Mervyn Johns, Edward Rigby, Marie Lohr, C. V. France, David Farrar
'At last, it seems, we are learning to make films with our own native material.'—*Sunday Times*
'It has the sinister, freezing beauty of an Auden prophecy come true.'—*James Agee*
'A refreshing, an exciting and an excellent film.'—*Documentary News Letter*

West Side Story
US 1961 155m
Technicolor Panavision 70
(UA) Mirisch / Seven Arts (Robert Wise)
The Romeo and Juliet story in a New York dockland setting.
The essentially theatrical conception of this entertainment is nullified by determinedly realistic settings which make much of it seem rather silly, but production values are fine and the song numbers electrifying.

w Ernest Lehman, *play* Arthur Laurents, after Shakespeare *d* Robert Wise, *Jerome Robbins ph* Daniel L. Fapp *m* Leonard Bernstein *ly* Stephen Sondheim *pd* Boris Leven

Natalie Wood (sung by Marni Nixon), Richard Beymer (sung by Jimmy Bryant), Russ Tamblyn, *Rita Moreno*, George Chakiris

AA: best picture; Robert Wise,
Jerome Robbins; Daniel L. Fapp;
Rita Moreno; George Chakiris
AAN: Ernest Lehman; musical
direction (Saul Chaplin, Johnny
Green, Sid Ramin, Irwin Kostal)

Western Approaches
🎞 GB 1944 83m
Technicolor / Crown Film Unit
US title: *The Raider*
Torpedoed merchantmen in the
Atlantic are used by a U-boat as a
decoy.
A fictional story is played to great
documentary effect by men of the
allied navies. One of the outstanding
'factual' films of the war years.

wd Pat Jackson *ph* Jack Cardiff
m Clifton Parker
'Without a doubt the best sea film
in existence.'—*Daily Mail*

'Two women helped him
    overthrow the most ruthless
    power in the west!'
The Westerner
🎬 US 1940 99m bw
Samuel Goldwyn
Judge Roy Bean comes to grief
through his love for Lily Langtry.
Moody melodramatic western with
comedy touches; generally
entertaining, the villain more so than
the hero.

w Jo Swerling, Niven Busch, *story*
Stuart N. Lake *d* William Wyler
ph Gregg Toland *m* Dmitri Tiomkin

Gary Cooper, *Walter Brennan*, Doris
Davenport, Fred Stone, Paul Hurst,
Chill Wills, Charles Halton, Forrest
Tucker, Dana Andrews, Lilian
Bond, Tom Tyler

AA: Walter Brennan
AAN: Stuart N. Lake

'Sister, sister, oh so fair, why is
    there blood all over your hair?'
Whatever Happened to Baby
Jane?
🎬 US 1962 132m bw
Warner Seven
Arts / Associates and Aldrich
(Robert Aldrich)
In middle age, a demented ex-child

star lives in an old Hollywood
mansion with her invalid sister, and
tension leads to murder.
Famous for marking the first time
Hollywood's ageing first ladies
stooped to horror, and followed by
Hush Hush Sweet Charlotte and the
other *Whatevers*, this dreary looking
melodrama only occasionally grabs
the attention and has enough plot for
about half its length. The
performances, however, are striking.

w Lukas Heller, *novel* Henry
Farrell *d* Robert Aldrich *ph* Ernest
Haller *m* Frank de Vol

Bette Davis, Joan Crawford, *Victor
Buono*, Anna Lee
'It goes on and on, in a light much
dimmer than necessary, and the
climax, when it belatedly arrives, is a
bungled, languid mingling of
pursuers and pursued . . .'—*New
Yorker*

AAN: Ernest Haller; Bette Davis;
Victor Buono

What's Up, Doc?
🎬 US 1972 94m Technicolor
Warner / Saticoy (Peter
Bogdanovich)
In San Francisco, an absent-minded
young musicologist is troubled by the
attentions of a dotty girl who gets
him involved with crooks and a
series of accidents.
Madcap comedy, a pastiche of
several thirties originals. Spectacular
slapstick and willing players are
somewhat let down by exhausted
patches and a tame final reel.

w Buck Henry, David Newman,
Robert Benton *d* Peter
Bogdanovich *ph* Laszlo Kovacs
m Artie Butler *pd* Polly Pratt

Barbra Streisand, Ryan O'Neal,
Kenneth Mars, Austin Pendleton,
Madeleine Kahn, Mabel Albertson,
Sorrell Booke
'A comedy made by a man who
has seen a lot of movies, knows all
the mechanics, and has absolutely no
sense of humour. Seeing it is like
shaking hands with a joker holding a
joy buzzer: the effect is both

presumptuous and unpleasant.'—*Jay Cocks*

'It's all rather like a 19th-century imitation of Elizabethan blank verse drama.'—*Stanley Kauffmann*

'It freely borrows from the best screen comedy down the ages but has no discernible style of its own.'—*Michael Billington, Illustrated London News*

Where No Vultures Fly

GB 1951 107m
Technicolor
Ealing (Leslie Norman)
US title: *Ivory Hunter*

Adventures of an East African game warden. Pleasantly improving family film, nicely shot on location; a sequel, *West of Zanzibar*, was less impressive.

w W. P. Lipscomb, Ralph Smart, Leslie Norman *d* Harry Watt *ph* Geoffrey Unsworth *m* Alan Rawsthorne

Anthony Steele, Dinah Sheridan, Harold Warrender, Meredith Edwards

'These expeditionary films are really journalistic jobs. You get sent out to a country by the studio, stay as long as you can without getting fired, and a story generally crops up.'—*Harry Watt*

'No one will wonder why it was chosen for this year's royal film show. It is not sordid, as so many new films are; it has a theme that almost everyone will find appealing; and the corner of the Empire where it is set is fresh, beautiful and exciting to look at.'—*Daily Telegraph*

Whisky Galore

GB 1948 82m bw
Ealing (Monja Danischewsky)
US title: *Tight Little Island*

During World War II, a ship full of whisky is wrecked on a small Hebridean island, and the local customs and excise man has his hands full.
Marvellously detailed, fast-moving, well-played and attractively photographed comedy which firmly established the richest Ealing vein.

w Compton Mackenzie, Angus Macphail, *novel* Compton Mackenzie *d* Alexander Mackendrick *ph* Gerald Gibbs *m* Ernest Irving

Basil Radford, Joan Greenwood, Jean Cadell, Gordon Jackson, James Robertson Justice, Wylie Watson, John Gregson, Morland Graham, Duncan Macrae, Catherine Lacey, Bruce Seton, Henry Mollinson, Compton Mackenzie, A. E. Matthews

'Brilliantly witty and fantastic, but wholly plausible.'—*Sunday Chronicle*

'Pick up the pieces, folks, Jimmy's in action again!'

White Heat

US 1949 114m bw
Warner (Louis F. Edelman)

A violent, mother-fixated gangster gets his comeuppance when a government agent is infiltrated into his gang.
This searing melodrama reintroduced the old Cagney and then some: spellbinding suspense sequences complemented his vivid and hypnotic portrayal.

w Ivan Goff, Ben Roberts, *story* Virginia Kellogg *d* Raoul Walsh *ph* Sid Hickox *m* Max Steiner

James Cagney, Edmond O'Brien, Margaret Wycherly, Virginia Mayo, Steve Cochran, John Archer

'The most gruesome aggregation of brutalities ever presented under the guise of entertainment.'—*Cue*

'In the hurtling tabloid traditions of the gangster movies of the thirties, but its matter-of-fact violence is a new post-war style.'—*Time*

'A wild and exciting picture of mayhem and madness.'—*Life*

AAN: Virginia Kellogg

'You are cordially invited to George and Martha's for an evening of fun and games!'

Who's Afraid of Virginia Woolf?

US 1966 129m bw
Warner (Ernest Lehman)

A college professor and his wife have an all-night shouting match and embarrass their guests.

As a film of a play, fair to middling; as a milestone in cinematic permissiveness, very important; as an entertainment, sensational for those in the mood.

w Ernest Lehman, *play* Edward Albee *d* Mike Nichols *ph* Haskell Wexler *m* Alex North

Richard Burton, Elizabeth Taylor, George Segal, Sandy Dennis

'A magnificent triumph of determined audacity.'—*Bosley Crowther*

'One of the most scathingly honest American films ever made.'—*Stanley Kauffmann*

AA: Haskell Wexler; Elizabeth Taylor; Sandy Dennis

AAN: best picture; Ernest Lehman; Mike Nichols; Alex North; Richard Burton; George Segal

'Nine men who came too late and stayed too long!'
'The land had changed. They hadn't. The earth had changed. They couldn't!'

The Wild Bunch

US 1969   145m
Technicolor   Panavision 70

Warner Seven Arts / Phil Feldman

In 1914, Texas bandits are ambushed by an old enemy and die bloodily in defence of one of their number against a ruthless Mexican revolutionary.

Arguably the director's best film, and one which set a fashion for blood-spurting violence in westerns. Undeniably stylish, thoughtful, and in places very exciting.

w Walon Green, Sam Peckinpah *d* Sam Peckinpah *ph* Lucien Ballard *m* Jerry Fielding *ad* Edward Carrere

William Holden, Ernest Borgnine, Robert Ryan, Edmond O'Brien, Warren Oates, Jaime Sanchez, Ben Johnson, Strother Martin, L. Q. Jones, Albert Dekker

'A western that enlarged the form aesthetically, thematically, demonically.'—*Stanley Kauffmann, 1972*

'We watch endless violence to assure us that violence is not good.'—*Judith Crist, 1976*

'The bloody deaths are voluptuous, frightening, beautiful. Pouring new wine into the bottle of the western, Peckinpah explodes the bottle; his story is too simple for this imagist epic.'—*Pauline Kael, New Yorker*

'One of the most moving elegies for a vanished age ever created within the genre.'—*Time Out, 1984*

AAN: script; Jerry Fielding

'The best ******* mercenaries in the business!'

The Wild Geese

GB 1978   134m
Eastmancolor

Rank / Richmond (Euan Lloyd)

Adventures of four British mercenaries in a central African state.

All-star blood and guts with a few breezy touches in the script.

w Reginald Rose, *novel* Daniel Carney *d* Andrew V. McLaglen *ph* Jack Hildyard *m* Roy Budd

Roger Moore, Richard Burton, Richard Harris, Hardy Kruger, Stewart Granger, Jack Watson, Frank Finlay, Kenneth Griffith, Barry Foster, Jeff Corey, Ronald Fraser, Percy Herbert, Patrick Allen, Jane Hylton

'That streetcar man has a new desire!'

The Wild One

US 1954   79m   bw
Columbia / Stanley Kramer

Hoodlum motorcyclists terrorize a small town.

Brooding, compulsive, well-made little melodrama which was much banned because there was no retribution. As a narrative it does somewhat lack dramatic point.

w John Paxton, *story* The Cyclists' Raid by Frank Rooney *d* Laslo

Benedek ph Hal Mohr *m* Leith Stevens

Marlon Brando, Lee Marvin, Mary Murphy, Robert Keith, Jay C. Flippen

'A picture that tries to grasp an idea, even though the reach falls short.'—*New York Times*

† 'What are you rebelling against?' 'What've you got?'—sample dialogue.

†† Sharpness of photography was achieved by the Garutso lens.

Wild Strawberries
Sweden 1957 93m bw
Svensk Filmindustri (Allan Ekelund)
original title: *Smultronstället*
An elderly professor has a nightmare and thinks back over his long life.
A beautifully paced and acted, but somewhat obscure piece of probing symbolism.

wd Ingmar Bergman ph Gunnar Fischer *m* Erik Nordgren

Victor Sjostrom, Ingrid Thulin, Gunnar Bjornstrand, Bibi Andersson, Naima Wifstrand, Jullan Kindahl

'The work of a man obsessed by cruelty, especially spiritual cruelty, trying to find some resolution.' —*Kenneth Cavander, MFB*

AAN: script

Winchester 73
US 1950 92m bw
U-I (Aaron Rosenberg)
Long-time enemies settle an old grudge.
Entertaining, popular, hard-riding, hard-shooting western of the old school.

w Robert L. Richards, Borden Chase, *story* Stuart N. Lake *d* Anthony Mann *ph* William Daniels *m* Frank Skinner *md* Joseph Gershenson

James Stewart, Shelley Winters, Dan Duryea, Stephen McNally, Millard Mitchell, Charles Drake, John McIntire, Will Geer, Jay C. Flippen,

Rock Hudson, Tony Curtis, John Alexander, Steve Brodie

The Window
US 1949 73m bw
RKO (Frederick Ullman)
A New York slum boy is always telling tall tales, so no one believes him when he actually witnesses a murder . . . except the murderer.
Classic little second feature, entertaining and suspenseful; unfortunately it had few successful imitators.

w Mel Dinelli d Ted Tetzlaff *ph* William Steiner *m* Roy Webb

Bobby Driscoll, Barbara Hale, Arthur Kennedy, Paul Stewart, Ruth Roman

'Logical, well-shaped, cohesive, admirably acted, beautifully photographed and cut to a nicety.'—*Richard Winnington*

The Winslow Boy
GB 1948 117m bw
British Lion / London Films (Anatole de Grunwald)
A naval cadet is expelled for stealing a postal order; his father spends all he had on proving his innocence.
Highly enjoyable middle-class British entertainment based on an actual case; performances and period settings are alike excellent, though the film is a trifle overlong.

w Terence Rattigan, Anatole de Grunwald play Terence Rattigan *d* Anthony Asquith *ph* Frederick Young *m* William Alwyn

Robert Donat, Cedric Hardwicke, Margaret Leighton, Frank Lawton, Jack Watling, Basil Radford, Kathleen Harrison, Francis L. Sullivan, Marie Lohr, Neil North, Wilfrid Hyde White, Ernest Thesiger

'Only a clod could see this film without excitement, laughter and some slight moisture about the eyes.'—*Daily Telegraph*

With a Song in My Heart
US 1952 117m
Technicolor
TCF (Lamar Trotti)

Singer Jane Froman is crippled in a plane crash but finally makes a comeback.

Romanticized showbiz biopic with the singer providing voice only. Adequate production and plenty of familiar tunes made this a successful mass appeal sob story.

w Lamar Trotti *d* Walter Lang *ph* Leon Shamroy *md* Alfred Newman

Susan Hayward, David Wayne, Rory Calhoun, Thelma Ritter, Una Merkel, Robert Wagner, Helen Westcott

AA: Alfred Newman

AAN: Susan Hayward; Thelma Ritter

'A big city cop who knows too much. His only witness—a small boy who's seen too much!'

Witness

US 1985   112m Technicolor

Paramount / Edward S. Feldman

A young Amish boy witnesses a murder, and a big city detective hides out in the community to protect him.

As much about the meeting of cultures as about cops and robbers, this is one of those lucky movies which works well on all counts and shows that there are still craftsmen lurking in Hollywood.

w Earl W. Wallace, William Kelley *d* Peter Weir *ph* John Seale *m* Maurice Jarre *pd* Stan Jolley *ed* Thom Noble

Harrison Ford, Kelly McGillis, Josef Sommer, Lukas Haas, Jan Rubes, Alexander Godunov

AA: editing

AAN: best picture; direction; Harrison Ford; original screenplay; photography; music; art direction

BFA: music

The Wizard of Oz

US 1939   102m Technicolor

MGM (Mervyn Le Roy)

Unhappy Dorothy runs away from home, has adventures in a fantasy land, but finally decides that happiness was in her own back yard all the time.

Classic fairy tale given vigorous straightforward treatment, made memorable by performances, art direction and hummable tunes.

w Noel Langley, Florence Ryerson, Edgar Allan Wolfe, *book* Frank L. Baum *d* Victor Fleming *ph* Harold Rosson *songs* E. Y. Harburg, Harold Arlen *md* Herbert Stothart *ad* Cedric Gibbons, William A. Horning*

Judy Garland, Frank Morgan, Ray Bolger, Jack Haley, Bert Lahr, Margaret Hamilton, Billie Burke, Charley Grapewin, Clara Blandick

SCARECROW (Ray Bolger): 'I could while away the hours Conversin' with the flowers, Consultin' with the rain. And perhaps I'd deserve you And be even worthy erv you If I only had a brain . . .'

COWARDLY LION (Bert Lahr): 'Oh, it's sad to be admittin' I'm as vicious as a kitten Widout de vim and voive; I could show off my prowess, Be a lion, not a mowess, If I only had de noive.'

GLINDA, the good witch (Billie Burke): 'Close your eyes and tap your heels together three times. And think to yourself, there's no place like home.'

DOROTHY (Judy Garland): 'If I ever go looking for my heart's desire again, I won't look any further than my own back yard, because if it isn't there, I never really lost it to begin with.'

DOROTHY, LION, SCARECROW, TIN MAN:

'We're off to see the Wizard, The wonderful Wizard of Oz. We hear he is a whiz of a wiz, If ever a wiz there was. If ever a wever a wiz there was, The Wizard of Oz is one because, Because of the wonderful things he does . . .'

'There's an audience for it wherever there's a projection machine and a screen.'—*Variety*

'I don't see why children shouldn't like it, but for adults there isn't very much except Bert Lahr.'—*Richard Mallett, Punch*

'As for the light touch of fantasy, it weighs like a pound of fruitcake soaking wet.'—*Otis Ferguson*

† Ray Bolger was originally cast as the tin man but swapped roles with Buddy Ebsen who was to have been the scarecrow. Ebsen then got sick from the metal paint and was replaced by Jack Haley. Edna May Oliver was originally cast as the wicked witch. For Dorothy MGM wanted Shirley Temple, but Twentieth Century Fox wouldn't loan her.

†† The sepia scenes at beginning and end were directed by King Vidor

AA: song 'Over the Rainbow'; Herbert Stothart
AAN: best picture

'His hideous howl a dirge of death!'
'Night monster with the blood lust of a savage beast!'
The Wolf Man
US 1940 70m bw
Universal (George Waggner)
The son of an English squire comes home, is bitten by a gypsy werewolf, and becomes one himself.
Dazzlingly cast, moderately well staged, but dramatically very disappointing horror piece which established a new Universal monster who later met Frankenstein, Abbott and Costello, and several other eccentrics.

w Curt Siodmak *d* George Waggner *ph Joseph Valentine m* Hans Salter, Frank Skinner *md* Charles Previn

Lon Chaney Jnr, Claude Rains, Warren William, Ralph Bellamy, Bela Lugosi, *Maria Ouspenskaya*, Patric Knowles, Evelyn Ankers, Fay Helm

MALEVA (Maria Ouspenskaya):
'Even the man who is pure in heart
And says his prayers by night
May become a wolf when the wolf bane blooms
And the moon is pure and bright . . .'

'It was the look in her eyes that did it. How could he resist? How could he know it meant murder?'
The Woman in the Window
US 1944 95m bw
International (Nunnally Johnson)
A grass widow professor befriends a girl who gets him involved with murder.
A refreshingly intelligent little thriller which was criticized at the time for a cop-out ending; this can now be seen as a decorative extra to a story which had already ended satisfactorily.
Good middlebrow entertainment.

w Nunnally Johnson, novel Once Off Guard by J. H. Wallis *d Fritz Lang ph* Milton Krasner *m* Arthur Lang, Hugo Friedhofer

Edward G. Robinson, Joan Bennett, *Raymond Massey, Dan Duryea*, Edmund Breon, Thomas Jackson, Dorothy Peterson, Arthur Loft

'A perfect example of its kind, and a very good kind too.'—*James Shelley Hamilton*

'The accumulation of tiny details enlarged as though under a district attorney's magnifying glass gives reality a fantastic and anguishing appearance.'—*Jacques Bourgeois*

'In its rather artificial, club library style an effective and well made piece, absorbing, diverting and full of often painful suspense.'—*Richard Mallett, Punch*

AAN: Arthur Lang, Hugo Friedhofer

A Woman of Paris
✂ US 1923   85m (24 fps)
✗ bw   Silent (music track
added 1976)
Charles Chaplin
A country girl goes to the city,
becomes a demi-mondaine, and
inadvertently causes the death of the
one man she loves.
Remarkably simply-handled 'road to
ruin' melodrama; its subtleties of
treatment make it still very
watchable for those so inclined.

*wd Charles Chaplin m Rollie
Totheroh, Jack Wilson*
*Edna Purviance, Adolphe Menjou,
Carl Miller, Lydia Knott*

'A thoroughly workmanlike
entertainment and a candidate for
honours and dollars entirely·
independent of the drawing power
built up by Chaplin in other
fields.'—*Variety*

'After five minutes of watching the
sparkling new print, the spell begins
to work. Chaplin is neatly turning
the cliches inside out, like a
glove.'—*Alan Brien, Sunday Times,
1980*

'Mr Chaplin as writer and director
has not done anything radical or
anything esoteric; he has merely
used his intelligence to the highest
degree, an act which for many years
has ceased to be expected of motion
picture people.'—*Robert E.
Sherwood*

'The plot is desperately simple,
but played with a control, a
complete absence of histrionic
vehemence, rare in the early
twenties.'—*Dilys Powell, Punch,
1980*

† Chaplin appeared unbilled as a
railway porter. The film was not a
commercial success and he withdrew
it for fifty years.

Woman of the Year
♉ US 1942   114m   bw
° MGM (Joseph L. Mankiewicz)
A sports columnist marries a lady
politician; they have nothing in
common but love.
Simple, effective, mildly
sophisticated comedy which allows
two splendid stars, in harness for the
first time, to do their thing to the
general benefit.

*w Ring Lardner Jnr, Michael Kanin
d George Stevens ph Joseph
Ruttenberg m Franz Waxman*

Spencer Tracy, Katharine Hepburn,
Fay Bainter, Reginald Owen,
William Bendix, Dan Tobin, Minor
Watson, Roscoe Karns

'Between them they have enough
charm to keep any ball
rolling.'—*William Whitebait*

AA: script
AAN: Katharine Hepburn

'135 women with men on their
   minds!'
The Women
♉ US 1939   132m   bw
° (Technicolor sequence)
MGM (Hunt Stromberg)
A New York socialite gets a divorce
but later thinks better of it.
Bitchy comedy drama distinguished
by an all-girl cast ('135 women with
men on their minds'). An
over-generous slice of real theatre,
skilfully adapted, with rich sets,
plenty of laughs, and some
memorable scenes between the
fighting ladies.

*w Anita Loos, Jane Murfin
play Clare Boothe d George Cukor
ph Oliver T, Marsh, Joseph
Ruttenberg m Edward Ward, David
Snell*

*Norma Shearer, Joan Crawford,
Rosalind Russell, Mary Boland,*
Paulette Goddard, Joan Fontaine,
Lucile Watson, Phyllis Povah,
Virginia Weidler, Ruth Hussey,
Margaret Dumont, Marjorie Main,
Hedda Hopper

'Smash hit of solid proportions for
extended runs and heavy profits . . .
a strong woman entry but still has
plenty of spicy lines and situations
for the men.'—*Variety*

'A mordant, mature description of
the social decay of one corner of the
American middle class.'—*Time*

'So marvellous that we believe

every Hollywood studio should make at least one thoroughly nasty picture a year.'—*New York Times*

'Whether you go or not depends on whether you can stand Miss Shearer with tears flowing steadily in all directions at once, and such an endless damn back fence of cats.'—*Otis Ferguson*

Women in Love

🎭 GB 1969 130m De Luxe ⚔ UA/Brandywine (Larry Kramer)

Two girls have their first sexual encounters in the Midlands during the twenties.

Satisfactory rendering of a celebrated novel, with excellent period detail atoning for rather irritating characters. The nude wrestling scene was a famous first.

w Larry Kramer, *novel D. H. Lawrence d Ken Russell ph Billy Williams m* Georges Delerue

Glenda Jackson, Jennie Linden, Alan Bates, Oliver Reed, Michael Gough, Alan Webb

'They should take all the pretentious dialogue off the soundtrack and call it Women in Heat.'—*Rex Reed*

'Two-thirds success, one-third ambitious failure.'—*Michael Billington, Illustrated London News*

AA: Glenda Jackson
AAN: Larry Kramer; Ken Russell; Billy Williams

Words and Music

🎵 US 1948 121m Technicolor
MGM (*Arthur Freed*)

The songwriting collaboration of Richard Rodgers and Lorenz Hart. Musical biopic which packs in a lot of good numbers and manages a script which is neither too offensive nor too prominent.

w Fred Finklehoffe d Norman Taurog *ph* Charles Rosher, Harry Stradling *md Lennie Hayton ch* Robert Alton, Gene Kelly

Tom Drake, *Mickey Rooney*, Perry Como, *Mel Tormé*, Betty Garrett, *June Allyson*, Lena Horne, Ann Sothern, Allyn McLerie, *Gene Kelly*, Vera-Ellen, Cyd Charisse, Janet Leigh, Marshall Thompson

'The story of a family's ugly secret and the stark moment that thrust their private lives into public view!'

Written on the Wind

🎭 US 1956 99m Technicolor ⚔ U-I (Albert Zugsmith)

A secretary marries her oil tycoon boss and finds herself the steadying force in a very rocky family.

The sheerest Hollywood moonshine: high-flying melodramatic hokum which moves fast enough to be very entertaining.

w George Zuckerman, *novel* Robert Wilder *d* Douglas Sirk *ph* Russell Metty */m* Frank Skinner

Lauren Bacall, *Robert Stack*, *Dorothy Malone*, Rock Hudson, Robert Keith, Grant Williams

AA: Dorothy Malone
AAN: title song (*m* Victor Young, *ly* Sammy Cahn); Robert Stack

'Torn with desire . . . twisted with hate!'

Wuthering Heights

🎬 US 1939 104m bw Samuel Goldwyn

The daughter of an unhappy middle-class Yorkshire family falls passionately in love with a gypsy who has been brought up with her. Despite American script and settings, this wildly romantic film makes a pretty fair stab at capturing the power of at least the first half of a classic Victorian novel, and in all respects it's a superb Hollywood production of its day and a typical one, complete who ghostly finale and a first-rate cast.

w Ben Hecht, Charles MacArthur, novel Emily Brontë d William Wyler ph Gregg Toland m Alfred Newman

Laurence Olivier, Merle Oberon, David Niven, Hugh Williams, Flora

Robson, Geraldine Fitzgerald, Donald Crisp, Leo G. Carroll, Cecil Kellaway, *Miles Mander*

CATHY (Merle Oberon): 'I don't think I belong in heaven, Ellen. I dreamt once I was there. I dreamt I went to heaven and that heaven didn't seem to be my home and I broke my heart with weeping to come back to earth and the angels were so angry they flung me out in the middle of the heath on top of Wuthering Heights and I woke up sobbing with joy.'

HEATHCLIFF (Laurence Olivier): 'What do they know of heaven or hell, Cathy, who know nothing of life? Oh, they're praying for you, Cathy. I'll pray one prayer with them. I'll repeat till my tongue stiffens: Catherine Earnshaw, may you not rest while I live on. I killed you. Haunt me, then! Haunt your murderer! I know that ghosts have wandered on the earth. Be with me always—take any form—drive me mad! Only do not leave me in this dark alone where I cannot find you. I cannot live without my life! I cannot die without my soul . . .'

'Sombre dramatic tragedy, productionally fine, but with limited appeal.'—*Variety*

'Unquestionably one of the most distinguished pictures of the year.'—*Frank S. Nugent, New York Times*

'A pattern of constant forward motion, with overtones maintained throughout the rise of interest and suspense.'—*Otis Ferguson*

'A strong and sombre film, poetically written as the novel not always was, sinister and wild as it was meant to be, far more compact dramatically than Miss Brontë had made it.'—*Richard Mallett, Punch*

AA: Gregg Toland
AAN: best picture; script; William Wyler; Alfred Newman; Laurence Olivier; Geraldine Fitzgerald

Y

A Yank at Oxford
GB 1938 105m bw
MGM (Michael Balcon)

A cocky young American student comes to Oxford and meets all kinds of trouble.

A huge pre-war success which now seems naïve, this was the first big Anglo-American production from a team which went on to make *The Citadel* and *Goodbye Mr Chips* before war stymied them.

w Malcolm Stuart Boylan, Walter Ferris, George Oppenheimer, Leon Gordon, Roland Pertwee, John Monk Saunders, Sidney Gilliat, Michael Hogan *d* Jack Conway *ph* Harold Rosson, Edward Ward

Robert Taylor, Vivien Leigh, Maureen O'Sullivan, Lionel Barrymore, Robert Coote, Edmund Gwenn, C. V. France, Griffith Jones, Morton Selten

'A draw picture for Taylor at a critical moment in his meteoric bid for fame.'—*Variety*

† A total of 31 writers are alleged to have worked without credit

Yankee Doodle Dandy
US 1942 126m bw
Warner (Hal B. Wallis, William Cagney)

The life story of dancing vaudevillian George M. Cohan.

Outstanding showbiz biopic, with unassuming but effective production, deft patriotic backdrops and a marvellous, strutting, magnetic star performance.

w Robert Buckner, Edmund Joseph *d* Michael Curtiz *ph* James Wong Howe *m* Heinz Roemheld *md* Heinz Roemheld, Ray Heindorf *songs* George M. Cohan

James Cagney, Joan Leslie, *Walter Huston*, Rosemary de Camp, Richard Whorf, George Tobias, Jeanne Cagney, Irene Manning, S. Z. Sakall, George Barbier, Frances Langford, Walter Catlett, Eddie Foy Jnr

COHAN (James Cagney) at end of vaudeville act: 'My mother thanks you. My father thanks you. My sister thanks you. And I thank you.'

COHAN: 'Where else in the world could a plain guy like me sit down and talk things over with the head man?'

ROOSEVELT (Captain Jack Young): 'Well now, you know, Mr Cohan, that's as good a description of America as I've ever heard.'

'Possibly the most genial screen biography ever made.'—*Time*

AA: music direction; James Cagney
AAN: best picture; original story (Robert Buckner); Michael Curtiz; Walter Huston

'They tamed a tropic wilderness!'
The Yearling
US 1946 134m Technicolor
MGM (Sidney Franklin)

The son of an old-time country farmer is attached to a stray deer.

Excellent family film for four-handkerchief patrons.

w Paul Osborn, *novel* Marjorie Kinnan Rawlings *d* Clarence Brown *ph* Charles Rosher, Leonard Smith *m* Herbert Stothart

Gregory Peck, Jane Wyman, Claude Jarman Jnr, Chill Wills, Clem Bevans, Margaret Wycherly, Henry Travers, Forrest Tucker

AA: Charles Rosher, Leonard Smith (and Arthur Arling)
AAN: best picture; Clarence Brown; Gregory Peck; Jane Wyman

The Yellow Rolls Royce
GB 1964 122m
Metrocolor Panavision
MGM (Anatole de Grunwald)

Three stories about the owners of an expensive car; an aristocrat, a gangster, and a wandering millionairess.

Lukewarm all-star concoction lacking either good stories or a connecting thread.

w Terence Rattigan d Anthony Asquith ph Jack Hildyard m Riz Ortolani pd Vincent Korda

Rex Harrison, Jeanne Moreau, Edmund Purdom, Moira Lister, Roland Culver, Shirley Maclaine, George C. Scott, Alain Delon, Art Carney, Ingrid Bergman, Omar Sharif, Joyce Grenfell

'Tame, bloodless, smothered in elegance and the worst kind of discreetly daring good taste.'—*Peter John Dyer*

You Can't Take It with You
♉ US 1938 127m bw
Columbia (Frank Capra)

The daughter of a highly eccentric New York family falls for a rich man's son.

A hilarious, warm and witty play is largely changed into a tirade against big business, but the Capra expertise is here in good measure and the stars all pull their weight.

w Robert Riskin, *play* George S. Kaufman, Moss Hart d *Frank Capra* ph Joseph Walker m Dmitri Tiomkin

Jean Arthur, Lionel Barrymore, James Stewart, Edward Arnold, Spring Byington, Mischa Auer, Ann Miller, Samuel S. Hinds, Donald Meek, H. B. Warner, Halliwell Hobbes, Mary Forbes, Dub Taylor, Lillian Yarbo, Eddie Anderson, *Harry Davenport*

GRANDPA VANDERHOF (Lionel Barrymore) offering a prayer: 'Well, sir, here we are again. We had a little trouble, but that's not your fault. You spread the milk of human kindness, and if some of it gets curdled, that's our look-out. Anyway, things have turned out fine. Alice is going to marry Tony. The Kirbys are going to live with us for a while. And everybody on the block is happy. We've all got our health—and as far as anything else is concerned, we'll leave it up to you. Thank you.'

'The comedy is wholly American, wholesome, homespun, human, appealing, and touching in turn.'—*Variety*

'Shangri-La in a frame house.'—*Otis Ferguson*

AA: best picture; Frank Capra
AAN: Robert Riskin; Joseph Walker; Spring Byington

Young and Innocent
🏃 GB 1937 80m bw
GFD / Gainsborough (Edward Black)

US title: *A Girl Was Young*

A girl goes on the run with her boy friend when he is suspected of murder.

Pleasant, unassuming chase melodrama with a rather weak cast but plenty of its director's touches.

w Charles Bennett, Alma Reville, *novel* A Shilling for Candles by Josephine Tey d *Alfred Hitchcock* ph Bernard Knowles m Louis Levy

Nova Pilbeam, Derrick de Marney, Mary Clare, Edward Rigby, Basil Radford, George Curzon, Percy Marmont, John Longden

Young at Heart
👯 US 1954 117m
Warnercolor

(Warner) Arwin (Henry Blanke)

The daughters of a small-town music teacher have romantic problems.

Softened, musicalized remake of *Four Daughters*, an old-fashioned treat with roses round the door and a high standard of proficiency in all departments.

w Julius J. Epstein, Lenore Coffee, *novel* Fannie Hurst d Gordon Douglas ph Ted McCord md Ray Heindorff

Doris Day, *Frank Sinatra*, *Ethel Barrymore*, Gig Young, Dorothy Malone, Robert Keith, Elizabeth Fraser, Alan Hale Jnr

Young Frankenstein

US 1974 108m bw
TCF / Gruskoff / Venture / Jouer / Crossbow (Michael Gruskoff)

Young Frederick Frankenstein, a brain surgeon, goes back to Transylvania and pores over his grandfather's notebooks.

The most successful of Mel Brooks' parodies, Mad Magazine style; the gleamingly reminiscent photography is the best of it, the script being far from consistently funny, but there are splendid moments.

w Gene Wilder, Mel Brooks d Mel Brooks ph Gerald Hirschfeld m John Morris ad Dale Hennesy

Gene Wilder, Marty Feldman, Madeleine Kahn, *Peter Boyle*, Cloris Leachman, Kenneth Mars, Gene Hackman, Richard Haydn

AAN; script

The Young in Heart

US 1938 91m bw
David O. Selznick

A family of charming confidence tricksters move in on a rich old lady but she brings out the best in them. Delightful, roguish romantic comedy, perfectly cast and pacily handled.

w Paul Osborn, Charles Bennett, *novel* The Gay Banditti by I. A. R. Wylie d Richard Wallace ph Leon Shamroy m Franz Waxman

Douglas Fairbanks Jnr, Janet Gaynor, Roland Young, Billie Burke, Minnie Dupree, Paulette Goddard, Richard Carlson, Henry Stephenson

'Sentimental drama, vastly touching and entertaining . . . has everything to ensure box office success.'—*Variety*

'It comes as a gentle breeze in the hurricane of hurly burly comedies that have hurtled across the screen of late.'—*Motion Picture Herald*

AAN: Leon Shamroy; Franz Waxman

Young Mr Lincoln

US 1939 100m bw
TCF (Kenneth MacGowan)

Abraham Lincoln as a young country lawyer stops a lynching and proves a young man innocent of murder.

Splendid performances and period atmosphere are rather nipped in the bud by second-feature courtroom twists, but this is a marvellous old-fashioned entertainment with its heart in the right place.

w Lamar Trotti d John Ford ph Bert Glennon m Alfred Newman

Henry Fonda, Alice Brady, Marjorie Weaver, Arleen Whelan, Eddie Collins, Richard Cromwell, Donald Meek, Eddie Quillan, Spencer Charters

'A dignified saga of early Lincolniana, paced rather slowly . . . lack of romance interest is one of the prime factors which deter the film from interpreting itself into big box office.'—*Variety*

'Its simple good faith and understanding are an expression of the country's best life that says as much as forty epics.'—*Otis Ferguson*

'Period details are lovingly sketched in—a log splitting contest, a tug of war, a tar barrel rolling match . . .'—*Charles Higham*

'Its source is a womb of popular and national spirit. This could account for its unity, its artistry, its genuine beauty.'—*Sergei Eisenstein*

'A film which indisputably has the right to be called Americana.'—*New York Times*

'In spite of the excitements of a murder, a near-lynching and a crackerjack trial, it remains a character study.'—*New York Sun*

'One of John Ford's most memorable films.'—*Pauline Kael, 70s*

AAN: Lamar Trotti

Young Winston

GB 1972 157m Eastmancolor Panavision
Columbia / Open Road / Hugh French (Carl Foreman)

The adventurous life of Winston Churchill up to his becoming an MP. Generally engaging if lumpy film which switches too frequently from action to family drama to politics to character study and is not helped by irritating directorial tricks.

w Carl Foreman, *book* My Early Life by Winston Churchill

d Richard Attenborough *ph* Gerry Turpin *m* Alfred Ralston *pd* Don Ashton, Geoffrey Drake

Simon Ward, Robert Shaw, Anne Bancroft, Jack Hawkins, Ian Holm, *Anthony Hopkins*, John Mills, Patrick Magee, Edward Woodward

AAN: Carl Foreman

Z

Z

✪✪ France / Algeria 1968
125m   Eastmancolor
Reggane / ONCIC / Jacques Pérrin

A leading opposition MP is murdered at a rally. The police are anxious to establish the event as an accident, but the examining magistrate proves otherwise.

An exciting police suspense drama which also recalls events under the Greek colonels and was therefore highly fashionable for a while both as entertainment and as a political *roman à clef*.

w Costa-Gavras, Jorge Semprun,
novel Vassili Vassilikos
d Costa-Gavras   ph Raoul Coutard
m Mikis Theodorakis

Jean-Louis Trintignant, Jacques Pérrin, Yves Montand, François Périer, Irene Papas, Charles Denner

AAN: best picture; direction

Ziegfeld Follies

US 1944 (released 1946)
110m   Technicolor
MGM (Arthur Freed)

In heaven, Florenz Ziegfeld dreams up one last spectacular revue.

A rather airless all-star entertainment in which the comedy suffers from the lack of an audience but some of the production numbers are magnificently stylish.

w various   d Vincente Minnelli
ph George Folsey, Charles Rosher
m various   ad Cedric Gibbons,
Merrill Pye, Jack Martin Smith

Fred Astaire, Lucille Ball, Bunin's Puppets, William Powell, Jimmy Durante, Edward Arnold, *Fannie Brice*, Lena Horne, Lucille Bremer, Esther Williams, Judy Garland, *Red Skelton*, *Gene Kelly*, James Melton, Hume Cronyn, Victor Moore, Marion Bell

'Between opening and closing is packed a prodigious amount of material, some of which is frankly not deserving of the lavish treatment accorded it.'—*Film Daily*

'The fastidious are advised to head for the lobby while Kathryn Grayson sings 'There's Beauty Everywhere' against magenta foam skies.'—*Pauline Kael, 70s*

Zorba the Greek

✪✪ GB 1964   142m   bw
TCF / Rockley / Cacoyannis

A young English writer in Crete is befriended by a huge gregarious Greek who comes to dominate his life.

A mainly enjoyable character study of a larger-than-life character, this film made famous by its music does not really hang together dramatically and has several melodramatic excrescences.

wd Michael Cacoyannis, novel Nikos Kazantzakis   ph Walter Lassally
m Mikis Theodorakis

Anthony Quinn, *Alan Bates*, *Lila Kedrova*, Irene Papas

'For all its immense length, the film never gets down to a clear statement of its theme, or comes within measuring distance of its vast pretensions.'—*Brenda Davies*

AA: Walter Lassally; Lila Kedrova
AAN: Best picture; Michael Cacoyannis (as writer and director); Anthony Quinn